D0539168

Huxley

Also by Adrian Desmond

THE HOT-BLOODED DINOSAURS
THE APE'S REFLEXION
ARCHETYPES AND ANCESTORS
THE POLITICS OF EVOLUTION
DARWIN (with James Moore)

Huxley:
The Devil's Disciple

ADRIAN DESMOND

MICHAEL JOSEPH

LONDON

MICHAEL JOSEPH LTD
Published by the Penguin Group
27 Wrights Lane, London w8 5TZ
Viking Penguin Inc., 375 Hudson Street, New York, New York 10014, USA
Penguin Books Australia Ltd, Ringwood, Victoria, Australia
Penguin Books Canada Ltd, 10 Alcorn Avenue, Toronto, Ontario, Canada M4V 3B2
Penguin Books (NZ) Ltd, 182–190 Wairau Road, Auckland 10, New Zealand

Penguin Books Ltd, Registered Offices: Harmondsworth, Middlesex, England

First published in Great Britain 1994
Copyright © Adrian Desmond 1994

All rights reserved.
Without limiting the rights under copyright
reserved above, no part of this publication may be
reproduced, stored in or introduced into a retrieval system,
or transmitted, in any form or by any means (electronic, mechanical,
photocopying, recording or otherwise) without the prior
written permission of both the copyright owner and
the above publisher of this book

Typeset in 11/12.5pt Monophoto Sabon
Printed in England by Clays Ltd, St Ives plc

A CIP catalogue record for this book is available from the British Library

ISBN 0 7181 3641 1

The moral right of the author has been asserted

Contents

Contents

Illustrations

Acknowledgments

I AM ESPECIALLY thankful to my home critic Nellie Flexner for reading reams of manuscript, and to Jim Moore for his usual incisive comments on the major portion of the book.

Angela Darwin, currently transcribing T. H. Huxley's and Henrietta Huxley's letters to his sister Lizzie, provided an endless stream of quotes, photocopies and comments, and put up with my even greater stream of queries. Her knowledge of family matters has greatly enriched this volume.

My main research was carried out on the Huxley letters at the Archives of Imperial College, London, and my thanks go to Anne Barrett, who was ever ready to help.

I used a splendid microfilm of the archive letters, furnished by Research Publications Ltd, P.O. Box 45, Reading RG1 8HF. Without these fifty-four reels of film – which allowed me to trawl through Huxley's 5,000 letters in the wee hours – I should never have been able to give this biography its full body. I am grateful to Cristina Ashby at Research Publications for her generosity.

Not that it is exactly *easy* to decipher Huxley's scrawl. His handwriting is notorious among scholars. When he was in a rush (which was always), it resembled one of his drunken crayfish which had fallen into the ink pot and staggered across the page to its doom. Compositors constantly complained of his writing, as did Huxley when they took enterprising guesses at his words. 'Your printers are abominable', he told the editor of *Nature*. 'They make me say that "Tyndall did not see the *drift* of my statement", when I wrote "draft" as plainly as possible'. After twenty years, my sympathy is still with the printers.

For information, discussions, offprints and translations I am indebted to David Allen, William Collier, Mario di Gregorio,

Acknowledgments

Antonello la Vergata, C. G. Gross, Boyd Hilton, John Laurent, Jim Moore, Robert Ralph, Evelleen Richards, Nicolaas Rupke, Richard Milner, Simon Schaffer, Jim Secord, Mary P. Winsor and Alison Winter.

Sir Andrew Huxley very kindly supplied photographs of portraits in his possession, as did Mrs Hilary Buzzard and Michael Huxley/ Richard Milner. And Angela Darwin made available pen-and-ink sketches from the family letters.

Sir Andrew also graciously consented to my publishing extracts from his grandfather's letters.

To the following archives and librarians I extend my thanks for access, help and hospitality, or for permission to quote from manuscript material: Howard Hague, Charing Cross and Westminster Medical School; John Thackray, the British Museum (Natural History); Ian Lyle, Royal College of Surgeons of England; Gill Furlong, University College London; Graham McKenna, British Geological Survey; Gina Douglas, the Linnean Society of London; N. H. Robinson, Royal Society; Virginia Murray at John Murray (publishers); Gillian F. Lonergan, Co-operative Union, Manchester; David Webb, the Bishopsgate Institute, London; Stella Newton, Oxford University Museum; Reg Fish and his successor Ann Sylph, Zoological Society of London; the British Library; Royal Institution Archives; Cambridge University Library; Wellcome Institute for the History of Medicine, London; King's College, London; University of London Library, Senate House; National Library of Australia, Canberra; and the American Philosophical Society.

My editors Susan Watt, Anne Askwith and Robyn Ayers offered a wealth of suggestions, and I thank them and the Michael Joseph team generally.

Smiting the Amalekites?

'MY GOOD & KIND agent for the propagation of the Gospel', Darwin called him, 'ie the Devil's gospel'. Thomas Henry Huxley became Darwin's Rottweiler, instantly recognizable by his deep-set dark eyes and lashing tongue. Where Darwin held back, Huxley lunged at his limping prey. It was he, not Darwin, who enraptured and outraged audiences in the 1860s with talk of our ape ancestors and cave men. Listeners were agog in a prim, evangelical age. These were terrifying, tantalizing images. 'It is not the bishops and archbishops I am afraid of', Samuel Butler once said. 'Men like Huxley . . . are my natural enemies'.[1] No one stirred passions like Thomas Henry Huxley.

Huxley was one of the founders of the sceptical, scientific twentieth century. We owe to him that enduring military metaphor, the 'war' of science against theology. He coined the word 'agnostic' – and gave the West its existential crisis. All of this makes him look so modern that we want to snatch him from his age. Today his agnostic stand seems obvious. But yesterday it was an immensely daring, motivated, ideological position. That plodding zoological autocrat, Richard Owen, called him a pervert with 'some, perhaps congenital, defect of mind' for denying Divine will in Nature.[2] Who can realize the prissy, patronage-based, undemocratic, sermon-dominated, Anglican-controlled, *different* society Huxley faced, and faced squarely?

He remains a saint to some, a sinner to others. He had a huge, multi-talented intellect and seemed to run ten lives simultaneously. 'Brilliant' was George Eliot's word for him, but even she wondered where this *agent provocateur* would strike next. He had a stiletto of a pen. 'Cutting up monkeys was his forte, and cutting up men

xiii

was his foible', the *Pall Mall Gazette* noted. The alternative, for Huxley, was 'to lie still & let the devil have his own way. And I will be torn to pieces before I am forty sooner than see that'.[3] He was built 'on the high pressure tubular boiler principle', and adoring students came from every continent to see this social engineer thundering onto society's mainline like an unscheduled express. George Eliot thought he was out of control half the time. The corpulent cosmic theist John Fiske travelled from America and understood him perfectly:

> I am quite wild over Huxley. He is as handsome as an
> Apollo . . . I never saw such magnificent eyes in my life.
> His eyes are black, and his face expresses an eager
> burning intensity . . . He seems earnest, – immensely in
> earnest, – and thoroughly frank and cordial and modest.
> And, by Jove, what a pleasure it is to meet such a clean-
> cut mind! It is like Saladin's sword which cut through the
> cushion.[4]

There was no alternative to '*seeing*' such people, Fiske said. 'Reading their books don't give you the flesh-and-blood idea of them. But once to see such a man as Huxley is never to forget him'. *Huxley* uses a 'ciné theory' of narration, with its historiography hidden, to conjure up a flesh-and-blood picture of T. H. Huxley.[5] It is an unashamedly *social* portrait, which pans across London's splashy streets to catch him in action – and it locates him firmly in a reforming, industrializing, urbanizing, Dickensian context, with its slums, its trade unions and its great debates on evolution, emancipation and moral authority.

Thomas Henry Huxley came from nowhere, proud, pushy, a new Luther looking for a pulpit. He was half mad at times, messianic at others. An outsider with a cutting tongue and a chip on his shoulder, he would claw his way from the dockside slums to the presidency of the 'Parliament of Science', the British Association for the Advancement of Science. He rose with the muddy-booted engineers, the industrial Dissenters hacking at the obstructive Anglican edifice. His life is a chronicle of the rising middle classes. It is also the tale of a society in crisis, out of which came today's technocratic world.

He was born into an age of bishops in cauliflower wigs deliberating on God's goodness in Nature. At the end he was riding a penny-farthing through a new world, of trains, telephones and electric lights. He left a secular society probing human ancestry, a society led by intellectuals proudly wearing his 'agnostic' badge.

The wrenches as England industrialized told in his gritty, tub-thumping, scientific life, with its hunger and pain, and its campaign for a new intellectual aristocracy. Beatrice Webb saw 'a strain of madness in him'.[6] Indeed the whole family had its ups and downs – scandals, traumas and asylums were as much a part of his private world as the medals, presidencies and praise.

There was a flawed perfection to Huxley as no other eminent Victorian. Contradictions wrapped themselves up in his tall, wiry frame: he was the great educational reformer who had next to no formal education; the sceptic who made Biblical phraseology his stock-in-trade ('Pope Huxley', the *Spectator* dubbed him); the materialist with a messianic streak. He tailored evolution to middle-class needs. He harangued, he applied it to man and mind, even worse he took it to the masses. And yet he had excruciating trouble assimilating Darwin's doctrine of Natural Selection himself.

'Extinguished theologians', ran one of his wonderfully blood-curdling slogans, 'lie about the cradle of every science as the strangled snakes beside that of Hercules'.[7] For a century histori-ans have debated, championed and denounced Huxley's 'war' on theology. But why did he rise like Saul to 'smite the Amalekites' – these enemies of his scientific Israel? And how are we to interpret the 'warfare' anyway? As rational science triumphing over holy obscurantism? At the dawn of the twenty-first century 'reason' seems a precarious, value-laden yardstick, and one which has an infuriating habit of changing allegiance. In Huxley's young day, it lay with the natural theologians. Not only is the 'warfare' image hackneyed; so is the reaction to it – the demilitar-ized history born in the 1970s, which smoothes over the Victorian conflict.[8] The point is not to deny the struggle, any more than to refight the good fight. It is to understand the social currents that carried this rapier-wielding doubting Thomas to power.

So this is no cardboard cut-out history, with Huxley the sheriff 'placed on Boot Hill to clean up the town' of stubble-chinned theologians.[9] It is the nuances that make history interesting, and it is the tableau that carries this ciné style of narration. We have to capture the rich texture of his emotional, religious, scientific life, trace his Unitarian friendships, his Christian Socialist backers, his broad alliances with an avant garde raging against the privileged

Anglican Church.[10] If we see him developing a rival profession of science, with its ideological roots in industrial Dissent, the antagonisms begin to clear up.

And we can only do that by prising open the closed areas of his life. The teenage Huxley is unknown: no papers have been published on his shadowy medical origins, no books entitled *Young Huxley*, no Ph.D theses on his opium-hazed teachers or his skew-hatted student days.[11] Darwin's gentrified opulence was never his. Huxley's birth above a butcher's shop spoke for itself. His was a world of sots and scandals, of debts and ne'er-do-wells. He was a man on the make, a 'plebeian', he said. We have to track him through the slums that made Dickens shudder, through a turbulent student world – of Gin Palace lowlife and fiery medical democrats. Understand the Church-baiting, reforming 1830s and 1840s and Huxley's public emergence in 1851, 'soul sickened and sceptical', makes sense.[12]

The newer approaches to science, emphasizing its class and social underpinnings, push us further in that direction. Only a backcloth of steam factories, professionalization, imperial expansion, liberal Dissent and *laissez-faire* will allow us to appreciate why Huxley's New Model Army of outsiders pledged its allegiance, not to the aristocracy and clergy, but to the captains of industry.

The *enfant terrible* scrambled to the top of his profession; indeed he *made* a profession of science. With him the 'scientist' was born. In Darwin we see an older ideal, the wealthy, self-financed gent whose home was his laboratory – and in Huxley twentieth-century corporate science in the making.

Bishops' wives were astounded that he wasn't a sort of scientific Jack the Ripper; 'and yet', one exclaimed, 'I hear that he is a devoted husband & an affectionate father'.[13] Behind the headlines lay this quieter Huxley, the family man, the teacher, the fossil expert who showed that dinosaurs were the ancestors of today's birds. Here too we see the *realpolitik*. Everyone knows of his clash with a purple-vested Bishop Wilberforce in 1860, when Huxley declared that he would rather have an ape for a grandfather than a bishop who prostituted his gifts. But who knew that the two were quietly working together in the Zoological Society, sacking drunken keepers and arranging exhibits?

Huxley was a new breed of star performer. He transported audiences to strange dinosaurian worlds, or conjured up alien pithecoid people. Bushy-bearded labourers with blistered hands flocked to his talks on our ancestry. He drew the sort of crowds that are reserved for evangelists or rock stars today. Two thousand were turned away from St Martin's Hall in London one Sunday when he delivered his sermon on material salvation (the outraged Lord's Day Observance Society promptly stopped the lecture series). He was the most scintillating scientific missionary to stand on a soap-box.

That Victorian shrine, the *Life and Letters of Thomas Henry Huxley*, is a splendidly cracked monument, like an old imperial statue, good in its day for inspiring the troops, but now covered in historiographic vines. In 1900 it did not matter that the letters were bowdlerized and contracted.[14] As we approach 2000 it does, and the new microfilm edition of his 5,000 letters, diaries and manuscripts housed at Imperial College in London has enabled me to retranscribe them – and to discover how many of Huxley's famous *bon mots* were Victorian misquotes.

The *Times* claimed that no one could 'estimate the forces which have been at work to mould the intellectual, moral, and social life of the century' without appreciating T. H. Huxley. It is crucial today, as the aftershocks of the great Victorian crisis of faith rumble on in the West, to understand this 'apostle Paul of the new teaching'.[15]

1825–1846

Dreaming my own Dreams

1

Philosophy Can Bake No Bread

THE LANKY 15 year-old sidled down fetid alleys, past gin palaces and dance halls. Sailors hung out of windows, the gaiety of their boozy whores belying the squalor around them. The boy's predatory looks and patched clothes seemed in keeping. But his black eyes betrayed a horror at the sights: ten crammed into a room, babies diseased from erupting cesspits, the uncoffined dead gnawed by rats. The scenes would scar him for life.

In 1841 young Tom Huxley was in a twilight world. For a highly strung, sensitive lad the degradation was numbing. Daily the drug-grinder's apprentice threaded his way through East London's hovels. He carried a little muslin bag, but his drugs proved useless when the people 'were suffering from nothing but slow starvation'.

The century's worst recession had left mass unemployment. It showed in the haggard faces of his patients. Each wretched garret brought sorry sights, of bedridden seamstresses with no better food than 'bread and bad tea'. How could he suggest a healthy diet? One deformed girl, nursing her sister, 'turned upon me with a kind of choking passion. Pulling out of her pocket a few pence and halfpence, and holding them out, "That is all I get for six-and-thirty hours' work, and you talk about giving her proper food"'. Tom trudged ahead of the Grim Reaper, unable to stay his scythe. He watched the paupers succumb, mortality statistics scratched on the 'ledgers of death'.

Night-time found him in his tiny dockside surgery, venting his anger. The wide-eyed boy who loved metaphysics and religion and dreamed his way into the immensity of geological time asked himself: how could a 'solitary Philosopher' be 'happy in the midst of poverty'?[1] The pleading faces were to haunt him for life. They put the moral fire into his drive for a New Reformation. Christianity had failed the starving. Politics had failed them. The young evangelical would look for a new sort of salvation.

Thomas Henry Huxley's was an ignominious beginning. Not for him Darwin's silver spoon; he had no fortune to inherit, no family tradition to uphold. He was born on 4 May 1825 above a butcher's shop in Ealing, a small village 12 miles west of London. His father was an 'active intelligent man', but intelligence hadn't gained him success. Tall and dark, George Huxley bequeathed to his youngest son a quick temper and a 'glorious firmness which one's enemies called obstinacy'. He passed on little else, except a talent for drawing, which would give Tom his eye for capturing a rainforest or a reptilian fossil. George had been teaching mathematics at Ealing School for 18 years when Tom was born. It was a minor public school, relying on Classics and discipline to stiffen the backbone of the Anglican nation, and already in precipitous decline. At the time of Waterloo it had boasted 300 pupils, and George had taught John Henry Newman (the future Catholic cardinal) before that. From the school the Newman brothers had acquired their intense evangelical bias. But the fall in its fortunes had left George Huxley penniless.

His father's neglect bred a bitterness in Tom and he compensated by doting on his mother. Rachel was 'a "Cockney" born within the sound of Bow Bells' (although of Devonshire descent) and already 40 when she gave birth to Thomas Henry, her sixth and youngest surviving child. The boy's love for her was 'a passion'. He 'laid awake for hours crying because I had a morbid fear of her death – her approbation was my greatest reward and her displeasure my greatest punishment'. From his mother came 'the tone of his inner spiritual life', a pious, moral, questing, questioning spiritual life, never content, never at rest. The boy's emotional submergence was total. He had his mother's slender build and black eyes, and even the twiddling movements of her fingers. Her lightning intuition was his: 'things flash across me', she would say. That trait would serve Tom well as he rose to become a star performer in the Victorian firmament. Maternal wit and paternal temper formed an explosive combination. They left Tom quick and sharp, with a short fuse and a low flashpoint.

This mental ferocity had its matching exterior. Tom's piercing eyes and penetrating stare were set off by a raptorial mouth. His boyhood years did nothing to diminish this predatory look. He grew lean and gangling, with straight black hair and a permanent sarcastic expression, signalling a lethal bite. It went with the mocking surplice, as the boy turned his collar back to front and preached 'to my mother's maids in the kitchen'.[2]

The Huxleys were a strange, impassioned family, permanently at odds, with no vice or virtue that was not exaggerated in the youngest member. Being 'much younger than the rest', Tom rarely saw his brothers and grew up 'while they were little more than strangers to me'. He was heroically alone, or so an inner voice told him – paternal neglect and poverty leaving him 'without [much formal] education and without friends of my own age, left to quench my own running thirst for knowledge as I but might'. A battling mentality gave him inner strengths, but the insularity bred a bitter streak. Cocooned in his mental world, he became introspective and 'one of the most secretive thin-skinned mortals in the world'.

Of his three brothers, James was four years older and 'the only one for whom I felt any inkling of affection'. Jim and Tom were lookalikes, the identical hot-tempered, hyperactive pair who 'can't take things easily'. Both were feisty, but Tom had the laconic edge. The oldest brother, George Knight Huxley, was the staid one, already on his way to becoming a barrister and businessman when Tom was a toddler. He would subsidize the others in their hours of need: 'my sage and prudent brother', Tom called him. 'The truth is . . . we are all three too much alike to get on well. Our intense though hidden selfishness lies at the root of each of our characters, and is the source of its good & its evil'. It gave them a 'determination & force of character'.[3] It also put the poison into their clashes. The third brother, William, was eventually estranged by one of these boiling feuds and Tom never saw him again.

The sympathy and security came from his raven-haired sister Lizzie. Indeed, 'of the surprising six people who sprang from our father & mother', Tom always told her, 'you and I are the only two who seemed to be capable of fraternal love'. Nine years older, she was a mother figure and adored accordingly. Like so many daughters in large households, she was the unsung heroine. She helped with Tom's religious training and, speaking French and German, fired the boy's interest in Goethe. Theirs was an intense bond, never to be broken. Tom was more detached from the elder sister, Ellen, and when her life took a disastrous turn he could only 'marvel' that she and Lizzie 'sprang from the same stock'.[4]

At the age of eight, in 1833, Tom started in his father's school, and a 'Pandemonium of a school' at that. Twenty-four months there was the only schooling he had in his life. By now Ealing School had dwindled to 40 pupils. The fall in standards was even more evident and the masters 'cared about as much for our intellectual and moral welfare as if they were baby-farmers'. Burly louts terrorized the younger lads, although 'bullying was the least of the ill practices'. He must have studied Ovid and Virgil, music and mathematics, but all he could remember was laying out the class tough, William Poideoin. The wiry Tom had always been victimized, 'but there was a wild-cat element in me which, when roused, made up for lack of weight' and, notwithstanding a black eye, 'I licked my adversary effectively'.[5] This David and Goliath image would become an emblem of a life's struggle in a hostile society.

The school's decline crippled Tom's father. His '28 years faithful service' counted for nought; his fees collapsed and in 1835 he abandoned teaching.[6] George, at 55, took the family north to his native Coventry, armed with a letter of recommendation from old boy Newman.

So Tom spent his early teens footloose in the silk-weaving city of Coventry. Here his grandfather had owned 'a large old inn' while raising his family on a farm a few miles from the city, but he had died in debt and both had been sold 30 years before Tom's birth. The city was small enough to amble around in an hour. Hemmed in by commons and landed estates, it had become ingrown and choked. Rows of half-timbered houses hid hives of congested courts containing most of the 30,000 inhabitants. Every house had its loom, turning out fancy ribbons for the lower classes. Down endless terraces Tom saw them, little bent men pressed against clattering looms, with women and children winding the silk.

George Huxley took over Coventry's new Savings Bank. This should have been a wise move, as retrenchment in Parliament was mirrored by penny-pinching in private life, and the 'old stocking gave way to the savings-bank'. Everywhere the ethic was evident: the Huxley family arrived to find the ribbon masters sweeping the Anglican gentry out of the Town Hall after the first civic elections, and selling the corporation silver to pay for reforms. The bank was no less a symbol of thrift and self-sufficiency.

But the weavers never trusted it. A leaked word from the bank about their savings and the boss might cut their wages. And anyway they had their own friendly societies, legalized in 1836. Dozens sprang up in local pubs; here the weavers kept their own company, as they downed a pint and paid in their pennies.[7] Not that they could make any deposits, with the onset of a recession in 1837. The Ealing boy became used to 'their dialect and ways', and to their sallow faces (the silk's delicacy allowed them no windows or winter fires), but he saw few in his father's bank.

With his father struggling, Tom was thrown on to his own devices. He had no more schooling, 'nor sympathy in any intellectual direction'. It left him with a biting resentment. His sisters eked out a living with a dame school. Six year-olds would attend for a year before becoming winders on their fathers' looms. But as the corner shops collapsed and families starved on one hand-out loaf a week – plus a little 'mother's mercy' (opium) to 'deaden the gnawing wolf within' – the pennies for education vanished.

Tom recoiled into a fantasy world, escaping into a secret realm of science, 'dreaming my own dreams'. At 12, rummaging through his father's library, he encountered James Hutton's *Theory of the Earth*, that aimless eternal earth, wheeling on, with no signs of a beginning and 'no prospect of an end'. Voyaging through the vastness, Tom became withdrawn, his emotions confused. From his nightly cosmic wanderings came 'Joys and anticipation', where daily reality brought only disappointment in 'all those whom I had reason to love and value most'. Cynical and sad, he saw 'absolutely nothing to bring me into contact with the world – and I hated and avoided it'.[8]

He could ramble over the surrounding commons, past villages 'black with coal dust . . . and broken by Dissent'. But each cottage showed the same sickly occupants. Peering through their windows revealed scenes of appalling filth, with pregnant 16 year-old daughters destined for a life of drudgery. Tom did not need to be told by the sour-stomached critic Thomas Carlyle that society had to be cleansed. But reading the essayist did give him a sense of religious mission which owed nothing to a decrepit theology. Young Tom learned that new heroes were needed – Great Men with a sense of destiny.

Carlyle also taught him the heroic quality of work. Play was not for Tom, nor any of the 'pursuits of boys of my own age'. Carlyle breathed the Alpine air of German romanticism and Tom took up the language. It was another fortification; scholarly airs could shield a sensitive soul. Friends found him 'pretending to make hay with one hand, while in the other he held a German Book!'⁹ The turgid tomes were mischievously hidden at picnics, but the ribbing only increased the boy's aloofness.

Intellectually stifled, he sought out older men, ribbon masters. But still this upstart David showed his slingshot mentality. Even among these manufacturers he 'was too proud to be treated as one whit of less importance than they'. But his mentors were indulgent and well versed, Unitarians and Independents, marginal men developing new forms of knowledge. Their Chapel science was based on natural causes rather than the Anglicans' miracles. Such materialism went with the wheeze-and-snort of steam. No supernatural lore to underpin the status quo for them: the ribbon masters' earthy science was to move society on. It was to usher in the cotton millennium. Power-looms went with dissent. Often they went with doubt: it was 'an age of darkness, and yet of brightness ... *Steam, iron, smoke, egoism, doubt*, and *distrust*, are all alike in colour'. In Coventry the future George Eliot lost her Puritan faith. And here Thomas Huxley's religious pilgrimage began.

In one businessman, George May, Tom found a sympathetic ear and an appealingly irreverent approach. The Lord's Day was not so much for observance as to argue the ground of all existence:

> Sunday. Hinckley. Had a long argument with Mr.
> May on the nature of the soul & difference between
> it & matter[.] I maintained that it cannot be proved
> that matter is *essentially* – as to its base – different
> from soul. Mr. M. wittily said, soul was the
> perspiration of matter – We cannot find the
> absolute basis of matter we only know it by its
> properties neither know we the soul in any other
> way ...[10]

This ethereal talk was set against a background clatter. Three new steam factories went up in Coventry in 1836–8. Steam power promised a new destiny. It might even have been Tom's. Stephenson's locos were speeding faster every year, too fast for Coventry, bypassed as the first London-Birmingham railway in 1838 took away its road trade. But it was electricity that fascinated Tom. He jotted memos in a hand-stitched notebook – 'make a galv. battery' or 'try the expt. of a simple galvanic current', wondering if he could crystallize carbon. He was always seeking components, causes, mechanisms. His imagination stretched to the heavens, looking for ultimate particles or 'speculating on the cause of colours at sunset'.[11]

But industry was not to be Tom's destiny. Every Coventry lad became an apprentice. It was a peculiar city, where only those who had served a seven-year indenture (in any trade) could become voters. For a boy fascinated by philosophy, his apprenticeship could only be in medicine. Even then he faced an ethical dilemma, studying while the poor starved. He justified himself with an epi-graph in his notebook: 'Philosophy can bake no bread; but it can pro-cure for us God freedom & immortality. Which now is more practical Philosophy or Economy'?[12] It was a question for life.

Both sisters married medical men in 1839. The urban build-up created an urgent need for doctors. The silk-paternalists had opened a second dispensary, where the weavers picked up their drugs for a penny-a-week subscription. An old part-timbered house was even being converted into Coventry's first hospital. Tom tunnelled the cheapest way into the cheapest profession, burrowing behind brother Jim. Lizzie's husband, 39 year-old surgeon's son John Salt, had already apprenticed Jim. Even before Ellen's mar-riage, her own beau John Charles Cooke was teaching Tom the trade.

Cooke was a beer-swilling, opium-chewing man of massive medical lore, a rambunctious entrepreneur who could teach any-thing for a fee: anatomy, obstetrics, pharmacy or forensic medicine. While training Tom he was editing a huge compendium of medical lectures. Not just *any* lectures, but those of the flamboyant John Elliotson: a fierce materialist who saw the brain pour out thoughts as the liver does bile – a *provocateur* whose outrageous Spinozaism took away the soul and the 'consoling' Christian hopes 'of the despised and the miserable'.[13] Elliotson was a brilliant innovator, whose mesmeric experiments were positively theatrical. (Too much so even for London's 'godless' University College, which sacked him after his hypnotized patients caused havoc.) Cooke never shied away from heresy or hard work.

Tom began at 13 under Cooke, not gently, in deference to his tender years, but traumatically. The lad entered a dissecting room to find a naked cadaver – a cold body and a dead brain which had once glowed with hopes and desires. His morbid curiosity 'over-powered all other feelings'. He stood for hours, transfixed by the gruesome probing as the corpse was dismembered. The human gore was emotionally shattering. He fell into a strange lethargy.

For weeks he deteriorated, 'poisoned' somehow, until he looked 'thin and ill'.[14] His distraught parents sent him to a friend's farm, where the catharsis of haymaking carried him back to an innocent past and worked its healing power. Farmyard smells would always remind him of his rebirth on those sweet autumn mornings, even if the scars never quite healed.

He began questioning the meaning of evil and death. How did it square with God's beneficence? It did not, according to Southwood Smith's *Divine Government*, that Unitarian bible which Tom read at George May's. This was a provocative book – a plea that poverty and distress were signs that society had taken a wrong turn and that reform was a divine duty. 'Agree with him partly', Tom jotted on 25 October 1840. But wouldn't the Unitarian's denial of Christ's divinity and miracles have an 'injurious effect on morals'?

Coventry exposed Tom to a biting sectarianism. He heard the shrieking denunciations of Anglican privilege – to tithes and church rates, to the Church monopoly on Oxbridge education and professional posts. These were the corrupt fruits of State endowment. Radicals saw the Church continuing to 'commit fornication, until the Dissenters tear her ... from her ILLICIT EMBRACE' with the State. Tom was among defiant, proud men whose resistance to the Church had been unprecedented. Some 50,000 summonses a year had been issued by the clergy to prise tithe money out of the Dissenters. After reading Southwood Smith, Tom had 'a long talk with my mother & father about the right to make Dissenters pay church rates – & whether there ought to be any Establishment – I maintained that there ought not in both cases'.[15] He was learning the morality of civil disobedience.

In the anatomy schools the sectarian factions were buzzing with discontent. 'I hate all people who want to found sects', Tom jotted. 'It is not error but sectarian error – nay & even sectarian truth w^h. causes the unhappiness of mankind'. Yet he could not keep his fingers out of the fire. In an age when students dabbled in immensities, he argued passionately about Creation. So intense were the discussions on 'medical metaphysics' during classes that one teacher was 'afraid that ... *common physic*, by which so many of us "live, and move, and have our being," will fall to the ground!'[16]

Now Tom had to think seriously about common physic himself.

*

At 15 he took his first real look at the Great Babylon. Both brothers-in-law had gone to London, Salt to practise, Cooke to teach. On 7 January 1841 he followed them down.

In Buckingham Palace the popular young Queen Victoria, three years on the throne and only 21, had just married Prince Albert. In Parliament peers still ruled and patronage guaranteed all things. Lord Melbourne was Prime Minister, and the great Whig salons held power – but only just. The reform drive of the 1830s – with its acts to widen the middle-class vote and democratize the town halls, and its bills to benefit Dissenters (who had even been forced to marry in Anglican churches) – had petered out. In 1841 Sir Robert Peel was set to put the Conservatives back on the government benches. Not that the 'benches' were much for Tom to look at, being in the patched-up portion of the Houses of Parliament, which had been gutted by fire in 1834.

London – haloed in a 'sublime canopy' of smoke, with its gas-lit streets and islands of gentrified opulence. Fashionable carriages paraded through Hyde Park flaunting their wealth. The world's largest city, a sea of 2 million faces, bred a numbing awe. One could drown in the 'ocean stream of life' flowing down Regent Street. Nothing matched the elegance of Mayfair, or Nash's stucco terraces around Regent's Park. Opulence, anonymity and round-the-clock activity gave the city an excitement unknown in the provinces.

But Tom saw little of this salubrious side. Cooke had apprenticed him to Thomas Chandler, a lowlife doctor in the East End. There the gloomy waves were of the hovelled poor, wallowing in filth and disease. He had entered a dark world, penetrated only by missionaries shocked by the 'moral degradation'. London had its vile excesses too.

That January Tom found himself alone in a tiny Rotherhithe surgery. The horrors he saw there were to mark him for life. The East London poor were as little known as 'the savages of Australia'. Yet no aborigine, he later remarked, was 'half so savage, so unclean' as these troglodyte tenement dwellers. Rooms were putrid from overflowing cesspools. Even sanitation pioneers such as Southwood Smith (who took Dickens to see the fever nests) needed a 'dose of fanaticism, as a sort of moral coca', to stomach the sights.[17] Starvation left the children emaciated and typhus killed them. Even death brought its own shame. Wasteland burials were so common in Rotherhithe that rotting bodies were thrown up with each new interment. It was a macabre winter.

Thomas Chandler was a reforming practitioner,[18] a former House Surgeon at University College Hospital and full of Elliotson's hypnotic techniques. Tom watched him mesmerize his delirious patients, passing his hands rhythmically over their faces, putting them into a calming sleep. The trance was a 'marvellous remedy' for gnashing fits and incurable tics, his speciality, and he had plenty of twitching maniacs to practise on.[19]

Tom must have sensed the shambles around him. Mesmerism, though it gave the underprivileged General Practitioners more power, was a two-edged sword. People were getting hold of it. Young girls sleepwalking on stage were turning the practice into a sexually charged side-show attraction. Street 'patterers' carried lurid placards announcing a new pamphlet 'The Diabolical Practices of Dr − − − on his Patient when in a state of Mesmerism'.[20] While reformers were trying to police medicine, circumscribing it in their own professional hands, lay performers were running amok.

In the nine years since the 1832 Reform Bill the medical ranks had been in revolt. They too wanted a widening of their power, a say in the running of the elite licensing bodies, the Royal Colleges of Physicians and Surgeons. General Practitioners were unionizing and attacking the knightly hospital consultants who ran the colleges like rotten boroughs. Chandler's mesmerists were milling with the rest outside the porticoes of the Oxbridge-Anglican Establishment. Tom was swept along, listening to the shouts for talent before rank, watching as his medical class tried to gain a say.

The turbulence tossed the boy about. A boy he still was. 'I have had my trowsers seated', he told his mother, 'but I have grown lately & they are outrageously short – the best wear I am sorry to say very badly – wear white & shabby – But Nelly inspected me the last time I was in London . . . & I dare say you have received an "*official*" account'.[21]

There were breaks in the gloom for Tom: Jim might arrive, or he would visit a theatre with 'Aunt Lizzy' (his mother's cousin Eliza Knight). But by day the youngster steeled himself for his slum rounds. His surgery was on Paradise Street, itself a sick joke. He was a hundred paces from the water's edge, traced down dark alleys between the warehouses and pubs. Here, on a sewage-slimy Thames, as belching smoke and river fog blended into choking pea-soupers, one drew 'gloom with every breath'.

The deformed garret-dwellers showed the need for a new kind of regeneration. The Church was a rich man's luxury, irrelevant here. 'I dare say there ain't ten out of a hundred gals what's living with men', a costermonger said, 'what's been married Church of England fashion'. The Bible held no hope and word-of-mouth ignorance acquired mythic proportions. But there was a dumb perspicacity on the streets, and a casual incredulity about rich folks' notions. One ragged girl had heard:

> that the world was made in six days: the beasts, the birds, the fish, and all . . . There was only one house at that time as was made, and that was the Ark for Adam and Eve and their family. It seems very wonderful indeed how all this world was done so quickly. I should have thought that England alone would have took double the time.[22]

A new foundation for living was needed, a new way of controlling mores and freeing people. Factory workers were marching, demanding the vote and annual ballots, uniting in support of the democratic People's Charter. Tom read Carlyle's *Chartism* on this 'bitter discontent grown fierce and mad'. Riot police were no solution; society had an obligation to the destitute. Duty to the working classes was *Chartism*'s message. Something had to step in where Christianity had failed. The seething slums, Tom said, gave 'a terrible foundation of real knowledge to my speculations'. Science had to pay social dividends.

He sat grinding drugs in his apothecary's shop, reading: 'in that little narrow surgery I used to work morng after morng & eveng after eveng', ploughing through 'that insufferably dry & profitless book Humes *History* [of Great Britain]. how I worked against hope through the series of thefts robberies & throat cutting in those three first vols'. The despair mirrored his surroundings. Rotherhithe was notorious for the knife-wielding gangs in its criminal slums, and its underbelly of 'whores, pandars, crimps, bullies'.[23] But the real obscenity was the middle-class indifference to this ocean of poor.

'*Cursed is the ground*' indeed. Engulfed by drunks and whores the boy became guilt-ridden. He anguished over the 'deep draught of abomination I took'. Remorse led to mental flagellation, that evangelical comfort: 'I confess to my shame', he said, 'that few men have drunk deeper of all kinds of sin than I'. He had to regenerate himself before he 'earned absolute destruction'.

Guilt came from being middle-class among the destitute. The starving were mostly decent people, whose only crime was poverty. 'I see no fault committed that I have not committed myself', he jotted (it was Goethe's aphorism). He remained a Puritan in this moral rectitude and resignation, but he could never accept the notion of innate depravity. There had to be hope. He moved closer to Southwood Smith's view of earthly salvation. Acquiescence in the face of such poverty was a sin; 'redeeming the people from a degraded condition is a duty', Smith had insisted. Welfare and educational programmes must bring society back in line with God's benevolent intent.[24] Tom had begun his own regeneration. Monastic study would put him on the road to redemption.

He spent nights tackling chemistry and history, then came Latin and Greek. He would work his way out of the quagmire. He set his sights on University College, that emblem of Dissenting aspiration, with its radical French sciences and Benthamite economics, all a snub to Oxford and Cambridge exclusivity. By April 1841 spare hours were devoted to algebra, geometry and physics. Letters went off to his mother: 'I got the books all right', but is 'there not a Latin Grammar at home, & an Euclid? I am glad my father sent Hutton for I like it much the best but the college requires Euclid'.

Lists tumbled out of him, read this, read that, followed by admonishing progress reports. By the summer he was deep in physiology, having dumped Hume's *History* 'in utter disgust & despair'. Like all self-improvers he had faith in book learning; education became a passion, as it did with so many radicals seeking 'bread, knowledge and freedom', convinced that self-improvement was a path to power. The new steam presses had caused prices to plummet, and with the newspaper tax down to a penny (the hated tax was a failed government initiative to crush the pauper press) the streets were awash with radical prints. Swamping them was the *Penny Magazine*, 200,000 subsidized copies a week to divert the masses with more innocuous knowledge. Tom flew high and low, ploughing through Müller's *Elements of Physiology* while picking up insect trivia in the *Penny Cyclopaedia*.

There was no wilier product of the 'Steam Intellect' society than Tom Huxley. His workbench discipline was extraordinary. Week in, week out he kept up a punishing schedule: on Tuesdays and Thursdays physiology, on other weekdays a 'chronological abstract of reigns', evenings of arithmetic, Saturdays devoted to chemistry and physics, with an hour's German each day. In between he grappled with Guizot's *Civilization in Europe* and built electromagnets. Always he pushed harder: 'I must get on faster than this', he chivvied himself as he fell behind in Ancient History, 'and let me remember this – that it is better to read a little & thoroughly than cram a crude undigested mass into my head'.[25]

With an intellectual head of steam Tom packed his books and escaped the ghetto late in 1841. He moved in with sister Lizzie and John Salt. At 14 Euston Place, next to the new Euston Station, they were close to University College Hospital. Tom and Jim, that identical pair, were living in tandem. As Jim left Salt's apprentice-ship and went to Gloucester Lunatic Asylum as dispensing chemist, Tom moved in. Lizzie was protective towards her little brother. She pushed him on, sure of his bright future.[26] Here family life was more congenial, and Tom adored her year-old daughter Jessie, who was just starting to walk.

Euston Place was a medical enclave. It saw the comings-and-goings of professors and swaggering students with their '"loudly" dressed' look. Tom's other brother-in-law John Cooke was a neighbour at No 18.[27] He had come down to teach across the road at a cut-price anatomy school, Sydenham College. This was among the last of the private schools, set up behind University College Hospital. 'Dingy purlieus' these places were, often converted houses, offering cheap courses to lure students away from the hospitals. They were breeding grounds for dissidents, their angry teachers engaged in a dirty war with the elite surgeons. The drop in student numbers during the depression only exacerbated this rivalry. Survivors like Sydenham College were clinging on at the bottom end of the market.

Tom took the affordable option. He enrolled at Sydenham College in October 1841. More floats from his brothers-in-law saw him through – £4 for the medicine course, £5 for chemistry, £2 for Cooke's forensic medicine class.[28] A 'mildewy appearance' marked his fellows: plaid trousers, long hair topped by stove-pipe hats, the reek 'of full-flavoured Cubas'. Add to this dissolute air a proud and opinionated voice, and that was Tom. At night deep-dish discussions grew slurred in the grogshops as the hot topics were aired: mesmerism, medical reform, Chartism, the poor laws, and not least the reflex arc – that new concept pioneered at Sydenham College (and slated by the medical barons as soulless and 'mechanis-tic', because the reflex jerk was not under conscious control: the body was acting as an automaton). Not to mention the eternal verities: *Punch* lampooned the students' tipsy forays into metaphys-ics, with skew-hatted reprobates prodding one another: 'What you say about Corporeity is all very well, but it presupposes the idea of

– (hic) – absolute spirituality and transcendental – (hic) – perfection . . .'[29] The topic was Tom's to a tee.

In these back-street schools flaming politics were fuelled by emancipatory science. The Dissenting teachers spat at rank and wealth; some worked in gin palaces or brought petitions for their pupils to sign. They made morals cultural products, they made thought a function of brain matter, and they claimed the entire mental realm for the new medical expert. They were tearing the spiritual halo from mind and nature and usurping the role of the priest. These angry Dissenters demanded professional parity with the State-supported clergy. No wonder Dr Arnold at Rugby School saw a generation of 'materialist atheists of the greatest personal profligacy' being raised in this Sodom and Gomorrah.[30] But most of all the firebrands screamed defiance at the 'medical aristocracy'.

That was even true of the urbane coffee-drinking Marshall Hall, founder of Sydenham College and discoverer of the reflex arc. As head of a radical ginger group, the British Medical Association, he damned the College of Physicians for its Anglican exclusivity:

> Can anything be imagined more preposterous, more
> iniquitous, more *immoral*, than this mingling of sacred
> things with profane, of religious with medical distinctions
> and privileges? Of religion it is a mockery; it is hypocrisy
> . . . it is intolerance; it is, in a word, the same fire which
> consumed the bodies of our fellow-men in Smithfield![31]

Tom heard the call for merit before Church privilege. Hall was trying to open up the top jobs to talent. He could be seen in college, dissecting turtles to prove his reflex arc, although outside his science and politics were derided by conservatives.

While the top hospitals trained the gentry's consultants – those 'plundering monopolists' who took the plum jobs at the Royal Colleges – Tom's school taught the humble GPs. These were destined for the inner cities. They were the new men who soul-searched about slums and sanitation, who used the new secular sciences as a tool for education and liberation. And for their pains, they were despised as a 'low born cell-bred selfish' mob. Tom was clearly gazing up from below.

The medical world wasn't all demos and debauchery. Of course the press and pulpit focused on those 'anencephalous abortions of the human race' found drunk in class, but usually billiards and smoking were the worst excesses. Even these were eschewed by Tom. He stood apart 'isolated among my fellows, in habits, in thought and still more by poverty'. Not 'by any means shy, in fact, quite t'other', but he was 'as sensitive as a woman, as proud as Satan and as poor as a church mouse'.[32]

Still, like *Punch*'s drunks he began 1842 grappling with imponderables. Studying muscles and bones only sent him soaring into the clouds. Trying to pigeon-hole all knowledge as either 'physical' or 'metaphysical', he stopped short at 'morality'.[33] The boy had been buffeted by so many winds that he no longer knew whether morality was a cultural product or God's gift; the former, he began to suspect. He had become a radical; long-haired still, but with a straight stovepipe and sober breath.

2

Son of the Scalpel

TOM NOW LOOKED THE part, a serious study in shabbiness, his cast-off clothes tailored to his cut-price school: 'a very pale, thin, lanky, ugly body with dreadfully long hair which no persuasion would induce me to cut, and a generally neglected style of attire'.[1]

But still Lizzie saw in her Bohemian brother the family's deliverance. 'My highest hopes are centred in that boy', she always said.[2] In April 1842 she was vindicated: Tom took his first certificates of merit at the Sydenham College awards.

Fortified, he pushed on after Easter, registering for the spring botany course. Or perhaps he was egged on by Cooke, an expert on medicinal plants. His new teacher, like so many in these parlous private schools, was an idiosyncratic outsider – or rather an insider turned out, an Oxford-trained clergyman who had lost his vocation and was looking to a new salvation. This was Richard Hoblyn. A kindly soul with a friendly face, Hoblyn was now eking out a living by writing chemistry manuals and books on steam engines, and teaching botany to top up.[3] (When all else failed he went into business with Cooke, cramming London University applicants for their entrance exams.)

Unable to afford the 3*d* bus fare, Tom strode the four miles from Euston to Chelsea to hear the nurseryman's son and University College lecturer John Lindley at the Physic Garden.[4] He hiked over two or three times a week, always finding Lindley ruddy-faced and hearty, in stark contrast to his students. Occasionally Tom was defeated in his trek. On 2 May 1842, two days before his 17th birthday, demonstrators taking the 30-foot Chartist petition to Parliament brought the capital to a standstill. Flyers went up everywhere, crowds waved tricolours. The depression was hitting London hard, with mass unemployment, and the 100,000 Chartists in a one-and-a-half-mile column blocked all routes. It was orderly, but ominous.

A different sort of flyer forced Tom's pace later in May. The Worshipful Company of Apothecaries announced its yearly competition for medals. (Apothecaries were the lowest of the disintegrating medical estates: drug compounders and General Practitioners, the shopkeeping class of medical men.) Tom looked 'longingly at the notice'. Salt urged him on, and Tom entered his name, telling no one else but Lizzie, fearfully ambitious but terrified of appearing vain. ('Virtue . . . aware of itself is sickly', he copied out of Carlyle.) He put in long hours for a young hand, from 8 am. until midnight.[5] He mined out Cooke's library and set into the nation's. Ten minutes away lay the British Museum. He marched past the Grenadiers guarding its entrance, past the rubble (the new wings were under a forest of scaffold), past masons sculpting stone colonnades, past horses turning giant cement mixers. He signed the visitors' book, glanced at the giraffes on the stairway, and headed for the library to lose more hours in the *Annales des Sciences Naturelles.*

For three summer months he kept up this regime. In the process he swept off Hoblyn's prize at Sydenham College, winning a book, *La Botanique.* As a diversion he pored over his homemade batteries, puzzling at the currents breaking up chemical solutions.[6] But the pace of each 'long hot summer's walk over to Chelsea' showed where his ambition lay – in the Apothecaries' medal.

On exam day, 1 August, he was a disembodied wreck. How he got to Apothecaries Hall in Blackfriars – 'Rhubarb Hall' to the students – he never knew. All he recalled was Lizzie throwing her slipper after him for luck. He sat, the youngest of six, at a long table, the candidates glaring 'at one another like strange cats in a garret'. Paper and plants were placed in front of each at 11 am. The invigilator opened his *Times* to read of the Chartist unrest. And there Tom sat, only the spine-tingling 'Scratch, scratch, scratch' disturbing the still air. At 4 pm. the others finished, but he and a rival asked to carry on, furiously competing, his fellow looking like 'an attorney's clerk writing for his dinner'. Tom, cramp in his hands, collapsed exhausted at 8 pm., his rival at 9 pm. It was his first public exam, an unprecedented eight hours of writing, and he would never forget it. Lizzie and Salt waited up, worried, and 'Great were the greetings . . . when I got home'.[7]

*

Brother Jim was muddling along at Gloucester Lunatic Asylum and the boys cogitated on their careers. Doubtless it was Cooke again who saw the opening. London's newest teaching hospital, Charing Cross, offered six free places a year.[8] Their father could scarcely afford the servant's-wage sum of £42 a year fees. So Jim and Tom, the identical hyperactive pair, continued their careers together: they both applied for free tuition.

Free scholarships were for the sons of destitute gents. Embarrassed vicars and surgeons applied for their boys, whose 'station in society gave them a just pretension'. Respectability was the watchword: two clergymen had to vouch that Tom's father was a distressed teacher 'unable to defray the expense'. Unlike the grubby back-street schools, Charing Cross was not prepared to open the floodgates to tinkers and chimney sweeps. Consultants feared the 'irruption of the Gothic hordes'. Even corner druggists were edging out the few labourers who had a foot on the slippery professional slope. Hospital managers looked into Huxley senior's 'station in society' and his sons' 'classical education' and 'moral character'.[9]

That August the 'Gothic hordes' were a sensitive subject. Tens of thousands were massing on London's commons; a General Strike paralysed the cotton towns as a protest against wage cuts. Demonstrators were shot in Preston, after a hail of stones stopped the Mayor reading the Riot Act. The clashes came closer, much closer: crowds jeered the columns of Grenadier Guards on their way to Euston Station to crush the northern strikers. Screams of 'Bloody Butchers' curdled the air. Outside Salt's house in Euston Square the troops had bayonets fixed. Yards from Tom's window baton-wielding police bludgeoned a path into the station. For a week in mid-August the family was besieged; daily the battalions ploughed their way in. Daily the crowds shouted 'Don't go and slaughter your starving fellow countrymen'. It was a confirmation that reform had failed the labouring classes. Subjected to workhouses and wage cuts, denied the vote or a decent living, they were clenching their fists. 'Nature, God, and reason, have condemned this inequality', announced the Chartist proclamation on 17 August.[10] It was a thought. What *did* Nature say of social inequality?

Through the uproar the boys continued to canvass the clergy's vote. Jim was safe in Gloucester, although even here a commotion arose as a demagogue was summonsed for a show trial. George Holyoake, young, fluent and provocative (or, in the *Times*' view, a 'miserable-looking lad' indulging in an 'absurd harangue') inflamed

Gloucester Crown Court by denying God. He added injury to the insult by suggesting that rich parsons go on half pay during the depression. In a nine-hour speech he toed the line of his gutter rag, the *Oracle of Reason* (penny trash which demanded a priest-free democratic society and used evolution to oust a patrician God). On 16 August the judge recognized the 'enormity' of Holyoake's blasphemy and jailed him for six months, leaving no doubt that cloth-cap atheism was taken as an attack on the Anglican State. There were no such scruples about the Church for Jim. He topped the clerical requirements by lining up five reverends as referees, which at least showed willing. But, like Tom, he was running up debts and had begun tapping Salt again. Charing Cross promised a career, he reassured Salt, and a chance to liquidate 'both principle and interest'.[11] Tom's thought exactly, with the country crumbling and the strike biting.

Salt and Cooke added their references, and stranger voices were heard. Father scrounged from his Ealing old-boys. The down-at-heel ex-master again doffed his cap to well-to-do pupils. By now there was no mightier High Church voice than that of John Henry Newman. He was enormously influential, fighting Church reform and reinstating Church ritual (even if he stood on a precipice, ready to jump over to Rome). The boys were a generation younger than Newman, born long after he had left Ealing. But their father still begged an endorsement for them, as he had once for himself.

Tom was happier pulling himself up by his own bootstraps. Everyone thought he had lost the Apothecaries' prize. Salt appeared one day with a dejected expression, having heard that the winners were University College men. 'Lizzie came to comfort me and I believe felt it more than I did'.

> What then was my surprise on returning home one afternoon to find myself suddenly seized and the whole female household vehemently insisting on kissing me. It appeared an official-looking letter had arrived for me, and Lizzie . . . could not restrain herself from opening it. I was second [and] to receive a medal accordingly.

The prospect of a silver medal on top of his Sydenham College prizes ensured his place at Charing Cross. On 6 September 1842 the managers took the unprecedented step of admitting both brothers.[12] So on 1 October 17 year-old Tom Huxley and superannuated Jim joined the sons of the surgeons and clergy as free scholars.

*

Charing Cross Hospital was solid and classical, shouting its philanthropic importance in the salubrious Strand. Building work had only finished in 1834, as the New Poor Law was put into place and the workhouses planned. At no time in the nineteenth century did sick paupers need more help. (The rich had their five-guinea consultants.) Fitting out the wards had taken the rest of the decade. These had been lean years for a charity serving London's swelling army of poor. When the Huxleys arrived the hospital was only just out of the red.

Decimus Burton's building stood on a small triangular strip, its main entrance on Agar Street (a short new road running off the Strand). Tom Huxley took rooms at No. 9, facing the porticoed entrance.[13] From here he could see the wan faces of the destitute crowding round the waiting room.

The plan had been grand: the first modern hospital, dispensary and medical school built as one. It sounded fine in the prospectus; in reality Huxley found only three upper floors finished and then some of the wards empty. The so-called 'medical school' was a few rooms in the basement between the morgue and the chapel. Frugality was the key. Cost-conscious managers ran it on a tight budget, as befitted a retrenching workhouse age. Huxley suffered with his patients: coal fires were extinguished at dusk as the gaslights went on. Budgeting even hit his canteen lunch. To 'avoid trouble and waste' it was always beef and it was always boiled.[14] No fish or pork was served, and no vegetables but potatoes and rice, each unappetizing platter saved by a little beer.

At least underground the din was muffled. The widened Strand with its new shopfronts was drawing Oxford Street's crowds, but nothing penetrated the sombre air of the morgue. Above was a crush of carriages, the clatter of iron rims on cobbles, so deafening that the Strand had just been experimentally resurfaced with wood. All around were entertainments, from gentlemen's clubs to the notorious Coal Hole, where carousers shouted their obscene 'evidence' during mock stage divorces. By day *Morning Chronicle* hacks rushed to their offices. At night revivalists preached at the 'profligate wretches' about them. They could be heard praising the Lord for reclaiming sots, or applauding missionaries from the heathen colonies. Well-meaning prigs, Huxley thought them; so many 'Stigginses', like the po-faced reverend in *Pickwick Papers*, wheedling money out of passers-by to provide 'the infant negroes of the West Indies with flannel waistcoats'. All life was here, from the hymn-singers of Exeter Hall to the 'gay' girls whistling a different tune outside. Huxley must have agreed with Dr Johnson: 'the full tide of existence is at Charing Cross'.[15]

Opposite on the Strand stood the rebuilt Hungerford Market. Its cavernous interior stretched down to the Thames, a jostling confusion of stalls and barrows, with women in bonnets and shawls shouting their wares. Huxley could rummage for old clothes, or fresh vegetables, or descend to the vaults for his whelks and fish – and coming out, he could pick up tea in the corner grocery.

The Strand improvements were not the only sign of civic pride. It was never as fashionable as Regent Street, but more interesting, with its kaleidoscopic facades. The real transformation was occurring in front of St Martin-in-the-Fields church. Nests of ramshackle houses had been cleared to make a huge open space. Huxley could stand on the site and look down Whitehall, or over to Pall Mall, or up to the new National Gallery. This was Trafalgar Square in the making. The people were being pushed out: imperial architecture and municipal pride had no place for the mangy poor.

The other end of the Strand was different. There the stench of social deprivation remained. Squalid, sewage-filled alleys made up the vile no-go rookeries around Drury Lane, whose sick and wounded swelled the hospital's casualty list – so much so that some gentlefolk saw the charity attracting this 'Lazarhouse of disease' back to the affluent end of town.[16]

For the hard-up pupils lured by the bright lights, there were non-medicinal leeches. Money-lenders clustered round the college, turning long-term students into long-term debtors.[17] Not that Tom needed them: Cooke could be tapped, and brother George was good for £30 floats.

At the hospital the surgeon daily walked the wards, dragging 'a miserable tail of a dozen joints'. By year's end the trailing students had seen a thousand patients from the rookeries and road crashes. Eight thousand were treated in Huxley's first year, gashes and building accidents, pouring in from every scaffolded site down to the Houses of Parliament (gutted by fire in 1834), not to mention the crushed limbs from the sewers being laid in the West End. Dickens, who had worked near by, was horrified by the 'ghastly appearance of the hapless creatures' in casualty. 'In one bed, lay a child enveloped in bandages, with its body half-consumed by fire', in another a woman 'in a heavy stupor', her face 'stained with blood'. One girl from the ghetto, thrashed so brutally by her man, died before his eyes. From these gin-sodden rookeries came endless stabbings and beatings. It was a sad fact that cases of 'personal violence' made up the third largest category of casualties.[18]

The 'Dame of the Wards' (matron) ensured a rigid regime, policing her untrained nurses and under-fed poor. Huxley withstood the spartan conditions and mercifully missed reveille: no patient was to be in bed after 7 am., all were to be scrubbed and ready for breakfast at 8 am., no swearing, no 'gross or filthy conduct' by staff or patients, no drunken visitors, no smoking. The squad of domestics doubling as nurses was drilled as tightly. They wore uniforms but they were poorly paid; the sots smuggled in gin for a tip, and fallen angels were regularly cast out. Huxley missed morning prayers in the wards, but not the vicar of St Martin-in-the-Fields on his rounds, performing his own spiritual surgery on the ungodly hovel-dwellers.

Just before 9am. Huxley fought his way through the out-patients (the waiting room was inside the Agar Street entrance), past the gaunt faces and emaciated bodies. Saddest were the hunchbacks and tykes with club-feet, come because the hospital specialized in deformities.[19] Others were dejected, turned away for simply being starving. Some did get in later, by the back entrance. They lay ready, boiled and flayed, for his 11 am. dissections. Unclaimed pauper corpses and workhouse dead were marked down for the medical school. This amid the outcry that, for the crime of being poor, the sentence was dismemberment:

> A worse than felon's doom! for when his life
> Returns to God! then, then the bloody knife
> Must to its work – the body that was starved,
> By puppy doctors must be cut and carved.[20]

And in the depths of the depression there was no shortage, particularly when the first snows fell.

Dissecting Drury Lane's dead was not for the squeamish. Huxley's teachers warned of this disagreeable duty, but he was becoming inured. Not so others, who fled in terror, faced by decapitated heads, hovered over by bloody scalpelled hands – the first fledgling reaction of ashen youths wanting to 'breathe again the salubrious atmosphere of the streets'.[21]

Huxley learned one lesson during these subterranean days. The *Lancet* rammed it home: nothing was to be seen except by dissection. While bad surgeons walked the wards reading 'from other people's bad books', life and death stared them in the face: 'medicine is a *trade*, and not a *science*', the *Lancet* insisted (jabbing at the elite consultants); the apprentice must learn by application.[22] Look for yourself – it was a motto he learnt for life.

On 9 November Huxley attended the Apothecaries' prize-giving 'and bore my share in both pudding and praise'. He collected his silver medal, querying the vanity of prizes. But he told himself that the real 'charm of success lay in Lizzie's warm congratulation'.[23] She in turn prophesied great things 'touching the future fortunes of "the boy"'. Her joy turned sour eight days later. At the height of the depression, with disease and starvation endemic, Lizzie's daughter Jessie died of scarlet fever. She was not two-and-a-half; it was Tom's first sight of death in the family and he was devastated. He could never look back on this period without 'Mental pain' erupting from the 'seething depths'.[24]

It was the beginning of his Charing Cross career and Huxley ground on in a gloom. He threw himself into work and derived inspiration from the strangest source: a godfearing teacher whose lectures were steely cold and whose former life had been too hot. This was the diminutive, lonely Thomas Wharton Jones. Every afternoon Huxley watched this drab, clerk-like man enter, wearing rusty broad-cloth. He stood at a table's edge, 'with downcast eyes, and fingering his watchchain', and talked a cold, clinical and enthralling physiology.[25] The Scots accent betrayed a haunted past. At Huxley's age he had been Robert Knox's assistant when the one-eyed, gold-waistcoated, civic-skewering Knox had the largest anatomy class in Edinburgh. Here, tragedy had turned to public notoriety. As the mob poets shrieked:

> Burke's the murderer, Hare's the thief
> And Knox the butcher who bought all the beef . . .

It had been Wharton Jones and two other assistants who opened the back door to Burke and Hare, unwittingly paying for their sacked-up murder victims. Knox barely escaped the mob after the chilling trial, nor were his assistants spared. A traumatized Wharton Jones fled, wandering from city to city for ten years. He specialized in eye surgery; but like Knox he always looked wider, studying the giant eyes of squids too. And he became an adept embryologist, making his name in 1835 by describing the nucleus in the human ovum (barely seven years after the unfertilized egg itself was discovered).

This had secured him the Charing Cross post. He had only been at the hospital a year when Huxley arrived. It was perhaps fitting that Thomas Wharton – named after the Chairman of the Board of Excise – should twiddle his chain and talk with a clerk's precision. 'Singularly dry and cold in form', Huxley called the lectures, 'but admirable in logical construction, and full of knowledge derived from personal observation'. Their breadth was remarkable. He had Huxley studying the teeth of foetal sharks, feather growth and the sutured jigsaw of the perch's skull. Wharton Jones 'never had any notes' but his talks could have been printed straight off.[26] He was a sad, solitary figure, but Huxley never felt 'so much respect for anybody as a teacher before'.

From such a man Huxley could learn the fastidious side of microscopy. He followed his teacher's interests, examining the formation of blood corpuscles. He kept abreast of the new German cell theory – that all living tissue was composed of discrete cells – and the debates on their central nuclei. He felt the excitement as anatomists finally described the egg's fertilization and the development of a 'rudimental embryo'.[27] So engrossed did he become that while others relaxed in the courtyard his head could be seen silhouetted in an upstairs window peering through an eyepiece. He was in an unused ward fitted up as a museum. The constant frame suggested to one beery wag a pub board, 'The Sign of the Head and Microscope'.

Even up here it was hard to concentrate. Financial crises had forced the hospital to sell some of its street frontage. Pubs and newsagents flaunting pornographic prints lined its sides. Next door conjurors performed in the 'Polygraphic Hall', and the audience's roar carried up to Huxley's museum. Then, after dark, the sleazy nightclubs on Chandos Street at the back opened up, their clientele of 'seedy Dick Swivellers' attracting the patrolling prostitutes. Old tutors knew the pitfalls. They fretted about students, doubled over dismembered corpses. They feared that this charnel-house work would blight the young bud and drive the tyro into these 'saloons to seek the company of harlots and drunkards'.[28]

Huxley's days dragged on. He struggled in for 9 am. chemistry classes, then dissections, with afternoons of physiology, medicine and surgery, followed by physics at 6.30 pm. The *Lancet*'s advice was never to burn the midnight oil. But 'I am like the owls', Huxley said, 'nocturnal natured, and as they can't mouse so I can't work at an other time'.[29] He lurched between backbreaking work and bone-idleness. Slaving at night left him doodling by day. 'I worked extremely hard when it pleased me, and when it did not ... I was extremely idle (unless making caricatures of one's pastors and masters is to be called a branch of industry)'. Quick-witted, he darted from subject to subject, endlessly questing, pursuing his fancy. 'I read everything I could lay my hands upon, including novels, and took up all sorts of pursuits to drop them again quite as speedily'. His intellect, 'rather acute & quick than grasping or deep', made the craft side of medicine a chore.[30] But in an age looking for certainty it was suited to the exactitudes of physiology and the cold logic of chemistry.

That logic was deftly chopped by Huxley's other favourite, George Fownes. He was fresh from Germany's best chemical laboratory at Giessen. He returned with a Ph.D. (a degree unheard of at home). He also returned with the latest German techniques to reduce proteins to their constituents and synthesize bodily byproducts. Chemistry was encroaching on the organic realm for the first time. Fownes was doing what once was thought impossible, making the materials of life. He committed Charing Cross to this laboratory-based 'organic chemistry'. The school's President talked of the science's 'grandeur', and Tom felt it. Fownes had him boiling egg albumen, adding alcohol, passing electric currents, simulating the body's chemistry. He dissolved flesh with alkalis and digested it with acids, like the Germans looking for the molecular basis of muscle activity.[31]

While his teachers used German methods, their overview remained quintessentially English. For them, every atom of the universe functioned perfectly because it was Divinely designed. Fownes was deep in his *Chemistry as exemplifying the Wisdom and Beneficence of God* while Tom was boiling flesh. The book argued that the proximity of Britain's iron and coalfields was providential. For Wharton Jones the body's perfect plan pointed to the same Celestial Draughtsman. 'Profound philosophy!' barked Knox at these 'design arguments' in 1843. Huxley heard the guffaws from the radicals who 'breathed a doubting theism'. Divine design was passé. A 'vile' joke 'peculiar to British physiology', cackled Knox, and 'downright nonsense' as a serious explanation. Wharton Jones, seeking absolution long after Burke was hanged, loathed Knox's stiletto wit. He praised the eye's camera design, and God as a sort of Supreme Fox Talbot. The Establishment applauded; Huxley's two mentors each received the 100-guinea Acton Prize of the Royal Institution, given for books on the Divine in nature.

But Huxley had moved with the cotton Dissenters and Unitarians. He could never accept chemical formulae as God's handwriting

– nor spiritual design as a satisfying explanation of life. He delved into the original German sources and emerged much harder-headed. Atop his student notepad sat a quote from the Zurich anatomist Jacob Henle:

> To explain a Physiological fact means in a word to deduce
> its necessity from the physical and chemical laws of
> Nature.[32]

But then hadn't a disapproving Carlyle noted this stark tendency in the age?' Freewill, he said, has 'withdrawn into the dark', and the 'spectral nightmare of . . . necessity usurps its throne'.[33]

But Huxley's fascination with the functional architecture of nature showed. Jim watched his young brother walk off with the awards. At prize-giving on 1 May 1843 Revd J. W. Worthington presented him with Fownes' chemistry and Wharton Jones' physiology medals, praising his 'extraordinary diligence'. As always the vanity of prizes left him cold, and he scratched on the back of Wharton Jones' diploma, 'Well, 'tis no matter. Honour pricks me on'.[34] This nervous indifference was no consolation for Jim, who had to be content with a good conduct note.

Spare hours were now spent a mile away, in the refurbished Royal College of Surgeons. The building was only five years old, yet Huxley marched past doric pillars already 'blackened with coal-smoke'. He sat in the magnificent 90-foot museum, sun streaming in through high alcove windows, lighting three-storey book-lined walls. Twelve thousand exhibits – endless deformities, surgical curios, pickled platypuses and chimpanzee parts – made it the richest vein of morbid and comparative anatomy in town: 'everything the imagination of man can conceive'.[35] In pride of place were fossil giants, ground sloths and huge armadillos. And facing them a skeletal notoriety, the human giant, O'Brien, snatched and skeletonized against his dying wish.

Restocking costs were still £3,000 a year, and it showed. In the library was every German source. Here Huxley delved into the latest French tome on the latest subject, 'electrophysiology', his interest piqued by Wharton Jones. Fools knew that electric shocks made hanged felons move, but their betters hardly knew why. Wharton Jones pictured muscles composed of stacked discs surrounded by nerve fibres. The current turned them into electromagnets, whose attraction caused the muscle to tighten. Given this breathtaking analogy, and the bravado with which steam-cranked society saw its designs in nature, one suddenly understands Huxley's delight in the 'mechanical engineering of living machines'.[36]

It was not only the 'engineering part of the business' he loved. The 'architectural' side appealed too – what he called 'the wonderful unity of plan' in the myriad 'diverse living constructions'. Medical London was a powerhouse of this 'philosophical anatomy'. All molluscs were reducible to a common blueprint, all vertebrates to another, insects and crustaceans to a third, starfish to a fourth: it was the law of the age, unity in diversity. Detecting the plan behind the varied fins, fingers and wings gave Gradgrind anatomists their *raison d'être*. This was *the* science in the great Babylon. The 'all-pervading unity' of life was 'one of the most sublime truths in nature'. Animals were not built by Creative whim, but constrained by morphological laws. Legislative Whigs combined with laconic radicals to hail this new zoology based on '*Law* and *Order*'.

Huxley joined them. The spiritual had lost its power. Leafing through his old Coventry notebook one day, he fell on his remark about the Unitarians' anti-miraculous nature injuring morals. 'God help you goose', he scribbled, laughing at his naivety.[37]

Like all great truths the Archetypes of Life could mean anything to anyone. Here, in the conservative College of Surgeons, the grave Richard Owen was beginning to put a new gloss on these groundplans. Owen was diffident, shy – his radical enemies said sly (by which they meant the pet of society patrons). Seven years the Hunterian Professor, he was a brilliant zoologist 'with brains enough to fill two hats'. Chimpanzee anatomy, platypus reproduction, giant moas – he was master of them all, and now turning to fossils. He had caught the public imagination by christening the 'dinosaurs'. He then provoked a gasp by proving that tiny marsupials lived alongside them. Huxley watched Owen escorting the greats around his museum, at once charming and obsequious. In a Chartist age he was the Tory favourite: a scourge of red Lamarckians (and the recipient of a £200 pension from Prime Minister Sir Robert Peel for his pains). It made him the darling of Carlyle's set. They delighted 'in Owen, with all his enthusiasm for fossil reptiles'. A 'tall man with great glittering eyes' was Carlyle's generous comment on Owen's goggle-eyed looks. More generous still, he claimed that he had learned more from Owen 'than from almost any other man'.[38] Owen was to please even more. He was planning to put a definitive shine on these abstract groundplans of life –

turning them into Creative Ideals, pure images existing only in the Divine mind. As the unknown Huxley sat in the library, watching, Owen was in his room upstairs planning his magnum opus on the vertebrate Archetype.

The College of Surgeons overlooked the leafy square of Lincoln's Inn Fields. Huxley would walk to it through the new Tuscan colonnades of Covent Garden market, slipping on the stew of cabbage leaves, weaving among the pie men and flower girls. In an evening he might wander through theatreland, watching the swells stream in to see Edmund Kean in his latest production.[39] Perhaps he stopped at the Bohemian Wych Street pub, The Shakespeare Head. The haunt of artists, hacks and students, it was owned by the editor of *Punch*. The publican was perfectly placed to lampoon medical low-life:

> Son of the scalpel! from whatever class
> You grind instruction just enough to pass

from Charing Cross you come, and every college, 'Thirsting alike for half-and-half and knowledge'.

> Though to cheap hats and boots thy funds incline,
> And light rough Chesterfields at one pound nine;
> Though on the virtues of all plants thou'rt dumb,
> Save the *Nicotina Tabacum*,
> (*Pentandria Digynia*! – Lindley – mum!)[40]

Not really Huxley. He bought his 'half-and-half' at the bar, even if he had not learned to puff cheap Chesterfields. *Punch* twitted the tyro surgeons, who drank themselves into a stupor while talking tipsy metaphysics. But Huxley's quest for the two valued commodities of the age – bread and knowledge – was earnest. And he knew more of Lindley's Physic Garden than its tobacco plant.

Only one route to the College of Surgeons made an indelible impression on him, and that was the shortest one, through the cesspit of courts and alleys around Drury Lane.

> Alleys nine or ten feet wide, I suppose, with tall houses
> full of squalid drunken men and women, and the pavement
> strewed with still more squalid children. The place of air
> was taken by a steam of filthy exhalations; and the only
> relief to the general dull apathy was a roar of words –
> filthy and brutal beyond imagination – between the close-
> packed neighbours, occasionally ending in a general row.

Thousands crammed these tenements, sometimes 20 to a room, six to a bed, with buckets as toilets and the stench overpowering. Among them 'the rotting, uncoffined bodies of the dead remain where they died'. A few days in a 'festering London August' and corpses were 'quivering with maggots', which at least kept them out of the puppy doctors' paws. One in four children died. The surviving urchins scraped horse manure off the Strand crossings for a living, to allow silk-chokered gents to pass unsullied. Huxley stole past twopenny doss houses, where the sexes slept together on filthy floors. Here the gangs made life difficult, and rats made it lethal. 'All this,' he puzzled, 'almost within hearing of the traffic of the Strand, within easy reach of the wealth and plenty of the city'. Here he was, a penniless scruff. 'Nobody would have found robbing me a profitable employment'. He passed the down-and-outs unmolested. But he did wonder why, in the depression with the Chartists inflaming passions, the hovel did not explode and the beggars go on a looting spree.[41]

While society forgot the poor, reformers were busy cleaning the middle-class Augean stable. Even the conservative College of Surgeons capitulated. For 20 years its 'self-perpetuating, tyrannical' council had withstood the wrath of Thomas Wakley's battling *Lancet*. But in 1843 the crochety councillors were finally subjected to elections. 'Old Corruption' was dying around Huxley. The new men, Huxley's men – GPs and Dissenting teachers representing the urban industrial areas – moved in with their gutsier science.[42] Talent and training were to replace rank and wealth. Huxley saw a new world in the making.

But still the poor were denied a voice and damned to their hovels. Gentlefolk assuaged their guilt by giving coppers to voluntary hospitals like Huxley's, which were left to pick up the pieces. Minds as well as bodies were healed at Charing Cross, which specialized in mental problems, of special interest to Jim Huxley. Students went free to hear the humane mad-doctor John Conolly at Hanwell Lunatic Asylum, and to see his unmanacled inmates (a libertarian approach Jim was to copy later).[43]

Tom was watching more corporeal surgery. The operating theatre was tiny; the patient strapped, screaming, the 'dreadful shrieks . . . resembling the bellowing of a wild animal' as the knife cut. A poor devil lay on the slab, gas lights above. The students clustered sweatily around, packed in tiers overlooking the table. The cutting was swift; it had to be with trauma the greatest killer. Buckets caught the dripping blood, the sawdusted floor mopping up the spurts. The event was almost as shaking for the students as for the patient. Elsewhere, Huxley's old teachers were pioneering painless approaches. Chandler was still exploiting mesmerism's *'tranquillizing* effect', greater than 'the largest "safe" dose of opium'. His flamboyant friend Elliotson had moved on to mesmeric surgery, giving 'painless amputations' his theatrical cachet.[44]

Jim was hearing different screams. He was doing well in midwifery, picking up a certificate of merit in 1844.[45] He had plenty of practice, in the maternity ward and at home, where Lizzie gave birth to another baby, Flory. Tom too was often around, the perfect babysitter who practically adopted the girl. He was strangely comforted by her cries, seeming to work best under domestic pressure.

Back in the Strand he found a new friend among the 1844 intake, Joseph Fayrer. And a new exotic horizon: Fayrer had sailed in from Bermuda. He was five months Huxley's senior but had seen the world. His father had commanded the largest steam ships sailing to New York. Joseph was a hardy hand: Trinidad, Havana, Jamaica, he had visited them all as a midshipman in his father's paddle steamers. As the freezing pea-soupers set in and the 'soft black drizzle' of soot cast its 'funereal pall' over Charing Cross, he fired Huxley with stories of sparkling Caribbean seas, 'where the water was clear as crystal' and 'the fish, corals, and seaweed were visible in its depths'.[46] He had been paralysed by poisonous sea-urchin spines and had swum among sharks. It was after seeing surgeons working on yellow fever victims in Bermuda that he had decided to come home and study medicine.

Like Huxley, Fayrer stood in awe of the great engineers. The students could always indulge their passions at the Adelaide Gallery. Here were chugging steam engines, and an 'oxyhydrogen microscope' that was said to magnify three million times.[47] Replica paddle boats sloshed up and down a 6,000 gallon tank. But the *pièce de résistance* was the ultimate deterrent: a Perkin's steam-operated machine gun firing 20 rounds a second down the 100-foot gallery.

Fayrer became a firm friend. The two often worked through the night, not that darkness brought quiet. Even at 2 am. the Strand reverberated to the drays dragging vegetable wagons from Waterloo Bridge to Covent Garden. Theatres were their only relaxation. They shunned the raucous student life: 'hardly anything would induce me to dance', Huxley said, or 'to go to such a thing as a party'.[48] While Fayrer fired him up with steam ships in hot seas, he tempted Fayrer with physiology. They sat side by side, watching the chain-twiddling Wharton Jones. In May 1845 Fayrer followed Huxley by taking the physiology prize. In fact he scooped the awards, winning a £15 scholarship for two years.

In 1845 all three of Tom's brothers married, leading to a certain matrimonial confusion. None quite agreed with the others' choices. William so disparaged George's Mary that Tom cut him dead (and they remained estranged for life). Tom's defence of Mary reached a point of passion. Every time he saw her 'she looked prettier than ever with just the same bright eyes and merry laugh'. He called the 'loveable little creature' his 'sister'. Confusion was caused by Jim's wife being another Mary, so George's wife became 'Polly'. Confusion turned to chaos for the girls. Tom was the spitting image of Jim, but Polly's problem was voices: she 'often fails to distinguish between my voice and George's for which I laugh at her immensely'.[49]

Tom's reservation was about Jim's wife. Jim was sharp, full of the world and its ways. But as to an intellectual match, 'I doubt whether he has married wisely'. She was 'a very good creature, and manages his house capitally, but she is nothing more'. No luminous wit to 'brighten a husbands path'. No bon viveur: 'Brought up in a remote country town, under the eye of her father an old clergyman, she has no notion of making her friends amusing'. After a while he sensed that even Jim felt 'frightfully uneasy at times'. Not that Tom – the last unmarried offspring – would make a better catch. He gazed wistfully into the future, only to see himself 'doomed to be a dreadful spoon of a husband'.[50]

Evidently in late 1845, a most extraordinary and unaccountable scandal broke around Lizzie and Salt. Whatever happened, it was hushed up; and so successfully that no historian has managed to penetrate it (few, indeed, have even known about it). There was clearly a fear of social disgrace and ostracism, with Tom more paranoid than most. His mother never forgave Salt for dragging 'your poor unfortunate sister' into the gutter, as she told Tom: 'believe me I can almost hate the man for his unprincipled conduct towards all who have befriended him'.[51] Jim broke off from Salt, and George considered himself compromised. Tom was the only one left to help Lizzie. Did Dr Salt administer some heroic drug overdose that killed a patient? Surely, in light of their eventual clandestine flight from the country, it was nothing so mundane as a financial scandal? (Medical men were well known in the bankruptcy courts, and it was hardly a crushing social stigma.) The event, whatever it was, was traumatic and terrible and would split the family for life.

Tom blotted out the horror, drowning himself in the gigantic surgical tomes now dropping from the steam-presses. By day he trundled on like an automaton, anatomizing his way through the animal kingdom. Insects and centipedes were teased apart. He became absorbed in snails and even more the extraordinary multi-generation lifecycles of flukes and jellyfish.[52] By now he was being invited to Wharton Jones' tiny town house. At home his teacher's outer crust cracked to reveal a volcanic interior. He veered from the sublime to the ridiculous, from germinal vesicles to jams and galoshes. He talked of his own huge unfinished text on eye surgery (to be praised and damned as gloriously definitive and 'absurdly pedantic'). The air was charged as he launched thunderbolts against rival embryologists. In an age of clashing intellects he was already embittered, a little man with a huge rage. Backbiting and infighting were occupational hazards before the rise of professional adjudicators. Huxley sat, sipping tea, listening to him rant 'with more energy than worldly wisdom'.[53]

Huxley continued his journey around the human body. He was still silhouetted in the museum window, measuring the layers in the hair follicle. All year he had been doing it, unable to believe his eyes, convinced he had found a new membrane. He had. The Germans had missed it: right up against the hair shaft, a single layer of cells, 'very delicate and pale'. He could even see their nuclei '1-2000th of an inch' long.[54] Wharton Jones wanted him to publish, suggesting the *Medical Gazette*, sober and sedate like himself (and a regular reporter of his lectures). So a short note was prepared; Wharton Jones polished the prose and Huxley perfected the drawing. Students regularly fired off missives to the medical press, grumbling about cantankerous surgeons or school costs. But rarely one 'On a Hitherto Undescribed Structure', in the human hair or elsewhere. The 20 year-old held his breath and posted his paper.

Huxley's years as a long-haired student were ending. Most boys went into practice at this point, but he still longed for the academic world. In August 1845 he walked down the Strand to London University's offices in Somerset House. Here, in a stark hall, he put himself through Part 1 of the Bachelor of Medicine exam. The affable University College physiologist William Sharpey was impressed, awarding him the gold medal for anatomy and physiology.[55] But Huxley never managed to sit Part 2. After three years he had finished his hospital training. His free scholarship had expired and he needed to pay his way.

At 20 he was too young to obtain a College of Surgeons' licence to practice.[56] He was deep in debt, having borrowed £2 a week for three years to cover food and rent. He owed sums to Cooke, and to dependable George. He had glittering golds but no gainful employment. He needed pay, and fast.

On 28 November 1845 he picked up an 8*d Medical Gazette* and there was his note on the new hair membrane. Wharton Jones was delighted. He incorporated 'Huxley's Layer' into his lectures and blew his protégé's trumpet. 'There's something for you at your time going down to posterity', chortled Jim.[57]

3

The Surgeon's Mate

HOW COULD HUXLEY MEET his mounting pile of debts?
The solution came from his nautical friend Joseph Fayrer. He
suggested the sea. The sick bay afloat had its appeal; Her Majesty
would pay, while his other liege lady, Nature, could be followed
lasciviously around the globe. The Navy fostered scientific assistant
surgeons. Look at the son of Kew Garden's Director, Joseph
Hooker, who had stepped off HMS *Erebus* in 1843 after his
Antarctic herborizations. Or the young crustacean expert Harry
Goodsir, not long gone with Sir John Franklin to the Canadian ice
packs, searching for the North-West Passage. So good did it sound
that Fayrer took his own advice; he enlisted himself.[1]

Huxley saw the benefits. An assistant surgeon's lot had improved
by 1846. He was now saluted as a subaltern, with pretty good pay
at 7s 6d a day. These were minor points, but medical reformers
had fought for them furiously, and they were still fighting on other
fronts. He would have to endure abominable conditions, and it
was a high-risk career; the death rate among surgeons' mates in
the West Indies and Africa was notorious.[2] But who else would
pay him to anatomize voraciously around the world?

Fayrer goaded him into writing personally to the Physician
General of the Navy, Sir William Burnett. It seemed 'rather a
strong thing to do', but a poor boy without patrons had little
option. A long confab on 31 January 1846 'ended in our concocting
a letter'. Huxley duly excused himself:

> Having a great desire to enter the Medical Department of
> Her Majesty's Naval Service and being at the same time
> totally unprovided with any friendly influence by which

the attainment of my object might be accelerated – I take
the liberty of addressing myself directly to you as the
Head of the Department . . .³

The entry requirements were stiff. He had the necessary certificates, everything from surgery to botany, proof of a year spent in human dissection, six months apprenticed in pharmacy and so on. He cut his hair and collected references: Wharton Jones told of his medals and Sharpey gave a 'very high opinion of his abilities'.⁴ Huxley added that a 'Silver Botanical Medal was awarded to me by the Apothecaries Company' and that the university had given him a gold. 'I have paid especial attention to Microscopical Anatomy' and he pointed Sir William to his discovery published in the *Gazette*. His credentials looked good.

And to the top brass. At the bottom of the acknowledgment from the Naval Medical Office was a note from Sir William to see him at Somerset House. 'I thought that looked like business', and so it was. Sir William, 67, had started as a surgeon's mate himself and had survived the battles of the Nile and Trafalgar to receive a CB and four war medals. He was a kindly reformer who had recently bettered the pay and position of the assistant. A spruced Huxley sent his card ahead. Sir William emerged, 'a tall shrewd-looking old gentleman, with a broad Scotch accent'. He clutched Huxley's card. 'The first thing he did was to return it, with the frugal reminder that I should probably find it useful on some other occasion. The second was to ask whether I was an Irishman. I suppose the air of modesty about my appeal must have struck him'.⁵ The Physician General was satisfied, and made arrangements to give the brash aspirant his final *viva*.

The College of Surgeons tested the Admiralty's medical men first, issuing 'fitness' certificates. He also needed a vicar's note vouching for his 'good moral character' and another testifying to his competence in the Classics.⁶ He had diplomas everywhere, his life summed up in pieces of paper.

But at least he was progressing. Salt himself had fled the country, leaving Lizzie, heavily pregnant, to have her baby and follow on. The shadow falling over the family was darkening. Tom was losing his favourite sister, who had pushed him on and thrown her shoe after him for luck. The backbiting intensified as Jim turned on Salt, leaving more bad blood. In secret one February day Tom took Lizzie and the children across the Channel to Antwerp. She went, babe in arms, with the maid holding Flory. The flight was precipitous: Lizzie had not even registered baby Edith, no one had booked accommodation and Tom had to tour the lodging houses.

He took the night ferry back. It docked at 7.45 am. on Thursday 19 February. He rushed to Charing Cross and by 11 am. had gathered up his certificates and received 'the order to go for examination before the College of Surgeons'.

It was hard to concentrate. He reassured Lizzie the next day that he was home 'safe and sound and without sea-sickness'. But the return had made him more paranoid. The pilot had asked him 'if I knew who it was that came over in the vessel who wanted private lodgings'. He had been at one of the residences Huxley had tried. 'Is it not odd?' Tom asked. 'I should advise you to keep to yourself and the children as much as possible out of the way of the people belonging to the Victoria [the English ship] – which lies not very far from you – and Elizabeth [the maid] should be particularly careful not to pick up any English acquaintance – she would not be a difficult person for anyone to pump'.[7]

Everything conspired to stop Huxley joining up. No Board examined at the College of Surgeons on the following Friday, 27 February, so he had to bide his time. He was now itching for his shillings.[8] His *viva voce* at the College on 6 March was a perfunctory affair and accordingly cheap at two guineas. He passed routinely.

A few days later he went before Sir William and, finally, on 13 March 1846, the pallid landlubber became a 'Jack Tar', a sailor. Officially he was put on the books of Nelson's old flagship, HMS *Victory*, that functional shrine in Portsmouth Harbour. Actually he was to take up residence in the largest hospital in the world, Haslar Naval Hospital in Gosport, across the harbour. He had what he wanted, 7s a day. 'So you see all the prophets' noses are rubbed the wrong way', he laughed to Lizzie.[9] At last he could chip away at his debts.

But nothing was so simple. He now added an 'agent' (a sort of finance company) to his creditors, borrowing to buy his kit. What with dress uniform, cashmere waistcoats, cocked hat, 'rich gilt town-made Sword, £4', and so on down to twelve boxes of boot blacking, he found himself forking out £46 2s 6d. That was four months' pay and money he could ill afford.[10]

Queen Victoria's Navy was 'the right arm of England', flexing its muscles before the world. The 'Senior Service' still gloried in

Nelson and Trafalgar as it policed the seas and upheld the *Pax Britannica*. It was opening up new colonies, helping to turn 'White Men's Graves' into hospitable little Englands. Reform was in the air; press ganging was dying and so were the disciplinarians. And the future held new challenges as iron-cladding, steam furnaces and screw-propellers ousted timber and sail. But behind the poster romance lay the usual 'drudgery, boredom, danger, and misery' below deck.[11] The assistant surgeon would find out for himself.

Haslar was a huge, century-old, red-brick hospital facing the sea. With three storey and wings 500 feet long, it could accommodate 2,000 patients in 80 wards. Fever cases had their own isolation units and a mad-house treated the Navy's insane with a new sensitivity. It was built on a promontory, with a jetty into the harbour, so that the casualties could be landed direct. From here Huxley could gaze across the grey waters to the wharves at Portsmouth, or watch the square-riggers being fitted out.

Huxley was swamped amid a torrent of surgeons fresh from their ships or awaiting commissions, and miffed that his new chief, Sir John Richardson, '"Old John," as we irreverent youngsters called him, took not the slightest notice of my worshipful self'.[12] Sixty year-old Sir John was a taciturn figure. In his day he had dressed gunshot wounds during the Peninsular War against Napoleon and sailed on Franklin's first polar expedition. Haslar's museum was his creation, and chocked with the spoils of countless voyages. Of course he had noticed his new assistant. Even as Huxley decried 'the churlishness of the chief', Sir John was trying to get him a good survey ship, or a better shore posting.

One day Sir John 'heaped coals of fire on my head by telling me that he had tried to get me one of the resident appointments, much coveted by the assistant-surgeons'. He wanted the brilliant microscopist in his own museum. 'I was within an ace of being appointed' too, Tom told Lizzie. But an Admiralty man 'put his spoke in the wheel on behalf of a friend of his & so I am out of it'. No favoured shore posting. 'However', said Sir John, 'I mean to keep you here till I can get you something you will like'. And that explained why Tom was not 'packed off to the West Coast of Africa like some of my juniors'. He had been spared the worst fever-ravaged posting in the Service. But packed off he would be: 'mother is not very well', he informed Lizzie, 'and the probability that I shall be off some time or other, instead of stopping here for a twelvemonth, does not brighten her'.[13]

*

Succumbing to the paranoia as the Salts fled, Tom addressed Lizzie's letters to 'Miss Knight'; 'let me know whether I may write to you directly', he said. Salt had taken the alias 'Dr Scott'. Every subterfuge was practised to keep the family skeleton from springing out of the closet. Tom even feared some tampering with the mail. Better not 'send any more letters to me', he advised his sister, 'in case of accidents'.

'Mrs and Dr Scott' moved to Cologne incognito. As Huxley looked to his own commission, Lizzie was worried sick, but still defiant. 'We did what the time compelled us to and believed it no concern of anyone's', she told him, sending greetings on his 21st birthday. 'They cannot judge fairly if they would'. Salt was having trouble scraping a living 'but we do not despair'. Where it would end she did not know. Emigration schemes were canvassed, but even finding travel information frightened her, for fear she would tip her hand and then 'everyone w^d know'.[14]

Huxley was facing his own uncertain journey. His destination too was some distant land, at the farthest reach of the Navy's long arm.

At Haslar he heard the stories of capricious sea captains. There were spit-and-polish men, sacrificing comfort to 'smartness and show'. The press depicted their 'perfect despotism', so out of keeping with the age. They were autocrats, for better or worse – and the worst forced their surgeons to suffer 'much vituperation, and abuse, without the power of retaliation' or, at least, not without being cashiered. At sea there was no come-back, as one irate surgeon wrote: 'I have seen a captain's fist . . . shaking near a subordinate's face, when, had it been on shore, and in plain clothes, the latter might have eaten him, boots and all'. For a headstrong Huxley holding his tongue would be a tall order. Even full surgeons lived in 'hot, narrow, and confined' cabins aboard frigates, 'like large coffins', close to the gun-room. And why? another asked: 'in order to give the captain's steward a large berth' aft. As he said, 'the captains will soon have half the ship to themselves'.[15]

Huxley began to wonder what his own captain would be like. But not for long. The Arctic and Indo-China surveyor, Captain Owen Stanley, contacted Richardson, hoping to pick up one of his best charges with a flair for science. It was Huxley's break, especially as Sir John 'has shown himself for some reason or another a special good friend to me'. It was 'an *exploring expedition* to New Guinea (not coast of Africa, mind)', Huxley reported to Lizzie in May; 'would I like that? Of course I jumped at the offer'. He had fallen on his feet – a captain with a penchant for science, who was not prepared to underrate his junior surgeon. And New Guinea, 'a place almost unknown'.[16] Tales were already rife about the mist-shrouded tropical island. Captain Francis Blackwood had just returned from the region in HMS *Fly*, with stories of suspected inland ranges, exotic birds and warlike natives.

With the Season in full swing the aristocratic Stanley was recruiting his officers in town. He trained back and forth, dividing his time between Portsmouth dockyard and the London soirées. Huxley was given leave to come up for an interview.

He was ushered into Stanley's presence. The captain was short and stocky and impenetrably reserved, like many a sea captain – a lonely, unmarried, grey-haired old man for his 35 years. Only occasionally did the brusque outer crust crack to reveal a kind, insecure soul. The saturnine Stanley had seen the empire forged at the sharp end. He had climbed the ranks as the Navy roamed the globe, his life a microcosm of imperial endeavour. At 15 he went to Patagonia, where he learned to survey. (His ships brought back the Fuegian 'savages' who were to return on the *Beagle* with Darwin and FitzRoy.) He had searched for the North-West Passage, and sailed the brig *Britomart* to north Australia (1837–43), planting the flag to pre-empt the Dutch. He had helped to secure New Zealand, seizing it from under the eyes of the French and out of the hands of the Maoris. He was seasoned to hot and cold. He had been crushed in the Arctic ice for ten months, and trapped in tropical Burma for longer.

It showed. He looked burned out. He was broody and suffered bouts of 'suicidal despair'. He flew high and low, sometimes reserved, at other times wild-tempered. He was a good surveyor, if unadventurous, and 'a thorough scientific enthusiast', Huxley noted. What Huxley did not know was that ambition had got the better of Stanley, whose 'bruised self-esteem' showed that he had never quite succeeded. He was ignominiously surveying British rivers when the *Rattlesnake* command came through.

In his two interviews Huxley began to get the man's measure. Stanley, like his father, was an 'aristocrat to his very finger-tips', from a line of heirs and heiresses. Or, as the mate put it, he was 'an exceedingly gentlemanly gentleman'.[17] The Stanleys were leading Whigs and liberal Anglicans, steering the ship of state, and ruling the waves as naturally. His father had loved the sea, but ended up on the 'Dead See', the bishopric of Norwich, given him by the Whigs and nicknamed for its dilapidated state. The family were noble Whigs all, tolerant of Dissent, full of *noblesse oblige*. With his brother Arthur leading the Anglican reformers at Oxford, and a cousin in Melbourne's ministry, the helm seemed Stanley's by right. But Huxley was constitutionally suspicious, however civil the skipper to his scientific young surgeon.

The *Rattlesnake* was to continue HMS *Fly*'s work along the cloud-covered shores of New Guinea. Huxley was promised full leave to collect New Guinea's exotic animals. 'Depend upon it unless some sudden attack of laziness supervenes, such an opportunity shall not slip unused out of my hands'. He had high hopes, as the skipper 'shows himself altogether very much disposed to forward my views in every possible way'.

Stanley was recruiting the veterans of Blackwood's three-year voyage. 'I am progressing with my list of officers', he reported, portraying them with Dickensian candour. 'Mr Suckling, First Lieutenant, an old and steady, good officer, though somewhat deaf. Mr Ince, a fat, laughing, good-humoured sailor, who was out with Captain Blackwood in the *Fly*, is Second Lieutenant. Mr Dayman, a very clever and intelligent person who went out with James Ross in the *Erebus*, is the Third Lieutenant, and assistant Surveyor. Doctor Thomson, a young man, fond of botanical pursuits, is the surgeon, and a Mr Huxley, a very good naturalist, is the assistant surgeon . . . ' He had, he said, 'every reason to be satisfied'.[18]

So had Huxley. He was reassured by Stanley's technical bent and saw promotion if he stuck to his scientific last. 'So that altogether I am in a very fair way, and would snap my fingers at the Grand Turk'. Stanley introduced him to the scientific lions: first, to the pride's imperious leader Richard Owen, whose new *Lectures on the Comparative Anatomy and Physiology of Vertebrates* started and stopped with fishes. Bring home fish brains was Owen's advice. Then to John Edward Gray, the British Museum peon, a closet taxonomist who twinkled at the sight of pickled invertebrates. He and Richardson were currently dividing up the spoils of Captain Ross' Antarctic Expedition; if any obscure barnacle was a desideratum, Gray would know it. Best of all was an opening to the irrepressible Edward Forbes at the Geological Survey.[19] Jokey and gangly, laughing as he threw his long hair back, Forbes was instantly approachable. His own survey had been to the Aegean; he was an expert on the starfish and sea slugs in the deep-sea dredge. There was no one better to show Huxley the ropes.

Huxley was dying to leave, to see the tropics, taste their fruits; not least to start dissecting and making a name for himself. He knew that he would suffer 'privations and petty vexations'. He had read the *Lancet* editorials deploring the assistant surgeon's lot. The marine officer straight from school messed in the ward-room with the lieutenants, walked their weather-side of the deck, and had a cabin and servant. Not so the junior surgeon. He could be the most educated man aboard, four years in medical school, and yet be barred from the ward-room and denied a berth, given only a hammock. Worst of all, he had to sling it in the gun-room with the midshipmen, boys all, 14 or 15 year-olds. The *Lancet*, wanting education rewarded, in the Service and out, was furious. The junior surgeon was dripping with 'professional diplomas'. And for what? To be 'thrust into a filthy, dark den, called the midshipmen's berth, among a set of noisy, half-educated school-boys'. Huxley would have to sleep, work and eat with the 'middies'. And the word was that these pranksters had 'a great antipathy to studious habits'. He looked at his armful of certificates and wondered if his good intentions were for nought.

An aristocratic high command pooh-poohed this 'namby-pamby, brooding discontent'. Gun-room discipline and class divisions were what counted. Why should the assistant surgeon mess with his 'better-paid superiors'? For the old guard it was not education but breeding that counted. As one peppery old gent said, before long the 'cook's-assistant' will be making demands![20]

Huxley sat in his room at Haslar, no pitching, no yawing, no hissing wind or shrieking middies. Before him a new £13 microscope (his first £37 quarterly cheque on 1 July was used for anything but settling debts). Here was the way to study a bee's muscles, quietly. He teased out the nerves of a slug. It was filigree work, requiring intense concentration.[21] How would he manage on a rolling ship, crowded and cramped?

The shillings continued to slip through his fingers. Charting unknown regions, he had expected a library on board. But the Admiralty supplied no books. He had '*carte blanche* from the Captain to take as many as I please', but they were 'ruinously expensive' for an assistant in hock, 'though a mere dewdrop in the general cost of the fitting-out of a ship ... A hundred pounds would have well supplied the *Rattlesnake*'.[22] And so went the rest of his cheque. The Service was proving somewhat expensive.

*

Her Majesty's Ship *Rattlesnake* was stripped to her timbers in Portsmouth dock when Huxley first saw her. She lacked the striking power of her reptilian namesake. Twenty-eight-gun frigates of her class were already obsolete. 'Donkey' or 'jackass' frigates they were laughingly called by the old salts who had seen active service. Nor did the surveyors have much clout. They might have the most hazardous jobs during peace time, but 'the officers of *"regular"* men-of-war, as they delight to be called, pretend to think surveying a kind of shirking – in sea-phrase, "sloping"'.

The ship was small, 113 feet and 503 tons, with a complement of 180 officers and men. She was 44 years old and her timbers showed it. Launched in 1822, she had seen hard service 'chasing pirates and privateers' and as a troopship in the Chinese Opium Wars.[23] Most recently she had been off New Guinea, only to return in a rotting state. The fastidious Stanley was supervising a massive refit.

His orders, in a word, were to secure northern Australia for British settlement and make the surrounding seas safe for British merchantmen. In practice this meant surveying the Torres Strait – the passage between northern Australia and New Guinea – which was used by ships returning home via India from Sydney and the South Seas. He was to mark channels through the reefs (notorious as a ships' graveyard), to enable square-riggers to beat through the Strait at night. He was also to assess sites for new British colonies. The Admiralty feared that foreign traders could pass unseen through the Strait; it wanted local garrisons and coaling stations, and regular patrols to keep watch for French ships. Imperial vigilance was a prime part of the mission.

With emigration peaking, propeller-driven steamships were expected to be a major part of future traffic, reaching Sydney via Singapore through the Inner Passage, inside the Barrier Reef. Here the steamers would be protected from the Pacific swell. Most ships still steered outside the reef because of the risk of wrecking. Certainly no merchantman out of the colony would chance the Inner Passage, with the sun's glare on the water ahead masking the white foam. The inner channel had to be 'well swept and its dangers marked out'. This was Stanley's second priority.

Also on the South Seas route – and awaiting exploitation by gold miners and whalers – lay the haunting island of New Guinea. Stanley was to chart its southern shores and the archipelago off its eastern tip. These were not such friendly waters, and the Sea Lords warned him to 'guard against the treacherous disposition of their inhabitants'. Huxley knew he would meet savages. The *Fly*'s men talked of charcoal-painted Papuans and scare stories of head-hunters abounded. What terrors awaited them behind the luxuriant camouflage at the water's edge no one knew. But the Admiralty realized the potential for exploitation. The *Rattlesnake*'s naturalists – like so many before them – were to send New Guinea's riches to the British Museum. Here 'zoological *patriots*' would christen and claim its rainforest inhabitants, on the gilded principle that 'once an animal is named and described, it becomes . . . a possession for ever'.[24]

By now all the 'unpeopled regions of the earth' were seen as British territory. The 'surplus' poor from the industrial slums were being shipped in huge numbers to the colonies, 400,000 a year during the depression. The figure was expected to rise with the Irish potato famine worsening; and with prospective steam lines putting Australia 'little more than a month's voyage' away that continent was looking attractive.[25] Surveying vessels were a bridge-head, opening up territories as well as maintaining links and policing the little Englands. The *Rattlesnake* was to act as banker as well, carrying £50,000 in gold coin for the Cape Colony and £15,000 for Mauritius.

The ship was commissioned on 24 September 1846, but the Sea Lords were tying up Stanley's refit with red tape. While waiting Huxley escaped to that peripatetic 'Parliament of Science', the British Association for the Advancement of Science, which was holding its jamboree at nearby Southampton. All his new contacts were there. Owen dominated the proceedings with his numbingly technical talk on the vertebrate groundplan or 'Archetype'. Here too was Forbes, the voice of the British Asses' 'Dredging Committee' (he had even dredged his way along the coast to the Southampton venue). There was an irreverence about Forbes that Huxley found appealing. Rollicking was the word; unlike Owen, Forbes was positively playful, sparing nobody with his *John Bull* squibs.[26] Forbes talked jellyfish and starfish. He even gave Huxley a prize, an *Amphioxus* dredged from the sand: a strange transitional creature, not a fish for it had no heart, nor a head proper, yet with a lamprey-like notochord and nerve chord running its length. Where it stood was a mystery, which increased when Huxley saw its invertebrate's blood.

Huxley's commission came through on 2 October. Still the *Rattlesnake* was unready, so he and his 'fellow prisoners' found themselves remanded in the Hulks, the penitentiary ships in the harbour. Now he understood Dr Johnson's quip, that 'being in a ship is being in a jail, with the chance of being drowned'. For generations these rotting warships had housed the Gin Lane reprobates on their way to Botany Bay. They were the staging posts for leg-iron men convicted of pilfering food or swearing trade union oaths. Their decks squelched blood and tears; in the air the crack of the cat-o'-nine-tails and stink of torn flesh. With transportation suspended, the sailors were left with the stench. Tom posted his brother George a maudlin cartoon of his cell under the motto 'Am I not a man & a brother?'

Aboard the *Rattlesnake* Stanley's rearrangements were drastic. He jettisoned some cannons and two actually ended up in his cabin. He was making the most of the available space; 'having only eight guns on the main deck, I have arranged all the officers' cabins and the Mess place there, the midshipmen occupying the gun-room below. A poop extending as far as the wheel gives us an excellent chart room, with plenty of light and air'.[27]

Coming aboard at last, Huxley was delighted to find that Stanley had planned the crew's quarters meticulously. Against all the prognostications, he had his own cabin (or rather an alcove off the gun-room), and a cot, while he could stow his books and set up his microscope in the chart-room. Even so it was not the lap of luxury. Given a berth six feet by seven, crammed with cot, clothes, desk, chest, cocked-hat box and rifle, there was scarcely room to turn. Nor to stand: 'I really doubt whether Jonah was much worse accommodated'. Huxley's 5 feet 11 inches left him disadvantaged, with 'the height of the lower deck . . . 4 feet 10 inches. What I am to do with the superfluous foot I cannot divine. Happily, however, there is a sort of skylight into the berth, so that I shall be able to sit with the body in it and my head out'.[28]

Thrust among 22 high-spirited youngsters, he appreciated the complaints. Surgeons' mates were 'the *dry nurses* of the navy', there to keep the boys in check. Stepping into the gun-room he saw why: two were troublemakers, another pair were the worse for wear after a fight. There was a mischievous glint in the eye of Philip Sharpe, the son of an old clergyman. But at least Tom could escape to the poop. 'In an ordinary frigate if a fellow has the talents of all the scientific men from Archimedes downwards . . . they are all lost. Even if it were possible to study in a midshipmen's berth, you have not room in your "chat" for more than a dozen books'. But Stanley had transformed the poop 'into a large chart-room with bookshelves and tables and plenty of light. There I may read, draw, or microscopise at pleasure'.[29]

The *Rattlesnake* was towed out of dock later in the month and moored in harbour. Here the work continued. She sported new cannons from Woolwich arsenal, and Stanley boasted that she had 'the best supply of instruments that a surveying ship ever sailed with'. Pride of place went to the 17 gleaming chronometers, for use in fixing longitude and the location of wrecking reefs. She carried a decked boat, the *Asp*, which could be hoisted on and off, as well as 'two gallies, thirty-two feet long; a very fine pinnace and two first-rate cutters, so that in the boat department we are well off'.[30]

On 21 October Stanley mustered the ship's company. Huxley now met his messmates for the first time. The officers seemed 'very gentlemanly', and he hoped that their shared interest in science would foster camaraderie. 'The requisite discipline is kept up', he told Lizzie, 'but not in the martinet style'. Common pursuits meant they had 'more respect for one another' than in men-of-war.

There seemed no lack of *ex officio* naturalists. The Navy's paid collector was the rugged, bushy-bearded ornithologist John MacGillivray. Only three years older than Huxley, 'Jock' MacGillivray was already a veteran. He had been with the *Fly* and was itching to go out again after only six months. Huxley had heard the tittle-tattle. Gray at the British Museum slated MacGillivray as an 'ignoramus', telling Cooke as much.[31] But his credentials were good: his father was professor of natural history at Aberdeen, and John was well-versed by the Zoological Society's bird artist and erstwhile Australian traveller, John Gould.

Among the supernumeraries was Stanley's personal collector, James Wilcox, on board to stock the museums in the bishop's Norwich diocese. But the man Huxley warmed to was the surgeon. 'My immediate superior, Johnny Thompson [sic], is a long-headed good fellow without a morsel of humbug about him'. Thomson was a rucksack and rifle man. He was another avid collector, keen to augment his cabinet and to record events, bringing his daguerreo-type camera for the purpose. He was a candid Scotsman, with an 'even and amiable disposition' to offset Huxley's hot temper. They would get on well. 'One friend on board a ship is as much as anybody has a right to expect'.[32]

Two weeks before sailing Huxley bade farewell. He stayed with George on Regent's Park and picked up last-minute tips from

Forbes. His brother threw a farewell party, with Fayrer making a speech and Tom *debuting* in his uniform. The real leave-taking was more poignant. He clasped his mother goodbye on 19 November; always embarrassed by emotional displays, he was choked by her 'gut tearing sentimentality'. His father was 66 and fragile, and Tom knew that five years could be forever.

The family he left was badly fractured. He had outgrown his parents and outdistanced his brothers. Lizzie's exile had taken her on to Bonn. Cut dead by James and the rest, she castigated their 'mental aberration on the subject of my husband'. Cooke's teaching had flopped and he was drowning his sorrows in beer and opium, and 'Ellen is not getting on better' (she too had hit the bottle). 'The ladies are not in the ascendent in our family', said Lizzie; nor, it seemed, were their husbands.[33] Tom's departure would only speed the break-up.

Back in Portsmouth the ship was a buzz. Ratings rushed around; everywhere smelled of polished wood and tarred rope. Chests of tea and casks of rum were coming aboard. The tub became a creaking Noah's Ark: crates of ducks and chickens, corralled sheep and yapping gun dogs, winched on to the sounds of the fiddler and accordionist practising their shanties. It was bursting with provisions and bristling with marines (sentries for the shore parties on hostile shores). Loved ones were coming and going in tears. But it was the last supernumeraries who added the incongruous note.

As Huxley had been warned, Stanley began commandeering half the ship. He settled his steward in a large berth and his butterfly collector in another. He made room for the Revd Robert King, son of his old superior in the *Adventure* and the *Beagle* in South America, Phillip Parker King, who was now living in Australia. Unknown to the Admiralty, Stanley had even planned to take his mercurial brother Charlie to Hobart, where he was to be the Governor's Private Secretary. Charlie, a Royal Engineer and social catastrophe, had just blighted the family name by marrying a banker's daughter, Eliza Clayton, who would have been *nouveau riche* had she had money ('No money *at all*' and worse, 'a voice like a vulgar person who wishes to speak *genteelly*'). Hobart seemed a suitable place for them. The plan only fell through because of the *Rattlesnake*'s delays, forcing the newlyweds to take a merchant ship. But Huxley found other Stanleys settling in.

A nice cruise to Madeira, the bishop believed, would do his recuperating daughter Catherine good. And of course she would need her sister Mary as a chaperon. Notwithstanding the crush,

Stanley gave over two more of his cabins. Huxley, squeezed in the ship's bowels like Jonah, watched in horror. One cabin was set up with cots as their sleeping quarters, another made into a pleasant dressing room, which the young ladies were decorating with pictures. The idiosyncratic Stanley again forgot to tell the Admiralty. Rough-cut swabs, wondering what sort of survey they were signed up for, saw the girls bring a little of the Bishop's Palace aboard: a sofa, and a piano which played Bohemian Quadrilles, and all the finery, right down to silver wine labels engraved with the Stanley crest, 'two for port, two for sherry, and two for Madeira – we mean to be very grand'.[34]

There was a criminal profligacy to it in 1846, as the Irish potato famine intensified. They were sailing as starvation ravaged the rural communities. Death now stalked the hovelled poor, who subsisted on bread and potatoes, forcing untold thousands more to America and the colonies. The ship seemed safely removed, a floating autocracy. Each man was at his station, protected by the *noblesse oblige* of the bishop's son on the bridge. On 27 November the bishop himself came aboard to bless their endeavour.

1846–1850

The Devil and the Deep Blue Sea

4

Men-of-War

HUXLEY SAILED ON 1 December 1846, leaving the *Lancet* campaigning for better conditions. Education demands rank: it was a cry dear to his heart. He was even being cited himself:

> Some of the best educated young men in the profession are at present acting as naval assistant-surgeons, and 'denizens of the midshipmen's berth' . . . On looking over the navy list, we find, that such men as the younger HOOKER, the botanist, and HARRY D. GOODSIR, are assistant-surgeons; and also several graduates and undergraduates of the University of London. Among these, we may mention, T. H. HUXLEY, a medallist of 1845 . . .[1]

But in an odd way Huxley preferred the middies' mess. Like MacGillivray, he was deep in debt and scrounging. Living was cheaper in the gun-room. He would only have to fork out 30s a month, barring drink. That would save a pound on the extravagances of the ward-room.[2]

The bishop's entourage accompanied the ship along the south coast, past Dorset's blue lias cliffs and Devon's smugglers' bays. The *Rattlesnake* put in at Plymouth, where the £65,000 treasure trove was brought aboard. Knowing the captain's commission, cocky Midshipman Sharpe calculated his 'nice little share' and reckoned it 'paid for his outfit'. The middies' impecunious minder, who had begged, borrowed and begrudged £46 for his, could only wonder at the corruption.

The bishop's farewell sermon was preached against the backdrop of Devonport docks. Workers poured out of the gigantic store-houses to hear it. Huxley was lost amid a thousand listeners: port families and 'rough sailors whose eyes were dimmed with tears'. Then he scribbled a farewell note to his mother. His cabin was homely with 'my gay curtain and the spicy oilcloth'. And he had his modicum of privacy. But then, Cooke's example notwithstanding, 'If I had no cabin I should take to drinking in a month'.³

With the world facing him, he sat in his berth making resolutions. On 10 December, after the treasure chests had been stowed and the instruments calibrated, he started a diary: 'Thank God! fitting out is at last over. We have no more caprices to fear but those of the wind – a small matter after having been exposed to those of the Admiralty'. Plans tumbled out of him. He was leaving England as a student, with one eye on pay and one on his 'future prospects', for careful 'observation may enable me to *become* a teacher'. He had to annexe some remote corner of the animal kingdom, as Victoria's Navy was annexing the world. Specialize, that was the trick. Study what nobody else could, the 'perishable or rare marine productions', the sort that rarely reach England – take them over and make them his own. He had in mind the delicate gelatinous animals, jellyfish and their relatives. These he could dissect, draw and discard as they sailed along. Simply naming and claiming new animals could be left to the closet taxonomists at home: 'what I *can* do and they *cannot*' is anatomize fresh filamentous corpses on the high seas.

He would make the most of the voyage: scoop out fish brains, as Owen advised, and, donning his hat as a philosophical anatomist, dissect every mollusc from cuttlefish to clam to see if they shared the same plan. He would dissect the trepang too, that huge commercially harvested sea slug of the Barrier Reef, and barnacles and worms and corals and fish parasites . . . He slapped his diary shut with a defiant flourish: 'All these are things which I can attend to myself and in which I neither interfere with nor need the assistance of any one else'.⁴ He had a dogged determination to go it alone. The young idealist, with an outsider's faith that talent could triumph, faced a new dawn.

The next morning, 11 December, the crew bade their farewells. Huxley cut his moorings. Great white shrouds of sail were unfurled and HMS *Rattlesnake* left English shores. The noise as the canvas caught the wind erased all thought of land: creaking joists, lashing waves, officers screaming and men shouting, the ensemble drowned by the wind in the rigging. Out in the Channel the tempests forced him to eat his words about the Admiralty and its blusterings. Nothing had prepared him for the Atlantic storms. As the weather worsened the *Rattlesnake*'s shoddy workmanship became evident. The scuppers, carrying run-off water from the decks, were inefficient. The gales sent thunderous waves crashing over her bows, and nearly every hatch leaked, leaving the main and lower decks flooded. For days the old tub was pitched and tossed. The provisions were ruined. Not that the middies cared for food, lying about groaning. Water sloshed from side to side carrying 'everything that was movable'. Huxley dodged the crashing debris. Desks 'were completely resolved into their elements', gun-cases smashed and even 'the unfortunate ducks were picked up dead in bucketfuls'. The *Rattlesnake* had been turned out in 'a disgraceful state'. He had expected the sturdiest ship for a dangerous survey. But the Sea Lords had provided 'the slowest, clumsiest' and leakiest ship ever to 'wear the pennant'.[5] The passage to Madeira was mercifully quick but remarkably uncomfortable.

The Portuguese island of Madeira, off the African coast, had been the traditional first stop on circumnavigations since Cook's time. The vineyards and whitewashed villas came as a welcome sight to the sailors standing on waterlogged decks, and a stopover allowed the crew to fix the leaks. Eight days out from a snowy December England, and Huxley was in a world of balmy breezes and banana plantations.

While Stanley took his sisters partying, Huxley sat in the pews of the cathedral. On Christmas Eve he watched the Catholic festivities, less with a sense of anthropological mission than with evangelical anger. To puritanical Englishmen Catholicism conjured up the miseries of the 'shiftless' millions in Ireland. It put the moral spite into their anti-Popery. The rationalist scorned this prostitution of human reason. To the young sailor priests and prostitutes were all of a piece, only standing on opposite sides of the sacred divide. At Mass the 'chanting' was 'of a most vile description'. It was 'difficult to say who evinced more indifference to what was going on – the choristers or the people and Santa Maria! ... I was glad to get away, even at the risk of being whisked off by some of the Portuguese pimps who hail you at every step'.[6]

Christmas Day was spent on the island, dominated by its volcanic cloud-covered summit and plummeting mist-filled ravines. Huxley and the ship's purser clambered up the Curral Mountain on horseback, along hair-raising ledges, 'with a perpendicular rock on our right and an equally perpendicular precipice on our left, our hold on terra firma being entirely confined to some five feet of rough stones'. He was concentrating too hard to be terrified. At the top he stood in awe, his 'enjoyment of the sublime and beautiful' marred only by a more primal hunger.[7]

'Mountain scenery is new to me', he mused, but it would become a lifelong obsession, and the signs of violence forced strange reflections. On 26 December, as the ship sailed on a warm breeze, Huxley dwelt on the dark, mocking disguises of Romantic Nature:

> Nature is a true tragedian – her most painful throes, her
> wildest struggles have all within them some element of
> beauty – even in death she covers her face, like Caesar,
> with a graceful mantle. So in this island, a huge monument
> of some awful volcanic phenomenon – made up of wild
> peaks and intervening deep gullies and ravines.

It was as if she was disguising the awful plunges with cotton-wool clouds. The picturesque town of Funchal overlooking the bay was the same. It seemed a fair 'whited sepulchre' city from afar, 'but all stinks within'. On mountain tops and in sherry-sipping society, the cynic saw superficial friendliness disguise a primal savagery.

Huxley's reverie was interrupted by the Master at Arms calling, 'Three bells, sir'. He was on his way. The lush tropics of Rio de Janeiro awaited.[8]

On the last day of the year, Huxley recorded a latitude of 21° 12' – they had crossed the Tropic. They ploughed on, through shimmering phosphorescent seas, caused by myriad luminous jelly-fish which he netted for dissection. The *Rattlesnake*'s sails caught the Trade Winds on 2 January 1847. Flying fish skimmed the water's surface. They littered the decks in the morning, but nothing else did: he searched in vain for the fine reddish dust that Darwin had reported on the *Beagle*'s deck 15 years earlier.[9] The long weeks of the Atlantic crossing were spent examining the haul from his tow net. One day it would be bristle-jawed arrow-worms, confusing creatures whose relationships were unknown. Another it was sea squirts (which shot water jets on being handled), and even droplets of water proved to be positively alive with pulsing water-flea-like crustaceans.

Huxley's microscope was set up in the chart-room. Here he was in familiar surroundings. His money had gone on books, which lined the walls: Buffon's natural history, innumerable novels, old student notebooks, tomes on zoology, German philosophy, Dante and Horace in Italian to teach himself the language, 'and there I sit' and work 'much as though I were in my rooms in Agar Street'. With the exception, of course, that he now had a growing audience. He watched the voracious arrow-worms swim around 'with their heads buried in some unfortunate' sea squirt. His microscope was an escape hatch; it transported him into an exotic world of beautiful diaphanous beings, pulsing and phosphorescing. The trouble was the queue of swabby faces wanting to peer down into it. It was true about the 'noise and frivolity' of the mess. Delicate dissections were hard enough on land. On a rolling ship, surrounded by prying eyes and practical jokers, they needed the patience of Job, or at least 'the toil and labour of a moral Sisyphus'.[10] His gawping middies wanted to see 'something pretty', and he bored them with incomprehensible microscopic sights so as to be left alone.

After passing the Cape Verde islands, 300 miles from tropical Africa, the frigate was rocked by a momentary earthquake, but little else shattered the peace. 'Our friends the flying fish have quite left us, and sharks, dolphins and pilot fish have taken their place'. The mugginess made it impossible 'to rake together any thoughts in this hot noisy berth'. In the calms the canvases flapped uselessly, and Stanley took the opportunity to take deep sea soundings, or try to. Spun yarn weighted with 384 lbs of lead shot, fed out for 38 minutes to a depth of 2,600 fathoms, still failed to hit bottom. At one point the obvious happened, and Huxley reported that, 'alack and alas . . . the splicing came undone and away went the lead minus line, to investigate for himself. He has however not yet returned to report, and strong fears are expressed that he has absconded'.[11]

Then they were buffeted by squalls, sheets of rain accompanied by thunder and lightning, with waterspouts visible in the distance. Again the water in his cabin was 'wish-washing about'. The sick list grew, the old salts with rheumatism and boys with puffy feet. They stood outside his sick bay, most of them illiterate, a gruff bunch scorned from the upper deck as 'degenerate, despicable, immoral, and barely distinguishable from the common criminal'. Huxley saw them no differently at first. 'What a precious pack I have to deal with', he mused as he lanced feet. 'Save the necessary courtesies of life, I shall make it my business to have very little to do with them'.

Worse was yet to greet him in the surgery. They crossed the

Equator on 13 January – 'usual tomfooleries observed', he jotted of the heathen Saturnalia. He and the doctor suffered first, being ducked and drenched, and Huxley dished out the same to 'the unhappy beggars who had to follow'. His infectious spirit struck the midshipmen and Philip Sharpe audaciously doused the captain. (Huxley was beginning to like their style.) But the ducking had tragic consequences. The sick list grew 'in consequence of the Neptunizing'.[12] Two novices contracted pleurisy, writhing with chest pains and fever for days. Huxley watched helplessly as one succumbed, the first death on a long voyage, and a terrible irony under the circumstances.

Into the southern Atlantic and he caught his first Portuguese man-of-war, the poisonous *Physalia*. These were the invertebrate yachts of the high seas, with their beautiful sails and long deadly tentacles. He picked up his specimen by its five-inch vivid blue float, careful of its poisonous tentacles (hence their name 'sea nettles'). He had a day to examine it, for in the equatorial heat it was 'semifluid & stinking' by the next morning.[13] But that was time enough to correct the 'horridly superficial' observations of the French zoologists. He was becoming his own man, and on the way to his first *Rattlesnake* paper.

A week later they approached Rio, sailing past golden sands and fringing palms. The harbour was crowded with everything from hollow-log canoes to 'felucca-rigged boats', with merchantmen standing off. Aromatic scents carried on the sultry air as Huxley came up to catch his first sight of the New World. It beats Madeira 'into fits', he burst out as he saw the city on 23 January; it must rival 'the Bay of Naples for the title of the most beautiful place in the world'. For a week they remained at Rio, the crew visiting its shops and squares, and the markets with their exotic fruit and fish. 'They must eat queer things', he said as he saw the cuttlefish and hammerhead sharks on the stalls. In 90° temperatures they examined the unhewn-granite buildings. The richer streets rivalled those in Europe, and 'feather-flower' bouquets of humming-bird plumes could cost a fortune.[14] Outside town the whine of the cicadas grew deafening, and Huxley marvelled at the colossal saxhorn snails clustering on pawpaw hedges and the enormous gaudy butterflies fluttering through the banana groves.

But the drawbacks were shocking. The stench on the beach was offensive, but even more overpowering was the moral stench of slavery. Along unsewered streets the blacks trudged, their backs glistening, pulling carts or humping crates. Gangs marched to the beat of a tin rattle. Some had iron collars, others masks of tin, padlocked from behind. MacGillivray was stunned at the 'extreme brutality' of the masters. Huxley was chastened by the blacks' resilience. 'I have a much greater respect for them than for their beastly Portuguese masters'. He compared the slaves to 'the corresponding class in England, the manufacturing and agricultural poor', the workers demanding their own 'emancipation'. It was a pity, he thought, recalling the horrors of the potato famine, that a 'few of the hungry Saxon millions now famishing in England' could not seize this 'vile, ignorant' nation and transform Brazil into a 'second Indian Empire'.[15]

Huxley and MacGillivray hardly escaped the stench of slavery at sea. The boat they hired to dredge the beautiful Botafogo Bay was crewed by slaves, who were made to work by 'dint of bribery and ridicule'. The genial Forbes had taught Huxley the trick of dredging, and what he lacked in equipment he made up for in ingenuity. Gauze meat covers doubled as sieves, and the results were spectacular. This was no choppy Southampton; the azure waters of the palm-fringed bay were 80° and the pair pulled up 45 species of molluscs, starfish, anemones and the primitive little sand-burrowing *Amphioxus*. They sat examining their catch against the spectacular backdrop of Sugar Loaf Mountain, the warm waters lapping at their feet.

Huxley made fast friendships, the first with MacGillivray. They explored everywhere together. Being 'Naturalists', *officio* and *ex-officio*, they 'had or pretended to have a more or less naturalistic' goals. But 'our investigations always took in the end a chemical turn, to wit, the examination of the nature and properties of a complex liquid called Sherry Cobbler. Oh Rio, thou Sodom-and-Gomorrha in one, town of stinks and beastliness, thou shalt be saved not because of one just man, but because of the excellence of the iced drink'. The sultry days saw them climbing the mountains. They gloried in the fierce tropical storms, watching the solid lightning bolts strike the peaks. Or they spent them dredging, decamping afterwards to a tavern to consume sherry and pigeon.

'Cobblers or no cobblers, however, our liege lady Nature was not neglected'. He examined the reproductive organs of the burrowing *Amphioxus*, and kicked himself for failing to make out the blood circulation. The pair dredged bivalve lamp-shells from the bay on sailing away from Rio on the morning of 2 February, and further out started hauling in nets full of jellyfish.

'By the way', he wrote to his mother (who had just moved down from Coventry to live with the Cookes), 'tell Dr. Cooke with my kindest regards that old Gray is a lying old thief. Many of the things he told me about MacGillivray e.g. his being an ignoramus in natural history etc. etc. having proved to be lies'.[16]

On the long haul to the Cape of Good Hope they took soundings daily and recorded the water temperature at depth. Albatrosses, gliding on long narrow wings, brought the men to the gun rails. 'We don't at all keep in mind the fate of the Ancient Mariner, inasmuch as whole broadsides of small shot and rifle bullets are fired at them daily, but they don't keep to their part of the affair, never coming "for food or play" to the mariner's holla'. Little else distinguished the days in mid-ocean. Huxley could only tell them apart by his harvest. Some days saw a passing armada of Portuguese men-of-war, or the purple-and-white-striped crests of penny-sized *Velellae* ('little sails'), with their tiny tentacled rims.[17] These 'siphonophores', or sea nettles, were jellyfish relatives and the oddest animals, seemingly simple but infuriatingly complex. Nobody could agree about them. Was each a single organism? Or was it a complex colony of many individuals united, one the gas bag, others modified as stinging tentacles, still more the food-ingesting or siphon polyps (hence the group's name), all specialized for single tasks and subordinated to the whole?

The sailing gas-bags had Huxley taking to a boat and trailing his net. Early on, he dropped his drawing book from the starboard quarter boat, and had to watch his unique record of this pelagic life sail away itself. There was nothing for it but to start his dissections afresh. Mercifully many thumb-sized seasquirts or 'Salpae were taken today in the towing net', he logged on 23 February. 'They were of the same kind as those of w^h. I had previously made (& lost!) drawings'. These sketches were of inordinate complexity. It could take a month to dissect every part of a man-of-war; even then the filigree work could be infuriating. And it all supposed a constant supply. In this perishable climate 'You get a day's work out of your specimen and on the morrow he is rotten'. He needed a regular supply of corpses. 'If Dame Nature will send me one every day I shall do'. Unfortunately she could be profligate one day and parsimonious the next. But at least light breezes in notoriously rough waters bought Huxley the time, and he planned a paper on the man-of-war, to be posted home from the Cape along with his first £40 savings.[18]

The light winds bore the *Rattlesnake* on 8 May into Simon's Bay, on the tip of southern Africa. With the ship moored the storms started to lash the Cape. The gales kept the crew in Simon's Town for a month, although Huxley put the detention down to the 'ball given by the Admiral [of the British Naval Headquarters] on the 7th [April]'. Not that the junior surgeon was to be left out. He too donned his £6 10s dress suit and attended the soirée. 'This was a very creditable affair', about the only one of their stay. 'The "fair Afrikanders" did honour in point of good looks to their native land and danced bravely'.

But it was his only light relief. Simon's Town was a 'dull, dreary' place dominated by the naval dockyards. 'Nothing but officials, stall-keepers and Malays to be seen'. The military installation itself was buzzing; the Boers had made their Great Trek into the interior, and the British were engaged in the 'Caffre War' against the natives, and planning their policy of segregation. But the war meant little to Huxley beyond extortionate prices in the shops. While the officers took coaches the 23 miles to Cape Town, Huxley's South African experience was reduced to foraging along the sea shore.

Still, his haul of molluscs dredged up in the dreary harbour paid dividends. He dissected their nerves and found Owen's descriptions to be wrong. Moreover the nerve patterns of diverse molluscs, from squids to mussels, suggested a common plan – and another paper was in the offing, one putting him up with the elite philosophical anatomists. A 'grand' unifying paper this time – a huge 'monograph of the Mollusca' 'based on examination of at least one species of every genus'.[19] It was hopelessly ambitious – even Huxley realized that 'my eyes are bigger than my belly' – but the Simon's Town stopover allowed him to anatomize his way through another branch of the animal kingdom.

His eyes were getting bigger all the time. The tyro was intent on restructuring the whole of invertebrate creation. He projected papers on jellyfish, sea anemones, siphonophores and the homologies of the heads of crustaceans, insects, spiders and millipedes ('Modest notion this and about enough for the five years in itself'!). It dawned just how much there was to do, with every microscopic dissection of a minute corpse taking days amid pitches and rolls. But it was good to have an obsession. 'I should assuredly go clean daft' aboard ship 'had I nothing to do'.

The man-of-war paper *was* finished. In it Huxley routinely made the sea nettle a single individual composed of 'organs', which he described minutely.[20] Stanley – who had a habit of wandering in to watch Huxley at work – suggested he send it to the bishop. The Whig Lords, before career 'scientists' controlled their own house, ran science as they did the State. Noblemen included trusteeship in their public calling. They ruled the faunal empire at the Zoological Society; they held the British Museum's natural treasures in trust for the nation. Even so, the societies were racked by dissension as the new radical democrats and capitalists swept in, demanding accountable specialists at board level. But the vestiges of rotten borough corruption persisted, with appointments the gift of Lords temporal – and abstruse papers recommended by Lords spiritual.

Bishop Stanley had for a decade been the figurehead President of the Linnean Society. Huxley let the captain send the paper, but he was quietly cynical. Probably 'the Bishop will get it printed in the *Linn. Trans.*, by no means on account of any inherent merit, but because it is the first fruits of his son's cruise'. Not that he really doubted the value of his work, but he hated nepotism. When Stanley sent it from Simon's Town, he told himself that the satisfaction was in the work – which was as well, because he would be ignorant of its fate for a long time. The bishop's people had it, and 'They may do as they like with it'.[21]

Finally, with the £50,000 in chests carried ashore to replenish Cape Town's war-torn coffers, and with the 'all engrossing "Caffre war" dinned into our ears from morning to night', the crew were happy to weigh anchor.

For 24 days they tacked across the Indian Ocean. Typically they experienced 20-foot waves, so that even on 'calm' days Huxley's microscope had to be lashed to the table. But occasionally the calm was shattered by north-easterly gales and mountainous seas, making work impossible for the hydrographers as much as Huxley. On 2 May 1847 the tropic birds heralded a nearby reef and before dusk the look-outs spotted Bamboo Mountain, their first sight of Mauritius. Darwin had rhapsodized in his *Journal* about the island's 'air of perfect elegance', and Huxley had great expectations. At night they could see bright moonshine on glittering sands. The *Rattlesnake* came round to the northern end of the island and Huxley awoke on his 22nd birthday to a brilliant blue sky, transparent turquoise water and the 'handsomest of tugs' to tow them into Port Louis harbour.

And yet, restricted to ship on his first day in this palm-fringed paradise, he fell into a black mood. He was still adrift and dispossessed in his nihilistic thoughts – thoughts of chance and circumstance:

Twenty-two years ago I entered this world a pulpy mass
of capabilities, as yet unknown and save for motherly
affection uncared for. And had it not been better altogether
had I been crushed and trodden out at once? Nourishing
me up, was as though one should pick up a stray egg,
unconscious whether dove's or serpent's, and carefully
incubate it. And here I am what a score of years in the
world have made me – such a bundle of glorious and
inglorious contradictions as men call a man.

In Port Louis harbour he stewed in his berth, suffering the stench
of putrefying jellies. He was an outsider aboard ship as much as in
scientific society. Yet he was looking for the way in, a way to
make his mark, a way to escape the religious and social chains of
the past: 'Morals and religion are one wild whirl to me – of them
the less said the better. In the region of the intellect alone can I
find free and innocent play for such faculties as I possess'. Only
uncovering the truth in nature 'allows me to get rid of the
"malady of thought"'. He had found a way in; he would share in
the democracy of intellect.[22]

The dislocated sailor perked up on finding his shore legs. The
island's sorcery worked a spell; the primitive charm he expected
from Saint-Pierre's Rousseauesque tale of love in paradise, *Paul
and Virginia*. Port Louis was a tropical splash of colour, an exotic,
ethnic mêlée. One passed 'silks and satins of the French lady' here,
'the richly embroidered drapery of the Hindus' there, and everywhere 'turbaned Musselmen, Cingalese, Chinese with their tails
carefully stowed away in their caps'. Urbane equestrian shows
were held against the spectacular mountain backdrop. Even the
Indian convict labourers had fiercely noble expressions. Bearded
Moors traded with Parsee merchants and young Creoles smoked
cheroots on street corners. Market stalls were crammed with a
hundred-odd species of brilliantly hued fish. 'In truth it is a complete paradise', he regaled his mother, 'and if I had nothing better
to do, I should pick up some pretty French Eve (and there are
plenty) and turn Adam'. She knew her Tom, but he reassured her,
'N. B. There are *no* serpents in the island'.

The isle was a Gallic temptress, which the stiff-lipped English
after 40 years of colonization had failed to subdue. And British
sensibilities were still shocked. MacGillivray was horrified to see
coolies and cane cutters working on the sabbath – although it
probably reinforced young Huxley's less parochial outlook. Here

too was a place to die, or at least to catch insects: the cemetery 'is one of the most beautiful places I have seen', with its rock tombs garlanded with fresh flowers, and graves overhung with acacia blossoms, buzzing with life.[23] The mêlée extended unto death. There was no sense of Christian universality, but Muslims and Confucians and Hindus each following their own rites.

Not that sentimentality got the better of Huxley. He made a determined show of keeping it at bay. If this curable romantic made a pilgrimage to the tombs of Paul and Virginia, it was only for the glorious hike. Down Saint-Pierre's lilting cabbage-palm avenues, that 'holy temple' where the young lovers admired 'an Intelligence that is infinite, all-powerful and the friend of mankind'. But still Huxley plucked two roses to scent his cabin.

The wiry Huxley was indomitable. Even in the heat he strode 35 miles to Chamarelle Falls and back, sustained by pork brawn and sardines. He took in tow the purser and Revd Robert King, the one having to be carried across streams because of his sore feet, the other adding to his burden by filling his bag with exotic snails. Not for Huxley renting a horse, or borrowing the Surveyor General's stately elephant, as Darwin had done. The subaltern's group 'trudged, full of life and spirits'. And every new vista, from mango plantations to the 350-foot jungle-chasm falls, indeed, 'the firm earth' itself after 'weeks reeling at sea, intoxicated me'. (His 'pocket pistols filled with strong waters' and wayside stops for 'vin ordinaire at sixpence a bottle' helped.) It was, he admitted red-cheeked, 'one of the most pleasant trips I ever had'.[24]

The ship sailed on 17 May with the captain, capricious as ever, carrying £4,000 in bullion for Hobart. This was at the Governor of Mauritius' request, but it meant Stanley disobeying Admiralty orders and delaying the survey. Of course, there was another reason, besides his commission; he could surprise his brother Charlie and Eliza in their colonial home. He plotted a course for Tasmania, 5,000 miles across the Indian Ocean. The *Rattlesnake* tacked south in the 'loveliest weather'. They passed great whales, one 50-foot finback rising majestically out of the water 30 yards away and showing 'his real size to us'. Again Dayman tried to take deep sea soundings, and Stanley even employed an ingenious scoop to bring up some hitherto unseen sea-bed. But to no avail; after feeding the line out for two hours, to a depth of almost four miles, it snapped. By the time they caught the westerlies they were so far south in mid-winter that Huxley was feeling the cold. The galley fuel ran short and the fires were quenched at four each afternoon.

The consequences were unthinkable to an Englishman: 'No hot grog, tea at half-past three, and other abominations'.

'I had one of my melancholy fits this evening', he recorded on 22 June. The blue devils had now turned into black depressions, and they were striking with ferocious regularity. It took him an hour and a half stalking the poop deck, adopting his usual remedy, 'a good "think" to get rid of it'. He looked to his inner strengths, his scientific work, and took comfort from his gelatinous conquests. An hour of planning cured him. Across the Indian Ocean he had been studying the most transparent, troublesome, 'strange and whimsical forms'. Or trying to: *Diphyes* was a ghostly creature, like the man-of-war but with the float replaced by two swimming bells. It was farthing-sized and all but invisible, 'so transparent, that in the water, one sees nothing of it . . . Taken out of water, it looks as if it were composed of two elegantly-cut pieces of very clear glass'.[25] Detach the two parts and they float off by themselves, raising again the question of individuality. Another paper was the tonic he needed, and he planned to post it home from Sydney.

On 24 June, after 28 days at sea, came a welcome sight, the 'jolly face and English tongue of the old pilot' who saw them into Storm Bay in Tasmania. Past the huge basalt pillars at the mouth of the estuary he guided them. Sailors at the gun-rails could spot warehouses in the coves, a tiny fort, and everywhere a patchwork of green and fallow fields. It seemed so quintessentially English. Six and a half months out of Plymouth, on the other side of the world, and the talk was of the furnished cottages, rosy children and real pianos. 'And this in a place where fifty years ago you would have seen nothing but naked savages or kangaroos'.

The next morning they could see the church spires of Hobart 'peeping out from among the trees'.[26] Of all the little Englands scattered across the globe, none recalled so much the mother country. It was all a sea-weary sailor needed.

5

An Ark of Promise

AS A PORT OF CALL Hobart was unscheduled. The captain surprised his brother Charlie on 25 June 1847. But he found Eliza as uncomfortable at Government House as she had been among the Stanleys at home, and rudely snubbed by the Governor's wife. Huxley had a grand view of these social manoeuvrings at the soirées. And there were plenty of these. In fact, Hobart was 'a round of lesser and greater debaucheries'.

Huxley walked Hobart's chilly winter streets, gazing up at Mount Wellington, with its thick eucalyptus cover. After so long at sea English tea and fireside chat were a godsend. Fresh from London he was lionized – which meant being invited into local homes, served by 'ticket-of-leave' men (convicts free to work as they please) and pumped for gossip. The poor boy, socially deprived as he saw himself, loved it: Tasmania 'was without question one of the best places we have sojourned in. The people are very hospitable – really hospitable'.

For a colony barely 40 years old and 12,000 miles from home, it was surprisingly *au fait* with medical developments. The local surgeons initiated him into the latest painless surgery. Mesmeric operations he knew all about, like Chandler's, using hypnosis as an anaesthetic. But as he left England word was arriving from Boston of a rival anaesthetic, ether. The anti-mesmeric surgeons were lauding it. It was a wonderful 'Yankee dodge' to dislodge Elliotson's populists and put the power back into the hands of the professionals. An equally theatrical 'etherial epidemic' was sweeping Britain, with druggists' placards blaring 'Painless Extraction of Teeth'. But it was here in Hobart, only eight months after the Boston announcement, that Huxley 'saw an ether operation for the first time'.[1] Populist he might be, but he was looking to professional rewards, and this procedure gave the surgeon greater command over his patient.

The reception in Hobart raised Huxley's expectations of New South Wales. Eight days later they made their way into Sydney's Port Jackson Harbour, past beautiful coves, their sloping shores surrounded by 'wattles and myrtles with glistening sheen of dark green leaves', the sapphire sea 'so clear, that at thirty feet below, the bed of white sand was visible'. Sailors pressed the gun-rail. To port was Woolloomooloo Bay with its bustling wharves, backed by terraces of stone houses with windmills on the hills. They stood off a neatly clipped park, no surer sign of English civilization. Here they anchored, in Farm Cove, alongside the merchantmen.

Huxley was excited at the 'prospect of obtaining news from home after seven long months of absence'. A boat came out 'with a cartload of letters and newspapers, but no line for me'. It heightened his sense of isolation, of friendlessness in a lonely port. 'I damned everything and everybody' and 'sat down to dinner in a temper that Satan need not have envied'.[2]

To make matters worse, he was kept aboard at first. He was put to work with the ratings, scrubbing and painting. Not for him Darwin's evening stroll through the salubrious part of town. (But then Darwin had travelled as the captain's gentleman companion, rather than a seven-shilling subaltern.) Huxley knew the treats in store. Darwin's *Journal* pictured the whirligig of Sydney life, with the broad streets a crush of smart carriages and starched livery servants. Nothing had prepared Darwin for this 'paradise to the Worshippers of Mammon'. What worried him was the indiscriminate wealth. Ex-cons once broken on the wheel could be worth tens of thousands, and this raised the awful impossibility of telling a man's respectability.

Huxley hardly shared Darwin's fears. When he did get ashore he found the fashionable quarter even more opulent after ten years. Civic pride now competed with colonial snobbery. There was a new architectural grandeur. Town houses of polished stone and red cedar looked important. They stood on gaslit streets. An elegant Government House had been built, along with new 'iron and brass foundries, shipyards, breweries and shops "emulating those of Bond Street"'. Even a university was talked of. But the seamy underbelly of the city was the same, and much better known to the Jacks. Cheap grog in the sleazy pubs on the Rocks drew all sorts. Stocking-capped sailors mixed with prostitutes and ex-cons, and everywhere cabbage-hatted squatters sat about, fresh from their sheep runs. Drunks lay around in fustian-jackets and 'rooskin caps, while their stockingless women smoked Irish pipes, or danced on beer-stained tables.

Drink remained the national pastime, occupying the gents no less than the Jacks, and the 'Gins' (aborigines) inhaled the same alcoholic haze. Ale houses and breweries were everywhere, explaining why half the government revenues came from alcohol sales. The stocks about town were well tenanted by the tramps unable to afford the fine 'for indulging too freely at the shrine of Bacchus'. But for all the 'likker', it remained a fascinating, irritating city, a 'maelstrom of crime and drunkenness, brutality, bigotry and snobbery', but no less of opulence, gaiety and colonial endeavour.[3]

Huxley made up for his own forced labour aboard ship by 'calling, and being called upon – Govt. Balls and the like'. The young officers were courted by the colonial ladies, eager for the gossip. Donning his dress uniform, he threw himself into Sydney's dissipations, soiréeing at the new Government House with his midshipmen. Lizzie heard of his gaiety: 'What think you of your grave, scientific brother turning out a ball-goer and doing the "light fantastic"?' Periodically it palled, as the high life caught up with him. 'I managed three balls and two dinners in the course of a week. I can't say I liked all this'. Outwardly he remained cheerful, explaining the 'method in my madness'. Lonely in a foreign port, where there was 'not a soul who cared whether I was alive or dead', he forced himself to 'pick up a friend or two among the multitudes of the empty and frivolous'. In private he was considerably more cynical. It was social ship-scrubbing, so much extra 'humbug', necessary perhaps, 'but on the whole it was a dog's life, altogether making a toil of pleasure'.[4]

With a 15-foot draft the *Rattlesnake* was too deep for close reef mapping. For this Stanley had inherited a shallow-draft tender left in Sydney after the *Fly*'s expedition, the *Bramble*. But it was so decayed that a lengthy refit was necessary, while a second tender was sold off as useless. Even more useless were the officers manning the boats. Stanley 'packed them all off home' and re-manned the *Bramble* with his *Rattlesnake* men.

For three months the ships were buzzing with fitters and joiners in Farm Cove. Nearby merchantmen unloaded British factory goods and took on wool for the return journey. Not all plied a colonial trade. Sydney controlled an empire within an empire.

Hundreds of tons of sandalwood were shipped to China for incense. And stranger cargoes could be seen: dried trepangs, the Barrier Reef sea slugs, destined for Chinese drug emporia.

Midshipman Sharpe reckoned that these months 'were about the best I ever had'. Bush picnics, Saturday fishing trips and soirées: sometimes with Captain Stanley, whose Sydney friends stretched back to his *Britomart* days, sometimes with Huxley, who enjoyed the junketings, despite himself.

Stanley stepped off the ship straight into a religious dispute. Like the Whig bishop, he saw no threat in Dissent, nor in its demands for equal rights with Anglicans; and fresh in port he agreed to chair a Dissenters' meeting to found a Seamen's Chapel. The High Church *Australian* damned him for joining their 'sacrilegious' ranks. What! Does he believe that any 'possessor of a black coat' can 'marry and baptize'?[5] And he, not merely an 'epauletted Son of Neptune', but an epauletted son of a *bishop*! Huxley, born into a sectarian age, watched the papers trade insults. Twelve thousand miles and nothing new: the same catcalls of 'bigotry'. Stanley backed out, leaving the *Sydney Morning Herald* to add injury to insult by concluding that he was spineless to boot.

Huxley spent his time more productively. He had caught more *Diphyes* coming up the coast and he began his new paper, 'far more considerable in extent' than the last. Its title, he informed Lizzie, would be the self-important 'Observations upon the Anatomy of the Diphydae, and upon the Unity of Organisation of the Diphydae and Phosphoridae'. ('There!' he added. 'Think yourself lucky you have only got that to read' that and not the paper itself!) Again he was using common structures to relate all these 'sea nettles' through one grand blueprint.[6] Three months gave him time to finish and it sailed off, like the last, to His Lordship at the Linnean.

It was followed by a letter to Forbes, announcing that he was corralling all the supposedly 'widely separated families' of polyp and medusa-bearing animals. He was uniting them all: the stinging hydras, sea anemones, sea nettles and jellyfish.[7] He was bringing them together in a new class; but such are the ironies of life that a Göttingen zoologist Rudolph Leuckart, barely two years his senior, anticipated him in an epochal book at precisely this moment, calling them all the 'Coelenterata'.

Away from the microscope the desolate partying continued. The lonely sailor was scouring the ballrooms for 'a few pleasant acquaintances'. He cruised the dance halls and crashed private parties. But rather than pick up a few shallow friends, he fell prey to a consuming passion.

She had hair of 'Australian silk'. Perhaps she was pretty, he could not decide. She did not know a fish from a frog but she had a ferocious talent, spoke German, loved poetry and philosophy, and the Polka. He first met Miss Henrietta Anne Heathorn at a party. She was leaving but he still waylaid her for a dance; 'my brother in law', she recalled, declared 'it impossible as his wife my sister had already gone to put on her wraps & the horses c^d not be kept waiting. Never mind said Mr Huxley – we shall meet again & then remember you are engaged for the 1st dance'. His deep-set dark eyes mesmerized her. They 'had an extraordinary way of flashing', she noted, 'when they seemed to be burning – His manner was most fascinating'.[8] While gadding about he had already met her brother-in-law, the businessman William Fanning. Fanning was married to Henrietta's half-sister Oriana and Henrietta herself kept house for them in New Town, 'a pretty house at Cook's River'.

The girl with silky hair was constantly surprised by her subaltern with flashing eyes. At the next Government ball, 'suddenly I saw him opposite me in a quadrille dancing with my sister. In the refreshment room we met & chatted so long that the man who brought me there had gone away'. Dances ruled the calendar in Sydney. They were social fortifications for a beleaguered elite, where matches were made and new arrivals could be mined. Two more passed; each time she scanned the blue-jackets for 'that delightful doctor', and each time she found him. The last was at the parsonage. 'What an eve of glamour it was'. He pinched a wishbone from his companion's plate and 'we pulled then wished & danced. He uttered magic words – before he left he begged of me the red camellia I wore'.[9] Huxley stole away, looking for all the world like a raven-haired romantic – indeed returning to his berth to preserve the bloom.

In his own diary he cloaked his emotions. The charade of interminable dances, he jotted, 'thank God, was checked by a serious . . . illness which lasted some three weeks'. His recuperation was inimitable, a 100-mile ride under shadeless gums up the coast past Newcastle. He was presumably invited by his outward-bound companion, Revd Robert, the fourth son of Captain King. The captain was a towering figure in the colony, the son of a former governor, and running an enormous farming and mining operation, the Australian Agricultural Company. Huxley rode to the company's estate at Port Stephens, where the Kings had a beautiful house called 'Tahlee'. The ubiquitous captain ran one of the colony's scientific salons. Frequently in London, he was as likely to be found bent over the barnacles in the Zoological Society's museum as discussing maritime affairs. (It was in the zoo that King had taught Darwin how to use preservatives.) King and Huxley had molluscs in common and the sea at heart, and they struck it off. The captain saw the surgeon away with packages, letters and another introduction to Richard Owen at home.

Huxley rode on with another son, Philip Gidley King, to his house at Stroud, 20 miles away. Philip had been one of the *Beagle*'s middies. At 30, he was running the company's stud farms and their approach to Stroud was heralded by fields of prize cows. Of course Huxley overdid the journey and paid for it. He was laid-up with chronic rheumatism in his foot, which kept him bedridden for days. The march was typical of the way he attacked everything, knocking himself out. And so there he lay, disgusted but grateful for King's 'kind-hearted attention'.[10]

His absence baffled Henrietta. Only later at a *Rattlesnake* picnic did she learn that he was ill up-country. Friends playing Cupid would constantly ask the middies 'whether Dʳ Huxley had returned'. She waited. 'Exquisite' picnics and parties passed. 'I began to think all that had gone before was my imagination & that his was just a sailors way'.

Arriving back, Huxley was 'glad to find that I had been inquired after by the New Town folks' – all 'instinct I suppose, for I could not have told myself why at the time'. Henrietta was way ahead of him.

In late September he found an excuse to call at Fanning's house, 'Holmwood'. Henrietta was caught unawares: she was upstairs when she heard hooves galloping up the drive and a servant 'looked out of the Bulls eye window & exclaimed Its Doctor Huxley'. Huxley joined her two half-sisters for lunch, but Henrietta 'was paralysed & cᵈ only get down' after they had adjourned to the drawing room. Even more paralysing, 'of all subjects the one under discussion', said Huxley, 'was my reception into the family'. It was coy, talk of '3 sisters . . . going about without a protector' and him offering his services to Henrietta. 'My heart leaped', Huxley said. 'But I thought to myself, Tom, you are a fool . . . and you have only seen one another four times'. He walked with them, twining flowers round her bonnet. She slipped on a branch and he pulled it away 'saying . . . so would I remove all hindrances from your path in life'.[11]

Impulsive in all things, he was as good as engaged at their fifth meeting. He had chanced his arm, and his life's course was plotted. The outsider, true to form, had found love in the colonies. The sober cynic, scratching the surface of a hollow pleasure-seeking society, had uncovered a heart as emotionally and intellectually full as his own. It surprised her; it certainly staggered him.

Nettie he called her, or 'Menen'. She was poetical, artistic, religious and well read. Two years' schooling in Neuwied on the Rhine meant they talked the same language. 'I had not the least idea of the true meaning of Science,' she admitted. 'Something of art, something of literature I knew but of science not an iota'. But 'the happiness of being together swallowed up everything else'. He drew her into an unimagined world, stranger than Australia. He unveiled the cosmos, explaining the elegant laws of chemical affinity and the unifying archetypes of animal life. He opened a door 'to undreamt of possibilities', revealing scientific dramas 'that were like fairy tales'.[12]

She would smooth the rough edges and soothe that 'scornful contempt for his fellow creatures'. Nettie was two months younger than 'Hal', having turned 22 on 1 July, 'but she is *in fact* as much younger than her years as I am older than mine'. He loved her 'Saxon yellow hair', although 'appearance has nothing whatever to do with the hold she has upon my mind for I have seen hundreds of prettier women. But I never met with so sweet a temper, so self-sacrificing and affectionate a disposition'. Her only folly was to leave 'her happiness in the hands of a man like myself, struggling upwards and certain of nothing'.[13]

But struggle and uncertainty marked the middle classes moving across the empire. Henrietta's family had been there: her mother's father had been a physician in Barbados, her grandmother (born on Antigua) had married three times and Nettie had been born in the West Indies (illegitimately, so she later discovered). She was an imperial outsider, a hardened match for Tom's marginality. She had been brought up in the hop-growing district of Kent by an aunt, her paternal grandfather having been a brewer in Maidstone. With 200 grog shops in Sydney, Australia looked like a Dionysian dream. Her father had taken over a 100-foot, three-storey flour and timber complex, Woodstock Mill, close to the village of Jamberoo, 90 miles south of Sydney.[14] He added a brewery, drawing water from the Minnamurra river, and converted the cooperage to produce beer barrels.

Nettie had followed her father out, arriving with her mother and half-sister before Christmas 1843. They travelled on a bullock dray from Wollongong to Woodstock, sitting on sacks stuffed with maize husks, stopping only to quench their thirst from sponge-like ferns in the tree forks. She had never seen such sights: 'gum-trees two hundred feet' high draped with 'snake-like' lianas, and 'lofty cabbage palms' whose canopy blocked out the sun.

For Nettie Woodstock was a steam-engine 'fairyland'. Like Hal she loved the 'whirr of machinery' and she crept into the mill to watch the ox-drawn cedar logs in the teeth of the saw, spraying perfumed sawdust.[15] But her mother wept bitter tears at the hardship, and Nettie was reduced to unpicking her own dresses. Not that she remained long. Her youngest half-sister Oriana came out two months later and was married to Fanning in the Woodstock parlour. The couple set up home in New Town, where Nettie joined them.

This is where Hal found her. Fanning's became a second home, evenings around the fire there reminding him 'of the happy old days at S[alt]'s'. Here he encountered Nettie's father, 'a curious man of strong natural talent evidently, but rather ingenious than sound'. With a French frigate in port, one final Government ball gave them the occasion to talk openly. Or rather not, as they paced about outside, pretending to take the air: 'No word of love was spoken but we understood one another'. Huxley, stiffly attired in his dress uniform, beat around the bush furiously, 'half mad with excitement'. And so ended his first Sydney spring, precipitously, with an engagement after six dances.

Huxley had his emotional mooring at last. In his unsettled way he was settling down, and away from the dance floor Nettie found quite a different soul, 'earnest and silent'. 'You have', he said, 'tied your fate to that of a young poor, I had almost said, friendless, man, rich in nothing but his love for you'. It focused his mind, and fitful nights worrying over his prospects 'brought on my old nervous palpitation'. They would marry when he made full surgeon. This he expected sometime after his return, accelerated by 'his scientific work, for this was the inducement held out by the Admiralty to energetic subalterns'. Science could still be his salvation. With renewed energy he dissected a simple relation of the cockles and mussels, *Trigonia*, and posted his findings to Forbes.[16]

Nettie's presence rekindled almost religious emotions in Huxley.

Absolved, he would rise, 'nobler and purer', 'banishing evil from my thoughts'. The long-haired student from the medical garret would start again, the font within cleansed. She had 'sweetened the very springs of my being which were before but waters of Marah, dark and bitter'. So began 'a new era', one 'of much more importance than all H. M. navy put together'. The three months up, he had to agree with young Sharpe: 'the most pleasant I have ever spent, and fraught with events'.[17]

The *Bramble* had already left port. Stanley wanted to test the tender and her 36 crew. He had kept on her commander, Lieutenant C. B. Yule, a 'very good fellow', whose knowledge of New Guinea 'will be invaluable'. At the Governor's request they sailed her 240 miles south to the whaling station at Twofold Bay, to survey the site for a new customs house. (The Sea Lords in London were monthly more infuriated by his idiosyncratic behaviour.) He found the landscape artist Oswald Brierly languishing there, managing the whaling works. Brierly was well salted, having sailed the world on an adventurer's yacht, and Stanley brought him aboard to record the *Rattlesnake*'s progress in New Guinea.

Dayman was taking soundings in Port Jackson to see if the channel could accommodate a battleship. The first major dry dock east of Bombay, big enough to berth a steamer or warship, was being built on Cockatoo Island, north of Sydney. With Britannia's need to secure the region for immigration and trade, everyone expected men-of-war to become common sights soon. As the *Bramble* and *Rattlesnake* joined up, the time of parting came. Hal left Nettie a miniature of himself, which she placed under her pillow, and he was gone.

At daybreak on 11 October 1847 they sailed out of Sydney Harbour to map the passage up to the Barrier Reef. He 'felt down-hearted'. The 'pain of parting from her was the feeling uppermost in my mind. But I am not one of those who "put finger i' the eye" and whine over the unavoidable'. He would look on the positive side and keep her 'ever present with me in my wanderings . . . an ark of promise in the wilderness of life'.

He might have been 'more outwardly content' now, but it did not stop him letting out 'a great general growl' about the shipboard separation 'as I walked up & down [with Dayman] during his watch'.[18] As they tacked north to the Inshore Passage, between the mainland and Barrier Reef, Huxley tried to get back to his thimble-sized comb jellies. But it proved difficult. They hit a squall, with terrifying lightning bolts, but the real maelstrom was in his mind. He wrote back to Nettie on the '5th day of the Hegira'. Sydney might have been his Mecca, his place of rebirth, but the prophet feared the impression he had left. He had been talking religion with her, the previous Sunday after church, leaving her under a dark cloud.[19] Now he forlornly tried to make amends, as the 'matter . . . so deeply interests us both'. But he still sounded like a Calvinistic product of London's low-brow anatomy schools. The student had emerged from the radical chaos of the 1830s and 1840s like so many, full of rational Dissenting ideas about nature, as non-miraculous and subject, as one Dissenter said, to '*Law* and *Order*'. He had pushed on, delighting in Sir William Hamilton's logic in proving that reason could not reveal God, because it could not tear aside the veil of phenomena (Hamilton used intuition for his evidence of the Divine). Huxley realized that the human mind was trapped by the limitations of thought and language, and hemmed in by physical evidence. Going beyond Hamilton, he refused to treat the Divine outside the reach of the senses as anything but an ungraspable dream.

How to explain it to Nettie? It is not *what* we believe, but *why* we believe it. Moral responsibility lies in diligently weighing the evidence. We must actively doubt; we have to scrutinize our views, not take them on trust. No virtue attached to blindly accepting orthodoxy, however 'venerable' – and certainly not for its social status (Anglicanism, as the State religion, still carried enormous privileges). Who could respect a person who would 'gratify a selfish ambition by adopting and defending the first fashionable error suited to his purpose'? Better to be 'one of those who would spend years of silent investigation in the faint hope of at length finding truth'. Huxley was on his way to defining a new relationship between Man and 'the great deep sacred infinitude' of Nature (as Carlyle had it), helped by the expanding vision of Victorian science.

He trod gingerly with Nettie. His was an honest doubt, he claimed. It was an admission that one could only go so far, stopping short of Genesis myths and miraculous interventions, Afterlife and Atonement. It *was* legitimate to 'doubt, in all sadness of heart, and from solemn fear to tread where the fools of the day boldly rush in'. But he repudiated the flaming atheists, the slum demagogues who were fired by socialist dreams. Those wretches used their politicized atheism to destroy the Anglican social fabric – 'those miserable men, whose scepticism is the result of covetousness & who pitifully exhibit their vain ingenuity for the mere purpose of . . . disturbing the faith of others'.

He ended with a powerful image of the Reformation, when protesters indicted the corrupt Papacy and sought a morally cleansed basis of belief. 'I can only say in Martin Luther's ever famous words, "Hier Steh Ich – Gott helfe mir – Ich kann nicht anders" ["Here I stand – God help me – I cannot do otherwise"]'.[20] At Holmwood, Nettie was not comforted.

The ship arrived at Moreton Bay on 17 October 1847. A local steamer had sunk in the south passage to this 20-mile-wide bay, drowning most on board, and Stanley's surveyors spent time marking a safer north entrance. Huxley went off shooting, tagged by two 'gentlemen in black', friendly Morton Islanders, bagging 'ten fine cockatoos, whose edible excellencies I mean to try at breakfast'. The sight of the flat munching faces of dugongs or sea cows caused excitement, no less than the aborigines harpooning them in Brisbane River. A new porpoise was also spotted, although killing it was a native taboo, and MacGillivray refused rather than 'outraging their strongly expressed superstitious feelings'. (Only later did he learn why. The aborigines worked with the porpoises to catch shoals of mullet – the porpoises driving them inshore, allowing huge numbers to be speared, themselves weaving safely in and out of the natives' legs.)

On board, the crew entertained the aborigines, the men and women all naked, save only a 'small fringe in front' on the young girls. The married women were evident by the loss of the last joint of the right-hand little finger.[21] The industrious MacGillivray started to build a lexicon of aboriginal sounds. Huxley set off with Stanley up the Brisbane River in the *Asp*. The blue-and-white flowering vines at the jungle's edge gave way to 'picturesque' country near Brisbane itself. This was a 'veritable Garden of Eden'. It was perfect pastoral land, and the squatters' wool was cried out for by the English mills. But the shifting sand banks made the Brisbane River a treacherous artery, and Stanley's brief was to find a safer way of transporting the wool to the waiting ships.

Stanley and Huxley parted in Brisbane, which had only recently been freed from its vicious military rule. Huxley hired a horse and a squatter guide and decked himself out. What with corduroys, 'a cabbage tree hat' and moustache, 'no one could have distinguished me from a genuine squatter'. (Darwin would have flinched. He dismissed the squatter as 'the horror of all his honest neighbours', the contemptible ex-con who 'steals a few animals, sells Spirits without a licence, buys stolen goods & so at last ... turns farmer'.) No such scruples for Huxley, setting off in squatter's guise for the Darling Downs. 'I shall not soon forget the exhilaration of my spirits as we rode through the bush', free from all worries about 'such things as ships'. Up the Brisbane River they galloped to see the wool depots. By the next day they had reached the Dividing Range, and on the third had 'the stiffest ride of all – forty-five miles', their brains baked and gullets dry. Through dense bush they rode, lassoed by vines, laughed at by kookaburras. The last pass proved 'one of the toughest climbs ... I ever had'. The scene at the top of the Darling Downs was worth it: majestic eucalyptuses, strangler figs built on flying buttresses, 'whimsical festooned creepers' hanging 'like a fantastic drapery', and 'a deep stillness reigned over all, broken only now and then by the sweet musical chime of the bell-bird'.[22]

Coming back was even sweeter. Nettie's first letter caught him at Brisbane. He sat reading it behind a sack in the *Asp*, stuck on a mudflat. She talked of her love, 'deepened and confirmed', and whatever her religious worries 'I have no misgivings'. 'Thank you, thank you a thousand times', he intoned, 'it is all, all I could wish'. He had not been romancing in a dream, 'the story of our love is a true story'.

Many a lonely sailor found love in town or among the rocks. Huxley was not alone in his affair. The *Bramble*'s surgeon Archie McClatchie had paid court to Nettie's best friend Alice Radford. At sea the shipmates had 'dreadfully long "yarns"' about the girls, with Archie tweaking Huxley about tying the knot on his 'struggling fortunes'.[23]

The *Rattlesnake* hauled off on 4 November. They sailed past coral islands colonized by breeding seabirds, stopping only to survey Port Curtis on Harvey Bay, near the Tropic of Capricorn. In London Gladstone had planned to turn this superb ten-mile-wide bay into the major port for 'North Australia'. (And to start a new convict colony to take the pressure off Tasmania.) A year earlier settlers had founded the town of 'Gladstone'. But before the first nail had been hammered, its fate had been sealed a world away. The Conservatives had been swept from office in 1846 and the incoming Whigs scotched the idea. Huxley entered a ghost town of eerie relics: piled bricks, posts marking the '"Government-house," wheel ruts in the hardened clay ... with a goodly store of empty bottles strewed about everywhere'.[24] As the grog-swilling settlers had pulled out, so an older life had returned, the emus and kangaroos leaving tell-tale tracks across the mudflats.

Aboard, the chart-room was quiet, the middies away, and Huxley pored over the mud from the dredge. It was full of fern-like *Plumularia*, branching colonies of tentacle-waving polyps, the 'sea firs' so abundant in these waters. And dragged from its burrow was a superficially clam-like *Lingula*, a sort of 'living fossil', its shell indistinguishable from those in ancient rocks.[25]

Then he and MacGillivray took off for Facing Island, out in the Bay. In 90° temperatures they waded the swamps and sedge grass, sending oystercatchers flying. Flocks of noisy blue mountain parrots flew between gum trees as the men cooked black duck 'bush fashion' for supper. The land was good only for game in the sailors' eyes, and MacGillivray returned to shoot a 22-pound Australian bustard for his messmates' supper. As always the ship was a sanctuary in these hostile waters; poisonous sea snakes infested the harbour, and enormous sharks would break surface to shred fish hooked from the *Rattlesnake*'s stern. But the towing net yielded treasures: endless jellyfish, including the two-foot *Cephea*, like an enormous all-seeing umbrella with its eight red eye dots.[26]

Three hundred miles further on a storm forced them into the Percy Islands. The sailors arrived on the main island to find the gum scrub graced by flocks of black and white cockatoos, and scattered turtle carapaces signalling aboriginal feasts. They left it smouldering. Someone set fire to the long grass, trapping the naturalists who barely escaped to the boats. On deck all they could do was watch the blaze for days until nothing remained. They pushed on to Captain Cook's Whitsunday Passage (near modern Proserpine). Ashore the lagoons were dry and cracked. Metallic flashes caught the eye as the crew searched for water in the brush. The captain's servant shot a yellow-breasted sunbird, with its steel-blue throat. MacGillivray too was out with his gun, hunting for the most extraordinary of birds, megapodes. In clearings these 'brush turkeys' could be seen scraping great mounds of vegetation, in which the females would lay their eggs and, unique among birds, let the fermenting greenery do the incubating.

The bizarre beauty of the place only emphasized their distance from home. On Saturday 11 December Huxley had been away for a year – 12 months that had seen black despair and a bright light. He had mastered the sea nettles, but not his feeling of alienation, and his loneliness only increased at the thought of Nettie. That day found the *Rattlesnake* off Cape Upstart (near today's Bowen) and the perfect present was yet to come. No water could be found. The pools located by the *Fly* were dry. In fact almost no fresh water had been detected anywhere inside the tropics and the crew were rationed to six pints a day in the heat. The captain had no choice but to stop surveying the reefs and turn the ship back. It was a 'red mark' day, Huxley scribbled. He would see his sweetheart again. 'Sydney in five weeks! Bravo'.[27]

But everything bedevilled them. A powerful trade wind battered the square-rigger; then they were becalmed. The *Asp*, charting inshore, found inaccuracies on the Admiralty map. Sheltering during a squall on Keppel Island led them to more unknown reefs, which had to be mapped. On Christmas Eve, Huxley came on deck for his 10 pm. constitutional, to be greeted by a cacophony of shouts as a poop officer spotted foam a cable's length ahead: ' "Breakers on the lee bow", screamed a lookout. "Hands about ship. Down with the helm", and round went the old ship like a whisk', past the prettiest coral reef. A few moments more and Christmas Day would have been spent as a castaway on Curtis Island. The mix of heart-stopping drama and slack canvas infuriated him:

> Christmas Eve! a time that one has been used to consider
> as . . . an occasion of pleasant meeting among friends.
> And here I am in this atrocious berth without a soul to
> whom I can speak an open friendly word. But it is all
> good discipline doubtless . . . for I find myself getting
> more and more satisfied and content with my own sweet
> society and that of my books.

The frustration was relieved by Carlyle and the teeming crustaceans. Carlyle was a bit of a crustaceous philosopher, whose books were devoured by Huxley as quickly as 'by the mighty hordes of cockroaches in my cabin'. Carlyle warned him against 'a dead brute Steam-engine' view of nature, built of mechanical checks and balances, pain and pleasure drives, utility and fatalism, with 'all soul fled out of it'. That way lay 'the black malady', scepticism. Contentment could only come from Nature's poetic praise of the Godhead.[28] But perhaps the greatest lesson he learned from reading Carlyle was that real religion, that emotive feeling for Truth and Beauty, could flourish in the absence of an idolatrous theology.

Christmas Day was shadowless under the Capricorn sun. Huxley was nostalgic for snowy mornings, church music and childish excitement.

> There shall be no more Christmas days or festive days of
> any kind for me in a ship. It is a cruel mockery to call a
> drinking bout among a parcel of people thrown together
> by the Admiralty 'spending a merry Christmas'. It is a
> more than Egyptian feast, for *all* the guests are skeletons.

Two years earlier he had been sitting by the fire with the family. That, 'alas! was but the last ray of a happy sun, followed by a dark night of misfortunes'. Lizzie's banishment preyed on his mind. It was now complete in its peculiar way. Word reached him that the 'Scotts' had crossed the Atlantic to New Orleans. Even here their hopes were fading, their plan to buy a farm and start afresh in some semi-civilized territory. Dreams require cash: Lizzie had done her best 'with G^{eo} to induce him to spare a trifle', but they had sailed empty handed. George still received 'pitiable' letters 'from America . . . in which *she* is made to appeal to my feelings to avert actual starvation', all because of 'her vagabond husband'. Tom's mother was crushed. 'God help them for . . . what can be the end of all his strange doings'? His doings became stranger: from New Orleans they had trekked to the backwoods – social ostracism sending them to the farthest reaches. And still there was secrecy; only Tom knew their final destination, Tennessee.[29] 'Oh Lizzie! . . . what endless misery hast thou seen'. The ship rolled along, his gloom accompanied by bumping waves; 'you and I were the only two I believe who really loved and therefore understood one another'. Her image seemed to fade, the sound of her voice drowned by the wind in the canvas: 'we may never meet again'.

As the year ended they blew into Moreton Bay and filled the kegs. All hands watched the *Bramble* return from Brisbane with the mailbags. That afternoon, 6 January 1848, the weather brightened. 'I got half a dozen letters, one from Sydney which was almost more than I had ventured to hope – and that I read first – so true is it that a man shall leave his father and his mother and cleave unto his – ah! would I could call thee – wife'. But Nettie was in black. The Governor's death had put the colony in mourning, and it turned her thoughts to their eternal destiny:

> I hope dearest that I may die before you . . . I was thinking
> I could not bear you to be taken and me left alone . . .

God forbid this and may the day be very far distant before
this dread separation shall come. May we love and grow
old together and dying may we meet again in Heaven.[30]

Heaven could wait; it was their earthly separation that frustrated
Hal. The next morning, the skipper brought equally welcome
news: 'that the [man-of-war] Paper had arrived, had been perused
by Prof. Forbes who was "delighted" . . . with it, and was to be
read before the Linnean Society'. Perhaps he was sailing into
glory.[31]

All eyes were now on Sydney. For five hours on 13 January 1848
this was literally true. The *Rattlesnake* lay becalmed, 'sails flapping
against the mast – in sight of the Heads'. 'Would that the good
ship *Rattlesnake* were the veriest old smokejack of a steamer', he
grumbled as a 'Hunter River steamer' chugged past, only an hour
from disgorging its passengers. It was a sign that the days of
canvas were numbered. The sailing ship *Rattlesnake*, by 'sweeping'
the Inner Passage, was ironically making the sea safe for the
steamers. He found the issue a talking point in Sydney the next
day. Plans were already afoot for a railway to siphon the flood of
steamer-born immigrants away from Sydney. How far away
nobody could tell, although an exploring party at that moment
was blazing a trail across the continent to the Swan River Settlement (Perth).

Given shore leave, he was 'off to New Town' to make up for
three months' separation. The two weeks were awash with colour
and excitement. Hal and Nettie, along with most of the colony's
50,000 inhabitants, joined the festivities as Sydney celebrated its
60th anniversary, culminating in a regatta on 26 January. Every
ship was dressed, lights sparkling; 'we gave a grand turnout', he
admitted, proud of his adopted city.

The euphoria ended on 2 February, when 'I found myself out at
sea again'. Stanley had set out for the Bass Strait at the new
Governor's request, to inspect the lighthouses between Tasmania
and the mainland. The smooth water of the Strait was cathartic
and endless *Oceanea* jellies left Huxley 'content with the world'.
He even dropped his mother a teasing note, suggesting he might
turn 'colonial' and leaving her to guess why.[32]

But as usual the warm glow turned into a hot stew. In the thick
mist at Port Phillip the thermometer topped 90°. But there were
compensations. Inside, the Port was alive with sails, acres of white
canvas and blue medusae. The magnificent harbour, wide and

deep enough for 'half a dozen navies', saw a fleet of merchant vessels ready to take on wool. And, on the ripple line, 'Vast numbers of a large "sea-jelly" (*Rhizostoma Mosaica*), gave the water quite a milky appearance'. Huxley was now blinkered by more than love. Dismissing the country, and writing off the seaside village of William's Town as 'a few weatherboard houses', he cocooned himself aboard, pulling up and drawing the football-sized, tentacle-less jellies.[33]

Only when the temperature fell by 30°F did he stir. He put ashore with McClatchie at a 'rickety pier' attached to a William's Town tavern. They lubricated themselves and took a mail cart the two miles to Melbourne. 'I must say I was very much surprised, knowing that the place had been not more than ten years in existence, to observe its size and the many tall chimneys which rose near the river – evidently indicating manufactories of considerable size'. These tallow works had attracted colonists and the city already boasted 12,000 people. 'There are several very good hotels. We went to the Royal, procured horses, [and] rode about the Town'. Everywhere were 'bullock-teams and drays recently arrived with wool'; everyone hurrying, with 'few loungers like ourselves in the streets'. It oozed prosperity. The talk was of independence from New South Wales (which was soaking up the revenues) and the creation of a self-governing state, Victoria. They arrived with a grand ball imminent, but Huxley declined this time; 'faith'! he exclaimed, 'I'm getting staid'.

The wind in their teeth, they sailed on 21 February to Tasmania's northern coast, dominated by Mount Valentine, 'bold and grand in its outline'. Huxley set off to explore the 'cheerful' region around Port Dalrymple. The effect of crossing the Bass Strait had been to bring them closer to home. 'Everything from the rosy-faced girls and children to the fruit trees bent down under their weight of apples or pears put us in mind of England'. He took the steamer up the 'picturesque' River Tamar the 40 miles to Launceston. It was 'exceedingly pretty country . . . very like some of the middle counties of England'. Yellow stubble fields greeted him everywhere, the harvest just in, and galloping down shady lanes left him with an exhilarating homesickness.

In Port Dalrymple everyone was busy. Dayman with his chronometers, MacGillivray shipping sunbird skins to John Gould at London's Zoological Society,[34] and below decks Huxley was finishing his most ambitious paper, based on his hundreds of jellyfish nettings.

The jellies had a simple stomach suspended under an umbrella-like bell. Microscopically the stomach wall appeared as two 'foundation membranes', an inner, ciliated one and an outer, denser one. Huxley made these layers and the gelatin-like mass sandwiched in between the defining features of medusae. Every jelly's muscles, sex organs and tentacles stemmed from a precise part of a membrane. Then he went on to relate the jellies themselves to the stinging *Hydra*-like polyps and men-of-war and plumularian sea firs. *All* shared this two-layer plan, their membranes only folding differently. To prove that the tentacles or sex organs of *Physalia* and the jellies were homologous he caught every growth stage, and then watched these parts emerge from the same layers in the embryo.

What did this say about jellies? They had been lumped by default with single-cell amoebas on one hand and starfish on the other in Cuvier's rag-bag group, the 'Radiata'. From 12,000 miles away the assistant surgeon was breaking into this 'lumber room' of ill-assorted creatures; he was regrouping the two-layer stinging animals into a great discrete class of their own. From down under he was turning nature upside down.[35]

Nettie, a sensible girl who liked Schiller and penned love poems, must have asked 'Why jellyfish?' And he must have led her self-importantly from these pulsing 'nastinesses' to the great problem of existence, contrasting his tiny truths of creation with the sand-castle sophistries for which men were willing to die. The tiny truths were real bricks which would build a palatial foundation to Truth. They were the stanzas of Nature's great poem; and only by reciting the ultimate sonnet could we gain a rational set of mores and a real meaning to life.

Huxley planned to post the opus to Sir William Burnett, to present to the Royal Society, not out of 'sycophancy', but because 'I owe the old man much, and would do this as a simple matter of respect'. He made it sound like a favour to the old gent. But in truth he was rationalizing his use of silver-haired patrons. The stakes were high. The Royal Society was the upper tier of English science, nigh-on 300 years old and able to confer enormous prestige. Curiously, at this moment it was suffering a corporate version of Huxley's own angst. His reluctant relations with the Burnetts and bishops reflected the wider antagonisms of British science. The Society's courtly days were ending. Its old loyalties to Crown and Church (typified by Burnett and bishop) were fading with the influx of capitalists, doctors and academics.[36] Its new backers were merchants and empire builders; its new gods utility and service to the state; its new priests, the technocrats and specialists. Men like Huxley were taking over, disdaining salon politics and society patrons, contemptuous of the spider-stuffing clergy and blue-blooded dilettantes. Half-way round the world he caught the metropolitan mood exactly, even if he had to swallow his pride and play the game for the moment.

This was to be his make-or-break paper, and on it his scientific fate would ride. If it succeeds 'I shall go on accordingly'. If it flops 'I will give these things up and try some other channel towards happiness for dear Menen and myself'.

At sea on 3 March an unprecedented $10\frac{1}{2}$-knot speed shook the scuttlebucket, 'jury-rigged as she was' for slow surveying. Huxley's tremors were inside. He thought on pride and vanity. A driven man, wanting scientific recognition, he was twisted by guilt, the fear of ambition. His volcanic moods were fuelled by thoughts of Nettie and the need to be noticed, and brought to flash point as he tweezered medusae. 'I am content with nothing, restless and ambitious . . . and I despise myself for the vanity, which formed half the stimulus to my exertions'. 'Oh would that I were one of those plodding wise fools who having once set their hand to the plough go on nothing doubting'.

Stumbling on the granite outcrops and 'mutton bird' burrows of Goose Island left him feeling a plodding fool. He was greeted at dusk by 'clouds' of these returning shearwaters, flitting past his head 'like spectres in the gloaming'. As darkness fell, and the crew set about clubbing the birds in a bloodthirsty scrum, he peered through Stanley's telescope, seeing a nebula for the first time and becoming lost in the blackness of space.

'I must say this for the skipper – oddity as he is, he has never failed to offer me and give me the utmost assistance in his power'. Stanley brimmed with *noblesse oblige*, but his kindness left Huxley uneasy. On the run up to Sydney Stanley came into the chart-room, watched him drawing medusae and offered again to post the paper to the bishop. It prompted Huxley into musing on his own attitude. 'I often fancy that if I took the trouble to court him a little we should be great friends – as it is I always get out of his way and shall do so to the end'. Huxley was his own man, his fierce independence bordering on social contempt, taking pride in his class and his talent. His dark eyes flashed defiance. Rank for him was earned by grit and ability, not appointed from on-high. He met social hauteur with intellectual snobbery. 'That same stiffneckedness (for which I heartily thank God) stands in my way with others, my "superior" officers'. Were he to kow-tow they 'would I am sure think me what is ordinarily called a "capital fellow" i.e. a great fool'.

It was nobody's fool who beat up the south coast. The fates of course mocked him. Just as the frigate tacked north for Sydney, the wind chopped to the east, lashing them with rain and forcing them in to Cape Howe. 'If I were a Catholic I would invest a little capital in wax candles to my pet saints'.[37] But Nature was no capricious dame, to be appeased by the gods. His life was now planned: to understand the eternal truths behind her superficial veil. Knowledge of a secular nature, there lay the new source of power. It was not to be delegated by episcopal patrons, but seized by plebeian hands.

6

The Eighth Circle of Hell

IT WAS A TIME of trysts. These were 'fairy days' for Nettie, when midshipman Sharpe 'was Mercury to me and Hal', carrying notes and arranging rendezvous. The ship's arrival in Sydney on 9 March 1848 had given them another seven weeks' grace.

Hal caught up with the gossip. He heard about the three clergymen who had deserted to Rome, leaving Nettie's church unattended. Distant Sydney was shadowing Oxford, as the Tractarians moved to more ritualistic Catholic practice. 'How very dreadful', she exclaimed, sharing his dislike of anything 'Romish'. 'I cannot imagine any sensible person turning Catholic, it is repugnant to common sense'.

Huxley could never escape the whirl of religion. 'What wonderful and beautiful sights have already met your view', his mother exclaimed, 'there is something so fresh and refreshing in your letters, so unlike the worldliness and care of everyday life'. She hoped that his chance 'to contemplate the wonders of Nature' away from the Church-haters and Chartists would fortify him, hoped:

> that whilst your mind is young & free to judge of the God of Nature by his Works and Providences, you may also find an inward witness to strengthen those same convictions e're you return to the Land of your Birth, and mix again, as you 'must do,' with the Scoffer and the Unbeliever. I say 'must do,' because they seem to me to stalk about more arrogantly than ever. May God bless you my dear Tom, for he alone can keep you from such Adversaries.[1]

*

86

The lovers were soon visiting the 'fine shops in George Street and Pitt Street, where French silks' were cheaper than in London. They strolled in the Domain (the public gardens), taking in the military band or watching Sydney's elite disport themselves in their expensive carriages. Then tea on the verandah, yellow loquats and peaches, so plentiful that they were fed to the pigs. The land seemed to Nettie an 'earthly Paradise'. And now she had her Adam, even if he offered more bitter fruit. But even that – Hal's scepticism – might abate with 'God's blessing'.[2]

But paradise was littered with ruined archangels. Huxley met his share of these sad souls, petty criminals spared the gallows, boys sent out for burglary. Transportation to New South Wales had been suspended, but this was still a prison colony. Iron gangs worked on the roads, their grey and yellow uniforms standing out. Convicts took on every wretched duty: on the sheep stations, in shops and as servants. Even as portrait painters: for all of Nettie's disdain she was painted in pastels by Thomas Griffiths Wainewright the Poisoner. (Actually he was transported for forgery. The sickly aesthete, now broken on the road gangs, had exhibited at the Royal Academy before trying to obtain his inheritance ahead of time.)

The servants were Nettie's bugbear. Decanters had to be locked up, and desk drawers. Once a drunken butler pointed a gun at Will and had to be led away struggling. Uppity maids and tipsy recidivists were all the gossip:

> Domestic troubles – a new housemaid arrived the night
> before, sent word before breakfast – she didn't think she'd
> like the place and forthwith left – all the other servants
> believing her crazed. Really I never knew such a
> discontented race.

'Of all the minor miseries of life there is in truth one transcending all, that of being dependent on your cook'. But having to brook the cook's wild turkey without bread sauce was nothing to Huxley's shock in the stable. He met the groom. The face was familiar, a bit older and hardened; it was William Poideoin, the bully who had given him a black eye at school. Poideoin was a rarity among the pilferers and prostitutes, but not the first public schoolboy Sydney had seen. He 'occupies the post of half clerk – half ostler to a stable man here. He recognised me and I commiserated [with] him greatly (from his own account) until I heard . . . that he had been "sent out" (colonial for transported which is impolite) and had one or two colonial convictions since'. Ticket-of-leave men were all on the make, and Poideoin, grubbing for references from 'Respectable parties', tried to tap Huxley 'for old school fellows sake', without much success.[3]

Tom told everyone at home. But his letters carried more startling news. He dropped his mother a line about the engagement. Lizzie learned of the romantic side, how they 'managed to fall in love . . . in the most absurd manner after seeing one another – I will not tell you how many times, lest you should laugh'. George's was a more jaded account: 'Jim is my great comfort', Tom joked of his medical brother, mad-doctoring again and a model of family virtue, complete with a baby daughter, Katy. Look at him, 'he committed a similar folly about the same time of life – with a coarse lookout and now le voilá', transformed into 'a respectable, corporative, bunch-of-seals sort of man' (a crack at Britain's growing civic pride and mayoral regalia). The vision was horrifying and appealing. 'You are right in imagining the astonishment of us people at your essay in the tender business', Jim replied, 'especially our mother, who . . . scarcely thought the world as yet contained the properly adapted article for you'.

Immediate marriage was out. He was not going to copy MacGil-livray, who was crushed by debt yet crazily rushing into marriage (love-sick sailors quickly succumbed in the colony). A Malthusian poor-house society showed no mercy on the improvident. Huxley was not prepared to sink in penury like his brothers-in-law (a sticky topic, with George now bailing out Cooke): 'were she Venus & the Graces rolled in to one I am not sufficiently fond of love in a cottage, to hurry into marriage upon a hundred & twenty seven pounds ten shillings and no pence per annum. Vice to be hated needs to be seen, they say. If poverty were substituted for "vice" the proverb would be more veritable – so we have made up our minds to wait like prudent folk'.

His hope remained science and the Service. He intended to 'write myself into my promotion' and 'I have the strongest persua-sion that four years hence I shall be married and settled in England. We shall see'.[4]

It gave his make-or-break paper a new urgency. This was not just jellyfish esoterica; it was his deliverance. If he could hold the Sea Lords to their word about rewarding scientific assistants, he could jump the queue to full surgeon – or, if not, obtain an academic post in London. Either way it was his future and he invested enormous energy in it. He talked incessantly of these hopes, but Nettie never fully understood. Living in the real world, of planters and brewers, she found the idea bizarre, that 'a description of a marine creature should win him fame', let alone the funds 'that would enable us to marry'.[5]

In mid-March the paper was ready. It went first to a beautiful new mansion, Elizabeth Bay House, the best scientific salon in Sydney. This was the home of the austere bachelor William Sharp Macleay, out in the colony eight years to help his father (a former Colonial Secretary). Huxley rated Macleay 'one of the first anatomists of the present day'. He was also 'the most extraordinary old fellow I ever met with ... talk of what you will from Church history to Colonial politics – on the number of joints in a beetle's hind leg – he is equally ready. And his black eyes twinkle in the midst of his yellow wrinkled physiognomy'.[6]

At Macleay's salon you could find Captain King and an enthusiasm for insects. Here was also heard more arcane talk. Long before, as an Embassy attaché in Paris, liquidating British claims at the end of the Napoleonic Wars, Macleay had devised a peculiar geometric arrangement for his beetles. He classified all organisms in sets of five, which he pictured on the circumference of a circle. He saw five classes of animals, joined in a ring, each class with five orders, ultimately ending up in myriad circles of five linked species. This elegant pattern was considered a piece of Divine neatness – or more commonly as Macleay's '*Quinarian* nonsense'. But it was no nonsense to Huxley, searching for the sublime patterns in nature. Macleay's 'circular system' would influence him enormously over the next decade.

Macleay had devised it in the aftermath of the French Revolution. As an Embassy attaché he had seen the social shambles caused by the ragged revolutionaries, and it was in this context of post-war Paris that his new science packed its ideological punch. The English upper classes blamed the Revolution on the poisonous philosophies of the Enlightenment. And the naturalist singled out for most venom, the man who 'vomited' his 'abominable trash' over a profligate Paris, was Jean-Baptiste Lamarck. Lamarck's evolutionary theory was damned as scientific excrement, fouling the wellsprings of society and subverting Church authority. Lamarck, professor of insects and worms at the Paris Museum of Natural History, had seen animal life rise unaided on the earth, one species transforming into another, rather than being Created miraculously. He envisaged twin evolutionary streams rising from the same base – one passing through the worms towards the insects, the other from polyps to molluscs. In the reactionary Regency, Macleay emasculated the system at a stroke. He bent Lamarck's two streams into a circle, destroying the force of his upward-moving nature (which ultimately made mankind an evolved ape), while leaving the idea of continuity intact.[7] He bastardized the system, sending nature round in circles. Mankind was spared a soul-destroying ape ancestry.

Huxley was set thinking by Macleay, pondering nature's geometry as he prepared his 'Medusae' paper. The circles appealed to his aesthetic sense. He had a 'strong appreciation of the Beautiful in whatever shape', and in Nature's circular symmetry the beauty seemed transcendent. Lizzie learnt that 'the celebrated' Macleay 'werry much approves what I have done'. It was a good signal and ended an autumn of optimism. 'I tell Netty to look to being a "Frau Professorin" one of these odd days, and she has faith'.[8]

Huxley was more modern than Macleay. He took a developmental approach to the classification of life. He would show the organs of jellyfish and men-of-war developing from the embryo in the same way, to prove that they were related. All had a common two-membrane structure – indeed, Huxley casually noted towards the end of his 'Medusae' paper, these jellyfish membranes bore the same physiological relation to one another as did the two cell layers in the early vertebrate embryo. And that was a breathtaking connection – sweeping across creation from the man-of-war to Man himself.[9]

As always there was the hoary problem of placing the paper. Oddly enough, George on business in Versailles had run into the Bishop of Norwich. There could have been no more inspired coincidence; nor a more agreeable tip-off. Tom's mother reported that they 'travelled in the same carriage . . . The Bishop identified His Name with yours immediately', leading to a bumpy conversation about sea jellies 'in which you figured most agreeably amongst the Bishops observations'. It was, said his mother, 'Honey to my Heart'.[10] And to Tom's. Now he knew that he was being noticed.

His qualms vanished. On Stanley's say so, he again targeted 'the Nautical Bishop – I want him to get [the new paper] read at the Royal Society . . . If a thing is worth any thing it's worth making the best of'. And on that principle he wrote to Sir John Richardson, asking him to back the bishop. George he dragooned even more shamelessly. 'As you have met the Bishop and know him would you mind calling upon him some time or other to ascertain the fate of my unfortunate . . . progeny?' He needed feedback. 'The Bishop will tell you what competent men say . . . and let me know "nothing extenuating["] I am not likely to "die of an article" a la Keats'.[11]

In the event Stanley sent it with his dispatch to Admiral Beaufort (the chief hydrographer), to be passed on to the bishop. Perhaps this was to make amends, to take the wind out of their Lordships' sails after his own peregrinations. Anyway the message went with it, that his young surgeon 'is very anxious to have [it] read out at one of the learned societies – the Royal in preference'.[12]

Would it share the fate of Noah's raven, never more to be seen – or was it his dove? With the paper gone, he girded his loins. Before him lay the long haul. Every man-jack would be a hirsute Noah before they finished on the reef, 'making straight the path of the steamers'.

> For the next ten months Her Majesty's Ship will be a kind
> of lay monastery – a floating hermitage – free from all the
> deceits of the world the flesh (save of a black & woolly
> nature) & and devil . . . For ten mortal months we shall
> do nothing but cultivate our beard – fry our liver – and
> make acquaintance with great numbers of marine
> unpleasantnesses.

But at least in the watery wastes he could show a profit: 'where there is nothing to be bought you can't spend . . . I shall have some seventy or eighty pounds in my pocket on our return & be able to pay off old scores'.[13]

The 'fairy days' were at an end. Nettie steeled herself for the uncertainties ahead. She was 'fearful lest you meet with attacks from the natives'.[14] No one underrated the dangers, or the fevers that swept the sick bay. She reconciled herself to long silences as the ship made its laborious way to Cape York, on the north-eastern tip of Australia.

Stanley now added a barque to his mini fleet of mother ship, deck boats and tender. The *Tam O'Shanter* carried an exploring party, destined to blaze the trail overland, through the hot, trackless bush all the way from Rockingham Bay (near the modern town of Ingham, in northern coastal Queensland) to Cape York, 600 miles north as the cockatoo flies. While the donkey-frigate earned its name, continuing to mark a channel for the steamships inside the northern stretch of the Barrier Reef, the overland party would cut its way through the unexplored bush, mapping, collecting plants and animals, recording aboriginal tribes and so on, to join up at the Cape.

Stanley had helped plan the overland expedition, qualified only by his sea captain's omniscience. The barque was packed with provisions, 28 horses, 100 sheep, wagons and every breed of hardy explorer. Led by the indomitable Edmund Kennedy, who had searched the central Australian deserts for rivers and knew the North Australian interior, the party included the botanist William Carron (Macleay's gardener), Thomas Wall the naturalist, a store-keeper, shepherd, three carters, four labourers and a Hunter River aboriginal guide, Jackey Jackey. There was enormous optimism about this trip. Kennedy was a good leader, religious, supportive and full of enthusiasm. It was to be a 'pilgrimage of discovery'.[15]

The *Rattlesnake* sailed out of Sydney on 29 April 1848. Immediately Huxley's tumultuous emotions overcame him. As the ship cast off he opened his diary with the refrain 'I have no heart to write'. It set the tone for the long voyage. It should have been a challenge as he entered the richest coral sea in the world. By his own admission the opportunities were 'such as none but a blind man would fail to make use of'. And he had plenty of time, for they were to map reefs by means of a monotonous series of triangulations and explore tropical islands for the 600 miles of the Inner Passage, between the Barrier Reef and the mainland.

Five days out, on 4 May, Huxley took stock. The flotilla had struggled 150 miles against adverse currents. The wind had died, the sea was a 'blue mirror'. He peered in, reflecting on life, or rather on the pulsing jellies, still hoping to claim this corner of creation. Medusae gave way to marriage. 'My birthday again. What an immense change has this twenty-third year made in me! Perhaps ... it will turn out to be the most important in my life. My first year of sea-life – my first year of scientific investigation ... my first year, last but not least, of love'. He reread Nettie's letters, and scooped out a 'beautiful' *Stephanomia*, a sea nettle with a whole column of swimming bells, and spent his birthday studying it.[16]

The 1,500-mile trip to Rockingham Bay gave him time to learn Italian, which he found easy. It took him away from the wretch-making smell. The meat packers had failed to seal the containers, leaving them with half-a-ton of putrefying flesh, which would have crawled over the side by itself had it not been fed to the sharks off Port Bowen. On 21 May they reached Rockingham Bay, an inlet

18° south of the Equator. The land was lush during the rains and the water holes full. For a few it was heaven. As the ship circled the bay – Goold Island – the Family Islands – Dunk Island – Doctor Thomson continually took off ashore. 'The time passes on very comfortably,' he nodded; every island had its collectables and shells. 'With a perpendicular sun the perspiration pours down off me and my clothes are as wet as if I had walked through a pond'. His dark-eyed assistant had a more pained expression. Huxley began niggling. 'Rain, Rain!' he growled:

> The ship is intensely miserable. Hot, wet, and stinking.
> One can do nothing but sleep. This wet weather takes
> away all my energies. I do not mind dry heat to any extent
> but to be steamed in this manner is too much for me. I try
> to pass the time away in thinking, sleeping and novel-
> reading, which last is a kind of dreaming.

He lay in his Turkish bath, lost in the anonymous *Ranthorpe*. (It was actually written by George Henry Lewes, later George Eliot's lover, both of whom Huxley would come to know well.) He identified with the wounded aspirations of its rough diamond hero. Through salty eyes he stared into a cracked mirror. It was a clichéd story, but for a moment he was back on the Strand. He was standing in Percy Ranthorpe's shoes – that sold-out dramatist and poet, hating himself for believing that 'merit unheralded wins no victory, unpatronised, gains no attention'. But deep down Ranthorpe, like Huxley, another 'poor, dreamy boy, self-taught, self-aided', knew that there was only real 'dignity in intellectual rank'. It left Huxley with a niggling self-doubt. 'Have I the capabilities for a scientific life'? If he had, there was 'something holy' in using them. But to strive with no gift, pushed on by patrons, 'no Bedlam fool can be more worthy of contempt'.[17] As he stewed in his sweat, the doubts boiled up in his brain.

Even the jellies lost their attraction. Only the natives now piqued his interest. Ashore he painted the aborigines, and they painted him, thumbing bars of red paint across his forehead. He felt their flat elongated beards. They stared back at his own facial adornment, only marginally less remarkable. He had grown 'a peak in Charles I. style', which gave a '*triste* expression to my sunburnt phiz'. Like most sailors, he was faintly bemused by the 'savages'; it was a jittery, nervous reaction. The young man from Ealing gave a condescending laugh at the sight of them struggling with pipe and baccy. He shared that sense of civilized hauteur, perhaps because they were unaccountably threatening, less physically than culturally. What did he make of these naked 'gins', who looked upon white men as '*marki*' or ghosts of their ancestors?[18] He stared into their eyes during painting sessions. Fads and taboos gripped every culture. But here the alterations were painfully physical; the right upper incisor was knocked out during childhood and the septum of the nose perforated for a bone; bodies were covered with extraordinary whirling cicatrices or ornamental scars, and there was no clothing but an occasional armlet or girdle of twisted human hair, perhaps with an opossum tassel.

Fierce currents forced the barque to stand off 500 yards. Kennedy's supplies were ferried over. The fiddler played a 'stamp-and-go' shanty as the horses were hauled over the gunwale and their heads lashed to a boat, ready to be swum ashore. On the beach the 89 surviving sheep were gathered by the shepherd. A ton of flour and 600 lbs of sugar were off-loaded; three carts, four tents, canvases, gunpowder, shot. The ferrying was endless. All the boats were involved: guns, blankets, books, axes, pack saddles, 40 chains, three kangaroo dogs. Nobody would say they came unprepared for a four-month journey through the bush.[19] The 13 hardened men helped by the crew set up camp close to a fresh water creek. Carron the plant collector wandered off to pick specimens, the storekeeper checked his mountain of provisions.

The team was to trek north between the Dividing Range and the coast to Cape York, where they would rendezvous with the *Rattlesnake* in October. Kennedy invited Huxley to join the reconnoitring party, to scout out the terrain for a few days. Loath to pass up an opportunity to see the natives, he set off with Kennedy's 'light party' on 30 May. He was desperate for a 'modicum of adventure'. At base camp 'we had a capital breakfast à la bush – damper [unleavened bread], tea and chops to wit – and by 9 o'clock were mounted and off, exploring and no mistake'. The four looked the part, billy cans dangling from belts. 'Each man had pistols in his holsters and a double-barrelled carbine slung by his side, cartridge belt and etceteras, so that, though I fear no sergeant would have marched though Coventry with us as "regulars", we should not have been badly equipped for a guerilla raid'.

They beat a path through the tall grass, but along the ridges the going got tough. Too tough; they began to realize how impenetrable the bush was. Irritating rattans – prickly palms – cut them at each turn, while huge buttressed trees and enormous screw pines blocked their way. Epiphytes or air-plants perched in the tree forks, but the hanging briers were ready to snare anyone who gazed up. Fenced in by ridges they beat their way back to base camp to try again the following morning. The next day was no better. Even following a river bank was fruitless, the forest was impenetrable. Aborigines appeared from nowhere at one point, only to scatter; but Huxley could hear the 'coo-eys' on all sides as they watched unnoticed, and he imagined the sensation 'produced by a spear between the shoulders'. They ploughed on, becoming bogged in creeks and tea-tree marshes, continually backtracking, constantly cut off by rivers. Eventually they bivouacked close to the shore. It might not have been successful, but it beat the tedium of dissection. And Huxley saw his aborigines: that night a group 'came very cautiously sauntering with their hands behind them'. He engaged them in a sort of self-mocking gesticulatory conversation. 'I bound my handkerchief round the head of one, and obtained in return some sliced edible root wrapped in a leaf. They invited me to their camp but I declined as Kennedy did not wish to have any close intercourse with them'.

Before the light failed the rains hit again, torrential downpours. They tried to dash back to base camp, but the rivers were rising. They floundered a third of the way over and retreated in face of the swirling waters, convinced that 'soaking was better than drowning'.

Two abortive attempts to penetrate the interior boded ill. The next day they started the last, up the coast, across open savannah, with red kangaroos scattering through the tall grass. But they were soon caught in the brush again. 'The same rope-like climbers, the same prickly rattans, the same dense high forest'. They hacked through for a mile, making impossible progress, only to find their way barred by a river. Kennedy decided to start the real expedition from its far bank and they returned to camp to prepare. He wanted Huxley to travel with them, and if

> the Service would have permitted I certainly should have
> done so – two or three months in the bush would have set
> me up in strength for the next three years . . . I rather like
> Kennedy. He is evidently a man of grand determination.

But a surgeon's mate was not his own man, and the skipper prevailed. After an evening carousing in Kennedy's tent, Huxley saw the party off the next morning. It was 5 June as the crew watched the exodus, some with foreboding, others seeing a moment in the continent's history. The exploring party disappeared in search of a promised land: a confident Kennedy at the head, the convoy of carts, sheep, horses, with 'the rear brought up by the indefatigable Niblet [the ticket-of-leave storekeeper]', the whole bearded procession 'patriarchal-looking and imposing'.[20]

Now Stanley's flotilla began its painstaking survey. The plan was to zig-zag the 600 miles up the Inner Passage to achieve an unbroken series of triangulations. The surveyors took theodolite readings, moving from island to island; the *Asp* charted the coastline, the other boats took depth readings near the reefs, while the *Rattlesnake* sounded the centre of the channel. It was to be the most exhaustive sweep, in every sense, taking four and a half months. And it gave Huxley an unparalleled opportunity to study one of the most exuberant seascapes on earth.

Before them lay an exotic world. Quiet emerald lagoons contrasted with Pacific breakers outside the Barrier. Along shallow coral banks the Jacks scattered. They paddled through tidal pools and combed the sparkling waters for trophies. In the lagoons they found themselves dwarfed by bizarre sea sculptures, giant sea fans and towering staghorn corals. Below them stony brain corals sat impassively. Everywhere were harlequin colours, dazzling flashes of butterfly fish, shocks of sapphire and yellow. Coral polyps waved orange and pink tentacles, and whole shoals of brilliant reef fish turned as if one, creating a bewildering optical illusion.

They landed on 37 coral islands, stopping hours here, a week there. Shooting parties went to one, scouts searched another for water. MacGillivray bagged birds, Thomson collected shells and the sailors searched for conches. Then they would move on, the look-outs blinded by the sun's glare off the sea, watching for foam ahead.

It should have been a lifetime's experience for a tyro setting out to conquer the invertebrate kingdom. The dappled shallows were shimmering with life. Hidden in the undersea forests enormous clams slotted between sea fans, octopuses lodged in crevices, feather stars walked on a thousand feet and feathery tube worms waved a thousand arms. Jewelled flatworms fluttered like marine butterflies. Here was the new world of echinoderms and molluscs – speckly sea cucumbers looking like deflating cushions and brilliant sea slugs, some a foot long. They would creep along the bottom, flaunting their crimson and yellow-red trimmings, or flounce through the water in blazing butterfly strokes.

But beauty turned into monotony, and the surveying routine

into a grind. Huxley's scientific notebook remained blank. It was too hot to sleep. He lay mouldering in his sweaty cabin. It wore him out just watching the cockroaches; 'a sudden unanimous impulse seems to seize the obscene thousands which usually lurk hidden in the corners of my cabin. Out they rush, helter-skelter, and run over me, my table, and my desk'.[21]

His creaking timbered world began to close in. Tiny nuisances preyed on his mind. Even when he was fired up, niggling problems ground him down again. Not that there was active opposition to his work.

> But it is a curious fact, that if you want a boat for
> dredging, ten chances to one they are always actually or
> potentially disposed of; if you leave your towing-net
> trailing astern . . . it is, in all probability, found to have a
> wonderful effect in stoping the ship's way, and is hauled
> in as soon as your back is turned; or a careful dissection
> waiting to be drawn may find its way overboard as a
> 'mess'.[22]

His diary entries became brief, lazy and late. He ignored the wildlife. And in the stultifying heat he ignored the most stunning coral on earth.

So began Huxley's descent, his dark gloom contrasting with the coral sea's brilliance. Off Dunk Island he lay listless, listening to the rain. He finished a novel as MacGillivray chased huge purple butterflies and gigantic black and gold spiders. Jock returned with five kinds of starfish and 12 crustaceans, some new, and flycatchers, ready to be shipped to Gould.[23] But Huxley could not be roused. It was the same at each stop. They sailed on to the Barnard Islands (near modern Innisfail), where MacGillivray found a gorgeous rifle bird, with metallic green throat and velvety black surround.

On the mainland Huxley and MacGillivray did run into aborigines, with 'necklaces, and cylinders through their noses', who 'seemed very desirous of making our acquaintance'. It shook Huxley from his apathy for a time. A new group appeared, with black paint across the eyes, bartering armlets for ship's biscuits. And nearer to Double Point the ship's team obtained a green-painted boomerang, never before seen in this region.

But Huxley's interest in the reefs was petering. Great lethargic gaps began to appear in his diary; in mid-June he passed the Frankland and Fitzroy Islands (off modern Cairns) without comment

No word about the huge headed flying fox with ringed eyes, even though MacGillivray found a rookery so full that branches were bending under the weight of bats. He shot dozens, their cries of pain like the 'squalling of a child'. Huxley stopped all notetaking. Many of his resolutions had come to nought: to collect fish brains, fish parasites and breeding barnacles. And the sad fact that, sitting on the world's finest reef, he was unable to shake his lethargy and look at the coral polyps could only have deepened his gloom. Sweltering on the sun-drenched beaches he sank further into despair.

The azure seas were teeming with reef fish. Small patrolling sharks would pass the paddling sailors. Ashore egrets dashed through the scrub snapping up skinks, past wild nutmeg, round screw-pines. The mound-incubating megapode birds could be seen scraping their huge fermenting nests. The brush turkeys were killed for the pot; pomegranates were picked, yams dug and coconuts were shot from the palm tops for drink. Naturalizing came easy; so much awaited discovery. MacGillivray collected unknown snails; indeed half the ship's company combed the beaches for cowries and spider shells, adding more ballast to the hold.[24] But the junior surgeon was never as committed a naturalist as MacGillivray. He had no interest in new birds or snail variations. His passion was the micro-structure of medusae, looking inside, not out, and the clammy heat had killed that.

The cloistered world within a man-o'-war's timbers was a prison – 'perfect isolation between the blue of the sea and the blue of the sky', a sailor lamented. 'The life without you is monotonous and empty', the life within becomes obsessional and dementing. 'Everywhere, the ship is the old Europe we are vainly trying to escape from'.[25] But no escape was possible. It was the familiar prison each returned to from the desiccating reefs.

Huxley craved human company. The months and steam-heat were taking their toll. He was lonely for Nettie. Nature was a soulless comforter. He had no interest in pickling new fruit bats and rifle birds to please the closet taxonomists at home. That wasn't serious science. Nor did he change when Nature came to him – in the shape of the unknown species of kangaroo that obligingly swam over to escape a dingo and lived on deck for a few days.

Craving human contact, he devoted pages of his diary to some sails sighted one day – more space than to all the siphonophores combined. Sails in this uncivilized region acquired a mystique, unrivalled by anything in nature. They meant humans and intrigue. A lifeboat with a shipwrecked crew? A cruiser with dispatches? A boarding party returned with tales 'of natives and attacks and wounds and distressed crews'. A 25-ton cutter, out from Sydney to search for sandalwood, had been ambushed off the Palm Islands. Huxley was ferried over 'laden with lint and bandages', and he listened to the story as he plastered the master's fractured skull: of a dawn attack by 30 aborigines armed with waddies and boomerangs, the fight with cutlass and pistol to regain the deck, and the turning point as the crew retook the swivel gun amidships. Such dramas were the making of legend. Huxley thought on the dying throes of the 'gentlemen in black', shot through the throat, with morbid fascination.

Life and death was everything and nothing out here. Shipboard life was a sort of sleepwalking for Huxley. Its surreal aspect was heightened by his immersion in Dante's *Paradiso* at night and 'three-water grog' by day (his quarter-pint rum ration).[26] Dante was his escape, his voyeuristic adventure. He mulled over sudden death, and survival, the stimulus of the minute. He still regretted not travelling with Kennedy, even though the overland party had failed to show at the rendezvous points. But he was too lethargic to think of it now.

It was a somnambulant period, as the flotilla moved its monotonous way up the coast. Up past the mangrove-lined Trinity Bay (site of modern Cairns), past swampy islands with huge salt-water crocodiles, along untold reefs, a haven for blue mantis shrimps with snapping jaws and sea urchins with spines like knitting needles. They made Low Island, with its signs of native turtle feasts. Nothing had induced him to open his diary for six weeks. Except now, on 7 July, when he scribbled the four strained words 'Anchored under Low Ids', only to snap it shut again.

He recoiled within, rereading Nettie's letters, thanking her a 'thousand times'. He told of his 'crisis' and 'fits of mental and bodily irritability'. Highly strung, like all the family, with a boiling intellect that teetered sometimes towards madness, he lay a prey to heat and worry. His mind became a maelstrom. There was no escape; even his clammy studies of the Low Island jellies and sea slugs disintegrated. The humidity left him prostrate. Thoughts of Nettie tormented him through the night. He wrote one long love letter for three months. 'Oh God this horrible absence! I cannot reconcile myself to it with all my philosophy'.[27] They passed Cape Tribulation, its name catching the mood, while the Hope Islands seemed a mariners' joke – except to Jock, who delighted in their *Halcyon* kingfishers.

At length the ship reached Cape Flattery in late July. Here Huxley escaped to scale the peak of Lizard Island 78 years to the day after Captain Cook himself had climbed it. Down below, MacGillivray found still more unique snails and came to the conclusion that every islet had its peculiar species. He returned armed with the 'showy golden blossoms' of a low-spreading tree *Cochlospermum*, bags of poisonous snakes and the porcelain shell of a Pacific cowrie, the first to be seen in Australia. Nor, he boasted, had he returned from any of the 37 islands 'without some acquisitions to the collection'.

His haul only emphasized Huxley's despondency. The heat addled his brain. Even teasing out the cowrie's nerves proved a strain, as sweat trickled into his eyes. For weeks one island blurred into another. Imagine 'months shifting from patch to patch of white sand . . . living on salt pork and beef, and seeing no mortal face but our own sweet countenances' obscured by long beards. The six weeks left 'a perfect blank in my memory'. At least Dayman's team had a job to do. They were 'living hard and getting fatigued every day', but the rest 'were yawning away their existence in an . . . orchis-house'.[28]

Boredom in paradise became the norm; or was it hell? Lizard Island had been his Mountain of Purgatory. On leaving it he swapped Dante's *Paradiso* for the more congenial *Inferno*. Expelled from the undersea Garden of Eden, with its eerie staghorns and stony brains, his soul descended through its own circles of despair. Dante provided a grim counterpoint to the ordeal on the reef. Sailing from Lizard Island, he heard the 'cries and shrieks of lamentation'; he heard the damned in limbo, stripped like himself of the beatific vision, separated from those he loved.

The medieval journey matched his torment. Off the mangrove-fringed Howick Islands, he was oblivious to the skies blackened by flying foxes and the shoreline traces of turtle feasts. But he had the smell of roasting flesh in his nostrils. Under the blazing sun the Pilgrim descended into the Eighth Circle of Hell, the awful *Malebolge* – the ditches stuffed with pimps and popes, the 'steaming stench . . . disgusting to behold'. The 'soles of every sinner's feet were flaming'. Even Huxley drew breath, the furnace air burning his lungs. 'I think I never read anything so horribly distinct' before. Dante 'describes Hell like a practical *Times* reporter'. 'I don't wonder at the Italian women thinking that he had actually been down to Hell'. The Pilgrim roasting on the reefs was trapped in his *Bolgia*, unable to escape, only to meditate on his sins.

All around great ungainly pelicans were plunging into the emerald waters. But he was in the infernal kingdom, watching black fiends fish sinners from the boiling pitch. He missed the real sport. Parties combed the Claremont Islands with a setter. Quail provided targets for the 'First of September' shooters, imagining themselves on the moors as the season opened. While the plump Torres Strait pigeons 'appeared on the table at every meal, subjected to every possible variety of cooking'. And signs of exhausted turtles dragging themselves up the beaches led to caches of leathery reptilian eggs for breakfast.

September wore on, with no sign of Kennedy at the rendezvous points. He too was being tested by fire.

Dante poked fun at the Pilgrim. 'May your guts burn with thirst that cracks your tongue'. And they did. No terrors in the *Malebolge* could match this damnable voyage. Caught between the devil and the deep blue sea, Huxley locked himself below. 'We are laying at present under Sunday Island . . . I have not been ashore and don't care to go, what's more'.

The circle was complete, for it was on Sunday Island on 30 September that he finished the *Inferno*. Like the Pilgrim, he finally emerged from this 'trench of misery'. He made his 'way back up to the bright world' and came ashore for the shoot at Cavin Cross Island, although the splattered entrails matched the worst excesses in Dante. 'The poor birds were very tame and the shooting was simple butchery . . . I had nothing to do but load and fire as fast as possible'.[29] The blood lust became so intense that one midshipman shot at the captain, thinking him fair game.

Four days later the *Rattlesnake* reached Cape York. The crew were weary, some had scurvy. Stanley was mentally drained. The isolation of command was beginning to tell. But he pressed on: keeping them at work, clearing out old wells on the beach and pumping aboard 75 tons of fresh water. Then came more soundings. The boats went off to map the coast. Others were ordered to Albany Island, off the Cape, which was being considered as a coaling station for the steamers.

Huxley met MacGillivray's 'old acquaintances', the Cape aborigines. Huge numbers arrived from the islands, 150 men, women and children, including Papuans who were friendly with the Cape people. MacGillivray, compiling his aboriginal dictionary, sat with them round a fire, eating their shellfish and mealy plums. Like

Huxley he was a smoker, but their smoke-filled bamboo pipe, three feet long and as thick as a man's arm, made him nauseous. More came in, bringing him a new phalanger, 'quite tame, and very gentle', with short, silky, grey hair and, the oddity, a bald tip to its tail.[30]

The steamy days ticked away with no sign of Kennedy. MacGillivray spent his time packing a crate for John Gould, a cornucopia of unknown birds, a riot of emerald, topaz and jonquil-yellow feathers, so important to a bird artist.[31] He went out shooting in the jungle, scouring the lush Asian palms, or searching the open eucalyptus valleys, moving between 12-foot high termite mounds. Glorious honey-suckers, sunbirds, purple-throated orioles and king-fishers splashed with 'sealing-wax red': all went off to the Zoological Society, packed with flying fox pelts and the pet phalanger skin.

The arrival of a provision ship from Sydney meant supplies – sheep, bread, limes to counteract the scurvy and, best of all, mail. Hal opened Nettie's first, but every letter was dominated by 'the news that a Revolution has again convulsed France'. She even feared that 'we shall be enveloped in War' and that he might be recalled. His mother reported that 'Louis Phillipe has abdicated ... and the "on dit" is that the whole French family are in England'.[32] Jim, a political animal like Tom, sent a blow-by-blow account: of Court corruption and the clampdown on liberty, resulting in a mob bursting 'into the Tuilleries'. 'There were 100,000 troops in Paris at the time – yet was it a bloodless revolution'. The democrats turfed the 'old rogue' 'out of throne & country', but the revolution devoured itself as provisional governments rose and fell, none finding 'favour in the eyes of the mob' until the 'representation [was] doubled & any blackguard of 25 is eligible to sit'. At this even Jim lost sympathy. 'They are in a terrible financial mess and the provisional Gov^t. has got the Herculean task of satisfying the many headed – wherein every class interest wants everything for itself'.

Huxley wondered if the London rookeries he had once walked had exploded. At 'present old England rides the storm in safety', said his mother, although there were 'fears for the immediate future owing to the frequent outbreaks of the horrid Chartists and other disaffected ones'.[33]

But Cape York was a world away. The late mail only prompted Huxley to wish that the revolutionaries 'who are going to make a democratic New Jerusalem of Europe would turn their attention towards the Anglo Australian line of packets, and reform them' first. From the bush the tumultuous events in Europe seemed remote. The civilized world might be tearing itself apart, but with news five months old no one really knew. And his mother still hoped that his exotic experiences were having a devout effect: 'enriching your mind and forming your Character for a high destiny both in this Life and that which is to come'.[34]

On 2 November they could wait no longer for Kennedy and weighed anchor. Huxley was beginning to be glad that he had not walked overland: 'Fancy my disgust at finding the ship gone'. The *Rattlesnake* tacked west, sailing across the Gulf of Carpentaria to the mangrove-covered bays of Port Essington (in what is now Arnhem Land). 'We dropped anchor opposite a high cliff . . . on top of which was perched a ruinous-looking block-house with a few pieces of cannon mounted on its top, the firing off of which would I verily believe have blown down the whole concern'. The sinking feeling was reinforced by the Commandant's gig which came out to greet them, bearing apologies that all the marine officers were ill.

The ten year-old settlement was as sick as its garrison. Stanley had been present at its founding in 1838, when the prefabricated shacks and Government House were erected. It was to have been the seed of a 'second Singapore'. 'Victoria' the colony had been christened, the first in honour of the new Queen. It was a government attempt to colonize the north coast – to control the Torres Strait traffic and provide for merchantmen poaching Dutch trade in the East Indies. Now it was a rotting shanty town. The buildings were termite-ridden. The Government House had been wrecked in a hurricane. Even the dogs had disappeared inside the giant crocodiles. It was the most 'miserable ill-managed hole in Her Majesty's dominions'. The settlement was too far up the inner harbour, away from the sea breezes. As such it was 'fit for neither man nor beast', the 'fearful damp depressing heat' leaving everyone 'a prey to ennui and cold brandy-and-water'.

In this decaying hothouse intrigues proliferated. The result was as much 'caballing and mutual hatred' among the troops 'as if it were the court of the Great Khan'. Orders came laced with vitriol. The 'commandant is a litigious old fool always at war with his officers, and endeavouring to make the place as much a hell morally as it is physically'.

Fevers were rampant, caused by bad food and unbroken toil, the men like mad dogs being worked in the midday sun. There was nothing in the *Inferno* to match: the poor squad was prodded by fiends and tortured by fire. Two years earlier 60 troops had arrived. At parade Huxley counted 'just ten men present. The rest were invalided, dead, or sick'. The hospital holding the fevered was a living hell. It was close by a putrid lagoon, positively steaming at 90° like a '*hot* salt bath'.[35] The roof leaked in the monsoons, forcing the surgeons to operate under tents. Abandonment of the settlement was imminent and the colonists prayed daily for deliverance.

It had no saving graces except its pineapples, growing like weeds. But the steaming shallows were 'a hotbed for medusae'. The harbour was alive with marble-like spherical jellyfish, *Bougainvillia* (named after the French explorer), and Huxley bobbed in his tropical bath plucking out specimens.

If he was suffering for his science, religion still plagued him and the symptoms again showed. A shipwrecked missionary, Father Angelo, had lived here a few months and tried to drive the spirits out of an aboriginal nature. MacGillivray knew the difficulties. He never doubted the natives' intelligence, although like all whites he judged them on their mimicry of Western ways. They had little to thank the settlers for, least of all the drink 'to which they have become passionately addicted'. But God was harder to imbibe than grog. That dogged explorer Edward John Eyre, the first white man to cross the empty immensity of the Great Australian Bight, developed a sympathy for these 'shadowy-characters of the never-never', but he had gone to New Zealand knowing that not a 'single real and permanent convert to Christianity has yet been made'.[36] Given the fact, the pragmatic MacGillivray placed Christianizing second to civilizing. The missionaries were at least rendering the shores safe for shipwrecked sailors.

The souls of the natives held no interest for Huxley. What intrigued him was the fate of the man sent to save them. As always he had his eye on the sects of his own culture. For months Father Angelo had learned the aborigine's tongue and taught his bemused charges Latin prayers. Huxley learned that the man was 'wholly without religious feeling, well acquainted with theology and a strong stickler for the doctrine of his church'. Nothing reinforced his prejudices about papism and its militia more. The priest was 'a *soldier of his church*, i.e. like most soldiers he did his duty religiously but cared not two straws for the quarrel in which he fought'. The military metaphor, honed by Huxley's anti-Catholicism and suspicion of the warring sects, was becoming pointed.

Like the buildings, the priest had crumbled in this hell-hole. Just before the *Rattlesnake* arrived he had died, as MacGillivray put it, blasphemously denying God.

All their minds were turning. In mid-November they beat a retreat and 'it was like escaping from an oven'. The *Rattlesnake* put to sea before the monsoon. The skies were already heavy, with lightning on the horizon at night. Bearing west again, they could make out the cloud-covered summits of the 'magnificent island' of Timor. They took the westward route round the Australian continent, 'listlessly and lazily'. It was a slow return, gruelling to even the hardened hands. Provisions ran low and each hungry man became an angry man. Even the good-natured Doctor could 'vomit forth a whole bellyful of bile against some unfortunate messmate, and what a pleasing relief followed upon this medical treatment'. His assistant sympathized, too often indulging in the treatment himself.

Both noticed Stanley's deterioration. His demeanour was changing with the strain. For 22 years, man and boy, he had been surveying hazardous shores. Like surveying captains before him, brittle perfectionists all – Pringle Stokes of the *Beagle*, who shot himself in Tierra del Fuego, and FitzRoy on Darwin's expedition, who broke down in Valparaiso – Stanley teetered on the brink. Emotionally drained, he was overworked and obsessive, refusing to delegate the simplest task. He had grown distant from his officers, 'constantly snarling at them from an ungovernable temper'.

It took them over two months to sail back to Sydney. Christmas Eve passed with Hal reminiscing again about 'dear Old England'. He was 'tossed and tumbled like a pea in a pill-box', and the loneliness left him with 'a great mind to take a dose of Laudanum tonight and sleep all through tomorrow'.[37]

By the time they reached 30° south they hit a revitalizing cool wind, 'and my energies, well nigh extinguished for some time . . . are beginning to be restored'. Suddenly released, he started taking an interest in the *Velellae* and *Physaliae* again, filling reams of paper. The captain sailed past the Swan River settlement (site of modern Perth), disappointing everybody by not stopping. But in the breeze Huxley was tweezering and probing and jotting. Out of the tropics he could think.

And in the cool he perked up. The penitent was being led by a beatific vision. Nettie's divine light would lead him out of limbo, up through the heavenly spheres to paradise. The Pilgrim's isolation, like Dante's, was ending. He was on his way 'home', to his Beatrice. A year earlier they had just met and his desires 'seemed a dream'. Now 'I have a "sober certainty of waking bliss" '.³⁸

The ships reached Sydney on 24 January 1849 in a deplorable state. Nine months in the tropics had left them rotting. A crawling mass of cockroaches blackened the rigging and crunched underfoot. They swarmed, shivered Midshipman Sharpe, 'over tables at meals, flying into candles, dropping and crawling all over you when asleep'. As a drastic remedy the *Bramble* was sunk in Mosman Bay for a week, then hoisted out, free, at least for a while. Huxley was not much healthier, arriving 'little better than a walking Lots' wife', and February found him 'chiefly engaged in putting a large supply of wholesome food into me'.³⁹

As the refit began, Huxley started three months' leave. The city was scorching. On the north shore 'a hot wind blew – a brick-fielder, so called because the wind passed over certain old brick-fields'. The girls wore cool white and the houses had closed shutters, with wet blankets behind. The cabbies had their own way of cooling off. Huxley limped back aboard one night. 'We did *not* get drunk', he explained to his mother, 'but our cabman did – and consequently your son was busily engaged about two o'clock this morning in extricating himself from a bouleverse'd cab by the windows'.⁴⁰

He was hit by a tidal wave of home news. 'Your picture of the present state of the family is like a Daguerreotype', he replied to George, 'but it is decidedly not flattering. Very few warm tints and a great breadth of shadow'. As always the impecunious Cooke looked portly in focus. He is 'growing quite fat', Ellen admitted, but 'I can't say he is growing rich'. Fat and floundering. His partnership with Richard Hoblyn, cramming students for their exams, was a flop, so that George was now bankrolling him too. 'The worst', grumbled George, 'is that he is not a whit the better while I am so much poorer'.⁴¹ Tom had heard it all before: the family seemed doomed to fall backwards off the financial fence; sinking fortunes were their fate. It mustn't be his.

His father was frail and Tom feared 'there is but small chance of my ever seeing him again'. His mother was as lively as ever, and fishing for information about his fiancée. He was now distant, and his prim responses made no bones about Nettie's place beside him. He sat down on 1 February to give her a full account of Henrietta – her hair, her uncertain looks, her 'womanly' mind:

> With my present income of course, marriage is rather a
> bad look out, but I do not think it would be at all fair
> towards Nettie herself, to leave this country finally without
> giving her a wife's claim upon me. I could not, in common
> delicacy, ask her to follow me to England without such
> were the case. But there are difficulties on all sides.[42]

The task was to convince George, who was financing successive
married Huxleys and loath to keep the last. Tom agreed that
marriage was a 'hazardous act' (MacGillivray had stepped ashore
to find himself a father). But he could not ask Nettie to England
unmarried, only to find himself posted 'to the West Indies or
China'. 'Ulysses endeavours to reach his Penelope would be nothing
to mine – and I have the additional disadvantage of not being a
hero'. So his idea was 'To marry just before we leave Sydney',
then to leave Nettie with her parents while he established himself
in London. They always had his '138£ a year'; it might not set
them up salubriously, but 'it will keep us both from the gutter'.[43]

Sydney was home from home; 'my friend Fanning's house is
as completely my home as it well can be', he told his mother.
'And then Nettie had not heard anything of me for six months,
so that I have been petted and spoiled ever since we came in'.
He had thought of jumping ship. But to do what? Become a
colonial doctor? London was the centre of the world and the
pivot of imperial science. That was where he had to be. 'It is
very unlikely I shall ever remain in the colony', he reassured
her.

While he was thinking of the future, Nettie was contemplating
marriage: 'Isy [her half-sister Isabel] is persuading me to get
married – and Willie [Fanning] won't say one way or the other –
and I – there are so many reasons for and against I know not what
to say'. Neither knew how long they would be apart after Hal left
for home. 'Much must depend upon how things go in England. If
my various papers meet with any success, I may perhaps be able to
leave the service'.[44]

But would they meet with success? At home Cooke had been
chasing around for news. He 'called both at the Royal and the
Zoological Societies', Tom's mother reported, 'but could not hear
tidings of your Papers'. George too was trying to track down the
'wandering scientific babes'. His shipboard brother feared that
'somebody has turned out the cruel uncle to them'. His need to
know had nothing to do with 'vanity': 'all my worries at present

are intensely practical' – and he spelt them out as brutal propositions.

> 1^{stly} that I am an Ass^t. Surgeon in the Navy, and by
> way of Lemma to that, that I might nearly as well break
> stones on the road; 2^{ndly} that I want to get my
> promotion when I get home or else get out of the
> service altogether & 3^{rdly} that I have no interest or
> visible means of making other people help me either to
> the one end or the other: 'arfal' as the clown says, I
> must help myself.

With no patronage strings to pull, his papers had to shout his name. He had no other way of jumping the Navy List to promotion, or of picking up a scientific job, or of bringing Nettie over. The logic was stark.[45]

All the while Hal was watching Nettie with Alice, Ory's three year-old daughter. She adored Ory's children, sighing 'If dear Alice were only my own'. Hal, now one of the family, stood godfather to Ory's new baby boy. It tied the cords tighter and the baby claimed a special place in Nettie's heart. 'The love that one has for a child is such a tender holy love', she believed. Hal teased her for it, while secretly knowing 'that I should love the mother of my children even better than my dear mistress'.[46]

If children had to wait, at least they were together for the moment. Not that the euphoria was to last. It was overshadowed by news from the north.

A schooner docked on 5 March with three skeletal survivors from Kennedy's overland party. Sydney was agog. At a court hearing they presented a pathetic sight, 'pale and emaciated, with haggard looks'. In a trembling voice, one of the survivors, Carron, told a horrifying tale of despair.

It had taken them six weeks just to clear the swamps of the base camp region. Straightaway it proved too much for the shepherd, who ran off and had to be hauled out of an aboriginal camp. As they hacked through the strangling undergrowth the horses collapsed, the sheep died from the wet of continual river crossings and the men came down with malaria. The three-horse carts crashed around on the tree-strewn jungle floor and had to be abandoned. Of the 800 lbs of goods packed into each, the axes, saws and specimen boxes were jettisoned and everything else crammed into saddle bags. By August the storekeeper Niblet was very ill; a month later midday temperatures were topping 100° and even one of the kangaroo dogs died of heat exhaustion.

Huxley listened as the story reached its horrifying dénouement. It took them five months to trek 400 miles. Only nine horses remained and the labourers humped enormous crates through the jungle on their backs. Behind them, where once was a flock, trotted a solitary sheep. On 11 November they killed it and shared the flesh in a last supper. Realizing the hopelessness of the situation, Kennedy left eight men under Carron at Weymouth Bay. He and Jackey struck out with the remaining three, taking seven horses, pushing on the last 150 miles to the Cape to fetch help.

Tragedy dogged their every step. Near Shelburne Bay one carter accidently shot himself in the shoulder; another was too ill to go on and both were left, cared for by the third. Kennedy and Jackey ploughed on alone. Near Escape River, not 20 miles from their destination, they were tracked for days by aborigines. Kennedy fell with a spear in his back. Jackey buried him amid the leaves of the scrub floor and walked on, taking the long route round the hostile tribe. Eight days later, on 23 December, Jackey, lame and exhausted, struggled into the Cape.

A rescue party found nothing of the three Shelburne Bay men but their clothes. At Weymouth Bay, Carron's group camped by a brackish creek, and waited. Where aborigines could live off the land, white explorers, carrying all the trappings of Western civilization, could only starve. One labourer, weak and emaciated, died on 16 November, a carter four days later. Gloom gave way to a sort of 'sluggish indifference'. In 110° temperatures the flesh of the last horse rotted within two days. They were surrounded by armed aborigines, sometimes taunting, at others bearing rancid fish, once attacking with barbed spears. Another week on, and the shepherd 'withered away . . . without pain or struggle'. Fate mocked them: they actually spotted the *Bramble* passing the bay one day, but frantic rocket-firing failed to attract it. The last vestige of hope dashed, they sank into a terminal lethargy. One labourer struggled to the creek and sat down to die on its bank. They found him the next morning but had no strength to dig a grave. On 28 December Niblet and the naturalist died and were covered with leaves.

The macabre scene had the air of a malarial hallucination, bodies bobbing in the creek, in the bushes. Nothing seemed real. They had lost their will and 'withered into perfect skeletons'. Jackey and the rescue team found armed natives everywhere, rotting corpses, and Carron and one labourer barely alive. Carron's elbow and hip bones were poking through his skin. Fearing an attack, they carried the botanist swiftly out of camp, clutching his seeds. He left his precious plants and his diary behind.

These poor souls had suffered and died for their science and their survey. Huxley thought of Kennedy, a 'fine noble fellow', and what might have been. To 'have perished by starvation or the spears of the natives . . . You may be sure I am not sorry to return home'.

The jolt served to strengthen his resolve. Like everyone he was haunted by the tragedy. A brig, searching Weymouth Bay, found Wall's and Niblet's skulls, which were taken to Albany Island for burial.[47] Kennedy's body was never recovered, only the half-chewed remains of his papers, buried by Jackey. These were brought to Stanley, but they only undermined his mental state more. Huxley steeled himself for the last leg of the survey, thankful to be alive.

1. (*Above*) The earliest known daguerreotype of Tom Huxley, as a medical student in the early 1840s.

2. (*Inset*) Huxley's self-portrait as a student: 'a very pale, thin, lanky, ugly body with dreadfully long hair'.

3. (*Right*) *Punch*'s satire on the dissipated 'sons of the scalpel'.

METAPHYSICS.

4. Charing Cross Hospital about 1840. It is the triangular building on the right, seen from the Strand.

5. The studious Huxley, aged twenty, possibly in his Agar Street lodgings.

6. Tom in 1846, already with his black-dog look.

"am I not a man & a brother?"

7. (*Above*) The newly-commissioned sailor in October 1846, billeted in the 'Hulks' (the old prison ships in Portsmouth harbour), while the *Rattlesnake* was fitted out.

8. (*Right*) Assistant Surgeon Huxley, RN.

9. HMS *Rattlesnake* off Sydney Heads.   10. (*Inset*) Henrietta Heathorn, a brewer's daughter in the convict colony. This portrait was painted by Thomas Griffiths Wainewright the Poisoner.

11. The *Rattlesnake* in the sweltering Louisiade Archipelago, off the eastern tip of New Guinea.

12. (*Inset*) The Portuguese Man-of-War. Huxley dissected endless sea-nettles and jellyfish during the voyage. This is an engraving from his *Oceanic Hydrozoa*.

13. Hacking through the snagging scrub with Kennedy's light party.
The nearest figure is Kennedy, the next Huxley.

7

Sepulchral Painted Savages

'Am I AT SEA or dreaming?'

The *Rattlesnake* left Sydney harbour on 8 May 1849 and sailed north, this time destined for New Guinea. Hal left Nettie a knot of grief and frustration. She had heard of the 'fierceness' of the Papuan natives and worked herself into a state, imagining Hal 'exposed to their attacks'.

The dreaming carried him up the coast. He settled into his somnambulistic routine, lost in Nettie's letters in the momentary calm, 'then comes a roll . . . the timbers creak, the pigs squeal, the fowls cackle, two or three plates fly with a crack out of the stewards pantry' and the cook's curses brought him back to reality.

He had a ruder awakening after Moreton Bay (Brisbane). Steering through the Coral Sea, the heavily laden ship was hit by a cyclone. The *Bramble* lost her stern-boat and separated from the *Rattlesnake*, which was itself 'plunging and rolling in the heavy seas like a log'. The shoddy caulking left the gun room and Huxley's cabin flooded. He sided with the men, blaming it on the officers, who should have been "tending to the ship, 'stead o' givin pic-nics in Sydney harbour'.[1] Then the tiller rope gave way and the ship broached to and was hit by three huge waves broadside.

Far from the cyclone, Nettie sat at home with his old letters:

> They are never-failing sources of comfort . . . Ah how I
> love him – with my whole soul – with all the truth and
> devotion that ever urged a woman's heart. My desire is to
> become good and excellent as the being he imagines me –
> my happiest dreams are of a peaceful home with him to

love and care for – my hopes, his advancement in temporal
and eternal blessings.

His own dreams returned with the glassy seas, and by June his
diary entries were taking a lyrical turn. He gazed at her picture at
night and then walked the deck: the 'little waves plish-plash with a
pleasant murmur against the side', but he was absorbed as 'a
thousand thousand thoughts chase one another through my brain',
and always Nettie became 'at last directly or indirectly the object
of my meditation'.

He huddled over his microscope. He had plankton enough to
keep him absorbed: sea urchin larvae, sea nettles and comb jellies,
a pulsating, flashing, jerking mass of life, a world within a world
seen through his eyepiece. And endless tiny stalked polyps, *Tubularia*, which turned up in every ocean at every latitude. He was
still listing them, only to discover one day when the tide dragged
his net under the hull that they were actually 'attached in large
masses to the ship's bottom!'[2]

Then the steaming downpours began. It was back to being
'sweated and stewed & bedeviled under the sun ... living like
romany d– – – [dogs] domiciled in a wooden hutch'. He sat
'melting though half-stripped' in his 'orchis-house'. But no orchid-
fancier had to endure this botanical sauna day after day. 'Hot,
wet, rainy, muggy', he logged on 9 June, as he shut himself away
with his increasingly exotic trawl, 'singular' sea butterflies (gaudy
swimming slugs) and bizarre crustaceans with long frontal spines.

The stewing heat drew out Stanley's insecurities. He suffered
morbid fears about the terrors of the interior. Cannibalism ob-
sessed him. Nor was it surprising with the lurid tales of New
Guinea's head-hunters. The dismemberment of Kennedy's men
had left them all with a nightmare.

Sight of the Louisiade Archipelago off eastern New Guinea on
10 June restored Huxley's faith that they were moving on: jungle-
covered mountainous islands obscured by clouds. The island chain
stretched away eastwards from New Guinea, and the *Rattlesnake*
followed it to the furthest tip, Rossel Island, which loomed up a
'rich, leafy mass, of all shades from indigo to grass green'. Even its
rugged peaks remained jungle-strewn, and shrouded all day 'by a
fleecy cloudy canopy'. Huxley knew 'nothing more beautiful than
a cloud resting upon a mountain peak, like the head of a delicate
girl resting on the broad shoulder of an old warrior'.[3]

On 13 June Stanley was 38 and logged: 'a better day could not be chosen for the commencement of our survey!' Proper charts would finally allow British merchantmen to sail these waters safely. On maps the Archipelago, like New Guinea itself, was a mass of blanks, vague shores, uncharted reefs and missing islands. Yet this was the trade route to the East Indies and the Pacific – the route taken long before by Captain Blyth with his precious bread-fruit plants.

Rossel Island stood at one end of a huge 30-mile lagoon. They could see coconut palms and huts, and offshore the sails of native canoes. They needed sheltered anchorage inside the lagoon, away from the Pacific breakers. But the only entrance was a narrow channel, 200 yards wide, with razor-like coral banks on either side. The *Rattlesnake* squeezed through, 'passing within a stone's throw of roaring breakers on either hand', the leadsman singing 'out his "Deep nine" or "By the mark fourteen"', with everyone holding his breath. They were safe.

Well, not all. 'The skipper's black dog "Native"', Huxley wrote, 'committed suicide last night, by walking into the sea out of the main chains. The skipper and his dog had this in common, that they liked one another, and were disliked by every one else'. Stanley's jagged nerves and bellowing rages were wearing – as were his jitters about the natives. Here they were friendly enough, turning up in their ten-man canoes with carved bows and outrigger. They bartered yams and coconuts for axes, pilfering the odd one like the most 'dexterous London thieves'.

The month was spent exploring the islands in what they called 'Coral Haven'. Huxley went with MacGillivray, Simpson and Brierly to see the islanders, waving green branches as the recognized sign of peace. His account of the first parleys was laced with parochial wit, giving it a mocking tone. His mixture of plebeian patter and derring-do disguised a deeper unease among these 'savages'. Having lured the fishermen to the beach by antics, he was greeted by 'one bright copper-coloured gentleman who appeared like Paul to be "the chief speaker" bearing a green branch in his hand'. Huxley laid down his gun 'and had a very interesting and polite interview with friend coppery and two other gentlemen who were quite black and had large fuzzy heads of hair with combs a foot long, narrow and very long-pronged, stuck into the front of their very remarkable coiffure. Brady had given me a red cap which was much coveted by all, but I made one of the fuzzy-headed gentry give me an ornamented chunam-gourd for it'.

Huxley was in an alien world and showed few of MacGillivray's anthropological insights. His reaction swung between astonishment, embarrassment and condescension, as it did for most European travellers. He identified two 'races', some natives being black and 'fuzzy-headed; others again were of various shades of copper colour' with close-cropped hair. 'Their only clothing was a long leaf curled up behind into a most absurd appendage like a bustle'. 'And the septum of the nose was ornamented – save the mark! – with a long white bone or some such thing stuck through it'.

But he excelled in his chatty accounts of an individual's quirks. He was the Ealing boy facing spirits from another world, wrestling for understanding. There was the 'old gentleman' who 'had lost his nose, which imparted an expression of soft and pleasing melancholy to his countenance'. Another's foot was swollen to gigantic proportions with elephantiasis (giving Huxley first-hand experience of diseases never seen by normal surgeons). He lampooned their 'ugly mugs', although 'some of the young nymphs were comely enough'.[4]

The mess buzzed at the sight of a 'blackie' with a human-jaw bracelet. This 'singular piece of *bijouterie*' had everyone offering hatchets, mirrors and handkerchiefs in exchange, but he would not 'part from it for love or money'. Like all sailors, wanting their trophies (on Darwin's *Beagle* in New Zealand it was shrunken heads), the *Rattlesnake*'s ratings were busy trading for human jaws. Otherwise it was jade hatchets and totem figureheads, swapped for axes and hats. On another island the natives wore necklaces of human vertebrae. Whether they were 'the memorials of friends or trophies of vanquished foes', the bleached bones were enough to make Stanley shudder.[5] It increased his morbid fear and made him reticent about any sort of contact. Huxley and Thomson saw it as a crisis of nerve.

Huxley and his messmates spent these sunlit days 'tucking up our duds' and wading the shallows. They picked their way through the mangroves, watching hermit crabs and 'queer little leaping fish' (mudskippers). His workload was light, although his duties were more exotic than any Charing Cross demonstrator's. No Strand surgeon had to treat a sailor writhing in pain after standing on a poison-spined frogfish.

On shore they watched sacred kingfishers and sulphur-crested cockatoos among the palms. The mound-incubating megapodes were common, 'running about the thickets, and calling to each other like pheasants'.[6] Shooters bagged them, a staple for the pot. Regular searches were made up mangrove creeks for water. On these Huxley was able to see the jungle's edge, with its pitcher plants full of sweet water and 15-foot tree ferns, although the scene had to be appreciated through swarms of biting flies.

By now he was having difficulty restraining his sarcasm about the skipper. Stanley went with Brierly and Huxley to sketch the tree-fern luxuriance of a creek. Huxley was a lightning artist with a good eye. But seeing Stanley's child-like sketch 'I nearly burst out laughing'. 'That he had neither smell nor hearing nor taste sufficiently refined to enable him to distinguish one sensation from another, sulphuretted hydrogen from Millefleurs, "God save the Queen" from "Old Dan Tucker" . . . I knew long ago, but now I find that his eye is equally defective'.

Huxley's bravado ashore disguised a deeper unease. At the centre of Coral Haven was 'Pig Island', named from an incident on 20 June. The larking sailors landed, 'looking well to our "ammunition of war"', and were surrounded by 40 or so armed 'hullaballooing' villagers. The crew knew nothing of native customs. The agitated villagers threw an appeasing pig at their feet, at the same time surreptitiously lifting Huxley's gun. 'I looked big and blustered a little, they drew together and scowled, handling their spears', wrote a tense Huxley, 'so I pretended at last to be satisfied, and forming in battle-array, Simpson as advance guard, Brierly and I carrying the pig, and MacGillivray as rear-guard, off we marched'. They broke into a nervous laughter 'at the absurdity of the scene'. And thus 'piggy and his carriers, squealing and laughing', hastily made for the boat.

But Stanley shied away from contact. Whatever his phobias, inland penetration was not his brief; indeed his orders were to 'guard against the treacherous disposition' of the natives. His quailing appalled Huxley and Thomson. When the captain did land he looked 'as stupid as a stockfish'. It was not only the skipper's sketching that Huxley impugned, but his savvy during the exchanges and, ultimately, his nerve. A reckless Huxley sneaked away from one beach bartering session and followed a jungle path, stumbling on to a native village. He returned to fetch a jittery Stanley. But the captain insisted on an armed escort, and even then was 'anxious to get away, wandering about in a regular fidget'. What incensed Huxley was the captain's boast about his 'communication with the natives' and that, having met them ashore, '*I don't think it necessary to go [again] myself*'. Huxley lambasted the 'little man' as a regular 'Sir Joshua Windbag'.

Sunday 1 July was Nettie's 24th birthday. That day her emotions got the better of her: Fanning passed on Hal's present, Schiller's works, 'with a note from dearest Hal. So surprised and overcome was I that I wept for many minutes . . . I longed that he were by to thank and tell how much how very much I loved him'. A thousand miles away Hal lay in his bunk, brooding, doubting. What was he? A man of massive knowledge to most people, a mixture of horse sense, street patter and profound philosophy set off by the sharpest critical faculty.

> I might have made a good critic, and an accomplished
> man. As it is what am I? A hotch potch of knowledge and
> ignorance, fact and fiction picked up from all the highways
> & byways of knowledge cheek by jowl with the most
> absurd ignorance at which a schoolboy might blush . . .
> There are few men who do not know a great deal more,
> and that in a better manner than I do, & there are very
> few books and still fewer men in whose learning I do not
> find some fallacy.[7]

The next day the *Rattlesnake* hauled off, zig-zagging west from reef to reef inside Coral Haven. Parties landed on each island, searching for water and bartering axes and cotton nightcaps for yams. The hold was filling fast. On Brierly Island (named after the ship's artist) 368 lbs of yams were swapped for 17 axes. Huxley, the unfulfilled engineer, watched the outriggers as much as the natives, sketching them and insetting details. He joined the barter parties and inveigled his way into villages, sketching scenes, sharing coconuts, amazed at the native's kiln technology and ability to turn out earthenware pots '18 inches across'.

On other islands more than deals were struck. Joannet's skirmishing natives sought to impose their own trading terms. Dayman's men opened fire and the 'crack and whistle of the shot' sent natives crashing over the galley's side. Huxley patched spear wounds and axe cuts. It was this 'treacherous attack' by friendlies known to have been out to the *Rattlesnake*, Stanley told the bishop, that firmed his resolve: no parties would be sent to the interior. No bird-of-paradise or exotic bloom was worth the 'sacrifice of one human life'.[8]

When the canoes deserted the frigate, there were other visitors. All hands came to the side one night to see the ship surrounded by swarming, fluorescing, 100-segmented worms giving off a 'brilliant greenish light'.[9] Huxley threw himself back into this pelagic life with gusto in the absence of native contact. He was now dissecting daily, minute worms and jellies and sea nettles; and if he got bored there were always parasitic crustaceans to pick off his catch. A few 'nastinesses' could keep him from 'utter stagnation'.

Nastiness was ever present. Tragedy lurked below decks. The ship's carpenter, whom he had been treating since Sydney, was buried on Middle Island on 2 August. Life seemed cheaper in the torrid zone, so far from home. The crew made a fire over the grave, to conceal it, lest his jaws end up as native ornaments.

> The traces of Death's hand at sea are soon obliterated;
> you die in the morning, and in half an hour your cabin is
> nailed up, and folks are speculating as to who will have
> your vacancy. You are buried or thrown overboard in the
> afternoon; the next day your traps are sold before the
> Captain, and the day after you are forgotten. There is
> hardly room for the living on board a ship, so that no
> wonder that the dead find no resting place in it.[10]

In mid-August, after sailing 300 miles from Coral Haven, they sighted a hazy 'blue mountain mass' on the horizon ahead – this was the awesome '*Dowdee*', the New Guinea mainland. For the first time they faced the real unknown. Few had seen it, none had explored it. It was, 'perhaps, the very last remaining habitable portion of the globe into which European cruisers and European manufacturers had not penetrated'.[11] Its north coast was un-mapped, and its south coast had to be charted before it could be opened up. On this huge, lush, jungle island were peoples uncon-tacted by the outside world.

The mountainous land was enveloped in dense white cloud, impenetrable and mysterious. Huxley, straining for a view, played the jaded Jack Tar. 'Time was when I should have made this a red day ... when I was young and a little enthusiastic'. 'There lies before us a grand continent – shut out from intercourse with the civilized world, more completely than China, and as rich if not richer in things rare and strange. The wide and noble rivers open wide their mouths inviting us to enter. All that is required is coolness, judgment, perseverance, to reap a rich harvest of knowl-edge and perhaps of more material profit'.

And 'a little risk'. The alluring rivers could seduce, invite them into dark creeper-strewn traps that would close in behind, a throttling jungle where alien eyes watched every turn. The cynic cut in: the poor boy, wondering why he should suffer, unrecognized and unrewarded. Too much was demanded of frontier science.

Where did it get Carron, plucked from his own private hell? Why take risks? Facing the shrouded mysteries of New Guinea forced strange reflections. Huxley started a deranged dialogue with himself in the sultry heat: what was 'the advancement of knowledge and the opening of wide fields for future commerce to my comfort'? The seven-bob subaltern was paid for bandaging boils, not breaking new ground; 'it's all very well for young fools' to talk of the nobility of knowledge, but 'You get no thanks for that' and the 'pay [is] just the same'.

He snapped out of his strange mood instantly. 'Admirable reasoning! but Cortes did not reason thus when he won Mexico for Spain nor the noble [Rajah] Brooke when he conquered a province [Borneo] in a yacht'. It was the leitmotiv of Huxley's young life: the need for danger money at the forefront of science. Trained explorers need to be recruited, as all specialists struggling with nature. Pay for the 'wounds and contusions' in the fight to advance knowledge. Push people to the limit, yes; but reward them.

'Mysterious currents' forced them to stand off for days, unable to anchor, the shrouds around the mountains tantalizingly visible on the horizon. Occasionally the clouds would clear to reveal stupendous green jungled summits; 'I never saw the like before', Stanley admitted, 'far more magical, far more sudden'. But he was not tempted to go in. For the last two weeks in August the *Rattlesnake* lay at anchor off Brumer Island.

The island looked glorious through the spy glass. From under dipping coconut fronds came a stream of natives in huge catamarans. The contact promised much; these boats were of a new type, three logs, anything up to 30 feet long, lashed together by rattan cords. The central log was exquisitely carved and painted red and white at the bow and stern. These Papuans seemed well disposed and were the first actually allowed on board the *Rattlesnake*. They shinned up a rope, their enormous hair combs appearing before their blackened faces, peering over the gun rail. They were impressive in their strangeness, with high white-striped cheeks, high-crowned skulls, flat circular earrings and a stick through the nose. In their canoes they seemed taller. On deck they shrank to five foot four, dwarfed by their ten-foot polished spears, and purple amaranth flowers in their hair hardly made them fearsome. On board they clustered, chewing betel nuts and spitting black saliva through black teeth, protesting their friendship by touching their noses while pinching their navels.

Eventually 100 a day were turning up, some carrying hornbill heads or cassowary feathers for trade. On board an 'amusing vagabond' would stick his cowrie shell necklace in his mouth, to heighten the effect of his charcoal face and white-painted brows, put on 'a grotesque attitude' and start beating a tin pot. To the laughter of the crew the drummer, fiddler and fife-player struck up a shanty and joined in. For Huxley the novelty superseded serious study. There were none of Darwin's probing questions, about their origins, about the enigmas of God's handiwork, or the meaning of savages for civilized, sherry-sipping man. For the moment Huxley was just another sailor laughing at their 'grimaces and antics'.[12] Not that he lacked the opportunity. He mischievously led one inquisitive Papuan down the hatch to the ward-room, where the officers were sipping wine. They might refuse a surgeon's mate his rightful place, but hardly his eerie sepulchral-painted guest, with nose sticks and hair comb, who was by now fearfully clutching Huxley's hand. So they seated him in an armchair and offered him a glass. And there he sat, nervously enjoying himself.

MacGillivray went on with his lexicon. There was plenty of time to question them on the names of common objects. Most days the canoes would arrive, with the natives bringing cooked yams as calling cards. They seemed kind and soon understood the Victorian proprieties. But kindness invited its own reward, and they were scurrilously cheated by 'Honest Jack' – and greeted by 'torrents of choice Billingsgate' (fishmongers' foulmouthing) if they reciprocated. Men brought boys to look at the strange ship. Out of a huge 27-man canoe stepped one venerable chief. Huxley thought him not 'unlike the Bishop of Norwich' (old chiefs apparently being the same everywhere). The skipper did his best to impress. He lit blue lights at night, giving the ship a ghostly glow, or fired rockets, and mystified them with scenes of civilized life on his £25 magic lantern.

Sometimes tattooed women came too, dressed in red-and-green-dyed grass skirts. The crew draped them in gaudy regatta shirts and they would 'dance for our amusement' on the quarterdeck. Huxley never considered the common denominator of his own stovepipe-hatted sex and the coppery-combed 'gentlemen', but he saw 'how perfectly women are women all the world over', with 'the same incessant flow of small talk'. 'And to complete the resemblance they all persisted in kissing and hugging an impudent young varlet of a ship's boy', then taking a 'roguish delight' in inspecting the black smudges on his white face. One aspect was not shared with civilized women and must have seemed barbarous to Huxley: MacGillivray noted that 'they appeared to be treated by the men as equals and to exercise considerable influence over them'.

On 19 August the cutters were dispatched to the island, with Huxley, MacGillivray and Thomson along. The captain's orders were to find water, but all were keen to see a village. With natives holding their hands, they marched up a snaking craggy path towards the island's central ridge. Led like blind men, they stopped at the top and for the first time saw a breathtaking view: high jungly hills on each side and spread out before them lush coconut groves and the 'curious gables of the native huts', set off by the 'wide ocean with a tremendous line of rollers' in the distance.[13]

The whole village turned out for the procession. Men in hair combs and cassowary feathers were beating out rhythms on drums or 'roaring' into huge bamboo pipes, so that it turned into the 'most hideous uproar imaginable'. Huxley moved freely among the huts, sketching the charcoal-blackened women. Here was a strange Arcadian beauty. Untouched people; not necessarily noble savages, but apparently happy ones. They lived in a land of plenty, ready to share their bananas and guavas and coconuts. They were to be envied their 'primitive simplicity and kind-heartedness'. Where was that 'malady of thought' afflicting industrial England? He realized that 'civilization as we call it would be rather a curse than a blessing to them'. Huxley knew the fate in store for them, slamming the 'mistaken goodness of the "Stigginses" of Exeter Hall, who would send missionaries to these men to tell them that they will all infallibly be damned'.

Stanley's timidity was now the talking point. He never ventured ashore. In two weeks parties were allowed to visit the island only twice, for a couple of hours each. There was no reconnaissance, no collecting. We 'have not been permitted to take the slightest advantage of the opportunities afforded' us, moaned Huxley. Proper exploration of the island could have provided a dry run, readying them for New Guinea. But no; 'we knew as much of its botany, similarly zoology, when we anchored, as we do now'. The New Guinea 'mainland was not half a dozen miles off and there appeared to be some promise of a large river. Not a boat was sent to explore the coast . . . if this is the process of English Discovery, God defend me from any such elaborate waste of time and opportunity'.[14]

With no exploration, Huxley had to content himself with sketching the canoes of inquisitive visitors. Or scissoring sea slugs. Nights would find him 'sitting in my hatch – which opens into the common den where the rest of the menagerie divert themselves', candle burning, sweat pouring, writing up his notes or reading the 'wonderful' *Wilhelm Meister*, Goethe's 'cold & glassy' reflection of life. He liked novels of disillusionment.[15]

Morale was collapsing again in the heat. September found them moving along the New Guinea coast. Days they spent 'coquetting with the shore', unable to find an anchorage. One moment they were in 100 fathoms, too deep for an anchor, the next in six and stirring up the mud dangerously. Nerves jangled as it became clear that Stanley was afraid to land. Some took to grog and vice: a seaman was lashed for drunkenness and a midshipman for 'unclean and indecent behaviour'. All hands were summoned to watch. The men were tied to the grating, with the surgeons behind. They were needed, with the 'cat' able to knock a man down and lacerate his back. Huxley's insubordination was more private. He kept his complaints about the failure of the 'little man's heart' to himself. He escaped Stanley's lashing tongue when others were verbally whipped. 'I am sick of the brute! He has been like a little fiend all day, snubbing poor old Suckling in the most disgusting manner, and behaving like a perfect cub to all about him'.[16]

With the crew on a knife edge, fights with the Papuans were flaring up. Huxley heard that the equally 'gallant and humane commander' Yule in the *Bramble* had fired at angry natives, who through a mix-up had given a pig and received nothing. Still, the continual barter was revealing some interesting items: on 5 September two live *Cuscus* were traded 'for an axe a-piece'. These rare phalangers – grey-coated, naked-tailed, opossum-like marsupials – now joined the ship's company. Gentle, slow and nocturnal, they lived curled up asleep in the corner of the hen coop by day, forepaws over nose. At night they came alive, eating coconut and lapping pea soup, their huge reddish-yellow eyes giving them good night vision. As Huxley strolled on deck for his 10 pm. constitutional, and Stanley smoked his cigar, the night-watch allowed the *Cuscus* to climb the rigging.

Between deals they scudded westward, slaking their thirst with hot rainwater streaming off the sails. ('It's what a wine merchant would call a "full-bodied" drink by the time we get it'.) The mugginess reminded them of a 'vapour bath'. 'It rains continually', Huxley complained, 'heavy clouds hang over the land in bands almost down to the shore, their white fleece shewing beautifully against the blue side of the mountains'. They pushed on past Cape Rodney in mid-September, never landing, remaining between seven and 30 miles offshore. Finally on Thursday 20 September they put in under some red cliffs. It was 'so like a place near Preston, to which I went the day Charlie was married', noted Stanley, 'that I called it Redscar'. On Sunday morning Huxley rose to the sight of sunrise over the majestic New Guinea summits. The range had been growing steadily as they sailed west; now it assumed spectacular proportions. It 'can hardly be less than 10,000 feet high', he guessed, and some 'thirty or forty miles inland'.

What did Huxley think of the 'little man' appropriating the entire New Guinea mountain chain? (It was christened 'Owen Stanley's Range'.) Naming might be 'possessing', but this was imperial arrogance run amok. Huxley was sick of Stanley's conceit. Too timid to step ashore, he sailed past claiming the distant mountains! Peaks and islands were called after the officers – parcelled out by the skipper. The assistant surgeon even found one of the 40-odd islands in the Calvados Group named 'Huxley Island'.[17]

The Papuans now were smaller, with hair 'frizzled up into a mop projecting backwards'. But their canoes stood off and no waving of red rags would lure them in. Nor were shore parties allowed. Everyone moaned as the chances slipped away. Even more galling, on 25 September, when the *Rattlesnake* moved a few miles along the coast, Papuans with pigtails tied with dog-toothed rosettes came out from a river's mouth to invite them ashore. They 'were civil enough', though heavily armed, and the fact that they were ignorant of iron showed that Stanley had an opportunity for virgin contact.

But no. The ships sailed on another 30 miles, to anchor off Yule Island, named in honour of the *Bramble*'s 'gallant' commander. Even this stopover lasted only a few hours. Buffeted by heavy seas, they were uncomfortable at anchor and finally, on 27 September, after six weeks cruising along New Guinea's coast, never once setting a foot on the mainland, Stanley plotted a course due west, across the Great Bight of New Guinea, back to Cape York in northern Australia.

It 'makes me sick', Thomson fumed. He considered the four months a fiasco. The French had passed these shores but not penetrated the interior. Here was the crew's opportunity to be 'considered discoverers; but this was denied us'. 'And now we have left this great *terra incognita*'. 'I cannot now conceal my chagrin'. Huxley was never able to collect the bird-of-paradise he had promised Lizzie's daughter Flory.

For four days they sailed across the Coral Sea, past islands on the northern extremity of the Great Barrier Reef – past Bramble Key, with its huge booby and noddy colonies. A resigned crew arrived at the benighted Cape York on 1 October, and Huxley scribbled his last dyspeptic note for two weeks: 'No provision ship, no letters. I won't swear'.

The provision ship arrived the next day with five months' mail. Nettie told him that the Fannings were moving to England. *Punch* kept him laughing and the *Times* was long out of date. Yesterday's news made him feel remote. Not *so* remote that his bank manager could not find him, even at the ends of the earth. Salting away his shillings had left him no richer. Still £140 in the red, he concluded that 'the sooner I desert and go to California the better'.[18]

Then came even more astonishment. After all the worrying, he had positive sightings of his intellectual offspring. He was over-joyed by his first direct message from Forbes on 'the fate of my scientific efforts'. 'They are it appears to be printed and he promises, in his own words, "to see that they are done justice to". At the same time he speaks of ... my establishing for myself "a high name as a naturalist"'. Huxley trumpeted the news to Nettie, knowing that a paper in the Royal Society's *Transactions* would increase his prospects.

A letter from Jim added more. He had spotted two notices of his brother in the *Athenaeum*: his two year-old paper 'On the Anatomy of Diphyes' had been read at the Linnean Society on 16 January 1849, and in the 10 March issue: 'Meetings for the ensuing week:- Zoological. "M^r. Huxley R. N. On the animal of Trigonia"'. Tom had waited to hear this for so long. Not even the Linnean paper being attributed to 'W. Huxley Esq' could dampen his euphoria. So, said his practical brother, your 'mind is bent on Scientific pursuits', how would it 'be converted into daily bread'?[19] Jim suggested he become a mad-doctor, bread before science, but Tom had fixed his sights.

Buoyed up, he sent Forbes another screed, arguing again that the lowly stinging animals were all of a kind, which he proposed to call 'Nematophora' (from the 'nematocysts' or stinging cells). He was the first to see that all the hydras and jellies and sea nettles and anemones were two-layered. His little truths were becoming bigger, as he began to corner whole chunks of creation. He suspected, too, that his stinging animals could be arranged in some sort of geometric pattern, to show their relationships. There must be 'a great law hidden in the "Circular System" if one could but get at it . . . but I, a mere chorister in the temple, had better cease discussing matters obscure to the high priests of science themselves'.[20]

Huxley's joy contrasted to Stanley's blank countenance. Ten days after recalling his brother's wedding at Redscar Point, he heard that Charlie was dead from a stomach infection, leaving Eliza widowed and alone in Tasmania. But Stanley's mind was turning; he made no mention of it, showed no grief. He was withdrawing, his reason becoming impaired.

The monotony of Cape life was suddenly broken two weeks later. Huxley was now to learn far more of the intimate details of aboriginal customs, and from an unexpected insider source.

The sailors were dumbfounded to see among the aborigines a 'white woman disfigured by dirt and the effect of the sun on her almost uncovered body'. They stood in disbelief, staring, as she came forward, slightly lame, with inflamed eyes, 'and in hesitatingly broken language cried "I am a Christian – I am ashamed"'. A cutter brought her out to the ship, accompanied by her 'brothers'. Slowly, over the days, she told her story 'in half Scotch, half native dialect'.

She was *Teoma*, which turned out to be Thompson, Barbara. She was only 20, a tinsmith's daughter from Aberdeen, who had come out with her father when she was eight. At 15 she had run away with a sailor to Moreton Bay. After marrying they had sailed to the Torres Strait to make a living scavenging off the wrecks. But a squall capsized their cutter, drowning everyone except Mrs Thompson, who was rescued by natives out turtling. As a white *marki* (ghost) she was adopted as an elder's reincarnated daughter. For five years, as one of the 'jumped-up-alive', she was treated well and lived on Prince of Wales Island in the Strait. She spoke the language of her 'brothers' fluently and adopted their manners so as to present 'a most ludicrous graft of the gin upon the white woman'. She had sung ballads to herself at night to try to retain her old language, but even now found it difficult 'to translate her native thoughts into plain English'.

Like all the aborigines, she had known of the *Rattlesnake*'s presence, and she told Huxley of Kennedy's death. Now MacGillivray had a 'native' translator to add the more awkward concepts to his lexicon. She poured out astonishing stories, of tribal attacks, the cutting-and-carrying of heads, the *marki* deities and animistic beliefs of her people. She gave Huxley and MacGillivray their first deep insights into aboriginal culture. *Teoma* joined the ship, settling into the captain's workshop, surrounded by calico presents. 'Poor creature!' said Huxley, 'we have all great compassion for her and I am sure there is no one who would not do anything to make her comfortable'.[21]

The naturalists set off ashore. Seaforthia palms towered 80 feet above them. Along the rivers they collected seeds of tiny banana and ginger plants for Sydney's Botanical Garden. MacGillivray found the 'play houses' of the bower birds, large stick-canopied tunnels, their entrances littered with attractive objects, where the male indulged in 'strange antics' to lure the female. He collected one precarious bower and actually shipped it lock-stock-and-barrel to the British Museum. He and Wilcox, the captain's collector, sent more imperial treasures to Gould: a trove of beautifully prepared kingfishers, *Cuscuses*, lovely wrens, flycatchers, honey-eaters, iridescent starlings and spectacular crimson-cheeked black parrots.[22]

But this wasn't for Huxley. He stole off for a month's adventure in the *Asp* to chart the islands around Bligh's Channel at the western entrance to the Strait. His party went heavily armed, hearing from *Teoma* that a renegade white man, thought to be an escaped convict from Norfolk Island, was leading a tribe on Mulgrave Island, raiding vessels and terrorizing the islands. This proved the need for a garrison settlement here, to make the Cape a port of refuge, a coaling station, a trading post and a missionary centre. Stanley brooded on the outrages. Before leaving the Cape he visited Albany Island and the graves of Wall and Niblet, or what remained of Kennedy's men. He was now obviously unstable.

Time hung heavily and Huxley spent the last steamy month at the Cape poring over fleshy sea squirts (or salps). He had hauled in hundreds of these flask-shaped creatures at Redscar Point, and here at the Cape 'the sea was absolutely crowded' with them. Alive they defensively spurted a stomach-ful of sea water at him; dead no kin readily claimed them. They were anomalies, apparently with no close relations. Tradition made them strange molluscs, and all the stranger for his observation that the free-swimming embryo of one, an *Appendicularia* from New Guinea, had tail muscles like a tadpole's.[23] (It was a hint of the most astounding relationship ever to be uncovered in the animal kingdom; the sea squirt larva would eventually be linked to the fish. Within 20 years it would be made the evolutionary bridge between the invertebrates and the backboned fish, reptiles and mammals.)

But the strange salps said something else to Huxley at the Cape. He always found two types together, so distinct that they looked like separate species. But they were not; one was actually producing the other, long chains of them could be seen emerging from it. The chains detached and inside each member a foetus developed – which itself grew into the original solitary form! This lifecycle was seen as an 'Alternation of Generations', just as hydras produce medusae, which breed hydras. But not by Huxley: at the Cape he argued that the first salp simply budded off the second. The chains floating away were not *individuals*, but detached reproductive organs, bits of the parent no less (zoöids he called them). These were the sex organs of the mother salp living independent lives!

Nothing was stranger, that an individual could exist in 50 free-swimming parts! So were the millions of aphids springing from one female by parthenogenesis nothing more than bits of her? A more provocative Royal Society paper was on the way.[24]

Nine weeks at the Cape were enough. Not that sailing would be better, with the *Rattlesnake* doubling back to New Guinea. But with *Teoma* aboard at least Huxley had a guide to aboriginal culture. They set sail on 3 December and that afternoon reached Mount Ernest Island in the Strait. Huxley got ashore and shouts of *Poud! Poud!* and offers of biscuits to an old man bought him his ticket to the local village. He passed a strange enclosure, with houses fenced in low bamboo, and was warned that it was 'a place to be feared'. (It was a sacred site, according to *Teoma*, for initiation into manhood, and any woman looking at it would be executed.)

The old man led them further into a magical clearing, 'arched over by magnificent trees and so shaded and cool, with a "dim religious light" pervading it'. The great canopy deflected 'the hot sun' and in the 'silence and the gloom' he imagined himself in a great cathedral. Huxley, always set pondering by religious expression, stood before 'a strange fantastic sort of monument in this savage sanctuary'. Through his mind flashed fantastic images of 'horrible savage rites' and alien gods, yet the clearing seemed so still and 'utterly peaceful'. A great screen of mat was adorned by reddened spider shells and at its base 'flat stones of all shapes carved and painted with hideous human faces'. In the shade he sat down to sketch this ancestral funerary monument, pleasing the old man by his attention. It was haunting. 'I never shall forget the beauty of the place; while in it I felt as if listening to beautiful music'.

He came even closer to the dead on Darnley Island. Stanley refused to come ashore, but Huxley penetrated the coconut fringe on the 'bright white beach', passed clumps of 'shimmering bamboos' standing sentry, and entered the beautiful village of Mogoor. He wandered among the 'whimsical-looking beehive-shaped' huts and picked up trophies. His native minder 'had no objection to pilfer his ancestors' skulls and basely sell them'. Nor Huxley to buy them, of course. He came away with three.

The people were 'gentle and polite'. The women were treated kindly, and so were strangers. Huxley was offered a *coskeer*, a wife; not that Nettie needed to be jealous, with polygamy the norm throughout the Straits. Still it was ironic, for this was about the closest he would come to nuptial bliss in the southern hemisphere. While he refused a wife, MacGillivray accepted a new species of *cuscus*, brought in tame in a 'nice bamboo spindle-shaped cage'.[25] The old man who parted with it pleaded that it be cared for properly, but MacGillivray skinned it nevertheless. Wives and *cuscuses*: the white *marki* ghosts were showered with gifts. They were higher beings, and such they must have appeared, striking lucifer matches and shooting birds from the skies.

Bramble Key was the last island before New Guinea. They remained there for three days, stocking up. Some raided the tern colony for eggs. Others collected spinach; and 17 turtles were taken during the night as they plodded, exhausted, back to the sea after egg-laying. The massive reptiles, 280 lbs apiece, were manhandled aboard ship to be kept alive for food. The terns' eggs were a treat. But Huxley called the spinach 'filth' and the island something worse. 'Its hot, damp, muggy, rheumatic, disgusting, and abominable'.

Christmas dinner was better, a turtle feast during the thundery monsoon off Redscar Point in New Guinea. Then a post-prandial stroll on deck to admire the mountains. Rolling in an awful swell they had to drop a second anchor. Table-topped Mount D'Urville at 13,000 feet seemed to be adversely affecting the weather, as the disintegrating Stanley was affecting the crew. None was unhappy to leave. The *Bramble* stayed on to finish the survey, while the *Rattlesnake* cast off on 29 December, sailing back along the coast. As the new year 1850 rolled in they scudded east, all eyes astern, as clearing skies revealed majestic jungle-covered mountains up to 120 miles away.

Duchateau Island natives came alongside at dawn on 8 January, 'confound them', said Huxley, 'for they disturbed my slumbers'.[26] He had lost interest. Stanley had too. He finally cut southwards, to Sydney. 'Today finishes eight months' away, Huxley jotted. 'A month hence we must be in Sydney. I dare not think about it'.

8

Homesick Heroes

THE BRITTLE PERFECTIONIST was cracking. Captain Stanley looked ravaged and no one questioned his cut-and-run policy. He had been racked for months. The flood of anxieties, about the reefs, the savages, the safety of his crew and the worth of his work, had pushed the 'little man' to the brink. The crash came with horrifying violence.

Sailing away from the Louisiade he had a seizure, leaving him partly paralysed. As he dragged his leg, his mind began to wander. Then came the vitriolic outbursts. His 'waspish' temper 'became unbearable' and Thomson showed alarm as Stanley snapped heads off. The doctor pleaded with him to relinquish command or he 'could not feel . . . responsible for his life'.

Stanley's fastidiousness deserted him. He seemed not to care anymore, his mind gone, his body paralysed, his brother dead. He ignored badly charted wrecking-reefs in the Coral Sea. This, as MacGillivray said, was practically criminal for a surveyor with 17 chronometers on board.

The run to Sydney was painfully slow. Light winds dogged them. 'We have made about 600 miles in the last fortnight', Huxley logged on 24 January 1850; 'we are about 800 miles from Sydney, and might be there in a week. But so we might a week ago. Uncertainty and suspense seem my lot. Patience! Patience!' On 4 February they were still lying becalmed, 30 miles off Sydney Heads. Only six hours away but no breeze to blow them in. He had not heard from Nettie for five months and the frustration was showing. 'The Fates can surely not tantalize any longer'.[1]

These were the moments that Nettie dreamed of yet dreaded, as the *Rattlesnake* hove into sight. In her 'bitter fancies' she feared that he would not step off, that 'a letter black-edged and sealed' would arrive in his stead. It was her recurrent nightmare. 'The gnawing of despair . . . Oh God, whatever I deserve, avert this evil from me'.

But the *Rattlesnake* arrived and once more Hal stepped lively ashore. He had survived New Guinea. So had *Teoma*, now transformed into Mrs Thompson once more. She was reunited with her parents and Hal expected to find her a '"Lioness" in the good town of Sydney and a source of great glorification & turkey-cock gobbling for us'. Others were less fortunate. Stanley looked haggard. Staggering on deck to take the mail from a sombre Robert King he received another body blow, word from the Bishop's Palace that his father had died the previous September. He showed no sign of shock, but his anguished inner cry was almost his final one.

The captain had done his work. He had proved the absence of any stray reefs off New Guinea. He had taken the first step in opening these regions to the whalers and gold prospectors. But it was never enough for a man consumed. One desire 'rules all his actions', noted Thomson, and Huxley understood it well, 'the wish to rank amongst the . . . *savans* of England'. Scientific pre-eminence was the intellectual badge of a gentleman. It 'fills his mind by day and is the subject of his dreams by night'. But the captain was to be disappointed, the doctor recognized, for he is 'a superficialist in all his knowledge'.[2]

Hal stepped into the Sydney sun to find everything changed. Holmwood was abandoned and the Fannings already on the seas to England. Nettie was in the next cove, lodging with Mrs Griffiths at Woolloomooloo. He would troop the few hundred yards across the beautiful public gardens to meet her. Then 'we descended to the little summer house on the rocks and talked even to my heart's content of our home and all that we would make it'.[3]

They watched the ships as Hal caught up with nine months' news. He heard of the balls, the races, and the day Nettie came home to find the boozy cook setting the house on fire, the butler drunk in the road, the children covered in soap-suds and the baby smashing eggs on the bed. But what could a brewer's daughter expect in a tipsy ticket-of-leave society? By the water's edge she briefed him on the events half-a-world away: 'War, nothing but war', with Louis Napoleon's march into Rome to restore Pope Pius IX. Hatred of the Catholic French put her in mind of the new clergyman, who looked like 'a romish priest'. But her father's financial troubles at the brewery seemed more immediate – as did marriage.

Huxley was glad to be off the ship. After being parboiled in the gun-room for months he could let off steam. He enjoyed a wild dash with shipmates to Parramatta. Darwin had cantered here ten years earlier, taking the Great Western Road on the south side of Port Jackson. But his was a civilized jaunt with the stream of 'Carts Gigs, Phaetons & Horses'. Nothing so sedate for Huxley; he rowed over to the north shore and then cracked the whip, scattering swarms of green budgerigars.

> You can't fancy what a mad ride we had out here. We
> came up the North Shore way (about eight and twenty
> miles) in about 3 hours & a half galloping, jumping,
> singing and shouting like four 'wilde jäger' Luckily its a
> very solitary road and I don't think there were any
> spectators of our follies. If there had been they would
> certainly have imagined us just escaped from Tarban Creek
> [the local lunatic asylum].[4]

He was not always a quiet hot-head. Parramatta was a small town, with 17 pubs (he stayed in the 'commodious' Woolpark Inn), a racecourse, barracks and the notorious Female Factory, which had successfully turned generations of pilferers into 'alcoholic sluts'. Ships' surveyors routinely brought their chronometers for checking to the observatory at Parramatta, but Huxley's was no staid party cradling precision instruments.

The home news was of the usual pecuniary disasters. 'Poor Cooke', wailed George, 'he is in a desperate state. He has clung to teaching till it has entirely failed him . . . they have the utmost difficulty to exist from day to day'. Rock-steady George was wailing about himself too. The crash of 1847 had wiped him out. Railway shares had collapsed, banks had folded, even the Bank of England was threatened: 'my fortune is gone', he told Tom. 'The panic . . . knocked down my property to half its value. The French revolution in 1848 gave me another blow, and the very large sum I have advanced to the different members of the family to start them in the world not being forthcoming I am completely crippled'.

Huxley's sources of income were disappearing. And the moral pressure was building; his parents were leaning on George and James, but Jim too had run into difficulty and was cutting his 'allowance to the old folk one-5th'. Mother thought Tom ought to start contributing. Her 'claim is a moral one equally on all of us', George warned, even as he fought Tom's corner and pleaded that 'it was not fair till you had time to get clear'. But Tom felt the pressure. He could *not* get married, he *had* to earn. He had heard the word: McClatchie, back in England and visiting George, reported to 'D^r. Tom that your Brother looks on your matrimonial Alliance (*at present*) as an imprudent speculation'.

George continued to root for Tom and his strange science. 'You will have heard of the Bishop's death. I must try & get at his execs & learn if they had any papers of yours'.[5]

While Hal watched his pennies, Nettie's worries were other-worldly. On the surface all seemed smooth. The Sydney Heads 'with a thousand sun-sparkles' looked 'tenfold more beautiful' with Hal beside her. But there were emotional undercurrents, and sometimes the swell broke surface. At moments their eternal life arm-in-arm no longer seemed so secure:

> Oh if I only . . . felt assured that Death would be to us but
> a dark gate which led us to eternal happiness, what peace
> would possess me . . . And my friends – my Father, my
> Mother, the one believes not and the other believing is not
> so mindful of heavenly things as I would she were – and
> he, dear Hal – God guide him to the perfect light for I am
> often very unhappy about his sentiments – I have so much
> need of leading unto holy things . . . that I fondly hoped
> he would have been the guide and instructor unto more
> perfect ways – but here my hopes have borne bitter fruit.
> Something has come over me of late; I cannot pray as
> fervently as I did.

Her sombre thoughts would fly away as he arrived at the door. On 7 March they attended a ball at Government House, Huxley in his dress uniform and cocked hat, Nettie breathless: 'to dance . . . with him it is bewitching – he holds me so that I scarcely touch the ground – I danced incessantly but never once felt tired'. Other nights were spent at home. On 12 March 'We all had a round game of cards in which Hal most provokingly won all from me and asserted that his influence over me was so constant that it was exemplified even in the smallest things – then he impertinently whispered in my ear, "Give me a kiss". How his eyes flash sometimes!'[6] Then he ran across the Botanical Gardens to the ship.

*

Stanley was aboard. At 38 he was a pathetic sight, wizened, 'prematurely old'. He had written telling his widowed sister-in-law Eliza 'to lose no time in joining the ship'. He had fitted up her cabin and was comforted by their shared grief. Now he looked to London and a shore posting. High things were expected – an Admiralty desk was talked of, perhaps even Beaufort's at the Hydrography office. Of the last 26 years Stanley had spent 22 at sea, which was enough for one lifetime.

At daybreak the next morning, 13 March, he was found unconscious on his cabin floor. He had suffered an 'epileptic paralytic fit' and fallen on his head. Huxley cradled him, but there was nothing he could do. Stanley died in his arms at 7.40 am.

Waves of remorse struck the men as they realized what Stanley had been suffering. He had finished his survey in torment. 'But he died', Huxley wrote, with 'the end attained', and his epitaph was the thanks of endless mariners who were to thread their way through the maze of coral reefs. 'Which of us may dare to ask for more?'[7]

Sydney society shuttered its windows on 15 March. Flags were flown at half mast. HMS *Rattlesnake* had 'her yards a'cockbill [disorderly] and topped in opposite directions, instead of being quite square and trim'. The coffin was lowered into the pinnace, which proceeded across the harbour to the north shore, followed by boats bearing the cream of Sydney society. A visiting ship in port, HMS *Meander*, fired a 38 gun salute, one for each year of his life. Ashore Huxley proceeded behind the coffin, the *Meander*'s band playing a dirge, and Revd Robert King read the service.

The next day, Huxley was in church again. On 16 March Nettie's half-sister Isabel was married. Nettie was somewhat disapproving, with Isy an old maid of 38 and her husband 20. But Hal acted 'Papa' and gave the bride away, even if he sat in the pew (as always foul tempered during church services) uttering 'the greatest absurdities in the gravest possible manner'. Here he met Nettie's mother for the first time, and 'so "snaked"' her 'that she was deep in her praises of him'.

It highlighted his own problems. Hal told his mother that he had made up his mind: 'I determined that we should be terribly prudent and get married about 1870, or the Greek Kalends, or, what is about the same thing, whenever I am afflicted with the *malheur de richesses*'. If sudden wealth, or at least a steady job, was the desideratum, then another piece of tittle-tattle raised his hope:

I heard from an old messmate of mine at Haslar the other
day that Dr. MacWilliam, F.R.S., one of our deputy-
inspectors, had been talking about one of my papers, and
gave him to understand that it was to be printed.
Furthermore, he is a great advocate for the claims of
assistant surgeons to ward-room rank, and all that sort of
stuff, and, I am told, quoted me as an example!
Henceforward I look upon the learned doctor as a man of
sound sense and discrimination! . . . I find myself getting
horribly selfish, looking at everything with regard to the
influence it may have on my grand objects.[8]

The time for leaving was drawing close. After Stanley's death the
last survey was abandoned. Huxley had his wish, to get home
early, but not in the way he expected. Yule had taken command,
with orders to proceed directly to England by the fastest route. His
appointment by the *Meander*'s captain infuriated Sydney's naval
commander, who considered this his prerogative. It left Yule
jittery and unsure of his position, and eager to be off.

The dam of pent-up emotion was continually breached in these
fraught days. A teasing Hal made Nettie cry by taking back his
miniature. ''Twas so mean of him'. 'I could cry that I shall not
clasp it tonight as usual'. He 'was tyrannizing – he knew I could
refuse him nothing'. Two days later a box arrived for her and
there it was, 'set in a pretty little locket which I could wear. I
kissed it again and again . . . I was so very very happy and yet I
could not stop my tears'.[9]

He was an emotional despot. But she was angelically susceptible
to 'those strange piercing glances which, odious snake, he has
never yet found to fail'. Glances like Medusa's own: 'I wish to talk
but your eyes wont let me', she once complained. 'Hal, dear Hal
. . . You draw out my thoughts and feelings – and appropriate
them most tyrannically – and yet 'tis perhaps one of the things
that has bound me with stronger love to you. You *are* a tyrant still
conquering by strength where influence fails'.

In their last weeks together the idyll was tainted by flashes of
the future. The frustration showed in his capricious moods, fitful
one minute, fond the next. There were stolen kisses as Mr Griffiths
went out to smoke his cigar, and more on a drive under the
pretext of taking the children out.[10] It was a time for parting
presents, a turtleshell comb from the islands, and a daguerreotype
taken by Thomson, showing Hal in his uniform.

He handed over his diary, his account of the Coral Sea inferno and New Guinea natives. 'It tells of the wanderings of a man among all varieties of human life', he explained, 'from the ball-room among the elegancies and soft nothings of society to the hut of the savage and the grand untrodden forest. It should tell more. It should tell of the wider and stranger wanderings of a human soul, now proud and confident, now sunk in bitter despondency – now so raised above its own coarser nature by the influence of a pure and devoted love'. But it was a history of the outer man, not of his inner soul.

One inner feeling now clouded his thoughts. It 'hangs like an incubus over me'. For two or three years they would not see one another, and the cloud would 'remain until the dreaded separation is over, and Hope has again become the only possible comforter'. She cried at the thought of it. 'Three years – they seem immeasurable – how often will my heart sicken and long to rejoin him and know it must wait and weary'.

At times they were paralysed by emotion. Doubt vied with desire. Hal would go gloomy, his moods swinging, fearing the failure of his scientific plans, fearing they might drift apart in the storms of life and love. He poured out his heart, worrying about 'having overrated his ability'. And should he fail, he asked Nettie 'if I w^d still . . . esteem him as before – for said he to be loved from compassion would be unbearable'. Money, he had to make the future promise it. It was the straw he clung to as the moment of parting came. Science had to pay.

Near the end they were constantly together, riding, dining, cuddling on the rocks. The storm clouds broke on Saturday 27 April, the 'bitter day'. A sailor brought word that the ship was to sail on the Tuesday. Hal led Nettie quietly into the drawing room to prepare her. 'I have not cried today', she jotted on Sunday 28 April, 'but the heaviness at my heart seems to weigh me down – and I am so cold'.[11]

They sneaked a few hours alone on Monday night. 'Every now & then as I sat talking,' Hal wrote, 'the thought that I had to part from you shot through me like a cold pain'. 'I could have fallen on your neck and wept like a child'. The next morning he sent gifts, more turtle combs, copies of Carlyle, 'a letter for you written in the days of desolation on the New Guinea coast', and a note declaring that 'I never knew how much I loved you, dearest, till last night'.

It was clear the sailing would be delayed but 'I . . . dare not come ashore again. If I did I should never leave you. I would have given the world last night to return and lay my head upon your dear shoulder once more, and give you one more long, long embrace'.

Nettie spent a tearful Tuesday watching 'the old ship from the verandah' through a glass. By night she could see the square-rigger out in the bay with 'all the little boats clustering like busy ants around it'. She watched the endless provisioning 'in a kind of stupor'.[12]

He broke his vow and ran over for the last time, on Wednesday night. But the moment of farewell was strained. Both knew the years of painful separation that lay ahead. They tried to smile and disguise the inner hurt, but 'there was something horribly absurd in our doing so'. Nettie handed him her diary – and he was suddenly gone, leaving her savouring his 'dear words and dearer kisses'.

Huxley ran from Woolloomooloo 'in a strange unnatural state of excitement'. Ran mindlessly, breathing fast, confused, fearing that he would miss the ship, wanting to. The 'exertion seemed cooling & calming to me and I was collected enough by the time I got on board'.[13]

Everything was chaos. The ship was crammed, with invalid marines from the abandoned Port Essington, the *Bramble*'s crew, wives and children. Mrs Charles Stanley in black was mourning the old captain, and Mrs Yule was accompanying the new. They were sailing overcrowded, with upwards of 230 people on board.

That night the loading continued. Officers barked, sailors swore, shouts of 'One, two, three – haul!' accompanied the crash of cargo in the hold. The last crates of goats, chickens and ducks were winched on. The frigate seemed more like a farmyard. Screeching cockatoos and parrots were brought aboard, and the usual quota of cats and dogs. 'All was in confusion – visitors, duns & dirt were everywhere'. An inebriated MacGillivray staggered 'on board in the middle of the night & was put under arrest – his wife and child came about 2 A. M. '

Hal went to bed only to toss and turn, and before he knew it 'about ½ past seven we began to get the anchor up'. He too was straining with his spy glass. 'I watched you in the verandah this morning', he jotted in one last note, handed to a departing boat. 'Good bye – God bless you my own darling'.[14]

It was a scorching morning on 2 May 1850 as they waved goodbye to the crowds on Farm Cove. The sea was glassy. Then a 'breath of wind came hot as from a kiln from the northwest, the sails were loosed and we were on *our way home*'.

'I went up on the poop and found several who like myself had come to take a last look'. There was Mrs Stanley, tall and sombre in black. The laden ship pulled out slowly. They passed Woolloomooloo Bay. Hal desperately trained his signalman's glass on the houses and saw Nettie on the balcony:

> with glass directed towards the old ship. Did she see me? I know not. All I know is that the figure stayed there until we were far down the harbour . . . I watched & watched until we were between the heads and then as the house now a white speck was shut in by the south head I turned away and saw no more of Sydney. I said to myself that I had done with looking back. Goodbye Sorrow, come Hope.
>
> And therefore I went down with Simpson to have a glass of champagne – &, silently, I drank to *our* success & happy reunion.[15]

He watched as first Port Jackson and then the coast itself vanished. 'I saw the last of the land of Australia . . . a dark grey line along the horizon backed by as splendid a sky as ever the setting sun lighted up'.

> We part friends, O land of gum trees. I have much, much to thank you for.[16]

Yule stood on the bridge, making haste to retain his bars. He still feared being intercepted and replaced. 'At sunset the lookout man was specially ordered to turn his regards astern – he could see no sail & I think that now Cap Yule begins to think himself safe & breathes easily'.

Huxley had become an old salt, pronouncing on the passengers like a hardened sea dog. With children running everywhere, he relished the squalls. 'All the women save Mrs Stanley below & all the children sick – thank God'. Perhaps not relished; his 25th birthday was a washout, with water slopping in his cabin. 'Such a vile night – half a gale of wind – the ship rolling heavily and no sleep to be had. Oh the vile odour, oh the noises!' The preserved meats were giving off a stench again, not that he could concentrate on this olfactory offence for the din of creaking bulkheads, screeching parrots and swearing sailors.

The talk was of them heading for Chile to fix the leaking sternpost. It might not sink the ship but it certainly spoiled the biscuits. The storms kept the 'ladies all thoroughly done up – or rather down & invisible'. But when they eased, one 'good lady' Mrs Crawford threatened more damage with her singing. The cacophony inspired the dogs and then the parrots joined in. The desperate middies got up a fiddle and fife session to drown her out, 'but the remedy was as bad as the disease'.[17]

To the old salts' disgust they had turned into a passenger liner. Some fell to the 'seaman's snare'. MacGillivray staggered the decks, clutching a bottle rather mournfully. Or he could be found 'moralising as he sat contemplating himself in his looking-glass. Ah Jock! You're up to your old tricks again tonight'.[18] It disgusted his old drinking mate.

The reality of sea life was ever present. On 6 May one of the forecastle men died of blood poisoning in Huxley's sick bay. He had scratched himself with a splint of bone on serving the beef. It seemed nothing, but he was dead within days. Huxley felt helpless as he reflected on the doctor's culpability: 'am I not more or less guilty of this man's death from want of knowledge? The responsibility of the physician is something fearful'. Who would doubt the need for a more practical physiology, or a greater reward to spur on its devotees? But for now there was an awful fatalism to his job. 'We shall have two or three more deaths before reaching England. It is distressing to pass men and know that their doom is already fixed, they, poor fellows, unconscious as sheep before the shambles'. Mercifully he was distant from the men. It was the same in the haybarn all those years ago, when he sat alone. Now it was so in the sick bay.

In his candlelit berth he sat in solitary splendour. He devoured the Whig historian Thomas Babington Macaulay's epigrammatic *Essays* in between drawing up classificatory charts linking all known invertebrates. Or he indulged in imaginary chit-chat with Nettie. A sleepless, gale-tossed 48 hours was lost reading her journal. He followed her innermost feelings, 'of the aching that gnaws within my heart . . . but you know dearest by your own heart all the agony I feel. Let us rather turn to the bright future than dwell over the sad present'. So violently was the tub rolling that the water was up to his knees. He 'did not have to go down "the rocks" to my bath in the morning but stepped out of bed right into it'.[19] The crew wanted to put 'into New Zealand to have this vile leak in the after gunroom stopped, but Yule is afraid of being intercepted I believe and wont take a hint'.

Huxley was now squelching in his shoes and joined the others in making a formal complaint. They had been due to sail past the mountainous cliffs on New Zealand's northern tip, but at the North Cape Yule relented and turned for the Bay of Islands, by Cape Brett. Albatrosses heralded their passage down the coast and after dark on 16 May they entered the Bay.

The next morning the ship anchored off Russell. It gave Huxley an unexpected look at New Zealand. The village was pleasant, with a luxuriant, fern-covered backdrop. (Its 30-odd houses were new, and this 'calm & peaceful' feel belied the fact that Chief Heki had gutted the original settlement five years earlier during the Maori War.) Ashore Huxley found the tattooed Maoris a fierce and 'athletic' people, although the women's 'gaudy cotton prints' looked incongruous. Eyre, drained of his 'warmth and colour' by the Australian wastelands, was Lieutenant Governor of the colony, but still sympathetic to the people and, indeed, married himself in a double Maori ceremony.

During recaulking Huxley's party took the cutter 11 miles up the high-banked Kidi Kidi river. For the last two miles a Maori boy guided them, or rather took a 'cross cut' through endless bogs, 'dancing on' ahead as they lumbered through the swamps. But the result was worth it: 80-foot waterfalls, with a huge cave sculpted by the pounding water, its floor and walls a dense carpet of luxuriant ferns and mosses.

But Huxley was more engrossed in the missions than the *manuka* bushes. He wanted to find out 'what missionary life was like' for himself. So he trudged on ten miles to the mission centre at Waimate. A forced pace in the 'chill & bracing' air, through 'fine country . . . covered everywhere with high ferns', put him there by moonlight on 18 May. It was a school and church station of 40 whites and many Maoris, including the great Heki himself. He was welcomed with '*tea unlimited* and a blazing fire' and was 'agreeably surprised' by the missionaries. He had expected a certain '*straight-hairedness* . . . & methodistical puritanism but I find it quite otherwise'. They were 'quiet, unpretending, straightforward folks desirous of doing their best for the people among whom they are placed'. Much of their straight-hair had been torn out, as they were outwitted by the wily Maoris. Old chiefs, prompted on the temporal benefits of Christianity, would reply, 'You've forgotten the big rats', the ships' rats running amok, a parry that appealed to Huxley. Still, with a log fire and a rat-catching cat on his lap, he found even a mission homely.

He returned to the ship in torrential rains, muddy and bedraggled, 'my horse & I went head over heels together' down a clay bank, he explained. But it did not dampen his enthusiasm: 'I like the look of New Zealand'.[20]

The *Rattlesnake* raced on south-east, towards Cape Horn on the tip of South America. No Homeric heroes, these, returning the adventurous way. Every man-jack wanted a hasty end to the ordeal. The homesick sailors had one thought in mind, English soil beneath their squelchy shoes. Spirits were buoyant. Huxley and Thomson paced the deck, lost in plans. Thomson was returning to the baby he had never seen, Huxley to uncertainty. After four years as surgeon and mate their heart-to-heart threw up the unspoken truths. Huxley had a great respect for the man, but 'my hot temper had not always permitted me to act with perfect justice towards him and though we never quarrelled, I felt as I told him that was more owing to his even & amiable disposition than to my deserts'.

Johnny Thomson met him more than half-way. He was awed by his assistant's cynical wit and cutting brilliance. Thomson faced down his own pride to admit, as Huxley wrote in his diary, 'that although placed by the service as my superior he had never forgotten that I had far the advantage in intellect and knowledge'. Huxley, flattered, disclaiming 'in sorrow how untrue it was', nonetheless recorded it. He was getting the measure of his worth.

But would the world recognize it? For days he planned his first London moves. It took gall for an assistant surgeon to dictate terms to the Sea Lords. He would go to Sir William Burnett and request a year's shore posting to write a book on his oceanic men-of-war. And still richer, 'I shall tell him that I cannot afford to lose a ... year's pay'. Therefore 'will he manage the matter so that I may be nominally attached to some naval Hospital'. In short, he wanted half pay for an indefinite leave, with no duties! Huxley for his part would ask this on condition that the great guns – Owen and Forbes – vouched for his work.

Of course, 'living in London may be a *poser*', certainly on three shillings a day. But nothing daunted, he could lodge with George. Who knew? By the end of 1851, when the *Rattlesnake* was originally due to return, he might have a book in press.

It was getting cold now. But the moon in June looked a little lovelier for the luciferous *Pyrosoma* 'shining like white hot cylinders in the water'. Millions of them – the 'fire-body' *Pyrosoma* was another sea squirt, with its hard cylinder wall covered by luminous buds. The ship ploughed through them, phosphorescing like 'lesser moons'. It induced a trance: the sea glowed and dimmed, as if approaching and receding. Waves of 'soft bluish light' spread out 'as far as the eye could reach on every side'. But the moment he dropped a net in 'they dived down' and, millions or no, he ended up with a single specimen.[21] Still that was enough to let him finish his sea squirt paper for the Royal Society.

As they approached Cape Horn the weather worsened. Hail pounded the ship. Snow fell on 23 June – the first seen by the voyagers in four years – light flurries to start, and then blinding sheets. Huxley had bounced from an orchid-house to an ice-store and expected to shatter. The bitterness was 'nipping me up into a sort of animated mummy'. He became bluer and stiffer with each league. The ship began to freeze; the decks disappeared under snow, and ice hung in 'great stalactites about our bows'.

They were to 'double the dread cape' in mid-winter. The sun struggled only 10° above the horizon and gave no heat. Huxley's teeth chattered; wrapped in Nettie's 'beautiful comforter & wristbands', bundled in his great-coat, he determinedly stamped the deck for two or three hours a day. Out there, in the snow, with a lashing spray, the wooden tub seemed a pitiful liferaft in the icy vastness. It was 'desperately cold' now, 22°, with a fierce wind from the Antarctic.

Mrs Stanley was confined to her cabin and he would pop in to check on her. She might have seemed a vulgar parvenu in the Bishop's Palace but, an upstart himself, Huxley found her cultured and well-read, which counted above blood-line. He cared for her budgerigars, and she lent him 'Lamartine's Histoire des Girondins to say nothing of "Mary Barton"', with its evocative 'descriptions of the working classes in manufacturing towns', which he knew so well from his Coventry childhood.[22]

After rounding the Horn against glacial blasts and ferocious waves, the *Rattlesnake* beat up the Patagonian coast to the most desolate of colonial outposts. They anchored in the Falklands on an icy 8 July. The 'Ultima Thule', this, 'and no mistake'. The bleakness of Port Stanley was heightened by a snow-blanket over the treeless wastes. 'How can I describe to you "Stanley" the sole town, metropolis & seat of government'? he asked Nettie. 'It consists of a lot of black low half weatherboard houses, scattered along the hill sides . . . One barn-like place is Government House', another was the squalid barracks of the pensioned Irish soldiers, 'fretting to death' and bitter at having been duped into serving in such a godforsaken hole.

Here was Captain Sulivan, Darwin's old messmate on the *Beagle*. He had surveyed the islands and was now settled here, trying to make a living raising cattle, while shipping Darwin South American fossils. He is a 'fine energetic man', Huxley admitted, but to bring his wife 'to such a desolate place' verged on cruelty. The town was an abomination. The weather was no better. It was one of the most savage winters on record. The thermometer fell to 18° at night and the water froze as the ratings swabbed the decks. 'The only thing to be done is to eat, eat, eat'. To keep body and soul together, 'You consume a pound or so of beefsteak at breakfast and then walk the decks for an appetite at dinner, when you take another pound or two of beef or a goose . . . By four o'clock it is dark night – and as it is too cold to read the only thing to be done is to vanish under blankets as soon as possible and take twelve or fourteen hours sleep'.[23]

To add to his misery he caught mumps as they sailed. He lay in his bunk for ten days, cogitating on existence and calculating his extortion of the Admiralty's coffers. Letter posting became a serendipitous affair. If the lookout spotted a ship Huxley scribbled one on the chance that it could be sent aboard. Off Montevideo on 8 August they passed the *Phoenician*, 44 days out of England and Sydney bound, and Hal rushed a dozen lines.

Late August saw them back in the tropics, 'bowling along at a fine pace'. Through great sheaths of floating gulf weed they ploughed, 'a world in itself', full of shells, pipefish and planktonic crustaceans. Hal was back where he started, pulling in purple Atlantic *Velellae*. England was now only weeks away. He could visualize the great Babylon. 'I long to be home'.[24]

By October 1850, after voyaging 40,000 miles, they were less than three weeks from Plymouth. Neptune blew a 'splendid westerly gale' and the ship buzzed with excitement. There was a spring in every Jack's step, packing and crating, preparing trophies and tall stories – and reflecting. Almost four years they had been away. They had seen the ends of the earth, stood on blistering coral sands, fought through snagging gum scrub, swum in Papuan lagoons, been greeted as *marki* ghosts. They were 'about the last voyagers', Huxley supposed, who would meet 'people who knew nothing of fire-arms'.

He gazed at his 'ugly phiz' in the mirror. It was sunburnt and bearded and told a tale. Every man was returning 'his own Columbus', with stories of 'a southern cloud-land full of strange wonders'.

They thought on friends who had not returned. In the sick room he had stared death in the face so often. He had seen sailors succumb to pleurisy, blood poisoning and disease. He had held dying men in his arms, the skipper among the last. And yet for all of medicine's grave responsibility, he was not committed to the healing art so much as to a helping science, and a more material way to salvation.

He thought of his early censure of the crew, and how unjust he had been: after all, 'they turned out very good fellows'. But it was a different ship now – Yule commanding, MacGillivray splicing the main brace, his middies grown men and looking to commissions of their own. But it remained a microcosm of aristocratic tyranny, like a floating Tsar's court in an age that had dispensed with despots. Still, the 'Service has done me a world of good by case hardening me – knocking me about until I don't mind kicks'. It strengthened his self-discipline, while years of waking up 'on a soft plank, with the sky for canopy and cocao and weevily biscuit the sole prospect for breakfast' gave him a new appreciation of the civilized luxuries.

Landlubbers knew nothing of sailors' privations: they who must 'submit more strictly than Dominican or Franciscan to the three monastic vows – who see for months no civilized faces, but their own tanned and bearded visages – who feast with the thermometer at 90°, upon salt-junk, and (*horribile dictù*) three-water grog'. Like any swab he had sunk to the depths; he had sailed through hell, only to be saved by the girl with hair of 'Australian silk'. He had suffered loneliness verging on desperation. He had gone for months without letters, without knowing whether England's rookeries had blown themselves apart in a Chartist Revolution. Now he was coming home to a settled land: Jim reassured him that the country had steered wide of the European revolutions and, what 'is vastly to the credit of our liberal system of government, has escaped all internal broils herself'.[25] The storms had blown over.

He had gone out 'sick of the world, of its petty intrigues, its lesser and greater selfishnesses & dirt-eating' and found kindness in the colonies. He had voyaged in search of security, and found it.

Nettie's emotional support came with a ray of Australian sunshine. Sydney had turned the introvert about. The long-hair who never danced and shunned parties left the city adept at the light fantastic. 'People tell me, that I am full of fun that they cannot look at me without imagining some joke is going on'. But 'they only see my head'; inside nothing had changed. The heart 'still belongs to the poor proud student and longs, surely longs for the quiet home – the wifes dear smile and all the prattle of the fire side'.[26]

The poor proud student gazed at more than his own grizzled phiz. Staring back were his three savage skulls from Darnley Island. Here was his most enduring memory: of naked Papuans, 'Man-eaters and sorcerers', as the old travellers said, 'among whom divels walke familiarly'. And so it seemed from their fiendish looks, the mop of 'frizzled hair' and 'huge plaited pigtail' strung with teeth. But whatever the sinister human-jawed armlets, Huxley had faced no demons. He had found only villagers, friendly and gentle. The Papuans' 'kind treatment of their women', their pottery and canoe building and the 'grace of design displayed in their carved works' showed a 'capacity for development'. Was this how the 'growing science of Ethnology' should deal with these charcoal-painted people, as 'essentially children' growing towards the civilized ideal?

He had fewer kind thoughts about Australia's 'hopelessly irre-claimable savages'. He recalled *Teoma*'s horror at the infanticide and decapitation, and thought darkly on the men who had killed Kennedy. Had the Papuans and aborigines sprung from the same peoples, who swept down from Asia? What to do with Australia's savages? He pondered this in a barbarous mood. He had no truck with the philanthropic evangelicals and their 'Aborigines Protection Society'. No good could come from these bleeding hearts peddling their paper, the *Aborigines Friend*. Australia's nomads were blind to the Victorian ideals of private property, free-trade and Piccadilly fashion. His squatter's morality was evident; his final solution smugly horrifying. Their 'elimination . . . from the earth's surface can be viewed only with satisfaction, as the removal of a great blot from the escutcheon of our common humanity, by all those who know them as they are, and are not to be misled by the maudlin philanthropy of "aborigines' friends"'.

Genocide and progress were ugly bedfellows. Yet this was the 25 year-old who lamented even more the missionaries' coming. The superficiality of his contact, which bred thoughts of genocide, also led to reflections on the gentle New Guinea people. He looked with 'sadness to the time . . . when the peaceful idyllic simplicity of a life without care and without reproach, such as glides along in these Papuan Isles – the very Paradise of Lotus Eaters – . . . shall be defaced by the obtrusion of the Polynesian "scourge of God" – the white man. To substitute what? "The blessings of civilization" – which means for the dark race, labour, care, drunkenness, disease, and ultimate subjection and extinction'.

As he peered into the future the arcadia vanished: the islands were 'one vast "witness," that it were better for the Papuans to "walk familiarly with the devils" they have' than face the white man's demons.[27]

Other mementos littered his cabin: the carved turtleshell, remnants of molluscs and sea ferns. The ship had gone out with treasure for the colonists and come back with the empire's riches. Its hold was crammed with sequined sunbirds and glorious honey-eaters, beauty enough to grace Gould's *Birds of Australia*. MacGillivray had his crates of bats and bowers, his pin-boards of butterflies, boxes of snails and a pickle-emporium of crabs and molluscs. All were ready to be described, named and claimed by London's zoological specialists. They were bringing back the biggest haul of tropical 'corrallines' ever to reach Britain – a mix of sea firs, plumed hydroids, stalked organisms with hundreds of connected stinging-celled polyps along their arms, and twig-like moss animals.[28] As the ship sailed on the Gulf Stream, Huxley pondered these composite creatures. The simpler the animals the stranger the question. Was the tiny tentacled polyp or the whole fan-like plume the individual? Were these colonies, or one individual with a thousand waving buds?

He had his knotty questions. He had his notebooks. He had gone out with his 'proud oversensitive, and totally undisciplined mind' and learned to knuckle down to hard work.[29] He had brought back 180 sheets of drawings, and page after page of salty, sweaty description of diaphanous sea nettles and planktonic molluscs, of the blood system of transparent crustaceans, of the anomalous bristle-jawed arrow-worms, of two new orders of sea squirts and 40 genera of jellyfish – enough for a career, but could a career be carved out of such things? Security came not only from love, but from intellectual success. Could he make enough money from science to bring Nettie over? And what *had* been the reception of the papers he had posted home?

He looked ahead with trepidation. The family news boded ill: George doubted he would 'see the Old Man again'. His father was

frail after 'an apoplectic fit' and not expected to live. The feeling
against the Salts was as strong as the day he left. Tom's mother
had lost all sympathy after Salt 'beggared Miss Knight' (borrowing
more money). Then Jim sent word that Lizzie and Salt had lost a
baby boy 'under very distressing circumstances'.[30] In four years
Tom had not had a line from America and he longed for news.

He hardly knew what England held. And he had 'been leading
such a semi-savage life for years past' that he wondered if he
would ever settle down. He was candid with his mother. 'Time
was when I should have looked upon our return with unmixed
joy; but so many new and strong ties have arisen to unite me with
Sydney ... You must not be angry, my dear Mother; I have none
the less affection for you ... only a very great deal for a certain
little lassie whom I must leave behind me'. 'We have ... a
thousand difficulties in our way, but like Danton I take for my
motto, "De l'audace et encore de l'audace et toujours de
l'audace"'.

And audacity brought him back to the Sea Lords. He was ready
to lay down the law to the gold braid. With the new meritocratic
ethos sweeping medicine, he was looking for promotion as a
reward for scientific excellence. He had to make money from
science to bring Nettie over. Few had done it before. Wealthy
gents were philosophers by vocation, disdaining pay with its taint
of trade. But times were changing; a new generation was coming
out of London's medical schools, out of the godless college in
Gower Street, the sons of industrialists, merchants and Dissenters,
defiant against Oxbridge and the old paternalist order. They could
turn a penny if they could make science a new profession.

As the ship scudded along Huxley's thoughts turned and turned
again to Nettie. He clung to her image, the only fixed point in his
shifting world. When would he see her 'Saxon yellow hair' again?
He reread her letters, red-lining them where her 'little heart speaks
out'. He also kept another secret memento, in memory of their
first dances: that wine-red camellia.

Zephyrs chased them across the North Atlantic, a calm end to a
tempestuous voyage. The gentle breeze 'bids fair to carry us
home'.[31]

1850–1858

Lost in the Wilderness

9

The Scientific Sadducee

NOT FOR HUXLEY the mariner's folly, flipping guineas into the deep to thank Neptune for deliverance. But emotionally he was just as extravagant. After the long homeward haul the very rigging quivered with excitement. All hands strained for a sight of industrial Devonport. At last, on 23 October 1850, its smoke-stacks appeared over the horizon. After 40,000 miles on a jury-rigged, rotting scuttle-bucket, through hell-and-high-water, past interminable reefs and endless little Englands, he was back.

That day he 'saw English green fields' for the first time in four years. Not that he noticed, firing off letters, asking 'news of a certain naughty sister of mine', Lizzie in Tennessee. By now Yule had a ship full of impatient souls. Beating up the Channel, they were dogged by contrary winds and chased by the blue devils.[1] But Huxley put the time to use, planning his naval blockade of the Admiralty.

Past the White Cliffs his spine stiffened. He drew up a report for the hydrographer Sir Francis Beaufort. Another went to Sir John Richardson listing his discoveries, asking about 'a nominal appoint-ment' to a Thames ship in order to write them up. Officers routinely went on half pay until they were recalled.[2] But what surgeon's mate had the gall to dictate stronger terms to the Sea Lords? He wanted to remain on leave, and on half pay until he had finished. Nothing less would do.

They put in at Sheerness docks, ten miles down river from Chatham. More dusty grainstores and cranes, bluecoats and bark-ing officers – and the first real feeling he had arrived: 'I was standing in the midst of a group busily talking . . . when I felt my arm touched and lo! there stood my brother James'. It was the same fierce-eyed Jim, mistaken by everyone on board for Tom, 'chuckl-ing at having been the first to see me'. His asylum was close by, in Maidstone, and he had caught the ferry down to intercept the *Rattlesnake*. 'I ran away with him for five minutes' and 'returned to the ship not quite sure whether I had been dreaming or not'.

Finally, on 2 November, after nine days slow hauling, the old frigate moved up to Chatham and to our 'joy, we found ourselves fairly at home'. Here were more friends; first to come aboard was his old friend Archie McClatchie, engaged to Nettie's friend Alice. He looked 'stout and is happy as the day is long', but then he had written for Alice to come, 'Happy Dog!' At McClatchie's another pinch roused Tom from his dream. A servant 'announced "Mr Huxley"' and in strode 'no other than my Brother George & Polly'. Polly was a sight for sore eyes, 'prettier than ever', clutching at him and fussing, lost in emotion and insisting that he come and live with them. The party migrated over to Jim's that night, where the celebrations really began. 'How we talked!' – and the question-ing, about the savages, Australia, but most of all Nettie. They were all ears for Tom's tales. Everyone agrees 'that the cruise has done me a world of good'. The sunburnt sea dog was 'voted by acclamation the *handsomest of the family* Ahem!' The mariner had returned, 25 years old, feeling considerably more ancient. The absence had affected his heart too; 'they seem to me to be more likeable than they used to', he said. But then he guessed that the change was 'chiefly in myself'.

His father had survived, although he hardly recognized his son. Nothing had prepared Tom for the sight. He went to London on Monday and found him 'dreadfully altered' and 'mentally an utter wreck'. 'It is painful to me to look at him'. Tom's mother had lost her front teeth and sunken cheeks aged her. Otherwise she was 'just the same amusing, nervous, distressingly active old lady'.[3]

Others recalled times past. The stories about Cooke were true: 'The Doctor is fat & bloated as a prize pig'. At 39 he was burned out. It pulled Tom up to see the plump doctor in lean times, working himself to death, easing his pains with beer and opium. 'I am told that for the past four or five years they have been on the verge of penury'.[4] It reinforced Tom's image of science as adversity; of London as a rich man's arena. With no jobs for men of science, few students enrolled in courses and poor teachers could not survive on the fees. Cooke was a sorry proof that professing science did not pay. Huxley saw the steep climb ahead.

*

Yet everywhere seemed more salubrious. Wide streets, white stone, the West End oozed prosperity. His old haunts were now full of imperial buildings: Nelson stood on his column in Trafalgar Square, Whitehall was becoming the hub of empire. The Gothic Houses of Parliament were positively exuberant. The new Lords was 'magnificent', 'it looks like an Indian Cabinet'. The modern Babylon thrived on its self-importance. A Great Exhibition was about to gloat on it, and the huge glass-curtain Crystal Palace housing the exhibits was already under construction in Hyde Park. Steam enveloped everything: King's Cross and Paddington stations were in the making. Travellers fought through the throng of 'gay' girls at the new Waterloo station to take their first train ride to the seaside at Brighton. Traffic might snarl up on smoggy November streets, but still everything was dizzyingly fast: having waited months for letters he could hardly cope with ten posts a day. After the loneliness of the sea Huxley faced tidal 'waves of people silently surging' down streets. Perhaps this faceless anonymity was worse. Certainly the 'solitude of men seems a greater threat than the wilds I have been used to'.[5]

He rushed with the crowd, calling at the Admiralty, cap in hand. Sir William Burnett was 'ready and willing to do anything' – which meant passing him along to Beaufort. Sir Francis was ready and willing, except to dip into the Admiralty's coffers. Huxley moaned that the Sea Lords 'approved my plans, patted me on the back' and turned him down flat. Where Darwin, the privately-financed companion to Captain FitzRoy, received £1,000 after a nod to the Chancellor from his Cambridge tutor John Stevens Henslow – enough to buy the experts to write his lavish five-volume *Zoology* of the *Beagle* voyage – the surgeon's mate was denied £300. Beaufort hoped he would write a book 'creditable to himself, to his late Captain ... and to Her Majesty's service'. Huxley choked on the words: 'Publish if you can, and give us credit for granting every facility except the one means of publishing'.[6]

How to move from surgery to pure science, with no means? He was not a member of the gentry, living off his railway shares, like Darwin. He had no Tory patrons, like Richard Owen. Huxley had to make his way on a servant's pay of 6s 6d a day. It would hardly buy him into big-time science. Even less would it subsidize a tome on the man-of-war, winning him a paying position and Nettie's passage over. Such treatises were inordinately expensive. The 150 engravings in Darwin's *Zoology* had soaked up his £1,000; Owen was to cost his work on the extinct giant sloths at £700. Six and sixpence would not even settle old scores – and this was the rub. Having sent endless cheques home, Huxley arrived to find himself *still* £100 in debt.[7]

Back at the ship came better news. It was from the breezy naturalist Edward Forbes, the Geological Survey teacher who had shown him how to dredge. Huxley warmed to the erratically brilliant Forbes, a man free from the 'besetting sins' of pedantry and jealousy. No mortal was a more curious mix: a mollusc expert who cheered Huxley's 'diametrically opposed' notions; an Anglican idealist who could sympathize with 'a wounded spirit tortured by unbelief'. He was a paradox, a bon viveur who straddled the divides. And Huxley welcomed his outstretched hand: 'Up to his eyes in work he never grudges his time if it be to help a friend on'.[8] Perhaps it was because Forbes had walked the mean streets himself. The son of a bankrupt banker, he had scrimped for a living, adding a post at the Geological Survey to his Botany Chair at King's College. Even now, crushed by work, his wife expecting a baby any day, he found time to sift though MacGillivray's spiral-shells from the Coral Sea – casually immortalizing his young admirer in the process. A minute new one, $1/24^{th}$ of an inch long with translucent whorls, he christened *Chelotropis Huxleyi*. It was the sort of immortality Huxley never mentioned. But it meant a lot.

This was the Forbes who invited Huxley to town. Up he went again, to hear about his papers, his doves, flown from the ark. Forbes overwhelmed him with news: the Medusae paper had been not only read but *published* in the Royal Society's *Philosophical Transactions*, 'the first scientific publication in England', Hal boasted to Nettie. There were cut-outs of his *Trigonia* paper, read by Forbes into the Zoological Society's *Proceedings*, abstracts of the Man-of-War paper communicated by the bishop to the Linnean Society, copies of the *Diphyes* paper. Even his Cape York letter to Forbes had appeared *in toto* in the *Annals and Magazine of Natural History*! Forbes showered him with offprints.[9] It transpired that his name had been appearing everywhere – or rather 'William Huxley's' as the Linnean had it!

Forbes took him to dine with the geological elite, which gathered regularly in one of the Strand's 'dingy but cosy dens', Clunn's Hotel. Here Huxley met the heroic hammerers who had cracked the chaotic old strata. Among them strutted the 'Silurian King', Sir Roderick Murchison, a self-aggrandizing military man turned geological imperialist. Cast in the Napoleonic mould, he had tracked his 'Silurian system' into the heartland of Russia, conquering scientific territory as British goods conquered the world. Of course the old soldier had 'too much Sang froid'. His 'great talent' was topped by his 'great conceit', which Huxley put down to his '3–4,000 a year and a house in Belgravia'. (No modest house at that: 'all grey & gold . . . with arabesques like those of Pompeii', which even Ruskin admitted was 'coming it rather strong'.) Very different was another diner, the bureaucratic Benthamite Sir Henry De la Beche, the man who had put his Geological Survey staff in uniform and paid them a wage. These knights of science lionized the young sawbones, but 'Didn't I feel a minnow among the Tritons!'[10]

Straight off the ship, Huxley found himself welcomed by the geological gentry. These were the men who had unravelled the oldest fossil-entombing strata. They were reaching back to the first Days of Creation. That in itself made their science modish and put it under public scrutiny. Although they had restricted their activities to mapping outcrops and plotting ancient environments, by 1850 dangerous new questions were being asked. How to explain the succession of fossil dynasties, from the Silurian trilobites to Owen's mighty dinosaurs, from the first Jurassic shrew-like mammals to recent humans? No one was more sensitive to this issue than Huxley's main companion that night, Charles Lyell.

Lyell was clubbable and cultured; a friend to peers and Prime Ministers, and recently made Sir Charles by Queen Victoria. He was a lawyer by training and a gentleman by status: he lived on his capital and made geology his vocation. For 20 years eight editions of his *Principles of Geology* had delighted and infuriated. It debunked the notion of cataclysms rocking the primeval earth. Here the past and present landscapes were sculpted by the same slow and steady forces. That was his foundation, but on it stood a wobbly superstructure. Lyell argued that life had not progressed at all. He feared that a grand ascent from acorn worm to ape to Anglo-Saxon would encourage a barbarous evolutionary explanation, the sort touted by artisan atheists. These street-corner socialists would make man only a better sort of brute. They would deny him recompense in a future life and make him fight for it in this. In the 1830s such vicious logic had scared the urban gentry. So Lyell the lawyer called in an expert witness, Nature: he tried to convince the jury that no progression had occurred. It was a brilliant tirade against a criminal transmutation. But it smacked of special pleading. And, as everybody asked, if birds and mammals had always existed, why were their fossils not found in the oldest rocks?

Most geologists thought the remedy worse than the threat. For Murchison the successive strata housed increasingly high lifeforms. Only if they 'found the print of an aldermanic Robinson Crusoe's foot' in ancient Silurian sandstones would he 'knock under'. The geological clergy wanted a Creative progression as a sign that God had continually advanced life. A directional fossil record was proof that man was in His mind from the start. It affirmed the onward march, from the first Day of Creation to the last Day of Judgment. Lyell's fossil fiction seemed perversely unchristian. And that, by a curious twist, was what made it appeal to his young listener at Clunn's Hotel that night. Lyell was 'a most agreeable man', admitted Huxley, and his obstreperous palaeontology even more appealing.

It was 'a delightful evening', Huxley's first among the elite. Forbes topped it off by telling him that the government was now granting the reformed Royal Society £1,000 a year to aid research and publication and 'that as much as I wanted could be provided'. Suddenly the cherry seemed within his grasp. Only days ashore and backing for his book seemed secure.

As always voices whispered, niggling about the taint of patronage. 'God knows I care little enough for distinction', he told Nettie, except 'as it bears upon our prospects'. And he still had to gain the time to write. Being the man of the moment only reinforced his bullish mood. 'An appointment for 3 or 6 months I could get now, but, true to my old habits I must carry my point and have the year I determined upon'.[11]

His last days aboard were all 'bustle and confusion'. Chatham bristled with activity. The supernumeraries escaped in their carriages, with them his black-laced favourite, Mrs Stanley. Crates were carried off, wives wept and a stream of sailors drank away their back pay. But Tom was lost in the letter he had wanted for so long, from sister Lizzie. It spoke of 'sorrow and misfortune'. He could visualize Tennessee, 'from the baking and boiling and pigs squealing' to the backwoods privations. But there was a new baby to 'efface the bitterness' of two losses. 'God knows, my dear sister, I could feel for you. It is as if I could see again a shadow of the great sorrow that fell upon us all years ago'. He offered to stand godfather 'though I fear I am too much of a heretic to promise to bring him up a good son of the church'. 'Tell Florry that I could not get her the bird with the long tail, but that . . . I will send her some pictures of copper-coloured gentlemen with great big wigs and no trousers, and tell her uncle loves her very much and never forgets'.[12]

On 9 November he was paid off and the pendant hauled down. It was a glorious day, with 'the bells ringing lustily'. 'And now', he regaled Nettie, 'I am a free man caring neither for blue coat nor red'. The sea was behind him; ahead lay a more uncertain course among the land sharks. He wrapped his skulls, packed his note-books, thanked his middies and moved from his creaking alcove to George's house. At 41 North Bank, just off the promenading Regent's Park, he would be close to his parents in St John's Wood, and to the crowds at London Zoo, come to see Europe's first hippopotamus and Tasmanian tigers. But tucked away on a back street the house was oddly quiet. 'I look out upon a garden where in the morning I see thrushes and blackbirds on the grass and no whisper of the roar of the great Babylon reaches my ears'. After years of waves and wind it took some adjusting. Not that he minded the fussing of the scampish Polly, who 'has taken posses-sion of me for a time'.[13]

The reunion with Fanning and Ory in their Paddington villa was ecstatic. Willie rushed up 'and snuggled onto my knee as if he had left it only yesterday'. Huxley became one of the family. He dropped in often, to sit at dinner feeling Nettie's arm 'stealing round my neck'. It brought them closer even as it twisted the knife.

In some ways he was happier with colonials. They were '*real* people free from humbug and affectation'. In an age of 'Steam and Cant', before the squires of science were ousted by the young Turks, he found sycophancy and pomposity on opposite sides of the class divide. But no bootlicking for him – 'I am under no one's *patronage*, nor do I ever mean to be'. It was the leitmotiv of his life, this former East End apprentice, fiercely proud of his self-made image. But his attitude brought massive insecurities. He needed bolt-holes, shields against the world; or rather a real home of his own. He craved security, 'some one in whom I can place implicit confidence, whose judgment I can respect, and yet who will not laugh at my most foolish weaknesses, and in whose love I can forget all cares'.[14]

What he called 'humbug', silver-haired gents knew as salon politics. For generations patronage had guaranteed all things: touching a Lord's arm tipped pounds from the public purse, access to an archbishop opened doors in the British Museum. But this world was dying. Huxley sensed it as he began his scientific rounds. He hardly needed his introductions to the great Richard Owen, having moved straight into Owen's Royal Society circle. Owen had a high cultural reputation as a brilliant comparative anatomist, and a relatively low status as Hunterian Professor in the College of Surgeons, at the council's beck-and-call. Contact between Huxley and Owen was inevitable, not least with Owen specializing in parthenogenesis. Owen symbolized an age in transition – he had come up through the ranks, using hard work and noble patrons, and grace-and-favour would come no higher than Queen Victoria's present of Sheen Lodge in Richmond Park. But he was turning Liberal like the country, and he too was looking for 'pudding' to substantiate the praise.[15]

On 20 November Huxley asked to be posted to the Guard Ship HMS *Fisguard* on the Thames at Greenwich. He needed time, and 'less than a year would be wholly insufficient to my purpose'. Everyone went overboard to help. 'Old John' drummed up Admiralty support. Forbes swore that 'more complete zoological researches had never been conducted during any voyage'. Owen wrote to the First Sea Lord. The Royal Society Grant Committee came out 'strongly in favour of my "valuable researches" (cock-a-doodle-doo!!)'. The society's secretary, Thomas Bell, was a modest naturalist, as easy describing Darwin's *Beagle* reptiles as monographing British crabs, but he shone as an administrator. He was breathing life back into the old lady after the savaging by reformers. He invited Huxley to dine 'and meet a lot of nobs'. Outwardly Huxley took it all in his stride; inwardly he was 'considerably astonished'. Even as he forswore patronage, the top brass were pulling strings. Hands that were feeding him would one day be bitten, but for the moment the bulldog pup was slavering. He was staggered at his reception 'among these grandees'.[16]

Such a salvo went off that the Sea Lords made signals to surrender. On 29 November they appointed him 'Additional Assistant Surgeon' to the Commodore's ship *Fisguard* – and then granted him six months leave on half-pay, renewable. Huxley knew whose broadside had hit the Admiralty's mizen. He told Thomson (back in Edinburgh acquainting himself with the three year-old he had never seen) that Owen's letter had done it.[17] That day too Owen heard from their Lordships that the insistent young subaltern had what he wanted.

His foot was on the first rung of the ladder. 'I wonder how

many steps I shall get up before I am either stopped or get a tumble'. The pay was nothing to get married on. Every mate griped that it would not 'permit him to keep two messes'. So he hoped for a speedy promotion; the average wait was over ten years, but a book would show that he wasn't average. Better still would be a job offer. 'Don't you feel I am on the high road to become a mighty "spider stuffer" as Fanning has it? If stuffing fleas will lead me to my end I am greatly prepared to stuff them'.[18]

So within the month he had it all – a local ship and extended leave if he worked at his science. The chance would be a fine thing; everyone wanted to hear his tales of jawbone-wearing savages. 'I am not naturally a gregarious animal', said the sailor, but the social whirl staved off loneliness. He enjoyed evenings with Fanning, dinners with 'Mercury' (Mr Sharpe) and his 'nice old clergyman' father, even a trip to Nettie's Aunt Kate to hear stories of her childhood. And night-time camaraderie came in the shape of Forbes' boisterous Red Lion Club (named after a pub). Its hell-raisers irreverently shadowed the starchy British Association and Royal Society. It was a tavern vent, a safety valve for the engines of Victorian pomposity. Here the tyros blew off steam. Songs and jokes sent them into a roar as they lampooned an unctuous stuff-shirt science with its plum-in-mouth sermonizing. (The power of sermons in Victorian society explains the pervasive 'cant' which Huxley so hated.) He revelled in its 'Pantagruelistic aspect', set off by Forbes' inimitable squibs, satirizing the official banquets with their ' "butter-boat" speeches'.

The endless engagements overwhelmed the landlubber. 'If people would . . . not invite me out to dinners and parties, I should be getting on very well'.[19] One more ball, he swore, then work, back to his fleshy squirts and fiery *Pyrosoma*, readying his paper for the Royal Society.

These should have been honeymoon days as Huxley found his shore legs. But he flew high and low. One moment he was cocky: 'I don't know and I don't care whether I shall ever be what is called a great man. I will leave my mark somewhere'. A moment later he was crushed, wearied by 'this sharp intellect . . . incessantly rolling the Sisyphus-stone of its own queries'. He was too eager: 'one must wait, wait patiently', he groaned. At times he feared he was going nowhere and dragging Nettie with him, and then his anger turned to misanthropic fury. Messmates envied his appointment, but he only hated them 'for congratulating me on my good fortune'.[20]

And underneath he *was* lonely. Nettie's absence was crippling him. He imagined her 'bright smile – a kiss – one of the thousand nothings that make life something'. The passing winter saw him turning paler and more cynical. His meteoric rise among the rich ironically destabilized him more – 'from money to friendship', he now reasoned, 'it is not so much getting as keeping'. An increasing pugnacity masked a deepening insecurity. Success was easy. The drug grinder hovering on the doorstep of the Royal Society had to turn it 'to account'. He stood at the castle drawbridge 'ready to fight . . . or be blown into oblivion'. 'I *have* drawn the sword, but whether I am in truth to beat the giants and deliver my princess from the enchanted castle is yet to be seen'.[21]

Nettie's letters were taking four months to arrive, even longer now, given events. The traumatic news was of her father's financial crisis and his arrest and acquittal in Sydney. Following this the family had trekked 120 miles to Bathurst – a township on the banks of the 'miserable' Macquarie. Here, in treeless sheep country 2,000 feet above sea level, where she found the winter numbingly cold, Heathorn had started brewing again.[22] It increased Huxley's sense of isolation. 'Morning and evening I think of you as I look up at your dear face hanging there in my room', he wrote on 1 February 1851. He was becoming obsessive. He saw her everywhere. She was the heroine of his novels; she had Jane Eyre's 'passionate nature hidden under a mask of self content'; her 'half tearful' look stared at him from Millais' Pre-Raphaelite paintings.[23] He could not escape her.

He was languishing in the shadow of the voyage. He reminisced with newly promoted Captain Suckling and heard that Dayman was taking his own ship to the Cape. Everyone was doing well; even MacGillivray was a driven man, writing a *Narrative of the Voyage of H.M.S. Rattlesnake*. Huxley supplied the drawings, but the camaraderie was gone. The bleaker moments still haunted him. Mrs Stanley sent a few books from the captain's *Rattlesnake* library. She even enticed him over to meet the family, but he called a halt to this hob-nobbing: back at home 'the old lady' was 'inclined to be patronising' and 'I don't put up with that from anybody'.[24] Freed from naval etiquette he no longer had to hold his tongue. Sardonic to the last, he mocked Yule's talk on the voyage at the Geographical Society. MacGillivray followed Yule, 'and I looked on, and laughed'.

He moved through the great Babylon with the air of a moral assassin, stalking his limping, humbugged prey. He had Thack-

eray's *Pendennis* in hand, that 'fling against powdered-head and
... plush breeches', as the *Athenaeum* put it. Huxley revelled in
this exposé of society's 'chaos of folly, vice, and charlatanry'. It
caught the mood, 'the Byronic despair, the Wertherian despondency' of the men fighting their way up. It portrayed an age of
greed and doubt after the fall of the old moral certainties – the
virtue-less mercenary void Huxley found himself floating in. 'You
would not like it', he warned Nettie, 'it reveals too mercilessly the
mean & selfish side of our life. But it is true'.[25] Others cheered the
'mocking Mephistopheles'. The book appealed to alienated spectators like Huxley, 'soul sickened and sceptical'. It evoked his Grub
Street anguish. Dickens was for dilettantes; he is 'not a great artist
and rarely dips much below the surface'. But *Pendennis* – that
captures 'more nearly than any book I know the condition of the
thirsting young men'.

Huxley sided with the thirsting men: men from the ranks, the
trades, the cotton towns, the Dissenting outskirts. Not for him the
medal-festooned Murchison – Major Pendennis incarnate – nor
the forelock-tugging Owen. Not for him the 'roaring young blades
from Oxbridge'. He gravitated to an earthier breed, chaps from
the anatomy theatres who saw science as a mission and self-
aggrandizement as a sin, new men with new values.

The *Dreadnought*'s surgeon George Busk and builder's son
Edwin Lankester were two such. 'They are people quite of my
sort', part of the Red Lion pride whose dens he favoured. (So
much so that Lankester's boy Ray came to worship Huxley as his
'father-in-science'.)[26] They were fellow medical men with a biological interest and social conscience. Lankester was a giant of a man
with a soft Suffolk accent. Like Huxley he was an apothecary's
apprentice who had left school at 12; and he had known garret
starvation. But he had fought his way to a Heidelberg doctorate,
and he was still fighting. Hack work and *Daily News* pieces on
medical reform had kept him afloat. At Greenwich, where the
Dreadnought was berthed, they talked with Huxley of public
health and science for the people. They translated pioneering
German works and enthused over the invisible oceans of life
opened up by the microscope.

They made good sounding boards. Busk was sifting the *Rattlesnake*'s haul of sea ferns (one of which he christened *Plumularia
Huxleyi*). Huxley continued to argue the toss over these creatures.
He still considered the man-of-war a single organism, its parts
only so many 'buds' – even if some of the buds swam away to

start life anew! (Busk shared his interest, having translated a Danish book on 'Alternation of Generations'.)

There was another attraction at Greenwich, Busk's wife Ellen. She stood apart from the run of whale-boned matrons; a naturalist, freethinker, sharp witted, a 'playful' soul who showed 'evidence of suffering'. He took her into his confidence, telling her alone of his 'fair-haired ladee'. She became his 'favourite and ally'. He portrayed her as 'tall very refined', 'with black hair' and 'a most singular pair of penetrating grey eyes'. A 'sort of Egyptian priestess I fancy her', he said, spellbound.[27] She was refined like Mrs Stanley, well-read rather than well-bred. In polite circles words were spoken about her. Whatever Thackeray's stab at the stigma surrounding socially inferior wives, Huxley could hear the odd disparaging remark, the odd closing door.

He liked gutsy rationalists; he was secure among the industrial intelligentsia (Lankester's wife Phebe was the daughter of a Manchester cotton king). For 15 years, since they had swept into the town halls, Dissenters had been prying the professional institutions out of Anglican hands. They resented the Church's privileges, its Oxbridge exclusivity, its divine justification of the status quo and its damnation for all who disagreed.

By 1850 the Dissenters and rationalists had moved in from the fringes to become London's avant garde – and Huxley would meet them all, men such as George Henry Lewes (author of *Ranthorpe*) and Herbert Spencer. 'Secularism' was their watchword, coined by the former firebrand George Holyoake who was now settling into cigar-smoking respectability with the literary radicals on Lewes' weekly, the *Leader*. Dissolvent literature was their rage, books that eroded the clerical cement in the Anglican edifice. They pitted the Dissenting vision of a reforming society against the bishops' rigid hierarchies. Everywhere Huxley felt the meliorist ethic – improvement on earth rather than redemption in heaven. These were the real Pendennises, breaking the old shackles. They wanted scientific standards for judging truth, standards in their hands, legitimating their own claim to intellectual authority. The 'crisis of faith' was a collision of creeds, a product of the rents and changes in an industrializing society. 'The result is everywhere the same', Huxley said. 'Every thinking man I have met with is at heart in a state of doubt, on all the great points of religious belief. And the unthinking men . . . are in as complete a state of practical unbelief'.[28] It was agonizingly congenial.

A dissident himself, Huxley was not afraid of the friction as he rubbed shoulders with the 'bigwigs'. He was closer to scientific peerage than he knew. The reformed Royal Society only admitted 15 new Fellows a year; fewer were aristocrats and more were active researchers. The Council was looking for seriousness and scientific commitment. For his part Forbes was looking to get Huxley in. 'I had no idea that it was at all within my reach', Huxley said in surprise, but his papers spoke for him.[29] His doves had found not only a new land but friendly natives.

Still he was hungry. Still he seethed about the lack of paid openings. Science should be a salaried meritocracy, not a dabbling ground for the foppish aristocracy. 'I am sick of writing, weary of longing. The difficulties of obtaining a decent position in England ... seem to me greater than ever they were'. It was a *cri de coeur*, as always aimed at Nettie. 'To attempt to live by any scientific pursuit is a farce ... A man of science may earn great distinction – great reputation – but not bread. He will get invitations to all sorts of dinners & conversaziones, but not enough income to pay his cab hire'.

Radicals had been shouting as much for 20 years. But his cry had a personal ring. Every delay set back the day when he would feel Nettie's 'dear arms round my neck'. He could not consult her; soliloquies were sent off into the blue. Five months later in the Bathurst brewery they were a faint echo. He tried to grasp 'the immense distance in time that lies between us' as he wrapped her birthday present months ahead – itself as ghoulish as a Papuan jaw ornament: his entwined hair with a rattlesnake clasp, 'equal to anything in Thebes or Memphis for symbolic meaning'.[30]

A world away Nettie never understood his goal. Who else saw his salvation in the Salpae? But salvation required working at. His new Royal Society paper was ready in late March. He squirmed in the Society's meeting room in Somerset House as the Secretary read it monotonally. Portly Lord Rosse, famous for the huge six-foot-reflector telescope at his castle in Ireland, looked incongruous in the President's chair, 'more like a gentleman farmer'. All around, his forerunners gazed down sternly from the walls. Members sat uncomfortably on 'cold benches', the tyros wishing themselves 'merry round the [Red Lion] table' instead. The old noblemen probably found Huxley sharp, uncouth, uncompromising and charming. He found the dullness of the occasion appalling. 'I had no idea it was half so painful a process to listen to your own productions'.[31]

Still he had to step up production, 'or this precious year of seed time will bring forth no harvest'. North Bank had its warmth: if he fell into one of his 'hypochondriacal fits' Polly was on hand to talk 'consolation in her simple way'. But it was 'altogether *too* comfortable'. On his own he could 'effect twice as much'. So he decided to 'emigrate to some "two pair back"', which shall have the feel and manner of a workshop'. He set out in April's sooty drizzle. He traipsed muddy streets, past horses 'splashed to their very blinkers'. Even grimier were the bedsits themselves. 'I want some place with a decent address, cheap and beyond all things clean. The dirty holes that some of these lodgings are!' And 'such servants with their faces and hands not merely dirty but absolutely macadamised'.[32]

Between landladies he dropped in on Forbes. It was mid April and the man was in a state. He was arranging fossils in De la Beche's splendid new Museum of Economic Geology in Jermyn Street. The museum, with its plum Piccadilly frontage, was being finished in time for the opening of the Great Exhibition. The Geological Survey had moved here, to be linked to a School of Mines, where Forbes would teach. The lot, run with factory discipline, would bring expertise to the mining industry. The Italian Palazzo building was the first 'in Britain which is entirely devoted to the advancement of science'. At last Huxley had found a sign of government initiative – a huge State investment to train the next generation of engineers, metallurgists and geologists. The last licks of paint were going on, the opening day barely a month away.

Huxley had called on the offchance, but the news left him elated. Forbes confided that he was 'all right' for the Royal: the *enfant terrible* had been elected a Fellow, the youngest of the candidates. He had beaten the hardy hands. He had beaten his examiner at Apothecaries' Hall all those years ago; more awkwardly, he had beaten his naval superior, the *Fisguard*'s surgeon. Told the news he 'looked as cool as a cucumber'. The poor boy was to take a seat in the upper house of science and 'sport a tail' to his name, FRS. Recognition came no stronger. But for 'all my cucumbery appearance', he confessed to Nettie, 'I could not sit down . . . after the news. I wandered hither and thither restlessly half over London'.

The cost of the Royal Society Fellowship, £14 a year – over a month's pay – seemed prohibitive, but he hoped 'to make it worth the money'. This was to be no plume in his hat. He would 'turn it to advantage'. Having infiltrated the old boys' world he intended to turn it upside down. 'Will you take this step my darling' as proof 'that I have not worked utterly in vain?' He was one stop nearer his goal, and 'by no intrigue'.[33] A child of the 1840s could say no more.

The moment of elation saw him into his own 'den' at the end of April. It was close by, on Regent's Park, a sitting room and bedroom, cheap at '13 & 6d. per week'. His landladies were 'three virgins, long of nose and spinsterful of aspect'. He suspected these daughters of darkness the second he scanned his lounge, an eye-opener on the foibles of spinsterly free-spirits left over from the Regency. 'On the mantlepiece are four statuettes two of Voltaire & Rousseau and two others of a little boy and a little girl in very scanty clingy garments'. Over them hung a great gaudy painting of Waterloo, with soldiers knee-deep in gore 'sticking one another through & through'. He removed this abomination and a non-plussed Nettie now gazed down on the nymphs. He arranged his books, stood his microscope 'in a commanding attitude upon the little table' and carried on dissecting.[34] He had his neutral bolt-hole, a place of refuge after taking on the world.

He was now on his own. His parents were near by, but his father was 'as one dead' and his mother's 'marvellous indiscretions' kept him distant. Lonely, he bought a piping bullfinch, only to suspect that it was painted; the poor bird refused to sing 'but moped and died and is a joke against me to this hour'. He gave a quiet inner scream, 'Oh I am so sick, so weary of this life without love'.[35] The one he did care for was as distant as ever. 'I have left you now a whole year,' he sighed on 2 May 1851. Twelve months to the day since he had sailed from Farm Cove on a hot breeze, watching Nettie's image fade. It was still fading.

His melancholy fits were arriving with monotonous regularity. The sea dog was having trouble settling down. A life of science seemed so much self-indulgence. It wasn't a proper job, it was 'utter vanity', or rather bedsit frippery. Sometimes he craved work that would 'involve sacrifice and danger' to prove that he was alive. The next day, 3 May, he was bucked up. He thanked Owen 'for the honour of the F.R.S.', but the taciturn Owen answered in his Lancastrian accent, '"No, indeed you have nothing to thank but the goodness of your own work." For about ten minutes I felt rather proud of that speech'. 'The only use of honours . . . is as an antidote to such fits of the blue devils'.

For ten minutes too he warmed to Owen. He cooled as quickly. Owen 'is a queer fish, more odd in appearance than ever'. He has been 'amazingly civil to me', but there was something in his manner, acquired in the town houses of the gentry. 'He is so frightfully polite that I never feel thoroughly at home with him'.[36]

On 4 May Huxley turned 26 and found Dante's devils at the door once more. He retired to his serpent's den, exploding in frustration: 'there is no chance of *living* by science'. Look around, University College's down-at-heel zoology professor Robert Grant takes home £39 a year! His counterpart at King's had long emigrated. Such poverty created a 'shabby-genteel' caste, as Dickens called them, teachers with frayed cuffs, slumming it with whores and thieves in Camden Town. Even the best looked a bit darned and patched. 'Owen who has a European reputation . . . gets from his office as Hunterian Professor £300 a year! which is less than the salary of many a bank clerk'. (Admittedly that ignored his crown pension and grants, which took it over £700, but Owen's perks were exceptional.) Such sums spoke volumes about the value of science, when a society doctor could earn £3,000, a good lawyer £15,000 and the Canon of Christ Church, Oxford £1,000 for no effort at all. What value now 'the beauty of Nature and the pursuit of Truth'? 'A man who chooses a life of science chooses . . . a life of *nothing*'. Huxley took comfort where he could: he *had* penetrated the *sanctum sanctorum*. He might lack a parson's riches, but 'I cannot blame myself. It is the worlds fault and not mine'.[37]

How to change the world? His plight was made more pointed by the economic upturn. The hungry 1840s were over. A new buoyancy was evident as middle-class incomes rose. Boom times lay ahead: the years of *Pax Britannica* and sterling imperialism. Hyde Park's 'great Exhibition of Exhibitions' gloated in this industrial promise. The Exhibition had just opened, a testament to commerce and consumerism. It was crammed with everything from the latest engines to collapsible pianos, a cornucopia of the new and astonishing. Ten thousand exhibits proved that Britain really was the workshop of the world. Viewing them, Prince Albert gave praise to modern science! – and here was Huxley, the scientific aspirant, unable to afford 'three pounds for a season ticket'.

Only when the gate price dropped did he buy a shilling ticket. He entered the colossal Crystal Palace, past the single 24-ton block of coal, standing homage to the source of Britain's wealth. The glass transept was loftier than 'the vaults of even our noblest cathedrals'; its sheer size beggared the imagination. Thousands stood in reverential awe. An age which had lost its faith found a new technological salvation. It was the 'great Temple of England', Nettie heard:

> 50,000 people worship there every day. They come up to it as the Jews came to Jerusalem at the time of the Jubilee. In the meantime their profound teachers are disputing about 'prevenient Grace' and whether they shall be taught at all unless they will swallow all 39 articles. If Satan can laugh I think he must do so at the perplexities of the English bishops at the moment. If they try to mend their house they know it will come about their heads – so their only recourse is to sit quite still, and get the world in general to do the same – rather a difficult tack in these days.[38]

It reinforced his view that a new scientific curia was needed, men who could preach rational science and real salvation.

Civvy street seemed brighter to a rising star with an FRS. Some days he woke up 'startled' at 'the wondrousness of life'. Others he woke with a hangover. A week's fling after receiving his Fellowship saw him at Lankester's and Fanning's, dancing 'till half past three'. Bleary mornings were spent reviewing books on starfish and daydreaming about his own Barrier Reef experiences with their kin, sea cucumbers (which defensively shot out their stomachs when handled). He wrote polemics to prove that the 'generations' of medusae from hydroid parents were really buds or 'zoöids'. (He posted one to Darwin, introducing himself. But the Kent recluse doubted whether 'creatures having so plainly the stamp of individuality as have many of your zooids will ever cease to be called individuals'.) Finally he rounded the week out at Lord Rosse's on Saturday, where he made his debut as a Fellow. 'Prince Albert was there and all the scientific nobs', a glittering array of medals and knighthoods. Everyone was kindness itself, even the 'King of Siluria'.[39] Murchison grasped Huxley's hand and said 'he was delighted to be of any service' in the grant matter.

Huxley's phenomenal rise did little to mellow him. At times his cynical mistrust seemed self-fulfilling. No sooner was his Fellowship announced than he lost his Royal Society grant. The Committee argued that, as a serving officer, he should be funded by the government. And so the grisly business began all over again. 'I am not disappointed', he said, for Lord Rosse and Murchison have offered to back 'any application I may make to the Treasury'.⁴⁰ But it began his second six-months leave on a sour note.

Others were faring no better. MacGillivray was by now struggling with the *Narrative*. Huxley was so badgered about the book that he made inquiries of the 'mud-volcano himself'. MacGillivray was in dire straits; 'old Suckling beat up his quarters lately' and was so struck by Jock's distress 'as to leave £5 for him'.⁴¹ At one point John Gould found the drunken MacGillivray in jail and had to bail him out. 'I have done all I can', said Huxley, asked by the publisher to pry chapters out of him.

Hal's strength came from Nettie. 'Cynic and sceptic as I am, by nature and by culture, what Thackeray has so justly & strikingly called a Sadducee – I cling by our love as a certainty, a mysterious reality'. Love had shown him that there was more to the world than 'need, greed & vain glory'. But need if not greed was the name of the game; so off he went to the British Association in July as a one-man pressure group. Everyone had given him the same advice. Richardson told him to get the 'British Ass' to 'untie the Treasury purse'.⁴² Forbes was blunter: he should stand on a soapbox and shout, or 'make myself notorious somehow'. That was no problem. He went to the meeting at Ipswich, a beautiful town of timber-framed Tudor buildings, not 'to advance science, but to be "advanced" myself'.

A world stood between this meeting and his last. Before the voyage in Southampton he had gazed at all the 'somebodies'. Now he was a 'somebody' himself, and treading the boards to tell of his *Rattlesnake* arrow-worms: 'I know all about the scenery and decorations and no longer think the manager a wizard'.

The company was good. He met a lean Orangeman, John Tyndall, an out-of-work physicist. There was a passion to Tyndall, as any Irish Protestant who had once thrilled to fanatics calling up the 'martyred sons of the reformation from their blood-stained graves'. He was self-consciously 'lower class', and self-made; the £1-a-week surveyor had saved enough to study under the great Bunsen at Marburg, the picturesque German town where Luther had stood his ground. He was five years Huxley's senior and still in debt after his Ph.D. – another second-class citizen damned by his career choice. Germany had turned him into a romantic pantheist; for Tyndall, as for his hero Carlyle, 'the universe is the blood and bones of Jehovah'.⁴³ Tyndall, making his own pilgrimage away from Protestantism, would take central place in Huxley's coterie, a friend for life.

Joseph Hooker completed the evangelical triad. He was an imperial botanist and the only one whose future looked secure. 'His father is director of the Kew Gardens', making him the heir apparent, Huxley noted in envy. Hooker's peripatetic existence had been even more exotic. Fired by Cook's epic voyages, he had spent six years bouncing 'like a glass tumbler' from snowdrifts to steamy tropics. He knew the attractions of Sydney, and life in an alcove stuffed with fermenting plants. Three summers in the Antarctic ice-smasher *Erebus* had only whetted his appetite. Not even an engagement to Frances Henslow, daughter of Darwin's mentor, the Cambridge professor of botany, could stop him setting off again to collect Himalayan plants. His capture by an anti-British ruler had a regiment marching in to annexe southern Sikkim for the Crown. 'Do you remember hearing of Hooker's being detained prisoner among the Sikhs?' Hal asked Nettie. His fiancée had waited four years. 'How I envied Hooker', Huxley sighed; 'at this very meeting he sat by her side. He is going to be married in a day or two'.[44] 'I know somebody who would go and be taken into captivity twice over if he thought such a happy termination would follow'.

The sea brought Huxley and Hooker together, naval surgeons who knew the ways of their 'Lords of the Foul Anchor'. But Hooker had the Kew advantage; as the director's son he had picked up an easy £1,000 to publish his *Flora Antarctica*. Even now he was on a £400-a-year Department of Woods grant to finish his New Zealand flora and publish his Himalayan findings.

At Ipswich royalty itself conspired against Huxley. As he walked out to talk on the 'brilliantly coloured' men-of-war and the little *Velella*, with its sails like two 'elegantly shaped piece[s] of cut glass', he counted 20 listeners. The Court retinue had caused an exodus; Prince Albert had arrived and 'turned the heads of the good people of Ipswich'.[45] He pressed on regardless, drawing sweeping circles to illustrate his classification of the stinging 'Nematophora'. (He knew now Leuckart had named them 'Coelenterata' but thought his reasons wrong and stuck to his own name.)

Huxley's 'trumpeting' paid off, with the 'big-wig' President (the Astronomer Royal, George Airy) lining up the Association behind the Royal Society on his grant application. But they all urged him to ease up. The President-elect Colonel Edward Sabine had him to lunch on Wednesday 15 July. Sabine was an unflappable 63 year-old, famous for his magnetic surveys of the globe (indispensable to a naval power; he was behind the *Erebus* voyage to the Antarctic. He 'spoke cheeringly, and advised me by no means to be hasty, but to wait'. Huxley did not have to wait long for more puffs from the irrepressible Forbes. The *Literary Gazette* reported his praise for Huxley's Man-of-War paper. 'Polly is so proud of it that she has been carrying it about in her pocket', Hal told Nettie; 'she means to send you a copy of it so I shall spare my modesty'.[46]

Friday's papers held out even more promise. A job offer on the first page of the *Athenaeum* jumped out at him. He dropped Nettie a note:

> Thomas H. Huxley Esq. F.R.S.
> Professor of Natural History in the
> University of Toronto

> How do you think that would look my pet? . . . As for
> myself I feel happier than I have since I left you for it
> seems to me as if the cloud had begun to lift.

Centrifugal forces were flinging the marginal men out to the colonial edges. He would join the thousands spreading across the empire, hard-up professors and hapless paupers – perhaps even friend Tyndall, himself applying for the physics chair at Toronto. By now Canada was only two weeks' steaming time from Liverpool. The university was new and the pay perfect; '350£ Halifax is something over 300£ English'. Forbes and Fanning told him to try for it; even cautious George was converted by Polly. His heart urged him on – it had been six weeks since he had heard from Sydney. In Toronto he could settle his debts and send for Nettie. He began 'to dream dreams' again. Wiser minds knew that nepotism usually decided these matters, but his head was in the clouds. The FRS spoke for him, and what it did not say the references from the best men would. Now, 'if they only have fair play'.[47]

Buoyed up, he threw himself at *Hydra* and sponges with renewed vigour. Then he swanned off to join Busk and Lankester on the Suffolk coast at Felixstowe, where the Lions were summering 'with their lionesses'. Dredging as usual gave way to satanic discussions with his 'Egyptian priestess', Ellen Busk. Huxley's fascination and fear of strong women showed. In an age that pegged ladies as crippled religious dolls, it came as a revelation that she combined 'womanly feelings' with a razor-like rationality. ('In fact', Hal told Nettie, 'I am not sure that your big dog is not a little bit afraid of her scratch'.) There was none of the 'Missionari-ness' of Victorian matrons about her. She knew doubt and 'its darkness'. She too saw the destruction of orthodoxy as 'the only hope for a new state of belief'. Huxley thrived on the sea-mist of rationalism, bewitched by Mrs Busk. He pushed such a view on Nettie, sidelined in Sydney. 'I do not say think as I think, but think in my way', he advised her. 'Fear no shadows, least of all in that great spectre of personal unhappiness which binds half the world to orthodoxy'.[48]

His Toronto references were accumulating into a 'Who's Who' of zoology. 'They are from the 16 first men in Great Britain & France' – from the towering Owen to the reclusive Darwin (who knew Huxley by reputation), from the Secretary of the Royal Society to the President of the BAAS. There was praise for his strident language as much as his mastery of the arcane. No competitor could match them, 'whatever private influences they may have'.[49]

But he knew how the game was played: old school tie, manners before talent. Not to be outflanked he had Eliza Stanley ask the head of the clan, Lord Stanley at the Foreign Office, to add a titled word. Huxley's forelocks were unaccustomed to such tugging. But His Lordship obliged, writing to the Earl of Elgin, Governor-General of Canada, who would choose a professor from the Senate's shortlist.

Thus ended 'another act in the Tragicomedy of my life', he wrote after posting his references on 16 October. He oozed confi-dence, even drifting into messianic musings – 'tracing my own life back I could almost fancy myself set apart ... for some special purpose': alone as a boy, isolated aboard ship, separated from his love and suffering his own 'forty days journey into the wilder-ness'.[50] Was Toronto the Promised Land? 'What does nature want with me'?

Whatever it was, nature had a crushing sense of timing. That night he heard from Fanning that the colonial Governor was planning a natural history chair for the new Sydney University. 'Old Mrs Fanning was quite enthusiastic about it and prognosticates that I am to be Professor at Sydney instead of Toronto'. So, off he went to the Colonial Office the next day, swearing that 'if they will give me £400 a year ... I am their boy'. Fanning continued to inquire about the 'spider chair for Botany Bay'. He boggled at Huxley's references: 'So many lies would almost get a devil into the kingdom of Heaven', never mind a scientific reprobate into the convict colony.[51] Hal could be back anatomizing jellyfish in Port Jackson, by Nettie's side. 'It almost takes my breath away'.

He could join the exodus, the hordes attracted by the gold strikes. Nettie talked of nothing else now. Finds of 16-ounce nuggets had drawn 2,000 to the 'diggins' near Bathurst. The Australian gold rush was turning it into a boom town. The bedlam was unnerving for a girl translating Schiller and practising the piano: everywhere 'busy hands & eager eyes, thirsting with an unquenchable thirst for the glistening treasure'.[52] Hal pictured her trooping off herself, 'pick on shoulder'. But her accounts grew fraught, talk of fights, price hikes (loaves a shilling apiece) and constables quitting with gold fever. Still, with the wealth flowing back to Sydney, a £400 chair looked increasingly feasible.

He no longer knew which way the empire would pull him. Colonial comings and goings were now part of life. In October Nettie's friend Alice sailed in to marry McClatchie. She stayed with George and Polly and this triggered old memories. Time was 'I never saw her without knowing that you were not far off', Hal reported back. Unnerved, he wondered when he would settle into his 'genial philosophical state again'.[53]

As his frustration grew his provocations rose. In his den with the three virgins he was working on the whimsical 'wheel-bearers', microscopic rotifers (so called from the crown of cilia at one end, whirling like wheels). At Busk and Lankester's Microscopical Society he used them as a miniature 'fulcrum whence the whole zoological universe may be moved'.[54] He was still smashing up Cuvier's rag-bag of invertebrates, the 'Radiata'. Since Huxley's rotifers resembled flatworm larvae, and since Johannes Müller had shown that starfish larvae were also worm-like, Huxley now put them together in another discrete assemblage of life. He called it the 'Annuloida'. He was lumping together all the worms, flat-worms, rotifers *and*, outrageously, starfish as a related group. He was practising his provocations in this tiny alcove of creation. But then had Forbes not told him to make himself notorious?

It was grinding night-and-day work, with no recompense. He felt as if truths were cranked out of him at no cost to society. He looked at his brother, leaving for the City at 10 am., and Polly's laughable way of 'cossetting him when he comes home – "poor fellow he is so hard worked". I work as hard again and get no cossetting!' But he was hooked. Science was his opiate, leaving him poor but wanting more. Whether it 'has been a poison which has heated my veins or true nectar from the Gods life giving, I know not, but I can no longer rest where I once could have rested'. Nature's shot gave him a 'sense of power'; and he needed the surge of strength as he kicked at society's door.

It opened an inch and he beheld the Holy Grail. On 7 November he heard that he had been 'within an ace' of getting the Royal Society's 'valuable gold medal'. In a tie-break the 50-guinea Royal Medal had gone to a raddled old worker, George Newport, a deft dissector who had shown that the sperm actually penetrates the egg in fertilization. Newport was a real craftsman, surely the only former wheelwright ever to graduate to the Elysium. Huxley could not begrudge the nugget to such a man, 'old enough to be my father'. Still he was flabbergasted: off the boat a year and glimpsing the gold that 'such men as Owen & Faraday are glad to get'.[55] For another brief second he was flying high.

The year had seen lurches and swings. Daily poverty gave the gold its glint; the daily grind gave him his short-term goals. To George the businessman young Tom seemed to be directionless: the City, industry, a medical practice, that was where one earned money. Yet Tom had fixed his sights. He would scrabble for any university chair that would pay him to practise science. Even the cynic softened occasionally at his sense of achievement. Twelve months to the day since the *Rattlesnake* was paid off, the angry young man looked back. Like some foreigner, awed by the waves of humanity in the great Babylon, the sailor still despaired of the scientific 'scratching to keep your place in the crowd'. Yet the FRS had put him 'at the pit door of this great fools theatre', and now starfish, rotifers and pig-headedness placed him 'not far from the check-taker'.[56]

10

The Season of Despair

CHRISTMAS FOUND HUXLEY climbing the walls of a new
den. The news from abroad left him 'as savage as a bear'. The
Sydney chair never materialized, and the mail on 29 December
1851 had him growling uncontrollably. A Canadian contact tipped
him off that nepotism would win out in Toronto. References from
the world's best paled beside the qualification of another candidate,
'a Brother of a Gentleman holding a high position in the Prov^l.
Govn^t'. 'Of course he will have it', snapped Huxley: merit meant
nothing.

He began his descent once again, shattered, wrecked on more
reefs:

> Into what lies I have deceived myself about devotion to
> Science and the cultivation of the Intellect . . . It is all a
> sham . . . I could stamp and cry aloud for powerless
> vexation.[1]

In a fit he tried to make a killing another way. Despite his debts he
borrowed more to flutter on his brother's gold-mining speculations.
The fever was infectious. Hadn't Pendennis' father made a mint on
copper mines and turned a brass-button gentleman, ignoring his
drug-grinding origins? These were boom and bust times. 'Fanning
himself is deep in an Australian Gold Mine', George was backing
a 'Californian Gold mine – the West Mariposa', but then he was
as 'wily as any fox – with a vast amount of experience to boot'
(which meant he had already 'made and lost one fortune'). But
Huxley's fever quickly broke and he swore he would 'never be
such an ass again'.[2]

Others were in the same boat, eyeing the same reefs. An impecunious Tyndall had applied for the physics chairs at Sydney and Toronto. The young Turks were shadowing one another. Huxley offered him introductions to his Sydney friends. And he supported Tyndall's nomination for the FRS, but he was losing his own faith in the fellowship's influence.

Only gents with a fortune seemed to be faring well. Look at Darwin in his manor at Downe, the 'complete Kentish hog'. He was the last of the virtuosi, his home a laboratory: a specialist in everything – worms, flowers, flukes, glaciers and volcanoes. (Huxley knew nothing of his covert work on transmutation.) Darwin kept to himself, with Hooker and Lyell his conduits to London society. Inherited wealth had allowed him to wander the world's unknowns, moving from distant lands to the deep recesses of man's mind, looking for the 'key to unlock those secret chambers where the great laws of his nature are revealed'. More mundanely it had bought him time to write on coral atolls and Andean uplift, and now to churn out tomes on every known barnacle. One 412-page volume had just arrived by post, a present from Darwin who realized that young Huxley was too poor to pay.

Darwin was another old salt who placed Sydney among the '100 wonders of the World'. He had even shot 'platypi' on his ride to Bathurst.[3] But his voyage had been a pampered cruise by comparison with Huxley's. No duties, no middies; he had been a self-financed companion to the aristocratic captain. He had collected at leisure and dined ashore with ambassadors. (Such preferential treatment had galled the *Beagle*'s surgeon-naturalist, who had quit and shipped home.) But for all that, Darwin had known the blue devils, and he had seen a new world in the making, a natural world.

Huxley was thinking about his own voyage again, revelling in MacGillivray's *Narrative*, which had just been published. Given the earlier *brouhaha* it was a 'very creditable' affair. But the illustrations! – 'they have murdered mine in the engraving'. He parcelled up a copy for Nettie, to remind her of more tempestuous days. It took him back to Sydney docks; it even tempted him back:

> I was talking seriously with Fanning the other night about the possibility of finding some employment of a profitable kind in Australia, storekeeping squatting or the like. As I told him any change in my mode of life must be *total* . . . I will not attempt my own profession. I should only be led

astray to think and to work as of old, and sigh continually
for my old dear and intoxicating pursuits. I wish I
understood Brewing, and I would make a proposition to
come and help your father.

Why try to soar to intellectual heights? Why not clip Pegasus'
wings and force him to trot like any carthorse? In bleak moments
Huxley even believed that his impoverished origins had 'unfitted
me for ever taking any very high position'. And what of Nettie's
sacrifice on his scientific altar? He saw her 'wasting her youth'
in 'cheerless suspense'. Yet how could he forgo his dream? To
emigrate now would be to fail 'in the whole purpose of my
existence'. It would be 'a sin and a shameful thing'.⁴

He clung to his successes. The glimpse of gold left an afterglow
in his eyes. Sabine told him again 'that a brilliant prospect lay
open for me here if I would only wait', but with the debts piling it
seemed hopeless. The blizzards in 1852 saw him in 'doubt perplex-
ity and utmost despair . . . I am neither Stoic nor Martyr, and even
if I were I can get no clear perception of what is right to be done'.
Personal ambition went with a stabbing need to raise the appreciation of science:

> My brothers understand ambition and profit. Fanning
> understands ambition. None, not even you Menen, seem
> to comprehend the noble love of intellectual labour for its
> own sake – as an end of life. Nay as I dont doubt that like
> the rest I should turn from it at the first temptation for
> the flesh pots, I had better say no more about it.⁵

Through the winter he drove on in a demoniacal haze, writing his
master work on molluscs, planned on the voyage and executed for
an eternity. With his *Rattlesnake* haul of sea butterflies and
pelagic periwinkle relatives he was equipped. He would show that
all molluscs – from squids to snails to whelks – are modifications
of a basic archetype or plan. He was creating order out of Nature,
making it a 'harmonious whole'; and in a Romantic age establishing the coherent pattern of Nature meant the possibility of drawing
moral conclusions, which could give science a new political po-
tency. For the moment, though, he was in his corner, simply
arguing that the squid's arm was a homologue of the snail's foot.
Not, he insisted, that his 'archetypal' mollusc had a real Platonic
existence. It was no effigy in God's mind, even if Owen had seen it
there. It was an abstraction. It summed up 'the most general

propositions' concerning molluscs. The paper was a model of diplomacy, the sort that would establish his credentials as a 'philosophical anatomist'. It has 'taken me a world of time, thought, and reading' and is 'the best thing I have done'.[6]

His exposure at the Royal Society was getting him noticed. He became that 'promising young man', spotted by the old scholar of Chinese Sir George Staunton, who treated him to a tour of the House of Lords. It even got him an invitation to talk at London's fashionable venue, the Royal Institution.

Here the Friday night lectures were glittering affairs. Smart carriages would line Albemarle Street in Piccadilly. The socialites flocked in, more for the soirée to come than its zoological *hors d'oeuvre*. The institution was part of the Whig educational empire, run by technocrats, the few who saw science as essential to an efficient society. Michael Faraday was there, dreaming sublime dreams of electromagnetic force fields. By now the Institution's utilitarianism was tempered by a crowd-pulling dilettantism, and on Fridays 400 was a good crowd. Huxley's talk was scheduled for 30 April. It was 'considered a "crack" thing' and his self-assurance grew in proportion: 'all the bigwigs Faraday Owen Lyell &c give these lectures' and he was 'ready to go in with any of them. "The wind is tempered to the shorn lamb" in my case means "impudence rises with the occasion"'.[7]

Impudence it would be. Here Owen had baffled the fashionable ladies with his talk on flukes and medusae, or rather, his account of their multi-generation life-cycles; and whomsoever Owen could baffle, Huxley could mystify. He took on Owen's knotty problem. The larval fluke inside a snail host can multiply asexually into 200,000 sporocysts, each of which releases a new sort of swimming larva to infect mammals, including humans. Here they reproduce in the blood or liver, laying eggs which pass out and start the cycle over again. So, were these generations of different *individuals*?

No. He would contradict Owen from the same platform. He would argue that these 200,000 are successive free-living parts of the original individual. They were so many independent buds. It was a hard line to toe. And Owen was not known for his grace in the face of contradiction. He was 'feared and hated' for his sledgehammer responses. 'The truth is he is the superior of most & does not conceal that he knows it', and this was his problem, an insecure nature masked by arrogance. Huxley was working on Owen's subject, '"*Parthenogenesis*" which he told me he considered one of the best things he had done!' The sneer showed his delight at playing David; his slingshot aimed at the six-foot Goliath protecting the dons and deans. Owen had given him a lot of help, and 'I am as grateful as it is possible to be towards a man with whom I feel it necessary to be always on my guard'.

So his public début – like his life – was to be on a point of controversy. He told Faraday that his approach would 'considerably modify the theory of Zoology'. 'I suppose', Faraday retorted, that 'if you are . . . to oppose anybody you have thought well over it'. Huxley had, and he had upped the stakes; 'a success may do me a world of good', equally a failure might see him roasted alive.[8] Given the sable-and-feather mix of scientific gents and society ladies he would take his 'profound subject, and play at battledore & shuttlecock with it, so as to suit both'. Owen was being forced on to court.

In fact Owen was forced to play a number of games at once. Huxley finished his paper on molluscs with a cryptic admission that he could trace no progression from one type to another. Indeed he could see no progression in nature *at all*. Privately, his bizarre image was of an immutable archetype at the centre of a Ptolemaic sphere, on which sat all the slugs, squids, whelks and mussels. They were all equidistant from the centre (and the whole cluster sat in galactic isolation from all the other archetypal clusters). This strange amalgam of Macleay's circles and continental archetypes showed a man groping for symmetry and order in nature.[9]

Exhausted, he crawled to the end of his mollusc paper, feeling like one of his sea slugs. To get it in print, however, would require 'a little manoeuvring on my part'. Paranoia now masked the pugnacity, understandably with him destroying Owen's best work on parthenogenesis. The melodrama played out in his mind. He told Nettie on 15 March that if it were refereed by 'my "particular friend" Prof. Owen . . . it will not be published. He won't be able to say much against it but he will pooh-pooh it to a dead certainty'.

Why? Because for 20 years Owen has been 'the great authority on these matters, and has had no one to tread on his heels'. He portrayed Owen nailing up 'No Poachers' notices around his preserve, barring trespassers. In truth Huxley wanted his own blood-soaked banner: 'you will smile at my perversity dearest. I have a certain pleasure in overcoming these obstacles and fighting these folks with their own weapons'. Hostilities would commence, with atrocities committed on both sides, the nastiest 30-year feud in Victoria's reign. But this was merely the reveille, waking the belligerents: Owen, nodding to cloth and gown, his Divine Archetypes a bulwark against rationalist attack, his Natural Law an edict from God. And snarling at him a frustrated Huxley, one of the new Puritans thundering against Anglican thraldom.

The struggle was symptomatic of a wider divide, a reflection of massive urban and industrial developments. But its fury came from Huxley's own rage.

There was the more immediate cause of his paranoia. The previous day, talking to Owen, Huxley's hot head had got the better of him. They were discussing the great Berlin zoologist, Christian Ehrenberg, an expert on unicellular animals, the protozoa. Huxley saw the man as 'a sham'. Ehrenberg denied that many of the protozoans he studied were in fact plants, algae; and he maintained in the same 'oppressive manner' that his single-cell amoebas were miniature higher animals, with granules corresponding to every organ. In Huxley's view the 'man's hobby-horse' had 'run away with him'. Owen rose to the defence. But then Owen was 'a man of (scientific) property himself', a Tory who had defended the realm with the Honourable Artillery Company during the Chartist years, putting down rioters bent on destroying the old order. Of course he 'takes the conservative side', snapped Huxley. When in the

> argument I showed up Ehrenbergs want of judgment and candour and above all, his unwarrantable sneers at every body else he saw that he could much better pardon Ehrenbergs injustice & severity, than that of any *young man* who should think fit to say sharp things about him. I saw the hint but didn't choose to take it. I laughed – Ah, I said, I see you are a great conservative. His reply was 'And so will you be after you are forty–' which let me into the whole secret of his advocacy of Ehrenberg – it was a fellow feeling – a sort of who knows what established authority these young men will attack next? We must put 'em down. I suppose if I say anything more about Ehrenberg I shall have him bearing down upon me – but I don't mean to stop or go out of my way for all that.[10]

Owen took this deft punch on the chin. He never did referee the mollusc paper, but neither did he damn it. Rather he read it with 'great pleasure' as a work 'after my own heart'.[11] He was still extremely polite.

*

Toil calmed Huxley down. He turned in a paper on zebra tape-worms to the Zoological Society. Everybody was 'amazed ... at his complete mastery'. He made a horribly complex subject easy, showing with lightning sketches how the parasite transforms as it migrates around the zebra's body. In the audience a young un-known, Alfred Russel Wallace, marvelled at his 'wonderful power'.

Huxley found that 'the more I work the better my temper seems to be'. The time was his own now. His parents had moved to Jim's asylum, where there was round-the-clock supervision for his father. Before leaving, his mother parcelled out the family keep-sakes and gave Tom an 'old fashioned broach' containing a lock of her hair for Nettie.[12] He teased her about these 'testamentary dispositions'; but she only responded by passing on the toys she had 'put aside for me – "When I had a nursery"'.

He was eking out an existence, translating, cataloguing the sea squirts in the British Museum. It was pin money and not enough. Nineteen plates for his book were ready to be engraved, but the £200 cost of this six-month labour intensive process was beyond him. He needed the grant. He harassed the Astronomer Royal; he harangued the First Sea Lord.[13] But to no avail. Still he met rejections across the board.

He reached another low ebb. He was 'half mad' with worry, and 'equally wild at thinking of the long weary while' since he had kissed Nettie. 'Help me darling', he cried time after time. Then came the crushing blow. On Wednesday 14 April a telegraph sent him to Kent to find his mother dead. She had suffered a heart attack and died at 4.30 that afternoon. Tom arrived near midnight, numbed, clutching his imbecile father. She had been so 'active and youthful' and at 66 'her bright black eyes and lively manners made her seem younger'. In his quivering state he thought of her pro-phetic parting gifts. Her pride, his success, they merged into one desperately reassuring dream. 'She loved me I believe better than any of her sons and fancied she had a right to be proud of me'.

> I am very sad ... this has opened the floodgates, and the
> whole meaning of existence has sucked out & drowns all
> other feelings. For me there is neither certainty of faith
> nor any consolation – but only a stern summoning of all
> my courage to bear what is inevitable. Belief and
> Happiness seem to be beyond the reach of thinking men in
> these days but Courage and Silence are left.[14]

The sons stood over her grave in Barming Churchyard on Monday

19 April. Tom was still in his 'hideous dream'. Father was there, paralysed and feeble. They 'feared the shock might kill him' but a 'vegetable existence' put him beyond feeling.[15] (He survived three more years in the asylum.) For days Tom tried to function. His Royal Institution début was looming. 'I cannot put it off, and yet I feel unable properly to collect my faculties'. He knew how proud his mother had been about it. It was too late to back out. He worked in a pall of gloom. He considered what it meant to be an 'individual' – as only an invertebrate anatomist could, used to parthogenetic aphids and men-of-war that come apart.

His nerves created waves in the nihilistic void and the lecture somehow shook itself together. He would stand alone, opposing every zoologist on the knottiest problem of the age. A letter from Nettie on the morning of 30 April was a good omen. But every passing hour brought a fresh desire 'to break down, and then go and hang myself'. That night he stood backstage, more anxious than 'I ever have been in my life', thinking of how his mother 'would have entered into my nerves!' The born sermonizer, the boy who had reversed his collar and preached to the kitchen maids, was awaiting his ordination. George and Polly were out there, and the Fannings – and in the front rows the cream of London science: Forbes, Faraday, Wharton Jones and a 'whole lot of "nobs"' besides. The hour struck. In he marched, 'heart beating like a sledge hammer'. Suddenly he knew the felon's fear before the noose tightened.

He took a breath and cast a spell. He conjured up a tropical breeze and slapping sails; they stood off the New Guinea coast, looking up at 'that hot and copper sky – and below into the deep blue'. No disgusting ocean where:

> Yea, slimy things did crawl with legs
> Upon that slimy sea.

That was Coleridge's poetic 'libel upon [its] delicate and peaceful inhabitants'. The modern mariner found beauty and truth in its depths; and a simplicity to its life that posed the profoundest problems. The audience watched men-of-war 'floating idly along', or 'whole fleets of the Velella – with its curious sail . . . twisting about with every breath of air'. He pulled in the towing net and everyone peered at its contents. They saw brilliant-hued floats. They watched a bit bud off and drift away as an offspring, and he teased them – 'Is it an animal? – or is it only *part* of an animal?'[16]

Few accepted that individuals could exist in two or 200 parts;

the applause at the end was more for his ingenuity, even if friends confirmed that he had 'triumphantly demolished' Owen's 'whole system of Alternation of Generations'. Nor was it a polished performance, judging by one letter which complained that, whatever he was good for, it wasn't lecturing. But his ordination was over, and 'Thank Heaven'. 'After the Royal Institution there is no audience I shall ever fear'.

He crashed to the ground afterwards, 'very very tired'. He collapsed and slept and grieved his grief without worrying about work. He did nothing but sleep for days, mooching in a nihilistic gloom. He roused himself with Keats' poem *Endymion*, 'the dreamiest of dreamy legends full of glorious imagery, and inspired by love'.[17] Now he only had Nettie.

Unreal weeks passed, his brain anaesthetized; 'my life rolls on – work – work – work – with very little to vary it'. He had become an expert in the arcana of life. He refereed articles on starfish and sea slugs. He corrected the proofs of William Benjamin Carpenter's *Principles of Comparative Physiology*. Carpenter was a Unitarian and the Professor of Forensic Medicine at University College, and his book – which denied any miraculous tinkering in nature – was to Huxley's taste.[18] Lunching with the 39 year-old Carpenter would have reinforced Huxley's sense of the value of his expertise. Carpenter was fighting to end society's dominance by Oxbridge. He wanted talent and training rewarded. The time had come to put London's science specialists into the top jobs. Huxley was Carpenter's sort of expert, and Carpenter was Huxley's sort of man.

Meanwhile the grant business turned from fiasco to Whitehall farce – a case of missing memorials, wrong doors, officious Under Secretaries. Sir Charles Trevelyan at the Treasury sent him to the Prime Minister; but the PM's personal secretary had lost the memorial from Lord Rosse, and by now the Royal Society had mislaid its minutes as well. He traipsed corridors and sat in antechambers, doggedly determined, however bootless it seemed, his mood summed up by the expression on his new photograph: 'horribly savage & sulky looking'.

Absence was making Hal's memory of Nettie grow fainter even as his heart grew fonder. His correspondence became tardy. He missed Nettie's birthday. Another link snapped when the Fannings shipped back to Australia in August. They twisted his arm to join them, join the 80,000 other emigrants this year, lured by the gold.

But the great, intoxicating, intellectual Babylon had spoiled him; no jogging existence would now do, with 'the great problems of existence set hopelessly in the background'. The last sight of a tearful Ory will, Huxley said, 'throw me into myself more than ever'.[19]

A sniff of 'fresh Professorships' kept him going. With a thousand visitors expected at the pretty new Queen's College during the British Association week at Belfast, he borrowed money from George to go, determined to keep his ear to the ground. And his face to the fore: more confident now, he took to the podium 'for about three quarters of an hour without break', chalky hands waving as he sketched an archetypal sea squirt on the blackboard.[20] Afterwards he steamed to the Giant's Causeway, taking secret pleasure in the swell which sent the mighty philosophers to the side. He strolled the shore with Owen, dwarfed by the huge basalt columns reaching into the Atlantic where giants had once stepped. Owen and Huxley: the giants were of intellect now, world experts divided over the rule of the animal kingdom. Here they stood together, polite and mistrustful, on the final balmy day before the long cold winter.

In September Huxley took a last trip into the past. Two days deputizing for his old teacher Thomas Chandler brought the memories back: the little East End drug shop, his privation and dissipation. Maudlin thoughts choked him: 'you cannot fancy', he told Nettie, 'what a deep draught of abomination I took. From drinking deeper ... my sweet one, you saved me'. He liked to think of himself reclaimed, his new life dedicated to nature and truth. But *real* dissipation was her visiting cousin Alfred, caught creeping out for nights on the tiles, 'addicted to drinking & only fifteen!'[21]

Sots and sad recollections characterized the period. His first job offer came from a struggling private medical school. It was one of the gasping survivors. Founded by an irascible surgeon, George Dermott – a political bruiser who dictated notes in a gin palace – it was a Dissenting relic with no future (it promptly died). But there could be no backstreet lecture-grubbing for Huxley. He wasn't going to be dragged down like Cooke. The 'spectre of a wasted life has passed before me'. He had a 'vocation', and no man of the cloth felt a greater 'duty to follow it'.[22] His rise in this 'boiling scathing world' left him demanding something better.

Nettie told him to follow his heart, and that was set on a university chair. The death of Jock's father, William MacGillivray, professor of natural history in Aberdeen, sent Huxley to Owen and Forbes for references once again. George chuckled at Tom's 'chimerical' desires, but he was determined to take his place in the new intellectual world. 'The past two years' had proved 'that the dreams of my childhood and the aspirations of my manhood were ... not mere fancies'. They 'were the expression of a hidden force'.[23]

On 7 November he was vindicated. It had been blowing a gale for weeks. 'I had a deuced bad cold ... it was a beastly November day and I was very grumpy'. But the word came: he had his 'scientific knighthood', the Royal Medal. It filled an enormous longing. It was confirmation of the poor boy's right to walk the public bridleway of science. It would raise his 'status in the eyes of those charming people, "practical men"', who sniggered at his intellectual aspirations.[24] The 50-guinea nugget was proof that science *could* confer prestige in a world looking to rank and wealth. As the downpours continued and Forbes contemplated building an Ark, Huxley had already found his Ararat.

Preparing to be garlanded, Huxley finally felt part of the English nation. The gloss of gold replaced the dross of alien detachment. A new chauvinism punctured his blasé exterior. He caught the mood of national pride, now erasing the class hatreds of the 1840s. Before his investiture he even revelled in the spectacle of Wellington's state funeral. Friends were aghast at 'the national extravagance of spending 400,000 on a dead man', an Iron Duke, hero of Waterloo or no.[25] But Huxley sat in an icy St Paul's Cathedral feeling an inner glow. There he stayed from eight until three, watching the Gothic beams play on the 'best of our people'.

His own ceremony at Somerset House was as much political theatre. At the Anniversary Dinner on 30 November Lord Rosse awarded the medal. Behind him the bewigged past Presidents looked more benign in their frames, and the faces of the 60 Fellows quite exuberant. Huxley told of his lonely years at sea and of his dove: 'it has this day returned not indeed with an olive branch but with a twig of the bay – and a fruit from the Garden of the Hesperides'.[26] He hinted at his portfolios of *Rattlesnake* drawings and vowed to justify the award when the government 'of this *great* country' ceased its great deliberation and afforded him the few pounds to publish.

On that litigious subject he was still fuming. Three weeks earlier he had waylaid Owen, requesting yet another recommendation, this time to shake up the Home Office. Time passed with no sign of it. He was livid. Then he met Owen:

> I was going to walk past, but he stopped me, and in the blandest and most gracious manner said, 'I have received your note, I shall *grant* it.' The phrase and the implied condescension were quite 'touching' – so much that if I stopped a moment longer I must knock him into the gutter. I therefore bowed and walked off. This was last Saturday. Nothing came on Monday or on Tuesday, but on Wednesday morning I received 'with Prof. Owen's best wishes', the *strongest and kindest testimonial any man could possibly wish for*! . . . I gave up any attempt to comprehend him from this time forth.

To be the butt of such hauteur was galling. Owen was a gentleman on the Civil List, now settled royally into Sheen Lodge, and he acted the part. 'How sad it is', someone wrote, 'to see great genius combined with such a want of generous feeling'. Forbes could only agree. Owen 'is certainly one of the oddest beings I ever came across', he told Huxley, '& seems as if he was constantly attended by two spiritual policemen, the one from the upper regions & the other from the lower'.[27] But well might Owen have been getting a little lax; Huxley's requests for references were arriving weeks apart! Owen was backing Huxley to the hilt and to what avail?

The rains continued. Rivers overflowed and lakes covered the patchwork south of England. The Thames was set to flood as Huxley steamed down to Greenwich for Christmas with the Busks. Busk and Huxley were joining forces, turning an honest penny by translating the latest German tome on cells and tissues, Albert Kölliker's *Manual of Human Histology*. As a student text it would pay about £180, enough 'filthy lucre' to make the drudgery bearable.[28] With his writing finally showing a profit, Huxley promised Lizzie something in Tennessee ('Scott' had never been able to practise among the whites; he could only get work treating slaves).[29] 'Don't expect anything vast, but there is corn in Egypt'. He had seen it.

Others had too. A query about sea squirts from the *Economist* piqued his interest. It led him to another schoolmaster's son, a political pamphleteer with cosmic aspirations, Herbert Spencer. Spencer was the sub-editor of the *Economist*, a bumptious man with a breathless vision of an upward-sweeping nature. All he lacked was the proof of this evolutionary progress. Owen disappointed him. Like any self-respecting secularist Spencer hated Owen's Archetypal Holy of Holies and ended his course in 'complete disbelief'. And so he had turned to Huxley. He needed information on the 'production of composite animals by the union of simpler ones'.[30]

Where better than the free-trading *Economist* to find an odd rapport? Huxley indulged Spencer's utopian flights, passing this former railway engineer over to Tyndall with a line from Faust, as 'Ein Kerl der speculirt'.[31] A learned pact bound the tormented trio, who bartered their souls for beauty and truth. Spencer too had known poverty. He had toyed with emigrating. When Huxley was walking the East End hovels, Spencer was donning his Chartist cap and decrying all 'despotisms, aristocracies, priestcrafts'. While Huxley was learning surgery, Spencer was dabbling in more emancipatory sciences, from self-help phrenology to cosmic evolution. With his own phrenological bump of 'self-esteem' he should have been a preacher. But like Huxley in a new age, his tub-thumping was to the glory of the great Unknown. Spencer's, like Huxley's, was a fratricidal relationship with theology. He penned the stodgy sermons as Tyndall led the pantheistic hymns and Huxley preached hell-fire warnings about the unpardonable sin of faith.

Spencer was another child of the 1840s who had learned his politics around the Lord's table. Derby-born into a Chapel culture, he had a searing distrust of the privileged, State-endowed Church. He was still carrying his Nonconformist placard demanding fair play and reform, only now he projected this moral imperative on to the universe. Change was guaranteed: the growth of civilization was 'all of a piece with the development of the embryo or the unfolding of a flower'.[32] Progress through open competition was a 'law underlying the whole organic creation'. It alone could bear 'Humanity onwards towards perfection'.

Huxley found a freethinker whose evolutionary ideals packed a moral punch. Spencer's 'Development Hypothesis' was hot off the press. It ran in the *Leader*, that radical standard born of the hopes of 1848, putting the libertarian in uneasy alliance with the socialists. Spencer was an anarchist who decried all State intervention, whether it was State education for the poor or State privileges for the parson. To Huxley the first was as chilling as the second was cheering.

So began a turbulent friendship. Huxley would end up bursting Spencer's overblown balloons, but a secular iconoclasm bound them at a deeper level. Huxley also had Spencer to thank for his entrée into London's avant garde – that brilliant, anguished group which converged on publisher John Chapman's weekly soirées in the Strand, opposite Spencer's office.

At its hub was the Svengali-like Chapman, mesmerizing with his Byronic looks and the more attractive for flouting convention.[33] Marian Evans (soon to be launched as the novelist George Eliot) was part of his tumultuous household, although her ménage with the philandering Chapman, his compliant wife and jealous mistress was understandably uneasy. Fears that free thought meant free love were hardly allayed by the likes of Chapman. He was a druggist's son and a medical radical in an age which bred them with fearsome dispositions. And he published sensational books. Howls rose with each title: Marian Evans' translation of Strauss' *Life of Jesus*, which made the Gospels a 'misty chaos of contradiction and uncertainty'; Francis Newman's harrowing account of his retreat from Christianity, *Phases of Faith*; the lapsed Anglo-Catholic J. A. Froude's *Nemesis of Faith*; Spencer's finger-wagging to government in *Social Statics*. The climax came with a real proclamation of atheism – for many readers their first encounter with the unimaginable – *Letters on the Laws of Man's Nature and Development* by Harriet Martineau and Henry Atkinson, whom even Darwin's relatives considered 'two criminals'.

The charismatic Chapman was headhunting in 1853. He had revamped radical London's quarterly, the *Westminster Review*. He was casting around for 'advanced thinkers', not to shock, but to 'sap and undermine' a lumbering orthodoxy. He approached Huxley, who offered an account of the lonely cockroach-infested life on the Louisiade. Huxley's review of MacGillivray's *Narrative* added a dash of exotica in a day when businessmen 'run over to India, or to Australia ... without remark'. It sounded creaking timbers, smelled of grog, sweated in the '*hot* Scotch mist' and fired six-pounders at Sea Lords and soul-savers alike. What Chapman could decipher of the illegible script he liked and he took it on spec, offering Huxley his own scientific column. Here at last was a chance to wield his stiletto pen. Only as an afterthought did he ask about the pay. Chapman was bankrupting himself financing the cause. He offered terms Huxley could not refuse – '12 guineas per sheet (ie. 16 pages)', Huxley whistled to Nettie, and it 'promises to be a guinea a page by and bye'.[34]

Spencer and Chapman drew Huxley into a web of radical friendships. At the soirées he mixed with the literary freethinkers.

He could gaze on Froude's melancholy countenance or savour Newman's 'angelic sweetness'. Here were fellow-travellers William Benjamin Carpenter, the philosopher John Stuart Mill and the convicted atheist George Holyoake. With Huxley 'becoming celebrated in London' his February début created a stir, as Marian Evans noted. He was a glass-case zoological anomaly, a sharp 28 year-old intent on making his way by pure science. For her part Evans was now standing beside G. H. Lewes, a smallpox-scarred veteran with a more political need to popularize science. So this was the dissipated spirit behind *Ranthorpe*. A stare of seeming malevolence made Lewes a 'sort of miniature Mirabeau'. But the good-natured critic, actor, Germanizer and *Leader*-writer struck Huxley with his dramatic tongue:

> I say . . . that if astronomy must destroy theology, it will
> . . . deepen religion. There is no man in whom the starry
> heavens has not excited religious emotion; . . . whatever
> may be the litanies most suitable to his mind, under some
> form or other, man cannot help worshipping when under
> the canopy of the 'cathedral of immensity'.

The talk was reasoned and outrageous: disestablishment, democracy, the tyranny of marriage, biblical criticism, evolutionism – every emancipatory 'ism' to destabilize Anglican society. Spencer's anarchic individualists debated with Holyoake's atheist socialists. Then all would join Lewes to demand a liberating theory of 'development', a hammer to break the creationist shackles. On this Chapman even quizzed Owen, intrigued by the ultimate mystery, the way in which 'successive species have been introduced'.[35]

Huxley landed feet first in the throng, but he soon shuffled off to the rim, no doubt with a disapproving glare. Carrying a cross for real science, he scorned the developmental crudities of so many Lotharios. A perceptive Marian Evans reassessed this aloof spectator, with his love of '*paradox* and *antagonism*'. She saw that his personality was reactive: 'its being beckoned in one direction may incline it to turn off in another'. At times he seemed driven by his own bull-headedness. But perhaps that was the price for such 'brilliant talents'.

Afternoons were spent with Spencer and Lewes at the zoo, evenings at the opera. Lewes seemed comfortably familiar, long-haired 'and rather worn-looking', full of *risqué* jokes: a 'loose-tongued merry-hearted being with more sail than ballast', Carlyle called him. It showed as he fell prey to Huxley's wit. At dinner one day Spencer's guests described the difficulty of writing, and Lewes announced, 'I get up steam at once. In short, I boil at low temperatures', only to have Huxley flash back, but 'that implies a vacuum in the upper regions'.

Huxley found a man swopping women and swopping Owen's Platonism for Comte's positivism, shearing science of its woolly theological coat and paring the corpse down to the factual bone. (Science for the French philosopher Auguste Comte rested on 'positive' facts constituted into a hierarchy of natural laws. Advocating a 'Religion of Humanity' and technocratic priesthood, he gave science its most sanctified sectarian ethos as the only True Knowledge.) Lewes' insistence on facts was only marred by his insistent factual blunders. As for his addiction to evolution, Huxley had 'no objection whatever' while it was *an hypothesis merely* – meaning he saw not a tittle of evidence. But others felt the way the wind was blowing. If evolution be true, Lyell reasoned, trying to gain a crumb of comfort, 'the whole geological history of the globe is the history of Man'. Radical London was reverberating to this new hymn. That Unitarian-turned-atheist Harriet Martineau (the *belle laide* once inseparable from Darwin's elder brother Erasmus) raised her eyes while translating Comte in 1853:

> We find ourselves suddenly living and moving in the midst
> of the universe – as a part of it, and not as its aim and
> object. We find ourselves living, not under capricious and
> arbitrary conditions . . . but under great, general,
> invariable laws, which operate on us as part of a whole.

The avant garde was struck by the startling reality. To this end Lewes, Spencer and Huxley began emasculating Owen's anatomy, even as the cloying *Quarterly* was lauding it. None doubted that Owen was 'the greatest living comparative anatomist'; it only made them more cynical about his Divine Archetype. This was no blueprint for Creation. Romanticism was *passé*. To a new breed it was a bad mixture of pomposity and mysticism. In Germany too it was dismissed by an atheistic underground. Carlyle's romanticism had been an escape from 'the evils of industrial and materialist society'.[36] But the men from the engine sheds and medical manufactories saw their salvation in the industrial order. They needed to strip off the metaphysical gloss and liberate science, leaving it supposedly value-free and serviceable to its new industrial masters. The three zoo-going rationalists were deconsecrating Owen's universe.

This brash crowd was making the world safe for Darwin, who was still sitting in silent agitation on his theory of evolution. Darwin emerged from his Kent retreat on 6 April 1853 to attend a Geological Society meeting, which is probably where Huxley first saw him: broad-set, beetle-browed, with a beaming face and Shropshire accent. Enthusiasm oozed as he declared himself 'a man of one idea', barnacles 'morning & night'. Normally a reticent gent, he offered Huxley his sea squirts from the *Beagle* voyage, and then prompted him: 'it is very indelicate in me to say so, but it would give me *great* pleasure to see my work reviewed by any one so capable'. 'Upon my honour', he exclaimed in his self-effacing way, 'I never did such a thing before'. And then with unaccustomed bravado he dropped Huxley a list of his oddest findings for inclusion.

The mollusc paper came in return. Darwin, from a line of freethinkers and Unitarians, swore by material causes. He too eschewed archetypal ideas as so much verbiage. He too detested the Platonic imagery of 'Owen, Agassiz & Co'. Visualizing an archetype 'in *your* sense', he assured Huxley, as simply the common denominator of all vertebrates or molluscs, 'is one of the very highest ends of Natural History'. But not *the* highest. Huxley supposed a fixed abstraction, but could he not imagine an archetype '*undergoing* further development'?[37] Think of it as a hypothetical *ancestor*, a generalized forerunner from which any number of specialized descendants could evolve. Huxley, the 'architectural' man, interested in anatomy and geometry, not fossils and geology, missed the point.

While Huxley slid in and out of the best social circles and gloried in the kudos, the struggle for a chair had turned into a killing drudge. It was made worse by the separation from Nettie – three years now. Without a job, merit and medal would mean nothing and 'my small light will be ignominiously snuffed out'. Toronto was officially given against him and Tyndall in 1853. Within weeks a chair at King's College in the Strand slipped from his grasp. 'I have got very old . . . in the last two years', he moaned. Continual bouncing from elation to depression meant that 'a good deal of the spring & elasticity has gone out of me'.[38] Mental collapses seemed to regulate his life and 1853 saw the final precipitous trough.

Yet to the world he was thriving. At 28 he was a Royal Medallist, lionized by the 'big wigs' at Royal Society soirées as much as by Lewes' radicals. He seemed brilliantly combative to George Eliot and dashing to Ellen Busk; he was hungry, determined, and they knew he was on the way up. With the young bloods, he was sliding into a position of power. The proof came with his elevation to that star chamber, the Royal Society Council. He also 'propped' Tyndall's 'faltering soul' by announcing his own Fellowship. In fact for a man with no work prospects he showed some brass in directing Tyndall to the top job, telling him he should be 'looking to Faraday's place'. Tyndall, the poetic pantheist, knew that these moves were 'guided by the gods'. He too had been crushed by rejections, but for once justice was done. He gave such fighting talks on magnetism at the Royal Institution that Faraday secured his professorship there. Providence, said Tyndall on hearing a whisper that he would even follow Huxley with the 1853 Royal Medal, evidently 'intends to build us a Toronto at home'.[39]

Huxley too was held by the gravitational pull of the great metropolis. He needed its vibrancy and shared in its self-importance. Here were bookshops on every corner and the treat of first nights. No colonial hideaway would do; science at the centre was 'discussion and debate, politics and action'.[40] The metropolis meant brimming museums and rich institutions; it meant legislating scientific laws rather than collecting local taxes. 'My course of life is taken', he announced. 'I will *not* leave London – I *will* make myself a name and a position'.

Quite how had yet to resolve itself. That perennial grumbler Charles Babbage (who had successfully fleeced the government of thousands to build his calculating machine) complained that science was not a profession. There was no educational standard, no scientific civil service, not even a word for its practitioners. Opportunities were scant. Zoology was still an adjunct of medicine, and its chairs were pitifully undervalued.

But change was coming. The adulation of Mammon during the 1851 Great Exhibition gave science a new set of values. Savants rushed to hitch their demands to Victorian consumerism. Another trooper drilled by De la Beche in the School of Mines, the chemist Lyon Playfair, saw the way ahead. For him 'searchers after truth' were not dreamy idealists. They were 'the "horses" of the chariots of industry'. Huxley loved the rhetoric, the more because it got results. In 1853 a Government Department of Science and Art ('Art' being Technology) was set up to oversee the training of science teachers. Huxley hoped that it would break the Latin stranglehold, so that a schoolboy would in future know 'the difference between . . . the contents of his skull and those of his abdomen'. Playfair, appointed the Secretary for Science, became an ally in place. Cultivate him, Huxley told Tyndall; he 'has great influence and will have more'.[41]

While the future looked up, Huxley's money worries were as immediate as ever. Turning a 'prose labourer' was the quick option. No longer the night-owl, he was up at 8 am., at his desk all day and slumped in bed by midnight, too tired for parties. Medical reviews, German translations, long articles for cyclopaedias and encyclopaedic articles for the *Westminster*: the list went on. He had become a 'penny-a-liner', his speed dictated by deadlines. He honed his prose, giving his brilliant *bon mots* their vernacular edge. As a 'scientific jackal for the public', he acquired a butcher's knack of displaying the flesh from disembowelled books as tasty morsels. Readers salivated at his political sprint through comparative anatomy. In one of his sharpest anonymous pieces, he talked of the fall of the 'ultra-speculative "red" biologists' Geoffroy and Oken, the old radicals who demanded a common archetype for all animal life (giving men and amoebas equality on good revolutionary principles). But a new generation had taken over 'the Temple of Science' and, true to British Liberal principles, given each animal class its sovereign archetype. The keenest social metaphor enlivened the driest *System der Thierischen Morphologie*.

His production line kept the wolf from the door. What little surplus it generated went to Lizzie, needier herself and now 'in possession of another possible President' (a new baby boy). Off went a draft for $135, amassed, he hastened to add, 'by mine own sword'.[42] He would collect later, say 'twenty years hence', when he would come over 'on the possibility of picking up something or other from one of my nephews at Washington'.

Huxley's translations were tuned to contemporary needs. Chapman's clique wanted to make man and morality as natural as climate and cosmos. It wanted laws that stretched from stars to society. But to find them it was forced to plunder the microscopic realm, Huxley's realm.

The key turned up in the work of a brilliant Estonian embryologist, who had trained at Würzburg and settled in St Petersburg. Karl Ernst Von Baer had described how the foetuses of chicks, lizards and dogs all diverged and specialized away from a common homogeneous 'germ'. The notion of specialization and division of labour was elastic enough to satisfy everyone. It became the watchword; it explained embryos; it explained evolution; it explained the co-existence of creatures in a habitat, like so many trades in the same tenement; it explained an industrial society based on division of labour – for Spencer it explained everything. Growth from homogeneous to heterogeneous was the 'law of all progress'.

It was even the flirtatious babble of lovers, Marian Evans' come-hither call to Spencer. She would, she swore, presently 'be on equality, in point of sensibility, with the star-fish and sea-egg ... You see I am sinking fast towards "homogeneity" and my brain will soon be a mere pulp unless you come to arrest the downward process'.[43]

The towering edifice rested on Von Baer. He was acquiring heroic status among the cognoscenti. But they were reduced to cannibalizing and recycling secondary sources. Von Baer's work rested in German obscurity. So Huxley set to, translating the relevant texts.

Huxley actually stuck to the letter of Von Baer's law, damning its extrapolation to heaven and earth. Yet even the cautious Owen was extending it to the cavalcade of fossil animals. Life's historical progression mirrored the growth of the embryo; it became increasingly specialized. To prove it Owen plotted the progress of the horse from its ancient five-toed antecedent to today's single-toed thoroughbred.[44] It was no 'evolution', no damnable 'Development', indeed how the Word became Flesh he did not know, except by a 'predetermining Will'. (Lewes did; in the *Leader* he appropriated Owen's fossils for his own evolutionary ends.) Huxley, loathing Owen and his progressive-incarnation mysticism, shied away.

Moreover he believed that Von Baer himself had pulled the rug from under this 'progressive development' nonsense. Von Baer's study of the embryos of the great groups – the vertebrates, molluscs, starfish and insects – had shown each to be based on a unique archetypal plan. They could not be stacked into a chain, none was 'higher' than any other. Nor could Huxley embrace the 'progression of animal forms in time'. Almost all geologists accepted a fossil ascent from fish to man. But not Huxley. His deconsecrated palaeontology was deeply nihilistic and defiantly anti-Creative: no progress, no meaning to fossil life, no Christian comfort. For Huxley, almost uniquely, man was no 'modulus and standard of the creation', no end point, merely an 'aberrant modification'.

He became absurdly provocative. Murchison wanted to see a footprint in ancient rock as proof that man had always existed? Well, Huxley said, with mammals turning up in Triassic beds, he soon expected 'to see a bit of palaeozoic pottery'.[45] He stood the joke on its head. Belief in Palaeozoic man, splashing among the trilobites, put him in a minority of one.

Black clouds heralded the summer's end, pulling a sombre veil over the year. An emotional monsoon was imminent. The first winds had buffeted Huxley in May 1853. He ticked off three years of desperation. He was at his wits' end, diverted into dreary reviewing, rocking himself neurotically to the refrain, 'I can get honour in science, but it doesn't pay, and "honour heals no wounds"'. The wounds were festering. The civility of the Sea Lords had worn thin and in June they refused another leave: six months would see him back in service. He railed at Nettie, thinking she doubted him. Her apparent misgivings gnawed at him until he broke down in July. In an outburst he branded their marriage 'no better than a mockery'. Twelve thousand miles away Nettie recoiled, pleading that 'your words cold & sharp as steel harrowed my very soul'.[46] Isolation and strain, like Stanley's on the bridge, were pushing him to the limit.

The rage gave his reviews a jagged edge. His first *Westminster* column blasted the craze for séances. It hurled the money-changers from the temple of science, that 'Witch *Sabbat* of mesmerists, clairvoyants, electro-biologists, rappers, table-turners, and evil-worshippers in general'. Spiritualism, which was sweeping across the water from pentecostalist New York to emasculate the secular movement, was fit for ridicule.

> If it were true that our poor souls, instead of retiring into their rest after the weary fight of this world, were to be at the beck and call of every tobacco-squirting 'loafer' who chose to constitute himself a medium, would not those of us who have any self-respect sooner become dogs, and perish with our bodies?

The expert was reclaiming the temple for the priests of reason. Rival vendors in the intellectual market were being condemned to Hades. There was only one true saviour: Science. The trumpet-charge of Huxley's campaign for a policed and professional science had been sounded.

Unfortunately he then blew a new tune, swung round, and

lashed his own camp followers. He brushed off Lewes' own book on Comte with a two-page list of errors. He was serving notice that the temple was off-limits as much to scientific amateurs. The jobless savant was lauding it over the dramatic dilettante, biting his head off with a clean carnassial chomp. He hauled Lewes' headless corpse over the coals, branding him a book-learner. It sent Chapman's group reeling. Marian Evans, the sub-editor (now Lewes' lover and about to elope with him to Germany), implored Chapman not to print 'such a *purely* contemptuous' piece. It was an 'utterly worthless unworthy notice', a jab at one of their own.[47] But it went out uncut, as much a comment on Huxley's mental state as Lewes' slipshod science.

At the height of this crisis came a new edition, the tenth, of the bestselling *Vestiges of the Natural History of Creation*. 'Time was', he exploded in the most savage review he would ever write, 'when the brains were out, the man would die'. *Vestiges* was brilliant journalism, a pot-boiling synthesis of the fringe sciences. It was cleverly crafted to unite the secular factions under the banner of 'Development'. But the science was second-hand and Huxley loathed the book's blundering pretension. It was also visionary, sweeping from the coalescence of planets, the first 'chemico-electric' generation of living globules, through the fossil fish and ancient reptiles, the 'vestiges' of the title, to the perfection of man.

Huxley knew that the anonymous book was pegged on the Edinburgh publisher of low-brow miscellanies, Robert Chambers. The pernickety expert who could not get a job choked on its sales. For nine years the bestseller had been 'greedily swallowed' 'to the great glory and no small profit' of its author. There spoke a bitter specialist living from hand to mouth.

In his foul mood Huxley snubbed the journalistic old-hand; he derided Chambers' talk of 'creation by law' as empty verbiage. These laws looked like spiritual movers behind the scenes, which left the fossil succession an act of God. Transmutation 'is a perfectly legitimate' idea, Huxley reaffirmed, but the will of God was no explanation. In a fit Huxley threw down the book as 'so much waste paper'.

With *Vestiges* citing Owen, Huxley sarcastically stepped in 'to save the learned Professor's reputation'. Owen, trying to balance his rejection of transmutation with acceptance of fossil progression, was crucified again. Ancient armoured fish were the pretext, but the whipping showed how much deeper it went. Huxley parted from *Vestiges* 'in a very bad humour',[48] and he parted from the year in equally bad grace, having upset Nettie, alienated Evans and infuriated Owen.

But the storm was passing and the sun could be seen on the horizon. Nettie's reassuring letters exorcized his fears and the first hints of a real job raised his self-esteem. 'You must pray', he wrote to her on 1 January 1854, 'that I may never have another year' like the last, 'or I shall become altogether as the nether millstone'. 'I have been unjust', he apologized, 'but will never be so again'.[49]

11

The Jihad Begins

> There is always a Cape Horn in one's life that either one
> weathers or wrecks one's self on. Thank God I think I
> may say I have weathered mine – not without a good deal
> of damage to spars and rigging though, for it blew deuced
> hard on the other side.

Huxley had rounded his Cape after three years of storms. Three
years in a 'set-teeth sort of mood' which had left a permanent
grimace; three years 'when Martin Luther's saying – "If there were
as many devils as there are tiles upon the housetops, I will go"– was
the only fit expression of my habitual temper'.[1] Now in 1854 one
coup after another eased the grimace into a more pleasing grin.

The new year was icy enough for the Cape. In sub-zero temperatures the Thames froze and snow drifts paralysed even 'this
monster of a city'. But 7 January saw a thaw and Huxley reached
a post box to send Nettie a cheery update. The job front looked
good. Wharton Jones was ending his stint as Fullerian Professor at
the Royal Institution and Huxley was tipped to succeed him. That
'is £100 a year', he said. And Forbes was expected to be called
away to Edinburgh. There the old professor, Robert Jameson, 50
years in the post, had withered into a 'baked mummy'. Now, 'too
ill to lecture but too stubborn to retire', he was wished on his
way.[2] Should Forbes go, Huxley anticipated his place in the
Museum of Economic Geology. He knew the slips 'twixt cup and
lip, but he was still a knot of excitement.

The thaw revealed his first *Westminster* number, already on the
news-stands. It cheered Darwin. There was Huxley's review of his
barnacle monographs, and praise for the recluse as brilliant 'an

observer of nature on the small as on the large scale'. Huxley described Darwin's discoveries: how the barnacle larva develops a huge hump like Mr Punch, which oozes cement and glues it to a ship's bottom. And how female stalked barnacles hide a host of degenerate males under their shelly skirts. Darwin was pleased and Nettie perplexed, but Hal told her not to bother with it as 'it is all science and will only bore you'.[3]

Even the calamities were turned to advantage. On the day of the thaw the Sea Lords finally ordered him back to active service. The call-up came as the international crisis deepened, and Huxley assumed 'they will try to get rid of me by ordering me to the Black Sea'. The Crimea was dominating events. The Turks had resisted Russia's demand to protect the Orthodox Christians in the Ottoman Empire. The Russians had swept across the Danube Delta. With the sinking of the Turkish fleet the press at home whipped up anti-Moscow hysteria. Britain had vast naval superiority, '114 effective war steamers' noted Huxley.[4] The public called for the nation to prove itself. In January 1854 the British and French flotillas entered the Black Sea. Assistant Surgeon Huxley RN of course expected a man-o'-war posting.

Not that he had any intention of resuming service. Science was his career now. And so began a cat-and-mouse game with the Sea Lords. He kept recalling their promises to scientific officers, they kept ordering him to Portsmouth. (In fact not to fight but to join the training ship *Illustrious*. 'However', he noted in February as the allies issued an ultimatum to Russia, 'once in their claws there is no telling what might become of me'.) He put his failure to finish his book down to their refusal to fund him. But 'their Lordships saw no reason to alter their decision'.

> *My* Lordship said to himself 'No more so do I' and stuck
> the order on his mantlepiece . . . Luckily for me the
> 'Illustrious' is in the Home station so nobody can accuse
> me of an objection to face the Rooshians.[5]

With hostilities inevitable, strange commissions came his way. Chapman wanted a report on Sultan Schamyl's guerrilla war against the Cossacks in the Caucasus, east of the Black Sea. Huxley knew 'no more about Schamyl than the man in the moon', but for weeks he pored over reports of the Islamic resistance, 'dreamt about it & woke up thinking about it'. He rallied to Schamyl's *jihad*, berating the Cossacks' attempt to replace the 'youthful vigour' of Islam with the 'degraded idolatry of the Greco-Russian Tsar worship, misnamed Christianity'. It fitted the Russophobia of the moment. But his slant was revealing. He pointedly sided with the Sufis, whose asceticism and striving for truth contrasted with Orthodoxy's 'gew-gaw saints' and its 'besotted priests' fawning over the patriarch as 'God upon earth'.

These were months of hawkish patriotism. The press was pitting English liberty against Tsarist tyranny, and Huxley put Schamyl 'beside our own Cromwell' as a religious liberator. The metaphor was unmistakable, writ large by a warrior launching his own holy war. Indeed Schamyl seemed strangely familiar, with 'his silent earnest ways, intense determination and love of knowledge'. There went Huxley in dervish clothes, a man apart, asking what Nature wanted of him.

Huxley himself was rising through the ranks to become a field commander in what he saw as science's 'war' against a corrupt theology. His reports of atrocity and sacrifice show how much of his image of science came from the real battlefield. War was a holy duty. Schamyl's cry became Huxley's *idée fixe*: fight or succumb. The Sultan was binding a Muslim nation through new ideals, and Huxley's 'scientific Young England' would play up an orthodox Anglican 'threat' in its own call to arms (rejuvenation through war was a British national theme after 1854). There was power in Schamyl's sword.

Huxley was not against Russian imperialism. Indeed the 'aggression of a nation of higher social organization upon those of lower grade' was one of the 'conditions of human progress'. That was a bloody ethic of the age, soon to be sanctified in Darwin's work. The point was to redirect the Russian bear's gaze towards the Asian 'wastes where his claws may find exercise advantageous to humanity'.

The work was to Huxley's taste and Chapman praised its 'vigour'. It is 'the best thing I have written'. And since 'I shall get £30 for it . . . I don't mind how much more of the same is offered me'.[6]

His gung-ho air belied the ominous developments on his doorstep. Being Huxley there was no silver lining that could not resolve itself into a cloud. Deep in 'Schamyl', he watched his brother George collapse as a financial scandal threatened ruin and imprisonment:

> the sudden and unexpected break out of one of the
> partners in a great London Bank – a man who twelve
> months ago was known to be worth £150,000 – has

> involved him in ruin and I fear still worse for it turns out
> that some of the people with whom he has been connected
> in trying to save themselves have made most improper
> uses of moneys with which they were entrusted. And my
> brother and others equally ignorant of all this are legally
> though of course not morally responsible for their acts.

Huxley's head swirled with memories of the Salt scandal. He had
struggled from the Inferno to see the stars, only to find another
'abyss opening under ones feet'. George knew the stigma a jail
sentence would carry and his mental state 'bordered upon insanity'.
Huxley cared nothing 'for the opinion of the world . . . but I know
its practical effects & I see one more difficulty thrust in a path
which assuredly needed not to be more rugged'. Being a banking
scandal it was hushed up, but it put the bristling indignation into
'Schamyl'. 'When you read it', he told Nettie, 'try to find any trace
of what was boiling in the writer's head'.[7]

The Russians crossed the Danube and Britain declared war on
28 March. Huxley was still fending off the Navy. He used every
delaying tactic, furious at their broken promises. Early in April
their Lordships threatened to scratch his name from the List. He
wished them to the devil and was duly struck off for disobeying
orders. He cocked-a-snook at their Lordships. His final judgment:
'they got the worst of it in logic and words, and I in reality and
"tin"'.[8] But without regular pay the tin was all-important.

As a civilian he could be funded by the Royal Society, which
now offered £300 to finance his book. He worked furiously,
becoming 'more & more anchorite every day'. Science required
factory discipline, 'steady punctual uninterrupted work'.[9] His
scientific-artisan image was being forged, a work-bench mentality
far from the leisured aristocratic ideal. After a day spent teasing
apart the intestines of bivalve shellfish (brachiopods) or probing
their 'hearts' (in fact reproductive organs, as he was first to show)
he would write 'for five or six hours' into the night.

But his spirits were rising. Word that Nettie's father was coming
over – and that Nettie would accompany him – gave Huxley the
final boost. Turning inside out like an emotional sea cucumber, he
found his bottomless pit of pessimism become an endless font of
optimism. He knew 'that we *must* after all these weary trials have
many happy years to go through together'. He marked four heroic
years by posting a coral broach. 'I little thought years ago that I

should only be able to send you symbols of my love on your birthday in '54. – I hoped rather to have waked you with a kiss'. Twelve thousand miles of separation was the ultimate Malthusian restraint: no marriage, no kiss, no spoken word in all that time. But then, as an upright young man in a society without safety nets, the parish-magazine mores were his: no marriage without means. The fear of grinding poverty with a succession of babies made it axiomatic. Even with Nettie coming, the engagement would have to continue 'so long as . . . we can't afford to be married'.[10]

Soon after his 29th birthday he talked at the Royal Institution again, hoping that it would 'earn the Fullerian Professorship for me'. He was desperate for the pay. The wealthy Directors of the Institution could barely credit it: 'what's the use of a hundred a year to him?' asked one. Huxley simply sighed, 'I suppose he paid his butler that'.

He had a gift on stage. He would bend the geometry of a man's arm to produce a bird's wing, or remodel a snail to reveal a squid, showing that all vertebrates, as all molluscs, were variations on a theme, just as the words hemp and *hennep*, or cannabis and *canapa*, were modifications of a mean. But was there a deeper unity to life? Could we connect men and snails the way that linguists connect the words hemp and cannabis, by using known letter changes among the Indo-Germanic races? Yes, by means of the embryo. Von Baer had depicted molluscs, vertebrates and insects starting 'their development from the same point', as similar foetal germs. Words and worms, life was a grand unity. It was awesome stuff for the fashionable audience (which included 'the fair widow Mrs C. Stanley'). The chair looked within his grasp and 'my 30th year begins well'.[11]

How well he hardly knew. The pace of events caught him out. Jameson died and Forbes was called away a couple of weeks later. He left the Government School of Mines in Jermyn Street precipitously, two lectures into his own natural history course. On 25 May Huxley just as precipitously took over, lecturing 'twice a week on Mondays & Fridays'. 'Called upon so very suddenly to give a course of some six & twenty lectures, I find it very hard work, but I like it & I never was in better health'.[12]

Offers now seemed to cascade down upon him. He tramped the circuit, débuting everywhere. As a government employee in Jermyn Street he had no trouble teaching a parallel course for the Department of Science and Art at Marlborough House in mid-June. In July he started at Albemarle Street's City rival, the London Institution, in its imposing Finsbury building – drilling the merchants and bankers with more esoteric lore. (It was founded by business-men looking to the commercial application of science.) His piece-rate pay began to accumulate. 'Six lectures x five guineas' at Marlborough House; 'ten guineas a piece' in the City.[13] Of course the pressure mounted with the money. The strain regularly drove him to bed, exhausted. 'Lecturing you find hard work'? Tyndall asked. 'So do I, no work harder'.

Occasionally the old pain and alienation told in these talks, putting the teeth into his deconsecrated Calvinism. They were bared before the unsuspecting crowds at St Martin's Hall on 22 July. His seemingly innocuous subject, 'The Educational Value of the Natural History Sciences', was in truth ultra-sensitive. He was vindicating in public what he had been forced to justify to George and Fanning in private – the worth of spider knowledge. Physiology promoted health and happiness. But what value worms? Huxley was justifying his existence. His 'Scientific Calvinism' was a modifi-cation of Southwood Smith's in the *Divine Government*, which he had read as a boy. For Smith the prevalence of evil showed that society had strayed from God's intent and needed to be reformed. For Huxley 'Pain and evil' came with a crushing inevitability. They were impartial and inescapable. The physical 'Government of this universe' meant 'that its pleasures and pains are . . . distributed in accordance with . . . fixed laws'. But people needed a wider purview to appreciate it. To see pain 'woven up in the life of the very worms' would help them face it with 'more courage and submission'. His Schamyl-fatalism rationalized a harsh reality. Science offered a 'Carlylean center of indifference', a way of bearing up to war's carnage or nature's wastage.

There was a brighter side, a Romantic ray to pierce the gloom. The overriding happiness and harmony of life were 'refutations of that modern Manichean doctrine, which exhibits the world as a slave-mill, worked with many tears, for mere utilitarian ends'.[14] The universe was one of order. The *Bauplan* of archetypes and the beauty of azaleas were part of its regularity. They were inexplicable in functional terms. Huxley owed a great debt to the Romantic morphology of the 1840s, when the radicals with their immanent archetypes and laws had challenged Owen's conservative idealists, who made them the Thoughts and Desires of a Divine Craftsman. For Huxley, standing at the deathbed of romanticism, *Bauplans* and beauty were secular aspects of nature. But beauty for its own sake? Darwin would say something about that.

*

Even as Huxley spoke the 'oceans of disgust' were receding, leaving an enriched soil. In late July the Director of the Government School of Mines, Sir Henry de la Beche, made his appointment as natural history lecturer permanent. After the years of drifting he had his institutional anchor, even if it 'would have given me £100 a year only'. But Forbes had two other posts at the school. At first the geology professor at University College agreed to take over Forbes' additional course, on fossils, and also his job as 'Chief Palaeontologist', in charge of the museum fossils.

'Happily for me', Hal told Nettie, the professor pulled out, struck by 'a sort of moral colic' as the university frowned on his split loyalties. Huxley wanted this palaeontology lectureship as well (to double his money), but no arm-twisting would induce him to accept the museum job. It was a prestigious post but beyond his interest. Fossils were crucial to a museum of economic geology: the Geological Survey crew mapping the country used them to identify strata and *that*, said a utilitarian de la Beche, led to coal finds and understanding soil types. In short it was a plum job going at the right moment. But not for Huxley, who saw fossil curation as a diversion. So Sir Henry reluctantly upgraded Forbes' blue-collar assistant John Salter, a brilliant drudge – a Gradgrind who knew each of the 10,000 Palaeozoic fossils in the museum – but a prickly evangelical, and unstable. Everybody thought it 'simply ridiculous'. Huxley got the second lectureship,

> and so in the course of the week I have seen my paid
> income doubled. Listen to my title little girl & be in awe –
> I am '*Lecturer on General Natural History at the
> Government School of Mines*' Jermyn S^t . . . So after a
> short interval I have become a Government officer again,
> but in a rather different position I flatter myself. I am
> chief of my own department & my position is considered
> a very good one.[15]

So Huxley found himself in that grand, three year-old palazzo building with its prestigious Piccadilly frontage. On the ground floor was a huge auditorium, lit by six enormous cathedral-like front windows. Upstairs were the exhibits and galleries. Though it had few pupils at first (schoolboys drilled in Latin were ill-prepared to enrol), Jermyn Street was to train an elite core of industrial chemists, metallurgists and engineers. It was run with workshop discipline. Its laboratories analysed ores and coal, its naturalists looked at marine stocks and resources, its geologists surveyed mineral deposits. Huxley, with his anti-utilitarian bent, found himself in the most utilitarian institution in the country. It was to be his Archimedean point, the position he would hold for life, from which he could move the world.

It was a good place to be as the world began to wobble. The whole social ethos seemed to be on the slide. Professionalization was becoming the key in every sector. The lions-led-by-lambs slaughter in the Crimea was to spark an outcry against an incompetent aristocratic high command. Like everyone else Huxley chafed at this 'imbecility' at the top. Why should birth guarantee leadership (and what value leadership with Lord Cardigan commanding the Light Brigade from his luxury yacht in Balaclava Bay)? The sale of commissions was damned; jobs-for-the-boys were damned. Talented men were needed, men honed by competition. A Commission called for Civil Service places to be made competitive. The Inns of Court began to set exams. The ethos affected science, giving technical education a new cachet. In an attempt to tap the 'reservoir of unfriended talent', the Mechanics Institutes were affiliated to the Society of Arts and exams introduced.[16] These years marked a turning point. Patronage was being replaced by opportunity; allegiance to Church and Crown by service to the State. Huxley's men were coming in from the cold.

He was in place, the new-breed spokesman for science, articulate, self-serving and patriotic, with a lashing tongue and laconic wit. Where once was a closed door, he heard creaking hinges. Out came beckoning fingers. He began accumulating posts like a clergyman collecting livings. But he was no absentee vicar. He galloped ceaselessly round his parishes even if, 'as the jockeys say, the pace is severe'. Each letter to Nettie totted up afresh, as if continual counting would prove them to be no phantasms: £200 from Jermyn Street; Marlborough House, 30 guineas; London Institution, 60 guineas; the *Westminster*, 40 guineas; £50 for 'additional Lectures in Jermyn S.'; student fees, '40 or 50£ probably', an offer to teach at St Thomas' Hospital. Then came books: a *Manual of Comparative Anatomy* promised to Churchill, the British Museum's sea squirt catalogue, his book on the oceanic men-of-war (which his friend Edwin Lankester's Ray Society – set up to publish these sorts of unprofitable monographs – had agreed to print). By the autumn he was reckoning on £500 a year. 'A hundred & fifty pounds or rather more will about clear off my old incubus of a debt', leaving enough to 'make ourselves happy in a small way'. It might not carry him far up the slope of gentility, even with income tax at 7*d* in the pound. In fact, a married man 'cannot live at all in the position which I ought to occupy under less than six hundred a year'. But it was an extraordinary turnaround.

Four years after the *Rattlesnake* voyage he had struggled ashore. He took a last backwards glance. 'It has been a strange history that of these past years, full of dreams & nightmares, but I feel now . . . that I have been right in doing as I have done, in spite of all the pain it has cost us'. 'So my darling pet', he ended his letter to Nettie, 'come home as soon as you will – thank God I can at last say those words'.[17]

It was a more confidant government naturalist who set off in August for a holiday in Tenby, on the South Wales coast. Back to the Atlantic spray, to the rich shores of the Pembroke peninsula, where he could banish 'dyspepsias and hypochondrias and all my other Town afflictions'. Three months in this picturesque fishing village saw the landlubber swopping his sallow skin for a suntan, and taking stock among the tidal pools.

Even Tenby became a paying proposition. He had intended to 'do oceans of work' on sea squirts, but Sir Henry – a dab hand at transforming holidays into reconnaissance trips – put him on a piece-rate to survey the depths. A £50 cheque showed that he could do no wrong. The company was good too. With cholera sweeping through Piccadilly (where samples from the contaminated Broad Street pump proved at last that it was a water-borne disease), the city emptied and the Busks and Carpenters joined him. They took a communal cliff-top house away from the fashionable end of town, with their own 'steps down the cliff face to the sands'. More tranquil now, he would rise before dawn to watch the sun appear over the Carmarthen hills. Out to sea the 20-ton smacks could be seen trawling for herring. By day he joined them, dredging in eight fathoms, eating the whelks and dissecting the sea slugs and sea squirts. Then at dusk a stroll to 'see the slant rays of the sunset tipping the rollers as they break on the beach'. It left 'even *me* at peace with all the world'.[18]

He found an unlikely ally in a local doctor, Frederick Dyster. Unstuffy aldermen with penchants for marine worms were not common, and Huxley relished his find. The two scoured the rock pools and the friendship was sealed when Huxley designated their new feathery-gilled tube-worm *Protula Dysteri*. Christian Socialist aldermen were even rarer. Dyster backed the labouring unions and promoted workers' education, and he did his duty with articles on popular science for the *Christian Socialist*. Like the movement itself, he was well-to-do; he had a French maid, a deaf wife and a wealthy practice where the poor were treated free. But Huxley was never able to take the gold chain seriously. Nothing could stop him proposing that the town-father put his paupers to work collecting worms 'at so much a species'. Nor, as they sat by the fire, could he refrain from playing the Devil's advocate, to wit, 'a horrible Sadducee & sceptic in matters moral & political'. It was the honest basis for a revealing correspondence.

Cold weather brought Huxley back, and London closed in. 'Chimney pots are highly injurious to my morals', he reflected, 'and my temper is usually in proportion to the extent of my horizon'.[19] The grind meant swirling his *Westminster* sword. All the great debates got his cutting treatment. He sliced through the 'hot controversy' over extra-terrestrial life, accusing both the Scots Presbyterians (for) and Anglican dons (against) of basing their views of 'the Heavens' on their understanding of 'Heaven'. The new geological worlds at home were more his arena now. The novice palaeontologist pushed deeper into this *terra incognita*. Here too he found the natives squabbling. Murchison's Silurian empire was annexing the strata below. He was incorporating Revd Adam Sedgwick's fossil-rich Upper Cambrian rocks into 'his Lower Silurians', enraging old Sedgwick. It taught Huxley that stratigraphy was a matter of consensus. With impudent delight the tyro who loved a fight played the consummate diplomat: he suggested that the arbitration of 'Brachiopods will be found better than bombs'.[20]

The quarterly column had its theme: the lack of any progress from 'low' to 'high' animals in the fossil record. And he made his reasoning clear. The old cosmogonists, as he put it, wanting a Divine beginning and Six Days of miraculous Creations, had based their geology on 'the Mosaic account – but churchman and layman now unite in admitting that, if Moses were ever really in possession of the laws of geology, they must have been written on the tablets which he broke and left behind on Sinai'. It was quintessential Huxley, sarcasm with a serious point. A landscape dotted with progressionist castles showed 'that the want which' Genesis 'satisfied still lives'. The Owens and Sedgwicks needed an ascent from Silurian fish to Victorian Anglo-Saxons, to prove that man was in the Divine mind at the outset.

But negative facts were shifting sands, and a poor foundation for these towers. No evidence of Palaeozoic people did not mean evidence of no Palaeozoic people. Only a fraction of the world's Silurian rocks had been sampled. True, they revealed an undersea garden of trilobites and crinoids. But no one could infer camels or condors or cities from Pacific dredge samples today. Nor would anyone see the panoply of ancient life until the Silurian continents had been discovered.[21] Huxley was still looking for his Palaeozoic pottery. For him there was no comforting ascent. The fossil record still had no Christian meaning.

Quarter after quarter he delighted and incited. He picked another hot potato. Were the human races cousins, 'varieties of one species', or different species? And did the latter legitimate slavery? The crisis over American slavery was building. 'Uncle-Tom-mania' was sweeping Britain (with $1\frac{1}{2}$ million sales since 1852, *Uncle Tom's Cabin* was the century's bestseller), and Huxley was musing on racial origins – that tinder-box that was shortly to ignite. In an increasingly racist age, when even the *Times* understood the economics of Southern slavery, Huxley was not joining the 'negro' cause. But he damned the scientific apologists of the murderous slave-owner Simon Legree in *Uncle Tom's Cabin*. Were 'the negro . . . a metamorphosed orang' it would not justify slavery. We are 'bound to put down the slave-holder', not because of his 'cousin-hood with his victim' but because this 'brutality . . . degrades the man who practises it'. He warned 'the Legrees of the south' that science would not sanction 'their atrocities'.[22]

Thomas Henry Huxley had emerged a public man. His pieces were hard sea-biscuits for secular consumption. But it was tough going alone. He was over-extended, dyspeptic and in need of a comrade with a barbed pen. He turned to Tyndall, convincing him to take over the 'critical analytical or anything else-you-please-ical' reviews of the physics books, egging him on with the ungratifying observation: 'What idiots we all are to toil & slave at this pace'.[23] Chapman, now bankrupt, had faced pressure to amalgamate the *Westminster* with the Unitarian *Prospective Review* (in which case Huxley would have resigned). To prevent it the atheist Harriet Martineau had put up a £500 loan, which kept the review afloat. Chapman, up and running again, enlisted Tyndall, and the *Review* took on a more uncompromising tone.

The success of Huxley's coterie showed in the way the Royal Society's medals were falling. After Huxley's in 1852 Tyndall was nominated in 1853, and now it was a draw between Hooker and Forbes. These were the champions of his 'scientific Young England', demanding standards and status. Huxley found himself in a 'queer position', faced with a choice between Hooker and Forbes. So he played 'a sort of Vicar of Bray' and voted each way.[24] The 'bauble' in the event went to Hooker, for his work on the distribution of plants, a sad choice given events.

For months Forbes had written from Edinburgh, telling of his huge class and glorying in 'the most wonderful scenery in Europe'. Then all went quiet. He sent one strained letter on 8 November, talking of pain and weariness. Ten days later Huxley found Forbes' brother in Jermyn Street, preparing to rush north. The next morning, 19 November, came a telegraph. Forbes had died in agony at 5 pm. the previous day.

So departed the jovial soul who had made the public Huxley: the man who had eased him into Jermyn Street and on to the British Association boards, who had taught him to dredge and to shout. 'I owe him so much, I loved him so well', Huxley lamented. The autopsy revealed 'a large *chronic* abscess in one kidney', he told Hooker. 'His life must have been hanging on a thread for years'. Huxley performed his cathartic duties, asking Hooker to pass the news to Darwin, writing an obituary for the *Literary Gazette*, collecting for a bust and a 'Forbes Medal' at the School of Mines. But really he was helpless. 'I think I never felt so crushed by anything before'.[25]

In this stunned state, he found himself targeted. A group of Edinburgh professors pressured him to fill his dead friend's shoes. The calls came with indecent haste, days after the death. Its suddenness had led to a scramble, with every 'eminence on crutches' hoping to compete. Not surprisingly, for it was the best-paid natural history post in Britain, an 'El Dorado', Lyell dubbed it. With classes compulsory for medical students, the professor could add £600 in fees to his £1,000 stipend. Huxley half-heartedly entered the list. Professors no longer had to pledge allegiance to the Church of Scotland, but the chair remained the object of sectarian feeling. Still, he told Hooker, 'there is a mortal difference between 200 & 1000 a year'.

'I dread leaving London & its freedom . . . for Edinburgh and "no whistling" on Sundays'. The northern Athens was in decline. Its own tartan army of graduates had marched south to found the London University, now a federal colossus drawing students from the four corners. For them, as for Huxley, London was 'the centre of the world'. As the race hotted up, he cooled even more. He feared turning from a 'genuine worker' into 'a mere pedagogue'.

> I feel much like the Irish hod-man who betted his fellow
> he could not carry him up to the top of a house in his

hod. The man did it, but Pat turning round as he was set down on the roof, said 'You've done it sure enough but bedad I'd great hopes ye'd let me fall about three rounds from the top' – Bedad I'm nearly at the top of the Scotch ladder but I've hopes.[26]

He did fall. He urged de la Beche to hire a 'competent Naturalist' (himself) for the Geological Survey attached to the School of Mines, someone to dredge the British waters. The Director's forte was reconstructing the ancient environments, and Huxley presented his 'Coast Survey' as an aid to this; after all, the distribution and depth of modern shellfish gave the best clue to the habitats of their archaic forerunners. Another £200, he said, and 'I shall be strongly tempted to stop in London'. De la Beche succumbed and persuaded the Board of Trade to give Huxley his additional post.

Huxley threw over Edinburgh. The extra £200 would leave him in comfort. He might have to 'renounce the "pomps & vanities"' on £700 a year 'but all those other "lusts of the flesh" which may beseem a gentleman may be reasonably gratified'.[27]

His brief – to assess Britain's marine resources – would enable him to become 'something better than a Caledonian pedagogue'. And his pay put him up with the top-earning 'British Cuvier', Richard Owen. Huxley's plans took on their own Cuvierian grandeur. He dreamed of his own faunal empire, of organizing networks of collectors and having 'every species of sea beast properly figured & described in the [Survey's] Reports'.[28]

Nettie had seen out the old year visiting ships, looking over the *Waterloo* and booking cabins. She had packed amid scares of Russian ships sighted off the Heads. She would sail past new harbour fortifications, leaving behind her old colonial life. Hal expected her in May 1855. 'I look forward to our marriage as the beginning of life in its proper sense', he wrote. And the beginning of their properly delineated roles. 'You shall teach me something of your gentleness and patience . . . and I will teach you something of the great problems that are stirring the world'.[29] He rented them a narrow terraced house, 14 Waverley Place, St John's Wood, ten minutes from George and Polly's. Three floors allowed plenty of space for his library and dissecting room. The *Eyre Arms* on the corner was a mixed blessing, but otherwise it was a quiet cul-de-sac and well placed, just off the Finchley Road, with its Atlas omnibus into town.

With Nettie sailing, Huxley launched into his courses. A new classification became their basis. He had dispensed with the classic four branches of animal life – the four endorsed by the old gods of the Elysium, Cuvier and Von Baer, and still taught by Owen. Huxley's *Rattlesnake* shufflings led to five sub-kingdoms. The single-celled animals were separated off as Protozoa (a category common in Germany); he was finally calling his jellyfish and men-of-war Coelenterata – their two membranes, now termed endoderm and ectoderm, being like the earliest embryonic layers of the next group, the Vertebrata; molluscs he left; and the last, the Annulosa, was stuffed with insects, crustaceans, spiders, millipedes, worms and starfish. But not even this questionable lumping stopped him denouncing Owen's 'thoroughly retrograde' alternative.[30] From day one his students were subjected to a provocative view of life, delivered in blistering tones.

His London Institution talks in February and March 1855 were no less radical. The syllabus promised to knock any number of comfortable conventionalities: 'Vital Forces' were placed at the molecular level, plants and animals were made identical at the nucleus level, individuals were made to exist in many parts, 'Progressive Perfection' was called a will-o'-the-wisp. One City stalwart, the librarian Edward Brayley, 'who knows a thing or two more than God almighty', thought it 'the most heretical Syllabus he has seen'.[31]

His City duty done, he declared himself 'sick of the dilettante middle class' and turned to the cloth-caps.[32] De la Beche, an 1830s radical swearing by merit and education, ran yearly lectures for artisans. On winter nights hundreds packed the huge ground-floor auditorium, paying 6*d* to sample each professor in turn. The plebeian thirst for 'bread, knowledge and freedom' had not abated, and the jammed theatre at night contrasted to its half-empty state by day.

Dyster put Huxley in touch with the Christian Socialist educator Revd F. D. Maurice, and Huxley sent a block of tickets to his Working Men's College in Red Lion Square. Others trying to tame socialism came to him. Charles Kingsley was a Hampshire rector famous for *Alton Locke* (an evocative novel of hovel life). His new book, *Glaucus; or, The Wonders of the Shore*, was a moral tale masquerading as a ramble among the Torquay rocks. It was muscular Christianity to fire the hordes on their first train ride to the seaside. Huxley was reviewing *Glaucus* when its author tapped on his museum door. Kingsley had scorned Lewes and the *Leader*'s overture, fearing the taint of 'bigamy and atheism', but he grasped Huxley's hand. These theologians had impeccable credentials. Maurice had been sacked from King's for demoting Hell to a temporary holding cell, and Kingsley was a votary at 'Nature's shrine'. He could turn science into poetry and a stammer into a 'brilliant flash of words'.[33] His Anglican unorthodoxy was appealing, even if he justified change to save the status quo, and if his 'clods' were taught that 'true socialism, true liberty, brotherhood, and true equality (not the carnal, dead level equality of the communist ...) is only to be found in loyalty and obedience to Christ'.

Huxley's audience was taught something different. The tub-thumper was preaching old-time hellfire. He damned this 'idola-trous age', this society,

> which listens to the voice of the living God thundering
> from the Sinai of science, and straightaway forgets all that
> it has heard, to grovel in its own superstitions; to worship
> the golden calf of tradition; to pray and fast where it
> should work and obey; and, as of old, to sacrifice its
> children to its theological Baal.

Evangelicalism fired his sermon. He was turning the heathen to righteousness, making Science the Path. Maurice's co-operators swelled his audience – working-class socialists who were becoming interested in spiritualism after failing in the 1840s to create a democratic, co-operative society, in the hope that the spirit forces would put the nation back on its Millennial track. 'The theatre holds 600 & is crammed full', he reported. 'I believe in the fustian & can talk better to it than to any amount of Gauze & Saxony'.[34] But his words were an exorcist's and branded the spirit-rappers.

Infidel socialism was rampant on the factory floor. The extent of working-class atheism told as parsons urged bosses to sack freethinkers, often to find that they were the entire workforce. It told in the census revelation that only half the nation went to church, and next to none from the ghettoes. It told in the three days of rioting this June against a Sabbatarian Bill to stop London's Sunday trading. But most of all it told in the pauper press. Utopian socialist editors attacked 'Priestcraft' and promoted democracy. Demagogues looked through Lamarckian spectacles at fossil life rising by its own exertions, pushing the animal chain 'from below' (a 'power to the people' metaphor). And atop the chain, they saw humans progressing towards a bright co-operative future.

Huxley's workers were familiar with this indigenous street science. On corners, vendor hawked *The London Investigator* in 1855, with its evolutionary propaganda on the 'Origin of Man'.[35] This was gutter science to smash the Anglican state. 'Knowledge is power' was no idle slogan bandied about in illegal prints. Agitators demanded a progressive, technical education to ready them for the day they took control.

Such artisans converged on the school. But its teachers were supplanting this street literature. Huxley genuinely wanted 'the working classes to understand that Science & her ways are great facts for them'. He too believed that science could reveal history's moral. It

> prepares the student to look for a goal even amidst the
> erratic wanderings of mankind, and to believe that history
> offers something more than an entertaining chaos – a
> journal of a toilsome, tragi-comic march no-whither.

Then whither? Not to Millennial Peace, a global Harmony Hall. He had 'no confidence in the doctrine of ultimate happiness'. Nor would nations cease their conquests. News of the slaughter at Sebastopol, flashed home by telegraph, was proof in point. The bitter Dr Knox (reduced to living as an itinerant hack after the Burke and Hare scandal) was doom-mongering about the 'inexorable laws of racial antagonism'. And even Huxley saw the Crimea as part of a centuries-long 'trial of strength' between the Turkish and Russian races 'now being finally decided'.[36]

On the other hand history did not sanction a clerical state, backed by a Bible as a sort of 'special constable's handbook', as Kingsley had it. An 'active scepticism' ensured against such tyranny; doubting was a duty when all knowledge was provisional.[37] Science was only knowledge well organized and well tested. And that made Nature's own education the best guide.

Physiological laws provided the precepts of behaviour. They demanded obedience from the masses, said Huxley pulling a corporation face (writing to Alderman Dyster). He would show 'that physical virtue is the base of all other, and that they are to be clean & temperate & all the rest, not because fellows in black with white-ties tell them so, but because these are plain & patent laws of nature' – in short, drunkenness brings its own destruction.[38] Nature was the new moral sanction. And the new professionals –

trying to transform values as much as the old priests – would ensure that the querulous classes were bound by its judgments. The switch from priests to professionals left the unemancipated almost where they were.

For Huxley, the only way forward was a competitive, technocratic society, with the science professionals at the helm.

Some workers argued back. Most were enthralled. A few complained of the gobbledegook, being used to the fiery clarity of their own orators. But it only aided the tyro in honing his technique. The plebeianizing of Huxley's prose would be a long, dialectical process.

He emerged from his courses exhausted, debt-free for the first time in 15 years, to find Nettie off the English coast. His anxiety gave way to 'desperation at the continuous East Winds'. But on 6 May 'a westerly gale' blew and his heart leaped at the thought of their meeting. It had been five years since that night in Sydney when he dashed for his ship. For five years they had not spoken. For five years they had not seen one another's face. 'I am another man altogether & if my wife be as much altered, we shall need a new introduction'.[39]

The westerlies brought them together, the ecstatic moment coming days later. They touched for the first time since 1850. They wrapped themselves in each other's arms, emotionally choked, together again. But the moment was overshadowed; his idealized image of her, forged from years of longing, was shattered. She *was* altered, terribly; her features were drawn. She had been ill in Sydney and badly served by a quack; and violent gales on the high seas had made her worse. 'Oh this life!' he groaned, the devil 'mingles with all our happiness'.

He installed her parents close by in Regent's Park, and settled her in at George and Polly's, where she could have rest. She needed only care. Dashes between lectures were now punctuated by visits to her. 'God help me. I discover that I am as bad as any young fool who knows no better'; but for the lectures 'I should be hanging about her ladyship's apron strings all day'.[40] As she improved his cynicism gave way to gaiety, leading students to wonder what had become of his 'philosophership'.

It was the best of times, as Nettie recovered and more of the world fell his way. '1000 congratulations' Hooker pealed, referring to Nettie but also welcoming the *enfants terribles* – Huxley, Tyndall and Busk – into the Philosophical Club (that dynamic dining-circle-cum-think-tank inside the Royal Society). Hardly *enfants* any more, terrible or otherwise; they were over 30 and becoming established. Hooker in May became his father's assistant, given a house next to Kew Gardens where he could 'plunge into the Haystacks' of dried Himalayan plants. And they were bending Huxley's 'scientific Young England' into shape. The learned bodies were awash with new blood and Hooker hoped that the infusion would 'resuscitate' even the comatose Linnean. He was fighting the obstructionist 'old fogies' here and complaining of their 'imbecility'. Plans were laid for the tighter vetting of manuscripts, open discussion of papers and dedicated zoological and botanical *Journals*.⁴¹ The gentlemanly ethos was doomed.

To confirm his meteoric rise, Huxley joined Tyndall at the Royal Institution. In July he took the Fullerian Professorship for three years, putting another butler's wage in his back pocket. 'May the gods continue to drop fatness upon you', Tyndall jollied him, and may the 'next great step' be all 'your . . . rebellious heart can desire'.

His rebellious heart was being tamed. With Nettie improving the bachelor was heard chanting, 'Oh that there were no such things as pots & pans'. On £800 they could marry and move into Waverley Place immediately. Phebe Lankester was overjoyed at seeing the tearaway 'tied up'. Carpenter sent his 'intense condolence' along with a *'walnut-wood* book-slide' and inquired 'the time fixed for execution'. 'I terminate my Baccalaureate & take my degree of M. A. trimony (isn't that atrocious?) on Saturday July 21', Huxley laughed. Even he shared the ubiquitous Victorian sense that the brute was being humanized. 'After the unhappy criminals have been turned off there will be refreshment provided for the sheriffs, chaplain & spectators'.⁴²

Sir Henry preferred his hammerers single, an unattached corps devoted to the rocks. But should the unfortunate happen, he was not averse to dispatching lieutenants on surveying honeymoons (both Forbes and Salter had put on boots and taken their brides to north Wales). The wheelchair-bound De la Beche had died in April, but the ethic lived on. Huxley told Dyster to expect the newlyweds in a Tenby dredge by late July, 'and I am ready to lay you a wager that your vaticinations touching the amount of work that *won't* be done, don't come true'. 'So much for wives – now for *worms* . . . '⁴³ With 63 year-old Murchison, the Tory 'King of Siluria', taking over the Survey, Huxley saw uncertainty ahead and advised Dyster, as his 'right reverend father in Worms & Bishop of Annelidae', to publish elsewhere.

Nettie had stepped off the boat straight into a brawl, the first in a line that would last her married life long. 'There is no doubt I have a hot bad temper', Hal had warned her. 'If I hate a man, I despise him', and he detested no one more than Owen. Huxley's slick whipping of Owen in the *Vestiges* review had caused everyone to draw breath. 'By Heavens', Darwin whistled, 'how the blood must have gushed into the capillaries when a certain great man (whom with all his faults I cannot help liking) read it!'[44] It did; Huxley and Owen toppled into a petty world of tit-for-tat. Denunciations flew thick and fast. Arcane anatomical disagreements over the lamp-shell's heart blew up as the wedding preparations proceeded and Owen's *Lectures on the . . . Invertebrate Animals* was published with a snipe at Huxley's 'blindness'.

'Busk and I *roared*' over Owen's 'absurdities', wrote Carpenter five days before the ceremony. He egged Huxley on, having no love of Owen's idealism. As a Unitarian Carpenter accepted immanent natural causes for all mental and physical events; and although his image of fossil specialization was like Owen's, *he* believed that life's progress would one day find its material explanation. Carpenter sent a swift warning of the slur so that, 'if you wish to call him out, you may do so *at once*, rather than after the honeymoon is over'. He offered himself as a second. The 'best proof you can give of your full possession of eyesight, will be to put a bullet into some fleshy part of your antagonist'.[45] No intellectual duel marred the event. But it was a foretaste of things to come.

The banns had been read at the local Anglican church, All Saints, on the Finchley Road. And so, after an eight-year engagement – during which they had seen one another for a matter of months – the day arrived. Saturday 21 July 1855 was a perfect summer morning. The dull and rather large church looked brighter for the flowers. In the pews sat everybody who meant anything to Tom: his brothers, the Heathorns, Fanning's parents. There were the haggard Ellen (and presumably an opium-hazed Cooke) and his scientific confidants Hooker, Carpenter and Tyndall. 'As we knelt at the altar, he holding my hand to his lips', Nettie recalled, 'a great beam of jewelled light fell upon us from the coloured windows'. The sweet moment was savoured. She gazed at her new name in the registry book through 'a mist of amazement'. At last 'we had reached the Promised Land'.[46] Her parents gave a quiet breakfast at North Bank and that afternoon the newlyweds set off.

It was a leisurely trip to Tenby, with lashings of summer rain. Via Oxford and Warwick they went, then down to Stratford to see

Shakespeare's tomb before crossing into Wales. At Dyster's for a fortnight Hal was so doting that the French maid called him *un vrai mari*. The couple took lodgings in August and became a regular 'Darby & Joan'. They looked the part: on warm mornings he would carry Nettie to the beach (she was too weak to walk over the rocks). But Darwin's warning that 'happiness, I fear is not good for work' was unduly pessimistic. Dyster lost his bet – by early August Nettie was a Survey widow as Hal took to the dredge. He left her with the visiting Busks, and she caught up with the lost years talking to Hal's Egyptian priestess.

No Darby and Joan were ever so bizarrely occupied. Each morning Dyster popped in 'and found us in the back verandah my husband, coat off & shirt sleeves tucked up dissecting' a dogfish, pulling a new tapeworm from its gut 'whilst I wrote down its description'.[47] She refused to be excluded, however incongruous a honeymoon it turned out.

To complete his Survey report Huxley taxed the quarrymen working the limestone 'bone caves'. But it was a nearby drowned forest, emerging at low tide, that provided the best opportunity for understanding the process of fossilization. He dug around the trunks, knee-deep in silt, studying plant interment and slicing sections for Hooker.

He sailed on two or three days each week, his tiny boat dwarfed by the trawlers. Reaching mid-Channel his catch piled up: a new flatworm, bristle worm, crustacean, tapeworm and sea squirt. Through heavy seas he pulled as the months turned chilly. At night he would trudge home cold, thinking it 'wonderful how light the house looks', ready to dissect his haul.[48]

A dissection mirrored his life, fast and brilliant. He assimilated in days what took others months, including Darwin. On 11 August a piece of flotsam drifted into harbour covered with goose barnacles, *Lepas*, their blue-tinged shelled bodies connected to the driftwood by a stalk. Barnacles were in the limelight. Not long before they had been ranked as molluscs (they did look like mussels). But the barnacle was, 'in reality, a Crustacean fixed by its head, and kicking the food into its mouth with its legs' – those wafting feathery feet familiar in the acorn barnacles on seaside rocks. The sedentary barnacles were related to the shrimps that scurried around them. Knowing this, Darwin had been reappraising the group since 1846. He had ended up with 1,100 pages of dense monographs and a reputation as the blinkered 'Professor Long' in a Bulwer-Lytton novel. Nine years' work brought a startling conclusion: that a duct leading from the stomach was an ovary and, even odder, that part of the ovary produced cement to glue the adult to its rock! He sent a sceptical Huxley his preparations. But two days with his flotsam *Lepas* and Huxley had detected the 'true ovaria' in the stalk.[49]

The heartaches were over. By 1855 the 30 year-old had achieved those goals that had inspired him for eight years – marriage and a job in science. Or three jobs; he had shot past his peers and was vying with the top earner Richard Owen, about to become the new £800-a-year head of the Natural History Collections in the British Museum. Huxley was brusque, daring, clubbable and energetic, rubbing shoulders with Lyell's knights of science at one level, pulling the bearded working classes behind him on another. His power was growing, on the council of the Royal Society, in the reviews, as the ubiquitous 'Professor' popping up on every platform. He was as sharp as his scalpel, Darwin said, 'a very clever man'. But Darwin did wonder where Huxley's *science* was going – it seemed to be directionless.

Darwin had been sending monographs intermittently, and using Huxley as a conduit to the German zoologists. They were still fairly distant, and only in 1855 did Darwin's address soften from 'My dear Sir' to a warmer 'Dear Huxley'.

Huxley's drift was worrying. The bulldog pup was straying in the wrong direction. Darwin chuckled at the 'exquisite & inimitable' way he handled 'a great Professor', but this back-slapping concealed more than it revealed. Owen's fan-like, ramifying image of fossil life actually suited Darwin's evolutionary purpose. It was Owen – not Huxley – who was unwittingly playing John the Baptist to Darwin's Christ. Darwin tried a gentle remonstrance. He thought Huxley 'rather hard on the poor author' of *Vestiges*. And Huxley's denial of any progress in the fossil record left Darwin positively 'grieved'.[50] Huxley was proving himself a brilliant disappointment.

It was time to invite the tearaway to Downe for a 'pumping' session.

215

12

The Nature of the Beast

HUXLEY'S EMOTIONAL TYRANNY turned to tenderness inside the family. *Un vrai mari* he was, upholding family virtues, disdaining Chapman's libertinism. Not that it was a conventional household: Waverley Place was unremittingly scientific, what with 'his occupation, his friends, his books'. Nettie 'attended little by little' becoming, like so many scientific wives, an unsung helpmate. She sketched, translated and proof-read. By morning she would blow up diagrams, then 'a hasty lunch, & [with] the cab at the door I would be just in time to get them hung at the Royal Institution'.

Thus the girl whose pleasure had been poetry entered a 'Fairy Land of Science'. She brought intellectual strengths. 'In this utilitarian day, when the old forms of spiritual existence which once ennobled mens lives are become effete', he agreed, one must 'cherish the ideal in the world of Art'. And wasn't Nature herself ultimately

> a poem; not a mere rough engine-house for the due keeping
> of pleasure and pain machines, but a palace whose
> foundations, indeed, are laid on the strictest and safest
> mechanical principles, but whose superstructure is a
> manifestation of the highest and noblest art.

Hal, more and more the mechanical engineer, trotted Nettie around the foundations, giving disquisitions on the unseen forces and eternal verities, and the universal truths embodied in the tiniest diatom. Bit by bit she came to understand 'the great problems that underlay the dissection of even a fish or plant, or the identification of a fossil . . . It was a revelation that ennobled the world I lived in'.

All the while she healed his emotional wounds, switching from invalid to nurse. Hal was crushed by headaches after lecturing. As he charged through the animal kingdom, clawing power by clawing knowledge, the stress built up. He was forced to spread himself wide over physiology, palaeontology and marine zoology, not knowing in 'what branch of science I should eventually have to declare myself'.

Money remained tight as he met his debts and paid his dues. 'Societies & Clubs' cost him 'a mint'. There was one more now, as he joined the Survey men, sitting as a block in the Geological Society. The squeeze threw Nettie onto her own resources:

> My bush life in Australia had taught me to turn my hand
> to anything so that I could cook, paper a room, polish a
> floor, and make a dress & make myself generally useful.
> Owing to this I was able to get on quite comfortably with
> two maid servants and [had] many a pleasant little dinner
> with just [a] few guests in my dining room. From the first
> Dr Tyndall was the most intimate and in a short time we
> were Brother John, brother Hal, and Sister Nettie to one
> another.[1]

Herbert Spencer lured Huxley out for walks; Hooker came with 'Bloaters & . . . Pears'. Mercury himself, now Lieutenant Sharpe, dropped by with feather flowers for Nettie in January 1856, recalling old Sydney days.

But word of another messmate was chilling. MacGillivray had 'damned himself', abandoning his wife and children and shipping back to Australia. He had been drummed out of the Service as an alcoholic and was living as a down-and-out. Huxley found his wife sick with consumption, on to 'her last shilling & contemplating the workhouse'. He collected £50 for her passage home. At least with parents in Australia 'there will be more hope for her children than in an English poor-house'. It was the decent thing, putting a little money into her hand and seeing her aboard ship. Later he heard that she had died two weeks away from Sydney.

The sight of social wrecks had him craving support. Home was a sanctuary, its traditional values his security. Hence Hal and Nettie's staid roles: he would lead, be 'your guide as well as your lover'. Hers was the soothing balm, to ease the pain as he battered at authority. He would smite the Amalekites and she 'help me . . . in my battle'.[2] 'Battle' said it all. His psychology was adversarial.

He had to confront some embodiment of evil. So past the portcullis of Waverley Place he rode, his lance pointing at Belial himself, Richard Owen.

The lance struck Owen's *Lectures*, to Carpenter's cheers. In a slashing review Huxley slated Owen's zoology as old hat and his self-glorification as unseemly.[3] Partly it was brinkmanship, the angry *parvenu* showing his superiority. Partly it was pique – his own work having been ignored by Owen and his protégés. Whatever, the die was cast. However much was 'good & kind' in Owen, Huxley would now draw out the worst.

Although in part it was personal animosity, in reality the brawling was a bloody repercussion of the ideological divide. Huxley's clique was carving a scientific profession. Old patrons were snubbed as the young Turks fought for self-determination, old theologians abused as they made a show of dissociation. It was to be a self-validating profession. No split loyalties would be tolerated: clerical geologists were like 'asses between bundles of hay', Hooker said. Hence Huxley's hatred of Owen's 'unscientific realism of "Archetypal Ideas"'. It turned Nature's patterns into God's thoughts and surrendered the lot to natural theology. The new men needed an enemy to give cohesion to their ranks. And the imperious Owen was perfectly cast.

Owen was settling into the British Museum in 1856. But onlookers jibbed at his plans. 'Of course Owen would be the Autocrat of Zoology & Palaeontology', Carpenter said. Patrician dictatorship was no model for professional science. He must be made accountable 'to a body of scientific men, who are competent to estimate and criticise his proceedings'.[4] Duty to colleagues as much as to facts was explicit in the call for higher standards. Old-style patronage had to be replaced by peer review and state sponsorship.

Owen was the best palaeontologist in Britain. He had written 100 books and papers on fossils alone, christening the dinosaurs, studying the first mammals, describing fossil reptiles, New Zealand moas and Australian marsupials. Palaeontology was approaching its Victorian apogee – in a few decades 40,000 fossil animals and plants had been named. It was the equivalent of finding a new continent of creatures, underground. The rise and fall of ancient dynasties was generating intense public excitement, making this subterranean world the place to be.

Huxley now swept into palaeontology too. At first he was

pushed by the job. On taking over, Murchison had found no proper fossil catalogues. Salter was ineffectual, prone to depressions and fits of 'self-righteous piety', which everyone blamed on his 'damned religion'. His assistant William Baily kicked 'at everything like order & discipline'. So Murchison asked Huxley to take on the work. Huxley set out to master the fossil collection over the winter so as 'to be *no* longer at the mercy of my subordinates'.[5] And so he ended up doing the palaeontologist's job that he had originally turned down.

In the *Westminster Review* Huxley kept nudging 'higher' life back in time, convinced that there had been no progression. He would hail the world's oldest reptile, found by Lyell in the Nova Scotia coalfields during his American tour.[6] Or he would show that ancient trilobites were just as complex as today's king crabs.

Darwin watched. The last straw came when Huxley mauled even his friend Carpenter's evidence for a progressing fossil life. Carpenter's ancient life was more generalized. And so was Darwin's – but his ancients were *real* ancestors. Transmuting through aeons of time, adult animals had gone on specializing while the embryos remained largely unmodified, retaining their ancestral looks.[7] To Darwin it made evolutionary sense.

He was worried enough to meet Huxley head on – to hear first-hand his doubts about fossil progress. Darwin canvassed a meeting at his Kent home. He organized these periodic 'pumping' sessions, when younger naturalists were taxed (but not told why). At Downe Darwin could control events without putting himself in jeopardy. Here society had to accept him on his own terms.

Others were lined up. The Hookers were to arrive on Tuesday 22 April 1856. Hooker was a long-time confidant, one of the few to be let into Darwin's belief in transmutation ('it is like confessing a murder', Darwin had told him in 1844, and given the gentry's fear that such a bestial science would aid the socialist levellers it must have seemed like a criminal betrayal). At first Hooker had dismissed transmutation. But after being bombarded by Darwin for ten years he was teetering. 'Oh dear, oh dear', he sighed, 'my mind is not fully, faithfully, implicitly given to species as created entities *ab initio*'. With some trepidation, he was coming round to Darwin's '*Elastic* theory'. At any rate, the idea of 'Creation' was 'no more tangible than that of the Trinity & . . . neither more nor less than a superstition'.[8]

For almost two decades Darwin had been sitting on his theory.

He had conceived it in 1837–9, during the tumultuous years of riot, recession and clergy-baiting, when the squires saw themselves holding a lid on a seething, slum-ridden cauldron. It was reforming Malthusian science for a reforming poor-house age. It was also revolting to a besieged Anglican elite. The creation of species was proof that God intervened in Nature, as through the clergy He was supposed to intervene in society, upholding the paternalist order. To deny God's intervention invited catastrophe. 'Once grant that species' mutate, Darwin himself wrote, and the 'whole fabric totters & falls'. His mentor Revd Adam Sedgwick blamed the French Revolution on such 'gross (and I dare say, filthy) views'.[9] The quiet, affable Darwin risked being branded a class traitor. It was a sickening dilemma. So the recluse had kept his peace for two decades, drafting his wife a note, asking her to publish on his death. Perhaps he would rather have died first.

The years had seen some changes to his theory. Barnacles had taught Darwin that species were *'eminently* variable'. He now knew that variation was the rule, rather than the exception. This meant that competition between the variants operated constantly, not only when the environment fluctuated. He also had a better idea of how a species splits into two. Just as factories employed a specialist workforce, nature favoured a division of labour. Competition pushed variants to seek new openings. They diversified like skilled trades in a market, rubbing shoulders but minding their own business. Darwin, a laissez-faire Whig with a portfolio of industrial shares, saw the same laws shaping the creation of wealth as the production of life. By 1856 his factory metaphor was complete.

The time was right for him to go public. Democratic reforms had put Dissenters into the Town Halls. Unitarians now donned mayoral regalia, advancing their rational, cause-and-effect views of nature, unlike the old supernaturalism. As the Duke of Wellington had feared, power was passing from the Anglican gentry to cotton kings and shopkeepers, 'many of them [Unitarians and] atheists'.[10] Accelerating production left the country feeling prosperous. Society was quiet, people were optimistic. The Chartist scare had evaporated, and with it Darwin's fear of being branded a traitor. The recluse, part-Unitarian himself, was emerging into a safer world. A world where *Westminster* reviewers hailed evolution and Huxley's clique was poised to take power. The moment was opportune. At this gathering he would test the waters.

Another to arrive was the rector's son Thomas Vernon Wollaston. He was a good barometer of conservative feeling: well-to-do, a Cambridge man, currently arranging his beetles in the British Museum. Studies on Madeira had shown him that isolation and climate change could cause beetles to vary. This limited 'power of self-adaptation' was the thrust of his new book *On the Variation of Species*. At Downe Darwin hoped to lead him further. Counterbalancing Wollaston should have been the Tory-hater Hewett Watson. A fierce radical, he was applying fashionable demographic techniques to plant populations. Watson would need no leading; like many atheists he was a transmutationist already, a 'renegade', in Hooker's words.[11] Only his failure to turn up prevented the sparks flying.

Huxley was squeezed for time, with a Royal Institution talk on Tuesday 22 April and a lecture on the Friday. Then there was the inaccessibility of Darwin's hamlet. Although only 16 miles from St Paul's, Downe was the 'extreme verge of [the] world', and chosen by Darwin for that reason. But Darwin promised his carriage at Sydenham station for the nine-mile drive. And with illness the norm at Downe, Emma added that Nettie 'sh^d. have a comfortable arm-chair in her bedroom, so as to live upstairs as much as she liked'.[12]

Hooker was eager to get Huxley along. But *he* wished to talk strategy. He wanted to bring 'about more unity in our efforts to advance Science'. They now had 'sufficient command over the public, as Examiners'. They were even penetrating rival headquarters. (The War Office had Tyndall and Huxley testing candidates for Royal Artillery commissions.) As he spoke their grip was tightening. Carpenter was about to become the new high-profile Registrar of London University. It meant resigning his Examinership in Physiology and Comparative Anatomy, leaving Huxley to step in.

They talked of a corporate shield to protect their gains. Professional status meant ousting the 'pitiful botchers'. It meant controlling knowledge through their own journal, getting science into the classrooms, forming a club – some 'intellectual resort' where they could sojourn.[13] Ultimately, it meant selling themselves as knowledge-brokers. The men on their way to Darwin's were marking out a profession. They were distancing themselves from the vicar-naturalists, sneering at the Cambridge old boys. And, incongruously, awaiting them at Downe was squire Darwin, Cambridge-trained for the Church and about to provide their legitimating philosophy, a naturalistic science of creation with a competitive edge.

The Huxleys travelled on Saturday 26 April, across the chalk Downs, less desolate with the arrival of spring. Their first visit found Downe a sleepy hamlet of thatch and timber, where farm hands doffed their caps. Near by stood a magnificent new mansion, 'High Elms', testifying to Sir John Lubbock's banking fortune. (Darwin would cajole Sir John, London University's first Vice-Chancellor, into backing Huxley as an Examiner.) Down House itself was an ugly brick building fronting on to a small lane, which Darwin had brazenly lowered to protect him from view. It was big enough for his brood of seven, and a perfect rustic retreat. The inside had a frayed, lived-in look. There was little opulence to show for Darwin's fortune; nothing to suggest that he had just sunk £20,000 into the Great Northern Railway, or owned a farm in Lincolnshire.[14]

To Darwin, Huxley was a man of jutting jaw and searing wit; brilliant on a podium, or so he had heard. True, he was no naturalist, no Gilbert White, however fearsome an invertebrate anatomist. Above all he seemed brash and self-assured. Darwin, for his part, was never quite what he seemed. Apparently hearty, he was invalided by incessant vomiting fits. Seemingly outgoing, he was always self-absorbed. And his days ran like 'clockwork' amid a chaotic mess of skeletonized pigeons and dismembered ducks.

Emma Darwin, his wife, was the granddaughter of the pottery patriarch Josiah Wedgwood. She was a little severe, religious, well educated and musically talented (having studied the piano under Chopin). At Downe she fulfilled her parish role, dispensing bread tokens to the poor and gin-and-opium concoctions to the sick. Their home too was a hospice, where she doctored her sick husband. That Saturday they dined at seven, with Emma shepherding relays of servants. The banker's son John Lubbock joined them – very much Darwin's protégé, already dissecting waterfleas and their eggs and following Huxley's work closely.[15]

The next morning came the pumping. Darwin sat in his study near the marble fireplace. Behind him was a book-lined alcove with tiers of pouches, into which he popped notes. At the window a mirror allowed him to spy visitors coming up the drive. Here he was secure, and he had his questions ready: why did Huxley not see fossil animals as more generalized? Trace back today's single-toed horse and we arrive at the small, three-toed Eocene herbivore *Palaeotherium*, with its full set of teeth.[16] Could he not imagine following it further back to some primitive five-toed mammal?

And why did he deny that ancient animals could be intermediate between living groups? Didn't the camel-like *Macrauchenia* that Darwin had pulled from a Patagonian cliff-face point equally towards modern llamas and tapirs?

No. Huxley's answers were inscrutable. He never shared Darwin's field approach, where competition led to progress – or his utilitarianism, which made every structure serve some end. In fact Huxley did not think in terms of *origins* at all. Geometry, not genealogy, fascinated him: the surreal beauty of nature's secret architecture. Species were not to be explained historically, by messy mutations and supposed progression. They had to be appreciated as abstract anatomical patterns. Even then his image of their configuration was bizarre. He pictured species clustered on the surfaces of spheres, each with its central archetype. No animal was nearer the centre; none was more general; fish, reptiles, birds and mammals were all equidistant from the abstract vertebrate type.[17] Molluscs had their distinct sphere, as did coelenterates. And with the spheres unconnected no trilobite could illicitly jump the gap to call itself a fish.

Darwin was nonplussed. He did not tip his hand, simply saying 'that such was not altogether his view'.[18] Huxley had constructed a cosmos of Ptolemaic perfection, of crystalline spheres, brittle and useless to Darwin. He was not thinking in historical terms at all, of bloodlines, family trees, lost ancestors and the kinship of life. His was a defunct world of sublime impenetrability. It might have given no concession to Christian apologists or rabble-rousing Millennialists, but it was no less absurd to Darwin.

After lunch came a walk. Darwin would lead the way in his great coat. It was a beautiful stroll, through acres of gardens. Ten year-old Georgy and young Franky charged about playing Crimean War games. As with Darwin, the gardens were never what they seemed. The greenhouse was packed with saltwater tanks full of seeds, pods and dead birds with stuffed crops, which took some explaining. It was one of his brilliantly humdrum experiments. He was proving what botanists had doubted: that seeds could survive the crossing to oceanic islands, to start the process of colonization.[19] They did not need lost continents to travel over. Summoning up some missing Atlantis (as Forbes had done) to convey British seeds to the Azores struck Darwin as ludicrous. He had pepper seeds surviving five months in brine, long enough for currents to carry them across.

Next door was his real pride, the fancy pigeons. Come, see

them, he said, 'the greatest treat ... which can be offered to [a] human being'. He had 90 birds and every British breed. The aviaries were aflutter with cooing tumblers and pouters with ballooning breasts. Darwin's quirkiness must have struck Huxley. With his hatred of pottering dilettantes, he hardly knew how to take this farmyard science. Pigeons were a labourer's hobby, Darwin admitted it. He supped with pipe-smoking fanciers in gin palaces, picking up tips, 'hand & glove', he said, with 'Spital-field weavers & all sorts of odd specimens of the Human species'. He had an ulterior motive. His Nature was composed of myriad tiny variations. He was showing how skilled artisans could accentuate the slightest variation through selective breeding, pinching and bustling to build new strains, turning an original dove into the equivalent of 'fifteen good species'.

To confirm it he measured beaks and bones. I 'am watching them outside', he explained ghoulishly, '& then shall skeletonise them & watch their insides'. Decaying carcasses were strung up, and a 'fetid odour' rose from rotting corpses in retchmaking potash solutions. Everyone's flesh was creeping, even Darwin's: 'It really is most dreadful work'.[20]

Darwin's reason for starting this grisly business would have struck Huxley as even more horrifying. Darwin wanted to show that hatchlings were 'more normal' than their coiffed parents, that they were more generalized and nearer to the ancestral form. He was working on the premise that individual development held a mirror to ancestral history – that history, like embryology, was a case of increasing specialization. The work was a direct rebuttal to Huxley himself.

The guests ambled on. Hooker and Huxley resumed their planning. Darwin tried to whittle away at Wollaston's faith in immutable species. But for Wollaston beetles only varied *within fixed specific bounds*. To suggest that they broke these bounds and transmuted into new species was 'monstrous'. Darwin's work posed a moral 'danger': it denied God's intervention, that guarantor of the Anglican status quo.[21] Darwin's hopes were dashed and he later recoiled bitterly. Nothing was so 'rich, considering how very far he goes, as his denunciations against those who go further ... Theology is at the bottom of some of this. I told him he was like Calvin burning a heretick'.

After the guests left Darwin unpicked Huxley's objections. Huxley himself came away with no inkling of Darwin's theory of natural selection, but he sensed change in the air. His next *Westmin-*

ster column praised Hooker and Wollaston. These pioneers were tackling the 'chaotic assemblage of facts' about animal and plant distribution. According to Hooker's *Introductory Essay on the Flora of New Zealand*, half of the 100,000 known flowering plants were probably varieties; and Wollaston had shown how malleable insects were. Could these variants continue changing until they became new species? Hairline cracks were ruining Huxley's spheres. For the first time he conceded 'that the whole subject of the influence of climate, habits of life, and other external conditions, as well as of the capacity for variation inherent in each type of form, requires a thorough re-investigation'.[22] It was a small step, the first in a long march to a new world – a world far more hospitable to a rationalist ideologue. Darwin noted it. He logged the 'change in Hookers & Huxley's opinions', and he planned to draw these young Turks further into his heterodox camp.

A garbled account of the meeting had Huxley shifting further. Lyell heard that the Sunday plotters 'grew more & more unorthodox'. Word had it that the entire group laughed at the notion of immutable species. But not so: transmutation for Wollaston remained morally dangerous, and for Huxley geometrically difficult. Others refused to believe that Darwin himself would stretch varieties too far. Lyell's in-law Charles Bunbury, another Cambridge-trained squire, doubted that Darwin would 'assert an *unlimited* range of variation: he would hardly, I conceive, maintain that a Moss may be modified into a Magnolia, or an oyster into an alderman'.[23]

He would. Three weeks later Darwin laid plans to publish his theory after the years of waiting. The world was tumbling. Lyell was desperately rationalizing the birth of humans from ape parents; and at the Philosophical Club he found Huxley, Hooker and Tyndall veering towards transmutation. It showed in Huxley's lectures, running in the *Medical Times*. They had a quizzical air: if each species came from a 'single pair', whence that pair? 'Created' – what does that mean?

> . . . we have not the slightest scientific evidence of such
> unconditional creative acts; nor, indeed, could we have such
> evidence; for, if a species were to originate under one's very
> eyes, I know of no amount of evidence which would justify
> one in admitting it to be a special creative act independent
> of the whole vast chain of causes and events in the universe.

And assuming a natural emergence 'there can be no doubt that some form or other of that hypothesis – not less abused by its supporters than by its opponents – called the "Theory of Progressive Development" will present by far the most satisfactory solution'. The words were published on 17 May, three weeks after the Downe meeting. Huxley realized he had been wrong-footed. He was turning, knowing that his secular needs could be well served by transmutation (which could be opposed to supernatural creation), even if it had no jot of 'demonstrative evidence in its favour'.

Could individuals be successively modified? After the Downe weekend he saw no reason why not. After all pigeon breeds differ 'as widely from one another as do many species'.[24] Darwin had taught him that.

Huxley's about-face warmed Darwin. He devoured the lectures. So did Hooker, who found them 'overwhelming', 'like the old Scotch wife who said, "Ae, it was a grand discourse, I couldna understand the ane half of it"'. But it was not their 'revolutionary' nature that struck Darwin. It was Huxley's gall. He mauled Owen in the lectures. Mere mention of his name had 'the old adam in T. H. H.' rising to fight, such 'is the nature of the beast'. Owen's 'Archetypal Ideas' were consigned to oblivion; his parthenogenesis was denounced and his classification derided. Then came a dig at Ehrenberg's 'pertinacity'. Every tyro, of course, had 'to raise his heel against the carcase of the dead lion', but Huxley was baiting the living pride. The lectures were 'too vehement' for Darwin who held to an older etiquette. Huxley had hoped to be put up for the Athenaeum Club, the haven for London's literati. But in Darwin's eyes the butchery made blackballing a real possibility, especially with Owen voting.

> Cannot you fancy him, with a red face, dreadful smile &
> slow & gentle voice, asking, 'Will [you] tell me what M^r.
> Huxley has done, deserving this honour; I only know that
> he differs from, & disputes the authority of Cuvier,
> Ehrenberg & Agassiz as of no weight at all'.

Brilliant science was not enough. The Athenaeum stood for talent and character, not talented character assassination. The lectures stayed Darwin's hand: 'we had better do nothing, to try in earnest to get a great Naturalist into [the] Athenaeum & fail, is worse than doing nothing'.[25]

The problem was 'the way our friend falls foul of every one'.

Darwin was thinking of another with his feathers ruffled. Hugh Falconer was fresh from the plaster-white City of Palaces – Calcutta, that 'belvedere of a ruling race'. The Director of the botanic garden in the imperial capital had made his name resurrecting a Miocene menagerie from the Siwalik foothills of the Himalayas, everything from gigantic giraffe-like *Sivatheriums* to the first-known fossil monkey. Darwin found the repatriated Falconer 'indignant' at Huxley's attack on the prince of palaeontologists, Georges Cuvier.

Cuvier had made function the be-all of animal structure, and British theologians then made perfect structure the proof of a Wise Designer. What of the common plan among vertebrates? Huxley taunted the old fossil hod-men. It had no function. He queried Cuvier's boast that, because all the body parts were functionally integrated, he could build an entire beast from a single bone. What if Cuvier had found a fossil bear's bone? Would he construct a flesh-eating polar bear or fruit-eating brown bear?

Falconer rose to the challenge, relating the teeth of his Siwalik bears to their different habits – then came fossil hogs and dogs. He showed in each case how the body's organs are correlated and co-adapted to a specific lifestyle. Pick any part and you can predict the rest. He finished with Cuvier's prize fossil from Montmartre: part of a crushed skeleton which this 'law of correlation' had shown to be an ancient opossum.

The raptorial Falconer talked 'as if he had eaten Huxley without salt & left no bones at all'. But Huxley's bony frame lodged in Falconer's craw. Huxley rammed his point home, that no one could predict the number of a lion's teeth from its stomach. One had to consult the feline blueprint; this had been built up methodically from a study of all the big cats, and 'no further reason' for this pattern could 'be given than for the law of gravitation' (ruling out a theological gloss). 'By Jove', chortled Darwin, Falconer 'will find this pungent'. And in his new Fullerian course, Huxley promised to take 'Cuviers crack case of the 'Possum of Montmartre as an illustration of *my* views'.[26]

Huxley was honing his skills as a controversialist. All knew it. The tyro was mugging the old men. It was a job he relished, trashing reputations and received wisdom – and perhaps essential work if Darwin's big book was to sweep the world before it.

Darwin himself ground on, terrified at going public, wishing '*most heartily*' that he had never started. He was on to the 'causes of fertility', a huge chapter which would stretch 'to 100 pages MS.' Huxley was taxed on hermaphrodite jellyfish. Did these cross fertilize, rather than impregnate themselves? Surely so, for inbreeding must doom an animal in the 'severe struggle for existence'. How then? Did sperm accidentally wash into the mouth? A ribald Huxley thought the 'indecency of the process' was 'in favour of its probability, nature becoming very *low* in all senses' among the jellies. It fitted Darwin's image of a profligate, wasteful nature, based on overproduction and struggle, with success going to the best variants or breeding accidents. Perfection, design, the old certainties were dead, along with a vicarage view of life's buzzing contentment. Nature's depravity and violence screamed against a sublime Providence. Huxley's reply had Darwin blurting out, 'What a book a Devil's Chaplain might write on the clumsy, wasteful, blundering low & horridly cruel works of nature!'[27] There was no 'might' about it. Darwin had donned his satanic surplice, his Bible for a new nature was under way, and some of Huxley's cynicism was rubbing off.

In August an exhausted Hal escaped with Nettie to the Alps, on the principle that recuperation came from a hard climb. Lectures were also racking Tyndall, who joined them. (A fellow teacher at Jermyn Street, the geologist Andrew Ramsay, should have gone with his young wife Louisa, but Huxley had so 'alarmed Louisa by ... his want of faith' that 'she worked herself into a fever' and they cried off, fearing what he might say half way up the Matterhorn.)

The crystal-tipped peaks served an aesthetic need, but the drive was initially intellectual: Huxley and Tyndall wanted to understand the veined structure of glaciers. And Huxley was fulfilling a dream. The sub-tropical Curral Mountain on Madeira had whetted his appetite and he was dying to see snowy summits. From Basle's cathedral belfry they espied the Alps, and with elated irreverence each scratched a line on its great bell:

> The biggest bell
> Twixt heaven and hell
> this tongue can tell.

At Interlaken they hired two donkeys, sat Nettie on one like '*Sancta Maria*', and with a fussing Hal '*der heilige Joseph*' marched to Grindelwald. They trekked on, the scenery breathtaking, through the Wengern Pass, stopping at a primitive wooden inn below the Eiger, where they lay awake listening to the booming avalanches.

By now Nettie, who was five months pregnant, was barely able to move, so they settled her back at Interlaken, while Hal and Tyndall took off for the Rhône Glacier. Alpine climbing was entering its heroic phase; the great peaks were unconquered; ropes and picks were rarely used, only an alpenstock (walking stick). But on the ledges Tyndall's wiry tenacity came into its own. He was one of the most 'daring mountaineers you ever saw,' said Huxley, so 'we have christened him "cat"'. Reaching the 'ice cliffs', they scaled an adjacent rise, crossed on to the glacial crags and ate their 'frugal dinner in a manner which made the pomp of emperors poor'; 'indescribable magnificence', was Tyndall's exclamation. Looming up was 'the mighty mass of the Finsteraarhorn', and behind it the Matterhorn 'rose like a black savage tattooed with streaks of snow'. The Irish pantheist was rhapsodic: 'the shadow of the Finsteraarhorn caused the vapours to curdle up, and to flow with great velocity into the valley of the Rhone. Here however the sun still shone, and the vapours were licked up as fast as they came'. Huxley was euphoric: the massive grandeur sent the psyche dwindling and giddy. The two kept climbing, until Huxley's shoes were 'knocked to pieces'. An excruciating 11-hour ascent to Riffelberg revealed 'the most glorious sight I ever witnessed', a cloudless view of the Matterhorn. The splendour carried him home, where he was 'monomaniacal on the subject'. It was 'one of the most thoroughly successful undertakings of my life'.[28]

The momentum swept him on. No sooner back than he tramped off again, through the fishing villages of north Devon and Cornwall, then over to Wales, studying raised beaches for his 'Report on the Recent Changes in Level in the Bristol Channel'. He thrived on it 'so long as I walk eight or ten miles a day'.[29] It kept him out of smoggy autumnal London, out of the fray. The Caldy cliffs energized him, put a spring in his step, a cocky note in his voice. And he sounded it on his arrival home.

'There is going to be a set-to at the Geological' on 5 November. 'The great O. versus the Jermyn St Pet, on the Method of Paleontology'. But on Bonfire Night Huxley found himself the Guy, caught in his attempt to blow-up Owen and Cuvier's autocratic parliament. Owen produced a precious inch-long jaw with three molars – all that was known of one of the first mammals, the Jurassic *Stereognathus* – and all that was needed to deduce its nature. Owen pictured it as a tiny pig relative, and then his tone changed.

Stereognathus was functionally harmonious and predictable because prehistoric nature was a progressive expression of Divine
Intelligence. That was the issue – life's wise design. He glared at
Huxley and the temperature rose. Deviants who denied it manifested 'some, perhaps congenital, defect of mind'. These were
deviants who perverted 'the Young'; 'Lucretian' misfits whose
'doctrine subversive of a recognition of the Higher Mind' threatened Anglican society and called for 'prompt exposure'.

Word of the flare-up reached Hooker, who told Darwin:

> Owen I hear committed a cutting telling & flaying alive
> assault on Huxleys adaptation views at the Geolog. Soc.
> & read it with the cool deliberation & emphasis & pointed
> tone & look of an implacable foe. – & H. I fear did not
> defend himself well (though with temper) & perhaps had
> not a popular champion in Carpenter who barbed him.[30]

The festering hatred meant that relations could never be normal-
ized, even without the ideological divide. The rolling scrap took
Huxley through the birth of his son. In the emotional build-up he
did resolve to make amends: 'to give a nobler tone to science; to
set an example of abstinence from petty personal controversies'. It
was New Year's Eve 1856. He was twiddling his fingers, full of
good resolution but directionless. For three years he must continue
mastering every branch of biology and geology:

> 1860 will then see me well grounded and ready for any
> special pursuits . . . In 1860 I may fairly look forward to
> fifteen or twenty years 'Meisterjahre,' and . . . I think it
> will be possible in that time to give a new and healthier
> direction to all Biological Science.
> Half-past ten at night.
> Waiting for my child. I seem to fancy it is the pledge
> that all these things shall be.
> Born five minutes before twelve. Thank God. New
> Year's Day, 1857.

His mother named the Christmas boy Noel. He had her looks,
'large blue eyes golden curls clear fair skin & regular features'.[31]
But would the pledges made in his honour be redeemed? '1860 will
show'.

14. The landlubber swanking down the Park Road in London. Success at last after receiving the Royal Society's Royal Medal in 1852 for his *Rattlesnake* researches.

His early scientific friends:
15. (*left*) Edward Forbes;
16. (*below*) George Busk;
17. (*bottom*) W.B. Carpenter.

18. (*Above*) The hawk-eyed Huxley in 1857.

19. (*Left*) Tom and Nettie on their honeymoon. Never a moment lost, Huxley spent it dredging in Tenby Bay, South Wales.

PICCADILLY FRONT OF THE MUSEUM OF ECONOMIC GEOLOGY.

20. (*Above*) The Museum of Economic Geology attached to the School of Mines in the heart of Piccadilly, where Huxley was to teach from 1854.

21. (*Opposite, above*) Richard Owen, the brilliant comparative anatomist, and Huxley's lifelong rival.

22. (*Opposite, middle*) Owen's weasel-like reptile *Galesaurus*. This fossil suggested that mammals had reptilian forebears.

23. (*Opposite, below*) Owen teaching in the auditorium of the School of Mines in 1857. He proclaimed himself 'Professor' here, causing Huxley to sever all relations.

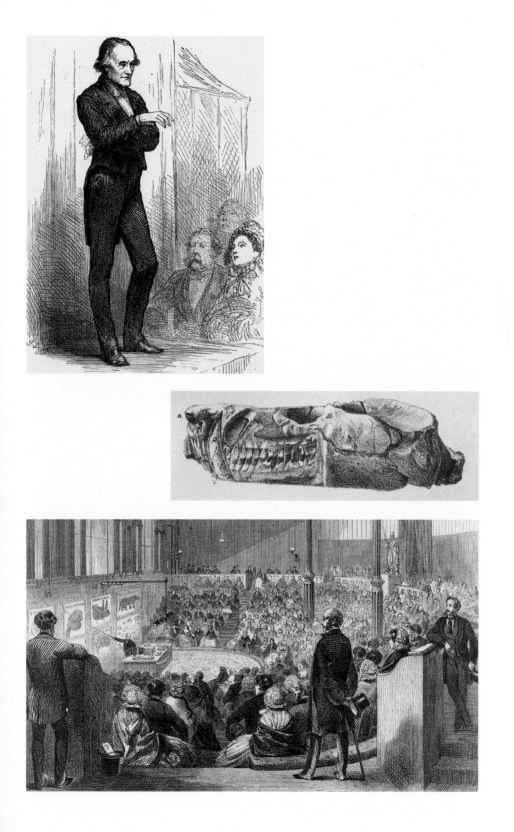

24. (*Above*) The gallery of Huxley's Museum in Piccadilly.

25. (*Opposite, above*) Huxley raging against the world - or at least the *Pall Mall Gazette*, with Tyndall looking on in trepidation.

26. (*Opposite, below*) The Irish physicist John Tyndall, whose own flamboyant pantheism caused a storm. Tyndall and Huxley 'formed a sort of firm' in the public mind.

27. Charles Darwin, shortly to start writing the *Origin of Species*.

13

Empires of the Deep Past

BABY NOEL WAS 'JOLLY to a degree'. But his father's resolution about avoiding controversy quickly crumbled. It couldn't have been otherwise. Huxley's cadre was moving into power, but everywhere they met Owen's imperious presence. What the scientific parvenus lacked in social strength they made up in moral posturing: hence Huxley's hallelujah, that finally 'the Lord hath given this Amalekite unto mine hands'.

Owen was to deliver guest lectures on extinct animals in Jermyn Street. His talks always attracted the Good and Great. It was galling to see them swan through the school, sundry lords, the Duke of Argyll, Dr Livingstone, fresh from the Zambezi, to be shown the 'intelligence of the Creative Power'. On the strength of this Owen announced himself as 'Professor of Comparative Anatomy & Palaeontology, Government School of Mines' in the *Medical Directory*. That was effectively Huxley's title and he took it as a slap in the face. 'Of course I have now done with him', Huxley seethed in January 1857, 'I would as soon acknowledge a man who had attempted to obtain my money on false pretences'.[1]

While Owen drew the socialites, Huxley retreated among the cloth caps. The flyposters for his working-class lectures were drawing crowds of 500, 'and the fellows are as . . . intelligent as the best audience', in fact 'they *are* the best audience . . . & they react upon me so that I talk to them with a will'. And he took pains to make them 'participants in my train of thought – not to shove information down their throats as if they were Turkeys to be consumed'.

Word of his lecturing prowess was out, the excitement, the controversy. His Fullerian audience doubled. Hooker sat in. So did

Herbert Spencer. Having published *Principles of Psychology*, which unashamedly embraced 'the genesis of mind in all its forms, sub-human and human', Spencer expected much from Huxley's topic, 'The Physiology of Sensation'. So much so that he did the outrageous for a man who absorbed facts through his skin: he bought a notepad.

'I will make people see what grandeur there is . . . in Biological Science', Huxley said of this course. And what uncertainty. He led his audience through a maze of dissected nerves and severed heads and abandoned them in a philosophical void. He taught that idealism (mind is the only reality), materialism (matter alone exists) and dualism (the two somehow interact through the human conduit) are all unprovable and irrefutable positions. 'I can fancy your turning round . . . as the Israelites did upon Moses and asking "Why hast thou led us out into the wilderness to die?"' But he was kicking away the philosophical crutches on which the gouty gents hobbled, those who castigated materialists as 'knaves'.[2] (They had their reason: artisan atheists, by denying a spirit world and abusing a corrupt clergy, had given materialism a seditious air.) Huxley was legitimating a responsible new breed of experts, the Tyndalls and Playfairs, Carpenters and Darwins, men who studied the material causes of culture and cosmos.

What interested him more and more now were fossils. He started another course for his students, but it took the inevitable toll. Headaches plagued him; 'its no joke', he told Dyster. 'My miserable body is getting shaky again notwithstanding early rising and a six mile walk every day'. 'Oh for a deep breath of a westerly gale on Caldy cliffs'.[3]

By the late 1850s fossils had become central to the debates over creation. Singular new ones were being construed in innovative ways. Owen set the pace. He had come to visualize a continuous creation, rather than so many separate acts. For him Divine Will animated Nature, pushing it forward continuously. 'Natural Law' was short for 'God's Fiat' and His writ runs smoothly now, as it has since the Beginning. Proof of its contingent action lay in life's rambling progression and spread into every niche. No transmutation could explain this, no inexorable Lamarckian ascent.

One fossil Owen hailed as spectacular: the metre-long amphibian *Archegosaurus*. This heavy, salamander-like creature from Bavaria's Carboniferous coalswamps was the most important find since the pterodactyl. Owen announced at Jermyn Street that it connected the fish and land vertebrates, 'linking and blending' them. He talked of the 'march of development' from lungfish via *Archegosaurus* to the first land-living amphibians.[4] This disclosure in Huxley's school on the eve of the *Origin of Species* shows how ready Owen's palaeontology was for an evolutionary gloss.

British expansion in South Africa allowed Owen to announce another surprise. After the Boers had trekked out of the scrubby Karroo plateau, army roadbuilders moved in. They found the region 'richer in fossil remains than it was ever thought'. Huxley was on the Geological Society Council when Owen exhibited one ferret-sized reptile skull with unheard-of features: nipping incisors, stabbing canines and chewing molars. This was a mammal's dentition! The 'weasel-reptile', *Galesaurus*, Owen dubbed it, admitting that the predator made a most 'suggestive approach to the mammalian class'.[5] It was the first hint of an unknown group of extinct mammal-like reptiles.

'Annectant' amphibians and progressive reptiles: these concepts fired the imagination. The age gave them life. As Owen envisaged a creative stream, so Spencer turned it into a torrent. From stellar development to steam power, all was a blur of forward motion. For millennialists biological development held the promise of future perfection. Many a night Huxley and Spencer walked home together, Spencer praising the 'beneficent necessity' of evolutionary and social progress. It was a stop-go walk as the cosmic philosopher was knocked down and 'continually got up again'.

Britain's own mood was buoyant. Industry and the 'economic miracle' left per capita income twice that of Germany. The export of machinery to the rest of the world was staggering, and when the railway engineer Robert Stephenson died his body was borne past throngs of silent mourners to Westminster Abbey. After the Indian Mutiny of 1857 the crown had annexed the East India Company's land. The Queen now ruled India. Great credit booms financed new companies, putting more people into work. Forty thousand commuted daily into London, which was already seized by traffic jams. As incomes rose Samuel Smiles proclaimed in his *Self-Help* that any virtuous Briton could become a gentleman. Social progress seemed inevitable, the end point of a cosmic evolutionary process.

Bold works shouted it. Henry Buckle's *History of Civilization* had society rising like fossil life, shaped by circumstance, subject to statistical laws. Buckle typified the revolt against an aristocratic history driven by Divine whim. 'Buckle the Great' (as Huxley mocked him) was another 1840s radical grown respectable, now speaking the *Westminster*'s language. He articulated its climactic belief in 'one glorious principle of universal and undeviating regularity'. Whether the vital phenomena of life or the vital interests of society, Huxley quipped, every 'disorderly mystery' was becoming an 'orderly mystery'.⁶

Buckle's was the first of the mythopoeic extravaganzas, a gigantic tome with its replacement naturalistic cosmogony. Spencer would perfect the technique, leaving Darwin and Huxley to fill in the fine texture and Tyndall to capture the cosmic warp and weave. Credos were becoming the rage.

Presidents of the Geological Society caught the mood. It affected spry 63 year-old Colonel Portlock (Huxley's backer for the fellowship). Portlock was a veteran of the 1812 War with the United States. He had a 'frame and nerves of iron' but no Iron Duke mentality. Acts of Creation were outmoded, he announced in his Presidential Address. Nature was no Absolute Monarchy, ruled by Divine caprice. God was a sort of Divine Samuel Smiles, helping Nature to help itself. Owen's 'march of development' suggested that new life was continually created by the 'action of physical circumstances'.⁷ With Presidents paying court, Owen looked supreme. An early *rapprochement* of his 'speculative Palaeontology' with Darwin's theory seemed likely.

The succession of species had to be explained, and Huxley was now as adamant as Spencer that transmutation was the only option.

At this point Darwin posted fragments of his 'big book', *Natural Selection* as he was set to call it. Odd pages arrived, glimpses that gave no sense of the whole. Darwin was 'like Croesus overwhelmed by my riches'. Each point – the overproduction of life, the random appearance of variants, their struggle for resources and the survival of the best (this sequence was the gist of his theory of 'natural selection') – would be bludgeoned home by bountiful examples. Through 1857 he ploughed, proving that 'large genera' (those with many species) are expanding and the 'manufacturing' sites of varieties. Nature was a superior Spitalfields weaver. He picks feathers, she screens 'every nerve, vessel & muscle; every habit, instinct, shade of constitution'. Nothing got past unless 'it gives some advantage'. Put less anthropomorphically, limited resources force the variants into a civil war. On the battlefront, the less fit are slaughtered and only those with an edge live to found new dynasties.

Such competitive individualism was part of the age. Tennyson's life 'red in tooth and claw' had wiped the smile off nature's face. Only from 'death, famine, rapine, and the concealed war of nature' could 'the highest good' come, 'the creation of the higher animals'. Perfect adaptation was a delusion, part of the defunct argument for a wise design. Individuals were blemished and locked in a struggle. A bloodthirsty leer crept over the face of Nature. Darwin's sickness seemed in keeping. The grind was racking him. The fear of breaking cover stretched him taut and occasionally he snapped. His retreats to a Farnham spa became more frequent, and the sanatorium doctors found him a pitiful sight, 'crushed with agony', sick and shaking.[8]

He would ask Huxley to verify a 'little point'. Did the specialized organs emerge first in the embryo? He would send the relevant pages without 'troubling you . . . in what way the case concerns my work'. (Not surprisingly with Darwin tying up embryonic development and evolution.) Darwin was still intimidated; nor did Huxley's mordant wit reassure him: 'The animal body is built up like a House', he replied, first the frame, not 'the cornices, cup-boards, & grand piano'.[9] Paragraphs were tricked out to inoculate *Natural Selection* against this sort of sarcasm.

Darwin did confide his 'heterodox notions', saying that classifica-tion should 'be simply genealogical'. For him reptiles, birds and mammals were the living tips of the vertebrate tree, whose dead trunk stretched back into the remote past; they inherited their common features from the same, extinct, fish-like ancestor. But Huxley – though looking at fossils these four years – still thought timelessly. He had trouble breaking away from the archetypes, those common-denominator abstractions around which all ani-mals, living and fossil, might be clustered. Classifying was not about 'pedigree & possible modifications', he replied. The 'pedi-gree business' had 'no more to do with pure Zoology, than human pedigree has with the Census'.[10] Classification was an arrangement for the living, not an appeal to the dead.

Huxley still had to be convinced by Darwin of a branching evolution. True, he held Darwin in high esteem. In class he called the 1,000-page barnacle book 'one of the most beautiful and complete anatomical and zoological monographs which has ap-peared in our time' ('you will turn my head', Darwin replied). But the monograph was descriptive. *Natural Selection* would be an-other matter, an evolutionary tome with a utilitarian core.

To sway an anti-utilitarian with a venomous bite was never

going to be easy. Huxley denied the 'doctrine that every part of every organic being is of use to it'. What of the hummingbird's lustre? It had no purpose, save to give nature's poem a beautiful cadence. Sea urchin shapes might tickle our geometrical fancy, but it was 'absurd' to think that they 'are any *good* to the animals'.

> Who has ever dreamed of finding an utilitarian purpose in the forms and colours of flowers, in the sculpture of pollen-grains, in the varied figures of the fronds of ferns?

Darwin had, and he cringed. So was beauty created for humanity's sake?, he asked in *Natural Selection*. That would 'be fatal to our theory'.[11] Are the fantastic shapes of rotifers for microscopists to admire? No, they are useful to their owners, or had been to their ancestors.

It was imperative to turn Huxley. He was a force in his own right, a charismatic leader. His *corps dramatique* was breaking into the old coteries. Huxley's presence in the societies was felt even when he was not a member, as at the Linnean. This had just moved to the prestigious Burlington House, near his Piccadilly museum. Before meetings he would dine with Hooker, Carpenter and Busk, the new secretary, to plan the old dame's facelift.

He was also helping to reshape London University, that educational 'Holy Roman Empire' with its catholic embrace of colleges. The science departments were fragmented and spread among Medicine and the Arts. But these time-honoured faculties of Arts, Theology, Law and Medicine were 'utterly inadequate' by 1858. No longer could 'Academic bodies' afford 'to ignore Science as a separate Profession'. With material progress the new Messiah, it was an emotive plea. 'What knowledge is of most worth?' echoed Spencer. 'The uniform reply is – science'. What do the ironworks cry out for? asked Carpenter – trained chemists. Tyndall, Lyell and Playfair were equally voluble. The pressure paid off. In 1858 the university created the first Faculty of Science and B.Sc. degree, complete with its progressive cachet.[12]

Huxley's word counted. His star was rising and about to twin Darwin's in the firmament. Together they were elected to one of the most prestigious scientific bodies in Germany, the Imperial Academy of Naturalists in Breslau, 'God forgive them', laughed Hooker. It was Darwin's first European accolade. Hooker told Huxley not to 'get intoxicated on the honour!' But that did not stop him from 'standing upon [his] head'.[13]

The 'cotton millennium' had found its scientific prophets.

Huxley and Tyndall were firing imaginations in a world 'where nothing need remain unknown' and everything could be bettered. They enthralled listeners, whose second sons with their B.Sc.s would keep Might enslaved to Right. Their prospering audience had grown up with steam, gaslight and change. They sped on 60 mile-an-hour expresses, their life a blur of motion, like Turner's *Rain, Steam, and Speed*, thrown out of focus by the hurtling engine.

Dickens inevitably linked 'science and the public good'. And in 'an age of express trains, [and] painless operations' 'such as our grandfathers and grandmothers never dreamt about', the telegraph was 'the most wonderful'. The major towns were connected. Submarine cables ran under the English Channel. Yet the ultimate challenge remained an Atlantic cable. In the summer of 1857 Dayman set off in the frigate *Cyclops* to fix the route. Huxley versed his surgeon on ocean-floor dredging.[14] Within weeks Huxley was examining the mud, a pale-coloured ooze from 12,000 feet (composed of myriad raspberry-shaped shells, all that remained of minute planktonic creatures called *Globigerina*). As he studied this shelly silt, wondering if he was gazing at the source of the world's chalk rocks, *Cyclops* and the 'Wire Squadron' set off in the first (unsuccessful) attempt to feed out an Atlantic cable.

A couple of weeks later Huxley arrived home from his second onslaught on the Alps, bedraggled but with his shakes steadied. Lightning trips were possible now, with a rail link depositing him at Geneva in 39 hours, 'weary but triumphant'. He had gone to confirm his doubts about the supposed fissures permeating glaciers. But it was an emotional sojourn among the ice cliffs. Tyndall was there, fraught himself, suffering a 'rascally brain'. With him was a mathematical friend, Thomas Hirst, dragged away after the burial of his young wife. Climbing had become a drug to ease life's pain, and it was 'a set of dirty sunburnt snowblind wretches' who emerged from their ascent of Mont Blanc. Or in Huxley's case two-thirds of an ascent; only days after arriving he was out of training and stuck at 10,000 feet, where he bivouacked 'on a pinnacle like S^t. Simon Stylites – & nearly as dirty as that worthy saint must have been'. Here he perched, alone for 17 hours, the desolate glory of the snowface sharpening his anxiety as the others became long overdue. Nettie heard how the madcap Tyndall had managed to conquer the summit in treacherous conditions. 'See what you gain by being a bachelor', she wrote to him. 'No vision of a wife to restrain you from glory – or a snowy burial'.[15]

Huxley charged at aphids the way he charged at the Alps, horns out, treating Owen as a great monolithic impediment.

One major article would wind up his invertebrate work (he was now moving wholly into fossils). Hooker and Busk wanted progressive papers on the Linnean agenda, and Huxley arranged his finale here on 5 November. It was a brilliant explosion on aphid parthenogenesis. 'Polemically', he told Dyster, 'it was . . . the most effectual smasher that has yet come down on the "neb" of my Eminent friend'. The languid-looking Owen was pelted for his 'ignorance writ large'.

It was another case of ideological worlds colliding. To Huxley and a generation of gutsy rationalists Owen's views were archaic. He accepted a residual 'spermatic force' in the female aphid, who continues to deliver (as do her offspring) without mating, until it is exhausted. Some attenuated force!, laughed Huxley, when the progeny of one aphid after ten generations could weigh (were they all to survive) more 'than the whole population of China!' Mystical forces infuriated him. These 'intellectual opiates' no longer soothed the scientific brain. Do gunners explain 'the propulsion of a bullet by saying it was "trigger force"?' Huxley saw the asexual broods on his geraniums as so many buds or zoöids, and their production curtailed by cold weather, not spent spirits.

The paper went off to Darwin, 'profiting by a weeks rest & hydropathy' at his spa. Having long done with 'life-forces', he loved this demolition work. But like all of literary London, he was agog at Huxley's temerity. In fact 'your Father confessor trembles for you'.

Tit-for-tat hatreds were now structuring every move. Huxley, as George Eliot observed, was inordinately reactive, and Owen as stubbornly responsive. Aphids might not amount to much on the cosmic scale, but Man was the measure of all things. Huxley and Owen, the mandarins of science, were moving towards the apotheosis. Lyell might have rationalized the first humans 'stealing quietly into the world', sired by apes, but Owen had not.

Darwin was deep in *Natural Selection* when Owen seized the initiative. Our brain was so distinct, he said in 1857, that he was divorcing mankind from all other mammals. Henceforth we would keep our own select company in a crowning new subclass, the Archencephala ('ruling brain'). Darwin, an unbudging relativist, wondered 'what a Chimpanzee w^d. say to this'.[16] More to the point, what would Huxley?

Owen was a senior statesman of science, fêted by Oxford University with an honorary Doctorate, decorated by the French with the Légion d'Honneur. No one knew more of apes. He had been dissecting London Zoo's corpses since 1830. The orang's foot showed that it could not stand erect and be counted a man, and the chimp's brain that it lacked the intelligence anyway. Every aspect of their prognathous faces and quadrumanous frames emphasized the unbridgeable chasm 'between *Man* and the *Ape*'. Only people were adapted to house 'a rational and responsible soul'.[17]

Owen was sensitive on the issue. Lyell was agonizing over an ape ancestry when the crunch came: news of a human-sized 'oak ape' *Dryopithecus* from French Miocene rocks. 'If Man was develop.^{d} out of any ape it was from the Dryopithecus', Lyell gulped, '& a million or more of years have been required for it'. The fossil was so human-like that 'tho' extinct perhaps for a million years' it might fool students in their College of Surgeons exams.[18] It didn't fool Owen. He was horrified, dismissing the creature as a gibbon and Lyell's suggestion as silly.

The burly Owen was built to stamp on such nonsense. He shared the fears of his Oxbridge patrons. Lamarck's suggestion that apes had only to move on to the plains, stand to see, free their hands and enlarge their brains to become men and women was execrable. What of morality? Was reason only the better part of brute instinct? The very hint would poison society. Moral responsibility was a gift carrying the promise of future rewards. Remove the fear of damnation and what is to stop the masses from rising up to redress their grievances? Species might turn over, but it was no self-creation. A caring Providence worked by other means.

The strains became visible with the début of a new ape. The gorilla, black and 'indescribably fierce', had not been known long. Owen himself had four tribal-fetish skulls obtained from an old ship's captain. They were daubed in sacred paint, making that 'scowling physiognomy' look even more menacing. But stabbing canines and overhanging brows were marks of the unreasoning brute.[19] These 'forbidding' beasts were not men in the making.

The militants on the streets were already heralding mankind's monkey origin. They learned about the latest finds in the pauper press and the worker-run Halls of Science in the industrial cities. Red Lamarckians saw life pulling itself up unaided – monkeys turning themselves into men, and men transforming their own social troop. There was no God on high delegating power through his clergy. Tory churchmen still saw Creation as the Divine sanction of the status quo. For this reason atheist demagogues – like Robert Cooper and the *Reasoner*'s sub-editor John Watts, who toured the country talking on the 'Origin of Man' – gloated over human ancestry.[20] Apes were paraded in their penny-trash papers and a new ape was grist to the mill. (The first gorilla seen alive had been sold as a chimp at Liverpool docks in 1855. It drew gawping crowds with Wombwell's travelling menagerie, the mistake only being discovered when it was stuffed.)

Hence the gentry's fears. Where would moral authority reside if man did not come from his Maker's hands? The squires looked to Owen. Britain's foremost comparative anatomist was well connected. He had seen his portrait hung alongside Cuvier's in Sir Robert Peel's gallery and he joined Gladstone for breakfast. Owen reassured them that no hideous parody could dull the lustre of the divine species. But a Cambridge don persisted: how does the anatomist explain human superiority? Is the hand or tongue really that different, 'or is the mind working on almost the same anatomy'?[21]

That was the problem. So Owen switched to a cerebral approach. Humans were moral agents and must have unique brains. In 1857 Owen (undoubtedly aware that Darwin was writing his 'big book') pointed to the huge cerebral hemispheres. They overlap the cerebellum, extending so far back, he claimed, that they divide into a unique third lobe. Into this extends a cavity (the 'lateral ventricle') with a peculiar 'posterior horn' and a singular structure projecting from its floor, the 'hippocampus minor'. No one knew what they were for, but apes, Owen claimed, lacked them. He seemed to have found the peculiar pieces to justify mankind's rational uniqueness.

Huxley was flabbergasted. Owen's classificatory edifice stood 'like a Corinthian portico in cow-dung'. Huxley's group believed that Owen had made a colossal error. They assumed that his preserved ape brains must have hardened into distorted shapes (although Owen was aware of the problem).[22] 'Man . . . as distant from a Chimpanzee' as 'an ape from a platypus!' exclaimed Darwin. 'I cannot swallow' that.

In 1858, as London Zoo received its first preserved gorilla in a cask, Huxley added a new lecture to his Royal Institution course. Not so much a lecture, 'The Distinctive Characters of Man' was a broadside which would prove decisive in the Darwinian debate. Behind him were pictures and brains, with humans placed ignominiously beside gorillas and baboons. Looking at them he made his provocative claim, shortly to become famous:

> Now I am quite sure that if we had these three creatures fossilized or preserved in spirits for comparison and were quite unprejudiced judges we should at once admit that there is very little greater interval *as animals* between the *Gorilla* & the *Man* than exists between the *Gorilla* & the [baboon] *Cynocephalus*.

Skeleton or cerebrum, it made no difference. The devil dared him and he proclaimed in public what Darwin thought in private.

> Nay more I believe that the mental & moral faculties are essentially & fundamentally the same in kind in animals & ourselves. I can draw no line of demarcation between an instinctive and a reasonable action.

True, in cultural terms the gap was 'infinite'. But it is speech, not some spiritual gift, which makes man 'a reason*able* being'. It was the source of our 'unlimited intellectual progress'. But that did not disguise the fact 'that to the very root & foundation of his nature man is one with the rest of the organic world'.[23]

Huxley finished his Royal Institution course croaky and 'bedeviled'. Morality and apes were now explosively mixed and awaited only a fuse. Darwin, ten chapters and a quarter of a million words into *Natural Selection*, was sidestepping human origins 'as so surrounded with prejudices'.[24] But Huxley ensured that mind and man remained in the polemical picture. His gladiatorial stand was not only pushing him into Darwin's camp, but on to its skirmishing defences.

His fearsome talents were still getting him noticed. He had hardly mellowed, but he now roared into the Athenaeum Club. Murchison put him up and wrote:

> I had a success as to you that I never had or heard of before. 19 persons voted & of these 18 voted for you & no one against you. You of course came in at the head of the poll; no other having i.e. *Cobden* more than 11.

It meant more money. 'Hoorar', cheered Hooker, conspiring to get Busk and Tyndall elected next – pay up quickly and come 'on

Monday night & help to swamp the Parsons & get Buckle in'. Buckle's science might have been 'bosh' (invited to dinner Huxley declined 'as I have too much of the Arab about me to eat a man's salt & then pitch into him'). But the whiff of a backlash had him rushing to Buckle's aid.[25]

The group still lacked a house organ, and Huxley kept thrusting his foot into doors. He did get his men a voice in the smartest weekly of the age. A column in the *Saturday Review* would align his scientific upstarts with Trollope and Bagehot. They were liberals; true, not of Mill's stamp, being wary of any democratic diluting of talent, but their assaults on plum-in-mouth pomposity had one preacher fulminating that 'man is born for the love of God and the hatred of the *Saturday Review*'. That was good enough for Huxley. He collected his own 'corps (d'elite!)' and signed them up. It should be 'a salutary influence in this quack-ridden country' gloated Tyndall at the Royal Institution, promising 'to perform my share of the business'.[26]

Only when Hal's own Royal Institution course ended in March 1858 did he find time to register his and Nettie's new baby, already six weeks old. After Noel he had wanted a girl, and Tyndall, more and more the atomic determinist, rejoiced: 'Pon my soul – I dont often swear thus – the gods are very kind to you. Things could not have happened more nicely if you yourself had been the patentee of the molecular architecture'. The devout Emma Darwin stood godmother. Jessie Oriana they named the baby, the latter after Nettie's sister. The Jessie spoke for itself; it had been 13 years since Lizzie's loss and Huxley was finally effacing the past. 'We could not make you a godmother', he wrote to Lizzie, although 'this is a better tie than that meaningless formality'.

But the past was always there, decaying in the shape of Cooke. Lizzie heard about the decline of 'Ellen & her husband'; 'she has not learned wisdom with age', he was drinking himself into an early grave '& now I think they cannot go much further'. Cooke died in September 'a bloated mass of beer & opium', 47, intestate and penniless.

'Chronic enlargement of the liver' the death certificate read, an epitaph for a life poisoned by drink. But Huxley thanked the man for his helping hand. And he knew the 'wear & tear of incessant occupation' that had driven Cooke to his grave. He was grinding down himself. The dissections were interminable, with nothing taken on trust: 'if Hal had but a little rest occasionally . . . ', Nettie lamented. But no. Waverley Place was a bustle. Toddler Noel was turning into a 'stout little Trojan', nothing like his raven-haired father in looks, but like him taking on the world 'as if he were its master'.

Huxley worked through the tears and tantrums. Herrings were examined for the Fisheries Commission, sea-nettles for his book. This he had picked up again, years late. It had a title now, *Oceanic Hydrozoa*. He pored over his 'travel stained cockroachy notebooks & drawings of 1847–8–9–50', that tropical aromatic memento from a world away. But a decade left him feeling 'like the editor of somebody else's posthumous work'. His changes since those barricade days reminded him of France, herself grown into a secure stodginess. Ten years had even sown a little silver in his hair. Otherwise his 'phiz' was the same.[27] Baby Jessie's 'nose is the image of mine', he lamented, and time has 'by no means softened the outlines of that remarkable feature'.

The old world passed away with Cooke, and Huxley threw his door open to the new. His dinner parties saw the rising talent. Guests were non-plussed to find the most formidable talents of the age, Tyndall, Spencer and Mill, facing them across the table. The Hookers would arrive, or the Carpenters. And the Busks, despite the gentle friction between Ellen and Nettie. Friction and jealousy produced a hint of electrostatic *frisson*: 'She was very gentle & kind & even called me "dear"', Nettie told Hal. 'She doesn't know how I'd love her if she were only straightforward about you'.[28] The prickly air was set off by their diametric temperaments. Tall, dark Ellen was 'quick and intelligent' with 'a self-possessed rather blunt but honest manner', a female Tom in truth; but, said Hirst, making his choice at dinner one day, 'she has not Mrs. Huxley's depth and warmth'.

Cooke's failure only highlighted Huxley's success. His 'Croonian Lecture' confirmed it. This was a gala night in the Royal Society's calendar, ill paid but well starred. On a midsummer evening, 17 June, Huxley stood in the Great Hall of Burlington House (the society's spacious new site). He was looking less shabby now in his frock coat, but just as fearsome, with scowling eyes and black hair swept over his ears. Richard Owen was in the Chair and the 'nobs' viewed Huxley – or rather his tongue – with some trepidation. His talk on the skull was clinical and slick. The insiders knew what he was up to: burying a wizened old morphology and giving a forceps delivery to the new. The birth of a new embryological anatomy was overdue and he dragged it screaming into a secular world to join its German *Bruder*. He focused on one superannuated belief: that the skull was made of distended vertebrae (an idea championed by Owen and the older anatomists in London). The Königsberg embryologist Martin Rathke had already noted the skull's distinct foetal origins, so it could not be a continuation of the spinal segments, each the embodiment of an Ideal Vertebra. Such mysticism was 'fundamentally opposed to the spirit of modern science' anyway. Huxley heroically refrained from mentioning Owen by name. But that was the least he could do with his crimson-cheeked protagonist fuming in the Chair.

Everywhere the old romanticism was in retreat: poets were rejecting Wordsworth's 'spiritualization of Nature'; anatomists were spurning life's Divine archetypal halo, and Huxley gave a hearty push to the cultural swing. He ceremoniously knocked off Owen's vertebral crown.

Spencer joined the regicidal clamour, making his own 'tremendous smash' of Owen's Platonism (like any ex-Unitarian). But Spencer was dextrously decapitating Owen while standing on his shoulders. He cut off the archetypal head but kept the progressive body. He still needed an image of progressing life, and he saw it evolving by the piling of '*adaptations upon adaptations*'. The specializations acquired during an individual's life were fixed and passed on. And this acquisition of skills carried over as cultural evolution in humans.

The day after the Croonian Hooker received a note. 'I wonder how Ricardus, "Rex anatomicorum", feels this morning', Huxley wrote. 'I am deuced seedy but that is just punishment for irreverent democrats'.[29]

Darwin was feeling worse. For 20 years he had been terrified of going public. Having finally screwed up the courage to write, he opened a letter from the Far East that morning. He scanned what seemed like a précis of his theory; 'all my originality', he cried in disbelief, has been 'smashed'.

It was from the affable Alfred Russel Wallace out in the Malay Archipelago. Wallace had occasionally sent jungle fowl skins, but he was a world removed in every sense: a hard-up collector gone native, shipping exotic butterflies and birds to a dealer, packing a 1,000 beetles per box to make it pay. He was a former builder's apprentice and surveyor, whose politics came from the socialist Hall of Science and evolution from *Vestiges*. He was another 1840s activist, outraged by wealth and organized religion. And his so-journ in the Indies had only increased his socialist faith in morality as a cultural product and mankind as an evolved animal.

Socialist spectacles gave his nature a pink hue. For him the environment expunged the unfit, not competition; and *his* evolution would realize the ideal of 'perfect man'. But Darwin had no inkling of this utopian vision. All he saw were a few rice-paper pages and an apparently identical theory: 'if Wallace had my M.S. sketch . . . he could not have made a better short abstract!'[30]

An emotional vortex sucked him down. Lyell and Hooker stepped in, acting the consummate diplomats, arranging a joint communiqué of Darwin and Wallace's theory of natural selection at the Linnean (where Busk and friends could control events). It was Darwin's first public pronouncement. But his concern was swept away by grief as his retarded 18 month-old son, Charles Waring, succumbed to scarlet fever. The baby was buried on the day of the reading, 1 July. The Darwins lined the graveside, leaving Hooker and Lyell to quell any rumbles among the Linnean fellows.

Huxley was not a member of the Linnean. But he worked behind the scenes. He vetted the documents establishing Darwin's priority. At last he had an overview of natural selection. He realized why he had been shown all those plumed, ruffed pigeons. Fanciers can spot nuances of colour or shape 'inappreciable to an uneducated eye', and tease them out by select breeding. Nature was only a more ubiquitous selector. Her feedback system was like 'the centrifugal governor of the steam engine', Wallace's letter said, 'which checks and corrects' automatically.

Darwin explained how. Human overpopulation was prevented by disease or famine. So it was with every species. Unchecked a pair of birds could multiply ten million fold in 15 years, or elephants overrun the earth in a thousand years. But predation and starvation take their toll. The grim reaper was vigilant, scything down the weak and ill-fitted. 'Only a few of those annually born can live to propagate their kind', Darwin argued. And in the scramble for resources a 'trifling difference' can 'determine which shall survive & which perish'.[31] The winners were those with some chance adaptation, fitting them to changing conditions (this was 'natural selection'). Only they thrived to breed, passing on their new trait. Since Silurian times 'millions on millions of generations' have transmuted this way. Huxley tried to assimilate the first thumb-nail sketch of Darwin's theory. Its whole naturalistic emphasis was glorious, but some details worried him, such as the relentless emphasis on micro-adaptations and the severity of the struggle. He thought it over.

As Huxley pored over the pages a 'panic-struck' Darwin fled to the Isle of Wight, taking his children away from the fever. Having broken cover he began a full article for the Linnean *Journal*. But the inevitable happened; it swelled uncontrollably. Anyway the 'subject really seems to me too large for discussion at any Society, & I believe Religion would be brought in'. Soon he was back to a 400-page book, an 'abstract' of *Natural Selection*, which he would call the *Origin of Species*. He turned down Hooker's offer of a Linnean grant. He preferred to go over professional heads and reach out to the public. For all his leanings Huxley delighted in empirical British achievement, and English gents came no more dogged than Darwin. His relentless utilitarianism – his demand that every curlicue and hue of the oddest orchid must function in order to be selected – made Huxley wince, but he relished Darwin's snatch at the supernatural:

> Wallace's impetus seems to have set Darwin going in earnest and I am rejoiced to hear we shall learn his views in full, at last. I look forward to a great revolution being effected. Depend upon it in Natural History as in everything else when the English mind fully determines to work a thing out it will do it better than any other.
>
> I firmly believe in the advent of an English epoch in science & art which will lick the Augustan . . . into fits.[32]

Spencer, lodging in the street next to Huxley's to aid their Sunday strolls, was also cranking up. Having broached the origin of mind in *Principles of Psychology* he mooted a ten-volume treatise on everything else. All knowledge was to be tackled in terms of development, or, as he was calling it, 'the evolution point of view'. The pair thrashed it out on their walks to the Finchley countryside. Huxley was notoriously 'chary in his praise', perennially pricking Spencer's theoretical balloons, but he backed his 'modern "novum organon"'.

Others were moving: even Owen in his pontifical address as President of the British Association in September 1858 assuaged conservative fears. The 'continuous operation of Creative power' need cause no fear, he announced. New species might emerge consecutively, but with Natural Law an expression of God's Will, 'our science' is still 'connected with the loftiest of moral speculations'. Owen loathed transmutation, and his notion of 'continuous Creation' would be critical in the years of Christian reconciliation.[33]

As Darwin geared up to publish, Huxley's banner was unfurling on another front. The move to fossil reptiles was inevitable. It was enough that Owen had charge of 'Nature's crowning race', the intimidating dinosaurs. Their Mesozoic empire was firing the Victorian imagination. It had come to light within living memory and assumed an apocalyptic aura, dramatized in John Martin's 'Gothick' paintings. To Tennyson the annihilation of these Brobdingnagian dinosaurs was a sobering reminder of earthly transience. His nature was indifferent, crushing individuals and empires indiscriminately. Dinosaurs were forcing Victorians to break out of their small, circumscribed world. But deep time, like deep space, Tennyson's 'terrible Muses', brought its own insecurity. Those 'dreadful Hammers!', Ruskin wrote of the geologists, 'I hear the clink of them at the end of every cadence of the Bible verses'. It drove some to despair, but left Huxley with his cosy alienation, secure in nature's 'vicious disregard'.[34] The High Churchman Henry Mansel was right in his *Limits of Religious Thought*: God could no longer be found in the rocks, only in revelation.

The Crystal Palace had its 'mausoleum to the memory of ruined worlds', stocked with Owen's life-size dinosaurs, 30-ton concrete models built like reptilian rhinoceroses. But Huxley took satisfaction in the news from America. In Connecticut huge three-toed fossil footprints were being ascribed to dinosaurs walking on their hind legs.[35] This was the most alien of concepts: bipedal creatures with 18-inch footprints and six-foot strides. It was the shape of things to come.

Huxley moved to the dawn of the 'Age of Reptiles'. He focused on the yellow sandstones of Elgin, in the north of Scotland. These were presumed to be Devonian in age – deposited as sediments when lungfish were life's apex and lush club-moss forests were spreading over newly emerged continents. The first discovery (in 1851) of a 4-inch 'lizard' skeleton had Lyell 'inebriate with joy'. Jubilant, too, were the Moray antiquarians led by the Minister of Birnie, Revd George Gordon, in whose parish this oldest of reptilian tombs lay. Such fossil firsts gave their Morayshire, 'the fairest spot on earth', an international importance.

It had locals scouring the quarries, but their next find, a

heavy-scaled creature, *Stagonolepis*, wiped the grin off Lyell's face. Its scutes were suspiciously like a crocodile's from the much later Mesozoic period. By 1858 Gordon was shipping regular consignments to Jermyn Street (thanks to Murchison's payments), keeping the preparators busy with friable limbs and jaw casts.

Huxley diagnosed another 'wonderful reptile', 15 feet long with a 'swinging tail'. And when he cried 'A tooth! A tooth! my kingdom for a tooth!' Gordon triumphantly obliged – allowing Huxley to confirm what his collectors suspected. *Stagonolepis* had socketed teeth, making it an advanced reptile, unlike lizards but like dinosaurs and crocodiles. Its spine and armour were indeed 'eminently crocodilian'. But crocodiles in ancient *Devonian* rocks?

Huxley introduced *Stagonolepis* at the Geological Society and left one overriding impression. Crocodiles must be reptilian Methuselahs, primeval creatures surviving little changed for untold aeons. He remained Lyell's heir. Spencer called the meeting 'a triumph for Huxley, and rather damaging for the progressive theory, *as commonly held*'.[36] Spencer was still trying to think his way round Huxley's obstacles. But what evolutionary view could Huxley accommodate?

His fossil expertise got him the Secretary's post of the Geological. More bureaucratic work, Nettie grumbled; he cannot stop, and he 'looks very tired & worn . . . for he never spares himself'. 'You cannot think what he has got through this past year'.

In 1858 Huxley stood on the threshold. He finally finished *Oceanic Hydrozoa* in September at a manic pace, as Nettie complained, giving it 'five weeks of 6 hours p^r diem during his seaside holiday (?!)'.[37] It ended an era of struggle, of furious highs and forlorn hope, of cynicism and crowning achievement. Had Huxley died on the eve of the *Origin* – of kidney-failure like Cooke, or crushed by a banking scandal like George who was wasting away with phthisis – and had friends collected his *Literary Papers* as they did for Forbes, he would have been remembered as a brilliant invertebrate anatomist who teased out the two layers of jellyfish, an idiosyncratic anti-progressionist, a prophet awaiting Silurian Man, an iconoclast, a scathing critic with a chip on his shoulder. How the world would really remember him the next few years would tell. The subaltern had risen through the ranks, competent in ever-expanding fields. The government officer was ready for whatever his 'scientific Young England' expected.

1858–1865

The New Luther

14

The Eve of a New Reformation

SIX YEARS EARLIER Nettie's sister Ory and her husband William Fanning had left Hal an insecure tyro. Now back from Sydney, they found a confident, hardworking teacher, but just as proud and pugnacious and doing what he had always prophesied, capitalizing on knowledge. The years had seen a transformation. Domestic anchorage gave him a new joy and stability. He doted on his little 'monkey', Noel. This 'bright eyed golden haired mannikin' was 'the apple of his father's eye and chief deity of his mother's pantheon, which at present contains only a god and goddess. Another is expected shortly, however, so that there is no fear of Olympus looking empty'.[1]

They also found him wielding power. Huxley's organizational flair was apparent. He was the whipper-in: 'it is no use putting any faith in the old buffers', he mused, 'hardened as they are in trespasses & sins'. With the *Quarterly Review* talking of moving the British Museum's natural history collection to a separate museum – giving Owen 'a temple of his own' – Huxley formed a 'Committee of Public Safety' and petitioned the Chancellor with alternative plans. His Danton was played to perfection. He expected 'oceans of trouble & abuse, but so long as we gain our end, I care not a whistle whether the sweet voices of the scientific mob are for or against me'.

His ginger group wanted a national museum, but not one under Owen's control. Theirs was to be a Temple of Reason. No republic had a more zealous Minister of Justice. Huxley arranged low-brow support for their people-friendly museum in Robert Chambers' *Journal* and high-brow coverage in the *Quarterly*. He even roused Prince Albert and *The Times*. 'Can you get at the

"Household Words"'? he asked Hooker. 'If only one knew that snob Dickens'.²

A national museum with research facilities would signal the changing ethos. They were no longer 'Gentlemen of Science', parsons and squires with their parish distractions. Quite what the salaried squad was no one could say for sure. Not 'Naturalists', any 'fool who can make bad species and worse genera is a "Naturalist"! save the mark!' Not 'Biologists', too 'foreign' and tainted by 'perversion' (Lamarck had coined the term). Nor 'scientists', an unfamiliar word. They were 'Scientific men'.³ Less gentle, but still with a duty to their own. The Committee showed its benign face as Hooker and Huxley set up a distress fund, a sort of Civil List for the stretched new man.

By January 1859 word was out about Professor Huxley's provocative night-time talks. Artisans flocked to them from all over London. Nobody talked so openly as Huxley; at least no 'nob'. Nobody dared say that humans and animals '*must* have proceeded from one another in the way of progressive modification'. This was now Huxley's firm line. Fired by their own infidel orators and Baptist evangelists, they quizzed him on the 'religious' implications. At a time when teachers were part of a tacit conspiracy not to ship intellectual arms across the class divide, Huxley's forthright response was eagerly reported in their trade journal, *The Builder*.

He fashioned a low-caste Dissenting image of science. The testimony of Nature was for all to hear. No priesthood had privileged 'access to her deepest secrets'. Every man his own pastor: it was a message for the Baptists as much as the democratic masses. Indeed every man must examine the 'mysteries' of existence for himself to keep Britain great; any nation 'hood-winked and fettered' by church dogmas and denying the 'free application of the intellect' would be 'rotten within'.⁴

Thirty years of Dissenting siege against a knowledge-monopolizing, State-supported Church had come to a head. But this was no attack on *religion* per se; a sceptical science merely purified theology by stripping off the concreting myths. Carpenter's Unitarians railed just as hard against Anglican supernaturalism and the State powers of the bishops. For all of them the Bible encoded history's moral truths. Huxley saw 'in these truths the result of a long & loving, if sorrowful, study of man's nature and relations – the stored wisdom of many generations ... Thou shalt love thy neighbour as thyself is the Law of Gravitation of Society'.

For 30 years the Anglican monopoly of the bench, the town halls, the hospitals and Oxford and Cambridge had been eroded, with the final disabilities on Jews being removed in 1858. During that time radicals had tried everything to undermine priestly power. Some had even deployed a self-sufficient Lamarckism to illegitimate the Creationist base of the Church (which was seen as God's pocket-borough, maintained, like Nature, through His personal intervention). Free trade was demanded in divinity as much as in corn. In 1859, with Britain poised to sign Cobden's epochal free-trade agreement with France, Huxley's scimitar was the latest cleansing weapon. He was undercutting the spiritual sanction of a rival profession, reforming God's rotten-borough. *Religion* was not the problem:

> My screed was meant as a protest against Theology &
> Parsondom . . . both of which are in my mind the natural
> & irreconcilable enemies of Science. Few see it but I
> believe we are on the Eve of a new Reformation and if I
> have a wish to live thirty years, it is that I may see the
> foot of Science on the necks of her Enemies. But the new
> religion will not be a worship of the intellect alone.

It would have the Christian ethics of love and duty – the old moral core, left after science had stripped off the mythic excrescences. The day the Whig Dissenters invaded the town halls in 1835 this scientific offensive was on the cards. Huxley, with his adversarial psychology, simply made it the more violent. Any new Unitarian Mayor could have said it, 'there is no safety in trying to put new wine into old bottles'. No 'disinterested Hebrew scholar', Huxley wrote, could render Genesis 'reconcilable with the most elementary . . . facts of Geology'. And if parsons think it 'permissable to turn and twist the Scripture phraseology' to ensure a fit, 'I for my part will undertake to prove that rape, murder & arson are positively enjoined in Exodus'.

The 'origin of man' had proved a cutting weapon in pauper hands. Now Huxley would appropriate it for his professionals. He had deliberately raised the subject, 'claiming my right to follow whithersoever science should lead'. 'After all', he told Dyster, 'it is as respectable to be modified monkey as modified dirt'.[5]

Dust of the earth or chimps in the trees – he had polarized the issue before the *Origin of Species* was out. Darwin had hoped to avoid the human question, but Huxley was making mud-or-monkey the fighting issue. At his spa, Darwin was tormented by a swimming head and 'severe vomiting'. (Worrying about the *Origin* 'is the cause', he admitted, 'the main part of the ills to which my flesh is heir'.) Reading Huxley's *Builder* article hardly perked him up. The parish gentleman feared an unseemly fray. He planned to reassure the *Origin*'s publisher (John Murray) that 'my Book is not more *un*-orthodox, than the subject makes inevitable. That I do not discuss origin of man. – That I do not bring in any discussion about Genesis &c'.

Darwin trudged on, in sickness and gloom. Through the domestic traumas at Downe, through the rages of Mrs Grut the governess, 'more "gruttish" than ever'. In March he sent Hooker a 90-page chapter on the spread of life. Even this was fraught.

> By some screaming accident [Hooker told Huxley], the
> whole bundle . . . got transferred to a drawer where my
> wife keeps paper for the children to draw upon – & they
> have of course had a drawing fit ever since. – I feel
> brutified if not brutalized for poor D. is so bad that he
> could hardly get steam up to finish what he did.

Darwin stoically set back his press date. 'I *have* the old M.S.', he calmed Hooker, 'otherwise the loss would have killed me!' From a distance Huxley turned the tension to farce, ordering Hooker to stand on his 'head in the garden for one hour per diem for the next week'.[6]

But how distant was Huxley really? Darwin spoke as if the *Origin of Species* would require religious conversion, so what of the evangelist on his own hellfire crusade? 'Hooker, who is our best British Botanist & perhaps best in World, is a *full* convert', Darwin wrote to Wallace. 'Huxley is changed & believes in mutation of species: whether a *convert* to us, I do not quite know'. But Huxley was 'a wonderful man'. He kept Darwin on his toes. 'When I feel myself chasing wild geese', Darwin said, softening Huxley up, 'you always rise before me'. Darwin was proving that homologous parts (say the hand, flipper and wing) derived from a common ancestor and were produced by 'real changes in the course of time'. It meant that Huxley's discrete subkingdoms were not so discrete any more – that his mollusc, vertebrate and medusa archetypes had themselves evolved from 'one primordial created form', and that his curious analogy between jellyfish and human embryonic membranes might be a sign of real affinity.

True to form Huxley pointed out a 'flaw' in Darwin's reasoning.

The tumblers and runts interbreed; fanciers had yet to pull their pigeons so far apart as to form real species, with sterile hybrids. But Darwin called his 'a mere rag of an hypothesis' with as many 'holes as sound parts'. The point was that 'I can carry in it my fruit to market'. Not that the naturalist, with his tortured 'prostration of mind & body', could walk much at all. Seeing his 'miserable' prose in proof, he had started rewriting until his health 'quite failed'. And through it all he feared that Huxley would give the rag 'such a devil of a shake that it will fall all to atoms'.[7]

'So do not be too ferocious', he quailed on 2 June 1859. His letter was opened by Huxley as he prepared for the Royal Institution. He was set to lecture on 'Persistent Types', 'living fossils', survivors from Silurian times like the club-mosses and burrow-living bivalve *Lingula*. It seemed that he was about to give Darwin's rag a shake. But no, he held it aloft to signal his change. For the first time he dovetailed their world views. He built an idiosyncratic half-way house, which he hoped would rise into a great temple. Like Solomon he saw nothing new under the sun, no new groups of animals since Silurian times. Therefore an evolutionary explosion must have occurred in the 'pre-geological' period, before the oldest Silurian rocks had settled as sediments.

The new Secretary of the Geological Society was taking on the empire's fossils in 1859, unpacking the crates from missionaries and explorers, governors and garrison commanders. The steamers were unloading increasing numbers, marked for the London museums. Huxley's work reflected the galloping colonization of the globe. Archaic amphibians from Australia, extinct tusked reptiles from the Cape, fossil penguins from New Zealand, he conquered them all. He was publishing as fast as his preparators could etch out the bones.

More Elgin reptiles came from George Gordon in Scotland. An excited Huxley himself sat down 'knife & chisel in hand' to reveal a six-foot, stout-limbed, plant-eater with a crushing 'pavement of teeth'. *Hyperodapedon Gordoni* he christened it, tickling the vanities to ensure more specimens. But the gesture disguised a blow to the Moray men, who had prided themselves on having the first created reptiles. Its kin were 'unquestionably *Triassic* forms'. Elgin's rocks were not ancient Devonian at all, but much later Triassic sediments, laid down during the 'Age of Reptiles'.

Huxley's suspicions sent Lyell to Elgin, and the region, he reported, 'more than justifies your scepticism'.[8] It was the final irony: Huxley, the palaeontological Peter, the rock of Lyell's non-progressionist Church, put the Elgin saurians back into a progressive sequence, back into the 'Age of Reptiles'. Huxley had hammered the last nail into Lyell's geological coffin. After 30 years defending the anti-progressionist faith Sir Charles accepted an ascending fossil series and looked to Darwin for its explanation.

A tortured Lyell began to tease at the issues with Huxley. The problem was to explain the great classes of animals. With no fossil intermediates connecting today's vertebrates and molluscs and insects, where was the proof that they had come from a common stock 'in the course of 1000^{ds}. of generations'? Was some 'creative' cause responsible for these huge jumps? Did transmutation only produce the variety once the great blueprints were established?

No, said Huxley – think of it another way. There were no intermediate forms, so perhaps '*transmutation* may take place without *transition*' – by leaps, leaving no string of middle stages (an idea that squared with his discrete crystalline spheres). Look at the sudden appearance of Ancon sheep, a long-bodied strain with 'short bandy legs', once bred in Massachusetts for the canny reason that they could not jump fences. Or hexadactyl humans (like Robert Chambers who, with his extra finger and toe, amputated at birth, joked that he was returning 'to the reptilian type'). Here were new forms appearing 'at once in full perfection'.

Natural 'monstrosities' ruled out any supernatural need. 'Creation' for Huxley was as much ideological effrontery as philosophical absurdity. Who, he asked Darwin and Lyell, imagined elephants flashing into being from their component atoms? It was contrary to experience, he told students. His atomic elephant was a clever caricature. Yet many who were branded 'Creationists' never thought in these terms. Owen's God worked to a Divine blueprint, the great groundplans of life, and His Word was made flesh by Natural Law (even if this was interpreted as a Divine Edict). Huxley had made straw men of the 'Creationists'. He had distilled his professional, dissenting strategy against the privileged Anglican Church into a Manichean Evolutionist *vs* Creationist slogan, us-*vs*-them, and he was now one of 'us'. Few saw him changing the rules of engagement.

Huxley's propaganda coup was not lost on Darwin. He ended the *Origin* by slating 'the blindness of preconceived opinion' – for who could believe that 'in the earth's history certain elemental atoms have been commanded suddenly to flash into living tissues?' Huxley had put the sting in the *Origin*'s tail.

Lyell braced himself to 'go the whole orang'. If evolution be true 'we shall in time discover extinct fossil varieties of Men', Miocene monkey-like men. But Huxley still wondered. What if mankind went back a long way? Couldn't Lyell imagine humans dodging Jurassic dinosaurs?⁹ What if people had existed since Silurian times? We would never find our monkey ancestors.

By now Huxley was trying to write his *Oceanic Hydrozoa* while reading other people's manuscripts. Putting the *Origin* proofs down, he would pick up Hooker's *Flora of Tasmania*, with its botanical support for Darwin. He finally finished his own preface in July 1859, eight years after the voyage. For five years all the plates bar two had been finished. During those years the Ray Society (which was to publish it) had been saved from bankruptcy – and during those years a succession of Germans had gone 'to the shores of the Mediterranean and made sad havoc with my novelties'.¹⁰ Huxley's first book, and the delay had cost him priority.

He posted the preface and the family left to spend August on the 'Paradise of Arran'. They took a Glasgow steamer down the Clyde and out to the Scottish island. Here, on the sheltered Lamlash Bay, with its smooth clear waters, Hal did what he loved, indulged in the lottery of the dredge. Carpenter had found the bay, with its 'treasure' of rare starfish and sea lilies. It was a teeming marine nursery, with larvae 'by *hundreds*': young worms and jellies.¹¹ It was a calming moment, time to draw breath before the coming storm. All sights were now on the publication of the *Origin*.

At home Darwin suffered a 'terrible long fit of vomiting' as he let go of his 'abominable volume'. The anxiety left him 'miserably unwell & shattered' and in no condition to face a hostile world. On 2 October he fled on a three-day journey to Ilkley on the desolate Yorkshire moors, there to hide out at a spa for two months until the furore over the *Origin of Species* had died down. Such absenteeism was to characterize his life from now on. The family joined him, only to sit out an early winter in 'frozen misery'. Darwin's internal exile was marked by hope and despair. Awaiting the first sight of his book he had 'an awful "crisis"', 'one leg swelled like elephantiasis – eyes almost closed up – covered with a rash & fiery Boils'. Now he understood Huxley's fascination with Dante. It was 'like living in Hell'.

He sought reassurance, touching his friends in letters. 'I shall be *intensely* curious to hear what effect the Book produces on you', he cajoled Huxley. 'I am far from expecting to convert you to many of my heresies; but if . . . you & two or three others think I am on the right road, I shall not care what the mob of naturalists think'.

The 'mental rumpus' affected Hooker no less in these weeks. He was moving house; with his wife and children away he 'avoided suicide' in the run up to the *Origin* and *Flora of Tasmania* by 'working extremely hard with my head hands & legs'.[12] His catharsis came from potting seeds.

Lyell was edging forward, desperately worried about a bestial human origin. ('It is this which has made me so long hesitate', he conceded.) He mooted to Huxley 'a race of savages at first with small cranial development & out of this the negro & white races ... being evolved'. But he was straining. His lingering need for the 'intervention of creative power' to supercharge the process made Darwin cringe: 'I cannot see this necessity', he replied. It would make his mechanism superfluous. 'Grant a simple archetypal creature, like the ... [lungfish] Lepidosiren, with the five senses & some vestige of mind & I believe Natural Selection will account for production of every Vertebrate animal'.[13]

In November Darwin faced his nemesis – the moment he had dreaded for 20 years. The world was about to peer into his soul. Here he was, a renowned naturalist, pillar of the parish, Justice of the Peace, fearing execration as an atheist. He was so over-wrought he didn't know what to expect. He knew that old Oxbridge friends would 'fulminate awful anathemas'; 'you will long to crucify me alive!', he told Falconer in his self-abasing way. He was now lame in his spa at Ilkley, with a swollen face that left him 'worse than when I came'. He clung to Hooker's enthusiasm and Lyell's support, and 'If I can convert Huxley I shall be content'.[14]

Huxley's copy of the *Origin* arrived in mid-November. For the first time he saw the book in its entirety. The remorseless emphasis on adaptation was still a shock. No student of Carlyle could be happy with crass utilitarian explanations, yet here life's chances were calculated on cost/benefit principles. It was a messy, competitive, individualistic approach, with the winners thrown up in the scuffle, at odds with his own search for innate developmental laws. Yet the book explained why modern life was based on so many set plans: these were inherited from common ancestors. And Huxley could salvage something of his old views. Natural selection did not demand that life continually progress, only that animals anchor themselves into niches. So his persistent types, 'living fossils', survived in niches which never changed.

But the details were never of overriding importance to Huxley. Whether or not the *Origin* pointed to a Golden Calf, it led his Israelites out of the wilderness. Huxley put it best in a parable:

> 'My sons, dig in the vineyard,' were the last words of the
> old man in the fable: and, though the sons found no
> treasure, they made their fortune by the grapes.

Any viable mechanism of life's succession would enable his professionals to reap a rich harvest. The *Origin* extended the natural realm; it increased 'the domination of Science', and the annexed territory required its colonial governors. Before them lay an unknown land. 'If we thought ourselves knowing dogs before you revealed Nat Selection', Hooker told Darwin, 'what d– – –d. ignorant ones we must surely be now'.

There was no more infuriating, enlightening book. It had no references, no illustrations. More an encyclopedia, to Huxley's thinking, needing endless readings for the meaning to seep through: an 'intellectual pemmican – a mass of facts crushed and pounded into shape, rather than held together by the ordinary medium of an obvious logical bond'. Exposition was not Darwin's *forte*, he was defeated by commas and daunted by grammar. But there was 'a marvellous dumb sagacity' to the man, 'and he gets to the truth by ways as dark as those of the Heathen Chinee'. Huxley worked his way through, annotating, and by the nth reading he began to transcend the 'humdrum and prosaic' and enter the 'vast and mysterious', awed by the terrible grandeur of Darwin's vision.[15]

As ill-luck would have it Huxley's *Oceanic Hydrozoa* came out within weeks of the *Origin*. As a short-print run, subscription-only Ray Society monograph, it was lost in the mêlée. All eyes were now fixed on the *Origin*. Darwin was on tenterhooks: 'I long to hear what Huxley thinks', he told Hooker on 20 November. The following day he heard. Huxley 'is vastly pleased with it', Hooker wrote. He was even thinking of turning over his next Royal Institution talk to the book. Darwin's mood brightened. How 'unspeakably grand if Huxley were to lecture on the subject'.

A public stand became imperative after the *Athenaeum* fired a 'contemptible' opening shot at the *Origin*. The book was a snub to the clergy and an insult to humanity. Was nihilism now to rule? What else could be said of a monkey-made-man? – he 'was born yesterday – he will perish tomorrow'. Darwin was furious at the way the reviewer 'sets the Priests at me & leaves me to their mercies'. It was crucial to play up the rival moral of evolution. To show progress through open competition, all that handicapped Dissenters had demanded in society. And Carpenter did: the 'War' in Darwin's Nature, he said, led inevitably 'towards the progressive exaltation of the races engaged in it'.[16]

'Since I read Von Bär nine years ago no work on Natural History I have met with has made so great an impression upon me', Huxley rallied Darwin. The dervish had heard the call and was 'prepared to go to the Stake' for parts of it. Like Carlyle's hero Mohammed he sharpened his 'claws & beak' to tear at 'the curs which will bark & yelp'. The new Reformation seemed closer than he had thought. He reminded Darwin that 'some of your friends ... are endowed with an amount of combativeness which (though you have often & justly rebuked it) may stand you in good stead'. Now Darwin was glad of it. Never one to enter the public fray, he needed a champion as Huxley needed a cause.

The two, so utterly unlike, seemed made for the occasion. Darwin's jubilation took a more traditional turn. 'Like a good Catholic, who has received extreme unction, I can now sing "nunc dimittis"'.

Having heard that his old Cambridge mentor, the blunt Dalesman Adam Sedgwick, 'laughed till his sides ached at my Book', Darwin clung to the *arriviste* men still more. He egged Huxley on. No more raised eyebrows at his savagery: 'What a joke it will be if I pat you on [the] back when you attack some immoveable creationist!'

He started arming Huxley with skulls and 'splendid *folio* coloured drawings' of fantails and runts for his lecture. Nettie produced her usual stockpile of pedagogical pictures. Those bizarre breeds held the illustrative key – 'those dreadful pidgeons', laughed Falconer, on which Darwin practised his 'leger-de-main'. Then Darwin sent parts of the precious *Natural Selection* manuscript, although he doubted if Huxley could 'make heads or tails of it'.[17]

The *Athenaeum* left a bitter taste. Huxley had a standing invitation to contribute to the new liberal *Macmillan's Magazine*. He plunged in, neutralizing the *Athenaeum* in the middle-brow monthly. It was an exuberant piece, out in two weeks, which praised Darwin's 'singularly original and well-stored mind'. Only the *Origin*, which had life stopping and starting as the environment stagnated or changed, could explain why the 'cockroaches of the carboniferous epoch are exceedingly similar to those which now run about our coal-cellars'. Huxley put 'the best thinkers of the day' on Darwin's side. He meant his group. Busk, Tyndall, Hooker and Carpenter all came over with the School of Mines lecturers. Hooker rallied the horticulturalists in the *Gardeners' Chronicle*, making nature a sort of Sublime Nurseryman, always weeding and improving. Carpenter roused the Unitarians, taking his line that miracles were absurd, God interrupting Himself. The Almighty's great law unleashed at Creation was wonderfully revealed in Darwin's world of 'order, continuity, and progress'. Darwin cooed at having 'got a great physiologist on our side. I say "our" for we are now a good & compact body'.[18] And he bubbled in his spa at Huxley's 'delightful & honourable compliment'.

The radicals were awed. Chapman thought the *Origin* 'one of the most important books of this century'. He too approached Huxley for an article. By now the *Westminster* was listing badly, and Huxley the lifelong debtor found himself in an unaccustomed role as creditor. But Chapman was planning a salvage operation, turning debts into shares in a new Westminster Publishing Company. He pressured Huxley about reviewing the *Origin*, which would cause a 'mental revolution', and about saving the *Westminster*, which had already done so.[19] So Huxley raised his credit limit and tailored a review for the avant garde.

Here the *Origin* emerged 'as a veritable Whitworth gun in the armoury of liberalism'. Britain, the world's mightiest industrial economy, was turning liberal as the Dissenters' ideals of free trade and fair competition became the cultural norm, and a gun-running Huxley was selling the *Origin* as a replacement for Dissent's old weaponry. He was tying the book to the forces of 'progress'. Such talk stirred the patriotic breast: in 1859 the *Origin* was vying for attention with Italy's war of unification and the home-grown Volunteers, the rifle clubs springing up in the panic over Napoleon's intentions. *The Times* resounded to Tennyson's booming voice:

> Ready, be ready to meet the storm!
> Riflemen, riflemen, riflemen form!

Darwin's muzzle-loader would keep Britain Great. And the *Origin* came highly recommended, said Huxley: 'bigots denounce it with ignorant invective; old ladies of both sexes consider it a decidedly dangerous book, and even savants . . . quote antiquated writers to show that its author is no better than an ape himself'. Perfect for the literati, who revelled in the shock of the new. The *Origin* underpinned the *Westminster*'s demand for fair play and the selection of the best. Complacent parsons could no more claim privileged status in society than inspired understanding of the universe.

> The myths of Paganism are as dead as Osiris or Zeus, and the man who should revive them . . . would be justly laughed to scorn; but the coeval imaginations current among the rude inhabitants of Palestine . . . have unfortunately not yet shared their fate, but, even at this day, are regarded by nine-tenths of the civilised world as the authoritative standard of fact . . .

Huxley was preaching to the converted when he called 'the cosmogony of the semi-barbarous Hebrew . . . the incubus of the philosopher'. No *Westminster* reviewer doubted it. The prophet looked to the sky for an omen: 'Not a star comes to the meridian at its calculated time but testifies to the justice' of the scientific cause. With this Heavenly sanction the Sultan of biology slaughtered the orthodox. And after the carnage he gave thanks, as 'Extinguished theologians lie about the cradle of every science as the strangled snakes beside that of Hercules'. The orthodox army of occupation was left 'bleeding and crushed if not annihilated'.[20] This was *Jihad* oratory, designed to raise a cry of 'Mashallah!' in the crowd.

Stump oratory was no place for caveats. Huxley was exuberantly endorsing the naturalism of Darwin's vision, not the fine points of his theory. Nothing was said of Darwin's infinitesimal variations, each selected for its adaptive advantage. Nor did Huxley mention that his own belief in large-scale mutations, his Ancon sheep, actually negated them. Or that the Home Counties rabbits which happily overran the Australian outback belied Darwin's vaunted adaptation. Then again, until spaniels and greyhounds refused to cross he considered Darwin's analogy between domestic breeds and wild species incomplete. And Huxley still had trouble with Darwin's genealogical approach to classification. 'Huxley demurs', Darwin confided to Hooker, '& says he has nailed his colours to the mast, & I would sooner die than give up, so that we are in as fine a frame of mind to discuss the point, as any two religionists'.

Huxley's bravura performance was in support of Darwin's evolutionary naturalism, not the minutiae of his mechanism. Darwin had created a new nature for the new professionals. And the more loudly Huxley applauded, the more heartily Darwin hailed 'my good & admirable agent for the promulgation of damnable heresies'.[21]

Others brought their own web of ideological beliefs to bear. Habituated to his workers' heresies, Charles Kingsley the Christian Socialist had come to see 'that it is just as noble a conception of Deity, to believe that he created primal forms capable of self-development'. But as for Darwin's mechanism – his ruthless competition between accidental variants – Kingsley could never allow 'chance and selfishness to rule the fortunes of the human race'. The *Origin*, he admitted to Huxley, 'startled many preconceived judgements of mine'. As muscular and militant in his own way, he thought that Huxley's *Macmillan*'s piece 'said what ought to be said' and would 'keep the curs from barking'. And for his part, he would continue to follow Darwin's 'villainous shifty fox of an argument, into what soever unexpected bog & brakes he may lead us'.[22] But it firmed up his view that 'Nature must be counteracted, lest she prove a curse and a destroyer', that co-operative human ethics stood outside, reflecting the sublimity of the City of God, not the savagery of the Roman arena.

The big question mark hung over the head of Richard Owen. A towering zoologist, his *basso* presence intruded everywhere. He will 'bitterly oppose us', Darwin guessed, for he seeks the good grace of 'the aristocratic world'. Owen stood apart ideologically. His 'continuous creation' and specializing fossil life might fit the bill. But he found Darwin's imperfect Nature, based on struggle and slaughter and chance and accident, simply repugnant.

Even after receiving a '*most* liberal note' from Owen, Darwin still suspected that he would be 'dead against us'. The shifting allegiances would ensure it, or rather Huxley's public stand. The Princes of Light and Darkness needed their celestial antipodes.

Darwin found out for himself. En route back from Ilkley in December he met Owen. Owen had now digested the book, where he found himself painted a reactionary. He was 'savage & crimson at my having put his name with defenders of immutability'. The elbowing had hurt, and Owen knew the culprit: he would have absolutely no truck 'with your Huxleys', he told Darwin, and he said it with such 'arrogance [as] I never saw approached'.[23]

Darwin's fraught daily life was relieved by the Boxing Day *Times*. The Thunderer, flag-bearer of the nation, carried an enormous review. Brilliant witticisms, bon mots, praise for the man whose barnacle books showed that he had 'not entered the sanctuary with unwashed hands' – it had to be by Huxley. It was, bar the opening. Huxley's tentacles now penetrated every literary crevice. The staff reviewer, daunted by the 'immensity' of Darwin's developing creation, against which

> The windy ways of men
> Are but dust which dries up
> And is lightly laid again

(meaning he was scientifically illiterate), had thrown up his hands and turned the rest over to Huxley.

> I wrote it faster than ever I wrote anything in my life – the
> last column nearly as fast as my wife could read the
> sheets. But I was thoroughly in the humour & full of the
> subject . . . I earnestly hope it may have made some of the
> educated mob who derive their ideas from the 'Times'
> reflect and whatever they do, they *shall* respect Darwin &
> be d– – –d to them.

Huxley's Dickensian knack for turning arcana into vernacular came into its own. Bank Holiday readers were taken to the Baker Street Bazaar to behold 'bloated preposterous pigs, no more like a wild boar or sow than a city alderman is like an ourang-outang'. Then to a Seven Dials feather club to see such *outré* pigeons that, were they 'known only in a fossil state, no naturalist would hesitate in regarding them as distinct species'. It was a streetwise exposition of artificial selection – or what people could do to change domestic breeds. And in nature where there were too many mouths to feed, a similar selection operated. Struggling individuals were 'like the crew of a foundered ship, and none but good swimmers have a chance of reaching the land'. Nature picked the best.

'The old Fogies will think the world will come to an end', crowed Darwin. 'I should have said that there was only one man in England who could have written this Essay & that *you* were the man'.

The *Times* flagged Huxley's continuing shift. The old fogies heard that the rocks housed a 'regular succession of living beings', and as 'a broad fact, the further we go back in time the less the buried species are like existing forms'. Where was the effrontery in Darwin's vision? All life is obviously related, he said, putting a new shine on his old embryological ware. 'Not only men and horses, and cats and dogs, lobsters and beetles, periwinkles and mussels, but even the very sponges' begin life as indistinguishable germs. Then they

> march side by side along the high road of development,
> and separate the later the more like they are; like people
> leaving church, who all go down the aisle, but having
> reached the door some turn into the parsonage, others go
> down the village, and others part only in the next parish.[24]

Outrageous perhaps, with the sponges arrested at the vestry while men and monkeys marched on, parting only later in their embryological journey.

Huxley had a provocative gift. He was marketing Darwin's ideas, becoming the recluse's 'hard-working unpaid agent'. Huxley's alignment kept Owen at a distance, and every insulting smack increased his alienation. 'Upon my life I am sorry for Owen', Darwin wrote, 'he will be so d– – –d savage; for credit given to any other man, I strongly suspect is in his eyes so much credit robbed from him. Science is so narrow a field, it is clear there ought to be only one cock of the walk!'[25]

With Huxley's *Westminster* review of the *Origin* posted off in December, the 'Committee of Public Safety' reconvened. Speculation was rife about that old dame, the *Quarterly Review*. How would it serve up the *Origin* to the fox-hunting squires? Lyell advised Murray (coincidentally also the *Quarterly*'s publisher) to give the review to a palaeontologist. Hooker said the same to the *Quarterly*'s editor, the cordial Norfolk rector Whitwell Elwin. (Elwin had actually refereed the *Origin*, quaintly advising Darwin to publish a coffee-table book on his 'delightful' pigeons first! More quietly he complained to Murray that 'between the ascertained facts & Darwin's conclusions there is a vast gulf which is bridged over by *unproved assumptions*'.) With the *Origin* out regardless, and Elwin lost for a reviewer, Huxley looked set to snatch the big prize.

But by the year's end he had 'heard nothing and I have my doubts whether Elwin & Murray will think me *tall* enough for the job'. Size was irrelevant; as Elwin told Murray, he wanted 'a really competent & *impartial* enquirer but I have some reason for thinking that Huxley is not that impartial'.[26] Nor would the shires have tolerated one of Huxley's secular sermons. In 1859 nature still had a moral force, and ruling on science remained the duty of their lordships, spiritual and temporal.

15

Buttered Angels & Bellowing Apes

THE *ORIGIN OF SPECIES* tantalized a prim generation. In the freezing weeks after publication it appeared in the unlikeliest places. Commuters coming to hear Huxley's lecture even snapped up the second edition on Waterloo Station. News-vendors, usually with nothing but trashy shilling novels, were touting this Royal Green 15s tome.

It was the 'Book of the Day', Owen conceded. Love it or loathe it, the *Origin* could not be ignored. Wollaston, Huxley's fellow visitor at Downe, felt a 'cold shuddering' and turned hostile. Though Darwin was careful not to say it, the *Origin* ultimately meant that man, 'with all his lofty endowments and future hopes, was . . . never "created" at all, but was merely . . . a development from an ape'. But without the promise of Heaven or the fear of Hell, why should we live a good life? Huxley knew that this was the crux, even as he trashed Wollaston's 'stupid review'.

For or against, the reactions were intensifying. One embarrassing old botanist told Darwin he would continue to read the *Origin* 'as I do the precepts of Christ & the parable of the prodigal son, till my eyes fail me'. The ecstatic highs were only matched by the abusive lows. Others damned the book, fearing that the loss of Creation's moral purpose would 'brutalize' humanity. They compared Darwin's fantastic mechanism to 'Bishop Wilkin's locomotive that was to sail with us to the Moon'.[1] With the stones 'beginning to fly', an agitated Darwin was relieved to see Huxley's *Times* review reprinted in the *Gardeners' Chronicle*.

The *Origin*'s sales galvanized conservatives. The *Athenaeum* demanded show trials to denounce Darwin in 'the Divinity Hall, the College, the Lecture Room, and the Museum'. It meant in

Oxford and Cambridge; wicked London was far too suspect. Indeed the School of Mines staff swung behind Darwin, giving him his first corporate support. They moved too fast for Murchison. But his 'sympathies were with the Conservatives', groaned Huxley, as his boss toyed with standing as London University's first MP (the seat itself symbolizing the growing power of Huxley's Dissenting technocrats). Murchison protested that he was in favour of any 'improvements which our advanced state of Society demands, provided they do not carry us into Democracy'.[2] But Darwin's book did not seem much of an improvement. No 'Silurian King' could accept a levelling theory that made a monkey of his kin.

The chief was outflanked in his own school. The geology teacher Andrew Ramsay had no stomach for a nature made of 'small miracles'. In the museum, Salter glued rows of Devonian and Carboniferous lamp-shells on to a board, copying the family tree in the *Origin*. Its 'beautiful branching gradation' staggered even Darwin, who viewed it on a visit to Huxley's museum one day.[3]

It raised expectations about Huxley's own Royal Institution talk. This was London's first major lecture on the *Origin*, at a West End venue, and delivered by the devil's disciple himself – 'you best & worst of men', as Darwin hailed him. Everyone expected an incisive flash, that explosive mix of provocation and perspicacity which marked his appearances.

Darwin plied him with pigeon skeletons. He even dispatched Huxley to a Piccadilly pigeon club, where velvet-waistcoated fanciers vied with their gaudy breeds. And despite his 'accursed health' he came to town to talk to him. There was no disguising Darwin's hopes for this lecture. Like a hyperactive Alpine goat Huxley had followed Darwin to the precipice and made the long leap – where even Lyell and Carpenter faltered – to a belief that all life stems from '*one* primordial form'. But few dared follow Huxley on human origins; even Lankester admitted that 'it was not given us to know how God first formed man'. Darwin now claimed Huxley as his 'warmest & most important supporter'.

Others too were lagging. Talking of Hal, Mrs Dyster wrote to Nettie:

> I was quite prepared for his siding with Darwins Views,
> & I can also believe that you enter also into these *with*
> your husband's help & spirit. *Mine* inclines greatly to
> [Darwin's] . . . theory, & I fear he is disappointed that I
> cannot like or understand it.[4]

A stirring patriotism shaped these weeks, moulding the very lecture itself. A grey-uniformed Huxley, gun slung over his shoulder, Tennyson's Arthurian epic *The Idylls of the King* in his hand, composed to the sound of trumpets. He had joined the home-grown Volunteers, the self-financed rifle corps composed of merchants and professionals. Napoleon's invasion scare and the Crimean fiasco had the *Times* demanding that the captains of industry and commerce be put in uniform, the proven best, thrown up by a cut-throat competition. Patriotism and liberalism locked hands as brigades of barristers and businessmen turned sharp-shooters. There were Civil Service Corps and Solicitors' Corps, and had Huxley had his way there would probably have been a Science Corps. It was no professional army, but it was Huxley's army of professionals.

Everywhere there was a warm glow in Britain's greatness. Tenny-son was evoking Camelot's past glory. Huxley, wrestling with the *Origin*, wallowing in the *Idylls*, portrayed science as an imperish-able Excalibur. No metaphor escaped him, and certainly not one tying science to a booming Britain. When he called the *Origin* a Whitworth gun in the liberal arsenal, he was evoking the national mood. 'I am drilling for [the] Rifles', he told Dyster after praising the *Idylls*, and will ' "pot" with my first shot the man who should dare to find fault . . . with any tittle of the book'.[5]

Huxley switched his drill day and on Friday 10 February 1860 faced his audience at the Royal Institution. He had distributed tickets to the Darwins, Spencer and Carpenter. They were all there, in the packed tiers of seats overlooking the little stage. The dignitaries occupied the front few rows. Owen was there, and of course Huxley spotted a bishop. On the walls were Nettie's blown-up pictures and on the table distorted and distended pigeon skulls. Darwin had even paid a fancier to bring in his curious coiffed breeds and there they were, show baskets full of puffing pouters, strutting fantails and 'pretty Toy Pigeons'.[6]

And this should have been the gist of his talk – the analogy between the fanciers' skill in drawing out tufts and top-knots, and Nature's mechanism for selecting the best wild variants. But no. Huxley spent too long defining a species and lost the audience. And when he did point to his pigeons ('in Mr Darwin's view the products of a long series of experiments in producing species') it was for another reason. He compared their origin from a wild dove to the descent of today's horses, rhinos and tapirs from the dog-sized Eocene *Palaeotherium*. Even then he threw in his *caveat*, that fanciers had yet to pull their pigeons so far apart as to produce real species; 'by & bye' they might, he admitted, but until then it seems 'to me impossible to admit that the doctrine of the origin of species by Natural Selection stands upon a totally safe & sound physical basis'.[7]

Darwin was nonplussed. He expected Huxley's Whitworth to be sputtering rounds with deadly precision, not to find the General leading a blundering Light Brigade. A fiasco, Hooker called it, which was a 'pity', as Huxley 'intended to have backed the book but unfortunately managed to damage it'. Not that the radicals noticed. It was Huxley's thrilling climax that moved a reporter from the *Reasoner*. He was used to street demagogues undermining Church and Creation, but to hear a man of science was astonishing. It was 'a most exciting and even solemn occasion'.

Huxley damned the sanctimonious meddlers who would stifle troublesome research. And, yes, Darwin's work meant that 'all living things & man among the rest must have arisen from one stock'. He railed against the moral cowardice that would prevent us from accepting it:

> And there is a wonderful tenacity of life about this sort of opposition to physical science. Always crushed it seems never to be killed, and after a thousand defeats it is as rampant now as in the days of Galileo.

The talk ended with an emotive flourish. The gun and grey dress were not only to bar Napoleon, but his priests – to make Britain safe, rational and great. Never was Huxley's sharpshooting more accurate. 'I had a Bishop & a Dean among my auditors', he explained, 'and, to please *them*, I wound up with the most energetic protest in favour of Science *versus* Parsonism that is likely to have reached their ears'. It had the desired effect. 'The High Church orthodox' sought the salubrious air outside. The bishop's entourage left comparing the 'building in Albemarle Street 1860 with the Paris Pantheon' in revolutionary 1791, a shrine to bloodthirsty atheism.

In his flag-waving finale, Huxley moved from 'the little Canutes of the hour enthroned in state & bidding the great wave to stay' to the scientific steamboats bringing a 'thousand treasures' on the rationalist tide. It was all 'very bold', Darwin muttered, as he listened to the gladiatorial metaphors that were his General's stock-in-trade.

For Huxley, Britain's destiny was to see a new Protestant reformation. The moral edifice would not collapse with these fresh truths. It would be undergirded. Britain

> may prove to the world that for one race at any rate
> Despotism & Demagogy are not the necessary alternatives
> of polity – that freedom & order are not incompatible –
> that Reverence is the handmaid of Knowledge – that truth
> is strength & that free discussion is the very life of truth.

Square up to science, he said embellishing this piece for publication. 'Cherish her, venerate her, follow her methods faithfully . . . and the future of this people will be greater than the past'.

> If you do otherwise I fear the day will come when our
> children will see the glory of England vanishing like Arthur
> in the mist & cry too late the woeful cry of Guinever:
>
> > It was my duty to have loved the highest
> > It surely was my profit had I known
> > It would have been my pleasure had I seen.[8]

Science was the real patriotism; it armed Britain with greater intellectual firepower. There spoke a man who had known a decade of debt, who had struggled to secure a science post, only to find it lacking in prestige. He was turning the patriotic tables, turning a reactionary Latinity into treason. Tying science to national salvation, in defiance of the other-worldly sort, was astute policy. If strength lay in Truth, then the country's well-being hinged on the expert's health. The nation needed him.

It was an intoxicating performance (even if Darwin doubted the value of patriotic poetry in an exegesis of the *Origin*). But there was little of Darwin's book in it, and nothing on selection. Darwin grew jaundiced.

> I succeeded in persuading myself for 24 hours that
> Huxley's lecture was a success. Parts were eloquent &
> good & all *very* bold, & I heard strangers say 'what a
> good lecture'. I told Huxley so . . . [But] after conversation
> with others & more reflection I must confess that as an
> Exposition of the doctrine the Lecture seems to me an
> entire failure . . . He gave no just idea of *natural*
> selection.[9]

Huxley was defending a rational explanation of life, not the nuts and bolts of selection. He was not equipped to talk on Darwin's ecological approach. He was no field naturalist juggling messy variables: he had no time for variation, survival rates and island isolation. He was rooted in embryology, with its belief in innate developmental pathways.

There were other obstacles in his way to accepting natural selection. Many critics saw in Darwin's Nature the 'sordid motives' of utilitarian society. Its core was naked survivalism: overproduction, struggle and death, a free-for-all with every individual clawing down his neighbour. In Darwin's 'horridly cruel' nature every part must serve a purpose or be cut down; only from death on a genocidal scale could the few progress. As Hell fell into disrepute, Nature was becoming more hellish.

Huxley wanted competition, but not this utilitarian shadow of workhouse society. He had never accepted Nature as a sweated 'slave-mill' run 'for mere utilitarian ends'.[10] His was a nobler vision of 'Harmonious order'. Raised within the romantic tradition and a rung lower than Darwin's great folks, Huxley had seen society at the sharp end. He could not afford to share his friend's heartless image. Even as he championed evolution, he softened selection.

Huxley's onslaught on 'Parsonism' simply raised the temperature. He was driving in his wedge, splitting off science for his men. He had turned the *Origin*'s factual arcana into an ideological arena. Not that Tory bishops – whose own science testified to a static, Created order – were unhappy with an ideological killing ground. They took up equally entrenched positions. What a 'sneer by the Bishop at Huxley', Darwin noted cryptically in a letter to Hooker. Within days of the lecture Lyell 'had a good half hour's argument with the B[isho]p of Oxford, Wilberforce', who thought Darwin's book 'the most unphilosophical he had ever read'.

Owen had 'gazed with amazement' at Huxley's diagrams comparing the origin of fancy pigeons with a evolution of horses and tapirs from a *Palaeotherium* parent. For years the languid giant had been shoved and goaded. This red rag finally sent him charging. Darwin was expecting 'many & bitter sneers from him', and Huxley ensured them. At the Royal Institution Huxley had mooted man's ape-like frame. Only he who was 'devoid of soul' and unconcerned 'about his own relations to a Creator' could find solace in a bestial human ancestry, raged Owen. And to claim that 'England owes her greatness' to such poisonous philosophy! More truly it 'parallels the abuse of science' at root of the French Terror.

Owen now came out bitterly against the *Origin*. He had received endless protests about it, from as far away as Livingstone in Africa, from as high as the Duke of Argyll in the Cabinet. As the senior statesman of science, his pronouncement was eagerly awaited. The *Origin* was a flash in the pan, he said, to be 'forgotten in 10 years'. The book might be, but Darwin hoped that with Huxley, Carpenter and Hooker on board 'the subject will not'.

Darwin was disheartened as the attacks began 'falling thick & heavy', despite Huxley's reassurance that 'the platoon-firing must soon cease'. In fact the conservative bullets began spraying ever wider. Even Huxley and Tyndall's Alpine climbs were made a laughing stock in the *Athenaeum*. It was a 'detestable article . . . about Tyndall – sneering at his veracity – & very disagreeable about Huxley', said Darwin. 'I look at the Editor as a spiteful old woman, who has taken, what my Brother calls her D.B. degree (ie damned bitch)'. Unable to fight his corner, Darwin relied on his Volunteers. Thank goodness, he told Hooker, for 'Lyell, yours, Huxley & Carpenter's aid'.[11] 'By myself I sh^d. be powerless'.

But this cadre, like the ill-assorted Volunteers, wrangled at the rifle range. All wanted to break the 'ecclesiastical domination' of Oxbridge to give 'the progressive sciences . . . fair play'. The urbane Lyell, writing a book on human antiquity himself, railed against the '30,000 [clergymen] who are sworn to read & interpret' Genesis 'in a certain way not favourable to geology, all paid by the State'. How to break the hold of the sermon? Get science into the classroom, Huxley answered; give schoolmasters a new vocational training, involving 'physical science & Nat^l Hist^y'.

But how, the old Unitarian persisted, to rationalize society at the very hearth place? Why were women barred from science? Radical Unitarians had already opened a 'Ladies' College in Bedford Square, where Carpenter taught. Lyell wanted to open the Geological Society as well. Let them into all the 'places of education to hear both sides discussed'. Wives might be proof-readers, translators, illustrators – like Nettie the best of help-mates. And for Darwin's Volunteers, who 'have a good deal of fighting to do', they kept the home fires burning. But this was it; Huxley saw science as masculine combat. Nor was the Geological 'a place of education', but a forum 'for adepts'. He began to look a rather ragged champion of fair play. In fact on women's rights Lyell thought he looked embarrassingly like 'the B[isho]p. of O[xford]'.

The coalition's seams were showing. The Unitarians talked emancipation, as Huxley's professionals strengthened their male meritocracy. Huxley – once furious at finding doors slammed in his face – now secured the inner sanctum. It would only be opened when daughters learnt something more than domestic skills at their mothers' knee. The school bench had to replace that maternal limb:

> I am far from wishing to place any obstacle in the way of the intellectual advancement and development of women. On the contrary I dont see how we are to make any permanent advancement while one half of the race is sunk, as nine tenths of women are, in mere ignorant parsonese superstitions. And to show you that my ideas are practical I have fully made up my mind . . . to give my daughters the same training in physical science as their brother . . . They at any rate shall not be got up as man-traps for the matrimonial market. If other people would do the like the next generation would see women fit to be the companions of men in all their pursuits.[12]

Women had to be schooled in science. And society had to lose its crippling prudery, to allow a more open approach to the body. The age's delicacy about even bee reproduction was notorious. (Rather than expurgate his talks Huxley refused to teach Bedford Square's 'virgins, young and old'.) Huxley himself planned a training programme. How hard he thought the task – or how much he underrated women's capacity – was shown by his eventual Ladies' course. It was a modified children's class.

When Huxley's *Westminster* review of the *Origin* appeared in April 1860 Owen found his divine archetype derided as 'verbal hocus-pocus'. Darwin was beginning to revel in Huxley's lethal pen, agreeing with 'Lyell that your extinguished Theologians laying about the cradle of each new science &c &c is *splendid*'. Who cared that the review hardly 'advances [the] subject'?

Of course it rebounded in Darwin's face. Days later the Huxleys arrived at Downe. They found Darwin bleary after losing a night's sleep. Owen's *Edinburgh* response was out. 'I am thrashed in every possible way', moaned Darwin. Twenty-five years' friendship lay shattered. 'I wish for . . . auld lang syne's sake he had been a little less bitter'. Anonymity could not cloak the review: 'Some of my relations say it cannot *possibly* be Owen's article, because the Reviewer speaks so very highly of Prof. Owen. Poor dear simple folk!'

They paced the grounds, talking over the German translation of the *Origin* (Huxley had all the contacts). Past the pigeon loft, now emptying, past the rabbit carcasses rotting comfortably. All the while they mulled over Owen's 'malignant' attitude. Owen had been hurt by the ape jibes, insulted by the 'preposterous' lampoon of animals flashing into existence. Darwin and Huxley had polarized the options: either rhinos were miraculously reassembled atoms or transmuted *Palaeotheriums*. Owen's continuous creation and transitional fossils had been shunted aside. For a Superintendent at the British Museum it rankled. Owen's overweening conceit demanded an overkill response. The newspapers egged Owen on. An *Athenaeum* reviewer scoured his new book, *Palaeontology*, for some pontifical pronouncement but found him 'hidden in the valley of dry bones'. Too cautious, it complained. Huxley has said enough 'to freeze us'. 'Is Prof. Owen, then, to be reserved'?

Owen abominated Huxley's soulless gorilla-ancestry. Was blood to run in the gutters as the 'Goddess of Reason' was installed in St Paul's Cathedral? (Aha! wrote Huxley's protégé George Rolleston, 'I have heard that allusion of his to the enthronement of the Goddess of Reason at Paris I don't know in how many Sermons'.) Gentlemanly onlookers were aghast. It was not *'becoming* in one Naturalist to be bitter against another – any more than for one sect to burn the members of another'.[13] But Huxley's sect, with its excommunications and conversions, its bible and corpus, indeed with Darwin's palpitating corpse, needed its stakes.

Through it all, Huxley continued teaching. He ran classes for schoolmasters at Marlborough House, now moved to South Kensington, as part of his plan to get science into the classrooms. He taught them to make the mundane exciting. And what was more mundane than a fishmonger's lobster? They crowded around as he fingered its segments, drawing back at his breathtaking conclusions on the unity of life. Before they exhaled he had whisked them away to glimpse its ancestors. To a time before men, before mammals or reptiles even; to an exotic land where its six-foot ancestor *Pterygotus* scavenged 'along the muddy shores of the Old Red Sandstone seas'.

Excitement was one way to inveigle science on board. Relevance was another. Such was the medieval mediocrity of Britain's public schools that Classics and mathematics were deemed sufficient for life. A Centurion's son from AD 400 'transplanted' into one of these moss-encrusted institutions 'would not meet with a single unfamiliar line of thought'. (A lovely touch, said Darwin, who hated the 'stereotyped stupid classical education'.) Yet 'modern civilization' was based on a scientific revolution. Deny that, Huxley said, and Britain's lead 'is gone tomorrow'. Science shows

> that the ultimate court of appeal is observation and
> experiment, and not authority . . . she is creating a firm
> and living faith in the existence of immutable moral and
> physical laws, perfect obedience to which is the highest
> possible aim of an intelligent being.

Authority was there, of course, in the Scientific Priest's robes. And morality rested in acknowledging his Laws. (Who is to wonder that Owen recalled the Temple of Reason, where *curés* were dragged to confess their charlatanerie?) Huxley's was an old En-lightenment gambit, and veterans as old as the Enlightenment had seen it fail before. George Grote, fêted for his *History of Greece* ('fetid' Carlyle thought more apt for this unspiritual outpouring) liked Huxley's Calvinism. Children should respect these 'immu-table moral & physical laws'. But what chance when the Bible in our 'schools, inculcates a faith not only different, but contrary'?[14]

Mundane work now meant crocodiles, to help Huxley fathom the Elgin fossils. He planned to look at Oxford's during the BAAS meeting there in June 1860. 'Your Bedroom is furnished as you desired!' his Christ Church disciple George Rolleston wrote. 'Your Crocodile's skull clear as driven snow'.

One ally amid the dreaming spires was more than any sadducee could desire, and Rolleston better than he dared hope. They had met in London, after the vicar's son had switched from his Classics course at Pembroke College to St Bartholomew's Hospital. A bit plummy at first, he toughened up in Huxley's *embrouillé* medical world. He scorned the shrouded symbolism of the Oxford Movement and spurned the mystical garb of Owen's archetype. By 1860 Rolleston was back at Christ Church, demanding reform, demanding the admission of Dissenters. Though a brain specialist, he still ran his papers past the master. In turn Huxley was backing him for Oxford's Linacre Chair of anatomy. Owen, of course, was

promoting a rival candidate, Rolleston reported, out of 'antagonism . . . to you'.

As 21,000 Volunteers paraded before Queen Victoria in Hyde
Park on 23 June 1860, Huxley was putting his rifle away. He
anticipated no target practice at Oxford. Nettie was to wait for
him at her sister Isy's in Reading. And so on 27 June Huxley set
off for Rolleston's 'Sash windowed Squareboxlike House' in Christ
Church. Here his reptiles lay ready in their Gothic haunt, scutes
polished and jaws in pieces.

His reputation preceded him. The *Westminster* essay on Darwin
had passed round High Table. Prompted by Rolleston, the progressive Vice-Chancellor Francis Jeune, another Pembroke man, had
read it 'to his own gratification'. He had passed it to that 'great
liberal large-hearted man' Henry Liddell, the Dean of Christ
Church, who was not big-hearted enough to appreciate Schamyl's
satire on the orthodox explanation of life – 'Mashallah! it so
pleases God!' But he considered the subject 'a "tremendous"
one'.[15] Pembroke's liberal phalanx treated Huxley to dinner that
night.

The British Association met for a week in a different town each
year, and each year Huxley found the meetings 'duller'. The public
flocked in, thousands of top-hatted gents and ladies in their new
tent-like, crinoline dresses. They milled around the venue halls, as
always impatient, wanting not only to see the scientific lions, but
to hear them roar. On Thursday morning, 28 June, huge numbers
gathered at the Zoology section. The Bishop of Oxford looked on.
There was an expectant buzz, a feeling that the Darwinian issue
would be aired. 'I determined to buck them', Hal explained to
Nettie. He refused to perform, even though called upon. 'I did not
think that a fit place to discuss the question. However, it was no
good, Owen got up and made a very clear speech attacking
statements of mine indirectly', and so 'I got up, and girding on my
armour, went at it'.

Owen had maintained that a gorilla's brain was closer to a
lemur's than a man's (denying Huxley's claim at the Royal Institution). And such distinct cerebral hemispheres, he implied, militated
against humans having evolved. The Glasgow anatomist Allen
Thomson had just dissected a chimpanzee's cerebrum and written
to Huxley confirming its 'extraordinary resemblance to the human
brain'. No Continental expert doubted it, and so Huxley jumped
up with a flat contradiction. Falconer had never seen 'such a set
down'.

'So you had been battling with the Archetype', Nettie replied, 'you were quite right to try to evade the fight', but under the circumstances 'he must be fought'. It was the bell for the longest knock-down fight over an anatomical point in Victorian times. Darwin heard of this tugging over his 'absent body'. He had stayed away, secure in his Richmond spa, where his body was falling apart unaided. Vomiting and headachy, he lived vicariously through the news. 'Your interests', Falconer reassured him, 'were most tenderly watched over by your devoted Elèves'.

'I am none the worse for being stirred up a little', Hal admitted. Life was no longer dull, but 'you could not expect to have a row every day of the week'.

By Friday Huxley was 'as tired as a dog'. He was 'eternally in a bustle', speaking at more meetings than he intended, 'but you know it is not easy for me to keep quiet when anything is going on'. He had given a convoluted paper on sea squirt eggs. That was the hottest topic he cared for: the source of the first embryonic cells to appear. (He tracked them back to the huge dividing egg-nucleus.) It was 'raining cats & dogs' and he was ready to quit and take the 4 pm. Saturday train to Reading.[16] Isy and Nettie promised better company than the Bishop of Oxford. The buzz was now about Saturday's session on Darwinism and society, where the rhetorical flourishes were expected.

On Friday he got out once in the rain 'to look at some of the chapels which are very beautiful'. He ran into the Edinburgh publisher Robert Chambers of all people, the author of the evolutionary *Vestiges* which Huxley had so savagely trashed six years earlier. When the BAAS had last met at Oxford, in 1847, Chambers had been humiliated by the Bishop of Oxford for the 'foul speculations' in *Vestiges*. He knew the pain a lashing tongue could inflict. Then the bishop had carried his scientific flock. But these were new times. With Church and science fractured into liberal and orthodox camps, the old smug consensus was dead. An avant-garde was prepared to lash back. Hence Chambers' 'vehement remonstrances' about Huxley's 'deserting them'. Chambers, once humiliated by Huxley himself, convinced him to stay on. By the time Huxley dined at the Vice-Chancellor's that night he was girding his loins again.

The Saturday meeting drew a huge public crowd, 700, some said 1,000, showing that expectations were high. So many in fact that it had to be switched to the long west room of Oxford's new Gothic revival museum. Hooker (yet to attend a meeting) 'swore as usual

I would not go in; but getting equally bored of doing nothing I did'. Huxley too sauntered in, beneath the angel guarding the entrance.

Inside a flood of light from the glass-roofed atrium played on the jostling crowd. Raucous students were packed at the back. Everywhere were dons and academics. The white chokers of the clergy dominated the centre: this, after all, was their 'temple', glorying in that holy Nature, through 'which the Author of the universe manifests himself to His creatures'.

The chairman was Hooker's father-in-law, Henslow. On the podium was the purple-vested Bishop Samuel Wilberforce, there as a BAAS Vice-President (a courtesy in his own see). He was a mathematician and ornithologist, and loquacious. But being in his own diocese did not guarantee him applause. To a few he was a 'finished Philistine'. The Church needed strong progressives, the liberal *Telegraph* said, rather than these 'old style Tories' who have not budged 'one iota beyond their ancient notions'.[17] Church liberals hated Wilberforce's hard line, as he condemned their softpedalling on miracles. He castigated the 'seven against Christ', the liberal Anglican contributors to the innocent-sounding *Essays and Reviews*, whose critique of the Genesis myth and biblical literalism inflamed more passions in a year than Darwin managed in a lifetime. The Darwinian boat was now bumping along on the ferocious waves already pounding the orthodox Church. But Huxley's reception was just as uncertain. His quips about 'extinguished theologians' alienated many, and there were murmurings about his 'irreverent freedom'.

Speeches and reports were dispensed with quickly. Student bellows rose. At times the crowd seemed to control the event, turning it into a piece of participatory theatre. Refutations of Darwin came and went; Huxley, called on, sarcastically admitted he held 'a brief for Science, but had not yet heard it assailed', and sat down. The crowd bayed for more; the bishop was called by name and finally obliged. He ranged widely, on the *Origin*'s unphilosophical character, on Egyptian mummies disproving change, on fancy pigeons, on the line between man and the animals. Then in a jovial mood, he tried to brighten two hours in a stuffy room with an ad-lib. Student laughter drove him on. In the heat of the moment no one could remember his precise words. But he twisted round and – referring to Huxley's gorilla put-down of Owen two days before – asked him whether the apes were on his grandfather's or grandmother's side.

It was a high-risk strategy. Sedgwick too had panned the *Vestiges* to protect 'our glorious maidens' from its wickedness. Maidens symbolized the chaste; the lurking evil was draped in the black cape of the bestial transmutationist. Wilberforce was playing on sensibilities, raising the inviolability of Victorian womanhood. Huxley could have made flippancy look like vulgarity. But he steered clear of the quagmire.

He waited, stage-managing the event just as much. And when the shouts for him climaxed, he rose. 'A slight tall figure stern and pale, very quiet and very grave' – 'white with anger', some said. He

> had listened with great attention to the Lord Bishops speech but had been unable to discern either a new fact or a new argument in it – except indeed the question raised as to my personal predilection in the matter of ancestry – That it would not have occurred to me to bring forward such a topic as that for discussion myself, but that I was quite ready to meet the Right Rev. prelate even on that ground. If then, said I the question is put to me would I rather have a miserable ape for a grandfather or a man highly endowed by nature and possessed of great means of influence & yet who employs these faculties & that influence for the mere purpose of introducing ridicule into a grave scientific discussion, I unhesitatingly affirm my preference for the ape.

That was enough for the raucous students. There followed

> inextinguishable laughter among the people, and they listened to the rest of my argument with the greatest attention. Lubbock & Hooker spoke after me with great force & among us we shut up the bishop & his Laity.
> I happened to be in very good condition and said my say with perfect good temper & politeness. I assure you of this because all sorts of reports were spread about e.g. that I had said I would rather be an ape than a bishop &c.[18]

'Soapy Sam' stood alongside Owen in Huxley's demonic Pantheon. He was everything the squad detested. Huxley's troops were hammering the wedge deeper between science and theology. They had not taken over the barracks to have a Tory bishop use 'his position & his lawyer faculty' to force them back into a moral harness. Huxley had an 'unmitigated contempt' for Wilberforce's tactics. What value science if it had to be approved by rank and wealth? What of integrity? This was not religious obscurantism blinded by a radiant science. If there was light, it came from the sparks caused by the political friction. Huxley oozed Puritan self-righteousness. He made the scientific man seem more principled, more earnest. Moral rectitude was his; 'truth' was defensively ringed by his New Model Army. And before it stood the embodiment of corruption, a purple-frocked bishop with a 'splendid nature debauched by society'.

Perceptions of the event differed so wildly that talk of a 'victor' is ridiculous. Huxley believed himself 'the most popular man in Oxford for full four & twenty hours afterwards'. But even Hooker thought that he had not managed to 'command the audience' and that in the electric air – when even 'Lady Brewster fainted' – it was *he* (Hooker) who subsequently 'smashed' Wilberforce 'amid rounds of applause'. And that it was *he* who was 'congratulated & thanked by the blackest coats & whitest stocks in Oxford' (the liberal clergy). In the chaos the punchdrunk combatants failed to see the jaunty Wilberforce leaving. He bore 'no malice', convinced that he had floored Huxley. He was punning happily as he saw the droll side:

> . . . now a learn'd Professor, grave and wise,
> Stoutly maintains what I supposed were lies;
> And, while each listening sage in wonder gapes,
> Claims a proud lineage of ancestral Apes.
> Alas! cried I, if such the sage's dreams,
> Save me, ye powers, from these unhallowed themes;
> From self-degrading science keep me free,
> And from the pride that apes humility![19]

The public relished the performance. Such acts it loved to see: intellectual tempests which swept away the 'the courtesies of life like a sou'-wester'. It was as stirring, the press said, 'as the Battle of Farnborough or the Volunteer Review'. At a party that night someone wished it could happen again, only to be pulled up by Huxley, 'Once in a life-time is enough'. But it was not. Darwinians needed victories to counter the bad press. The fight was talked up, each time with bloodier results. And not only by the Darwinians. With the furies raging over *Essays and Reviews*, liberal Churchmen like the Vice-Chancellor thought the bishop 'got no more than he deserved'. Rolleston, the meeting's organizer, shared his contempt. He intended to have his own 'slap at the Base Bishop', he told

Huxley, 'before he recovers the cudgelling you have given him'. Wilberforce was being pushed towards the slag heap of 'extinguished theologians'.

In his rest home, Darwin heard from Falconer 'how the Saponaceous Bishop got basted and larded by Huxley'. Darwin chivvied Huxley for his version. Drained by the howling reviews, he revelled in Huxley's retelling. 'I have read [your letter] twice & sent it to my wife & when I get home shall read it again'. 'But how durst you attack a live Bishop in that fashion? . . . Have you no reverence for fine lawn sleeves?' Darwin delighted in the witty repartee, even if it blotted out all talk of runts and tumblers.

Only one thing did Darwin enjoy more: Owen's 'basting'. They all suspected Owen of backing the bishop and making 'him strike whatever note he liked'. Owen, lodging at the bishop's palace, obviously chatted about Darwin's book – and Huxley's review. But knowing his faith in 'continuous creation', and his tree of life with its archetypal roots and fossil forks, he might have been coaxing Sam beyond the Six Days to a more informed opposition. But he suffered by association as the bishop resorted to 'round-mouthed, oily, special pleading'.[20]

Exhausted, Huxley crept to the station the next morning to catch the Reading train. He left an ally in place. Rolleston became the Linacre Professor and pledged 'never to give you cause to regret the share you have had in my promotion'. And as proof he started a home mission:

> I tell my friends here that if they would only believe that
> God is Almighty there would be no difficulty in reconciling
> Darwin with the established Creed. But people will not
> believe in this, the Second Article of the Apostles' Creed;
> and they persist in binding down Omnipotence to such a
> line of operation as they, poor mannikins, think they
> could carry out.

Rolleston still had 'a great deal of Oxford slough to shed'.[21] But Huxley thought it helped him blend in among the vipers.

Back in London's secular air, Huxley began a paper to claim the human domain. 'On the Zoological Relations of Man with the Lower Animals' was a landmark production that summed up the Victorian condition. Or exacerbated it, some said. What *were* man's ties to Nature?

> Theologians and moralists . . . impressed by a sense of the
> infinite responsibilities of mankind, awed by a just
> prevision of the great destinies in store for the only earthy
> being of practically unlimited powers . . . have always
> tended to conceive of their kind as something apart,
> separated by a great and impassable barrier.

But anatomists,

> discovering as complete a system of law and order in the
> microcosm as in the macrocosm . . . have no less steadily
> gravitated towards the opposite opinion, and, as
> knowledge has advanced, have more and more distinctly
> admitted the closeness of the bond which unites man with
> his humbler fellows.

Did it matter? For whatever mankind's parentage, whether archan-
gel ruined or ape risen, 'his duties and his aspirations . . . remain
the same'. No claim to Divine parentage will

> change the brutishness of man's lower nature; nor, except
> to those valet souls who cannot see greatness in their
> fellow because his father was a cobbler, will the
> demonstration of a pithecoid pedigree one whit diminish
> man's divine right of kingship over nature; nor lower the
> great and princely dignity of perfect manhood, which is
> an order of nobility, not inherited, but to be won by each
> of us, so far as he consciously seeks good and avoids
> evil . . .

Hooker thought these remarks would be 'balsam to many short
witted & honest but timid enquirers'.[22] Actually it looked as
though they were aimed at Lyell. At least they were more comforting than Darwin's crumbs. Darwin could offer Lyell no such
'"consolatory view" on the dignity of man'. Darwin, ever the
relativist, demoted man and deprivileged the present. His vision
was cosmic and shocking. Nineteenth-century gents stood at no
special point in geological time in his view. 'I cannot explain why',
he tweaked Sir Charles, 'but to me it would be an infinite satisfaction to believe that mankind will progress to such a pitch, that we
sh[d]. be looked back at as mere Barbarians'.

Huxley the essayist became Huxley the anatomist. From imponderables he switched to resolvables. All he could really clear up, he
said, were the claims about anatomical uniqueness. So he delved

into the neural arcana. Each of Owen's esoteric points about the 'unique' human cerebrum was refuted; every known expert was subpoenaed to prove that apes possess the cerebral lobes and bumps of their human betters. Rolleston sent dissection notes. So did others, while pleading to be kept out of 'controversy with the great potentate'.[23]

Brains, apes and human destiny wrapped themselves up in one disconsolate package and deepened the crisis already racking Victorian intellectuals. By now every review did what Darwin dreaded – extended evolution to humanity in order to slate it. Lascivious stories sold tabloids. Hacks wanted evidence that man 'came forth, in his complete humanity, from the womb of an ape'. Such carnality was a self-refutation. Even Owen was pestered on the point. One Episcopalian, writing a reprisal article on 'The Creative Week' for Wilberforce's *Replies to 'Essays and Reviews'*, asked him. Was Adam produced 'supernaturally ... *through* the ... womb of the Ape'?[24]

The Tory *Quarterly* – the review of the *Origin* that Huxley had angled for – had not fallen to an impartial critic. Hooker was staggered at Murray's eventual choice, Bishop Wilberforce. It might have been what the worried shires wanted, but hadn't the age of arbitrating bishops passed? 'The Article itself is astounding': where should he begin, with its 'appalling ignorance of the rudiments of Science, or incredible blunders'? What was Murray doing 'entrusting a Scientific book to an ignorant intemperate Reviewer'?

Darwin scribbled 'rubbish' in his copy. Against the sentiment that 'all creation is the transcript in matter of ideas eternally existing in the mind of the Most High', he jotted 'mere words', Owen's – the sort that sounded hollow to Darwin's Unitarians and secularists.[25] Not that it mattered. Huxley's scientifics were capturing the liberal press. And the story of 'Huxley, the Bishop & the Ape' was spiralling into legend. One rector, quick off the mark to use natural selection in his study of Saharan larks, was so angered at Darwin's deification by 'his prophet Huxley' that he recanted and rejoined the bishop. Huxley, that dark avenging angel, Darwin's 'good & kind agent for the propagation of the Gospel ie the Devil's gospel', was partitioning the world along his own lines. The burst from his Whitworth was scaring the rectors back to their own trenches.

He made a show of ousting those with a dual calling – clergymen with a scientific bent. If it meant denigrating, so be it. The professional demarcation dispute hit a low note as Huxley's pugnacity rubbed off on others. Why should science play host to the 'ignorant priest'?, asked Hooker. 'I say ignorant advisedly, for I hold' the clerical geologists 'to be as really *ignorant* of the fundamentals of Natural History as I am of Church History'.[26]

At this moment a journal dropped into the group's lap. The Dublin-based *Natural History Review* was crashingly unsuccessful. Worse, it was broadly anti-Darwinian. The proprietors wanted to sell it and Huxley drooled. Given his pool of talent it could be provocative; turn its orientation, make it 'mildly episcopophagus', and it could even pay. He roped in Lubbock and Rolleston, those 'plastically minded young men' (meaning Darwin's men). Then the older hands, Busk and Carpenter, were brought on board. Hooker, knee-deep in his own botanical 'midden-heap', was too busy, but he nominated his 'plastic' young assistants who would join for the glory of it. With this line-up, Huxley told him, 'you & Darwin & Lyell will have a fine opportunity if you wish it of slaying your adversaries'. Sobering up some months after Oxford, he was more circumspect. He wanted 'articles *for* & *against*' the *Origin*, he said, so as to leave no doubt 'that the review is a "Champ libre"'.

Darwin and Lyell, those wealthy virtuosi whose living rooms were laboratories where they could lavish time on innovative tomes, called it madness. Original research was what counted, carrying the imprimatur of a gentleman. Yet all around them the academic world was compartmentalizing. It needed specialist journals. To Huxley, a penny-a-liner on other people's papers, a rushing ideologue, with a talent for organization and a desire for power, the prospect of his own journal was appealing. But even Hooker was 'aghast' at the extra donkey work and told him to get a '*paid* subeditor'.[27] But there was no money in the kitty; indeed there was no kitty. Lyell prophesied that Huxley would end up carrying the load – 'quarterly mischief' he called it.

True, the piles were mounting. Starting was easy, but Huxley was finding it 'more & more difficult ... to *finish* things'. His fascination with one of the first vertebrates to have appeared on the earth, the bizarre armoured fish *Pteraspis*, was driving him to study all Devonian fish. (Brilliant work this: he traced the coelacanths back to a flourishing Devonian group of lobe-finned fish – 'Crossopterygians' he called them, archaic fish which, he hinted in a flash of insight, probably had lungs.)[28] Nights were spent drilling, although why the 'volunteer-soldiering ... does not kill you',

Darwin puzzled, 'I cannot understand'. If the rifles didn't, everyone expected that the journal would.

Torrential rains heralded the start of Huxley's holiday in August. He took the six-week break at home to clear the backlog. Here his only plague was a curly head poking round the door, wanting to play. Noel, three, was articulate and inquisitive, Jessie was toddling and precocious, 16 month-old Marian completed the blond conspiracy. Nettie, five months pregnant, looked forward to her next Christmas baby. There was a new togetherness as Hal's first holiday at home turned into a second 'Honeymoon'. Evenings were spent proof-reading Spencer's *First Principles* (the start of his ten-volume 'synthetic philosophy'). Hal passed the pages to Nettie, who liked their calm tone.

She read of the 'Unknowable', that mysterious reality beyond the reach of the senses. The 'web and woof of matter and force' had woven a 'veil which lies between us and the Infinite', in Hal's words. Huxley delighted in tracing the concept of the 'Unknowable' to the High Churchman Henry Mansel's *Limits of Religious Thought* (published in 1858). Since man's finite mind could never contact God directly, Mansel argued, we are in no position to question His inspired Word. Mansel was supporting Revelation, but Huxley saw him sawing through the plank on which he was sitting. So did Spencer, and in *First Principles* the 'Unknowable' replaced God Himself.

Nettie took Spencer's book in her stride. She had plunged into a society in crisis, 'destitute of faith, yet terrified at scepticism', as Carlyle had it. She saw it torn by Dissent and teased by the avant-garde. She lived with a devout man and found (as the same Carlyle said) that his 'deep sense of religion was compatible with the entire absence of Theology'. No husband 'manifested more of the moral presuppositions of a Puritan evangelicalism'. Yet, her Hal admitted, '99 out of 100 of my fellows would call me Atheist'. All around her values were transforming – no longer was worth linked with birth; or virtue with the Anglican communion. Nor did morality rest in using church creeds – about the created hierarchies in Nature and Society – to maintain the status quo.

She took the toddlers to Christ Church in Lisson Grove each Sunday. Here Kingsley's friend the Christian Socialist, Revd Llewelyn Davies – Church reformer, female emancipator and co-founder of the Working Men's College – drew intellectuals from far and wide. Nettie sat with them amid its giant Corinthian columns, listening to Davies' reforming sermons. She was happy with Davies (and Davies thought Christianity could only learn from the evolutionary movement). Nettie knew the mood as she scanned Spencer's sheets on the 'Unknowable'. Huxley surprised Spencer by thinking them quite good. Someone had to publish the big evolutionary picture, and only Spencer had the cosmic gall.

'I have not been away this autumn & don't mean to from being very well & jolly', Huxley told the Tenby folk on a wet 9 September. 'My wife is as well as N° 4 will permit . . . N°s 1, 2 & 3 are flourishing'.[29]

Six days later the bottom fell out of his world. On Thursday 13 September little Noel lured him out of the study for a romp. Then it was off to bed, and Noel kissed his father goodnight. Later he woke up, 'sick & feverish'. They soothed him back to sleep, but by morning Hal found him 'very ill', headachy, with a flushed face and a rash. Jessie too showed scarlet fever symptoms. But Noel had no sore throat, and the doctor thought the violence pointed to 'gastric fever'. Jessie was only mildly affected and the baby escaped. Noel's rash reddened and erupted and peeled. The frightened tears gave way to shivering as his pulse quickened and the 'little fellow gradually became delirious'.

Hal could not understand the virulence. 'It was as if the boy had been inoculated with some septic poison'. Nettie was frantic and Hal beside himself as Noel's 'restless head, with its bright blue eyes and tangled golden hair, tossed all day upon his pillow'. Desperation gave way to trauma as they stared the unimaginable in the face. All Saturday he thrashed in his bed, deranged, burning up. His father began to see 'typhoid symptoms', confusing him the more. They sat by the bedside, watching helplessly, hopelessly, mopping his brow. At 7 pm., just as the sun was setting, there was a sudden violent attack. It lasted two hours. They were an instant and an eternity. And then 'we had a dead child in our arms'.[30]

Nettie was crushed and bewildered. Two days earlier her 'hope & darling' had been horse-playing, his eyes twinkling. Those blue eyes now stared, vacant and fixed. A hysterical collapse gave way to numbness, a mindless incomprehension of this outrage on Divine justice. She subsided in agony, her head 'one hot patch of pain'. Hal saw her going out of her mind. Stoically he walked Nettie 'up & down outside the house to let the rain fall' on her 'burning head'. Then she retreated to her room.

Hal's grim resilience got him through the hours, but then came a deep sadness: 'we have lost our poor little son, our pet and hope'. 'The four corners of my house are smitten and I stand face to face with base patience & resignation'. That night Hal gently carried Noel into his 'study, and laid his cold still body here where I write'. He began to slip back into the inferno. Outside the gales continued, but inside a mental tempest left him groping for a stable rock to cling to.

> I could have fancied a devil scoffing at me ... and
> asking me what profit it was to have stripped myself of
> the hopes and consolations of the mass of mankind? To
> which my only reply was & is Oh devil! truth is better
> than much profit.

The rock became the bedrock of knowledge, and Nature laid her healing hand. Like Job he took solace in his religious stand.

> I have searched over the grounds of my belief and if wife
> and child & name & fame were all to be lost to me one
> after the other as the penalty still I will not lie.

He sat in the study facing the tiny body. His emotions were unleashed as he looked back to that New Year's Eve 1856, when he had sat at the same desk and pledged on his son's birth to give 'a new and healthier direction to all Biological Science'. He had found redemption on his son's death. There was no blame, only submission to Nature, and that brought its own catharsis. Therefore, 'I say ... without bitterness -- Amen, so let it be'.

Old friends were away: Hooker was examining the cedars on Mount Lebanon and Spencer composing chapters in Scotland. But Tyndall joined the funeral procession at 11 am. on Tuesday, 'stunned & bewildered'. Just as he worked alongside Hal now as Jermyn Street's Professor of Physics, so they stood together in their 'holy leave-taking'. Hal had bought a plot beneath an oak in St Marylebone Cemetery, Finchley and paid extra to have Noel buried 12 feet deep. As he watched the tiny coffin lowered the huge depth the sublimated anger turned to outrage at an insensitive Church. The minister was not at fault, but he

> read as a part of his duty the words 'If the dead rise not
> again let us eat & drink for tomorrow we die' I cannot
> tell you how inexpressibly they shocked me – [the
> clergyman] had neither wife nor child or he must have
> known that his alternative involved a blasphemy against

all that was best & noblest in human nature. I could have
laughed with scorn. What! because I am face to face with
irreparable loss ... I am to renounce my manhood, and
howling grovel in bestiality? Why, the very apes know
better, & if you shoot their young, the poor brutes grieve
their grief out & do not immediately seek distraction in a
gorge.[31]

Catharsis also came from writing letters, but only Kingsley's
brought such an emotive reply that Huxley opened his heart.
Kingsley, settling in to the Chair of modern history at Cambridge to
combat the 'Spinozaist tendency of the time', thought Huxley's ordeal
'something horrible, intolerable, like being burnt alive'. But the 'void'
would 'be refilled' hereafter, while in our earthly years we must 'make
ourselves worthy of the re-union'. Noel would be reborn.

Our physical body was irrelevant, Kingsley urged: 'I dare say I
am descended from some animal from whom also the chimpanzee
has sprung. I accept the fact fully, & care nothing about it'. What
mattered was our 'moral nature w[h]. can ... initiate the noble, the
beautiful, the merciful, the just'. This moral self was 'nearer to a
God than to a Chimpanzee', and if Nature's scythes 'can kill the
Chimpanzee, they cannot ... kill me'.[32] The self survives, Noel
survives in the Lord's sight, awaiting their reunion.

This emotional blackmail provoked Huxley's 'savage, splendid,
and sympathetic' reply. Belief was sacred, he responded, and that
put a moral premium on assessing all the evidence, whether it was
for Immortality or Evolution. For Huxley, science taught the
Christian truth 'of entire surrender to the will of God' – one had
to accept the teachings of Nature and give up all prior prejudice.
'Sit down before fact as a little child', he urged Kingsley. 'I have
only begun to learn content & peace of mind since I have resolved
at all risks to do this'.

Huxley's epistle to the Cantabrigians made belief in immortality
a sin in the absence of evidence. He warned of the delusion that
the 'moral government of the world is imperfect without a system
of future rewards & punishments'. Every bit the religious visionary,
he made heaven and hell a part of Nature itself. Theft or murder
bring their own penalty on the earth, inasmuch as they damage the
moral man. 'The gravitation of sin to sorrow is as certain as that
of the earth to the sun'.[33] He was weaving morality into the very
fabric of the cosmos.

*

Through the daily sorrow he trudged, leaving a stricken Nettie upstairs. He busied himself with distractions. He readied the *Natural History Review* for its launch on 1 January 1861. At least with subscriptions 'coming in very lively' he was 'sanguine of success'. Darwin proofed Huxley's trumpet-blast 'On the Zoological Relations of Man' and trilled 'Your term "pithecoid man" [ape-like man] is a whole paper . . . in itself'.[34] That bugle call would signal the *Review*'s new direction.

It was Kingsley who continued to bring Huxley back to life. Huge epistles passed between them, as the muscular moralists hacked to the bedrock of one another's being. Their frankness was almost embarrassing. Kingsley knew that 'Theology, metaphysic & the rest of it are actually dying' as 'the thinking portion of mankind' takes to the scientific high ground. He himself yearned to join the crusaders of science. 'Them I love, them I trust, with them I should like, had I my wish, to live & die'. But the more he strained for the new, the more he sought the moral gem in the old. He too was locked in 'struggle of w^h. I never talk . . . I never opened my mind to any one as I have now to you'.

It reanimated Huxley's 'useless carcass'. By October he was sleeping again. Outside the miserable rain battered the windows. After three months of ruined crops every pulpit echoed to prayers for fine weather. But not Kingsley's; he fired a national debate by refusing 'to ask that God should alter the course of the universe'. Instead he prayed for spiritual 'light', tapping the moral realm. Huxley believed that moral intercession was as questionable as a fair-weather 'blessing'. But he turned down Kingsley's request to write on prayer for *Fraser's Magazine*. More controversy and he feared he would 'break down'. The endless work in editing the review and liaising with printers and writers was draining him; although he still had enough spark to send Kingsley a prospectus 'with a prayer for help if you can give us any'.[35]

He knew he would have to 'drift into the stream again'. Indeed, hearing that Hooker had returned, sworn to a new serenity, he remonstrated that 'for men, constructed on the high pressure tubular boiler principle, like ourselves', that meant 'to lie still & let the devil have his own way. And I will be torn to pieces before I am forty sooner than see that'.

He was already being torn by the sight of Nettie. Emotional winds were buffeting them both. On 11 December at 9.45 pm. she gave birth to another son. It helped to ease the pain even as it turned the knife. Leonard, she called him, 'because it held our lost boy's name'. Another son was 'a great blessing', but she remained crushed. For his part, Hal scarcely knew whether 'it was pleasure or pain. The ground has gone from under my feet once & I hardly know how to rest on anything again'. Nettie could see the dagger twisting and conspired with Tyndall to get Hal away. That meant one thing. In unprecedented Boxing Day frosts, when the thermometer plummeted to − 17°, Busk and Tyndall marched him off to the rarefied air of the Welsh mountains, reaching Snowdon on 28 December. The grandeur of it matched 'most things Alpine'.³⁶

He arrived back on a sombre 31 December. It would have been Noel's fourth birthday and he found Nettie no better. She 'mends but slowly', he sighed to Hooker.

The next morning the first number of his *Natural History Review* was launched. 'What a complete & awful smasher (& done like a "buttered angel")', Darwin crowed as he imagined the effect on that 'canting humbug' Owen. Huxley sent Wilberforce a copy, marking his paper as 'justification for the diametrical contradiction with which he heard Prof. Huxley meet certain Anatomical Statements' at Oxford. (His Lordship typically received it with 'great pleasure'.) Huxley's polemic carried the review. As Lyell said, the 'public will at present devour any amount of your anthropoid ape questions'. Lyell persuaded the Athenaeum Club to subscribe. Hooker thought it could even sit on coffee tables – but for one dread, 'Anatomical' pictures. No one dared flick a page for fear of what 'will turn up next', mortified by the thought that 'it may be a Uterus'. Who could run the risk of the 'children, guests &c' glimpsing it? So pander to the prudes 'who regard Anatomical Plates as repulsive', Hooker said.³⁷ Cut them out.

Proprieties ruled society. Huxley acknowledged the point in his reply to Hooker. He mooted christening Leonard, and even more sheepishly asked Hooker to stand godfather.

> You know my opinions on these matters . . . So if you
> consent, the clerk shall tell all the lies for you & you shall
> be asked to do nothing else than to help devour the
> Christening feed, and be as good a friend to the boy as
> you have been to his father.
> My wife will have the youngster Christened although I am
> always in a bad temper from the time it is talked about until
> the ceremony is over. The only way of turning the farce into
> a reality is by making it an extra bond with ones friends.

At times one had to live a lie to live at all. Hooker and Darwin (a godfather as well), were as willing to be hung for sheep as lambs and swore in person to 'renounce the Devil & all his works'.[38]

Nettie came downstairs for the first time on 5 January 1861. Grief had left no room for elation at Leonard's birth, and with Hal back to his punishing schedule she was back to brooding. She forced herself out of the house on 8 February to hear him at the Royal Institution, but it was by 'the grace of god & her own will'.[39] Her pitiable state shocked the Darwins, who saw in her face the agony they had felt on their own Annie's death ten years earlier.

Darwin offered a fortnight's rest in Kent. His image of Downe life in all its morbid glory was alluring. Convalescent gloom shrouded the family. The house 'is dreadfully sick & melancholy. My wife lies upstairs with my girl & she would see little of M^{rs}. Huxley, except at meal times'. Eighteen year-old Etty, still weakly a year after catching typhoid, was attended by a bevy of nurses, with a teary Emma trying 'not to give way to despondency'. Nor would Nettie see much of Mr Darwin himself, so stomachy 'that I never spend the whole evening even with our nearest relations'. Treat it 'as if it were a country inn', he insisted; or, better still, a sanatorium.

So in March a grieving Nettie, three tiny children, trunks and a nurse set off from the new palatial, glass-roofed Victoria Station. They found Down House an infirmary where no one got well; here illness was the norm and health a strange affliction. Emma Darwin was a ministering matron, soothing with physic and spiritual balm in her rest home. She was pious, a little distant at first; or, as Nettie said, 'a dear kind soul' in a rather 'unobtrusive way'. Emma was as pained by Charles' ethical departure from Christianity as Nettie had been by Hal's professional hostility. So there was comfort in her words – and strength in her faith that 'suffering & illness is meant to help us to exalt our minds & to look forward with hope to a future state'.

Left to herself in this strange sanatorium, where the family turned up like guests for their evening meal, Nettie still brooded on Noel. She wondered if she would ever 'be clear minded again', or love her other 'darlings as I did him'.[40]

16

Reslaying the Slain

> Cook had got up some chops . . . for me in wonderful
> style last night, when I went home after my Lecture. Said
> Lecture let me inform you was very good – Lyell came &
> was rather astounded at the magnitude & attentiveness of
> the audience.

Huxley stayed in town, polishing his 'Rifle & Bayonet' and honing
his intellect. These Thursday nights in March 1861 saw the Tory
nightmare realized as he taught the great unwashed of their gorilla
ancestry.

The fliers for his new course brought the artisan élite in droves.
Lyell, preparing his *Antiquity of Man*, squeezed incongruously
among the carters and was astonished.

'My working men stick by me wonderfully', Hal cheered Nettie
at Downe. 'By next Friday morning they will all be convinced that
they are monkeys'. The cloth-caps needed no persuading. For
decades their gutter presses had proclaimed man's bestial origin.
By now the *Reasoner* was arming infidels with facts on fossils and
flints to counter 'Theological Theories of the Origin of Man'. Its
running mate, the *National Reformer*, was shattering the 'man and
beast' dichotomy. Huxley was riding a crest. The pauper presses
were devouring the *Origin* as they had the *Vestiges* and French
Revolutionary tracts before it. All were grist to their mill. Red
Lamarckians saw the '*divine* origin of man' as a supernatural
sanction to keep '*the masses in the mud*'. Of course they rallied to
any professor who would connect man to the 'under-world of
life'.[1]

These flaming atheists had a biting cynicism; 'life is nothing and nothing life', ran a slogan knocking the pretensions of the port-swilling squirearchy. Privately Huxley distanced himself from these 'cynics who delight in degrading man'. The 'absolute justice' he saw in nature was invisible to the demagogues (as it was to Darwin). But he needed the working-class constituency. So he tailored his talks, luring the cabbies and costermongers. First came a little iconoclasm, then praise for their sceptical spirit. He peered into the chimpanzees' cage and came 'face to face with these blurred' mirror images. The apes forced a sudden 'mistrust of time-honoured theories' about our own vaunted place. 'It is as if nature herself had foreseen the arrogance of man', he said in his best broadsheet style, 'and with Roman severity had provided that his intellect by its very triumphs, should call into prominence the slaves, admonishing the conqueror that he is but dust'.

Six hundred packed his great theatre in Piccadilly each week, with many more turned away. Men fresh from the workshops; at least here their place had not been 'usurped by [the] smug clerks' who had overrun the Mechanics' Institutes. They sat 'rapt & still'. Huxley was not the 'phrase-making *poseur*' they usually saw on the rostrum. This was serious. There was a breathless silence; then at the end came 'thunders of applause', which rumbled on after the professor had gone for his chops.

For his workers evolution was self-betterment. The race was hauling itself up by its hobnailed-boot straps. The image conferred dignity on humble origins. As one firebrand put it, from the 'progress of the past we look forward, with inexorable confidence to the achievements of the future'. Theirs was a co-operative march towards the millennium. But Huxley's Elysian metaphor was a mite different. He likened society's stuttering advance to an insect's ecdyses: periods of repressive restraint, Dark Ages, broken by dramatic moults when the old integument was cast off. For fleeting moments the old constraints vanished and the cultural grub puffed itself up in the rationalist air. The Renaissance and the French Revolution had seen such moults, and the creaking showed that another explosive showering of old shell was imminent. On Huxley's metaphor, history was not rambling, open-ended and Darwinian but guided on its own embryonic track with a set destination, when the chrysalis opened to reveal an adult butterfly. But this goal was less a socialist New Jerusalem than a scientific New Reformation. Maybe the butterfly 'state of Man' was 'terribly distant', he told his men, but every moult moves us closer.

Unlike the scoffers he believed that there was a sanctity to mankind. People might have arisen *from* brutes, but they are 'assuredly not *of* them'. An ape ancestry implied no 'brutalization', he said, his eye on Lyell perched warily among the weavers. We can 'leave the brooding' over degradation 'to the cynics and the "righteous overmuch" who, disagreeing in everything else, unite in blind insensibility to the nobleness of the visible world'. In fact,

> thoughtful men, once escaped from the blinding influences
> of traditional prejudice, will find in the lowly stock whence
> Man has sprung, the best evidence of the splendour of his
> capacities; and will discern in his long progress through
> the Past, a reasonable ground of faith in his attainment of
> a nobler Future.[2]

At Downe Emma Darwin 'was very kind & sympathising', and she eased Nettie's 'great pain'. The Darwins took to precocious Marian, now almost two. Being her father's daughter she 'wins golden opinions, but will not be tempted into any demonstrations of affection'. As Nettie relayed the day's doings to Hal, Marian would sit on her lap 'holding a dry pen' and trying to draw Pater, while complaining that 'I can hardly make a man'.

The misery of the place was wonderfully infectious. Hal advised Nettie not to 'go strolling too far carrying great babies', but she had little opportunity. It was blustery and wet and everyone had colds. Trapped inside, the children became trying. Downe sent Jessie into a 'most capricious & irritable mood'. Darwin took it heroically, at least until the Tennyson poems came out.

> Only fancy, M^r. Darwin does not like poetry & prophesies
> that you will get over your liking for it [Nettie wrote to
> Hal]. I fear he has not so good an opinion of you since I
> mentioned your taste for it. Let us pray for his conversion
> & glorify ourselves, like true believers.

Almost nightly Nettie gave readings, joined by Emma and sickly Etty, who ventured downstairs for an hour. But 'M^r. Darwin doesn't think anything of it! I suppose he has worked his poetry into his life, for I cannot believe he has no poets corner in his heart'. Shortly Darwin took to hiding upstairs.

Do stop 'subjecting poor Darwin to a savage Tennysonian persecution', Hal joked. 'I shall see him looking like a martyr & have to talk double science next Sunday'.[3]

The science was ape brains and more to Darwin's taste. It was also a public talking point. As Hal praised his workers as the sons of monkeys, the presses were rolling on Saturday's *Athenaeum*. The adventurer and gorilla hunter Paul du Chaillu was touring England, exhibiting his grisly haul of decapitated heads. (Faithful to Owen, he sold most of them to the British Museum.) His theatrical depictions of the majestic manlike-ape caused a sensation. He showed the proud beast, charging, pounding its chest, falling in a hail of bullets. Owen capitalized on du Chaillu's talk at the Royal Institution, following him on stage to point out that the gorilla's brain lacked a human-like cerebrum and hippocampus. The *Athenaeum* ran his reassuring words. Huxley responded with rapier speed, publishing a rebuttal to Darwin's cry 'too civil'. 'It is a good joke that since Owen attacked me, I . . . feel more inclined to clap anyone on the back, than to cry hold hard!' That reassured Nettie: 'To think that the mild Darwin should hurrah'![4] The public awaited each week's lunge and parry, wondering what would become of society if apes were found with hippocampuses.

Huxley rushed to get the April *Review* out. He worked harder with the *Gardeners' Chronicle* calling it 'a capital Review badly edited'. (They should 'thank God it is no worse', he piped up, still trying to juggle ten things at once after the tragedy.) Rolleston's refutation of Owen went in. But his proof that apes had a hippocampus was so chivalrous that Hooker thought him frightened 'of giving offence to God, Oxford, Orangs & Owen'.[5]

In the middle of it all Hal brought Nettie home. Seven months since Noel's death and she was still 'ill & weak from fretting'. The Darwins had been a release, but seeing the old house and Noel's bedroom she began 'running back again fast'. Hal was at his wits' end and now 'alarmed about her'.[6] Another spell away was the answer; borrowing the Folkestone home of the Secretary of the Royal Institution, Hal turned Nettie round. On Saturday 6 April 1860, as the *Athenaeum* ran Owen's haughty reply, he took her with the three children and two nurses to the Kent coast.

Londoners' jaws were agape. They watched Hal wind up the slanging match 'in disgust' the following Saturday. 'Life is too short' to go on 'slaying the slain', he finished. And with that the squibs started. One whimsical nonentity found its way into *Punch*:

> Says Owen, you can see
> The brain of Chimpanzee
> Is always exceedingly small,

> With the hindermost 'horn'
> Of extremity shorn,
> And no 'Hippocampus' at all.

Ending up

> Next HUXLEY replies,
> That OWEN he lies,
> And garbles his Latin quotation;
> That his facts are not new,
> His mistakes not a few,
> Detrimental to his reputation.
> 'To twice slay the slain,'
> By dint of the Brain,
> (Thus HUXLEY concludes his review)
> Is but labour in vain,
> Unproductive of gain,
> And so I shall bid you 'Adieu!'[7]

A touchy burlesque had finally raised Huxley into the public consciousness. What began in earnest ended in satire, releasing the valve on a fraught situation. The squib's authorship leaked. 'I would give you fifty guesses & you should not find out', he prodded Hooker. Darwin too was astounded. It was Owen's patron, a Church-and-State stalwart in the House, Sir Philip Egerton, well known at the School of Mines for his fossil fish cabinet – 'and the fact speaks volumes for Owen's perfect success in damning himself'.[8]

Every Saturday Hal went to Folkestone. At first Nettie was 'too weak to move off the sofa', but in a couple of weeks the sea air had raised her spirits. She began to walk, sometimes with Hal along the white cliffs, looking out towards France, or with George and Polly. Everyone hoped that her renewed strength would 'relieve the tension of her mind'.

Hal rushed back each Monday, into the office for more lectures and meetings. By now du Chaillu's gorillas were a tabloid obsession. Macabre tales of ferocity circulated, and salacious stories of women-snatching. Here was a giant black ape walking upright, 'stopping at intervals to beat his huge breast and roar'. The beast exerted a 'terrible fascination'. The gorilla became overloaded with sinister symbolism – *Punch* made every Irish patriot a Mr G. O'Rilla fit to be shot down. Du Chaillu returned to Africa to catch Owen a live gorilla. Huxley met with du Chaillu before he left, but he was unimpressed, finding nothing but 'inexplicable confusion' behind the hunter's mask.[9]

Respectable society had never been so provoked over its beliefs. What was it to be human? Were anatomists and butchers to be the new sages? The old sage was horrified. Huxley called on Thomas Carlyle on 30 April. Having spent the radical years slaying material- ist dragons, the hard-bitten hero was not about to tolerate prepos- terous monkey-men. But with the multi-authored *Essays and Re- views* questioning the existence of miracles (the book, out for a year, was still kicking up a storm), the bickering over brains left everyone wondering who were the true interpreters of humanity. Onlookers forlornly tried to disentangle the issues. Owen's backers saw the 'absurdity' of the hippocampus debate, when next to nothing was known of cerebral functioning. Huxley's Broad Church colleagues agreed. For Rolleston our 'diviner life is not a mere result of the abundance of our convolutions'. Nor did cerebral similarities say anything about ancestry. But the attorneys were playing to the crowd. Owen tried to swing support by blackening Huxley as an 'advocate of man's origin from a transmuted ape'.[10] He made human ancestry hinge on the cerebral point. Therefore Huxley's proof of the hippocampus in apes seemed a vindication of mankind's bestial origin.

'People are talking a good deal about the "Man & the apes" question', he informed Nettie. 'Some think my winding-up too strong'. Darwin called it 'truculent' (even though he himself was now 'demoniacal about Owen'). But how else to expose those who 'prostitute Science'? No wonder that it was thought 'strong – it was very', she replied.

> I think had I been at your elbow when you penned it I
> would have asked you to omit it, not from any fear – or
> least thoughts of injustice – but as a matter of policy –
> however Owen did certainly want a word or two of most
> severe censure from a man of courage, after starting what
> he must know to have been false.[11]

Huxley deliberately reduced the question to one of 'personal veracity'. He was fighting for the moral high ground, but he also knew that moral courage was the issue consuming the Anglican mind in the wake of *Essays*.

The *ancien régime* was being eroded from the inside. Liberal *Essay*ists, condemning miracles as atheistic (for breaking the links in God's causal chain), shared Huxley's belief that morality lay in the search for evidence. One *Essay*ist, the ultra-liberal professor of geometry at Oxford, Baden Powell, argued that an unbroken chain back to Creation was evidence of Divine intent. The *Origin* was a theological crutch; grasp it, he urged, and praise 'the self-evolving powers of nature'.

Wilberforce's mace forced the *Origin*'s and *Essays*' supporters into an uneasy alliance. Huxley, Hooker and Carpenter even had Captain Stanley's younger brother, Revd Arthur Stanley, the Canon of Christ Church, elected to their elite Philosophical Club, where he might be enlightened on the heat of a moon-beam or the existence of fossil humans. Stanley believed that the Bible should be interpreted like any other historical book. It led to a close camaraderie; a brotherhood of the beleaguered that might not have survived fair-weather conditions. Stanley confided to Huxley that the enthusiastic *Edinburgh* review of the *Essays* was his, which sent Huxley rushing to the Athenaeum library. The article struck him as 'a very clear defence', even if 'it would not be difficult to make mince-meat of it'.[12]

Wilberforce and twenty-five bishops wrote to the *Times*, complaining of the *Essays* and threatening to indict the authors for heresy. Lubbock started a counter-petition, which praised the book for trying to put the Church's teachings on a 'firmer' footing. Lyell, Busk, Carpenter and Darwin signed. But at Oxford Rolleston refused, no lover of *Essays*. So did Huxley, Hooker and Ramsay, who actually agreed with the hard-line bishops that 'the position of the Essayists [*was*] untenable for Clergymen'.[13] As astute strategists, they knew that this reconciliation wrecked their professional strategy, which relied on confrontation.

Hal dreaded Nettie coming 'back to the old scenes', fearing another of her 'relapses'. Mrs Hooker suggested a house move, in fact that he 'cut Sᵗ John's Wood altogether' to break the morbid connection. The Waverley Place rent was paid until March 1862, but Tyndall and Hirst came to the rescue and took over the lease. By mid-May Hal had found a larger house near by in Abbey Place, big enough for a growing family and a retinue of domestics. He was determined 'to put the top on her cure'.[14]

So in June 1861 a reinvigorated Nettie returned to a new home. Because of the move, money problems remained critical. Nettie's mother settled in, while Mr Heathorn sailed to Sydney to sort out the £35,000 debts resulting from his brewery's collapse. But Hal was 'only too happy to feel a little free from sorrow' at last. Apart from 'a lunatic neighbour', life was returning to normal. Becoming hectic, in other words; more and more of the *Review* was falling on his shoulders, as Lyell had predicted. Unless he watched over everything 'it goes wrong'. The 'paper is bad, the cover is bad, the type is bad, & the general get up loose shabby & dogseary'. He sacked the printer and upgraded everything. 'We must fly high if we mean to do well'.[15] He lost hours proofing, only to rush home to fix the overflowing cistern and catch the water dripping through the ceiling. But that was life.

By now the Darwinians were on top of every aspect of human origin. While Huxley dissected apes, Lyell prepared his *Antiquity of Man*. Sir Charles had toured the archaeological sites in England and looked at the hand-axes excavated by the customs official Boucher de Perthes in France. These had convinced him that early man had indeed used flint weapons to kill extinct hippos and hyaenas. Lubbock was publishing on Stone Age shell mounds in Huxley's *Review*. Falconer was excavating flint knives in a Brixham cave, on England's south coast. Here he had found his famous bear's arm-bone sharpened as a stave. Like an ageing professor, Lyell was gathering up all this evidence for his book.[16]

But where were the humans who had hunted cave bears? A beetle-browed skull cap had turned up in 1857 in the Neander caves near Düsseldorf. Before anyone had seen it, wild rumours abounded – Spencer had heard that 'this skull, mark, *is intermediate between that of the gorilla and that of man!* ... After this, anything else would be bathos'. Its swept-back forehead and massive brow ridges pointed to a brutal 'Neanderthal Man' as the bear hunter. Or so the anatomist Hermann Schaafhausen speculated when he described the skull. This and the stout limb bones had illustrators depicting 'horrible' prognathous cave dwellers, squat chimp-men wielding axes and sipping half-warmed pots of hyaena blood. Busk translated Schaafhausen's paper for the *Review*, and even he set Neanderthal Man's overhanging brows in outline beside a chimpanzee's skull.

Lyell began omnivorously collecting information on this too. He tapped Huxley, wanting him to illustrate the skull's peculiar features. In exchange Sir Charles acted as go-between with its owner, the school teacher Karl Fuhlrott. He sent Huxley's list of questions and received back photographs, measurements and a cast.[17] Huxley inexorably moved on to study fossil man, as if he had the time.

*

There were not enough hours in the day. By now he was deep in his winter courses and rushing between council chambers. Nettie hardly saw him. In a blue moon he might take her to a Jenny Lind concert. But otherwise his presence was a passing blur and he became known as the 'lodger' at home. Even his Saturday nights were spent in Jermyn Street, initiating students in the 'First Principles of Physiology'. He had become a 'mere lecturing pump eternally pouring out floods of discourse'. It was draining him. 'If one had but two heads', he said, '& neither required sleep!'

The one he had did not know which way to turn. The hares he set running darted in every direction. And around every corner he found them breeding furiously. By now Britain's mining operations had become vast. Coal fired the furnaces of the industrial north, and the black-face and 'black-lung' miners digging into these swamp seams disinterred their inhabitants. The Carboniferous corpses – most from the ironstone under the coal – came to Jermyn Street. Huxley checked consignments for fish and continually found something else: squat crocodile-like creatures, 'labyrinthodonts', the earliest amphibians (named after the labyrinthine folding of their tooth enamel). Industry was shining a light on the first vertebrates to lumber out of the methane-bubbling swamps – archaic armoured salamanders 'which pottered, with much belly and little leg, like Falstaff in his old age, among the coal forests'. In spare hours Huxley polished 'coal vertebrae' and shiny skulls, christening them appropriately. 'Anthracosaurus is a good name', Lyell wrote on hearing the latest arrival from Airdrie's Iron and Steel works. And so fish gave way to amphibians.

Lyell wished 'we could multiply you by five'.[18] Huxley's own production was indeed on an industrial scale. But everything had to be squeezed around the lectures. Fuhlrott's Neanderthal package arrived as Huxley was leaving for Edinburgh. It had to wait until he had given his man-and-apes pep-talk to a tough tartan workforce.

He came alive at these confrontationist moments. He never really expected to 'be stoned and cast out of the city gate'; he knew his working men too well. He packed the Queen Street Hall in January 1862, breaking all records (and the Philosophical Institution's run of safe, arty lectures). Among the querulous classes he found 'sinners enough in "Saintly Edinburgh"'. The evangelical *Witness* never understood this fustian enthusiasm. It was appalled at the applause when 'their kindred to the brute creation was most strongly asserted'. But Huxley talked their language. If great truths began as blasphemies, then he intended to blaspheme. Here was a new sort of intellectual hero, emulating the old agitators, 'flouting the novelty of his views instead of smuggling them in'. Edinburgh's workforce loved it.

It was a gentle blasphemy. 'I told them in so many words that I entertained no doubt of the origin of man from the same stock as the apes'. The *Witness* went into spasms. This was the 'vilest and beastliest paradox ever vented in ancient or modern times amongst Pagans or Christians'. Huxley revelled in the kicks and sent clippings to Lyell, Hooker and Darwin to prove 'that my labour has not been in vain'. There was an exuberance in this mock martyrdom. 'I made 'em listen', he boasted to Dyster, '& only after I was gone did the 'Witness' visit me with large & liberal cursing. Life has its joys, my son, if we earn them!'[19]

With the profanities pealing like bells he returned to the fossils. Even more did cave humans whet the public appetite. What were they? What were *we*? Semi-apes wielding hatchets? The cognoscenti's excitement was seeping through to the public. Here were the Ice Age humans that many said never existed. Huxley was looking at the first shattered skulls.

Lyell obtained another, the Engis skull, from the Meuse valley in Belgium. It was as old as the mammoths and yet modern in shape. What could Huxley say? – 'a fair average human skull, which might have belonged to a philosopher, or might have contained the thoughtless brains of a savage'. He turned back to the massive-boned and scowling-browed Neanderthal. That was different.

He settled in to the College of Surgeons. Here was London's chief stockpile of skulls, gruesomely stacked in a shrine to ethnic exploitation. He contrasted endless aboriginal relics with Neanderthal's 'degraded' cranium, pioneering new ways of bisecting and measuring skulls for easier comparison. 'The *Neander-thal skull*' emerged as an '*exaggerated modification*' of the lowest of the '*Australian skulls*'.

Ape brains and Neanderthal bones had the making of an esoteric bestseller. By the time he stood on the Royal Institution podium on 7 February 1862, his talk 'On the Fossil Remains of Man' was the teaser for a book. There never was a more startling lecture 'bearing on the *great question*', someone in the audience remarked. An august audience it was, as usual. Even the Catholic Cardinal Wiseman sat among the dignitaries, which led the wisecrackers to expect that, after such illumination, he would grant Huxley an ' "Indulgenza plenaria"!!!'[20] What Wiseman actually granted was less generous than absolution. And anyway Huxley relished his sins.

Huxley was a power in the School of Mines. He cruised over the Director's head and contacted the Chairman of a Commission looking into its running, setting out his views on curriculums and examinations. The school was a model state enterprise of hard-core intellects, all of a mind on the *Origin*, *Essays* and money for merit. The loose set of dogs had become a tight pack, and Huxley expected everyone to pull his weight. Salter had degenerated into a technician in his own department, and Huxley considered him 'the veriest "filius canis" I ever had to deal with'.[21] Salter's outbursts grew worse. 'Damn your eyes', he once shouted, taking a swing at Huxley, who had found his fossils left out overnight! The unhinged evangelical, despised by everyone from the doorman to the Director, was sacked. He picked up his Bible and fossil books and descended into madness; deserted by his wife, he eventually jumped into the Thames.

Huxley took over every menial role. He was prodigiously active in the school, and a good meeting organizer in the societies. What was drudgery to others had an urgency for him as he set about restructuring science from the base up.

His vulturine eye locked on to the Zoological Society, with its exotic cadavers. His swoop was swift and silent. Made a Fellow in 1860, he joined Wilberforce as a Vice-President in 1861. Huxley and the bishop sat together to sort out finances, sack drunken keepers and oversee a stream of imperial acquisitions. Every telegram – such as Wallace's on 19 March 1862 to say that he was returning from the Malay Archipelago with two living 'Paradise Birds' – set them into motion. Through the public shrieking this quiet collaboration continued, unheralded, unknown.

Noble prelates saw the government of science as part of their civic duty, and they provided links to the Zoo's society patrons. Wilberforce came to the council meetings, but not the separate scientific sessions, so he missed Huxley's talk on the Zoo's dead spider monkeys – their brains sectioned to show the hippocampus. Then again he missed Owen's on the peculiar Madagascan aye-aye, with its Fagin-like middle finger, long and scimitar'd for grub-hooking. This was perhaps as well, for whatever Owen's doubts about Darwin, he quietly admitted here 'that the attempt to dissipate the mystery which environed the origin of species' could only bring 'great collateral advantages to zoological science'.[22] This was realpolitik; the workaday reality behind the Manichean headlines, unseen through the smoke of battle.

At the Geological Huxley's rise was as fast. As Secretary he read reports and arranged meetings; his own papers on the earliest fish and amphibians seemed more like spirited '*viva voce* account[s]' to Lyell's in-law Charles Bunbury. Huxley was no hammerer; indeed geology, once the proud Queen of the Sciences, had become a concubine in his view, her purpose simply to help zoologists 'reconstruct the history of past life'.

The President, infirm and in Florence, asked Huxley to deliver the 1862 Annual Address. It was vintage Huxley, aimed at the fogies to 'flutter their nerves'. As always he set off to support Darwin, to demand of his critics: 'Now, Messieurs les Palaeonto-logues, what the devil *do* you really know?' And as always he skewed off.

The night showed him at his idiosyncratic best. Darwin's ramify-ing tree-image of evolution still had not sunk in. In fact the talk had nothing to do with Darwinism. Huxley did not try to trace newts and lungfish back to their common Devonian ancestor. Instead of concentrating on origins, he harped on the sharks' and crocodiles' long unchanging history. He could not shake his ten-year-old belief that the fossil record showed no progress. His talk, like so many, was a brilliant flash, and when the audience regained its sight 'there were many private protests'. Old Bunbury got the message, that 'the resemblances [of past and present life] are much greater' than the differences.[23]

So did Darwin. Huxley's claws risked maiming his friends. His fossil papers left not the slightest hint that he was Darwin's bulldog. In Edinburgh's museum he had found more labyrintho-donts mixed with the fish; that they were mistaken for one another should have suggested something to Darwin's right-hand man. But no. He used *Anthracosaurus* to show that amphibians had passed through prodigious periods unchanged. It was the greatest irony that those closest to Darwin could not give him the fossil back-up he needed – while it was Owen who was investigating the similari-ties between lungfish and amphibians.

'I want you to chuckle with me over the notion I find a great many people entertain', Huxley wrote delicately to Darwin, 'that the address is dead against your views'. But Darwin didn't chuckle at this strange exhibition. Even if natural selection could account for life standing still, Huxley's synopsis seemed so one-sided. 'I cannot help hoping', Darwin remonstrated, 'that you are not quite as right as you seem to be'.[24]

Huxley returned to his book. He peered at humans and apes from every side: he rounded up the best eye-witness accounts of living apes and examined embryonic growth. By the red letter day, 5 May 1862, he had a title, *Evidence as to Man's Place in Nature*. He had polished his stunning working-class talk for inclusion. The edge was deceptively shiny, but still jagged enough to draw blood. And it gushed out with his stab at Owen's cackhanded talk of the 'ordained continuous becoming of organic forms'. To the new rationalists Owen's clumsy words sounded quaintly evasive (Owen meant that a Prescient Intelligence produced new species by natural law – which he accepted as an expression of Divine Will). Huxley extracted his capital from Owen's metaphorical mystification. The 'first duty of a hypothesis [is] to be intelligible', he wrote, 'this may be read backwards, or forwards, or sideways, with exactly the same amount of signification'.

On that auspicious 5 May Hal's daughter, Rachel, was born at 1 am., raven-haired like him, the first to defy the blond conspiracy. Some hours later her proud father posted the first two chapters of *Man's Place* to Williams & Norgate for setting.[25]

Huxley was about to utter the greatest profanity since Copernicus moved the earth from the centre of the universe. He would move man from the centre of creation. But it was hard to be provocative with friends like Kingsley. So what? said Kingsley, hearing that his forebear

> was the ancestor of a gorilla – if so, I compliment my ancestors on having had wits enough to produce *me*, while my cousins have gone & irremediably disgraced themselves, by growing *four* hands instead of 2; & not being able to do the 3 Royal R's to this day.

But Cambridge professors of this stamp were rare, and Huxley expected a rougher ride from a prim society in the midst of an evangelical revival. He was writing the third chapter, on fossil men. Here was the heavy-browed Neanderthal. Huxley cut through the chimp-man nonsense and assessed its 'ape' features as entirely superficial. The brain was the normal size for a 'savage'. Its stout limbs suggested a cold-climate adaptation to glacial Europe, like one of Darwin's Patagonians. 'In no sense' was it 'intermediate between Men and Apes'. Provocation for Huxley took another form. If Neanderthal does not take us nearer the ape, 'Where, then, must we look for primaeval Man? Was the oldest *Homo sapiens* pliocene or miocene, or yet more ancient'? How much further back must we go to find the 'fossilized bones of an ape more anthropoid, or a Man more pithecoid'?[26] He was preparing the world for ancient semi-humans.

With work and travel he had no time for more than a three-chapter book. No multi-volume doorstopper for him; no *System of Philosophy*, nor even a 500-page *Origin* – but a pithy set of pamphlets, tracts for the times. He took the manuscript every-where. It wasn't only his wife who saw a blur these days; no one had him in focus. He lived a life based on express timetables. His was the first generation able to move with whistle-stop speed. He could open 1862 with a flying visit to Edinburgh, and after the 'frightful blackguarding from the "Witness"' plan to set the 'Irish Holy Willies' straight in Dublin.[27] In July he thought the Matter-horn would cure his rheumatism. In August he tramped Scotland for the Fisheries Commission. Then he tramped the British Associa-tion at Cambridge on his own business, and he topped off the year with a lightning trip to the Isle of Wight. The criss-crossing railways had not only transformed the land, putting every town within earshot of the chuff-and-chunter, but also accelerated the pace of life. Huxley trained 4,000 miles this year without taking time out of a hectic schedule. No one in history had commuted like this and still held down a regular job.

Or rather two. The vicar of science with his plural livings was incapable of turning down a new parish. Especially a plum parish like the Royal College of Surgeons, with its rich, cadaverous museum. It had been 20 years since the long-haired student had first seen Owen there – walking between the cow-sized armadillo and giant ground sloth, colossal fossils at the entrance which stood testament to Owen's fame. Now Owen's old job fell into Huxley's lap. It was a sweet turn, which capped the anti-Platonic swing at the college.

Huxley had already helped the stolid 30 year-old Crimea-veteran William Henry Flower become Conservator in the museum. A brewery owner's son (and how Huxley sympathized), Flower was a Broad Anglican in the Baden Powell mould. Indeed, Powell was his wife's brother-in-law and William had kept a three-day vigil at Powell's deathbed in 1860. Flower too praised evolution as a cleansing solvent, dissolving the dross which had 'encrusted'

Christianity 'in the days of ignorance and superstition'. Like Powell and the Unitarians he called miracles atheistic for breaking God's causal chain. (Tellingly, Rolleston was always asked the same question when he lectured on Darwinism, 'Was I an Atheist or a Unitarian'?) Darwin had restored the Divine Government's 'greatness and grandeur'. Flower stood with Rolleston, not exactly happy with Huxley's 'combative character', but backing him to the hilt, convinced that Owen offered nothing 'like a theory of creation'.[28]

Huxley supported these liberal Anglicans who disdained the Archetype's 'antique dress'. He had Rolleston elected a Fellow of the Royal Society. 'I go bail', Huxley told Darwin, drumming up support for Flower's FRS, for his 'being a thoroughly good man'. Huxley was consolidating his hold on a broad Darwinian party.

Hence it was Flower, only months in the College of Surgeons himself, who reported the news to Huxley,

> that 'there's not a man in all Athens that can discharge Pyramus' (*i.e.* the Hunterian Professorship) but you . . . I am exceedingly rejoiced myself at the prospect of the new 'Hunterian Professor,' though I don't know what *our* illustrious predecessor will say.

After two decades, Owen had made the college one of the most prestigious in Europe. German princes had it on their itinerary. The world's biggest – dinosaurs and extinct New Zealand moas – were born in his little room upstairs; here the 'Age of Reptiles' took hold, Jurassic mammals came to life and the amphibians found their origin. The college's acquisitions were the most prized anywhere, from platypus eggs to chimpanzee brains. But Owen could only watch as Huxley's supporters moved in. This abrupt transfer of power was a sign of the times, signalling the collapse of his empire of 'Archetypal Ideas'.[29] In five years the Royal College turned from a bastion of Platonism into a bulwark of Darwinism.

Huxley received the news of his Hunterian professorship in Switzerland and took a detour on his way home to look at Dijon's giant armadillo *Glyptodon*. He was already planning his inaugural address on the Surgeons' own showpiece skeleton.[30]

Not that he could sit still when he arrived home. He packed *Man's Place* back into his bag and turned around for Scotland. Playfair had co-opted him for the Royal Commission on Fisheries (his first Royal Commission). So his August holiday was spent steaming up the squally Scottish west coast, talking to the drift-netters at loggerheads with the trawlers' crews. He was looking at ways of increasing yields, and whether stocks could be sustained if fry were taken. The old fishing villages had barely changed for centuries, and it left him acutely aware that he held the livelihoods 'of a great many poor people' in his hands.[31] Of course, his book came home in September, a bit salty but not a word longer.

Man's Place fired the final shot at Owen's misshapen ape brain. Courtly souls were appalled as Huxley accused the intransigent Owen of perjury. But he had to 'get a lie recognised as such'. He needed a spectacle to expose that 'mendacious humbug'. 'I will nail him out like a kite to a barn door', he promised, 'an example to all evil doers'.[32] He was smashing the post-Waterloo consensus which made man sacrosanct and any science touching him a reverent and special case.

At the Cambridge BAAS in October, Huxley – as Chairman of the Zoology Section, 'King in Section D', as Kingsley had it (the section that had seen Wilberforce speak two years earlier) – had an ape brain brought in and Flower dissect out its hippocampus. The nailing was to be a public crucifixion. Of course the news-papers were full of it: everyone wanted more on the 'tremendous issues of life'. Huxley gave Darwinism its exposure and the papers reported him:

> The Times in its leader sailed as near the wind as they
> dared [noted Lyell]. The satire about the Chinese
> ennobling remote ancestors was keen enough . . . Lady
> Bunbury went home from the discussion with Kingsley &
> asked him if he did not think they had been too hard on
> Owen. He said no, I think he deserved the thrashing he
> has got.[33]

A deflated, self-opinionated Owen had his own explanation of Huxley's needling. 'Do you remember the story of the clever young Athenian who had an itch for notoriety?' Owen asked the Oxford professor of medicine. 'He sought the Oracle, and asked "What shall I do to become a great man?" Answer: "Slay one"!'[34]

Hooker thought the proofs of *Man's Place* 'amazingly clever'. Lyell too was dazzled by them. The old Unitarian had been buffeted by the Darwinian gale and hardly knew where he stood. Talk of human evolution titillated and tormented him. The pages were 'a great treat', even though he had been terrified of seeing their like for 30 years. But Huxley's jibe about an opposing army of '*emasculate* monks' was in atrocious 'taste & will do no good'. Lyell urged him not to send 'these *dangerous* sheets to press without Mrs Huxley's imprimatur'. The 'naughty' phrases were struck out. Lyell wanted him to go further, to camouflage his scepticism so as not to ruffle 'peoples feathers'. Do not write as if you were 'running counter to their old ideas'. It was a tall order, effectively a countermand to the militant strategy of the young guard. Nor would Huxley contemplate pandering to the 'peace & make-things-pleasant party'.[35] That was collusion with the peers and parsons, and Huxley promised collaborators a 'hot locus in the lower regions' if he became 'Commander in Chief in their universe'.

He stoked the furnaces too energetically for many. Having set the moral tone he was astonished to find Owen proposed for the Royal Society Council in November. Since 'one of us two is guilty of wilful & deliberate falsehood', he told the Secretary, William Sharpey, 'I did not expect to find the Council . . . throwing even a feather's weight into the scales against me'. But even-handed, genial Sharpey was not blinded by moral outrage; while he saw the 'surpassing beauty' of Owen's archetypes, he thought that Darwin's explanation can only 'exalt our conceptions of creative wisdom'. Owen's appointment was routine. No, stormed Huxley, the question was 'whether any body of gentlemen should admit within itself a person who can be shown to have reiterated statements which are false & which he must know to be false'.

The accusation 'is a *very painful* one', said 74 year-old President Sabine, the chivalrous soul who had helped Huxley in the lean years. The new men had over-stepped the bounds of taste even as they drew in the bounds of science. But Huxley's hounding was deliberate. If 'Truth' legitimated the group's right to self-determination, it had to be seen to be the final arbiter. A gentleman's pact not to pursue the matter was no good. They had to expose the 'grossest piece of scientific knavery ever perpetrated' to undermine Owen's whole toadying counter-ideology.[36]

Owen was appointed to the Council but lost his stature. The world knew it when the papers praised his 'chivalric devotion to error'. And Huxley had proved his point with a tenacity that cost him votes. His tenaciousness raised cheers among the gutsy new breed. But the conservative press saw truth in veneration and decency and experience, not in anatomical facts. Owen's posterior lobes took second place to Huxley's posturing. See how he 'crows and struts', the religious papers sneered. 'Here, then, we have the highest authority in England – the so-called British Cuvier', the *Patriot* railed, 'publicly contradicted by his juniors'. No dirty war has its winners, but the social dislocation and changing values of an industrializing, secularizing society left very real casualties.

Rumours began to fly that Huxley ate babies for breakfast. Some saw only his scything intellect, as if he were a religious vandal and home wrecker. 'And yet', whispered Mrs Tait, wife of the reforming Bishop of London, 'I hear that he is a devoted husband & an affectionate father'. It was an awful incongruity for the orthodox, who equated domestic virtues with Christian principles and equated atheism with immorality. In the old world, science had sung a Divine hymn and supported the Anglican status quo. Huxley represented the new order, whose science offered a new set of upright non-Anglican values. In his own mad pugilistic way, he was proving that evolutionary heterodoxy did not equal moral delinquency.

Still his moral campaign flummoxed the old men. 'Huxley is an exceedingly clever man, and rather an agreeable one; and I believe a good man', old Bunbury recognized, 'but I cannot take very cordially to one entirely without veneration'.[37] Huxley's devotion was of a messier, more modern and ill-defined sort, to the architecture of nature and melioration of ills, but there was no lack of feeling as his eyes filled with tears before the shrine of reason.

His theatrics drew the crowds, happy to see 'their boy' take a poke at the high and mighty. Workers turned up in droves, awed by an intellect able to conjure up exotic pasts, dilate on future glories and maim the hated orthodoxies in between. And Huxley did not disappoint. He drilled through the muddy accumulations of untold aeons to show them the evolution of life. He had his hodmen sink an imaginary shaft beneath the school's foundations, through the gravel beds with their elephant remains and cave tigers ('Rather curious things to fall across in Piccadilly!'). Through the London clay, littered with tropical palms, past turtles, which had paddled in warm lagoons where his workmen now sat on a chilly November night. Through hundreds of feet of sea-floor chalk, with its snapping ichthyosaurs, those reptilian dolphins, down to the deepest beds and first fish. The chain-gang exercise was carried off with plebeian panache.

Huxley was rushed, with no time or inclination to polish and publish these lectures, and such 'a 'umble minded party' that he never imagined that they would sell anyway. But his workers thrived on piracy. An enterprising hack took shorthand notes and rushed the pages to Robert Hardwicke's shop at 192 Piccadilly. Hardwicke was a dab-hand at cost-cutting and 'adventurous' publishing, and he distributed the printed lectures in fourpenny weekly parts.

Piracy was a long and dishonourable tradition. What quicker way to make money while democratizing knowledge? Times were more sedate now and there was a careful gentility to Hardwicke's move (he even asked Huxley's permission). Incomes were rising, steam presses and steam trains were sending cheap books country-wide, and Huxley found his lectures peddled enthusiastically to the elite mechanics and alert clerks addicted to the new *Popular Science Review*. (The sixties saw an explosion of low-brow miscellanies, including Hardwicke's *4d Science Gossip*.) Huge bundles were shifted in the Socialist Hall of Science in the Tottenham Court Road. The radicals loved Huxley's 'spirited, lively, familiar' style; the more so as he was 'confirming our own view of the universe'. But for Huxley it was galling. 'Now, I lament that I did not publish them myself and turn an honest penny', he groaned. Hardwicke 'is advertising them everywhere, confound him'.[38] He ended up having to buy his own pamphlets to post to Darwin.

Week by week they hit the news-stands. No one seemed put off by the top-heavy title, *On Our Knowledge of the Causes of the Phenomena of Organic Nature*. Huxley was making the profoundest science exciting to workers – something that the haughty gents who 'are far above receiving, or earning, weekly wages, have ... failed to attain'. He was plebeianizing the *Origin*.

By 8 December the professor had worked his way right into the crevices of Mr Darwin's thought. After two years of groping and rationalizing, Huxley finally made his back-alley fanciers connect with Darwin's 'struggle for existence'. Their own pigeon selection simulated Nature's weeding and sifting. Huxley tried to use 'struggle' guardedly, 'because some people imagine that the phrase seems to imply a sort of fight'. But in his vivid allegorical way he only heightened the bloody impression. He pictured Napoleon's rag-tag army retreating from Moscow. It arrived at the Beresina river, demoralized, 'everyone heeding only himself, and crushing through and treading down his fellows' to get across, the fittest alone making it – 'every species has its Beresina', he said. Whatever his workers thought of this bleak image, Darwin clapped.

The pamphlets were 'simply perfect', and with Huxley coming round Darwin threw them down

with the reflection, 'What is the good of my writing a
thundering big book, when everything is in this green little
book so despicable for its size?' In the name of all that is
good and bad I may as well shut up shop altogether.

Like all bootlegs they acquired a mystique. With a flourishing low
scientific culture they chalked up impressive sales. Appleton even
had a New York edition out within months, with *On the Origin of
Species* astutely prefixed to the title. Lyell was horrified at Huxley's
loss of royalties and in January 1863 advised him 'to rescue the
copyright of the third thousand'.[39]

But with Christmas past Huxley's mind was on *Man's Place*.
That too was about to hit the stalls.

17

Man's Place

'HURRAH THE MONKEY BOOK has come', Darwin cheered on 18 February 1863. He was driven to distraction by Lyell's *Antiquity of Man* and its strangulated efforts to come to terms with the *Origin*. Huxley promised better things. Lyell 'never rises to the magnificence of Huxley's language', Hooker had to agree. You can read *Man's Place in Nature* '1000 times with fresh delight'.

It was a bad time to publish. The American Civil War had closed Lancashire's cotton mills and the transatlantic book trade was depressed. And Gladstone's economic forecast only put the publishers 'more out of spirits'. With science books aimed at city dwellers and the industrial midlands, everybody prophesied an appalling season.

Not that Williams & Norgate was known for its hard sell. *Man's Place in Nature* sat on a specialist list, appealing to Oxbridge Latinity more than Yankee liturgies. The publisher's titles ranged from Arabic grammars and Sanskrit studies to catalogues of Silurian fossils and (after Huxley's arm-twisting) Spencer's *System of Philosophy*. But Huxley was happy to be wedged between the Old Testament exegetes. And being the *Natural History Review*'s publisher, Williams & Norgate did have the trade contacts.

Huxley's name and the inflammatory subject sold the book. His clever frontispiece itself set teeth chattering. Here was 'skeletonized Man' tripping ahead of his 'grim relatives', the loping train of 'grovelling apes' 'as gleesome as if they were going in procession' to the Palace. This was to become a skeletal icon, caricatured to this day as an ad-man's dream. But that belies its shocking début. It put off the high-brow reviewers. Worse, the book was no technical tome, with its delicacies shrouded in Latin, but written in punchy street prose. That prickliest subject, humanity's origin from ape-like ancestors, was being broached first among the people. And they loved it, even at six shillings. The shops were doing a roaring trade, finding these 'fairy tales of science . . . as eagerly demanded' as Wilkie Collins' sensationalist thrillers.

Within a week the publishers were preparing a second thousand, and Huxley called in corrections from 'Miss Henrietta Minos Rhadamanthus Darwin' (sickly Etty, the Darwins' literary stylist). Darwin himself never ceased 'to admire the clearness & condensed vigour' of Huxley's prose. As for the rousing finale of the working-class lecture, 'I declare I never in my life read anything grander'. Like a fine day, a book should end with this sort of 'glorious sunset'.[1]

January's new liberal weekly was the *Reader*, run by Kingsley's Christian Socialist comrade Thomas Hughes, author of *Tom Brown's Schooldays*. It was a new pie which left Huxley looking for an unoccupied finger to poke in. Not finding one he co-opted Dyster's. Tenby's alderman duly wrote his first review, taking his tone from Hal's letters (why should we prefer to be 'modified mud rather than modified monkey') and was gratified to hear Lyell call it 'the best thing that had yet appeared' on *Man's Place*.

Engels tipped off Marx (who knew all about Huxley's workers' lectures), telling him *Man's Place* was 'very good'. Old troopers joyously ran extracts in the *National Reformer*. In full-page editorials they talked of Italy's bloodshed 'to destroy long-standing abuses' and America's war against slavery – and in England the mightiest 'revolution' of all, 'a revolution of mind' signalled by *Man's Place*. The *Reformer*'s was real class warfare with the 'hideous and ugly' Church, a 'war to the death' against 'the tyrants of the mind' and property.[2] Huxley found himself drafted by some coarse drill sergeants.

He dodged the draft and shook this disreputable army. He looked for a gentlemanly engagement with orthodoxy. But for a moment the press seemed stunned into silence by his atrocities. (Wilberforce thought them so extreme as to have saved the Church from self-destruction.) And what response there had been showed an unaccountably 'just appreciation' of the evidence. Polite Oxford was positively diplomatic. The dons were delighted 'to find how very long it must have been . . . since we were "Pithecoid"', not that they believed 'we got here by that road'. And Rolleston was 'simply enraptured'.

Huxley was 'astonished to find how little abuse the book has met', only the evangelical *Morning Advertiser* 'having opened fire as yet'. Soon enough the religious tabloids started up. Neanderthal was the '"man" who is without the "living soul", spoken of in Genesis', reckoned the *Advertiser*. The Quakers' *Friend* doubted that he had 'any closer connection with ... Adam than have the possible inhabitants of the Moon'. Even so they knew that Huxley was defiling 'the sanctity ... which enshrouds our being'. But these barking 'dogs of St. Ernulphus' were as politically toothless as the radical ranters. What mattered was the urban middle classes, living off the fruits of industry, prosperous, aspiring. Huxley's material explanation of life accompanied the inventions that were changing it so fast. He published as the first underground railway opened at Paddington and London's gigantic new sewage system was set to flush out the medieval diseases. In the world's largest city people were small and life was hectic; change was becoming the norm, and here, in its Piccadilly heart, *Man's Place* dug up the last medieval obstruction. It put modern society at the end of a long whirligig of historical progress.

Huxley's 'lowly-origin, noble-future' image made no sense to the aristocracy. Where was 'our heraldic pomp, our vaunted nobility of descent'? But it summed up bourgeois destiny. Our rise 'reads very much like a Law Lords pedigree in the Peerage', someone saw: 'a remote ancestor' in William the Conqueror's day. 'Seventy fourth in descent a Wig-maker – and then the full-blown Chancellor or Chief Justice'.[3]

Nor did the book do the Huxleys any harm. They were rising past the wig-maker stage themselves. A month later the Court physician was making discreet enquiries about Mrs Huxley's maid Fanny Moore, as a wet nurse for Princess Alice's baby. Hal even found himself paraded alongside the 'other worthless individuals' in Lovell Reeve's *Men of Eminence*. George Grote saw him going to the top – President of the British Association, no less. With the appreciation came the demands: institutes wanted Neanderthal casts. An old shipmate, Revd Robert King, who had jellyfished off the *Rattlesnake* stern with Huxley, wanted ancient flints.[4] And he fished in deeper waters for information on how gorilla-men were to be squared with Genesis.

But the book's rationale still flummoxed many. The 'compensation of future progress will be poor comfort to most of your readers blinded, I suppose, as I am "by traditional prejudices"', was old Lyell's gentle lament. 'I forget the exact words of Popes line about the angels "who view a Newton as we view an ape"'. But angelic future archaeologists looking back on us as savages was cold comfort. We have lost the 'noble pedigree which we dreamt of'.[5]

That was the tone of the reviews, a muted howl; 'candid though heretical', groaned the *Athenaeum*. Some did wonder how he could leave mind and speech out of the story, since it was these which gave Professor Huxley 'that power to instruct, amuse and illustrate, by which he is raised immeasurably above the cleverest ape'.

In the reviews Lyell's *Antiquity* was often roped to *Man's Place*, the one making man 'a hundred thousand years' old, the other giving him 'a hundred thousand apes for his ancestors'.[6] Some lashed these books to the *Essays* as well, with their re-evaluation of Genesis. Society was being swept by tidal waves of dissolvent literature. Old worlds and old documents: the same scientific and historical techniques were being used in their interpretation.

The *Essays* recognized it. Even more extraordinarily, so did the Cornish Bishop of Natal (that new imperial see, created in the lush veld of Africa). The erudite John William Colenso's flock included ostrich-feathered Zulu princes. He stood up for Zulu rights. He allowed converts to live polygamously. He compiled a Zulu-English dictionary – but when he tried to translate Genesis and explain its contradictions he ended up doubting its truth himself. His *Pentateuch* was a sensation; a six shilling tome like Huxley's, but 10,000 were snapped up on publication (showing how much more the Genesis myth meant than the Neanderthal reality). Colenso was derided as a nigger-lover whose charges had paganized him. He was ridiculed for his anti-imperial faith that all men stood equal before God ('what, then, is the good of being a Christian?').[7] In the new Cape Town cathedral he was about to be publicly deposed as bishop. Even now he was in London, appealing against the sentence.

A Zulu bishop who doubted Genesis certainly appealed to Huxley, the more so when he spotted his ruddy face in his own college congregation. (Times *had* changed; Owen had counted Wilberforce's in his.) Colenso listened as Huxley broke up the invertebrates into ever more primary groups, seven now, escaping further from Owen's giant archetypal clusters which seemed such a block to evolution.[8] Or he examined Flower's dissection of a gibbon brain, displayed on a table to show the supposedly absent hippocampus. Intrigued, Huxley visited Colenso's house off Hyde Park (a far cry from his Pietermaritzburg cathedral opening on to the veld). *Man's Place* and the *Pentateuch* seemed odd bedfellows. But they were whipping the 'whole country' into controversies, the *Telegraph* said, over which the Wilberforces 'have lost their hold'. Who doubted a changing world when these books 'are torn from the hands of Mudie's shopmen as if they were novels'? Church heterodoxy was keeping pace with scientific heresy. The realignments told as Rolleston and Stanley petitioned Parliament to end Oxford's Anglican exclusivity and Colenso offered his mitred service to the *Reader*.[9]

The sparks from Huxley's and Lyell's books rekindled the embers of the ape-brain debate, which sputtered like a damp squib. The most sensible commentary on it came in a riotous broadsheet (littered with knowing touches). In this tavern farce, a couple of 'bone and bird-stuffing' costers Tom Huxley and Dick Owen were hauled up before the beak. The scruffs had been caught scrapping, with Huxley yelling you 'lying Orthognathous Brachycephalic Bimanous Pithecus'.

> LORD MAYOR. Are you sure you heard this awful
>   language?
> POLICEMAN X. Yes, your worship . . .
> LORD MAYOR. Did you see any violence used?
> POLICEMAN X. Yes, your worship. Huxley had got a
>   beast of a monkey, and tried to make it tread on
>   Owen's heels – and said 'twas his grandfather . . .
> LORD MAYOR. Did Owen appear much annoyed by this
>   outrage?
> POLICEMAN X. He behaved uncommonly plucky, though
>   his heart seemed broke . . . Never saw a man so mauled
>   before. 'Twas the monkey that worrited him, and
>   Huxley's crying out, 'There they are – bone for bone,
>   tooth for tooth, foot for foot, and their brains one as
>   good as t'other . . .
> As there appeared to be no case against Owen, he was
> allowed to be sworn. Hereupon, Huxley demanded to
> be sworn likewise, but Owen objected, declaring that it
> was impossible to swear a man who did not believe in
> anything . . . Owen, however, was directed to take the
> book in his right hand, whereupon Huxley vociferated,
> 'He does not know a hand from a foot' . . .

'Tom Huxley and his low set', known to include the escaped convict, alias 'John William Natal', played on in the pauper press. On trotted Hooker, 'in the green and vegetable line', 'Charlie Darwin, the pigeon-fancier, and Rollstone', cheering on their barrow boy.[10] Nor did the drunks in the stalls miss the punch-line. Big Dick Owen was one of 'these here standstill Tories', but a nip from 'Uxley's monkey got him going!

The farce, in all its serious forms, toured the globe. At each stop Owen's fortifications were strengthened by the established power brokers. In America the Yale geologist James Dwight Dana thought that our arms were freed for intellectual 'and spiritual service'. Clasped hands were the reverent concomitant of an overarching cerebrum. Wiser Germans hedged their bets. The embryological old-hand Rudolph Wagner supported Owen's ideology and Huxley's facts. But then he believed that brains held no evidence of evolution and science had no impact on faith. And he hoped that getting Huxley into his Göttingen Royal Society sent no message about Darwinism.[11] None wanted to see Huxley suck any Darwinian sustenance out of Owen's brain, but the neural nutriment always seemed to be rising up the straw.

The farce ended in the antipodes, where it played to Melbourne's packed houses. Fresh out from Britain, Owen's protégé George Halford introduced himself as professor of medicine with a talk on the ape's grasping toe. It endeared him to Melbourne's exclusives. With patronage controlled by the Presbyterian Church and an anti-Darwinian Governor he ingratiated himself with the claim that *Man's Place* 'might have been written by the devil'. Huxley's supporters (one straight from Jermyn Street) relayed this 'vulgar claptrap'.[12] As the *Athenaeum* had run pieces on the head, so the Melbourne *Argus* publicized debates on the foot. Halford's pamphlet *Not Like Man* was shipped to London to complete the world cycle. Here the *Lancet* abhorred its coarseness, the one aspect that had not changed during its 25,000 mile trip.

But the serious political appropriation began on the Continent. It was the barking dogs which had German insurgents pricking up their ears. Huxley had always been one of the few British zoologists spared the 'contemptuous comment' of German critics. The barricade socialist Carl Vogt – exiled to Geneva after the 1848 revolution – applauded *Man's Place* as a 'beautiful little book'. He even requested Busk's Stone Age skull illustrations for his own *Lectures on Man*. This would blend Darwinism with his belief in the separate origins of the human races. It would also scrape the depths, with 'simious' skulls from the Dark Ages scurrilously labelled 'Apostle skulls' on the fancy that they belonged to retarded monks. Vogt remained a bruiser. He reported that a 'crowd of young savants had come out' for Darwin in Germany and 'we must support the battle against all the champions of the old school'.[13]

By the time the arch-materialist (and member of Vogt's 1848 corps) Ludwig Büchner asked if he could translate *Man's Place* in July, he found that Victor Carus had done the job.[14] And the *Stellung des Menchen*, out within months, caused a sensation.

Russian militants were even more enthusiastic. Revolutionary politics in the Tsarist autocracy gave Darwin and Huxley an underground cachet. The socialist awakening in the early 1860s saw a stream of banned books smuggled in – easy enough with a bungling censor and so many exiles wandering the West. The student lawyer Vladimir Kovalevskii came to London in 1861–2 to look for books to 'awaken the masses'. He was devoted to the émigré activist Alexander Herzen, and the Russian secret police spotted him at the anarchist Michael Bakunin's London home.[15] He returned to St Petersburg to set up a press specifically to translate Huxley's working-class lecture *On Our Knowledge*, along with books by Darwin, Lyell and Buckle.

But the real interest was in *Man's Place*. Nihilists saw ape origins mock Orthodox spiritualism and relativize moral values, undermining the Tsarist state. They had two separate editions of *Man's Place* in preparation before a Russian *Origin* had appeared. They might have had difficulty with Darwin's competitive, weak-to-the-wall ideology, but Huxley gave them no qualms.

With no despot in Buckingham Palace, the surge of messianic materialism was less splenetic in Britain. But there was a hardening of attitudes as the authorities chased the *Essay*ists and Colenso. Tyndall himself was turning into a glorious cosmological force, gobbling up the ancient heavens in an alarming manner. He swept to the stars, then turned to the Delphic atoms for ultimate answers. Huxley aped his incurable determinism, summing up John's favourite query: 'Given the molecular forces in a mutton chop, deduce Hamlet or Faust therefrom'.

Tyndall's dramatic demands only grew. The one-time pantheist saw us all as souls of fire and children of the sun. He turned atomic evolution and the conservation of force into breathtaking conundrums. The *Origin*, he teased Nettie, merely reflected the ephemera of life.

It is only nibbling at the great question and until Darwin
shews intellect, genius, morality & religion to be latent
among the molecules of a quartersize loaf, and until he is
able to express human affections – the love for example
which you bear to that unhandsome Hal . . . in terms of
the combustion of a tallow candle, I shall take the liberty
of treating his literary productions with sovereign
contempt.[16]

These new explorers were colonizing a vast depersonalized galaxy.
Colenso did not hold a candle to the real dilemma of the age,
Huxley told Kingsley. 'Whether the Gospels are historically true or
not' was a matter of 'small moment in the face of the impassable
gulf between the Anthropomorphism (however refined) of Theology & the passionless impersonality of the unknown &
unknowable'.

As Tyndall flew higher, Hal planted his feet more firmly on the
ground. He matched Tyndall's endless cosmic optimism with
boundless scepticism. 'I know nothing of Necessity, abominate the
word Law', he said in his regular sparring with Kingsley:

I don't know whether Matter is anything distinct from
Force. I don't know that atoms are anything but pure
myths. Cogito, ergo sum is to my mind a ridiculous piece
of bad logic[,] all I can say at any time being 'Cogito'.
The Latin form I hold to be preferable to the English 'I
think' because the latter asserts the existence of an Ego –
about which the bundle of phenomena at present
addressing you knows nothing.

'Is this basis of ignorance broad enough for you?' Whether it was
Kingsley's souls secreting matter, or Mr May's matter perspiring
souls, Huxley had been thrashing at these clingy gossamer cobwebs
masquerading as knowledge since he was a boy. The only sensible
'axiom' was that *'materialism and spiritualism are opposite poles
of the same absurdity'*. Huxley shifted the emphasis from the
ground of existence to the 'great game being played' on it:

the wiser among us have made out some few of the rules
of the game . . . We call them 'Laws of Nature' and
honour them because we find that if we obey them we
win something for our pains. The cards are our theories
. . . But what sane man would endeavour to solve this

problem: given the rules of a game & the winnings to find whether the cards are made of pasteboard or gold leaf?[17]

By shifting from reality to the rules, Huxley was stacking the deck in his own social poker game. And Kingsley knew it.

The coarsest attacks on *Man's Place* were closest to home. As the American Civil War raged the doom-mongering about racial conflict inspired a charismatic reactionary with a Ph.D, James Hunt, to found the Anthropological Society. Hunt and fellow Confederate sympathizer Charles Carter Blake damned bleeding-heart liberalism and missionary philanthropy; with equality 'a mere dream', they abominated talk of black suffrage (and Huxley's fellow-traveller John Stuart Mill *was* talking about it), and the socialist environmentalism which spawned the 'rights-of-man mania'. The society was set up in 1863 to measure and maximize racial differences. In their white supremacist view, humanity was so many warring species. They denounced all talk of common ancestry; black and white men, Hunt proclaimed, came from different 'species of apes'.

Hunt was hissed at the BAAS for his slaving views. But he hit back from his racist base and used Nature's 'ironclad laws' to keep the slaves in chains. In the wake of *Man's Place*, ancestral purity was an emotive issue. White men had their own bloodline and Blake accused Huxley of polluting it and using his 'eloquence' in 'lowering "Man's place in nature"'. Naked racism was endemic in the age: even Lyell had balked at the thought of black ancestors: wasn't it repugnant to 'nearly all men'? Surely to teach it 'w[d]. ensure the expulsion of a Prof.'? Huxley proved him wrong but that did not stop the hate mail. Darwin himself was pelted by 'those of us who respect our ancestors & repudiate ... the contamination of Negro blood'.[18]

The first number of Hunt's *Anthropological Review* carried Blake's 'coarse attack' on *Man's Place*. Huxley instantly resigned his Honorary Fellowship and dismissed them as 'quacks'. The battering continued in the *Edinburgh Review* as Blake compared Huxley to his rabble, holding aloft d'Holbach's inflammatory *System of Nature* (that inspiration to the democrats during the French Revolution).[19] He saw Huxley sliding into a cesspit of 'absolute materialism' and 'atheism' from whose boggy depths the cosmos was 'quite unintelligible'.

The war had thrown up a rival faction which threatened the

Darwinian hegemony. Huxley switched to the 20 year-old Ethno-logical Society (a more benevolent, protectionist forum whose adepts had always looked to a single origin for the races and environmental causes of their diversity). In the old abolitionists' stronghold Lubbock took over the Presidency, and Busk backed him on the Council, as did Huxley, not that he had much truck with the old philanthropy.[20] The religious and racist complexities of human origins were leaving Huxley's clique feeling more be-sieged than ever.

Summer days saw him snowed under with manuscripts, with a glacier's weight of labyrinthodonts and fish crushing him. The added burden of the *Natural History Review* finally overcame him. Realizing that it had failed to 'appeal to the masses' he lost interest and had the 'Commissariat' hire two editors. 'In spite of working like a horse', he explained to Darwin, 'or if you prefer it, like an ass' 'I find myself scandalously in arrear'. He had publishers hanging on his every promise, and each was promised a textbook. Williams & Norgate were announcing his students' *Atlas of Comparative Osteology* (that medical sepulchre of skulls, broken down to illustrate his ideas on their homological parts). Churchill was publishing his College of Surgeons' lectures as a book. *That* 'will be out very shortly', he boasted to Hooker. 'N.B. This is not one of my ordinary book promises in which shortly may mean 7 years'. He was pestered by magazine editors for articles 'which you know you can knock off in a moment'. Giant armadillos, evening lectures on zoology and trips to provincial institutes took up any spare hours, while 'Colensoism and botheration about Moses' filled in the minutes.[21] The back burners were steaming, the front burners boiling over, and uncooked morsels sat in pots all over the stove.

And there they remained as he traipsed around Tyneside on fisheries business (Huxley was diligent in his commission duty, although the pay eased his way). His return only saw matters made worse. He talked to Macmillan about turning his Saturday night physiology lectures into a textbook as well.

Every publisher's advance brought him nearer a break-even point. But still he reckoned without more family tragedy.

'My poor old brother & I never had an angry word in our lives', he sobbed as he oversaw the undertakers. George had been support-ive from the day Tom stepped down the *Rattlesnake* gangplank;

the one who had loved little Noel as his own and made North Bank a home-from-home. To Tom the loss was 'larger than I had imagined'. George had gloried in his brother's rise; eating his words as Tom made his name – and his pay – by science. But he had 'been at deaths door' with tuberculosis for years and, although only 53, had wasted pitifully. The 'horror of the thing was the way of his death', Tom said sadly. Brother Jim was isolated in every sense in his asylum. He was becoming withdrawn himself, leaving Tom to carry the load.

George's business affairs were in a mess, and Tom had to let 41 North Bank, with all its memories. Then he made the final sacrifice for the brother who had given him so much. He sold his most treasured possession, the memento that had ironically proved to George that there was money in science. Tom sold his Royal Medal. Its £50 gold value cleared the debt.

The role of family banker and educator had already devolved on Tom. His sister Ellen, Cooke's widow, was drinking away his annual allowance. Then came her 'pathetic letters' begging for more. The nagging fear that 'some awful scandal' would break around her always kept Tom on edge. He was paying for Ellen's daughter Alice to study at Nettie's old finishing school in Germany. (She was expected to be a governess.) He sent Lizzie cheques in America. Brother Jim's daughter Katy, now 16, was also dependent on the family purse. Jim's first marriage had been a disaster 'and ended in a virtual though not a legal separation'. After Katy's mother died, Jim had remarried another 'woman who was much his inferior in social position & education'. The stepmother disliked Katy and virtually cast her out. So Hal and Nettie opened their door. 'She is really a very good girl', and her situation was very sad, Hal admitted, but his salary was stretching thinner all the time. This retinue of dependants left huge worries. With his massive output he had earned £1124 7s 10d in 1862 and he still ended the year £227 in the red.

The care of George's widow Polly and Heathorn's brewery debts now increased the burden. With the birth of baby Nettie on 21 September 1863 Hal had five children of his own and they were 'a devouring fire, eating up the present and discounting the future'. Given their mother's pernicketiness, there was also a fast turnover of cooks, nannies, maids and nurses (they trooped in regularly from an agency, and just as regularly out again).

It wasn't only with a heavy heart that Tom had George buried alongside Noel. It was with a realization that so many now depended on his science. Professionalism and power were no longer a tyro's ideal. They were the family's bread-and-butter. He trudged back to Tynemouth, borne down by 'sorrow & worry of every description'.[22]

He was counting the pennies again in March 1864 as Churchill published his *Lectures on the Elements of Comparative Anatomy*. The book's turnaround staggered everybody; Huxley had devised, dissected and delivered his Hunterian lectures on the classification of life, and cast them into a 300-page book, all within 12 months.

Before anyone had read it he was deep into his 1864 course. He burned the midnight oil, studying the college's skeletons or bottled embryos in his top-floor room. Flower watched him dissect: nothing flashy or 'finikin', but rapidly going 'to the point he wished to ascertain with a firm and steady hand'.[23] In the still of the night – as the gaslights played eerily on the giant's skeleton – he was the only soul about. In his quiet 'oasis', only the bell of Lincoln's Inn Chapel reminded him of the passing hours.

The next day would see him announcing his findings 'in that famous black gown with the red facings'. Scott 'will recollect [it] very well', he told Lizzie proudly. In Scott's day it was draped about Owen. Huxley was now delivering Owen's lectures as well as his own in Jermyn Street. He was driving himself into the ground. 'How often I have wished that he had some capital that he might do only original work', Nettie sighed, '& that he might rest, when he did not feel well'. The leisured Darwins were cruising along nicely on £10,000 a year interest. Nettie had seen them: the squire pottering, poking at his seeds, strolling around the Sandwalk; Emma reading Huxley's *6d* pamphlets to 12 year-old Horace, and ending with the refrain: 'I wish he would write a book'. Not *Lectures*, a proper book, 'something that people can read; he does write so well'. But a huge tome was the product of freedom and fortune. Everyone sympathized. 'If he had leisure like you and me', Lyell wrote, 'what a position he would occupy!' It was hard for Nettie not to be envious, seeing Hal 'eaten up with work'. 'Had he like Darwin ... private means – what work in his own special line' he might accomplish. 'But is of no use wishing for the impossible'.[24]

Huxley had hoped to generate income in America. But with war tariffs and a new US income tax sales were slow. He tapped Spencer's contact Edward L. Youmans, an energetic evolutionary salesman and go-between for English authors. Huxley's Appleton

editions of *On Our Knowledge* and *Man's Place* had met with
enthusiasm from 'earnest progressives', Youmans reported, but

> they were shamefully abused by the majority of the papers
> in which they were noticed. Agassiz the scientific autocrat
> of this continent led off in his organ the Atlantic Monthly
> . . . and the signal being given from the Cambridge
> watchtower the clergy echoed and re-echoed it . . . from
> one end of the land to the other.[25]

The war in America was spreading its hardship. With cotton
supplies interrupted, famine raged in Lancashire. But for Lyell and
Darwin the price was cheap. 'If the result . . . could be the
abolition of slavery by the year 1900', Lyell said after Lincoln's
Emancipation proclamation, 'it would be worth a heavy debt and
many lives'. Tory doom-mongering about a black insurrection
made it a hard line to hold. Even Huxley's *Saturday Review* expected a slave revolt of 'unrelenting ferocity'. It pushed much of the
British press on to the Confederate side, to the uncomprehending
dismay of New Yorkers.

Support for the North ranged from Darwin's warm sentimentality to Huxley's cool politics. Huxley was from the cynical generation which scorned the 'nigger philanthropists'. True, the abolitionists had appeal. They escorted fugitive, chain-rattling slaves to
mass rallies to whip up support for the North. But in the 1860s
they faced a harder racism. It was reinforced by the Arthurian folk
myths of national character. And the evangelical revival fostered a
new ethnocentrism, with its image of the 'unregenerate savage'.
The onus switched from breaking the slave's chains to saving his
soul. Stiggins' ideal of Christianized negro gentlemen seemed to be
receding.

Huxley had to fight for his pro-North principles with a cold
logic. He was up against a hysterical war propaganda, with the
Tory *Standard* tarring his North-loving, nigger-releasing traitors
as

> Atheists, Socialists, advocates of 'free love', or universal
> licentiousness, of women's rights, and every other
> abomination or absurdity which found favour in infidel
> France, in philosophical Germany, and in democratic
> America, but which religious and loyal Englishmen abhor
> and loathe.[26]

In another way Huxley trod on eggshells. Lizzie was now in

Montgomery, Alabama. Her husband, Dr Scott, was practising again, having been employed as the post surgeon. His Confederate forces had been routed in Tennessee after Grant's victory at Chattanooga. Their 15 year-old son Tom – the boy Huxley had never seen – was assisting his father in the army hospital. Lizzie's agonizing accounts had Tom's 'warmest sympathy, so far as the fate of the south affects you'. 'My heart goes with the south', he explained, but 'my head with the north'. There was none of Darwin's fury at the slave's plight; the shifting attitudes told in Tom's words:

> I delight in the energy and self-sacrifice of your people;
> but for all that, I cannot doubt that whether you beat the
> Yankees or not, you are struggling to uphold a system
> which must, sooner or later, break down.
>
> I have not the smallest sentimental sympathy with the
> negro; don't believe in him at all, in short. But it is clear
> to me that slavery means, for the white man, bad political
> economy; bad social morality; bad internal political
> organization, and a bad influence upon free labour and
> freedom all over the world . . .
>
> All this must jar upon you sadly, and I grieve that it
> does so.[27]

He had been fighting the point publicly for months, after raising it in his Hunterian Lectures. There was nothing in the anatomy of blacks to justify slavery, and only absurdity in the belief that they were a separate species. The smoke of battle wafted through the College of Surgeons. He spoke as no egalitarian, but he held that slavery was corrupting and the North is

> justified in any expenditure of blood, or of money, which
> shall eradicate a system hopelessly inconsistent with the
> moral elevation, the political freedom, or the economical
> progress of the American people.

He waved Hunt's ugly parody of a paper, 'The Negro's Place in Nature'. Its 'preposterous ignorance' spoke volumes about 'the slaveholding interest'. He ripped into its idiocies: that ape-like blacks had elongated heels and could not stand upright, and hair that originates in three follicles! One African doctor James Horton wondered if Hunt had actually seen a black man. An escaped slave, William Craft, made sure that Carter Blake had; he stood upright at the 1863 BAAS, his 'handsome presence' contrasting with the 'mean-looking' Blake, and chopped up his ape-comparisons to rapturous applause. Huxley's anti-slavery rationalizations weren't too strong for the Ladies' London Emancipation Society, which repackaged them in a penny tract.

Hunt, that 'low bred ill instructed imposter', was loathed by the Darwinians. 'I dare say the brute is paid by Confederates to lie as he does', Rolleston seethed. He actually was. The Anthropologicals had a Confederate agent on their Council, who used a slush fund to channel money from the Richmond government.

Huxley never rested his liberation case on anatomy. But the *Reader* applauded his 'doctrine of freedom' and concluded that he had made 'his physiological definition of the Negro's place among men equivalent to an earnest plea for Negro emancipation'.[28]

Huxley made the most of the surgeons' resources. His workroom was a charnel house strewn with peeling lemur muscles and gorilla tendons. But the topic everyone wanted to hear about was cave men. In class he insisted that Neanderthal was no more a 'missing link' or 'midway' to an ape than someone who walked '1 mile [up] the North Road was midway between London & York'.

So where were the ape-men? Wallace was for sending dyak-led expeditions to Borneo to find them. The region was in imperial hands and being opened up as a coaling station on the India-Sydney run. Its lignite deposits had been shown in Huxley's lab to be perfect steam fuel, and Lyell agreed that Borneo's caves might contain equally precious deposits of 'extinct ourangs, if not the missing link itself'.

What fossils existed were being wrenched this way and that. Carter Blake considered the Neander man a deformed hermit who hid out in the caves. Others made him the first non-sapient human – *Homo neanderthalensis*.[29] Or even a distinct genus, a semiconscious being languishing in 'brute benightedness', ape-like and without any conception of his Creator.

Such extremes were unlikely. Huxley obtained a cast of Neanderthal's brain, and it was much bigger than expected. So big that it 'might have contained the brains of a philosopher', said the Duke of Argyll, the Lord Privy Seal who took as much interest in Nature's laws as Palmerston's and clung to any proof of a more exalted past. But the public's mind was set. As Busk worked on a second Neanderthal skull in the summer of 1864, from a quarry in the Rock of Gibraltar, the press pictured a brutish ape-man. Despite squashing this gothic fiction, Huxley could not resist dashing off a sketch of the hairy new *Homo Herculei Columnarum*, with grasping toes, brutal stoop and tail stump![30]

He was 700 miles north in August 1864, passing huge granite outcrops screaming with sea birds. Leaving the Orkney Islands off the north Scottish coast he headed to the Shetlands on the clanking Fisheries vessel *Salamis*. He gripped the rails as it churned through the North Sea swell. Always he was a distant Londoner, and the local fisher-folk were reticent about talking to Commissioner Huxley. But he did his best, investigating net-meshes, fry and the damage done by beam-trawling.

The Shetlands wilderness gave a new perspective to life in the bustling metropolis. The horizons closed in as his train chugged past 'miles of house-tops'. Three million people now lived in London's sprawling terraces. Huxley was back to the traffic jams and rush hours, 'hideous, vicious, cruel, and above all overwhelming', as Henry James exclaimed of this 'dreadful, delightful city'.[31]

In November 1864, after years of abortive efforts,[32] Huxley finally created an invisible club. He brought together a robust group, all of a mind on Darwinism and Colensoism. He needed to pull his cadre together. Work was a centrifugal force pinning them to their posts. We 'have not seen your ugly old phiz for ages', he would write to Hooker, 'and should be comforted by an inspection thereof'. Hooker's father at Kew was ailing, and he himself was rushed off his feet by 'concerns domestic, scientific, social & official'. He stopped setting the teachers' botany exams for the 'Science & Tarts Department'. Huxley swore by science exams as the best form of accreditation; he was even trying to get them extended to middle-class schools, spreading science's power base right into the heart of the classroom. With the Oxbridge classicists condemning any concession to the industrial middle classes as 'a dangerous state of things', he needed Hooker's help.[33]

Huxley called a meeting at St George's Hotel, close to the Royal Institution, on 3 November. The greatest constellation of New Reformers came together. Hooker was lured in, and the omnipresent Tyndall (he and Hal had become 'a sort of firm' in the public mind). There was Hirst (about to take the physics chair at University College), Busk and Lubbock, and Spencer too. The group was completed by Edward Frankland (Tyndall and Hirst's fellow student at Marburg, and the new chemistry professor at the Royal Institution). These men had grown up on the perimeter, in London's medical schools, German universities or around the midlands Chapel; Lubbock being the oddity as an Old Etonian. None was Oxbridge educated; but this *was* an elite. They were the new intellectual clerisy, slim and fit after an evolutionary sauna. Not all the members were academics – Spencer lived by the pen, Lubbock by the ledger. And to the eight the mathematician and Queen's Printer William Spottiswoode was later added. In club-bable London this was the most elite club of all, with nine members and a closed entry book.

'Amongst ourselves there is a perfect outspokenness', Hirst said. And they showed it. Militancy was increasing on all sides, and they met as the conservative outrage grew at *Essays and Reviews'* non-miraculous Christianity. Two of the *Essays'* authors had been convicted of heresy. When the judgment was overturned on appeal, 'dismissing hell with costs', there was uproar in the parishes. Wilberforce drew up a petition declaring that 'the whole Canonical Scriptures' was the literal 'Word of God', and almost half the nation's clergy signed. He presented it to the Church Convocation, which formally condemned the book.

A group of evangelical chemists, led by Capel Berger, the Plymouth Brethren paint manufacturer, took their own petition to the BAAS, demanding that the Association 'maintain a harmoni-ous alliance between Physical Science and Revealed Religion'. They were sick of Huxley's 'dangerous clique' baiting parsons with the glee 'a small boy feels when he is tying a tin kettle to a dog's tail'.[34]

Wilberforce's Convocation and Berger's petition put the fire into Huxley's night conclave in November. All present shared a 'devotion to science, pure and free, untrammelled by religious dogma'. And that explains some noticeable absences. The older Unitarians Lyell and Carpenter were out.

No other nine-member Club could have written 'a scientific Encyclopaedia'. No other nine members could have staffed a German Technical University. But that was not the most significant point. This was no longer an outsider cadre trying to break in, but an insider caucus spreading out. For all its scientific exclusivity, the club had direct access to the City, Parliament, medicine, industry and the liberal Church – to the cultural heart of the country. Huxley's irregulars had become a National Force.

Various clever names were canvassed, none cleverer than Huxley's 'Blastodermic Club'. (It sounded like hellfire but referred to the germ of 'future organization'.) Anonymity suggested '*x*' to Mrs Busk (that unsung hero, one of the background wives – or *yv*'s, as the joke went – occluded from view). The image of mock freemasonry appealed and 'X' was adopted. As the masters of cultural politics, they would snatch Science from noble patrons' hands and put it on a par with Medicine and the Church. They would dine at 6 pm. on the first Thursday of each month, and then take a post-prandial stroll to the Royal Society, which met at 8.30, where their plans for altering Council procedures would soon tip the balance of power.[35]

Liaising with them were Flower and Rolleston. The liberal Church was still pacing liberal Science. Stanley was now '*the* Dean' to the group: the new Dean of Westminster. He was godfather to the Flower children and invited them to romp in the warm Deanery after chilly services. The Abbey opened its doors to the X. When Tyndall wrote against miracles in Lewes' new *Fortnightly Review*, Stanley – having to conduct a cattle plague ceremony – asked him to devise a 'prayer in which the heart might express itself without putting the intellect to shame'. And, finding a Roman sarcophagus in the crypt, he brought Huxley in to verify that its occupant was genuine.

It was Stanley who recommended the *Antiquity of Man* to Queen Victoria, although presumably not *Man's Place*. But Huxley's tome was finding its own royal by-way. In Berlin Lyell learned that the Princess Royal of Prussia was 'very much *au fait* at the "Origin" and Huxley's book'.[36] Whether or not the Queen was amused, profane fingers were touching the throne. The Dean even invited Ramsay to investigate the Abbey's Coronation Stone; like the zoologist who would dissect a nightingale to understand its song, the hammerers analysed the sandstone to cut through its myth-shrouded origin.

Ahead lay peaks to be scaled. The Xs were an indomitable bunch, used to Alpine faces – Huxley and Tyndall had introduced Lubbock to the exhilaration of the climb a couple of years earlier, marching him 12,000 feet up the Galenstock in five hours. But the deepest crevasses lay in Piccadilly. As their first act, the Xs readied the Royal Society's 'ancient olive crown' for Darwin. Awarding him the Copley Medal would raise the 'stock of moral courage' in the ranks. But the old gents bridled at 'crowning anything so unorthodox as the "Origin"' and nominated his old Cambridge teacher Adam Sedgwick instead. The Xs did secure it for Darwin, but President Sabine doctored his speech and removed the *Origin* 'from the grounds of our award'. 'Lord have mercy on S. ', was all Hooker could say as a furious Lubbock, Huxley and Busk tore

Huxley

into him. Huxley now mooted cutting the President's election term.

As the ruffled feathers subsided, Darwin – his stomach heaving at a hint of controversy – had Busk pass the medal to his worldly brother Erasmus, who found it 'rather ugly to look at, & too light to turn into candlesticks'. But it came with Huxley's blessing. And that, replied Darwin, was 'the real medal to me & not the round bit of gold'.[37]

The X's second act was to issue a notorious manifesto. The opportunity arose with another paper. Tom Hughes, working with Nettie's Revd Llewelyn Davies and about to become Lambeth's Liberal MP, wanted Huxley to shake up the loss-making *Reader*. Tyndall joined Hal on the board, as did Darwin's statistical cousin Francis Galton, eager for experience of 'seamy' hack work. The editor Norman Lockyer was a born organizer, as befits a clerk in the War Office. He had 'his heart in the business' and his 'science already in the right groove'. The weekly would become a stump for science, bigger than the *Westminster*'s, better than the *Saturday Review*'s; a proper publicist's soap-box, putting science right up with the *belles-lettres* in British culture. The *Reader* might be a 'pig in a poke', but the Xs could pull him out '& make him a comely grunter'. It was revamped and recapitalized, with Spencer touting £100 shares. Hughes and Davies paid up, as did five X-Clubbers. By late November they had 'it in hand'. Huxley was 'a director of the Reader C°. (limited)'.[38]

Circumstances shaped the conditions for Huxley's manifesto. The buy-out coincided with Disraeli's exotic performance in Oxford's Sheldonian Theatre. What with Darwin, *Essays*, Colenso and Huxley, 'Materialism', Disraeli knew, was 'in the ascendant'. To his cherubic delight it left the bishops' privileges teetering on the truth of the Old Testament. That had the Church's Jewish defender flouncing around in an outrageous wideawake hat, winding up the Tory faithful: 'Is man an ape or an angel?' he asked Wilberforce. 'My Lord, I am on the side of the Angels'. The Xs relished *Punch*'s depiction of this Jewish angel, even if it did dignify a 'disgrace to the country'.

Further afield, the conservative mood was hardening. In Europe, liberalism meant emancipation, anticlericalism, unfettered science and freedom of conscience. There was a romance to it: London's Whig Duchesses adored the Italian liberator Garibaldi, whose victories did so much to unify Italy, on his 1864 visit. Mobbing crowds of 500,000 equated liberalism with liberation. No one could deny the mood. One man tried: a good, inept, undiplomatic soul, Pope Pius IX. Horrified at events (not least the threat to the Papal States from Italian troops) he issued an encyclical and Syllabus of Errors. It damned the 'evil' age, with its 'free progress of science'. He refused to reconcile Rome with such 'progress, with liberalism, and with modern civilization'. Political impotence was sending the Pope towards a proclamation of Papal infallibility.

No one doubted that His Holiness had Darwin in mind. Nor that Huxley was a spectre. Not, anyway, after Cardinal Wiseman issued a Pastoral denouncing those who would put 'a solitary cranium . . . in the scale' against Scripture. And hadn't Huxley given men 'the matured intelligence' and women the 'ripened graces' of baboons? But the Pope had attacked English liberalism, and Britannia whipped her skirts behind the Whitworth gun, to flirt with fusilier Huxley. The 'Pope is a glorious old ass', he smiled, 'and I trust he may live a thousand years to go on doing us good'.[39]

It dictated the *Reader*'s snorting response. The covert policy was one of 'slashing attacks to right and left'. As the proprietors took turns to write anonymous leaders, the grunter's broad backbone creaked. With Huxley's on 31 December 1864 it snapped. His rival 'encyclical' on 'Science and "Church Policy"' sent his Anglican partners into a spin. The Church Policy was of course Disraeli's, and the editorial a thunderous attack on his 'electioneering' buffoonery. Huxley damned 'political intriguers', and none more than Disraeli, whose 'grotesque' pandering to the political bishops left him 'patronizing Science for its froth and scum' – its steam engines and telegraphs – while 'scorning its essence and the foundation of its human worth'. He pilloried Disraeli's belief that 'the scoffing light-horsemen of the eighteenth century have been beaten off, and the old traditions have emerged from the smoke not much hurt', when truly 'the broken squadrons of Voltairean cossacks fly only to disclose the heads of solid columns of warriors, disciplined', armed and ready.

The military metaphor got its edge from these party political tensions. This was no church-baiting in a social vacuum. Nor was religion at issue. Her 'unshakeable throne' was in the 'deeps of man's nature', and from it comes our sense of awe at nature's grandeur. But Genesis, the 'old traditions', the incarnations of gods, Disraeli's angels – 'theology' in a word – that was a debased branch of history, amenable to test, indeed tested and found wanting. As such, science had no 'intention of signing a treaty of peace with her old opponent, nor of being content with anything short of absolute victory and uncontrolled domination over the whole realm of the intellect'.[40] Never had such a demand been heard in a respectable weekly. It stretched the Xs' ecumenical alliance to the limit.

Rolleston withdrew his support. The ' "old Traditions" are' *not* 'likely to be absorbed or superseded' by science. And the 'Unknowable' was a provocative misnomer, when God 'has partly revealed Himself' in Jesus Christ.[41] The fainthearts were dropping away, Huxley told Darwin, but 'the revolution . . . is not to be made with rose-water'.

Huxley's scepticism ran deeper than even this piece let on. During the evangelical revival, with atheism execrated as a social evil, he built a camouflaging stockade with philosophically defensible supports. Look again, he urged Rolleston. 'The fact is that you have read into the article what you know or think you know of my opinions . . . there is not a word in that article opposed to any forms of belief in a revelation of the Unknowable . . . All that I affirm is that all these beliefs & traditions will have to find a scientific basis & that those which cannot . . . will have to go'.[42] Huxley was not reaching for common ground, but annexing it.

Darwin twigged that the 'capital' piece was Huxley's doing. On receiving Huxley's New Year photograph the next day he replied, 'it makes you look too black & solemn as if facing a bench of Bishops'.[43]

Huxley's son Leonard was not to be lost in a 'harem of sisters'. Another boy was born two weeks later, on 14 January 1865. 'He is to be our Benjamin the child of our old age'. Hal and Nettie were coming up for 40, with six children, and Henry, as they called him, was to be 'positively the last – and a counterpoise to his brother who would otherwise be ruined by the worship of his mother & sisters'. Or Hal hoped the last. But, he told a clerical friend, the 'trees of the Lord are full of sap'.

Nettie was flourishing, 'bless her old heart'. She had her work cut out, organizing a house full of domestics and children, always entertaining and always pregnant. She had returned to her old 'energetic' state, Hal reported. 'And she had need [to]; for what with Servants & what with the price of butcher's meat the mother of six children has a severe struggle in life'. And she had to minister to Hal. The 'lodger' spent his nights among the workers or 'amidst the "lights" (& livers too)' of his lab, only to stagger home late, moaning 'Lectures, Lectures, lectures till I am well nigh lecture mad'.[44] And she would apply 'hot iron & mustard poultices' to ease his aching shoulders.

Those scapulas were overworked as he waved diagrams in his huge auditorium. In 1865 his interests were shifting again. As he demonstrated his skull-bisecting innovations to the Ethnological Society he moved further from ape origins to the living races. Having made human history open-ended with *Man's Place*, raising new possibilities about the origin and antiquity of today's peoples, he became the target for barrow excavators and midden-mound explorers.[45] Archaeologists sent boxes of skulls, and expats shipped aboriginal relics to compare with Neanderthal man.

As usual he tested his new course, 'The Races of Mankind', on his Monday night workers first. (He brought his own reporter this time.) His working men were adoring. One would crave an autograph 'to show my mates'; cabbies refused his fare ('proud to have driven you, sir'). All felt that he has 'done me and my like a lot of good'. Street atheists were delighted that 'science was still marching in their direction' and that the professor was 'among the first friends of our faith'.[46]

Others lacked his savvy with this sort of audience. At times the grave Owen seemed to lack any political sensitivity. When *he* lectured the radical Quakers in industrial Newcastle and

> kept the whole assembly waiting for a long while, he
> apologized by saying, 'I have been detained at
> Ravensworth Castle'. Lord Ravensworth being a strong
> Conservative this Flunkeyism greatly disgusted the self-
> made men who received Gladstone as a King & have
> covered the Tyne Banks for 20 miles with Alkali works &
> Ship Yards.[47]

But Huxley was more sensitive. His workers even took up a collection once, thinking he was not paid for his talks. He sometimes looked as though he needed it. Rheumatic arms were nothing to the poisoned fingers as he grasped nettles. After our animal ancestry, race and class were the new emotive issues.

Emancipation and citizenship were the great questions, for black slaves *and* oppressed whites. But he faced a hardening climate. Even the *Saturday Review* pictured the Bethnal Green hovel-dwellers as a permanent 'caste apart'. The pauper was stuck in 'the condition in which God has placed him, exactly as the negro is expected to remember the skin which God has given him'. Enslaved blacks and downtrodden whites were coming to be seen as 'perpetual inferiors', fit only 'to toil that another may reap the fruits'.

At times the exotic faces on Bloomsbury and Piccadilly streets belied this denial of any faculty for improvement. Hindus were graduating in medicine from University College. (And, the ultimate irony, its first ever prize in English Law was taken by a Trinidadian ex-slave.) Japanese students were sitting chemistry classes there in 1865.[48] Nor did Britain's own 'under-world' see itself perpetually bonded. Huxley's workers expected nothing short of millennial progress culminating in the vote.

Between the expectations of labour and race and the fears of the elite Huxley's was the mediating voice; the judicial interpreter of Nature's discriminatory laws. The rights of working-class women – the slaves of the slaves – only pushed liberalism harder. The education of women was a pressing problem. He knew it. His own cook was illiterate and he had to read recipes 'to her *slowly*'.[49] Huxley turned 40 on 4 May 1865 as Lee and the last Confederate generals surrendered in America. 'The question is settled', the slaves were freed, leaving the 'laws of social gravitation' to operate unhindered. Stability was ensured, he wrote in his *Reader* piece 'Emancipation – Black and White', for it is

> incredible that, when . . . our prognathous relative has a
> fair field and no favour . . . he will be able to compete
> successfully with his bigger-brained and smaller-jawed
> rival, in a contest which is to be carried on by thoughts
> and not by bites.

That was his line – on workers, on blacks, on women – freedom for the oppressed, with the oppressor reassured that 'Nature's old salique law will not be repealed, and no change of dynasty will be effected'. To each side he pleaded natural laws and Cobdenite fair competition, making his the priestly mouthpiece of power broker-age. Of course women's education had to come. The booms as the persistent young Elizabeth Garrett hammered on London University's door had an awful echo. Let them graduate, injustice should not be added to inequality, he urged, and 'the "golden hair" will not curl less gracefully outside the head by reason of there being brains within'.[50] Let them have careers – Nature will hold them to a new station.

Incitement for one side, soothing balm for the other; Huxley made 'Nature' speak through his new priesthood. Black ancestors, workers' unions, women's education – it was a frightening time for timid souls. With the Church-sanctioned hierarchies shattered in Heaven and on Earth the old certainties were gone. Huxley was inscribing Nature's laws on the Tablets now. Obedience to his science was the Word from the Mount, keeping the command structure intact.

This was not power to the people. It was power to the professionals.

1865–1870

The Scientific Swell

18

Birds, Dinosaurs & Booming Guns

HUXLEY'S LABORATORY WAS a necrophiliac's delight, with its peeling tendons and pickled brains. And the 'General', as his students nicknamed him in the late 1860s, was positively intimate with his bones. He would hang his arm over the shoulder of a skeleton and take its hand as he talked. Then, turning to the blackboard, with a flash of strokes and smudges, he would transform one animal into another before their eyes.

Everybody's pupils became his protégés. His science was modern and tinged by the controversial. His responses were fast and as often as not Biblical. The ornithologist Alfred Newton, shrieking from the surgeons' gallery that he had found extinct great auk's eggs, would hear Huxley's shout that Newton 'was like Saul who went out to seek his father's asses and found a Kingdom'. A pugilistic fame put Huxley in the papers almost weekly. As the General organized flanking attacks on a posturing Disraeli or plodding Owen, or moved against the cotton racists or reactionary church, as he strove, above all, to put science's Whitworth gun at the front of Britain's cultural armoury, he grew in legendary status among the students.

University men migrated over for his lectures in Piccadilly or Lincoln's Inn Fields. They talked of his 'agreeable voice', and his homely style, which made abstruse subjects sound 'natural'. Flashes of 'caustic humour' would put 'an extra gleam in his bright eyes', or a 'gravity of look' would give a point depth. He 'never posed, was never starched, or prim' and it made the difference. Proficiency had come with age. No longer did he get up to speak with 'my tongue cleaving to the roof of my mouth'. Nor did he cling to his manuscript 'as a shipwrecked mariner to a hencoop'. Practice had given his public talks the fluidity of poetry readings – hence Dickens' joke, putting a false book-back on his shelf, marked '*The Collected Poems of T. H. Huxley*'. Of course Huxley's 'lucidity' had all the 'legerdemain of the performer'. Off-the-cuff ease required working at; like his writing, its didactic simplicity was the result of hard labour. But all the students agreed that the General had no equal.

Rarely, however, did he moot evolution in class. Nor, despite those fathers 'who dreaded sending young men to him, fearing lest their [sons'] religious beliefs should be upset', did he broach theology. Only occasionally did he lapse (and the students waited for those moments). He might point to the heart's mitral valve, 'so called', he said, 'from a supposed resemblance to a bishop's mitre. You know the thing I mean – a sort of cross between a fool's cap and a crown'. And since no student could remember which side of the heart the valve was situated, he introduced his mnemonic aid, 'a bishop's never in the right'.

From students they went on to become devoted assistants and his wickedest critics. But only Sharpey's gold medallist at University College, the fast-tongued physiologist of radical Baptist stock, Michael Foster, dared call the proofs of Huxley's *Lessons in Elementary Physiology* too dense, 'no offence I trust marm'.[1] Having pioneered the plebeian prose and cloth-cap homily, Huxley was expected to churn out racy textbooks too.

One student turned out a sadder antagonist. The tormented liberal Catholic St George Mivart was already a lecturer at St Mary's Hospital in Paddington. Mivart was well-to-do, born in his father's Mivart Hotel – later famous as Claridge's – and brought up among its noble clientele. He caught the excitement, studying lemurs with Huxley in the wake of *Man's Place*. Huxley proved 'a good friend indeed – firm, generous, energetic, loyal and affectionate'. Mivart was captivated by those 'dark eyes, bright and full of expression'. They would 'light up' as the two strode home for dinner, deep in philosophy and Darwinism and 'the possibility of the medusa having been an ancestral form of man'. But Huxley's Puritan chat of the violation of evidence and the 'sin of faith' troubled his pupil.

In Jermyn Street the courteous Mivart sat adoringly at the master's feet. For a time Mivart felt himself 'a thorough going disciple of the school of Mill, Bain & H. Spencer'. But the convert to Rome was racked in these encyclical years. Between the reactionary Pope and the militant Darwinians he found little solace. The

General hardly helped by visiting Catholic seminaries, darting admiring glances at the hard-line Jesuit militia – *our* 'great antagonist', he called it, 'which is able to resist, and must, as a matter of life and death, resist, the progress of science and modern civilization'.

Huxley's 'moral mischief' put his Catholic admirer on the spot. Mivart agreed that a dead chimp was comparable to a dead human. But man's 'moral & religious nature', with its hopes and aspirations, its promise of immortality and salvation, sets him further from a gorilla than the 'Ape differs from a lump of granite'. The split was to open up into a devastating divide. Mivart was not to genuflect much longer before bishop Huxley.[2]

Huxley's protégés were sliding into place. He pushed 'tooth & nail' to get them into chairs from Galway to Casale. He had them fighting in Melbourne. He had them in Glasgow's Hunterian Museum, undermining the old Whigs – that dying breed, like Prime Minister Palmerston himself, 'opposed to "new fangled things"'. Enrico Giglioli was back in Italy as professor of natural history at the Tecnic Institute of Casale, looking for a brave Italian publisher for *Man's Place*. Near by in Turin, he reported, the Catholic zoologist Filippo de Filippi was mining out the book and championing 'our descent from "Apes"', at least as far as our material bodies went. But like all of the old boys Giglioli was nostalgic for his youth under Huxley and desperate to get back to London 'in the midst of the scientific movement'.[3]

The Xs were beginning to control that movement. Off duty they took their YV's on moonlit trips down the Thames, stirred by Huxley's renditions of Tennyson. Darwin was a sort of corresponding country member. Old Sir Charles Lyell was sidelined, the more because he had obviously 'plundered' Lubbock's paper on prehistoric shell mounds for his *Antiquity of Man*. (Sending Lubbock, 'like all quiet & mild men', Huxley told Hooker, 'about twice as "wud" as Berserks like you & me'.) But there was another very telling grudge.

Ellen Busk had a rapier-intellect which rather spiked the tradition of religiously demure wives. So while Sir Charles regularly 'pumped [Busk] dry of his knowledge', Lady Lyell cut Ellen dead. She would not call, though they lived down the street, nor invite the Busks to her parties. The Huxleys resented it. Hooker saw Mrs Busk as 'a most thoroughly accomplished clever person', and 'more of a Lady' than all the fluttering socialites who flocked 'to

Lady L's soirees'.[4] It was a further reminder of the X-Clubbers' socially inferior origins. Ellen's was a new world, of gutsy George Eliot novels with their trader and surgeon heroes, a world which saw Elizabeth Garrett return from Paris the first woman Doctor of Medicine. Talented women were forcing their own way into the new aristocracy.

But Sir Charles' generation was moving aside. The Xs were the new power. With the death of Hooker's father in 1865 the State bought his herbarium and library, making Kew a public institution and Joseph Dalton Hooker its Director. Lubbock became Sir John on his own father's death and looked to a Parliamentary career. Hooker flinched at this 'awful waste of time, of energy, of brain, of life'. But Huxley backed him.[5] Not that it helped. Midway through Lubbock's first West Kent campaign in 1865 Williams & Norgate brought out his *Prehistoric Times*. It flummoxed the hop-growers, who thought familiarity with stone-age rubbish tips not the best qualification in a candidate. He lost handsomely.

Huxley knew that progressive science would eventually find its voice in the House. It was finding it everywhere else. Rationalist books were dropping off the presses. Man's aboriginal savagery, man's rise, man's rational goal, nothing seemed taboo after *Man's Place*. As a sofa-bound invalid, Darwin had his long-suffering wife recite from William Lecky's *History of Rationalism*. Huxley had to like Lecky's saga of disappearing miracles. It 'just missed being a first class work – But the man is very young & I have great hope of him bye & bye'. Hooker added Lubbock's and Edward B. Tylor's *Early History of Mankind* as the year's 'really excellent works'. Both turned the empire's savages into stone-age relics, like Huxley's 'living fossils' trapped out of time in the colonial backwaters. These people provided snapshots of our primitive past. This wasn't Darwinism with its adaptive spread into richly unique niches. Tylor's single ladder was climbed by all cultures; we had hauled ourselves nearly to the top, while aborigines were on the lowly rungs, reminding us of our past.[6] The idea resembled Huxley's ontogenetic track. It suited the empire's growing image of its native 'children', to be tended by white 'adults'. The Xs took to this Quaker's son who declared war on the savage superstitions surviving in his own culture. And Tylor shared the X-Clubbers' terrible need to emancipate us from our superstitious past.

The club's own rationalist efforts weren't doing as well. The *Natural History Review* had become too technical and inward-looking; this specialist biological journal with its Darwinian bent was foundering. It never did appeal to the masses, as Huxley had wanted. He was long 'out of concert with it & wash my hands of it. My share of the loss is £25.0.0 & I can't afford luxuries of that kind'. He was still roping in the best talents for the liberal *Reader*, with its wide arts, literature and science coverage – and the brightest was that physiological Turk Michael Foster, who impishly called Huxley 'Captain'.[7] But with too many Captains and precious few crew, the *Reader* ship was doomed too. It had listed after Huxley's cannonade at the Church, when the Christian Socialist commodores took to the lifeboats. Now it headed for the rocks.

Worse was in store when the new navigator came on board. Huxley's militancy had only encouraged a more aggressive take-over. One of Hunt's henchmen Thomas Bendyshe was angling to buy it out. 'I should be very sorry to see the Reader pass into his hands', Huxley told Lockyer. They halved its cover price to 2d and boosted the adverts, but to no avail. By autumn 1865 the ailing paper was 'bound over to Satan'. The wealthy Darwin was worried about getting his money back as the ship went down for good. A poor Huxley was sorrier about the lost opportunities. 'The N. H. R. & the Reader are the first & last journals I . . . ever mean to be connected with'.[8]

There was no ignoring the 'Cannibal Club', as Hunt's rival dining élite dubbed itself. By the end of the Civil War they were a wretched power in literary London. Theirs was a phenomenal rise, with the notorious specialist in Arab erotica Richard Burton aboard. They revelled in their repugnance. A savage's skeleton hanging in the window announced their rooms. Inside, meetings were brought to order with a negro's-head mace, and in an unsavoury reaction to the prudery of the age (and to the Ladies' nights at the Ethnological) their erotic excursions verged on the pornographic. They explored phallic symbols and sexual taboos with a freedom unknown elsewhere. They out-marginalized the Darwinians, and out–numbered them, and in their struggle for hegemony threatened to impose their own rival ideology of 'man's place' on society. They claimed '700 to 800 Fellows and a yearly income of £1,500 to £1600' (only later was it realized that they were cooking the books), three-fold the Ethnological's numbers. Lubbock and Huxley's society was bringing in barely £320 a year. The Darwinians might have seemed a model of family propriety by comparison, but they were alive to the danger posed by the cult's extremists.

With the Confederacy in tatters Hunt's men had lost their *raison d'être* and seemed tempted to submerge their infamy. Huxley too was weary of infusing life into the Ethnological. He called the warring factions a 'scandal'; and, as the *Saturday Review* saw, his authority to talk on human origins would be sapped so long as the experts were seen to 'quarrel among themselves'. A takeover was imperative to foster an image of solidarity. Huxley even put up a pontoon bridge for his regulars to march over. In his lectures he ceased referring to 'races', and used 'stocks' to cut through the preconceptions, and talked of them as 'persistent modifications'. But Hunt – that 'Turkey Buzzard', as Rolleston labelled him – feared that Huxley was out to 'crush' them, a qualm increased by the killing look in Lubbock's eye.[9]

In a topsy-turvy world Wallace the 'emancipating' socialist spelled out the main reason for uniting. The Ethnological – that philanthropic crowd-puller with its bevy of anti-slavery ladies – crimped his style. He saw the men-only Anthropological as 'a good protest against the absurdity of making the *Ethnological* a *ladies'* Society. Consequently many important & interesting subjects cannot possibly be discussed there'.[10]

The pulpit delicacy of Victorian sexual mores gave Huxley his own troubles at the Ethnological. With the straitlaced matrons he had to guard his tongue: no mooting the body to bring a flushed cheek, no sexual customs (a fainting subject) – so many taboos made his own culture an absurd subject for study. They certainly made a mockery of serious 'Ethnology'.

He rose to the challenge. He countered the pulpit's sway with his own 'lay sermons'. They drew the ladies; in fact they drew unprecedented crowds now. The Sunday League's flyer announcing that he was to launch its 'Sunday Evenings for the People' sent London into a flurry. The poor were admitted free and others fought for tickets. And who could object to the 'wonders of science' instilling a new 'reverence' in those who did not attend worship?

Two thousand milled about Covent Garden on the night of 7 January 1866, finding St Martin's Hall full. Inside was 'packed to suffocation'. 'Every part of the great Hall was crowded – every foot of standing room was occupied'. Fifteen months earlier Karl Marx had founded the First International here, when it rang to the cheers of Parisian workers. His daughter Jenny had waltzed in the Hall at communist meetings. Now she squeezed in again. With the 'leading names in science, Huxley (Darwin's disciple) at the head' setting the sabbath alight, 'dull England' did not seem so dull any more.

'Sacred Music' played Huxley in, a booming church organ pumping out Haydn's 'Creation' to heighten the sense of awe. ('You may live to see me a Bishop yet', he told Dyster.) With its echo fading he began his hymn. Science was tearing through the 'fine-spun ecclesiastical cobwebs' to behold a new cosmos, in which our Earth is merely an 'eccentric speck' – a world of evolution 'and unchanging causation'. It invited new ways of thinking. It demanded a new rationale for belief. With science's truths the only accessible ones, 'blind faith' was no longer admirable but 'the one unpardonable sin'. Huxley was sacrificing the old authority on nature's 'altar of the Unknown'.

His vision of science promised intrigue and exotic horizons. It was imperial and expansive. He knew he could move multitudes, and he carefully carried his congregation. He guided them 'through a new country', breathlessly, 'like a skilful charioteer', the *Leader* said, 'pulling up with the utmost ease' to show 'magnificent views of the broad and fertile kingdom of Natural Knowledge'.[11] It was a revivalist meeting with its ecstatic highs; the 'Kingdom of Nature' was at hand, and 'a nobler discourse on a nobler theme was never delivered'. Lost amid the hallelujahs was its serious function, as Darwin's laity imputed the old moral laws to the cosmic fabric itself.

Jenny Marx exulted in this 'genuinely progressive' sermon, at a time 'when the flock are supposed to be grazing in the house of the Lord'. Huxley was reclaiming those whose sabbaths had been spent 'bawling a hymn to "Jesus, Jesus, meek and mild"' or passed 'in a Gin Palace'. The sermon cascaded into a tear-jerking finale, and an outraged clergy watched Huxley depart with the audience brought to tears by the 'Creation'.

The womenfolk loved it. Here was the handsome Huxley, greying at the temples, black eyes flashing, the Puritan tease. Evolution to a prim generation was titillating. Ladies young and old were flirting dangerously. 'My mother (aged 75) is delighted with your sermon', Lewes wrote, running it in the *Fortnightly*, '& foresees a change in Religion coming'. (Huxley had made up with Lewes and often dined at the Priory, Lewes and George Eliot's rose-clad house in familiar North Bank. Still, Hal told Tyndall, you could always tell a Lewes review: 'nobody else could be so clever & so ignorant'.)[12]

Huxley's 'Lay Sermon' brought a catcall 'Atheist' from the *Spectator*. He wearily responded that 'Atheism is as absurd, logically speaking, as polytheism' – incapable of proof or disproof – but he clearly needed some alternative label to license doubt and throw the opprobrium back on to the 'sin of faith'. Owen berated these 'extremist views'. Having hoodwinked costermen into believing they were chimps, Huxley was arousing their wives. His 'contemptuous relegation' of the 'Supreme creative Will' was not for pretty ears.[13] Nor did the Lord's Day Observance Society think so. Incensed by this sabbatarian mockery, it stopped the 'Sunday Evenings for the People'.

The rush of the night seemed a hallucination the next day. In the cold light Huxley huddled over black bituminous amphibians. He had the 'scent of . . . carboniferous corpses'. From Irish collieries he ferreted out amphibians, sinuous eel-like creatures, with tiny legs and flat shield-shape heads for slithering through the shallows. In six years he had etched out more of the earth's first land vertebrates than any man living. With the Devonian land insects turning up – mayflies and grasshoppers – one could hear the buzz and snapping jaws of this ancestral fauna.[14] By night or day, it was the time to be alive.

Technical papers streamed from the press, and honours replaced the obloquy. From Paris' Société d'Anthropologie to St Petersburg's Imperial Academy, via the appreciative German academies, foreign fellowships came Huxley's way. He even felt a prophet in his own land, or at least a Sassenach sage, as he travelled to Edinburgh on 2 April 1866. He met up with Tyndall, escorting the wild, sleepless Carlyle; and there, with Carlyle fortified by a nip launching into a 90-minute extemporization, all three were awarded honorary Doctorates of Law. But the mixed feelings for Huxley told in the 'cheers and slight hisses'.[15]

Edinburgh's boos were drowned by the sound of the universities on the march. The oldest dames were donning new clothes; a bill before Parliament would even permit non-Anglican fellows at Oxford and Cambridge, presaging the fall of the entire Church monopoly. These moss-encrusted institutions, 'half-clerical seminaries', he called them, 'half race-courses', were modernizing. To his goading question, 'What are the Universities doing for Science?', a Cambridge group responded by founding a *Journal of Anatomy and Physiology* and demanding a contribution. Cambridge was rushing to catch up with London. With a chair of zoology founded in 1866, it was barely 40 years behind. But the capital kept its lead as Huxley dissected his way through the animal kingdom. In 1866 he began on the whales. Outside the classroom he added the evolutionary lustre:

> No doubt whales had hind legs once upon a time . . . my friend Flower the Conservator . . . will show you the whalebone whale's thigh bones in the grand skeleton they have recently set up. The legs, to be sure, and the feet are gone, the battle of life having left private Cetacea in the condition of a Chelsea pensioner.[16]

Huxley's annexation of London science capped his academic career. Capped was correct. This year he put another hat on. He took the Fullerian Professorship at the Royal Institution again. It was his third concurrent London professorship, a unique feat and probably never to be equalled.

Audiences flocked to hear him. The journalist Eliza Lynn was 'intoxicated' by Huxley's talks in his 'Court of Paradise', the Royal Institution. Here and in the School of Mines and College of Surgeons Huxley continued to collate the world's peoples with the surety that came from imperial conquest. With the navy patrolling the seas he could order the human parts he wanted, treating Her Majesty's Ships like zoological privateers. Occasionally the grave robbery called for Britannia's tact. Captain Watson would sail in with Patagonian chieftains' skulls plundered 'as privately as possible in order that the Natives might not know that any of the Graves of their ancestors had been disturbed'.[17] Or the *Nassau* would sail out with Huxley's shopping list of Fuegian skulls, and a reminder to pick up fossils of a rhinoceros-sized guinea pig (*Toxodon*) spotted at the Straits of Magellan.

Plunder of skulls was one thing, his old Charing Cross classmate Joseph Fayrer's offer was another. Rather than lecturing on indigenous races, come and see them: Fayrer, in the Indian medical service, invited Huxley to the City of Palaces, Calcutta, to compare a sample of all the Asian peoples rounded up by the Asiatic Society of Bengal. Brazen collation was the goal, as if stamping and ranking the races would result in a more orderly empire. For one mad moment the round-up seemed feasible. With railway barons laying tracks to rush troops to the Indian troublespots, Fayrer could transport his ethnological zoo; and Calcutta was rife with bureaucrats, ready to photograph and process. You 'do things on so grand a scale in India', Huxley replied in surprise, but what with lectures and little ones his own participation was out of the question.

Baby Henry had not been the last. Nettie, coming up for 41, already suffering from swollen veins and the stress of her extended family, had added 'another small humanity to the six who already pervade this house'. Abbey Place was bulging as the cots came out and new nurses arrived to look after newborn Ethel. Jim's daughter Katy was still with them for the holidays (during term time she was at Nettie's old German finishing school, paid for by Hal). Nor was life eased by the builders and dust and sheaths of scaffold as they were forced to build new rooms on top to accommodate the growing horde.[18]

So India was out. Barring a weekend dash to Dublin to finger black coal fossils, it was all the *pater familias* could do to catch up with the 'miles of work in arrear'. His age was telling. He knew it when Edith, the newborn baby that his sister Lizzie had carried on her precipitous flight 20 years earlier, had a babe of her own. 'How do you feel as a Grandmother?' he asked Lizzie. In Montgomery they had struggled through the war, robbed by itinerants after the slaves' emancipation. Lodgers made up their earnings. One who was put up after the siege of Atlanta was Albert Roberts, a young newspaper man come to work on the *Montgomery Mail*. His first sight was of Dr Scott, 'a distinguished gentleman in uniform', and 'a beautiful lady, likewise English'. Mrs Scott (Lizzie) 'was adorable', but the attraction for Edith proved greater. 'Give our love & congratulations to Edith', Tom wrote after hearing of her and Albert's baby. 'I read her husbands articles with great pleasure'.

Intrigue still surrounded Scott. Huxley had answered an executor's notice in the *Times*, inquiring after relatives of a deceased Mrs Salt. Her son John had been unknown to her for two decades; the estate came to only £250, but it was a lifeline in post-war Montgomery. After a rigmarole proving his relationship they had their inheritance. It took Tom back to the dreadful days when the couple fled. And here was his favourite sister an 'adorable' grandmother.

> I can quite understand all your feelings. Jess is but eight
> but I talk savagely . . . about my prevenient hatred of the
> long-legged puppy whom she will some day or other think
> more of than of her father & mother.[19]

Huxley was ending his own racial round-up at the Royal Institution in June 1866 as Germany's war of unification began. The Prussian advance 'swept on like a heavy spring tide', trapping his translator Victor Carus in plague-ridden Leipzig. One of Huxley's fellow examiners was with the Prussian troops as they surged across 'nearly the whole of northern Germany'. Do 'you want any Teutonic skulls' he asked, 'with perhaps a rifle bullet included'? More than the odd bullet. The Prussian needle guns proved decisive. Austria was defeated in July at the Battle of Königgrätz. With the peace, Carus finally got a letter out to ask Darwin and Huxley for their biographies to include in a German encyclopedia, now to cover a greater Germany. Everyone wondered how much greater. As the English went over for the 'Annexation Rejoicings', they found a new world power in the making.[20]

The propagandists of Germany's brand of *Darwinismus* knew it. Darwin's doctrines were spreading with British liberalism,[21] as free trade and secularism were taken up by radical unifiers in Italy and Germany trying to forge strong national identities.

The bombastic Ernst Haeckel at Jena was transmuting the *Origin* into a patriotic form. He had been evangelizing the Germans ever since standing up for Darwin at the Congress of Naturalists at Stettin in 1863. Haeckel had made Jena a 'citadel of Darwinism'. He cut an extraordinary figure. In his early 30s, he had a passion for nature's beauty that was religious and a fiery rhetoric that was inspirational. He would escort flocks of students through the Thuringian hills, dilating on the splendours of nature and *Darwinismus*. This Extraordinary Professor of Zoology at Goethe's old university, Huxley told Darwin, was 'one of the ablest' in Germany.[22]

Haeckel stretched Darwin's struggle for existence to society itself. This was the punch in his *Generelle Morphologie*, a 1,000-page double-decker, written to drown his sorrows after the death of his wife. *Darwinismus* drove the best 'peoples irresistibly onward', he insisted. It presaged a new Teutonic destiny. Neither 'the weapons of the tyrant nor the anathemas of the priest' could stop German progress now. Like all radicals, he saw a supine nobility wiped away in the struggle – dogs and aristocrats, he snorted, were all the same in the womb. His *Darwinismus* sanctioned a strong state, with free speech and free trade invigorating its people.

Jena's comparative anatomists were busy drawing evolutionary trees. But Haeckel's was something of a magical wood, with the missing ancestors modelled on living embryos. Huxley beat through the book's thicket of makeshift trees. Each of Haeckel's family trees was a racially related group sharing a common ancestor, born of the same warring struggle as the new Germany – or what he called a 'phylum'. All creatures in a phylum are bound together, the fit survivors, sharing a common bloodline purified by battle. It consecrated his Messianic ideal of the German *Volk*. 'While the booming of guns at the Battle of Königgrätz in 1866 announced the demise of the old Federal German Diet and the beginning of a splendid period in the history of the German Reich', he said welcoming Bismarck to Jena, 'here in Jena the history of the phylum was born'.[23]

For the moment Huxley could only browse through the book. As usual he faced a torrent of lectures, three waves combined into a 100-foot breaker which hit him as it had the gale-tossed *Rattlesnake*. 'If I could only break my leg', he sighed, 'what a lot of scientific work I could do'.[24]

In England things were moving fast. The British Association meeting in 1866 was a triumph. With Huxley, Wallace and Galton pulling strings, Tylor tracing civilization to its savage roots, Hooker satirizing the primitive tribe which had led the British Asses by the nose until 1860, the papers saw Darwin's theory 'everywhere in the ascendant'. Even the President, physicist and barrister William Grove, pleaded that gradual evolution was constitutionally sound; it obviated the threat of revolution and was in the best interest of the State.[25] Suddenly the reform of Nature sounded frightfully British.

A Harrow schoolmaster struck another chord. Revd Frederick Farrar proclaimed that 'the important question for England was not the duration of her coal', but her stock of science teachers. That was Huxley's sort of talk. Farrar was part of the liberal fallout from Maurice's Christian Socialist explosion. He was a science sympathizer whose work on the evolution of language tickled Darwin enough to recommend him for an FRS (and to send him Huxley's 6*d* pamphlets as a bonus).

Farrar and Huxley got up a Committee to force the issue of science in public schools. With Farrar's contacts and Huxley's know-how they intended 'knocking on the head' the excessive Latin versing.[26] If there were no texts Huxley would write them. If the most important facts of life concerned one's body, his *Elementary Physiology* would provide a fillip. Huxley, cheated of the best years of schooling himself, would ensure that his 'scientific Young England' fared better.

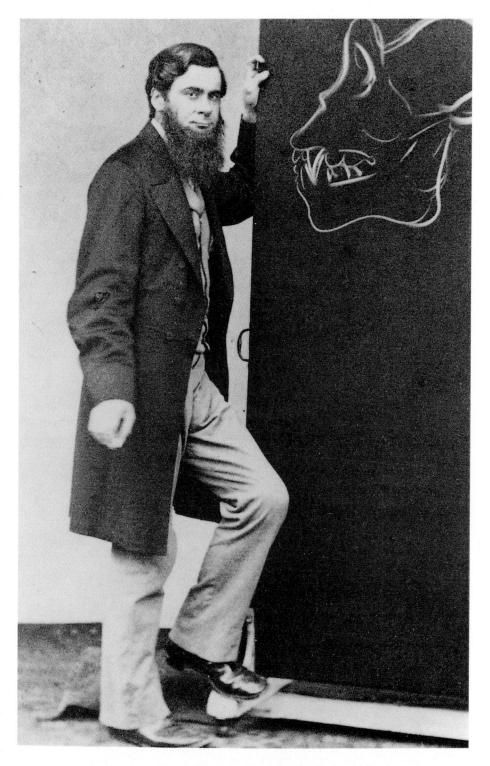

28. The young bearded lecturer at work, drawing a gorilla skull.

29. A 'grim and a grotesque procession', the Duke of Argyll called this skeletal troop, the clever frontispiece to Huxley's *Man's Place in Nature* in 1863.

30. The first known skull cap of Neanderthal Man. Huxley was given the cast by its discoverer Karl Fuhlrott.

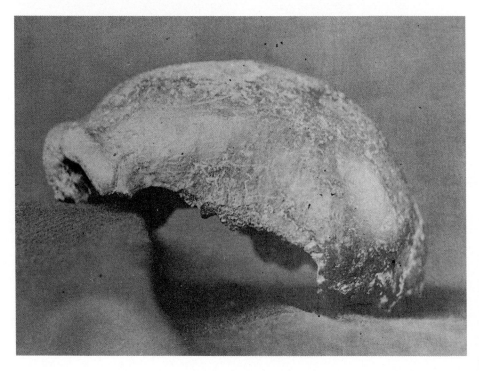

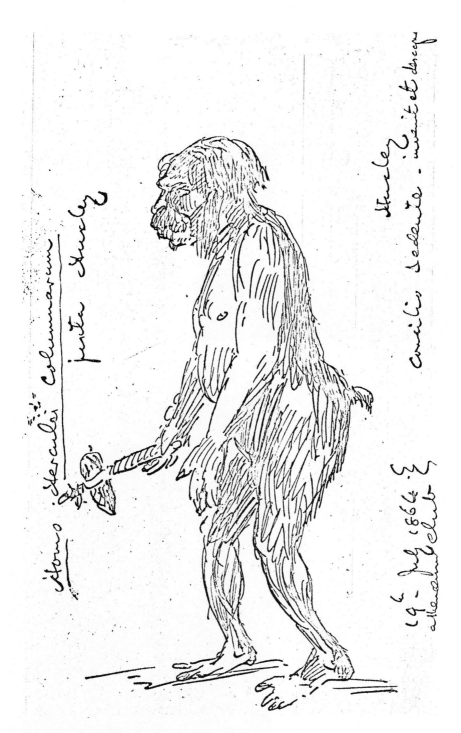

31. Not so grim: the discovery of another Neanderthal skull at Gibraltar in 1864 elicited this sketch of a hairy ape man. It was a joke: in reality Huxley was the first to show that Neanderthals were not 'ape men' at all, but large-brained humans adapted to a cold climate.

32. (*Left*) Nettie and 33. (*below*) Hal.

Now even Harrow toffs with Latin-filled heads looked on an alien 'wire-scape', as telegraph wires criss-crossed the skyline. They read of reptilian empires more exotic than the Roman, of human antiquities more ancient than the Bible's, of evolution more stirring than Genesis. Daily the newspapers played up the living dramas, as Brunel's gigantic *Great Eastern* paid out the enormous tonnage of telegraph cable from Ireland to Newfoundland. They lived when the first electrical messages crossed oceans at 288,000 miles a second. The revolution was being forced on the old seminaries, its lusty cries drowning out the morbid echo of dead voices.

At the BAAS Huxley had gained the 'Anthropologists' a limited hearing and it paid off in the merger negotiations. The duplicitous Hunt, presumably seeking legitimacy, even offered Huxley the presidency of the amalgamated society.[27] But events overtook the power brokers. The deal was in the final stages when a black uprising in Jamaica blew back in Huxley's face. A local revolt in the cane-cutting colony had been ruthlessly crushed. Jamaica was a patchwork of ramshackle estates, owned by absentee landlords and eyed by the destitute blacks. Eyre was Governor, the man once admired by Huxley for crossing the Great Australian Bight. But the gold-braid-encrusted Lieutenant Governor of New Zealand had become the stiff-necked Governor of this half-evacuated colony. Grievances about high prices, social injustice and squatters' rights had sent machete-wielding militants into Morant Bay's courthouse to hack the hated magistrates to death. White fears flashed back to the atrocious massacres in Haiti and the crackdown was brutal. Eyre's troops were loosed and 439 blacks were cavalierly shot in passing or hanged after impromptu court hearings.

The reprisals went on for weeks, culminating in the half-caste demagogue of Jamaica's Assembly, William Gordon, hanging from a yard arm. This Native Baptist minister might have been a 'poor type of small political agitator', Huxley admitted to Kingsley, who knew Eyre, '& very likely was a great nuisance to the Governor', but 'English law does not permit good persons, as such, to strangle bad persons, as such'. Huxley had done with Carlyle's Great Men as sacred makers of History. There had to be equality before the law. Eyre's 'preposterous subalterns' had illegally executed a man. The Governor approved and was as

> responsible for Gordons death as if he had shot him
> through the head with his own hand. I daresay he did all

this with the best of motives, & in a heroic vein[.] But if English law will not declare that heroes have no more right to kill people in this fashion than other folk, I shall take an early opportunity of migrating to Texas or some other quiet place where there is less Hero worship & more respect for justice.[28]

'The sight of heaps of dead bodies in Demerara' sent shivers down the liberal spine. Spencer's father died hallucinating about Eyre's atrocity. Anti-slavers found new hackles rising. Mill's liberals called it murder, and Huxley was asked to join their Jamaica Committee, formed to prosecute Eyre and wipe the blood from Britannia's robes.

But it was a divisive issue. Had Eyre not prevented a white bloodbath? Or a worse fate for the colony's 'tenderly nurtured women'? Lurid images blended with a belief that English law did not apply to a '*naturally* wild . . . inferior race'. Out of this potent concoction came the Eyre Defence movement. It put a strain on old friendships. Hal watched Tyndall join, and Nettie heard 'brother John' turn down a dinner invitation because he was pledged to the repatriated 'Eyre and his wife'. The cracks began to show. It was the only moment in Huxley's and Tyndall's life when 'each of us would have been capable of sending the other to the block'. Kingsley too called the prosecution 'detestable' (his grand-father, a Barbados judge, had been ruined by emancipation). And even Hooker thought that any population dangerous to the empire must be 'subject to the same nemesis'.[29] The *Pall Mall Gazette* despicably pinned Huxley's 'nigger' politics on to his 'peculiar views' of ancestry. No one who saw a hairy chimp 'as "a man and a brother"' would balk at giving blacks the same 'sympathetic recognition'.

The taunts pushed Huxley to the front of the Jamaica Commit-tee. He served with Mill, Francis Newman, Tom Hughes, Spencer and that veteran Rochdale radical turned Birmingham MP John Bright. Behind them in this alliance of philanthropy and reform stood Lyell, Darwin and Wallace. Authority was not absolute in Jamaica, any more than it was in Oxford. No man was above the Civil Law, as no Wilberforce could invoke powers above the Natural Law.

One enterprising ex-slave, Moses Moore, read of Huxley's talks in the *Antislavery Reporter*. Moses had worked his passage from Guiana and was living at the West India Docks, speaking on

SUNDAY EVENINGS FOR THE PEOPLE

WITH THE APPROVAL OF

Sir J. BOWRING, LL.D., F.R.S.
Prof. BEESLY, University College.
THOS. HORLOCK BASTARD, Esq.
FRANCESCO BERGER, Esq.
SIR JAMES CLARK.
W. B. CARPENTER, M.D., F.R.S.
M. D. CONWAY, Esq.
W. S. COOKSON, Esq.
I. F. CLARK, Esq.
ERAS. DARWIN, Esq., F.R.S.
CHAS. DICKENS, Esq.
W. H. DOMVILLE, Esq.
JOHN DILLON, Esq.
THOS. HENRY FARRER, Esq.
Prof. FRANKLAND, F.R.S.
F. J. FURNIVALL, Esq., M.A.
HENRY F. FARBROTHER, Esq.
Dr. J. E. GRAY, F.R.S., &c.

THOMAS GRAHAM, Esq., F.R.S.
W. B. HODGSON, Esq., LL.D.
JAMES HEYWOOD, Esq., F.R.S.
Prof. T. H. HUXLEY, F.R.S., &c.
Prof. A. W. HOFMANN, Ph.D. F.R.S.
FREDERICK HARRISON, Esq., M.A.
GAVIN HARDIE, Esq.
Prof. THOS. H. KEY, F.R.S.
Rev. THOS. KIRKMAN, M.A., F.R.S.
Sir CHAS. LYELL, Bart., F.R.S.
Sir J. LUBBOCK, Bart., F.R.S.
A. H. LAYARD, Esq., M.P.
J. BAXTER LANGLEY, Esq., M.R.C.S.
R. B. LITCHFIELD, Esq., B.A.
VERNON LUSHINGTON, Esq., B.C.L.
GODFREY LUSHINGTON, Esq.
JOHN STUART MILL, Esq., M.P.
Prof. HENRY MORLEY.

Rev. Prof. J. MARTINEAU.
Prof. RICHARD OWEN, F.R.S., &c.
WM. SCHOLEFIELD, Esq., M.P.
H. J. SLACK, Esq., F.G.S.
WM. SHAEN, Esq., M.A.
HERBERT SPENCER, Esq.
SPENCER SHELLEY, Esq.
P. A. TAYLOR, Esq., M.P.
Prof. J. TYNDALL, LL.D., F.R.S.
Rev. Prof. J. J. TAYLER.
Rev. CHAS. VOYSEY, M.A.
Sir JOSHUA WALMSLEY.
Prof. WILLIAMSON, Ph.D., F.R.S.
E. P. WOLSTENHOLME, Esq.
W. H. WILLS, Esq.
HENSLEIGH WEDGWOOD, Esq.
Sir J. G. WILKINSON, D.C.L., F.R.S.
ERASMUS WILSON, Esq., F.R.S., &c.

· The Sunday, as a day of rest and leisure, when the thoughts of men are released from the engrossing labour of mere existence, is the time most fitted for the exercise of the reflective faculties: and the Winter Sunday evenings would be so employed, if opportunities were afforded, by large numbers of those who at present do not attend places of worship, who would listen to discourses on science and the wonders of the universe, thus producing in their minds a reverence and love of the Deity, and raising up an opposing principle to intemperance and immorality.

A SERIES OF DISCOURSES IN

ST. MARTIN'S HALL, LONG ACRE,

WILL BE COMMENCED ON

SUNDAY EVENING, JANUARY 7th, 1866,

BY

PROFESSOR HUXLEY, F.R.S.,

"THE DESIRABILITY OF PROMOTING NATURAL KNOWLEDGE."

To be followed by (Jan. 14) Sir J. BOWRING, LL.D., F.R.S. : "Religious Progress outside the Christian Pale, among Buddhists, Brahmins, Parsees, Mahomedans," &c. ; (Jan. 21st) W. B. CARPENTER, Esq., M.D., F.R.S., " The Antiquity of Man ;" (Jan. 28th) W. B. HODGSON, Esq., LL.D., "Many members, but one body :" JAMES HEYWOOD, Esq., F.R.S., Rev. J. MARTINEAU. Prof. OWEN, F.R.S., CHAS. DICKENS, Esq., and many other gentlemen who have nobly offered their services.

To the many kind friends who have voluntarily tendered pecuniary help the Committee offer their thanks, and, at the same time, their assurance that to make the Sunday Evenings for the People " self-supporting " will be their study. A portion of the Hall will be free, so that the poorest may not be excluded; other parts will be reserved for holders of tickets.

Sacred Music will precede and follow each Discourse, and thus a social, moral, and really beneficent purpose will be served.

R. M. MORRELL, *Hon. Sec.*,
108 Great Portland Street, W.

34. The flyer for Huxley's 'lay sermon' in 1866. Two thousand were turned away and the hall was packed to suffocation. His talk was called atheistic and the Lord's Day Observance Society stopped these 'Sunday Evenings for the People'.

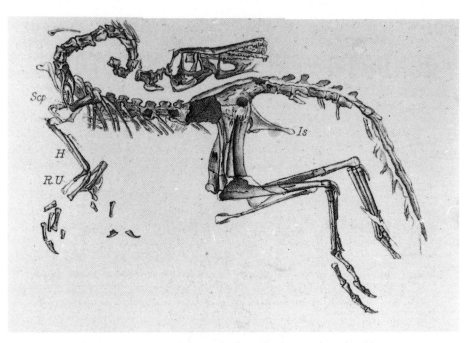

35. The tiny dinosaur *Compsognathus*, which walked on its long hind legs. It was crucial to Huxley's presentation of dinosaurs as the ancestors of birds.

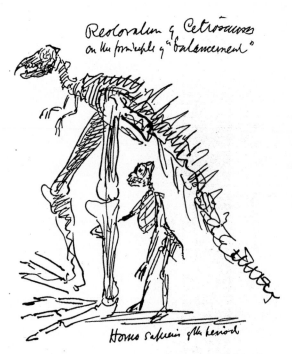

Restoration of Cetiosaurus on the principle of "balancement"

Homo sapiens of the period

36. The concept of bipedal dinosaurs was novel in 1868. When John Phillips unearthed a five-foot *Cetiosaurus* thigh bone, Huxley dashed off this caricature. The arms were unknown; in the sketch Huxley shrank them by a corresponding amount as a tease. Note the ape-faced 'Homo sapiens of the period': Huxley had long believed that humans lived alongside dinosaurs.

37. Huxley as President of the British Association for the Advancement of Science in 1870.

38. An unusual portrait of a smiling Huxley, known to his students as the 'General' and to the press as 'Pope Huxley'.

plantation life to raise the money for an education. He sent his 'thanks Sir as emanating from the heart of a "genuine negro"'. (The racists claimed that clever blacks were not pure 'Africans' but of mixed blood.) He wished Huxley's sense would prevail among the planters, 'who have placed the negro race as only two removes from apes'. A slave's praise highlighted Huxley's distance from the hardliners. He would give subject peoples the same rights under English law. But Hunt's cannibals lambasted the Government for recalling Eyre and Huxley for arraigning him. Jamaica revealed the political chasm again and the merger was aborted. Not that Huxley was 'personally sorry to be free of them'.

Race and class were emotively linked by Hunt's clique. It claimed that equality was as bad for a savage as a street arab. A little education would breed dangerous aspirations. The vote would be lethal. The 'nigger' is in 'Jamaica as the costermonger is in Whitechapel ... a savage with the mind of a child'. By contrast, Huxley was not only talking on ethnology at the Mechanics' Institute, but ending with a collection to ease the 'appalling distress' of the East End jobless, Hunt's Whitechapel 'savages'. Vivid were Huxley's memories of the dock slums, although a long 25 years had elapsed since he had sidled past the derelicts to his Jamaica Street surgery. He put his pennies into an open-top skull on the table, and the cranial vault was soon brimming with coins. It infuriated the reactionaries. The Anglo-Saxon gentry needed to be vengeful masters. The underworld cauldron had to be contained, by martial law if necessary. There could be no charity or freedom for these irreclaimables. The issue was sensitive, with reform on the agenda in 1866. 'We do not admit of equality even among our own race', Hunt's anti-democrats ranted.[30]

But why? radicals countered. Old Chartists and new trade unionists were uniting in a Reform League to push for suffrage. Even Gladstone, impressed by the Lancashire weavers' stoicism during the Civil War layoffs, thought that workers had earned the right 'to come within the pale of the constitution'. Mill's Committee swung its weight behind reform. Mill himself had taken Westminster for the radicals at the 1865 election, Bright was barnstorming in the north, and the Jamaica Committee bumped along on the reform bandwagon. These nights Huxley would sit around with fellow mountaineer and failed ordinand Leslie Stephen, 'denouncing God, Eyre and the British aristocracy by the hour'. The 'Jamaica Row' is rumbling on, he told Lizzie on 1 December, and 'there is to be a Reform demonstration on Monday of 200,000 people – So times are lively'.[31]

In January 1867 a craggy, long-bearded Darwin descended from Olympus and turned up in Jermyn Street. He was viewed as Zeus by the surprised students, and he looked the part as he toured the building with Huxley. The Royal School of Mines now led Britain in applied science education. Huxley's lectures towered over University College's, where that Restoration relic Robert Grant still taught a defunct 1830s zoology in a frayed swallow-tail coat. The small intake belied the school's importance. It was a 'seeding' establishment. Out of it came a select group of industrialists and academics, and its galleries were a shining example 'of what a museum ought to be'. Darwin had pulled his coddled youngest son Horace out of Clapham School. The boy had a mechanical turn and his father browsed though Huxley's prospectus.[32] Huxley himself would shortly put his own nephew 'young Jim' through the school, acting *in loco parentis* as Jim senior became more mentally muddled, shut away in his asylum in Kent.

Haeckel had toured the galleries three months earlier. Afterwards Huxley had wined and dined this Coryphaeus among German naturalists, and the Abbey Place troop kept a 'lively memory' of their larger-than-life guest. Huxley and Haeckel were like conspiring generals, with Hal 'as deeply interested' in the *Morphologie* as Haeckel was 'in his ape-theory'. The camaraderie came from a shared combative attitude; but Haeckel, used to the barricade socialist Carl Vogt's scurrility, found Huxley's 'Attic wit' of a 'much finer grain'. No doubt, too, the dinner conversation turned on their other mutual interest, jellyfish (it had to, with Haeckel calling his own house 'Villa Medusa'). Hal introduced him to the Xs. And Haeckel seems to have undergone something of a mystical experience on meeting the 'Jove-like' Darwin. The venerable patriarch stood silent and slightly flabbergasted, with a flowing beard like Moses on the mountain, as Haeckel boomed his embarrassing, gushing greeting in German.[33]

New Year 1867 saw Darwin 'swearing at each sentence' of Haeckel's *Generelle Morphologie*, hoping Huxley would arrange a translation. 'The German is too difficult for ordinary mortals', Darwin moaned. Even Huxley with his fluent German found it 'uncommonly hard'. Huxley had bullishly resisted Darwin's genealogical approach to classification. But now Haeckel was sending him 'genealogical tables' as well. Haeckel's evolutionary 'trees' were based more on embryonic relationships than Darwin's messy field approach, and they finally converted Huxley. 'Whether one agrees or disagrees' with Haeckel, he said, it was 'more profitable to go wrong than to stand still'.[34]

Even on holiday Huxley could not escape Haeckel's influence. Like all middle-class families the Huxleys trooped off to the seaside each summer. In 1867 it was the quaint village of Swanage on the south coast, six hours away by train and bumpy omnibus. And not content with seven children from ten years to 18 months, with attendant nurses and maids, they were joined by Haeckel's barnacle-specialist, Anton Dohrn. Haeckel's pupils venerated Darwin and Huxley. Like the master, Dohrn recalled 1859 as the turning point of the century, with the Italian War of Unification and the end of the Papal States counterpointing the intellectual bombshell of the *Origin*. Dohrn was shortly to found a unique marine laboratory at Naples, where European zoologists could study the larvae of the warm Mediterranean waters and solve the ancestral riddles.[35] But for the present Huxley and Dohrn fished in cooler Swanage seas. They all remembered it as a time of laughter. Up early for lobster breakfasts, then out with the dredge, while at night the herd of seven children was taught 'bovine vocalisations' by the affable Dohrn, leaving Harry toddling round the house shouting 'Mroo'.

The laughter continued at Haeckel's lamentable jokes about a 'gaseous' God.[36] But the *Morphologie*'s big message about racial ancestries had its impact. It finally forced Huxley to connect his ancient lung-bearing Crossopterygian fish with the first labyrintho-dont amphibians – in other words, to show how fish grew limbs and slithered out of the water.[37] He had caught up with Owen. But Huxley's next innovation would overhaul his enemy dramatically. It was the most unexpected piece of ancestor-hunting yet.

Birds and reptiles had interested Huxley for some time. His work-ing men were always the first to know of his innovations and they heard about the chicken's relationship with the tortoise in Novem-ber 1866. He taught them that the scaly-legged birds were an 'extremely modified and aberrant Reptilian type'. The stork and the 'snake it swallows' sat together in the professor's new verte-brate 'province', which he called the 'Sauropsida'.[38]

In spring 1867, his 24 lectures to the surgeons were devoted to this great reptile-bird ground plan. But that did not make ostriches and crocodiles any likelier-looking bedfellows. However odd to the cloth-caps, it was odder to Owen, who denied it. But Huxley made it seem more reasonable at a stroke. He suggested that dinosaurs had a bird-like heart and lungs and even 'hot blood'.[39] (He probably got the idea from a young palaeontological Ishmael and former piano-tuner's apprentice Harry Seeley, who had proposed that pterodactyls were 'hot-blooded'.)

But Huxley was only thinking in terms of ground plans. His ideas had no evolutionary twist yet. Nor did they on 7 April 1867, when he completely reclassified the birds on the basis of their palate bones at the Zoological Society.[40] Even now he thought that birds were not *literally* modified reptiles, simply that both were based 'upon one and the same ground-plan'. He was still thinking in static structural ways.

Then came the conversion. He finished the last of his Royal Institution lectures on 8 June 1867 and finally had time to give Haeckel's *Morphologie* its due. He studied the book assiduously and the impact was profound. The racial lines and fossil roots transformed his thinking – his notebooks blossomed with avian classificatory trees, a riot of snaking lines and crossings-out.[41]

Linking the living birds into a 'tree', he informed Cambridge's professor of zoology Alfred Newton – a dedicated ornithologist despite his hip disease and walking sticks – was just a step 'in the progress towards the ultimate goal, which is a *genetic classification*', a real blood line, showing how fossil and 'living beings have been evolved one from the other'. He had once told Darwin that was impossible; now it seemed obvious.

He narrowed his sights to partridge and pigeon heraldry, demonstrating how, on 'the Evolution theory', it could be depicted 'by a genealogical tree, or *phylum* as Haeckel calls it in his remarkable "Generelle Morphologie"'. He traced the birds to 'a single primitive stock', like a nobleman following his birthright to the Norman barons.[42] It had taken Huxley a gruelling seven years to come to terms with the most profoundly historical aspect of Darwin's *Origin*.

Having got rid 'of my incubus' – meaning the bird paper, but he might as well have meant his anti-genealogical millstone – he could march faster across the new land. But it was an accidental find that determined his direction.

Huxley was still immersed in fossil reptiles. From every little England the coffins came. As one of his suppliers George Gordon said, his Elgin reptiles 'in days of old must have had cousins scattered over the face of the earth as widely as Queen Victoria's subjects are at the present day'. Her Majesty's colonists were busily despatching them home. From Bengal had come bizarre two-tusked reptiles (dicynodonts). Even better had come from a postman with rounds along the Cape's Orange River. His box of bric-à-brac, 'as in Pandora's', had its treasure at the bottom. Here Huxley found broken 'thigh bones of a great Dinosaurian reptile as big as Megalosaurus and probably nearly allied to it'.[43] This was the first definite dinosaur from Africa. And with only thighs, what else could Huxley christen it, but *Euskelesaurus*, the 'good-legged dinosaur'?

But hind limbs did not a dinosaur make. What did this giant really look like? Owen's life-size dinosaurs in the Crystal Palace grounds stood like scaly rhinos.[44] But this image, like the concrete models, was cracking.

Huxley was in Oxford's museum on 24 October 1867, looking at the dinosaurs made famous by the late William Buckland (the hyaena-keeping, practical-joking Oxford geologist who had introduced the first 'giant reptile' *Megalosaurus*). He noticed a misplaced bone among the 'precious relics'. Having spent a year surrounded by bird skeletons, he saw that this was part of the pelvic girdle, the ilium, and so bird-like as to be astonishing.[45] The avian-shaped hip had never been noted before. It was the catalyst that set him on to the most spectacular of all pedigrees – a dinosaur ancestry for the birds.

His escort that day was Buckland's successor. Old John Phillips had been rather brushed aside by the Darwinians; the faster they rushed, the more he seemed a fuddy-duddy. His review of the *Origin* had been 'weak, washy, stilted stuff', and Huxley had condemned him 'to that part of Hell which Dante tells us is appointed for those who are neither on God's side nor on that of the Devil's'.[46] But in 1867 he was proving himself a live old buzzard, always able to come up with the right fossil bone, and equal to Huxley's quips.

With Phillips' bones, Huxley started pushing the birds back towards the dinosaurs. He dismantled Owen's rhinocerine bulwarks, rebuilding the monsters to avian specifications. Huxley was doing what the critics had demanded: transmuting one major class into another.

His excitement was muted at first. Just as he began, scarlet fever swept through the Abbey Place household. For three months they were 'like lepers'. Nettie was fraught, her mind numbed by the memory of Noel's death, her body 'pretty nearly worn out with nursing day & night'. On 25 November her 'little black eyed girl Rachel was attacked, just as we thought we were safe', but she was the last. Michael Foster's 'prescription of sal ammoniac' did wonders and, Hal told him, 'my wife blesses your name continuously'.[47]

Free of lectures and the fever, Hal spent Christmas in the British Museum's valley of bones, reassembling a powerful, 30-foot herbivore, *Iguanodon*, as a biped. The novelty of a full-size dinosaur up on its hind legs struck him. 'The restoration looks wonderful', he told Phillips, 'a sort of cross between a Crocodile & a kangaroo with a considerable touch of a bird about the pelvis & legs!'[48]

He also looked at that fabulous feathered fossil *Archaeopteryx*. This primitive reptilian bird had been bought on Owen's orders in 1862, to enhance his museum's European reputation (and to enable him to describe it). A bird with a long bony tail and four unfused fingers caused a sensation; 'startling', the papers called it – and the exorbitant £400 price-tag only increased its notoriety. Huxley's ethnological friend John Evans, manager of a pulp mill and a flint expert (a man who 'knows the wickedness of the world and does not practise it', and what better reference coming from Huxley?), detected a jaw with teeth, and then the brain case. After that, friends expected him to find 'the *fossil song*' as well, 'impressed by harmonic variation on the matrix'![49] Evans declared that the fossil's bearing on the 'Origin of Species must be evident to all'. It was enough to have Lyell pleading with Huxley as early as October 1862 to examine the fossil.

But Huxley had trouble with Owen's Jurassic bird. He never said much about it and only examined it at Christmas 1867 to show that Owen could not tell the right foot from the left.

Ironically, *Archaeopteryx* ruined Huxley's neat line between tall ostrich-like birds and giant strutting dinosaurs. With his lingering belief in the 'persistence' of animals, he looked for evidence of *oldest* birds – and Hitchcock's Triassic footprints suggested that big moa-like birds were already living alongside bipedal dinosaurs. For Huxley, *Archaeopteryx* was in many ways 'more remote from the boundary line between birds and reptiles than some living Ratitae [flightless birds] are'.[50]

But dinosaurs were huge – the three-ton *Iguanodon* was much too big to be a bird ancestor. And even more mountainous creatures were coming to light. Phillips' new *Cetiosaurus* (the aptly named 'whale reptile'), removed from local Jurassic rocks in 1868, had thigh bones as tall as a man, making it the 'largest animal that ever walked upon the earth'. Huxley might 'hunger & thirst' after such a 'Frankensteinosaurus', but these monsters could hardly have evolved into birds.[51] There *were* tiny dinosaurs in existence. Haeckel's colleague at Jena, Carl Gegenbaur, noted the delicate bird-like leg and ankle of the first – and tiniest – of them, the chicken-sized *Compsognathus* (from the fine lithographic slates of Solnhofen that had preserved the traces of *Archaeopteryx*'s feathers). Huxley pushed *Compsognathus* into the limelight as the 'missing link' between birds and dinosaurs and wondered if it was itself feathered.

He pulled all the evidence together on a wintry evening, 7 February 1868. The Royal Institution socialites entered his lush world of Jurassic palms. 'Those who hold the doctrine of Evolution', he began with a new confidence, 'and I am one of them', believe that today's discrete classes of animals – including birds and reptiles – have come from a common stock. But to find it we have to go back to a balmy Jurassic past, to a lagoon at Solnhofen. Flapping clumsily overhead was a heavy *Archaeopteryx*. And at the water's edge, a diminutive dinosaur, hopping like a bird, neck bobbing, snatching prey with its small arms.[52] The talk was a *tour de force*. At last one could visualize how tiny dinosaurs with long hind limbs passed by degrees into ancient flightless birds (of which kiwis and rheas are their 'scanty modern heirs'), and these via *Archaeopteryx*'s kin into the song birds heralding today's dawn.

It was the crowning moment of his palaeo-work. His first constructive use of the past had revealed a sensational pedigree. (Or one of his most 'sensational tricks', Owen growled.) The midbrow papers responded to the propaganda coup. His triumphalist talk was run in the new *Popular Science Review* and *Geological Magazine* as well as the faithful old *Annals and Magazine of Natural History* (Darwin's bedtime reading). Huxley, the anatomist interested in the laws and proportions of form, had taken the decade to adjust to Darwin's emergent evolution. He had moved from life's abstract geometry to its dynamic ancestry.

But he had come round and he carried the world with him. In New Jersey bipedal dinosaurs were also turning up. An ambitious, 26 year-old Quaker, Edward Drinker Cope, had resurrected a fearsome, 20-foot reptile, with a 31-inch thigh but only 12-inch upper arm. This was his 'leaping' *Laelaps*, named after Diana's hunting dog, turned to stone in mid-jump. Cope, who would initiate America's own dinosaur boom, immediately accepted its avian affinity. Even 68 year-old Phillips was convinced. 'The more

I reflect on the monsters', he told Huxley, 'the more grows my faith in their struthious [ostrich] affinities'. But he could hear his predecessor turning in his grave. 'What would dear old Buckland have said' to his terrible reptiles being cousins of the robins?[53]

Two weeks after the Royal Institution triumph Huxley wrote to Haeckel:

> I am engaged [in] a revision of the Dinosauria, with an eye to the 'Descendenz Theorie'. The road from Reptiles to Birds is by way of Dinosauria to the Ratitae [flightless birds]. The bird 'phylum' was struthious, and wings grew out of rudimentary forelimbs.
>
> You see that among other things I have been reading Ernst Haeckel's *Morphologie*.[54]

19

Eyeing the Prize

'IF HE HAS A FAULT, it is that, like Caesar, he is ambitious'. The *Spectator* was right, of course. The poor boy was still scrambling out of the ghetto. His ascent had been like a furious alpine climb. But by 1868 Huxley had scaled his way to the summit. He had come a long way since his birthday above a butcher's shop.

He was a new middle-class hero, whose wit tingled with patriotism and whose wisdom served the Dissenting elite. His ferocity was a reflection on the intransigent old order. Unable to call up professional backing, refusing to tug on patronage strings, he had forced his own way into society, pinking the old gents and pushing them aside with 'that slashing rapier of his': 'cutting up monkeys was his forte, and cutting up men was his foible', the *Pall Mall Gazette* observed. But the immovable grindstone of society had honed his blade.

There was another public side, and 1868 was a watershed there too. Thirty years earlier, the long-haired apprentice had been horrified by the dockland degradation. These no-go areas of starving wretches continued to haunt society. But Huxley's outstretched hand had turned the menacing labourers into backers for his Great technocratic Britain. 'I am a plebeian', he reassured them, 'and I stand by my order'.[1]

The 'plebeian' became Principal Huxley in 1868, head of his own Working Men's College. His benefactors were Maurice's ubiquitous Christian Socialists. There could be no more concrete proof of their good intentions, however questionable Huxley thought their co-operative politics. On 4 January he inaugurated this small South London college, which was situated across the Thames, on the Blackfriars Road. Lubbock and Tyndall sat on the council, while John Ruskin and Tom Hughes provided the library. To the classrooms were added a coffee lounge where burly mechanics could pore over their *National Reformers*, or touts could offer tickets for Monday nights in Jermyn Street:

> Sixpence for the course – a penny for a lecture by Huxley!
> You have never heard anything like it, my boys. Only
> remember the theatre holds but six hundred, so be in time.

Evening classes for women were planned, and a kindergarten for the tots who were usually written off as gutter-urchins.

In '*your* College', a wellwisher assured him, 'Scientific training' could only lead to 'the greatest literary excellence'. The workers saw it preparing them for power. And Huxley, inaugurating this 'South London Working Men's College', did nothing to disabuse them. There is not a pin to choose between 'your average artisan and your average country squire', a local paper reported him saying. The country would be no 'worse off under one regime than under the other'.

He was swinging the masses behind his professionals. He spoke to them in parables, rationalizing his pitch for power. His opening speech took the form of a game-playing metaphor. If life was a chess match, school should teach us the rules:

> The chess-board is the world, the pieces are the
> phenomena of the universe, the rules of the game are what
> we call the laws of Nature. The player on the other side is
> hidden from us. We know that his play is always fair, just
> and patient. But we also know, to our cost, that he never
> overlooks a mistake, or makes the smallest allowance for
> ignorance. To the man who plays well, the highest stakes
> are paid . . . And one who plays ill is checkmated –
> without haste, but without remorse.
>
> My metaphor will remind some of you of the famous
> picture in which Retzsch has depicted Satan playing at
> chess with man for his soul. Substitute for the mocking
> fiend in that picture a calm, strong angel who is playing
> for love, as we say, and would rather lose than win – and
> I should accept it as an image of human life.

Huxley's romantic personification of Nature had a dramatic punch. It needed to, for he looked on an extraordinary audience: behind the Christian Socialists sat rows of hard men, straight from Southwark's jam factory and engineering site. Leather traders and felt-hat makers dotted the scene, probably some Baptists and Methodists, but mostly freethinkers. A 'brigandlike' assembly, or so it seemed, with 'fine massive foreheads' draped in wideawake hats. These 'great bearded fellows with the signs of labour on their horny hands' had no time for philosophical niceties, and he gave them none.[2]

He made an angel of Darwin's anthropomorphic Natural Selection. Man's challenger was no longer God, but Darwin's godlike Nature, which scrutinized every gambit, every move. Only the scientist was investigating Nature's rule book; only he could be society's new schoolteacher.

Away from the sea of wideawake hats, Huxley was also wooing the other side. His address was spruced up for *Macmillan's Magazine* (itself synonymous with Christian Socialism at times). He persuaded bosses that it was in their interest to educate workers. Only an awareness of Nature's moral order could tame the political passions, and nothing less would stabilize capitalist society. The founding of the Trades Union Congress in 1868 gave his words their force. Widespread agitation had led to the second Reform Bill only months before, giving the better-off workers the vote. Across the Channel France was racked by strikes on the eve of the Commune. Touchy manufacturers heeded his plea for the democratization of knowledge. Investment in this sector would yield social dividends.

> A workman has to bear hard labour, and perhaps
> privation, while he sees others rolling in wealth and feeding
> their dogs with what would keep his children from
> starvation. Would it not be well to have helped that man
> to calm the natural promptings of discontent by showing
> him, in his youth, the necessary connection of the moral
> law which prohibits stealing with the stability of society –
> by proving to him, once for all, that it is better for his
> own people, better for himself, better for future
> generations, that he should starve than steal? If you have
> no foundation of knowledge, or habit of thought, to work
> upon, what chance have you of persuading a hungry man
> that a capitalist is not a thief 'with a circumbendibus?'

Like a line of parsons stretching back to Paley, Huxley was reconciling man to his place. It was a self-serving plea, hitching the nation's progress to his élite's; and such had the social centre of gravity shifted that his was now the voice of moderation. The 'true voice of Jacob', Tyndall called it, so 'different from either howling radicalism or hidebound, stupid Toryism'.[3] The Dissenting middle classes who put technology at the social hub had put Huxley there too. His Evolution had become the ameliorating ideology of the industrial order.

Lines of parsons awaited Huxley. Having squeezed them from science, he had no scruples about stretching its cosmic moral to their domain. Indeed, he was asked to. At last he had 'the chance of preaching just one sermon to the parsons in exchange for the thousands they have preached to him', joked the *Saturday Review*.

Farrar invited Huxley to lecture the City clergy at their antiquated conference centre, Sion House. It was a 'very odd meeting' in 'as odd a place'. Not even Londoners had heard of this anonymous building near the medieval city wall. What better than to have Huxley put some fire into its moribund meetings? Rows of vicars undoubtedly fidgeted as he undermined the biblical chronology ('6,000' years was chalked on a slate beside him). They heard him take the story back past Joseph, past the Pyramids, past their Nile mud limestones, past their nummulite fossils to an immense antiquity. And, according to the conciliatory *Saturday Review*, they received the Word with equanimity (apart from 'two eccentric parsons' who denounced geology as the devil's work), and proved it afterwards with 'a pleasant half-hour over muffins and tea'.

The *Review* was a mite eager. One vicar apologized the next day for the City clergy's 'rudeness & roughness which stood in painful contrast with the calm dignity, & gentlemanly quietness of your own manner'.[4] Evidently it was just short of a genteel tea. But even he agreed that Huxley was jeered for stating 'conclusions which no competent judge doubts'.

It showed the changing temper of the times. But so too did the Xs' link-up with Maurice's men. Tyndall 'could hew' the orthodox 'to pieces before the Lord in Gilgal', but the Stanleys and Kingsleys 'are so gentle & noble'. And Christian culture's *rapprochement* with science lay with these churchmen. More than Christian culture was tinged by the new science. The Hebrew scholar, the Berlin-educated Marcus Kalisch, exiled in Britain after 1848, asked Huxley to proof-read his *Commentary on Leviticus*.[5] Everyone now consulted this expert on pre-Adamite creation.

On holiday in 1868 at that 'out of the way place' Littlehampton, on the south coast, Hal could be seen strolling along the sands with Nettie, reading her his paper 'On a Piece of Chalk'. The Sussex resorts were now the holiday haunt of the London bourgeoisie, with mothers, maids and children settled into the new boarding houses during the week, joined by their husbands at weekends. Crinolined ladies in their multi-layered, bustled skirts watched the couple saunter past, Nettie, the perfect layman's advocate, stopping to criticize a point of style, or suggesting a better colloquial expression.

Then Hal left to deliver it at a BAAS fringe meeting. In 1868 the delegates gathered in 'the ancient city of Churches', Norwich. A quaking Hooker was President, his resolve strengthened by Tyndall, who told him it was 'a duty that the gods have laid upon you'. Norwich must 'have been as wicked as Gomorrah', a wag observed, for there was surely 'a Church to every family'. Now it was set to receive the real 'Priesthood of Science', as the *Reasoner* dubbed Huxley's arrivals.

Huxley lured the Continentals over: Carus from Leipzig and Carl Vogt from Switzerland. Indeed, Vogt's scurrility and the *Reasoner*'s anticlericalism seemed to set the tone, and not only on the fringe. Hooker in his presidential pulpit lambasted 'that most dangerous of all two-edged weapons, Natural Theology' (with its attempt to deduce God's attributes from nature). 'Rank infidelity' was becoming synonymous with Darwinism, the *English Churchman* noted in sadness.[6] The jargon of factory infidels and emancipating Dissenters had become the stock-in-trade of an under-valued and under-capitalized Science.

Huxley was a whirlwind. He promoted his bird-like dinosaurs, and paid his dues on that score. Re-examining his mid-Atlantic ooze, brought back by Dayman ten years earlier, he detected specks of jelly with his latest high-power microscope. With Haeckel guessing that an amorphous albumen was the primordial living matter, Huxley saw himself looking at the primal slime life of the abyss. He christened his inchoate jelly-creature *Bathybius Haeckelii*. The exuberant Haeckel fired up Huxley, who went on to depict a pulsating film of protoplasm carpeting the 'whole sea bottom from the Persian Gulf round Cape of Good Hope & away by S^t. Helena to England'.[7] Haeckel assumed that this primal life was chemically generated in the depths. Huxley doubted it, but the striking image of a 'continuous scum of living matter' circling the globe seemed to cap the materialistic world view.

Darwin's 'reign was triumphant' at Norwich, said the *Guardian*. Certainly the 'terrible "Darwinismus"' 'crept out when you least expected it'. Even the Hindu-temple expert and Calcutta factory owner, James Fergusson, 'Stolid as an Assyrian Statue' himself, stirred it into his discussion of Buddhist stupas. 'I am preparing to go into opposition', Huxley joked to Darwin about the dwindling number of adversaries. 'I can't stand it'.

More accurately, it was an evolutionary naturalism that stole the show: a visionary naturalism in Tyndall's case. Tyndall was blasting the 'Tories . . . who regard imagination as a faculty to be feared'. His own was positively rioting. Flabbergasted workers were teased with his techno-vision of conscious robots and laboratory-built babies. There was a futuristic beauty to his cosmos. Like a religious visionary, he *saw* the life-giving atoms 'and felt their pushes and pulls'. In his galaxy all forces were convertible and even consciousness had its 'correlatives in the physics of the brain'. This poetic materialism was enough to drive the mild Mivart to damn Tyndall's 'creed – "I believe in One Force"'. But there was a magnificent determinism to it: an awareness that we are all children of the Sun, and that love and pain were 'once latent in a fiery cloud'.[8] It was the stuff of dreams.

Huxley's talk at Norwich was no science fiction, but just as fantastic. In the Drill Hall he initiated his workers into the sea bed's surprises. By now the style was the man; perfect, pellucid. He took his navvies through 'the masonry of the earth's crust' to find the source of the chalk in the carpenter's breeches. For 90 minutes he never halted. He pictured the rain of dead *Globigerina* building up 1,000 feet of chalky sea-bed over the Cretaceous aeons. Then the huge swimming reptiles vanished, and the ocean floor rose up in the 'whirligig of time' to become the lush land where Norwich's fossil elephants would roam. Huxley's best lectures were odysseys, and he ended with the option, Evolution or Creation, as he always did when reaching out ('Choose your hypothesis; I have chosen mine'). It had an impact in this workers' stronghold. The Professor was like the Methodist fanatics, playing to the bushy beards. They yearned for an emotionally expansive science in their secular world, and he was a fisher of souls.

A man got up and said 'they had never heard anything like that in Norwich before'. Never 'did Science seem so vast and mere creeds so little'.[9]

The sermon itself had an oceanic feel. The *Reasoner* ordained Huxley's men to the 'Priesthood' in recognition of this mythopeic vision and Puritan zeal. They were the new brimstone pastors. Enemies saw them retaining the Old Testament benefit of a 'scientific hell', into which 'those who persist in rejecting the new physical gospel' might be cast. Huxley, that 'Roundhead who had lost his faith', conveyed enormous power and urgency.[10] No bearded listener doubted that this sceptical priesthood carried the blood-stained banner of the Reformation.

By the end of the decade Huxley's essays were breaking all records. They were carrying the *Fortnightly*. His electrifying piece 'On the Physical Basis of Life' in February 1869 sent it into an unheard-of seven editions, and the cheques kept coming in. 'No article that has appeared in any periodical for a generation' caused such 'a sensation', said John Morley, the new editor keen to make evolution the *Fortnightly*'s creed.

It was based on a lecture that itself consummated the decade. 'Physical Basis' had inaugurated a Sunday Evening series in Edinburgh, and eye-witnesses confirmed that it was just as sensational. That night Huxley made 'Protoplasm' a household word.

It was the stuff of plant and animal cells, indeed of the slimy depths themselves, but his gothic image of 'quivering disembodied life' took it beyond the mundane. 'Science is almost sublimated into poetry', someone said of protoplasm's 'rushing and roaring' maelstroms inside the cell. It was the unifying matter of life, common to men and algal mats. Huxley showed bottles of smelling salts and carbonic acid, the constituents of protoplasm. Even though living protein was a strange manifestation of these chemicals, it was no more to be explained by a mystical 'vitality' than hydrogen and oxygen becoming water was to be explained by some occult 'aquosity'. The audience sat rapt, and 'you might have heard a pin drop', such was 'the *intense* interest'.

Accept this, he goaded them, and 'you are placing your feet on the first rung of a ladder which, in most people's estimation, is the reverse of Jacob's'. For if the 'dull vital actions of a fungus' are the properties of its protoplasm, so *all* of life's activity is the result of its molecular forces – even the lecturer's thoughts as he talked. Pious Presbyterians knew he was trenching on the sacred. The timid, he continued,

> watch what they conceive to be the progress of
> materialism, in such fear and powerless anger as a savage
> feels, when, during an eclipse, the great shadow creeps
> over the face of the sun. The advancing tide of matter
> threatens to drown their souls . . .

The audience seemed 'almost to cease to breathe, so perfect was the stillness'. Then he released them. Matter and spirit were only imaginary states, raised into ideological spectres. Materialism involved a 'grave philosophical error' because ultimate reality was undiscoverable. It was no more fathomable than the politics of moon-men. He was having his cake and eating it: using 'materialistic terminology' while abjuring 'materialistic philosophy'. The gasp gave way to a burst of applause, its intensity for the 'impressive earnestness of his tone' as much as anything. A listener familiar with the scientific greats, not only 'of this country, but also of France & Germany', announced 'that Mr Huxley surpassed them all'.[11]

The Xs lapped up 'the "lunar politics"'. Morley lapped up the lucre, as the *Fortnightly* presses kept rolling. New York's tabloid *The World* ran a screaming headline 'New Theory of Life'. Melbourne's printers pirated the *Fortnightly* as 'proteinaceous' fever struck the colony, and enterprising restaurateurs offered luncheons of the 'best cooked' 'Physical Basis of Life'. The religious appreciation was sparse, even if protoplasm 'makes the whole world kin', but refutations from three continents appeared 'more times than there are copies of his article'.

After that triumph Huxley planned to combine his essays into a book. 'The public may thank me', Nettie said, 'for I have long been urging Hal to collect & publish them'. It could only be called *Lay Sermons*, with its exultant vision of the new scientific cosmos. It too would break the bounds as an intellectual bestseller. 'People complain of the unequal distribution of wealth', Darwin declared, but it was a far greater 'injustice that any one man sh^d. have the power to write so many brilliant essays . . . There is no one who writes like you'.[12]

Everywhere his writings were having an effect. As a besieged Pope was about to declare himself infallible, *Man's Place* appeared in Italy. Mivart was travelling to Rome at the time. He had begun to 'execrate' Huxley's use of the *Origin* 'as a means of impeding Man's advance towards his "end" whatever may have been his "origin"'. What he witnessed reinforced his view. He was 'amazed and saddened', he told Darwin, 'to see our friend Huxley's "Man's place in nature" for sale at most of the railway stations amongst a crowd of *obscenities*'.[13] Clearly the pauper-press fascination extended all the way to Milan.

With Parliament finally looking at scientific education, Huxley stepped up his agitation. Whither a nation which sent its school-leavers into medicine and industry armed with a knowledge of Jewish history and Syrian geography? He wanted an all-embracing 'earth knowledge' taught, to keep Britain ahead of Germany.

Nothing of its kind was known, so the General interrupted a hectic schedule to develop a course, calling it 'Physiography' (a sort of physical geography). He launched it at the London Institution, before an enthusiastic audience of boys and masters, among them Jess, Leonard and Marian.[14] Hal had a magical touch with children; he took them on an imaginary journey down the Thames, explaining the waters, the breezes, the hills – indeed the planet – as an interconnected whole. No schoolboy could kick a stone again without knowing the prehistoric tale it had to tell.

Hal's own brood was growing. Darwin would drop into Abbey Place occasionally to 'demoralise' his favourite Harry.

> I often think of your little man & can fancy I see him now
> with the spoon sticking perpendicularly out of his mouth
> & his eyes as roguish eyes as those of an angel. As Mrs
> Huxley won't sell him she might loan him to us & I w^d
> return mine with his manner highly polished.

Harry's big brother Len was his mother's 'great darling'. At nine he was still under a private teacher. He needed 'hardening physically by contact with boys', but like his father he was 'a clever, cool, imperturbable lazily persevering fellow', and 'very affectionate'. The older girls showed the passing years. Jessie was 'a fine strong limbed healthy girl', and at 11 already tall, 'only half a head shorter' than her mother.

They softened up the cynic. The children 'ripen wonderfully and make life ten times better', Hal had to admit. The house was a hive; 18 year-old 'young Jim' was seconded to the family for three years. (His father's health was 'shattered'; Jim was pensioned off from his asylum and now struggling even to pay the Jermyn Street fees.) Young Jim paced down Baker Street to his chemistry classes with Uncle Hal every day, cool and confident like all the young Huxleys, 'a very charming fellow & steady punctual & hardworking'.

Uncle Hal was 'definitely getting older', when he had 'time to think about it'. He finished the 1860s as he had begun the 1850s, ploughing through 'more work than is good for him'. He cried out for 'two heads or a body that needed no rest'. But all he got were more marching orders. Even on holidays he had to dart away to one institute or another. Or he was pinned to his desk, breaking only for a 15-mile afternoon hike.[15] He was coming up for 45, his hair silvering, a little fatter-faced. The famous physiognomy was losing its fierceness even as it gained a higher profile.

In 1869 the king-maker ascended the presidential thrones himself. Not one, of course; being Huxley, he had to run a gamut of societies simultaneously.

The old generation was handing over the sceptre. Poignancy marked Huxley's Presidential Address to the Geological Society on 19 February 1869. Murchison was absent, mourning his wife. 'My battle of life is nearly fought out', he sobbed the day before. He had wanted to attend, 'the more so as the 19 Feby is my birthday when I complete my 77th year & when I anticipated to be able to testify to the apostles how exalted a Chief you make'. It was a touching gesture to the new 'Chief'. 'May you live long to advance science'.

The neuralgic Lyell, 72 himself, advised Huxley on protocol, acting as his Parliamentary Private Secretary. To his own inauguration Sir Charles had invited the Archbishop of Canterbury and Sir Robert Peel '& both of them came'. That was a world before, and Huxley seemed unlikely to add an Archbishop or Disraeli to his list. Still someone had to say grace and Lyell suggested one of Huxley's radical clerics.

The times showed in his choice. After Huxley charged his glass to the Queen, John Bright was put down to toast the 'Commons', Dean Stanley the 'Church' and Tyndall the 'Physical Sciences'.[16] There was no more unholy, uncomfortable, pleasant party.

Bright was a spellbinding orator, the only one who 'ever really held me', Huxley admitted. But that night he had come to hear Huxley. Like a good radical speech, his was the cry of the underdog tyrannized. In his address Huxley defended Darwin against the holier physicists of Scotland. Darwin had reckoned on hundreds or even thousands of millions of years for natural selection to work in. Sir William Thomson, one of the dazzling Victorian intellects, propounder of the laws of thermodynamics, the entrepreneur who oversaw the laying of the Atlantic cable, deplored this cavalier call on time. Thomson calculated from the earth's rate of cooling that only 100 million years had elapsed since crustal condensation. And that was 'preposterously inadequate' for Darwin's higgledy-piggledy build-up of chance variations, added Thomson's cable-laying partner Fleeming Jenkin.

Huxley revelled in his role of defence counsel. 'Biology takes her time from geology', he retorted. Whatever the earth's age, and the accumulated rock strata suggested that it was immense, Nature has worked her results in it. His air infuriated another Thomson colleague, Peter Tait. The 'dashing' Huxley was like his 'Trades-Unionists', with a 'handloom-weaver's' hatred of the machines brought in to help him. His 'crab-catching' science should welcome the data-crunching might of the physicist. And so saying, Tait dropped the earth's age to a trifling *'fifteen* millions'.[17] That, at least, made Darwin realize 'how devilish a clever fellow Huxley is', for goading the engineers into refuting themselves.

Only 18 days later Huxley delivered another sweeping address. As the new President of the Ethnological Society he turned his attention to the empire. For years he had been showered with rice-paper letters, telling of hairy Burmese, or bizarre uses of the feet, or enclosing photos of Victoria's far-flung tribes. Huxley's colonial network of correspondents grew yearly, and at Sir Gilbert Scott's new, ornamented Colonial Office, Lord Granville talked of his plan to photograph the natives of every dominion.[18]

He streamlined the Ethnological and restricted women to special events. The journalist Eliza Lynn, 'intoxicated' by Huxley's revivalist science and accepting his view of women's 'natural' limitations, found herself excluded and complained bitterly. But it brought the Ethnological into line with the other male bastions. Huxley's own hardliners were purged and, with Hunt's death in 1869, he was free to move against his rivals. The rats were already deserting the Anthropological ship as the cooked books came to light (and a £1,000 debt). Huxley had a mole in place: a friend, the coral expert (and former Mayor of Colchester) Martin Duncan. The urbane Duncan, a little out of place among this 'rough lot', tipped Huxley off about each closed-door session, down to its 'prehistoric Billingsgate', or foul-mouthing.[19] But the merger and the clean-up were on track.

As he ascended the Presidential thrones, Huxley traded in his other chairs. His heir-apparents had been groomed. That loyal prince Michael Foster took over the Royal Institution domain, while Flower was told to 'make thy shoulders ready for the [Hunterian] gown, and practise the goose-step in order to march properly behind the mace'.[20]

The Xs marched behind him. The club was back in formation, their strange freemasonry having survived a civil war.[21] By 1870 the key positions were in the Xs' grasp. (With Faraday lying in Highgate Cemetery – no hallowed ground in Westminster Abbey for this simple man who had made the modern age with his electro-magnets, although the Xs were trying to place a monument there[22] – Tyndall now stood in his shoes at the Royal Institution.) To these key posts they added a key journal, a successful one, finally, after all the abortive efforts. It had a magazine-format, *Reader* or *Saturday Review*-style, but was dedicated to science. It was sustained by adverts for books, binoculars and toothpaste. Lockyer was the liberal editor, Macmillan the liberal publisher; the price was pegged at 4*d*, and the title fixed. 'What a glorious title, *Nature*', a mathematician rejoiced. 'It is more than Cosmos, more than Universe', it took us to the heart of 'mind and matter'. This was Huxley's long-time dream. Experience kept the weekly popular to start. To that end he opened the first number on 4 November 1869 with Goethe's aphorisms:

> Nature! We are surrounded and embraced by her:
> powerless to separate ourselves from her, and powerless
> to penetrate beyond her.
>   Without asking, or warning, she snatches us up into her
> circling dance, and whirls us on until we are tired, and
> drop from her arms.

The opener was purple and pantheistic and seemed to Darwin 'as if written by the maddest English scholar'. Huxley was still out to confound. It was a Nature that gloried in protoplasm and dinosaurs; a Nature that transcended the specialisms of science. This *Nature* was to be a broad cultural forum. It was a winning format; and it won despite piracy in America and competition from an Oxford-based monthly, the aloof *Academy*, with its call for German-style research (its first number carried Huxley's review of Haeckel). 'Darling Hal is as busy as usual', Nettie grumbled, 'I may say rather more so [because] two new Periodicals are just starting "Nature" & "The Academy" in each of which he has an article'.[23] But it was *Nature* that spoke for the London new wave.

Still this group had no label. Huxley dodged 'Atheist', 'Materialist', even 'Nihilist' for his know-nothing response to reality. But the label that proved hardest to peel off was 'Positivist'.

   Positivists recognized the sensory limits of knowledge, and they were a devouring force in 1869. Morley was with them, and Lewes. Mrs Llewelyn Davies' brother was one, as was her brother-in-law, the history professor at University College, Edward Beesly. Theirs was a ritualized secularism. They were turning Comte's philosophy into a Religion of Humanity. It was a surrogate theology which recognized no God, but gratified a religious need: a kind of Roman Church with mankind as its object of adoration. (The positivist pontiffs Richard Congreve and Frederic Harrison had been educated among Oxford's Anglo-Catholics, which made them doubly suspect.) Huxley, dining with Beesly and Harrison at George Eliot's house, was dismayed at their talk of restricting research to social ends. Who could predict the fruits of science? Once 'practical men' had laughed at philosophers for asking 'why a frog's leg twitches . . . and yet therein lay the bud of the electric telegraph'.

He saw his liberated science under the thumb of a new set of social jesuits. Mankind's emotional needs were not to be satisfied by empty ritual, but by the real awe of Nature's deep mystery. He had no time for Comte's 'superstitious infidelity'. 'Catholicism *minus* Christianity', he called it, which promptly became the *bon mot* of the age. A squealing Beesly lamented Huxley's 'hard & damaging blow . . . From almost everyone else this would not matter. But from a man of your eminence and known emancipation it amounts to something like putting Comte on the Index Expurgatorius'. Comtists had seen themselves facing the same orthodoxy, 'blunting the enemy's steel', ready for Huxley's lunge. Beesly had never expected Huxley's long knife in his back.

But with archbishops already associating secular knowledge with positivism, Huxley had to distance himself. The ersatz Church was putting the ritual into unbelief, luring converts from Huxley's ascetic scepticism. The 'very air' seemed 'full of Comtism' to Kingsley.[24] Huxley was trying to make it seem like a bad smell.

Huxley's scientific civil service needed its own brocade banner. 'Atheist' was out, there being no disproof of God; and anyway, it was a red republican flag, a political weapon to smash the spiritual basis of privilege. On Mondays he had his share of agitators demanding the unfrocking of priests. He could not be seen to countenance the destruction of the entire Anglican cultural fabric.

The lack of a label became embarrassing when Huxley exhibited himself at that theological zoo, the Metaphysical Society. James Knowles, architect-about-town, and the Poet Laureate Tennyson, whose hideaway cottage he was designing, were gathering living specimens of every sect, the most distinguished dialecticians of their age. Nowhere but in liberal London could Anglicans and Catholics, positivists and pantheists, Unitarians and unbelievers sit down in a grand gesture to debate God's existence. Lubbock approached Huxley in April 1869.

There is to [be] a preliminary dinner on Wednesday (21st.) next at Willis' Rooms at 7 Oclock

There will be about a dozen there, including [the Catholic] ArchB. Manning, Dean Stanley, Tennyson, [Harriet's Unitarian brother James] Martineau, [the Anglo-Catholic W. G.] Ward of the Dublin Review, [Walter] Bagehot of the Economist & [the religious critic R. H.] Hutton of the Spectator.

I have been asked to invite you, will you drop me a line to say if you can & will come.[25]

Nothing could keep him away. By the time the Metaphysical met in Willis' (a venue for literary lectures), Huxley had rejected everybody else's clothes and felt naked. All about him 'were -*ists* of one sort or another; and . . . I, the man without a rag of a label to cover himself with'.

What could he call himself? He was shifting power to an élite whose authority rested in right reasoning, not mythical realities. He had already dropped the 'Unknowable' as the last remnant of idolatry. (It had begun to acquire its own mystique. And when the *Spectator* apologized for rendering it 'Unknowable God', the term obviously had to go.) Yet in Willis' Rooms a cacophony of voices proclaimed that they 'had attained a certain "gnosis"', like the second-century gnostics who professed sparks of divine knowledge. That night he came up with '*Agnostic*'.

It was another pitch for his professionals. It switched the emphasis to the scientific method and its sensual limitations. Agnosticism was made for the moment. Even in his own camp it was necessary. The Cromwellian head of Darwin's New Model Army found his Ranters and Levellers pulling apart: some voted for Haeckel's monistic materialism; others watched Wallace turn to séances and spiritualism. (Wallace was the latest disillusioned socialist to appeal to the spirits to put society back on its millennial course.) Agnosticism enabled the Protector to stand aloof as he surveyed his forces on a neutral parade ground.

He could also lecture the clergy with clean hands. He portrayed agnosticism not as a rival 'creed', but as a method of inquiry. The sciences, he told the Young Men's Christian Association, 'are neither Christian, nor Unchristian, but are Extra-christian', in a word, 'unsectarian'.

That, too, filled a need. Since his slum days he had blamed a divisive sectarianism for the world's ills. His was a sect to end all sects: an attempt to clamber on to a higher moral plane, to escape the priests and paupers, Comtists and Christians. Agnosticism was a many-coloured philosophical cloak, allowing him to mask his deep doubt and indulge in moral brinkmanship. The word would push alienated intellectuals off the defensive for the first time since the French Revolution.

The sceptic's air of 'moral infallibility' flummoxed the opposition. The irony of an Infallible Head of the Church Agnostic was not lost on the *Spectator*, which dubbed him 'Pope Huxley'.[26]

As the social axis shifted in late Victorian times, agnosticism was to become the new faith of the West.

Huxley now faced archbishops as an equal across the Metaphysical table. But Catholic qualms about debating with the Devil were as nothing to those of the British Association for the Advancement of Science about choosing an agnostic pope as President.

The 'General Council' met in a fraught session on 23 August 1869. The outgoing President, Disraeli's confidant and North Devon's Tory MP, Sir Stafford Northcote, had invited Huxley to stay at his country seat during the 1869 Exeter meet. But even he hoped to thwart Huxley's succession. He tried to engineer a palace coup, offering the chair to another Tory grandee Lord Stanley, whose constituency was near Liverpool's 1870 convention site. When word leaked out the press damned this 'ignoble piece of Philistine hypocrisy'. But His Lordship refused the ignominy of being trounced by Huxley on a vote. Twenty years earlier surgeon Huxley had grudgingly nodded to another Lord Stanley. Now the nobleman grudgingly nodded to him. Rank moved aside for 'the mouthpiece of English science'. Northcote was forced to announce Huxley's presidency, even if, the *Times* noted, he 'seemed to feel some little doubt of the perfect wisdom of the choice'.

Hal was at home when the news came. Stanley 'repudiated their having any P. but a Scientific man', Hooker crowed, and 'Lubbock seconded [your nomination] with spirit'. Like everything else, Hal's presidency was born in controversy.

The *Times* feared that Huxley would act the wild partisan and shatter the BAAS's history of deference and consensus. He would 'be in as difficult a position as Mr. Bright in the Ministry'. However 'discreet' Huxley 'may be in the absence of opposition', it concluded, 'his best friends tremble for him'. 'The Times & Co regard you as a wild bull', Tyndall laughed; 'the Times & Co are I fear somewhat asinine'.[27]

The presidency was the acme of Huxley's young career. It crowned a decade which had seen more intellectual turbulence than any since the Regency. Darwin's statesman was to take the dispatch box in the 'Parliament of Science'. Twenty years earlier Huxley had marvelled at the 'big wigs' running the show, now he was a 'big wig' himself. At last he could write his own 'Queen's Speech', and he promised to 'show how pretty-behaved I can be'.

The papers poked fun at the *Times*. So, 'Mr. Huxley is very "indiscreet"', laughed the *Spectator*. And, 'even worse', is inclined 'to talk English'. What! would Northcote smother 'the one grand controversy now raging among cultivated men' over 'whether the Supernatural exists at all' and 'go on telling decorous little lies'?

'If only we had an "indiscreet" Archbishop! – but that being impossible, let us be thankful that we shall next year have an indiscreet President of the British Association'.[28]

Poor boys rarely became president, but then devil's disciples were not often elected pope. It was a testimony to Huxley's biblical dexterity and agnostic astuteness that he could juggle so many soubriquets and still not be pinned down. The Holy Father revelled in his title as the thinking nation genuflected. The Church's prestige was passing to his evangelical professionals, and the pay and power would sustain the first generation of career 'scientists', trained, standardized and accredited. Henceforth men of letters would assess him with a proviso: he 'is really a most agreeable man', said Leslie Stephen, 'considering that he is a scientific swell'.

Huxley remained an 'angry, humorous, unbalanced' soul. And he still toiled like three men, even without three professorships. It seemed he had to, and that only the centrifugal force of his Geological, Ethnological and workers' rounds kept him from caving in. His financial and mental health was underpinned by perpetual motion. Not so for brother Jim, retired, crumpling, although no one yet called him mad. Adversity was Hal's drug; he thrived on it – he had never hit the bottle like Ellen, or fled like Lizzie. It catapulted him out of the sty, and the passing images of a bloated Cooke and exiled Scott had only shot him faster. Old friends had dropped away. MacGillivray was gone: two years dead, 'alone and destitute' in a Sydney hostel, a drunken hobo, 'father and mother unknown' it read on the death certificate.[29] Fate had strange ways, turning one into a tramp and the other a president.

The real wonder was that Huxley came out secure. Marriage

had been his 'heroic remedy'. It was his addictive defence against the world, and it beat 'opium eating'. Abbey Place gave him the energy for his tub-thumping forays. The enchanted castle had turned into a rather stodgy family fortress, and the maiden Nettie into a rather harassed mother with haemorrhoids. But inside its walls he was a different man. The contentment showed as he sat on the sofa and teased his 'special pet' Ethel. If 'you [could] see him with his seven children . . . playing with them as heartily as if he were a child himself', Nettie told Lizzie.[30]

'You cannot think how stout he is getting', Nettie added. The changes in the mirror matched the self-important shape of his city. He marched across a new London. The festering river of his dockside days now ran through the smart imperial capital, bounded by an elegant Thames Embankment. The shapeless city of that soulless era had a new focus in Whitehall and the growing temple of intellect in the west, South Kensington. While the new palazzo complex off Downing Street, the Colonial and Foreign Office, was a reminder of Britain's growing empire.

It had been an imperial progress to match Hal's own. He had seen it at the sharp end. He had shown his 'jacket blue & the beautiful cockade' in steamy ports. Crates of bones and rocks now marked the path of his graduates as they surveyed their way across continents. This wealth of fossils had enabled Huxley and Owen, those competing Hammurabis codifying the laws of life, to reveal the origin of birds and mammals – even if neither accepted the other's conclusions. But Owen now stood aside like an embarrassing old Prime Minister. Huxley was the focus of attention in 1870. 'In his great genius, of which his . . . good-humour is the most conspicuous feature', even the *Spectator* could feel 'a cordial pride'.[31]

The publication of *Lay Sermons* took him into the world of *belles-lettres*. He was a breathtaking essayist, whose seemingly simple prose silhouetted the immensity of his subject. With his 'common-sense cleverness', he could concoct a world on the back of a *Globigerina*. People saw him not merely as the apologist of the evolutionary vision, but as the visionary. By 1870 science *was* Professor Huxley. He made the pace of evolution as exciting as a Waterloo express. He was naturalizing morals and vitalizing molecules, imputing justice to Nature to enable his X-men to bask in its glory. The riddles of existence that had racked the pauper presses in his student days now tantalized his respectable audiences.

This man from nowhere had made science fashionable and himself indispensable. Even Oxbridge masters consulted him about new posts. On his agnostic, neutral ground he could shake hands with university modernizers and church reformers, literary radicals and dissident artists. These were the emerging intellectuals captivated by his discoveries of primitive man, and discovering 'how much of man, not least his religion ... was still primitive'. They were the vanguard, seeking to fuse the best of Christian ethics with the beauty of modern science.[32]

Britain's new intellectuals would become aloof. But not Huxley. The 'plebeian' never really escaped grub street (not, at least, while Ellen was drinking away '220 p^r an.' of his hard-earned cash, or while seven children and sundry nieces remained a consuming fire). He was never to know the opulence of 'literary leisure'. 'But', Nettie sighed, 'we must submit'.[33] For all of that, his witty uncouthness served him well. It let him move from mechanics' meetings to Lewes' lunches, and still enjoy tea with Matthew Arnold at Harrow.

He continued to slide between worlds. His Liverpool Presidency in 1870 had its salubrious side, and a certain lording was necessary as he attended banquets and toured the city in the Mayor's stately coach. But he slipped away with Lubbock to look at the Liverpool no one wanted him to see. Into 'thieves' dens, doss houses, [and] dancing saloons' they dived, to be accosted by a bloody-nosed drunk in one. Thirty year-old ghosts haunted him as he moved among the 'unwashed, unkempt, brutal people' of this Atlantic trade port. He was back in docklands again.

Why did they not riot and loot the shops 'before the police could stop and hang a few of them'? It seemed an obvious question in the month that Paris fell to the revolutionaries. But his detective escort was lackadaisical: 'Lord bless you, sir, drink and disease leave nothing in them'. Epidemics silenced the starving in their insanitary slums. The angry apprentice rose up in Hal. It reanimated his ideal of a reformed Nature in an educated Britain knitting the nation together. The professor returned, shaking, to upbraid the toffs who gathered for a glimpse of him. You talk

of political questions as if they were questions of Whig and Tory, of Conservative and heaven knows what [the *Liverpool Mercury* reported him saying]; but beneath there was the greater question whether that prodigious misery which dogs the footsteps of modern civilisation should be allowed to exist . . . He believed that was the great political question of the future.

Huxley on the presidential platform was sedate. No panegyric on Darwin, no pounding of the clergy. On a serious subject he could be serious. The Franco-Prussian War was raging, but its toll paled besides the tens of thousands killed yearly by scarlet fever in the 'bloodiest of all wars'. Perhaps he was thinking of his own curly-headed Noel, who still brought a tear after ten years. He talked humbly of yeast from spores, multiplying in fermentation vats, and of the possibility of spore-like germs explaining these explosive epidemics. Science, he promised, would end this 'massacre of our innocents'.[34]

Philosophy could bake no bread. And it was the sober reflection of 30 years that it could not prove God or immortality either. But the revelations of science were assuming the lineaments of the Divine. And as the philosopher fingered the bread, and looked at its active yeast, he could promise freedom: freedom from disease and misery. 'Pope Huxley' was still offering salvation.

Abbreviations

CORRESPONDENTS

CD	Charles Darwin
CK	Charles Kingsley
CL	Charles Lyell
ES	Eliza Salt, later Scott (sister)
FD	Frederick Dyster
GR	George Rolleston
HAH	Henrietta Anne Heathorn
HS	Herbert Spencer
JH	Joseph Dalton Hooker
JT	John Tyndall
MF	Michael Foster
RIM	Roderick Impey Murchison
WBC	William Benjamin Carpenter

MANUSCRIPT SOURCES

AD	Huxley family letters being transcribed by Angela Darwin
APS	American Philosophical Society
BL	British Library
BM (NH)	British Museum (Natural History)
CCH	Charing Cross Hospital Medical School, Minutes of School Committee of Management
CUL	Cambridge University Library

Abbreviations

GSM British Geological Survey, records of the Government School of Mines

HH T. H. Huxley–Henrietta Heathorn Correspondence, Imperial College, Huxley Archives (catalogued in Pingree, *T. H. Huxley: Correspondence with Henrietta Heathorn*)

HM T. H. Huxley Manuscripts, Imperial College, Huxley Archives (catalogued in Pingree, *T. H. Huxley: List of his Scientific Notebooks*) HM series : volume : folio

HP T. H. Huxley Papers, Imperial College, Huxley Archives (catalogued in Dawson, *Huxley Papers*)

LS Linnean Society of London

OUM Oxford University Museum

RCS Royal College of Surgeons of England

ZSL Zoological Society of London

PRINTED SOURCES

CCD F. Burkhardt and S. Smith, eds, *The Correspondence of Charles Darwin* 8 vols (Cambridge, Cambridge University Press, 1985–1993).

CE T. H., Huxley, *Collected Essays* 9 vols (Macmillan, 1893).

Diary J. Huxley, ed., *T. H. Huxley's Diary of the Voyage of H.M.S. Rattlesnake* (Chatto and Windus, 1935).

LCK F. Kingsley, ed., *Charles Kingsley: His Letters and Memories of his Life* 2 vols (Kegan Paul, 1881).

LHS D. Duncan, ed., *The Life and Letters of Herbert Spencer* (Methuen, 1908).

LJH L. Huxley, ed., *Life and Letters of Joseph Dalton Hooker* 2 vols (Murray, 1918).

LJT A. S. Eve and C. H. Creasey, eds, *Life and Work of John Tyndall* (Macmillan, 1945).

LLD F. Darwin, ed., *Life and Letters of Charles Darwin* 3 vols (Murray, 1887).

LLL K. Lyell, ed., *Life, Letters and Journals of Sir Charles Lyell* 2 vols (Murray, 1881).

LRO R. S. Owen, ed., *The Life of Richard Owen* 2 vols (Murray, 1894).

LTH L. Huxley, ed., *Life and Letters of Thomas Henry Huxley* 2 vols (Macmillan, 1900).

MLD F. Darwin and A. C. Seward, eds, *More Letters of Charles Darwin* 2 vols (Murray, 1903).

Narrative J. MacGillivray, *Narrative of the Voyage of H.M.S. Rattlesnake, Commanded by the late Captain Owen Stanley, R.N., F.R.S., &c.*

during the years 1846–1850 including discoveries and surveys in New Guinea, the Louisiade Archipelago, Etc 2 vols (T. & W. Boone, 1852).

SM   M. Foster and E. R. Lankester, eds, *The Scientific Memoirs of Thomas Henry Huxley* 5 vols (Macmillan, 1898–1902).

Notes

SMITING THE AMALEKITES?

1. H. F. Jones, *Butler*, 1:385; *CCD*, 8:316.
2. Owen, 'Affinities', 4–8.
3. TH to JH, 19 Dec. 1860, HP 2.79; Hutton, 'Pope Huxley', 135–6; Haight, *Eliot Letters*, 8:89–90.
4. Fiske, *Personal Letters*, 121–2.
5. For a justification of the 'ciné theory' of narration, see Moore, 'Metabiographical Reflections'.
6. Webb, *My Apprenticeship*, 25.
7. *CE*, 2:52.
8. Jim Moore's *Post-Darwinian Controversies* in 1979 was the acme of this harmonious history, born, as he admits, out of the Anti-Vietnam War movement. But Moore has moved progressively to a gutsier political analysis of the Victorian 'crisis of faith', culminating in his superb paper on 'Theodicy and Society' in 1990.
9. Shortland, 'Book Reviews', 113.
10. Gilley and Loades, 'Huxley', and Barton, 'Evolution', provide the best studies of his politico-theological context, and Paradis, *Huxley*, the intellectual milieu. Bibby, *Huxley*, has studied his educational endeavours; Jensen, *Huxley*, his rhetoric; and di Gregorio, *Huxley*, his science.
11. Roos, 'Neglected', has made a start.
12. TH to HAH, 7 Sept. 1851, HH 164.
13. HAH's Reminiscences, HP 62.1.
14. Desmond, 'Darwin, Huxley'.
15. *Daily Chronicle*, 1 July 1895; *Times*, 1 July 1895.

1 PHILOSOPHY CAN BAKE NO BREAD

1. Huxley, 'Thoughts & Doings', HM 3:123, f.10. This notebook has been transcribed with an excellent commentary by Roos, 'Neglected', 416. *LTH*, 1:15–16; sensitive: TH to HAH, [?27 Mar. 1850], HH 79–80.
2. *CE*, 1:2–5; 'tone': TH to HAH, 7 Sept. 1851, HH 163; 'passion', 'active':

4–7 May 1851, HH 147; *LTH*, 1:1–4; 'Cockney': ES to HAH, 16 Mar. 1883, AD; Bibby, *Huxley*, 1–4; Ker and Gornall, *Letters*, 5:267; Murphy, 'Ethical Revolt', 802.

3. TH to HAH, 18 Aug. 1851, HH 162; 'sage': 31 July 1851, HH 160; 'can't': 14 Mar. 1851, HH 140; 'one': 23 Nov. 1848, HH 40; 24 Dec. 1850, HH 134; 16 Oct. 1851, HH 169; Paradis, *Huxley*, 19.

4. TH to ES, 27 Mar. 1858, HP 31.27; 'of the': TH to ES, 8 June 1876, HP 31.44; Bibby, *Huxley*, 4–5; *LTH*, 1:35; Davidoff and Hall, *Family Fortunes*, 281; Angela Darwin, pers. comm.

5. *CE*, 1:5–6; on Poideoin: TH to George Huxley, 24 Apr. 1848, HP 31.47; curriculum: Ker and Gornall, *Letters*, 1:4, 6–9, 31; *LTH*, 1:5, 8–10; 2:145.

6. Ker and Gornall, *Letters*, 5:267.

7. Prest, *Industrial Revolution*, 73 passim; Davis, *Every Man*, 3–4; *Diary*, 333; Gaskell, *Mary Barton*, 5; Eliot, *Middlemarch*, 122; 'large': ES to HAH, 16 Mar. 1883, AD.

8. TH to HAH, 23 Nov. 1848, HH 40–1; *LTH*, 1:6, 35; 2:145; opium: Gaskell, *Mary Barton*, 22, 53; Paradis, *Huxley*, 19–20.

9. K. Jaggard to TH, 11 May 1852, HP 19.13: *LTH*, 1:8–9; Bibby, *Huxley*, 6–7; Huxley, 'Tyndall', 3; 'pursuits': TH to HAH, 23 Nov. 1848, HH 40; Turner, 'Victorian Scientific Naturalism', 330, 340–1; Carlyle, *Heroes*; Prest, *Industrial Revolution*, 1, 71.

10. Huxley, 'Thoughts & Doings', HM 3:123, ff.6–7; *LTH*, 1:6; Gallenga, 'Age', 4; Thackray, 'Natural Knowledge', 678–87; *LTH*, 1:35; Haight, *Eliot*, 19–24, 36–9; 'was': TH to HAH, 23 Nov. 1848, HH 40.

11. Huxley, 'Thoughts & Doings', HM 3:123, f.2; Prest, *Industrial Revolution*, 20, 48–9; Rolt, *Victorian Engineering*, 68; *LTH*, 1:7; *CE*, 1:6–7.

12. Huxley, 'Thoughts & Doings', HM 3:123, f.2; *LTH*, 1:36; Tugwood, *Coventry Hospital*, 1–12; Prest, *Industrial Revolution*, 28–9.

13. Robertson, 'Elliotson', 205, 257; Elliotson, *Lectures*; sacking: *Lancet*, 1 (1838–9), 561–2, 590–7; on Cooke: Allen, 'Huxley's Brother-in-Law'; *London Medical Directory. 1845*, 36; *LTH*, 1:15.

14. K. Jaggard to TH, 11 May 1852, HP 19.13: *LTH*, 1:8; *CE*, 1:7–8; Richardson, *Death*, 30ff; cf. Audubon's reaction, *Audubon*, 1:146; farms and other times: Gaskell, *Mary Barton*, 3; F. Smith, 'Darwin's Ill Health', 455.

15. Huxley, 'Thoughts & Doings', HM 3:123, f.4–5; T. S. Smith, *Divine*, viii; 'commit': Epps, *Church*, 3; Halevy, *Triumph*, 150; Cowherd, *Politics*, 155.

16. 'Seat of the Soul', *Medico-Chirurgical Review*, 12 (1830), 461; Desmond, *Politics*, chap. 4; Huxley, 'Thoughts & Doings', HM 3:123, ff.7–8, 10.

17. *CE*, 9:217; Poynter, 'Smith', 389; Briggs, *Victorian Cities*, 311–15; Engels, *Condition*, 73–4; Norton, *Victorian London*, 17–18, 35–6; Raumer, *England*, 2:111.

18. I assume it was Cooke's doing. Both Cooke and Chandler had worked with John Elliotson, Cooke as co-editor of Elliotson's *Lectures* in 1839, and Chandler, House Surgeon at University College Hospital in 1834–5, as a mesmerist: Chandler, 'Cases of Mesmerism', 189; *London Medical Directory. 1845*, 31.

19. Chandler, 'Rheumatism', 81–3. He used mesmerism to cure epilepsy, tics, fits and insanity: *Zoist*, 1 (1843), 174; 2 (1844), 373; 3 (1845), 189, 486.

20. Mayhew, *London Labour*, 104; Winter, 'Island', 19–24; Parssinen, 'Professional Deviants', 113–14.

21. TH to Rachel Huxley, 23 Apr. 1841, AD.
22. Mayhew, *London Labour*, 48, 51, 174; *LTH*, 1:15–16; Tristan, *London Journal*, 7.
23. Chesney, *Victorian Underworld*, 105, 378; 'in that': Huxley, 'Thoughts & Doings', HM 3:123, f.9; Roos, 'Neglected', 416; *LTH*, 1:15; Carlyle, *Essays*, 6:110.
24. T. S. Smith, *Divine*, 104; 'I see': Huxley, 'Thoughts & Doings', HM 3:123, f.10; 'deep': TH to HAH, 28 Aug. 1852, HH 222; 'I confess': TH to CK, 23 Sept. 1860, HP 19.176; *LTH*, 1:220; Chesney, *Victorian Underworld*, 105, 378. By 15 Huxley had only a residue of Calvinistic 'moderate' evangelicalism left in him (in Hilton's sense, *Age*, 8–11) but growing rationalist and romantic streaks.
25. Huxley, 'Thoughts & Doings', HM 3:123, ff.9–13, 30; Weiner, *War*, 171; Vincent, *Bread*, 114ff; Desmond, *Politics*, 120; Sheets-Pyenson, 'Popular Scientific Periodicals', 550; 'I got': TH to Rachel Huxley, 23 Apr. 1841: AD.
26. *Diary*, 94, 97; *LTH*, 1:17, 19, 36; James Huxley to John Salt, Aug. 1842, HP 31.55–7.
27. Cooke was here by 15 December 1840, when two fellow teachers at Sydenham College, Sigmond and Heming, put him up for the Linnean Society: Certificate of Fellowship, LS. Sydenham College was in Grafton Street, off Gower Street. Cope, 'Private Medical Schools', 106. Cooke taught anatomy and physiology here in 1840–1: 'Sydenham College', *Lancet*, 1 (1840–1), 14. 'loudly': Thackeray, *Pendennis*, 330.
28. 'Sydenham College', *Lancet*, 1 (1841–2), 15, 61. It enrolled about 175 pupils: *Lancet*, 2 (1838–9), 176; 'dingy', *Lancet*, 1 (1842–3), 29.
29. 'Metaphysics', *Punch*, 2 (1842), 149; Dickens, *Pickwick*, 493.
30. McMenemey, 'Education', 145; Desmond, *Politics*, chap. 4.
31. 'Poverty and Religious Bigotry of the College of Physicians', *Lancet*, 1 (1840–1), 556–8; 'Sydenham College – Experiments on the Nervous System in the Turtle', *Lancet*, 1 (1837–8), 166–7; Manual, 'Hall', 139–51; Desmond, *Politics*, 124–34; Hall, *Memoirs*, 4, 60, 87–8, chaps 4–5, 145, 150, 157–9.
32. TH to HAH, [?27 Mar. 1850], HH 79–80; 'isolated': 16 Oct. 1851, HH 169; *Lancet*, 1 (1842–3), 29, 100–2; *Medico-Chirurgical Review*, 17 (1832), 574.
33. Huxley, 'Thoughts & Doings', HM 3:123, ff.14–16.

2 SON OF THE SCALPEL

1. TH to HAH, [?27 Mar. 1850], HH 79–80.
2. *Diary*, 94; *LTH*, 1:17; prize-giving was usually in April, e.g. 'Sydenham College', *Lancet*, 2 (1838–9), 176.
3. 'Sydenham College', *Lancet*, 1 (1841–2), 15; *LTH*, 1:17, 19 n. Cooke joined the Council of the Botanical Society in 1844. He taught materia medica at University College Hospital and elsewhere: *London Medical Directory. 1845*, 36; Allen, 'Huxley's Brother-in-Law', 191–3; David Allen pers. comm. Cooke–Hoblyn partnership: Rachel Huxley to TH, 15 Mar. 1847, 13 Sept. 1848, AD.
4. *Diary*, 95; Harte and North, *World of UCL*, 37; Goodway, *London Chartism*, 49–51. Omnibuses: Mayhew, *London Labour*, 347.
5. *Diary*, 95; Jackson, *Scharf's London*, 96–101. On the Apothecaries:

Holloway, 'Medical Education', 307–17; Waddington, *Medical Profession*, chap. 3. Carlyle: Huxley, 'Thoughts & Doings', HM 3:123, ff.17–18.

6. Huxley, 'Thoughts & Doings', HM 3:123, f.22; *LTH*, 1:19n; *Diary*, 95.
7. *Diary*, 95–6; *LTH*, 1:34.
8. Huxley's Sydenham College teacher, George Sigmond, had been physician at Charing Cross Hospital (before being sacked for financial irregularities): Sigmond was Cooke's friend and proposer for the Linnean Society, 15 Dec. 1840, LS Archives; Minney, *Two Pillars*, 66–7. Golding, *Origin*, 64–5 on the scholarships. *Lancet*, 1 (1842–3), 24, on the fees.
9. Charing Cross Hospital Regulations for Applications for Free Scholarship, 1842, HP 31.97; Golding, *Origin*, 64. 'The Pharmaceutical Society', *London Medical Gazette*, 28 (1840–1), 726–30, on the druggists; Desmond, *Politics*, 154, 196, on the move to drive out the working classes.
10. Jenkins, *General Strike*, 95–104, 165–71, 270–2; *Illustrated London News*, 20 Aug. 1842; Goodway, *London Chartism*, 51, 106–11.
11. James Huxley to John Salt, 11, 22 Aug. 1842, HP 31.55, 57; *Times*, 17, 18 Aug. 1842; Holyoake, *History*; Moore, *Religion*, 340–50; Desmond, 'Artisan Resistance', 85ff.
12. CCH, Vol. 1, f.330; *LTH*, 1:19–20; *Diary*, 97; TH to W. Burnett, 31 Jan. 1846, HP 11.194.
13. On the hospital: Golding, *Origin*, 41; Minney, *Two Pillars*, 46–77.
14. Minney, *Two Pillars*, 51–3, 56–7; Hart, *Roots*, 18; Golding, *Origin*, 60; Hunter, *Historical Account*, 194.
15. Minney, *Two Pillars*, 24–6; Jackson, *Scharf's London*, 74–5; Hilton, *Age*, 206–7, 270; Stigginses: *Diary*, 224; Dickens, *Pickwick*, 449, 452, 729.
16. Hart, *Roots*, 14; Jackson, *Scharf's London*, 28–9, 58; Minney, *Two Pillars*, 23–4.
17. *Lancet*, 1 (1842–3), 28. Debts to Cooke and George: HP 31.5–6.
18. Casualties: Golding, *Origin*, 75, 175; *Lancet*, 2 (1846), 138. Dickens, *Sketches by Boz*, 286–7; Minney, *Two Pillars*, 61; Jackson, *Scharf's London*, 72; 'miserable': 'Advice to Students', *Lancet*, 1 (1837–8), 20.
19. Minney, *Two Pillars*, 30, 53, 91; Hart, *Roots*, 9, 17–22, 25–6.
20. Richardson, *Death*, 265. The Strand's workhouses supplied more corpses for dissection than almost any other London parish: Durey, 'Bodysnatchers', 218.
21. This was a common reaction: Audubon, *Audubon*, 1:146. In 1843 the School's President W. D. Chowne warned of the unpleasantness of dissection: *Lancet*, 1 (1843–4), 17.
22. 'Advice to Students', *Lancet*, 1 (1837–8), 18–22; also 2 (1844), 20.
23. *Diary*, 97.
24. Huxley, 'Thoughts & Doings', f.51, HM 3:123; Jessie Rachel Salt, Death Certificate, 17 Nov. 1842: General Register Office, London.
25. Huxley in 'Thomas Wharton Jones', *British Medical Journal*, 2 (1891), 1176; Godlee, 'Wharton Jones', 97–105; Lonsdale, *Life*, 97. Lecture times: *Lancet*, 1 (1842–3), 24. Mob poetry: 'Dr. Knox', *Medical Times*, 10 (1844), 245–6.
26. Huxley in 'Thomas Wharton Jones', *British Medical Journal*, 2 (1891), 1176; CE, 1:9; Godlee, 'Wharton Jones', 99. On Wharton Jones' appointment in May 1841: CCH, Vol. 1, f.306. Huxley's student notebook, c. 1845, HM 3:124 (misdated '1847' in Pingree, *Huxley. Scientific Notebooks*, 62),

shows him studying shark's teeth (ff.22–3, using Richard Owen's *Odontogra-phy* as a guide), feather ontogeny (ff.24–7, after Theodor Schwann and Frédéric Cuvier), and the perch (ff.46–79, following Georges Cuvier and Achille Valenciennes).

27. Jones, 'Development', 261; Huxley's student notebook, c. 1845, HM 3:124, ff.11–15 for Henle, Rudolph Wagner, etc. on blood corpuscles; ff.34–6 for Theodor Bischoff on the ovum; f.83 for Albert Kölliker on nucleoli. These German anatomists based their work on Schwann's cell theory and accepted a mechanistic explanation of cell growth. On the increasingly mechanistic outlook in Germany during the 1840s see Lenoir, *Strategy*, chaps 3 and 4; and Jacyna, 'Romantic Programme', for the cell theory's reception in Britain.

28. McMenemey, 'Education', 138–9, 145; Chesney, *Victorian Underworld*, 7, 398; Minney, *Two Pillars*, 59, 89–90; *LTH*, 1:21.

29. TH to HAH, 2 Dec. 1850, HH 132; *Lancet*, 2 (1844), 19; 'Charing-Cross Hospital School', *Lancet*, 1 (1842–3), 24 on his classes.

30. TH to HAH, 8 Feb. 1848, HH 7; *CE*, 1:8–9.

31. Fownes' former teacher, Justus von Liebig, was now breaking protein into amino acids. Huxley was reading Liebig's journal, *Annalen der Chemie und Pharmacie*, while breaking up albumen himself: Huxley's student notebook, c. 1845, HM 3:124, ff.3–9. President: *Lancet*, 1 (1843–4), 18. Fownes was at the school from 1840–3: CCH, Vol. 1, ff.284, 347. On his 9 am. lectures: *Lancet*, 1 (1842–3), 24.

32. Huxley's student notebook, c. 1845, HM 3:124, f.1. Huxley quoted more from Henle's *Allgemeine Anatomie* (*General Anatomy*) (1841); but the tenor of Henle's piece, as Nordenskiöld, *History*, 398, shows, was mildly anti-vitalist. Rowe, 'Life', 423–4, 432; Godlee, 'Wharton Jones', 102; Lonsdale, *Life*, 402; Knox, 'Contributions', 501, 529. For the radical satires on 'design': Desmond, *Politics*, 56, 73, 110–17, 181–2. Fownes took the first Acton Prize in 1844; Wharton Jones the second in 1851.

33. Huxley, 'Thoughts & Doings', HM 3:123, f.18.

34. *LTH*, 1:23; CCH, Vol. 1, ff. 331–2, 336–7, 341; Hunter, *Historical Account*, 195. The exams were held on Monday 17 Apr. 1843.

35. Knight, *London*, 3:200–3; Carus, *King*, 60; Desmond, *Politics*, 251–3; Richard Owen's testimony: *Report from the Select Committee on British Museum* (Parliamentary Papers, 14 July 1836), 10: 44–6; *LTH*, 1:15–16; Richardson, *Death*, 57–8 on O'Brien.

36. *CE*, 1:7; Jones, 'Muscle', 77 (this was his introductory lecture on 3 Oct. 1843); Huxley's student notebook, c.1845, HM 3:124, ff.37–43.

37. Huxley, 'Thoughts & Doings', HM 3:123, f.4; '*Law*': Carpenter, *Animal Physiology*, 2:viii; Grainger, *Observations*, 47–8; Fletcher, *Rudiments*, 1:78; *CE*, 1:7. Recent research has shown how powerful philosophical anatomy was in London around 1840: Jacyna, 'Principles'; Desmond, *Politics*.

38. Monk, *Journals*, 113, 138; *LRO*, 1:197; 'brains': W. Broderip to W. Buckland, 27 Dec. 1844, BL Add. MS 40,556, f.314. The young Owen is discussed in Sloan, *Owen*, 3–72; Rupke, *Owen*, chaps 1, 4; Desmond, *Politics*, chaps 6–8. Hugh Torrens, 'When did the Dinosaur', suggests that Owen did not introduce his 'dinosaurs' until 1842.

39. Fayrer, *Recollections*, 22; Jackson, *Scharf's London*, 86–8; Dickens, *Sketches*, 60–2.

40. 'The Medical Student', *Punch*, 2 (1842), 71; Minney, *Two Pillars*, 27. J. Browne, 'Squibs', 166 for a wonderful study of this 'counter-culture of caricature'.

41. *LTH*, 1:15–16; Minney, *Two Pillars*, 26–7; Mayhew, *London Labour*, 284; Chesney, *Victorian Underworld*, 3–5; Richardson, *Death*, 278; G. M. Young, *Portrait*, 17, 20–1.

42. *Lancet*, 1 (1830–1), 4; *Medical Gazette*, 29 (1841–2), 117–20; Desmond, *Politics*, chaps 3–6, 9.

43. CCH, Vol. 1, f.333, 334; Hart, *Roots*, 12.

44. Elliotson, 'More', 490; Chandler, 'Extraordinary Effects', 3; Winter, 'Ethereal Epidemic', 1, 6–11. Chandler was now experimenting with phreno-mesmerism. With his patients in a trance, he would touch the 'bumps' on the skull to have them sing, fume, dance or whatever (touching the Veneration bump produced clasped hands): Chandler, 'Cures', 376; Cooter, *Cultural Meaning*, 150. Operating theatre: Harte, *University*, 38.

45. CCH, Vol. 1, ff. 341, 350; *LTH*, 1:36.

46. Fayrer, *Recollections*, 10; Tristan, *London Journal*, 7; Dickens, *Bleak House*, 49.

47. Altick, *Shows*, 377–80; Jackson, *Scharf's London*, 95.

48. TH to HAH, n.d. [?27 Mar. 1850], HH 79–80; Jackson, *Scharf's London*, 86; Fayrer, *Recollections*, 21–2. Fayrer's prizes: CCH, Vol. 1, f.357; *Lancet*, 1 (1845), 545.

49. TH to HAH, 16 Nov. 1850, 2 Jan. 1851, HH 129, 134; Bibby, *Huxley*, 4.

50. TH to HAH, 14, 23 Mar. 1851, HH 140, 141.

51. Rachel Huxley to TH, 23 Aug. 1849, AD.

52. Huxley's student notebook, c. 1845, HM 3:124, following George Newport on the myriapods and scorpions (ff.89, 135), Meckel on snails (f.106), W. B. Carpenter on shell structure (f.111), Edward Forbes on echinoderms (f.129). His readings on 'Alternation of Generations' (to be taken up so controversially later), especially Steenstrup's book, are on 118ff (cf. Winsor, *Starfish*, 61).

53. He was attacking Martin Barry, himself a leading importer of German embryology: Huxley in 'Thomas Wharton Jones', *British Medical Journal*, 2 (1891), 1176; Jones, 'Development', 258–9; Godlee, 'Wharton Jones', 98, 105; 'Mr. T. W. Jones's Manual', *Medical Gazette*, 39 (1847), 1046.

54. Huxley, 'Hitherto Undescribed Structure', 1341. The original MS, with his draft letter to the *Gazette*, is in HM 3:122 ff.1–6. For the research behind it see his student notebook, c. 1845, HM 3:124, ff.16–17. 'Thomas Wharton Jones', *British Medical Journal*, 2 (1891), 1176; *CE*, 1:9.

55. Sharpey's testimonial, HP 19.85; TH to W. Burnett, 31 Jan. 1846, HP 11.194; *LTH*, 1:23; *CE*, 1:9; Harte, *University*, 92, 101.

56. Candidates had to be 21: *Regulations of the Council Respecting the Professional Education of Candidates for the Diploma of Members* (15 Aug. 1843), i, RCS Library; *LTH*, 1:20; *CE*, 1:9; TH to W. Burnett, 31 Jan. 1846, HP 11.194. On his bills: HP 35.1.

57. James Huxley to TH, 30 July 1848, AD.

3 THE SURGEON'S MATE

1. CE, 1:9–10; Desmond and Moore, *Darwin*, 313, 326; Fayrer, *Recollections*, 23.
2. 'Assistant-Surgeons in the Navy', *Lancet*, 1 (1847), 685; also 1 (1840–1), 869; 1 (1841–2), 630; 2 (1840–1), 639, 933. 'Surgeon's Mate' was by the 1840s a colloquialism for assistant surgeon, who was in effect the junior surgeon aboard. Compare Huxley's 7s 6d a day (£138 per annum: HP 31) with a seaman's 26s a month: Rasor, *Reform*, 104.
3. TH to W. Burnett, 31 Jan. 1846, HP 11.194 (misdated in Dawson, *Huxley Papers*); Fayrer, *Recollections*, 24–5; CE, 1:10.
4. W. Sharpey's testimonial, 7 Feb. 1846; Wharton Jones's, 9 Feb. 1846, both HP 19.85. TH to W. Burnett, 31 Jan. 1846, HP 11.194. On the Navy's requirements: 'Naval Medical Service, Regulations', *Lancet*, 2 (1846), 342. Candidates also had to be between 20 and 24 and unmarried.
5. CE, 1:10.
6. *Lancet*, 2 (1846), 342.
7. TH to ES, 20 Feb. 1846, AD; also ES to TH, 20 Oct. 1846, AD, on the family fights; Clark, *Huxleys*, 14–15.
8. TH to W. Burnett, 25 Feb. 1846, HP 11.193a; Court of Examiners Ledger, 6 Mar. 1846, f. 51, RCS Library; Ian Lyle, RCS Library, pers. comm.
9. TH to ES, 20 Feb. 1846, AD; Clark, *Huxleys*, 15; CE, 1:10; date of enrolment and pay: HP 31.5; landladies' bills: HP 31.9–12; debts and drafts, HP 31.6; Cooke's £16 debt was repaid during the voyage: HP 21.181.
10. Gillot's bill, 7 Apr. 1846, HP 31.13; *Diary*, 351. He mentions borrowing from an agent to buy the outfit in TH to HAH, 21 July 1851, HH 159; *LTH*, 1:118n. The agent was Goode & Lawrence: HP 21.181.
11. Rasor, *Reform*, 10–12; *Lancet*, 2 (1840–1), 482.
12. CE, 1:11–12. One of his messmates was his later physician Andrew Clark, at Haslar from 1846–1853. On Haslar Hospital: Coad, *Royal Dockyards*, 295–7.
13. TH to ES, 22 Apr. 1846, HP 31.15; CE, 1:11; *LTH*, 1:25. On the West African postings: 'Naval Assistant Surgeons', *Lancet*, 2 (1840–1), 639.
14. TH to ES, 22 Apr. 1846, HP 31.15; TH to ES (addressed to Miss Knight), 12 Mar., 3 May 1846, AD; ES to TH, postmarked 12 Apr. 1846, AD.
15. 'Naval Assistant-Surgeons', *Lancet*, 2 (1840–1), 875–8, 935.
16. *LTH*, 1:25; CE, 1:12; Lubbock, *Stanley*, 163, 170–1.
17. *LTH*, 1:25; Lubbock, *Stanley*, 2, 19–24, 28, 33, 39, 72–5, 90, 119, 144, 148–9, 152, 155, 169, 278; CE, 1:12.
18. Lubbock, *Stanley*, 163, 170–2; *LTH*, 1:25.
19. *LTH*, 1:25, 27. On Owen: *Diary*, 16; Rupke, 'Owen's Hunterian Lectures'; Desmond, *Politics*, chap. 8. Wilson and Geikie, *Memoir*, 61, 250–1, 274, 359; On Forbes: Mills, 'View'; Rehbock, 'Early Dredgers', and *Philosophical Naturalists*, chaps 4–5; Browne, *Secular Ark*, chap. 6.
20. 'Naval Assistant Surgeons', *Lancet*, 1 (1840–1), 869; 2 (1840–1), 283, 444–5, 525–7, 767, 875–8; 1 (1841–2), 628–30; 2 (1844), 302; 2 (1846), 280, 306; 1 (1847), 288, 293, 345, 680, 685. Some middies were the sons of sea captains, being shown the ropes, such as Philip King on Darwin's *Beagle*; others were

placed in the gunroom by the Captain's friends, such as Philip Sharpe in Huxley's mess.

21. HM Notebook R1, ff.3–5, 24–5 July, 27 Sept. 1846, on bee, slug and snail nerves; £13 15s microscope, HP 31.6; 1 July pay, £37 7s 7d, HP 31.5.

22. Huxley, 'Science at Sea', 100; *LTH*, 1:27; on his book buying, HP 31.6, which also lists his mess bills, which averaged about £5 a month.

23. Lubbock, *Stanley*, 169; Huxley, 'Science at Sea', 100, 108.

24. Kirby, 'Introductory Address', 2, 5; Desmond, 'Making', 168, 174–5, on imperial London zoology. *Narrative*, 1:2–9; Huxley, 'Science at Sea', 102–3.

25. Matthews, *Emigration Fields*, vi–9; *Narrative*, 1:3–6.

26. Wilson and Geikie, *Memoir*, 190–202, 399; Rehbock, 'Early Dredgers', 323–40; *Amphioxus: SM*, 1:4–5; *LTH*, 1:28.

27. Lubbock, *Stanley*, 179, 182; *LTH*, 1:26; on his 2 Oct. commission, HP 31.8; 'Am': TH to George Huxley, n.d. 'The Hulks', AD; Lloyd, *British Seaman*, 209; Hughes, *Fatal Shore*, 138.

28. *LTH*, 1:26, 491; see the illustration in *Diary*, 177.

29. *LTH*, 1:27; 'Naval Medical Intelligence', *Lancet*, 2 (1846), 306; Lubbock, *Stanley*, 180–81; on Sharpe: TH to HAH, 2 Dec. 1850, HH 132.

30. Lubbock, *Stanley*, 170, 179–80; *Narrative*, 1:16 reports that the *Rattlesnake* carried 15 government chronometers and 2 private ones, although Lubbock gives the total number as 28.

31. TH to Rachel Huxley, 24 Mar. 1847, AD; Allen, 'Huxley's Brother-in-Law', 192. Gray was apparently piqued because many of MacGillivray's specimens from the *Fly* expedition failed to reach home: Ralph, 'MacGillivray', 185–9; *LTH*, 1:26, 33; Lubbock, *Stanley*, 171, 180; Whittell, *Literature*, 110–11, 465; *Narrative*, 1:179.

32. *LTH*, 1:32; *Diary*, 305, 326, 364; Whittell, *Literature*, 110–11.

33. ES to TH, 20 Oct. 1846, AD; 'gut': James Huxley to TH, 20 Nov. 1846, AD; E. Forbes to TH, 11 Nov. 1846, HP 16.151; Lubbock, *Stanley*, 182–6; Fayrer, *Recollections*, 24–5.

34. Lubbock, *Stanley*, 174–6, 181–3. On the Kings: Nicholas and Nicholas, *Darwin*, 130–8.

4   MEN-OF-WAR

1. 'Degradation of Naval Surgeons', *Lancet*, 1 (1847), 680. Jim sent out reports of the *Lancet*'s fight for the assistant surgeon's 'right of space cabins & the wardroom': James Huxley to TH, 30 July 1848, 22 Apr. 1849, AD.

2. *Lancet*, 2 (1840–1), 876; Ralph, 'MacGillivray', 188–9.

3. *LTH*, 1:28; Lubbock, *Stanley*, 183–5; Coad, *Royal Dockyards*, 15 pl.7, 136–8.

4. *Diary*, 15–17; *SM*, 1:198.

5. Huxley, 'Science at Sea', 100; *Diary*, 362–3; *Narrative*, 1:10.

6. *Diary*, 18; Seaman, *Victorian England*, 233.

7. *Diary*, 19; *Narrative*, 1:13.

8. *Diary*, 17–18.

9. Darwin, *Journal*, 4; Barrett, *Collected Papers*, 1:199–203; *Diary*, 18, 22.

10. 'The Naval Medical Service', *Lancet*, 2 (1844), 302; *Diary*, 22–3, 141; arrowworms: HM R1 Notebook, f.11; *LTH*, 1:32. One notebook from his Charing Cross days that he had aboard is in HM 3:124, see ff. 155–72.

11. *Narrative*, 1:14–15; *Diary*, 19, 23.

12. *Diary*, 24, 27, 363; Rasor, *Reform*, 16–22; *Narrative*, 1:16; Lubbock, *Stanley*, 187; *LTH*, 1:31–2.
13. HM R1 Notebook, ff.11–14; *Diary*, 26.
14. *Diary*, 27, 29–30; *Narrative*, 1:17–21; *LTH*, 1:31.
15. *LTH*, 1:32; *Diary*, 30; *Narrative*, 1:23; Lorimer, *Colour*, 101–3 on the comparison of blacks and the English agricultural poor.
16. TH to Rachel Huxley, 24 Mar. 1847, AD; ES to TH, 6 Dec. 1846, AD; Allen, 'Huxley's Brother-in-Law', 192. *Amphioxus:* HM R1 Notebook, f.16; *Diary*, 28–31; *Narrative*, 1:22–5, 329.
17. *Diary*, 28–31; *Narrative*, 1:24–7; Gould, 'Ingenious Paradox'.
18. TH to Rachel Huxley, 15 May 1847, AD; 'Salpae': HM R1 Notebook, f.17; *Diary*, 31–3.
19. *Diary*, 34–5; *Narrative*, 1:29–30; HM R1 Notebook, ff.35–45.
20. *Diary*, 32–6. MS, 'On the Anatomy and Physiology of *Physalia*', HP 34.1; abstract, *SM*, 1:361–2; HM R1 Notebook, ff.21–5, 31–2; Winsor, *Starfish*, 61–2.
21. *Diary*, 36; Gage and Stearn, *Bicentenary History*, 36, 43, 47. On the aristocrat's role in science: Desmond, 'Making of Zoology', 224–43; *Politics*, 135–7, 145–51, 223–34; MacLeod, 'Whigs'. Morrell and Thackray, *Gentlemen*, 25–9, on Bishop Stanley and liberal Anglican science.
22. *Diary*, 37–8, 40; *Narrative*, 1:30–33; Darwin, *Journal*, 570.
23. *Diary*, 39–40; *Narrative*, 1:34, 36, 38; *LTH*, 1:34.
24. *Diary*, 40–3, 45–9; *LTH*, 1:34–5; Darwin, *Journal*, 573; *Narrative*, 1:35–6; Saint-Pierre, *Paul*, 65.
25. HP 30.14; *Diary*, 37; HM R1 Notebook, ff.46–72; *SM*, 1:363–4.
26. *Narrative*, 1:41; *Diary*, 44–5, 49; Lubbock, *Stanley*, 188–9; Keynes, *Darwin's 'Beagle' Diary*, 406–7.

5 AN ARK OF PROMISE

1. *Diary*, 81; Winter, 'Ethereal Epidemic', 18–23; Lubbock, *Stanley*, 191; *CCD*, 1:490; Keynes, *Darwin's 'Beagle' Diary*, 406–10.
2. *Diary*, 81; H. A. Huxley, 'Pictures', 770.
3. Marshall, *Darwin*, 10–15; Nicholas and Nicholas, *Darwin*, 23–4; Lubbock, *Stanley*, 86–7; Darwin, *Journal*, 515–16; Keynes, *Darwin's 'Beagle' Diary*, 395–6; *CCD*, 1:482–5, 492; Desmond and Moore, *Darwin*, 175–6; *Diary*, 81.
4. *Diary*, 81–2; *LTH*, 1:37.
5. Lubbock, *Stanley*, 197–200; *Narrative*, 1:98n, 117; *Diary*, 98.
6. *LTH*, 1:33; HM R1 Notebook, ff.73–6.
7. TH to E. Forbes, [Sept. 1847], HP 16.154; Winsor, *Starfish*, 66, 76, 88.
8. HAH's Reminiscences, HP 62.1; *Diary*, 81, 338.
9. HAH's Reminiscences, HP 62.1; H. A. Huxley, 'Pictures', 781; Hughes, *Fatal Shore*, 344.
10. *Diary*, 81–2; P. P. King to TH, 30 Apr. 1850, HP 19.154. Nicholas and Nicholas, *Darwin*, 130–3. On King, Darwin and zoology: Desmond and Moore, *Darwin*, 109, 178–9; Darwin's notes on preserving specimens, DAR 29.3:78ff, CUL; *Report of the Council and Auditors of the Accounts of the Zoological Society of London* (London, Taylor, 1832), 9–10; Desmond, 'Making', 169n. Darwin also visited Captain King in Australia: *CCD*, 1:481, 483.

11. HAH's Reminiscences, HP 62.1; *Diary*, 82–3.
12. HAH's Reminiscences, HP 62.1; *LTH*, 1:37; Clark, *Huxleys*, 21; TH to HAH, 31 July 1851, HH 160 on her German school.
13. TH to Rachel Huxley, 1 Feb. 1849, HP 31.60; *LTH*, 1:38; Lubbock, *Stanley*, 198.
14. Bayley, *Blue Haven*, 20–3; Henrietta's Kent ancestry, HP 62.18; Clark, *Huxleys*, 21; her mother's ancestry, HAH to ES, 15 Jan. 1891, AD.
15. H. A. Huxley, 'Pictures', 772–4, 779–81.
16. *SM*, 1:6–8; HM R1 Notebook, f.77 (dated 'September' 1847); 'You': TH to HAH, 6 Oct. 1847, HH 1; *Diary*, 84–8; *LTH*, 1:37.
17. *Diary*, 80, 88.
18. TH to HAH, 16 Oct. 1847, HH 2; *Diary*, 88–9, 294, 303; *Narrative*, 1:43–4; Lubbock, *Stanley*, 197, 200, 214. Comb jelly *Cydippe* (= *Pleurobranchia*): HM R1 Notebook, ff.79–81.
19. In her first letter to him (14 Oct. 1847, HH 5) she pleaded: 'There is but one thing in our short acquaintance that I look upon with pain. It is our conversation last Sunday Afternoon. I cannot review it without sadness. I have thought over all you said and though in your presence unable to reply I may say almost without the power of reflection I have since weighed all your arguments yet cannot think you right. Do not I beseech you let years role by and still find you unfixed. Give much of your thought to this important subject, and oh whatever your ultimate convictions God grant they may be right, not alone in your eyes but in His.'
20. TH to HAH, 16–17 Oct. 1847, HH 2–3; Bainton, *Here I Stand*, 144; *CE*, 5:235–6; Carlyle, *Heroes*, 10. '*Law* and *Order*' were the words of the Unitarian W. B. Carpenter, *Animal Physiology*, 2:viii, later to become Huxley's ally in London. On Carpenter's deterministic physiology and theology, Desmond, *Politics*, 211–22. Paradis, *Huxley*, 92–3; Lightman, *Origins*, 96–7.

    Since so little is known of Huxley's early scepticism, and since it reflects so strongly on his later scientific and agnostic stand, I quote this passage to Henrietta in full:

    > I have thought much of our afternoon conversation, and I am ill at ease as to the impression I may have left on your mind regarding my sentiments. If there be one fact in a man's character rather than another, which may be taken as a key to the whole, it is the tendency of his religious speculations. Not by any means, is the absolute nature of his opinions in themselves a matter of so much consequence, as the temper and tone of mind which he brings to the inquiry. Opinion is the result of evidence. From a given amount and strength of evidence, as cause, a certain belief must, in all minds, always follow as effect. The intellect here acts passively, and is as irresponsible for its conclusion as a jury, who convict a man on the strength of certain evidence are irresponsible for their conclusion should that evidence turn out to have been unworthy of trust. For the verdict they are not responsible, for the manner in which they found it they are deeply & heavily so. It is the same with individuals. The opinion a man has, once more, neither is nor can be a matter of moral responsibility. The extent to which he deserves approbation or reprobation depends on the mode in which he has founded his opinion – and of this the Almighty search of hearts can alone be the efficient judge.

May his fellowmen then form no judgment upon the point? Surely they must and will do so, and so long as they confine themselves to their proper sphere of judgment nothing can be more fit than that they should do so. But let them not judge him by his agreement or disagreement with their own ideas however venerable and raised the latter may appear to them – let them rather inquire whether he be truthful and earnest – or vain and talkative – whether he be one of those who would spend years of silent investigation in the faint hope of at length finding truth, or one of those who conscious of capability would rather gratify a selfish ambition by adopting and defending the first fashionable error suited to his purpose.

Whether again he be one who says I doubt, in all sadness of heart, and from solemn fear to tread where the fools of the day boldly rush in – or whether he be one of those miserable men, whose scepticism is the result of covetousness & who pitifully exhibit their vain ingenuity for the mere purpose of puzzling and disturbing the faith of others.

On grounds of this kind only can a judgment be justly formed. On these my own dear one must you form your judgment of me.

As for my opinions themselves, I can only say in Martin Luther's ever famous words, "Hier Steh Ich – Gott helfe mir – Ich kann nicht anders". Perhaps after all they are not so different from yours as you may imagine . . .

Had I space I would write you much more on this matter which so deeply interests us both . . .

21. *Narrative*, 1:48–9, 168; TH to HAH, 18 Oct. 1847, HH 3.
22. *Diary*, 89–91; *Narrative*, 1:45; Nicholas and Nicholas, *Darwin*, 56; Hughes, *Fatal Shore*, 441. 22.
23. TH to HAH, 14, 17, 27 Nov. 1847, HH 4; HAH to TH, 14, 17, 23 Oct. 1847, HH 5.
24. *Narrative*, 1:50–3, 56–7; Lubbock, *Stanley*, 201; Hughes, *Fatal Shore*, 551–2.
25. HM R1 Notebook, ff.82 and 85 (Sertularidae); f.84 Brachiopod *Lingula*.
26. HM R1 Notebook, ff.86–97; *Narrative*, 1:54–8.
27. *Diary*, 91–2. Megapodes and sunbirds at Port Molle: *Narrative*, 1:59–63. Whittell, *Literature*, 111; J. Gould, 'On New Species', 201.
28. Carlyle, *Heroes*, 93, 209–10; Huxley, 'Tyndall', 3; Turner, 'Victorian Scientific Naturalism', 329–34; *LTH*, 1:237; *Diary*, 92–4; *Narrative*, 1:63–6; HM R1 Notebook, f.97.
29. Eliza Knight to TH, 27 Jan., 3 Apr., 11 May 1847, AD; 'with': ES to Rachel Huxley, 20 Dec. 1846, AD; 'God': Rachel Huxley to TH, 26 Oct. 1847, AD: 'from': George Huxley to TH, 27 June 1847, AD; *Diary*, 92–4. The 'Scotts' had sailed two months after Tom, on 27 January 1847, the only private passengers on the US merchantman *Thomas Wright*, landing in New Orleans on 21 March.
30. HAH to TH, 23 Dec. 1847, HH 6; *Diary*, 98–9.
31. *Diary*, 32. The *Physalia* paper was read at the Linnean Society on 21 November and 5 December 1848, but attributed to 'Willm. Huxley': LS Minute Book; HP 34.1; abstract: *SM*, 1:361–2.
32. TH to HAH, 6, 10 Feb. 1847, HH 7–8; *Diary*, 99–100; *Narrative*, 1:66–7. HM R1 Notebook, ff.108–17 for the Strait's jellyfish.

33. HM R1 Notebook, ff.123–8. *Narrative*, 1:67–8, 71; *Diary*, 100–1.
34. *Diary*, 100–6; *Narrative*, 1:68–70; Whittell, *Literature*, 111–12.
35. *SM*, 1:9–11, 23; draft MS, 'On the Anatomy and the Affinities of the Family of the Medusae', HP 34.127; *LTH*, 1:36, 39–40; *Diary*, 66–9; Winsor, *Starfish*, 61, 75ff; di Gregorio, *Huxley*, 5ff.
36. MacLeod, 'Whigs', 56–7, 70–80; Crosland, 'Explicit Qualifications', 179–83, Desmond, *Politics*, 222–34, 393–4.
37. *Diary*, 103–9; *Narrative*, 1:73–4; Lubbock, *Stanley*, 205–6; on his obstinacy: TH to HAH, 8 Feb. 1848, HH 8.

6 THE EIGHTH CIRCLE OF HELL

1. Rachel Huxley to TH, 26 Oct. 1847, AD. On Sharpe: *Diary*, 315; HAH to TH, n.d., HH 97; priests: 25 Feb. 1848, HH 13.
2. HAH to TH, 6 Feb. 1848, HH 10; H. A. Huxley, 'Pictures', 771; George Street: 12 Apr. 1848, HH 15.
3. TH to George Huxley, 21, 24 Apr. 1848, HP 31.47; *CE*, 1:6; *Diary*, 275–6; W. Poideoin to TH, n.d. postmark 4? Apr. 1848, AD; gun: HAH to TH, 17 July 1848, HH 29. Hughes, *Fatal Shore*, 163, 299–300, 307, 347, and 340, 487, 635–6 on Wainewright.
4. *LTH*, 1:37–8; TH to George Huxley, 21 Apr. 1848, HP 31.47; 'You': James Huxley to TH, 22 Apr. 1849, AD; Ralph, 'MacGillivray', 188, 190. George financing Cooke: George Huxley to TH, 27 June 1847, AD. On Britain's growing civic ceremony: Best, *Mid-Victorian Britain*, 82.
5. HAH's Reminiscences, HP 62.1.
6. TH to George Huxley, 27 Apr. 1849, HP 31.52; *LTH*, 1:38.
7. Quotes from Desmond, 'Making', 161–4, which also deals with the ideological impact of Macleay's system; Macleay, *Horae Entomologicae*, 1:332–3; Winsor, *Starfish*, 82–97; Stanbury and Holland, *Mr Macleay's Cabinet*, 19–34.
8. *LTH*, 1:38; 'strong': TH to HAH, 1 July 1849, HH 70.
9. *SM*, 1:24; the MS (HP 34.127) was endorsed 'Finished & sent to R. S^y in April 1848' (f.157 on jellies and vertebrate germs); *LTH*, 1:40; *Diary*, 69; Macleay was not so happy about Huxley's developmental approach: Winsor, *Starfish*, 92.
10. Rachel Huxley to TH, 26 Oct. 1847, and Rachel Huxley in George's letter to TH, 27 June 1847, AD.
11. TH to George Huxley, 21 Apr. 1848, HP 31.47; TH to J. Richardson, n.d., HP 25.68.
12. Lubbock, *Stanley*, 205–6.
13. TH to George Huxley, 21 Apr. 1848, HP 31.47; *CE*, 1:13.
14. HAH to TH, 14 Oct. 1847, HH 5.
15. *Narrative*, 2:119, 133; *Diary*, 125; Lubbock, *Stanley*, 209–14; Bassett, *Behind*, 24–5.
16. HM R1 Notebook, f.133–7; *LTH*, 1:38; *Diary*, 125–6; *Narrative*, 1:77.
17. *Diary*, 128–9, 363–4; Lewes, *Ranthorpe*, 68, 110–11, 351; *Narrative*, 1:78–80; Italian: TH to HAH, 22 May 1848, HH 20.
18. *Diary*, 126–7; MacGillivray, *Narrative*, 1:125, 145–6; *LTH*, 1:44.
19. *Narrative*, 1:83, 2:119–25; *Diary*, 127–8; Lubbock, *Stanley*, 217.

20. *Diary*, 129–36; *Narrative*, 1:82–3, 2:123–33; 'the Service': TH to HAH, 28 May 1848, HH 23.
21. Huxley, 'Science at Sea', 112; *Narrative*, 1:84, 106.
22. Huxley, 'Science at Sea', 108.
23. J. Gould, 'On New Species', 111, 201, and Whittell, *Literature*, 112; *Narrative*, 1:85–6, 90; *Diary*, 128.
24. *Diary*, 135–8; *Narrative*, 1:90–91, 93–6, 2:377–8. MacGillivray's efforts were rewarded, Forbes later named his new snail *Helix Macgillivrayi*. J. Gould, 'On New Species', 109–10, for the flying fox.
25. Huxley, 'Science at Sea', 104–5.
26. Huxley, 'Science at Sea', 99; Rasor, *Reform*, 82–3 on the rum; *Diary*, 138–42; *Narrative*, 1:93, 97–9, 112, 123; TH to HAH, 26 June 1848, HH 24.
27. TH to HAH, 2 July–27 Oct. 1848, HH 35–7; *Narrative*, 1:100–4; *Diary*, 141; HM R1 Notebook, ff.153–61; HM B 43.2, 46.1.2, 56–7.
28. Huxley, 'Science at Sea', 112; *LTH*, 1:44; *Diary*, 141–2; *Narrative*, 1:106–8; cowrie *Cypraea*, HM R3 Notebook, f.112.
29. *Narrative*, 1:110–16, 120; *Diary*, 143–5; Dante, *Inferno*, 233, 235, 240, 269–70, 347, 353, 383.
30. *Narrative*, 1:121–32; J. Gould, 'On New Species', 110–11; Lubbock, *Stanley*, 208; Huxley, 'Science at Sea', 109.
31. J. Gould, 'On New Species', 109–12 (1849), 200–1 (1850); ZSL Minutes of Scientific Meetings, 13 November 1849, f.15; 23 July 1850, f.59. Beauty was crucial to Gould, whose sales reflected the exotic splendour of his birds. The names he chose, like *Ptiloris Victoriae*, Queen Victoria's rifle bird, also implied conquest; and associating 'this lovely denizen of the Australian forests', shimmering in iridescent green, 'with our most gracious Queen', added to the bird's imperial appeal (p. 111).
32. Rachel Huxley to TH, 22 Feb. 1848, AD; HAH to TH, 21 June 1848, HH 26; Bassett, *Behind*, 30.
33. Rachel Huxley to TH, 31 May 1848, AD; James Huxley to TH, 27 Mar. 1848, AD.
34. Rachel Huxley to TH, 31 May 1848, AD; 'who': TH to George Huxley, 27 Apr. 1849, HP 31.52.
35. *Diary*, 136n, 146–9; TH to Rachel Huxley, 2 Feb. 1849, HP 31.60; *LTH*, 1:43–4; Lubbock, *Stanley*, 90–6, 108–11; *Narrative*, 1:135–9; Bassett, *Behind*, chap. 5.
36. *Narrative*, 1:153–9; Morris, *Heaven's Command*, 302; HM R3 Notebook, ff.33–51; *Diary*, 148; *SM*, 1:33.
37. TH to HAH, 24 Dec. 1848, HH 39; *Diary*, 150–2, 364–5; *Narrative*, 1:157–60.
38. *Diary*, 146, 152–3; HM R3 Notebook, ff.67–99.
39. TH to George Huxley, Apr. 1849, HP 31.50; Lubbock, *Stanley*, 243–4.
40. TH to Rachel Huxley, 2 Feb. 1849, HP 31.60; H. A. Huxley, 'Pictures', 771.
41. George Huxley to TH, 27 June 1847, AD; Rachel Huxley to TH, 13, 22 Sept. 1848, also 15 Mar., 12 May 1847, AD; TH to George Huxley, 27 Apr. 1849, HP 31.52.
42. TH to Rachel Huxley, 1 Feb. 1849, HP 31.60; *LTH*, 1:39; 'there': TH to George Huxley, 27 Apr. 1849, HP 31.52.
43. TH to George Huxley, 27 Apr. 1849, HP 31.52; Ralph, 'MacGillivray', 190.
44. TH to Rachel Huxley, 1 Feb. 1849, HP 31.60; *LTH*, 1:39, 45; *Diary*, 298.

45. TH to George Huxley, 27 Apr. 1849, HP 31.52; Rachel Huxley to TH, 7 Dec. 1848, AD.
46. *Diary*, 293, 328.
47. Lubbock, *Stanley*, 240–1; *LTH*, 1:44; *Narrative*, 1:82–3, 162–6, 2:133–276; *Diary*, 111–12, 244; Bassett, *Behind*, chaps 7–9.

7 SEPULCHRAL PAINTED SAVAGES

1. *Diary*, 172–3; *Narrative*, 1:166, 181; Lubbock, *Stanley*, 244; 'then': TH to HAH, 10 May 1849, HH 57; 'fierceness': HAH to TH, 21 Jan. 1849, HH 46.
2. *SM*, 1:33; HM R5 Notebook, f.16 *Tubularia* (f.99 ship's bottom); f.27 *Echinus* larvae; f.29 Diphydae; f.31 comb jelly. *Diary*, 174, 296.
3. *Diary*, 175–9; *Narrative*, 1:4, 183; Lubbock, *Stanley*, 177, 246–50; 'sweated': TH to George Huxley, April 1849, HP 31.50; HM R5 Notebook, f.33 *Pteropoda*; f.35 spiny crustaceans.
4. *Diary*, 182–5, 191–200; *Narrative*, 1:168–73, 186–91, 201, 277; Lubbock, *Stanley*, 245.
5. Lubbock, *Stanley*, 246; *Narrative*, 1:200, 208; *Diary*, 191–2; Huxley, 'Science at Sea', 117; Desmond and Moore, *Darwin*, 174.
6. *Narrative*, 1:189, 196–8, 208–12, 243–4, 246; *Diary*, 184–6, 188, 190.
7. TH to HAH, 1 July 1849, HH 70; *Diary*, 186–98, 209, 297–8; TH to HAH, 26 Apr. 1849, HH 51; *Narrative*, 1:4; Lubbock, *Stanley*, 256–7.
8. Huxley, 'Science at Sea', 112; *Diary*, 190, 197–207; *Narrative*, 1:215, 223, 228–37, 280–1.
9. HM R5 Notebook, f.50; also f.56, 65 crustaceans; f.62 worms; f.72ff, jellies and sea nettles; Notebook HP 51.1; *Diary*, 156, 209.
10. *Diary*, 209–10.
11. Huxley, 'Science at Sea', 115; *Narrative*, 1:238, 248.
12. *Narrative*, 1:254–84; *Diary*, 212–30; 'I never': Huxley, 'Science at Sea', 115–16 quoting Stanley's journal.
13. *Diary*, 215, 218–20, 223–9; *Narrative*, 1:233, 255–6, 260–4, 271–4; Lubbock, *Stanley*, 252.
14. *Diary*, 223–5, 231–2; *Narrative*, 1:283.
15. TH to HAH, 1 Sept. 1849, HH 71; 'sitting': TH to Rachel Huxley, 17 Sept. 1849, AD; HM R5 Notebook, ff.20ff; Notebook HP 51.12–22.
16. *Diary*, 211, 232–3; Lubbock, *Stanley*, 253; *Narrative*, 1:285. On the euphemisms 'unclean' and 'indecent', and the dying use of the 'cat': Rasor, *Reform*, 49–51, 98.
17. *Narrative*, 1:241, 285–90; *Diary*, 154n, 235–8; Lubbock, *Stanley*, 255; naming: Kirby, 'Introductory Address', 5.
18. TH to Goode & Lawrence, Navy Agents, 11 Oct. 1849, HP 181. *Diary*, 239–40, 366–7; *Narrative*, 1:293–301; HAH to TH, 31 Aug. 1849, HH 68; *LTH*, 1:64.
19. James Huxley to TH, 22 Apr. 1849, AD; TH to HAH, 6 Oct. 1849, HH 71. The Linnean paper was only published in abstract. Forbes read Huxley's notes on *Trigonia* at the Zoological Society: *SM*, 1:6–8, 363–4.
20. *SM*, 1:33–5; Winsor, *Starfish*, 77–8, 87ff; Huxley, *Oceanic*, 1.
21. *Diary*, 241–8; *Narrative*, 1:301–7, 2:277; Lubbock, *Stanley*, 258–61; Bassett, *Behind*, chap. 11.

22. *Narrative*, 1:317–26; J. Gould, 'On New Australian Birds', 276–9; Whittell, *Literature*, 116.

23. 'Sketch of a Classification of the Ascidians', HP 34.168; *SM*, 1:69–74; Redscar: HM R5 Notebook, f.100; HP 74; *SM*, 1:38–9.

24. *SM*, 1:38–53; Winsor, *Starfish*, 64; *Diary*, 56–60. What he did not set out to publish were his diagrams, drawn at the Cape, slotting the 'Nematophora' – indeed all animal life – onto Macleay's circles (HP 50.3).

25. *Diary*, 165–6, 248–62; *Narrative*, 1:307–8, 318–20, 2:8–15, 35–49; Lubbock, *Stanley*, 261–3; TH to HAH, 20 Oct. 1849, HH 73.

26. *Diary*, 262–5; *Narrative*, 2:29, 35, 49–66; Lubbock, *Stanley*, 265.

8   HOMESICK HEROES

1. TH to HAH, 4 Feb. 1850, HH 74; *Diary*, 265, 367–8; *Narrative*, 2:67; Lubbock, *Stanley*, 265–8.

2. *Diary*, 301, 368; Lubbock, *Stanley*, 261, 266–7; *Narrative*, 2: 67–9; 'Lioness': TH to HAH, 20 Oct. 1849, HH 73.

3. *Diary*, 288, 294, 302.

4. TH to HAH, n.d. (endorsed Feb. 1850), HH 75; *Diary*, 276, 281–2. On Darwin's trip: Keynes, *Darwin's 'Beagle' Diary*, 396–400; Nicholas and Nicholas, *Darwin*, 3, 13, 23–5, 68–9. Hughes, *Fatal Shore*, 262–3.

5. George Huxley to TH, 3 Nov. 1849, AD; Halevy, *Victorian Years*, 197; Rachel Huxley to TH, 30 Jan. 1848, AD; 'my': James Huxley to TH, 30 Jan. 1848, AD; 'D': A. McClatchie to TH, 24 Sept. 1849, HP 22.119. Cooke resigned from the Linnean Society because of 'circumstances which I cannot control' (presumably financial): J. C. Cooke to LS, 31 Jan. 1848, LS Archives.

6. *Diary*, 290, 299, 302.

7. Huxley, 'Science at Sea', 103; Lubbock, *Stanley*, 266–9.

8. *LTH*, 1:46; *Diary*, 303; Lubbock, *Stanley*, 270–1.

9. *Diary*, 303–5, 312; HAH to TH, n.d. [20 Mar. 1850], HH 78; *Narrative*, 2:86; Lubbock, *Stanley*, 270n.

10. *Diary*, 305–10; HAH to TH, n.d., HH 91.

11. *Diary*, 265–7, 308–13.

12. HAH to TH, Tuesday noon, Tuesday evening [30 Apr. 1850], HH 94, 95; TH to HAH, Tuesday morning [30 April 1850], HH 92.

13. Huxley's MS Diary, HH 128, f.1; *Diary*, 313, 317–18.

14. TH to HAH, [2 May 1850], HH 99; Huxley's MS Diary, HH 128, ff.1–6; *Diary*, 318–20; Whittell, *Literature*, 116; *Narrative*, 2:86.

15. Huxley's MS Diary, HH 128, ff.2–4; *Diary*, 317–19.

16. Huxley's MS Diary, HH 128, f.4; *Diary*, 319.

17. Huxley's MS Diary, HH 128, ff.4–8; *Diary*, 312, 319–22, 323.

18. Lubbock, *Stanley*, 272. On alcoholism in the Service: Rasor, *Reform*, 81.

19. TH to HAH, 14 May 1850, HH 101; Huxley's MS Diary, HH 128, ff.8–10; *Diary*, 322–3, 336; diagrams: HP 50.20–2.

20. TH to HAH, 18, 21 May 1850, HH 103–5; *LTH*, 1:52–3; *Diary*, 313, 323–5; *Narrative*, 2:87–94; Morris, *Heaven's Command*, 302–3; rats: Huxley, *West. Rev.*, 63 (1855), 252–3. Cf. Darwin's view, Desmond and Moore, *Darwin*, 174–6.

21. HP 51.63–70; *SM*, 1:53–9; *Narrative*, 2:95–6; Huxley's MS Diary, HH 128, ff.15–16, 19; *Diary*, 326–9.
22. Huxley's MS Diary, HH 128, ff.20, 24–6; *Diary*, 329, 332–3; *LTH*, 1:54.
23. TH to HAH, 12 July 1850, HH 111–12; *LTH*, 1:53–4; *Narrative*, 2:99–107; Desmond and Moore, *Darwin*, 336–7; *CCD*, 2:109–11; 3:109–26.
24. Huxley's MS Diary, HH 128, ff.28–30; *Diary*, 334–5; TH to HAH, 8 Aug. 1850, HH 115; siphonophores: HP 63.1–14; *Narrative*, 2:112–13.
25. James Huxley to TH, 22 Apr. 1849, AD; Huxley, 'Science at Sea', 98–9, 104, 106; *CE*, 1:12–13; 'Service': TH to HAH, 27 Mar. 1850, HH 79–80; *Diary*, 24, 338, 350.
26. TH to HAH, 27 Mar. 1850, HH 79–80; 'sick': 8 Feb. 1848, HH 7–8.
27. Huxley, 'Science at Sea', 117–19. The Quaker physician Thomas Hodgkin and William Wilberforce's heir in the anti-slavery movement, Thomas Fowell Buxton, had formed the 'Aborigines Protection Society' in 1837, and published the *Colonial Intelligencer and Aborigines Friend*. Hodgkin was guardian of an aboriginal boy brought to England by Eyre: Rose, *Curator*, 31–8, 104–17; Stocking, 'What's', 369–72.
28. *Narrative*, 1:343–402, 2:387–95.
29. TH to HAH, 28 Aug. 1852, HH 222; *LTH*, 1:57.
30. James Huxley to TH, 22 Apr. 1849, AD; Rachel Huxley to TH, 23 Aug. 1849, AD; George Huxley to TH, 3 Nov. 1849, AD.
31. Huxley's MS Diary, HH 128, ff.26, 55; *Diary*, 333, 350; *LTH*, 1:45, 54.

9   THE SCIENTIFIC SADDUCEE

1. TH to HAH, 16 Nov. 1850, HH 129; *LTH*, 1:60; Desmond and Moore, *Darwin*, 189.
2. *Lancet*, 2 (1840–1), 552–3; *LTH*, 1:57–8.
3. TH to HAH, 16 Nov., 24 Dec. 1850, HH 129, 134; *LTH*, 1:60, 63.
4. TH to ES, 21 Nov. 1850, AD; *LTH*, 1:61.
5. TH to HAH, 1 Mar. 1851, HH 139; Tristan, *London Journal*, 1–2; Norton, *Victorian London*, 31, 55, 73; Best, *Mid-Victorian Britain*, 51, 76; Huxley 'had a grand view of some of the celebrities' (including Disraeli) in the Commons: TH to HAH, 1 Feb. 1851, HH 136.
6. *LTH*, 1:56; 'approved': TH to HAH, 16 Nov. 1850, HH 129; Huxley, *Oceanic*, ix–x; Desmond and Moore, *Darwin*, 226–7; *CCD*, 2:26, 34, 37–9.
7. TH to HAH, 21 July 1851, HH 160; *LTH*, 1:118n; Desmond and Moore, *Darwin*, 226, 292, 396; Owen's paper: E. Sabine to TH, 30 Oct. 1853, HP 26.6; Desmond, *Archetypes*, 28. £120 pay per annum: HH 145.
8. TH to HAH, 31 Mar. 1851, HH 143; *LTH*, 1:95, 116; Forbes, *Literary Papers*, 119; Mills, 'View', 372–85; Wilson and Geikie, *Memoir*, 480. On C. *Huxleyi*: Forbes, 'On the Mollusca', 385.
9. TH to HAH, 16 Nov. 1850, HH 130; *CE*, 1:14; *Diary*, 354; 'Willm Huxley': LS Minutes, 21 Nov. 1848; HP 34.1.
10. TH to HAH, 16 Nov. 1850, HH 130; 15 June 1851, HH 153 on Murchison; *LTH*, 1:62–3; Secord, 'King'; 'Sang froid', 'Pompeii': Secord, *Controversy*, 43ff, 118–23; Stafford, *Scientist*, 7; Secord, 'Geological Survey', 233; 'dingy': Geikie, *Memoir*, 30.
11. TH to HAH, 16 Nov. 1850, HH 130; MacLeod, 'Royal Society', 325ff; Geikie, *Life*, 1:118–19; Geikie, *Memoir*, 197; Lyell, *Manual*, vi–viii; Bowler,

Fossils, 75; R. Porter, 'Gentlemen', 824. Lyell's fears: Desmond, *Politics*, 327–31; Desmond, 'Artisan Resistance', 108–9; Bartholomew, 'Lyell', 263–9; Bartholomew, 'Non-Progress'; Bartholomew, 'Huxley's Defence', 527–8; Lyell, *Principles*, 2:20–1. Lyell's palaeontology: Rudwick, *Meaning*, 181ff; Gould, *Time's Arrow*, 137ff. As President of the Geological Society, Lyell was preparing his final address on the subject of fossil stasis (Lyell, 'Anniversary Address').

12. *LTH*, 1:60–1; TH to HAH, 16 Nov. 1850, HH 129.

13. TH to HAH, 16 Nov. 1850, HH 129; n.d. [pre-30 Jan. 1851], HH 137; HP 31.115 for his zoo season ticket. Thylacines and hippopotamus: *Reports of the Council and Auditors of the Zoological Society of London, Read at the Annual General Meeting, April 29th 1851* (London, Taylor, 1851), 14–15.

14. *LTH*, 1:61–3; G. M. Young, *Portrait*, 7; TH to HAH, 28 Nov. 1850, HH 131; 16 Nov. 1850, HH 130.

15. Rupke, *Owen*, 21; Desmond, *Archetypes*, 40; W. S. Macleay to R. Owen, 28 Apr. 1850, BM(NH) OC 18.331; G. M. Young, *Portrait*, 76–7.

16. *LTH*, 1:59–62; TH to Admiralty, 20 Nov. 1850, HP 30.1. On Bell: MacLeod, 'Whigs', 77; Desmond, *Politics*, 393–4.

17. J. Parker to R. Owen, 29 Nov. 1850, BM(NH) OC 21.135; *Diary*, 353; *LTH*, 1:60; Huxley's official notification came on 3 Dec. 1850, HP 32.1.

18. TH to HAH, 2 Dec. 1850, HH 132; *Lancet*, 1 (1840–1), 869; 2 (1840–1), 876, 878.

19. *Diary*, 353; TH to HAH, 24 Dec. 1850, HH 133–4; 2 Dec. 1850, HH 132. Geikie, *Memoir*, 145; Huxley, 'Tyndall', 6. G. M. Young, *Portrait*, 13 on sermonizing. TH to J. Goodsir, 20 Jan. '1850' [1851], HP 17.72.

20. TH to HAH, 16 Dec. 1850, HH 133; 'Sisyphus': 28 June 1851, HH 155; *LTH*, 1:63.

21. *LTH*, 1:64; TH to HAH, 1 Feb. 1851, HH 135; 16 Dec. 1850, HH 133. This fight or succumb theme occurs in Thackeray's *Pendennis*, 306.

22. HAH to TH, 17–27 July 1850, HH 113–14; 5 Sept., HH 116; TH to HAH, 2 Jan. 1851, HH 134. Keynes, *Darwin's 'Beagle' Diary*, 403–8; Darwin, *Journal*, 527–8; Nicholas and Nicholas, *Darwin*, 63–4.

23. TH to HAH, 30 Apr. 1852, HH 200–1; Jane Eyre: n.d., HH 137 (also HH 184); 'cares': 1 Feb. 1851, HH 135.

24. *Diary*, 355–6; TH to HAH, 24 Dec. 1850, HH 134; 1 Feb. 1851, HH 135; Mrs Charles Stanley to TH, 12 Feb. 1851, HP 26.253.

25. TH to HAH, 1 Feb. 1851, HH 136; 7 Sept. 1851, HH 163–4. Tillotson and Hawes, *Thackeray*, 14, 46–7, 90, 107–8; Sutherland, *Thackeray*, 46; Hardy, *Exposure*, 12. *Pendennis* was dedicated to Chandler's friend John Elliotson.

26. Bibby, *Huxley*, 184; *LTH*, 2:423; Goodrich, 'Lankester', x; English, *Victorian Values*, chaps 1–5; 'my sort': TH to HAH, 7 Sept. 1851, HH 163; 'blades': Thackeray, *Pendennis*, 225.

27. TH to HAH, 7, 23 Sept. 1851, HH 163–5; 'fair': 15 Mar. 1854, HH 266; Jensen, *Huxley*, 39. Busk translated Steenstrup's *Alternation of Generations* in 1845. Busk, 'Account', 388, on *P. Huxleyi*. Thackeray, *Pendennis*, 106–7.

28. TH to HAH, 23 Sept. 1851, HH 165; Thackeray, *Pendennis*, 646–9; Murphy, 'Ethical Revolt', 800–11; on Holyoake, Desmond, 'Artisan Resistance', 107–8. For newer socially based approaches to the Victorian crisis of faith, see Moore's 'Crisis', 59–68; 'Freethought', 279–89; and 'Theodicy'.

29. TH to HAH, n.d. HH 138; *LTH*, 1:66–7; MacLeod, 'Whigs', 72–4; Crosland, 'Explicit', 181–2.

30. TH to HAH, 14, 23 Mar. 1851, HH 140–1; *LTH*, 1:66; Geison, *Foster*, chap. 2, on the parlous state of experimental physiology in the 1850s and the lack of paid openings.

31. TH to HAH, 31 Mar. 1851, HH 142; *SM*, 1:38; Geikie, *Memoir*, 145; 'farmer': TH to HAH, 15 June 1851, HH 153.

32. TH to HAH, 14 Apr. 1851, HH 144; 1 Mar. 1851, HH 139; *LTH*, 1:65; 'splashed': Dickens, *Bleak House*, 49.

33. *Diary*, 356–7 (Thomson's reply, HP 27.328); TH to HAH, 15 Apr., 6 June 1851, HH 144, 152; *LTH*, 1:67, 96. Museum: Geikie, *Memoir*, 184–5; Wilson and Geikie, *Memoir*, 447–9, 452, 469–70, 485–7; Flett, *First Hundred Years*, 65; Secord, 'Geological Survey', 227, 257–8; R. Porter, 'Gentlemen', 833. Huxley was elected FRS with the physicists G. G. Stokes and William Thomson, chemist A. W. Hofmann, and Admiral FitzRoy: Hall, 'Royal Society', 155.

34. TH to HAH, 22 Apr., 4 May 1851, HH 145–7.

35. TH to HAH, 4 May 1851, HH 146; 'sick', 28 June 1851, HH 155; 'bullfinch', 31 Mar. 1851, HH 142; *LTH*, 1:67–9.

36. TH to ES, 20 May 1851, AD; 'I said': TH to HAH, 4 May 1851, HH 146; 'utter': 28 June 1851, HH 155; *LTH*, 1:67–9, 95.

37. TH to HAH, 4 May 1851, HH 146; *LTH*, 1:67–9; Grant's pay: Desmond, *Politics*, 392 n.59 (358, on Owen's total income of £700); Desmond, 'Grant's Later Views', 396; Council Minutes, vol. C, f.135 (1839): King's College London Archives; Dickens, *Sketches*, 313; Beddoe, *Memories*, 32–3; Harrison, *Early Victorian Britain*, 131–2; Best, *Mid-Victorian Britain*, 107–9; G. K. Clark, *Making*, 119; *LLL*, 1:161.

38. TH to HAH, 23 Sept. 1851, HH 165–6; *Diary*, 356, 358. The family even took his imbecile father to see it (HP 31.62). Harrison, *Early Victorian Britain*, 173; Briggs, *Victorian Things*, 34; D. Thomson, *England*, 99.

39. TH to HAH, 15, 28 June 1851, HH 153–5; *SM*, 1:104–20; *CCD*, 5:49.

40. TH to HAH, 8 June 1851, HH 152; *Diary*, 358; *LTH*, 1:72. Huxley's request for funding, 26 May: HP 30.2. MacLeod, 'Royal Society', 328–9.

41. *Diary*, 357, 359; Ralph, 'MacGillivray', 191.

42. J. Richardson to TH, 24 June 1851, HP 25.70; TH to HAH, 8 June 1851, HH 152; 28 June 1851, HH 155; Thackeray, *Pendennis*, 648; *Diary*, 358; *LTH*, 1:87n.

43. Barton, 'Tyndall', 124–8; *LJT*, 1–2, 6–7, 17, 21–34; Huxley, 'Tyndall'; Turner, 'Victorian Conflict', 363; 'I know': TH to HAH, 12 July 1851, HH 156–7; *LTH*, 1:88–90; *SM*, 1:98.

44. TH to HAH, 12 July 1851, HH 156–7; 31 Mar. 1851, HH 143; *LTH*, 1:88–90. *LJH*, 1:62, 66–71, 122–3, 167, 219, 223, 312; Hooker, *Himalayan Journals*, 2:206. Dayman had been a mate on Hooker's *Erebus* voyage. The *Erebus* and its sister ship the *Terror* were subsequently lost during Franklin's expedition in search of the North-West Passage. At Greenwich Dayman was to show Huxley over 'the Search Ship that went out after poor Sir John Franklin and his comrades': TH to HAH, 16 Oct. 1851, HH 169.

45. TH to HAH, 12 July 1851, HH 156–7; 'An account of researches into the Anatomy of the Hydrostatic Acephalae', HP 37 ff.13, 35; *SM*, 1:98–101;

Winsor, *Starfish*, 77–9, 93–7; *LTH*, 1:89; *LJH*, 1:347–50, also 39–40, 161, 170.

46. TH to HAH, 16 July 1851, HH 158; *LTH*, 1:90–1; E. Sabine to TH, 14 July 1851, HP 26.1.

47. TH to HAH, 12 Oct. 1851, HH 168; 31 July 1851, HH 160; 'happier', '350£': 21 July 1851, HH 159. Sharpey (HP 26.64) warned him that 'local interest' would win out. *LJT*, 35. Morris, *Heaven's Command*, 202. Writing to the Bursar of Toronto University (18 Aug. 1851, HP 28.27) Huxley scratched out 'R.N.' and put 'F.R.S.' after his name. That tailpiece, as he had promised, was talking for him. It was a symbolic switch, and diplomatic, since an officer could not apply for a job! (HP 26.254). Bell (18 Aug. 1851, HP 10.274) even had the printer rush his new Royal Society paper so that he could send out the sheets.

48. TH to HAH, 23 Sept. 1851, HH 165–6. He continued: 'They say "how shocking, how miserable to do without this or that belief!" Surely this is little better than cowardice ... The intellectual perception of truth and acting up to it, is so far as I know the only meaning of the phrase "one sees with God". So long as we attain that end does it matter much whether our small selves are happy or miserable?' 'Missionariness': G. M. Young, *Portrait*, 2–3; Jensen, *Huxley*, 39–41; 'In fact': TH to HAH, 1 Feb. 1852, HH 185; *Diary*, 359; *Hydra* and *Spongilla*, HP 63.16–28.

49. TH to HAH, 12 Oct. 1851, HH 168; 16 Oct. 1851, HH 169; *LTH*, 1:78. The testimonials are printed in HP 31.68.

50. TH to HAH, 12, 16 Oct. 1851, HH 168–9. TH to the Bursar, Toronto University, 17 Oct. 1851, HP 28.31. C. Stanley to TH, n.d., HP 26.250; TH to Mrs Charles Stanley, 15 Oct. 1851, HP 26.254; Lord Stanley to the Earl of Elgin, n.d., HP 26.256; TH to Elgin, 6 Nov. 1851, HP 30.47. *Diary*, 361.

51. W. Fanning to TH, 23 Oct. [1851], HP 16.5; 'Old': TH to HAH, 16 Oct. 1851, HH 170; Marshall, *Darwin*, 117–20.

52. HAH to TH, 22, 31 May, 2, 9 June 1851, HH 148–51; 'pick': TH to HAH, 7 Sept. 1851, HH 164; Schiller: TH to HAH, 26 Oct. 1851, HH 171. Hughes, *Fatal Shore*, 561–2.

53. TH to HAH, 12 Oct., 7 Nov. 1851, HH 167, 172.

54. *SM*, 1:140–4; 'Arrangement of the Radiata', HP 37.43; G. Allman to TH, 28 Sept. 1851, HP 10.46; Winsor, *Starfish*, 102–17.

55. TH to HAH, 7 Nov. 1851, HH 172–3; *LTH*, 1:69–70; TH to W. S. Macleay, 9 Nov. 1851, HP 30.3; *LTH*, 1:91; MacLeod, 'Of Medals', 83.

56. TH to W. S. MacLeay, 9 Nov. 1851, HP 30.3; *LTH*, 1:91.

10   THE SEASON OF DESPAIR

1. TH to HAH, 29 Nov., 25, 31 Dec. 1851, HH 175–7. 'Brother': P. McGill to TH, 10 Dec. 1851, HP 22.129; TH to W. S. Macleay, 9 Nov. 1851, HP 30.3; *LTH*, 1:91, 100.

2. TH to HAH, 7 Nov., 11 Dec. 1851, HH 173, 176; Thackeray, *Pendennis*, 45.

3. CCD, 1:481–92, 2:345, 5:74; Keynes, *Darwin's 'Beagle' Diary*, 395–403; Desmond and Moore, *Darwin*, 124, 176–8; Nicholas and Nicholas, *Darwin*, 20–1, 45–54; Burstyn, 'If Darwin', 62–9; 'key': Gallenga, 'Age', 3. On

Tyndall: JT to TH, 2 Dec. 1851, HP 1.1; TH to JT, 4 Dec. 1851, HP 9.1; *LTH*, 1:79.

4. TH to HAH, 1, 6 Jan. 1852, HH 178, 181; 'purpose': TH to ES, 9 May 1852, HP 31.20; *LTH*, 1:80–2, 100; *Diary*, 360. For details of the *Narrative* copy inscribed 'H. A. Heathorn from T. H. Huxley 1852 & bound for her 1894' I am indebted to Mr William Collier.

5   TH to HAH, 1, 10 Feb. 1852, HH 185–6; 'that': 6 Jan. 1852, HH 181.

6. TH to HH, 15 Mar. 1852, HH 191; *SM*, 1:153, 173, 176–7; TH to W. Macleay, 9 Nov. 1851, HP 30.3; *LTH*, 1:91; Paradis, *Huxley*, 4ff. The Unitarian Joseph Maclise made the archetype a 'mathematical axiom': Desmond, *Politics*, 368; and the positivist G. H. Lewes ('Goethe', 498–9; Desmond, *Archetypes*, 49) derided its Platonic reality. For a rival idealized conception see Broderip and Owen, 'Generalizations'.

7. TH to HAH, 1, 27 Feb. 1852, HH 185, 189; n.d., HH 138; Berman, *Social Change*, chap. 4; G. Staunton to TH, 5 Feb. 1852, HP 26.274.

8. TH to HAH, 27 Feb. 1852, HH 189; TH to W. S. Macleay, 9 Nov. 1851, HP 30.3; *LTH*, 1:93–4; Owen, 'Metamorphosis', 12–16; Flower, 'Owen', xiii.

9. *SM*, 1:190–2; Huxley, *West. Rev.*, 63 (1855), 242–3; Ospovat, 'Darwin'.

10. TH to HAH, 15 Mar. 1852, HH 191. This letter was bowdlerized in *LTH*, 1:97–8; Desmond, 'Darwin, Huxley', 595. The Ehrenberg paragraphs were shorn, leaving the impression of gratuitous aggression on Owen's part (so successfully that Bibby, *Huxley*, 25, believed that an 'increasingly jealous Owen' *had* 'tried to prevent publication'!). The missing paragraphs are proof that Owen's heels were being nipped by the bulldog pup, as revisionist historians had suspected: Ruse, *Darwinian Revolution*, 142–4; Desmond, *Archetypes*, 21, 28–9. On Ehrenberg: Winsor, *Starfish*, chap. 2.

    Huxley (taking his cue from Siebold) attacked Ehrenberg in *SM*, 1:89; 'man's': *West. Rev.* 63 (1855), 558–60; and 'Lectures', *Medical Times and Gazette*, 12 (1856), 507, where he broke up Ehrenberg's Polygastria, removing the algae and combining the amoeba-like forms with the Foraminifera, sponges and Gregarinidae in the new sub-kingdom 'Protozoa'.

    On the Anglican and Coleridgean view of nature, law and society: Jacyna, 'Immanence', 325–6; Desmond, *Politics*, 114–15, 254–74, 358–72. Ibid, 331–2, and *LRO*, 1:167, 321 on the Honourable Artillery Company.

11. R. Owen to TH, 15 Mar. 1853, HP 26.6. Forbes and Bell refereed the paper.

12. TH to HAH, 15 Mar. 1852, HH 192; 'nursery': 16 Apr. 1852, HH 195–6; TH to ES, 17 Apr. 1852, HP 31.17; *SM*, 1:197; Wallace, *My Life*, 1:323.

13. TH to the Duke of Northumberland, 28 Mar. 1852, HP 30.10; TH to G. Airy, [Mar. 1852], HP 30.9; Admiralty to TH, 24 Apr. 1842, HP 30.12; *LTH*, 1:72, 100.

14. TH to HAH, 5, 16 Apr. 1852, HH 195–6, 218; *LTH*, 1:81.

15. TH to ES, 17 Apr. 1852, HP 31.17; 'hideous', 'She': TH to HAH, 16 Apr. 1852, HH 195–6; J. Barlow to TH, 24 Apr. 1852, HP 10.229; B. Vincent to TH, 24 Apr. 1852, HP 28.73.

16. 'Animal Individuality' draft, HP 38.10–13, 15; *SM*, 1:146; Jensen, *Huxley*, 56; 'heart', 'whole', 'break': TH to ES, 3 May 1852, HP 31.17; *LTH*, 1:98–100; 'ever': TH to HAH, 30 Apr.1852, HH 200; Flower, 'Reminiscences', 285.

17. TH to HAH, 30 Apr., 23 May 1852, HH 200, 206; 'triumphantly': G. Allman to TH, 30 May 1852, HP 10.63.

18. Carpenter, *Remarks*, 2–3; Carpenter, 'Dubois', 203; Desmond, *Politics*, 210–22; WBC to TH, HP 12.61–6; referee: TH to T. Williams, 7 July 1852, HP 29.45; TH to T. Bell, n.d., HP 30.9; 'my': TH to HAH, 13 June 1852, HH 209.

19. TH to HAH, 23 May, 13, 24 June, 5, 11 July, 5 Aug. 1852, HH 206, 209–10, 215–18; *LTH*, 1:81; also on the grant: HP 30.12–16.

20. His archetype was based on the sedentary adults. He was now dismissing his tadpole-like larval 'Appendicularia as an aberrant form': 'Sketch of a Classification of the Ascidians', HP 34.168; HP 35; *SM*, 1:194; 'fresh': TH to HAH, 28 Aug. 1852, HH 221. He earned his keep by reporting the 1852 BAAS meeting for the *Literary Gazette*.

21. HAH to TH, 11 May 1852, HH 203; 'deep', Owen: TH to HAH, 28 Aug., 16 Sept. 1852, HH 222–3; T. Chandler to TH, 12 Sept. 1852, HP 12.166.

22. *LTH*, 1:83; C. Aldis to TH, 8 Sept. 1852, HP 10.33; J. Bishop to TH, 6 Sept. 1852, HP 11.3; Cope, 'Private Medical Schools', 105–6; Clarke, *Autobiographical Recollections*, 128–32; 'boiling': TH to HAH, 30 Oct. 1852, HH 229. On Dermott's school, which changed its name to the 'Hunterian' after he died: Desmond, *Politics*, 166ff.

23. TH to HAH, 30 Oct. 1852, HH 229–30. HP 10.212, 16.168, 23.245, 24.107, 27.281; *LTH*, 1:79, 107.

24. *LTH*, 1:101, 105; C. R. Weld to TH, 7 Nov. 1852, HP 28.230; 'scientific knighthood': Desmond, *Politics*, 232; MacLeod, 'Of Medals', 83, 92. Floods and Forbes's Ark: R. Austen to E. Forbes, 29 Nov. 1852, HP 10.179.

25. R. Austen to E. Forbes, 22 Nov. 1852, HP 10.177; *LTH*, 1:102–3; Briggs, *Victorian People*, 9–10, 62.

26. Draft of Huxley's reply, HP 31.139; E. Forbes to TH, 16 Nov. 1852, HP 16.170; *LTH*, 1:103, 105.

27. E. Forbes to TH, 2 Dec. 1852, HP 16.174; 'I was': TH to E. Forbes, 27 Nov. 1852, HP 16.172; TH to R. Owen, 17 Nov. 1852, HP 23.247; 'How': L. Horner to E. Forbes, 17 Nov. 1852, HP 18.224, referring to Owen's miserable *Literary Gazette* obituary of Gideon Mantell. Owen's callousness cost him the chair of the Geological Society: W. Hopkins to E. Forbes: 4 Dec. 1852, HP 18.224; Desmond, *Archetypes*, 26–7, 208 n13; Benton, 'Progressionism'.

28. G. Busk to TH, 16, 22 Nov. 1852, HP 11.210–12; TH to HAH, 20 Dec. 1852, HH 238; A. Kölliker to TH, 31 Dec. 1852, HP 19.276, reply, 278. Huxley tried to interest Longman in a translation of Karl Theodor Siebold's book – presumably his and Friedrich Stannius's *Lehrbuch der Vergleichenden Anatomie* – on which see Huxley, *West. Rev.*, 61 (1854), 583; W. Longman to TH, 8 Mar. 1852, HP 22.9.

29. TH to HAH, 10 Feb. 1852, HH 186; Angela Darwin, pers. comm.; *LTH*, 1:106.

30. HS to TH, 25 Sept. 1852, HP 7.94; *LHS*, 64–5; Spencer, *Autobiography*, 1:368, 402, 2:24; Desmond, *Archetypes*, 97–9; Kennedy, *Spencer*, chap. 6.

31. *LHS*, 65, also 35, 41, 45, 49, 56, 61; Irvine, *Apes*, 10; Spencer, *Autobiography*, 1:201, 218–21, 227–8, 237, 246; Spencer, 'Theory'. On phrenology's use to the outsiders: Shapin, 'Phrenological Knowledge'.

32. Peel, *Spencer*, 97, 132; Wiltshire, *Social*, 66; R. M. Young, 'Development';

Desmond, *Archetypes* 96–8; Desmond and Moore, *Darwin*, 393; C. U. M. Smith, 'Evolution', 59–60; R. J. Richards, *Darwin*, 246ff.

33. Haight, *Eliot and Chapman*, 3–4, 14–23 and *passim*; Poynter, 'Chapman', 4–5, 18–19; Spencer, *Autobiography*, 1:347, 386–8, 394–5, 2:33; *LHS*, 40, 60, 65; Desmond and Moore, *Darwin*, 379.

34. TH to HAH, 9 Jan. 1854, HH 261; J. Chapman to TH, 12 Aug., 23, 26 Oct. 1853, HP 12.168–70; TH to Chapman, n.d., HP 12.169; Van Arsdel, 'Westminster Review', 547; Poynter, 'Chapman', 6–8; Spencer, *Autobiography*, 1:226, 372; Moore, *Religion*, 432; Huxley, 'Science at Sea', 99, 107, 112, 119.

35. J. Chapman to R. Owen, 13 Jan. 1848, BM(NH) OC 7.26; *LRO*, 1:390; 'I say': Huxley (quoting Lewes) in *West. Rev.*, 61 (1854), 257; Haight, *Eliot and Chapman*, 68; Haight, *Eliot Letters*, 2:89, 8:89; Desmond, *Archetypes*, 29–32; Spencer, *Autobiography*, 1:347–8, 377–8; Poynter, 'Chapman', 5; Ashton, *Lewes*, 4, 72; Bell, 'Lewes', 277.

36. Ashton, *German Idea*, 94–101, 126; Gregory, *Scientific Materialism*, 2, 29ff; Lenoir, *Strategy*, 197ff; Broderip and Owen, 'Generalizations', 80–1; 'greatest': Lewes, 'Goethe', 481, 498–9; Bell, 'Lewes', 288–94; Wilson, *Lyell's Journals*, 54–60; 'We find': Burrow, *Evolution*, 106; 'speculation': Huxley, *West. Rev.*, 61 (1854), 255–6; zoo: HS to TH, n.d., HP 7.96; *LHS*, 63; Ashton, *Lewes*, 96; Spencer, *Autobiography*, 1:348, 377, 403; '*paradox*': Haight, *Eliot Letters*, 8:89–90.

37. *CCD*, 5:130–1, 133–5; Desmond, *Archetypes*, 49–50.

38. TH to HAH, 20 Dec. 1852, HH 236; the King's chair: HP 11.215, HP 24.5, HP 16.178, HP 12.67–71, HP 23.126, HP 21.175, *LTH*, 1:79, 84, 107.

39. JT to TH, 22 Feb., 5 Mar., 11 Nov. 1853, HP 1.4, 6, 8; 'looking';: TH to JT, 25 Feb. 1853, HP 9.5; *LJT*, 38–41, 45–9; *LTH*, 1:79–80, 114–15.

40. Irvine, *Apes*, 32; MacLeod, 'Visiting', 2–3, 8–9; *LTH*, 1:84.

41. TH to JT, 25 Feb. 1853, HP 9.5; 'difference': Huxley, *West. Rev.*, 62 (1854), 255; Cardwell, *Organization*, 80–1, 87–9; Bibby, *Huxley*, 124; Secord, 'Geological Survey', 255.

42. TH to ES, 22 Apr. 1853, HP 31.21; *LTH*, 1:106–7; Hardy, *Exposure*, 69–70; Thackeray, *Pendennis*, 335; 'jackal', 'red': Huxley, *West. Rev.*, 61 (1854), 260–1; *LTH*, 1:85, 104.

43. Haight, *Eliot Letters*, 8:51; Paxton, *Eliot*, 19; Spencer, 'Progress', 448–9; Spencer, *Autobiography*, 1:377, 384; *LHS*, 61; C. U. M Smith, 'Evolution', 58; Desmond, *Archetypes*, 97; Ospovat, 'Influence'; Ospovat, *Development*, chap. 6; di Gregorio, *Huxley*, 28; Gould, *Ontogeny*, 109–14; E. Richards, 'Question', 134ff; R. Richards, *Meaning*, chap. 5.

44. Broderip and Owen, 'Generalisations', 50, 56; Owen, 'Lyell', 449; Ospovat, 'Influence', 10, 17–24; Ospovat, *Development*, 117–40; Desmond, *Archetypes*, 44.

45. Huxley, *West. Rev.*, 61 (1854), 581, 585, 593; 'aberrant': 62 (1854), 247; Geikie, *Life*, 1:119.

46. HAH to TH, 10 Sept. 1853, HH 250; 'honour': TH to ES, 22 Apr. 1853, HP 31.21; *LTH*, 1:73–4, 106–7.

47. Ashton, *Lewes*, 143–7; '*purely*': Haight, *Eliot Letters*, 2:132–3; 'Witch': Huxley, *West. Rev.* 61 (1854), 255–6, 266, 268; Barrow, *Independent Spirits*, chaps 1–2.

48. Huxley, 'Vestiges', 425–33, 438–9; Secord, 'Behind the Veil'; Bartholomew, 'Huxley's Defence', 526–8. Huxley listed *Vestiges'* howlers in HP 41.57–63.
49. *LTH*, 1:85–6; TH to HAH, 1 Jan. 1854, HH 259.

11 THE JIHAD BEGINS

1. TH to HAH, 3 Sept. 1854, HH 286; 'Cape Horn': *LTH*, 1:117.
2. Sheets-Pyenson, 'Horse Race', 464; 'baked': Geikie, *Memoir*, 165; 'monster', '£100': TH to HAH, 9 Jan. 1854, HH 260–1; 30 Apr. 1854, HH 275; *LTH*, 1:86; Godlee, 'Wharton Jones', 102.
3. TH to HAH, 9 Jan. 1854, HH 260–1; Huxley, *West. Rev.*, 61 (1854), 264.
4. Huxley, *West. Rev.*, 63 (1855), 562; TH to HAH, 9 Jan. 1854, HH 260.
5. TH to HAH, 16 Feb. 1854, HH 262–3; Seaman, *Victorian England*, 101, 127–9.
6. TH to HAH, 8 Apr. 1854, HH 271; 15 Mar. 1854, HH 267; J. Chapman to TH, 5 Mar. 1854, HP 12.171; Huxley, 'Schamyl', 491–2, 496, 500–17; Moore, *Post-Darwinian Controversies*, 19–100, on the 'warfare' with theology; Briggs, *Victorian People*, 62–4; 'Young England': TH to JH, 5 Sept. 1858, HP 2.35; *LTH*, 1:160 – this was a play on Disraeli's exercise in popular Toryism, the 'Young England' movement, designed to bolster the Church and Crown, for which Huxley would substitute Science and State.
7. TH to HAH, 15 Mar., 8 Apr., 12 Oct. 1854, HH 267, 270, 288.
8. *LTH*, 1:117; Admiralty: HP 30.18–27; TH to HAH, 8 Apr. 1854, HH 270.
9. TH to HAH, 8 Apr. 1854, HH 271; brachiopods: *SM*, 2:325; HM Box B:8.2–17; A. Hancock to TH, 23 Apr., 11 May 1854, HP 17.271–3.
10. TH to HAH, 15 Mar., 30 Apr., 4 May 1854, HH 266, 275–6; HAH to TH, 30 Dec. 1853, HH 258; Harrison, *Early Victorian Britain*, 139–40, 170; Davidoff and Hall, *Family Fortunes*, 222 passim.
11. TH to HAH, 30 Apr., 4 May 1854, HH 275–6; *SM*, 1:281; *LTH*, 1:138–9.
12. TH to HAH, 3 June 1854, HH 277; *LTH*, 1:108; E. Forbes to TH, 2 July 1854, HP 16.181.
13. TH to HAH, 3 June 1854, HH 277–8; Bibby, *Huxley*, 124; Hays, 'Science', 148, 151, 160; *Historical Account of the London Institution*; 'Lecturing': JT to TH, 31 May 1854, HP 1.11.
14. *CE*, 3:60, 62; Paradis, *Huxley*, 24–5; TH to FD, 10 Oct. 1854, HP 15.38; *LTH*, 1:113.
15. TH to HAH, 30 July 1854, HH 280; *LTH*, 1:109; E. Cardwell to TH, 20 July 1854, HM 3:121:38; TH to RIM, 17 May 1862, HP 30.63; GSM 1/7.141–2. John Morris was the University College professor, a good field palaeontologist well known for his *Catalogue of British Fossils*. On his decision: JH to TH, 1 Aug. 1854, HP 3.3; E. Forbes to TH, 31 July 1854, 16.183. Secord, *Controversy*, 271–2; Secord, 'Salter', 63, 65–6, 72; Secord, 'Geological Survey', 233, 243–50; 'simply': J. B. Jukes to TH, 1 June 1862, HP 19.110.

    Huxley's autobiography has been misunderstood. He recalled that Sir Henry

    offered me the post vacated of Paleontologist and Lecturer on Natural History. I refused the former point blank, and accepted the latter only provisionally, telling Sir Henry that I did not care for fossils, and that I should give up Natural History as soon as I could get a physiological post. (*CE*, 1:15)

This has been taken to mean that he wanted nothing to do with palaeontology. But he did want the palaeontological *lectureship*, and only turned down the museum job.

As for giving it up for a physiology post, the letters show only enthusiasm for his new job. He quickly saw the post as permanent, so much so that when Forbes tried to lure him to Edinburgh two months later 'to take part of the duties of the Professor of Physiology there who is in bad health, with the ultimate aim of succeeding to the chair', he turned it down, telling Nettie that he was fixed in 'London [and] I hope to remain there for my life long in *our* house': TH to HAH, 12 Oct. 1854, HH 287.

16. Cardwell, *Organisation*, 81–5; G. K. Clark, *Making*, 43–4; Briggs, *Victorian People*, 71–2, 85–7; G. M. Young, *Portrait*, 81; Turner, 'Victorian Conflict', 363ff; Stafford, *Scientist*, 18; 'imbecility': Huxley, *West. Rev.*, 63 (1855), 563.

17. TH to HAH, 30 July, 3 Sept., 1854, HH 280, 285; St Thomas': R. G. Whitfield to TH, 22 Aug. 1854, HM 3:121:114; Marlborough House: H. Cole to TH, 21 Sept. 1854, HP 12.265; *LTH*, 1:117–18. Earnings generally: Best, *Mid-Victorian Britain*, 110; Harrison, *Early Victorian Britain*, 131, 136.

18. TH to FD, 10 Oct. 1854, 5 Jan. 1855, HP 15.38, 46; TH to HAH, 30 July, 3 Sept. 1854, HH 280, 285; *LTH*, 1:109, 113. A. Hancock to TH, 8 Sept. 1854, HP 17.275, on his nudibranchs; HP 35 for the ascidians; Huxley, 'Report on Tenby Bay', n.d., HP 43.149. Secord, 'Geological Survey', 237–8; English, *Victorian Values*, 67–70. Tenby was no fortuitous choice. It had been De la Beche's headquarters when surveying Wales, and his director, Andrew Ramsay, had started as an assistant there: Geikie, *Memoir*, 28, 31–3.

19. TH to FD, 10 Oct. 1854, n.d., 5 Jan., 6 May 1855, HP 15.38, 42, 46, 62; *SM*, 1:337; *LTH*, 1:113, 121–2. HAH's Reminiscences: HP 78.81–3; Raven, *Christian Socialism*, 126, 159, 376.

20. Huxley, *West. Rev.*, 62, (1854), 574; 'Lower': 64 (1855), 568; Secord, *Controversy*. Other worlds: 61 (1854), 593–4; 62 (1854), 242–6; Brooke, 'Natural Theology and Plurality'.

21. Huxley, *West. Rev.*, 62, (1854), 575–6; Bartholomew, 'Huxley's Defence'; Desmond, *Archetypes*, chap. 3.

22. Huxley, *West. Rev.*, 62 (1854), 249, 253, reviewing J. C. Nott and G. R. Gliddon's *Types of Mankind*; Lorimer, *Colour*, 51, 72, 82–6, 123.

23. TH to JT, 17, 22 Oct. 1854, HP 9.12, 15: *LTH*, 1:85n, 120–1; Van Arsdel, 'Westminster Review', 458–9; Haight, *Eliot and Chapman*, 75–9.

24. TH to JH, 6 Nov. 1854, HP 2.7; JH to TH, 7 Nov. 1854, HP 3.13; *LTH*, 1:110–11; *LJH*, 1:416; *LJT*, 45–9.

25. TH to JH, 19 Nov. 1854, HP 2.1; subscription: HP 40.265; TH to FD, n.d., 24 Nov. 1854, HP 15.40–2; 'His': TH to JH, 24 Nov. 1854, HP 2.4; *LTH*, 1:116–17; E. Forbes to TH, 2 July, 8 Nov. 1854, HP 16.181, 192.

26. TH to FD, 5 Jan., 13 Feb., 1855, HP 15.46, 50; *LTH*, 1:117, 119, 122; TH to JH, 24 Nov. 1854, HP 2.4; Sheets-Pyenson, 'Horse Race', 465, 468.

27. TH to FD, 13 Feb. 1855, HP 15.50; *LTH*, 1:119, also 109, 123–4; Geikie, *Memoir*, 224. TH's Report to the Director of the Geological Survey, 3 Nov. 1854, HP 44.1. Geological justification: TH to RIM, [April–June 1855], HP 23.143; GSM 1/7.159–63. Edinburgh fell to his friend George Allman (G. Allman to TH, 20 May 1855, HP 10.71). And Huxley was right in his fears, Allman all but gave up original work: 19 Dec. 1855, HP 10.76.

28. TH to FD, 1 Apr. 1855, HP 15.56; *LTH*, 1:124. He tried unsuccessfully to marshal local helpers: A. Hancock to TH, 7 Apr. 1855, HP 17.280.

29. TH to HAH, 22 Nov. 1851, HH 174; HAH to TH, 3, 5, 18 Nov. 1854, HH 289–90; HAH's Reminiscences, HP 31.84; Mayhew, *London Labour*, 347.

30. Huxley, 'Lectures', *Medical Times and Gazette*, 12 (1856), 431–2, 483–4, 563; Winsor, *Starfish*, 117–19; di Gregorio, *Huxley*, 14. George Allman coined the terms 'ectoderm' and 'endoderm' for Huxley's two layers in 1853.

31. TH to JT, 13 Feb. 1855, HP 9.20; Tyndall replied 'I breakfasted with Owen a few days ago and ventured at the time upon one or two of your "heretical" remarks' (14 Feb. 1855, HP 1.233). *London Institution. 1855. Syllabus of a Course of Six Lectures on The General Laws of Life … by Thomas H. Huxley*: HM 3:122.7 (8 Feb.–29 Mar. 1855). Hays, 'London', 100; Hays, 'Science', 151, 160.

32. TH to FD, 27 Feb. 1855, HP 15.54; Wilson and Geikie, *Memoir*, 497, 517; Geikie, *Memoir*, 196; Secord, 'Geological Survey', 230–1, 258.

33. LCK, 1:184, 201, 313–17; Backstrom, *Christian Socialism*, 37; Raven, *Christian Socialism*, 343–60; 'Nature's': Huxley, *West. Rev.*, 64 (1855), 240–55 (reviewing *Glaucus*); Allen, *Naturalist*, 125–37. On Dyster's role in connecting Huxley with the Christian Socialist leaders F. D. Maurice, Charles Kingsley and J. M. Ludlow see, TH to FD, 30 Nov. 1854, 6 May, 28 June 1855, 29 Feb. 1860, HP 15.42, 62, 66, 110. F. D. Maurice to TH, 19 Dec. 1854, HP 22.200; Hilton, *Age*, 271. Huxley himself gave lectures in Red Lion Square.

34. TH to FD, 6 May 1855, HP 15.62; *LTH*, 1:138; 'idolatrous': Huxley, *West. Rev.*, 63 (1855), 562; spirit-rappers: 64 (1855), 254–5; *CE*, 3:61.

35. 'Origin of Man', *The London Investigator* 1 (1854–5), 8ff; Desmond, 'Artisan Resistance'; Johnson, 'Really Useful Knowledge'; sacking: Cooper, *Immortality*, 76; Briggs, *Victorian People*, 36, 90; Seaman, *Victorian England*, 17; G. K. Clark, *Making*, 149–50.

36. Huxley, *West. Rev.*, 63 (1855), 250, reviewing Robert Latham's *Native Races of the Russian Empire*; 63 (1855), 563 on Sebastopol; E. Richards, 'Moral Anatomy', 391–6; 'confidence', 'working': TH to FD, 10 Oct. 1854, 27 Feb. 1855, HP 15.38, 15.54; *LTH*, 1:113; *CE*, 3:59.

37. He was too astute not to see that 'our knowledge is the knowledge of our time – that absolute truth is unattainable – that all our theories, however well founded, and however grand, are but myths, which enable us to grasp for awhile that fragment of the incomprehensible universe which has presented itself, – to float thereby on the surface of the great abyss until some larger fragment come within our reach and the old is deserted for the new': Huxley, *West. Rev.*, 63 (1855), 559; 'special': Backstrom, *Christian Socialism*, 29.

38. TH to FD, 27 Feb. 1855, HP 15.54; *LTH*, 1:87–8, 138; Shapin and Barnes,

'Science', 37, 39, 48, 52–4. Huxley's lectures, says Paradis, *Huxley*, 42, were old morality plays with new props.

39. TH to FD, 6 May 1855, HP 15.62; *LTH*, 1:126.

40. TH to JH, n.d., 7 June 1855, HP 2.10–12; *LTH*, 1:127–8; Angela Darwin, pers. comm.

41. JH to TH, n.d. [Oct. 1854], HP 3.5; n.d. [Oct. 1855], HP 3.18; Gage and Stearn, *Bicentenary History*, 49, 53; *LJH*, 1:352, 355; F. Hooker to TH, 11 May 1855, HP 3.30; '1000': JH to TH, n.d., HP 3.15; 11 May 1855, HP 3.30; TH to JH, n.d., HP 2.10.

42. TH to JH, 6 July 1855, HP, 2.14; *LTH*, 1:126, 128; 'intense': WBC to TH, 6 July 1855, HP 12.76; 'Oh': TH to FD, 28 June 1855, HP 15.66; 'May': JT to TH, 4 July 1855, HP 1.19; Fullerian chair, 3 July 1855, HP 32.2.

43. TH to FD, 9 Apr., 6 May 1855, HP 15.60–2; *LTH*, 1:125; Wilson and Geikie, *Memoir*, 444–6; Secord, 'Geological Survey', 237–8.

44. *CCD*, 5:213–14; 'blindness': Owen, *Lectures*, 493; di Gregorio, *Huxley*, 37–9. Owen had complained (W. Sharpey to R. Owen, 12 [?Feb.] 1855, BM(NH) OC 23.376) of Huxley's error concerning the brachiopod (lamp-shell) heart, which underrated his own work, forcing Huxley into a retraction (*SM*, 1:335); 'There': TH to HAH, 8 Feb. 1848, HH 7.

45. WBC to TH, 16 July 1855, HP 12.78; Ospovat, 'Influence'.

46. HAH's Reminiscences, HP 31.79–80; *LTH*, 1:128–9; Pevsner, *Buildings*, 326; Angela Darwin, pers. comm.

47. HAH's Reminiscences, HP 78.81–4; tapeworm *Tetrarhynchus*: HM 3:125:2; also *Chondracanthus* (fishlouse), HM Box C 39 and HM 3:125:7; *CCD*, 5:442; 'Darby', TH to JH, 16 Aug. 1855, HP 2.16; *LTH*, 1:130.

48. TH to JH, 16 Aug., 14 Dec. 1855, HP 2.16, 198; *LTH*, 1:129–30; Notes on dredging specimens, 6 Aug.–6 Nov. [1855], HM 3:125:1–12.

49. 'Determined the develop[t]. of the true ovaria in the peduncle & made out that the "true ovaria" of Darwin are not ovaria at all': Notes on dredging specimens, HM 3:125:1 (12–13 Aug. [1855]); Huxley, 'Lectures', *Medical Times and Gazette*, 17 (1857), 238–9; Richmond, 'Darwin's Study', 389, 398; Desmond and Moore, *Darwin*, 368–9, 408–9; *CCD*, 5:200, 262, 281. Huxley dropped Darwin a note about his findings: *CCD*, 5:441–2. Darwin's views were shortly undercut still more: *CCD*, 6:301–2 n10; Huxley, *Manual*, 257.

50. *CCD*, 5:351; *LJH*, 1:375; *SM*, 1:300. On Owen's and Darwin's science: Bowler, *Fossils*, chap. 5; Desmond, *Archetypes*, 69; Desmond, *Politics*, 360–72; Ospovat, *Development*, 137–9; R. Richards, *Meaning*, chap. 5.

12 THE NATURE OF THE BEAST

1. HAH's Reminiscences, HP 31.84–5, 95–6; HP 62.1–5; 'what', TH to ES, 27 Mar. 1858, HP 31.24; 'In this': TH to HAH, 26 Oct. 1851, HH 171; *SM*, 1:307–12. FGS, 9 Apr. 1856: admission form, Geological Society of London.

2. TH to HAH, 14 Apr., 22 Nov. 1851, 27 Feb. 1852, HH 144, 174, 189; 'Bloaters': JH to TH, 14 Dec. [1855], HP 2.198; *Diary*, 314–15; MacGillivray: TH to JH, 17 Nov. [1855], [19 Nov. 1855], HP 2.196, 110; J. Gray to TH, 17 Mar. 1856, HP 17.109; *LTH*, 1:232; Ralph, 'MacGillivray', 192, who states that Hooker's father put up the money.

3. Huxley, 'Owen & Rymer Jones', 26–7; WBC to J. Chapman, 1 Sept. 1855, HP 12.80. Huxley also slated Owen's protégé Thomas Rymer Jones, 20 years professor of comparative anatomy at King's College, London, for his failure to keep pace with research: Huxley, *West. Rev.*, 65 (1856), 261–5.

4. WBC to TH, 22 Oct. 1858, HP 12.94; Desmond, *Archetypes*, 38–40. *LTH*, 1:93; *LJH*, 1:520; 'unscientific': Huxley, 'Lectures', *Medical Times and Gazette*, 12 (1856), 432; Turner, 'Victorian Conflict'; Wiener, *English Culture*, 15–16 on the destructive cleavage of the middle class caused by professionalization.

5. TH to RIM, 15 Oct. 1855, HM 3:125:8; [c.April–June 1855], HP 23.143; *LTH*, 1:132–3; Geikie, *Life*, 1:190; Secord, 'Salter', 66; *CE*, 8:274.

6. Huxley, *West. Rev.*, 63 (1855), 243–5; 64 (1855), 571; CL to TH, 29 Aug. 1855, HP 6.9; *LLL*, 2:183, 185–6; R. Richards, *Meaning*, 116, 148.

7. Darwin, *Origin*, 329–33, 435–50; Darwin's notes on Huxley's review of Carpenter's *Principles of Comparative Physiology*, DAR Box B.C. 40f, CUL; Ospovat, 'Darwin'.

8. *CCD*, 3:2, 211, 5:201, 345, 372; *LJH*, 1:474.

9. Napier, *Selections*, 491; Barrett et al., *Darwin's Notebooks*, C76; *CCD*, 3:43–4.

10. Holt, *Unitarian Contribution*, 132; Darwin, *Origin*, 56, 380; Schweber, 'Darwin', 212; Browne, *Secular Ark*, 210–16; Kohn, 'On the Origin', 250. Barnacles: Darwin, *Monograph*, 2:155; *CCD*, 4:344; Ospovat, *Development*, 85.

11. *CCD*, 3:211, 336–7, 5:403, 498–9, 6:66, 361; Browne, *Secular Ark*, 65–8, 77–80; T. V. Wollaston, *Variation*, 186, 189.

12. *CCD*, 2:324, 352; 6:66–7, 74.

13. JH to TH, [4 Apr. 1856], HP 3.23; n.d., HP 3.21; TH to JH, [31 Mar. 1856], HP 2.21; HP 31.142; WBC to TH, 9 July 1856, HM 3:121.93; *LJH*, 1:368–9; *LJT*, 60–3; *LTH*, 1:111; Harte, *University*, 102.

14. Atkins, *Down*, 97 passim; Desmond and Moore, *Darwin*, chap. 20, also 296, 397; *CCD*, 2:324–5, 6:113–14; Harte, *University*, 82–3.

15. *CCD*, 3:345, 6:74, 87, 197; J. Lubbock to TH, Dec. 1856, HP 22.53–7.

16. Owen, 'Lyell', 449–50; Owen, *Fossil Mammalia*, 55; Ospovat, *Development*, 134–9; Rachootin, 'Owen'; Stauffer, *Natural Selection*, 384; Desmond and Moore, *Darwin*, 145, 235; Desmond, *Archetypes*, 44; Bowler, *Fossils*, 102ff; *LLD*, 2:26–7.

17. This was an idiosyncratic mix of Macleay's circles and von Baer's archetypes: Huxley, *West. Rev.*, 63 (1855), 242–3; Darwin's notes on this interview: DAR Box B.C. 40e, CUL; Ospovat, 'Darwin'.

18. *LLD*, 2:196 for Huxley's wrongly dated recollection of this meeting.

19. *CCD*, 5:83, 338–9, 363–7, 370, 374–5, 477, 483, 500, 6:122; *LJH*, 1:494; *LLD*, 2:26–7; Barrett, *Collected Papers*, 1:255–8, 261–3, 264–73; Browne, *Secular Ark*, 196ff; Desmond and Moore, *Darwin*, 418, 423–4, 444.

20. *CCD*, 5:352, 386, 492, 508, 6:58, 152, 236; Darwin, *Expression*, 259; *LLL*, 2:213; Wilson, *Lyell's Journals*, 54; Secord, 'Darwin and the Breeders'; R. Richards, *Meaning*, 151–2; Ospovat, *Development*, 156–7.

21. Wollaston, *Variation*, 35, 186–9; *CCD*, 6:134, 147; Desmond and Moore, *Darwin*, 434–6.

22. Huxley, *West. Rev.*, 67 (1857), 281–2; *LJH*, 1:367; *CCD* 6:100.

23. Bunbury, *Life*, 2:90, 99–100; *CCD*, 6:89, 91 note 7; *LLL*, 2:212.

24. Huxley, 'Lectures', *Medical Times and Gazette*, 12 (1856), 482–3; Wilson, *Lyell's Journals*, 54–60.

25. CCD, 6:103, 106–7, 109–12; 'old': TH to JH, 30 Jan. 1858, HP 2.29; *LTH*, 1:157; JH to TH, [Oct. 1855], HP 3.18; *LJH*, 1:375; Huxley, 'Lectures', *Medical Times and Gazette*, 12 (1856), 430, 432, 484, 507. CE, 2:12. The savaging of Owen was deliberate policy: TH to JH, n.d., HP 2.77.

   Huxley was also demolishing Louis Agassiz's evidence for progression. Agassiz saw fish maturing equally in geological and individual time. His argument involved changes in fish tails. He believed that in the embryo, as well as in ancient fish, the tip of the backbone turned up ('heterocercal'), whereas living adult fish have 'homocercal' tails, where the vertebrae fuse and rays come off as a uniform fan. But Huxley dissected perch and mackerel embryos and found them to be homocercal from the first: *West. Rev.*, 63 (1855), 244–6; *SM*, 2:271.

26. TH to JH, 3 Apr. 1857, HP 2.23; *LTH*, 1:149; JH to TH, n.d., HP 3.66; *LJH*, 1:427; CCD, 6:112, 147, 175–6; Huxley, 'Method of Palaeontology', 43–5; CL to TH, 13 July 1856, HP 6.11; Falconer, 'Huxley's Attempted Refutation', 476–90; Morris, *Heaven's Command*, 267–71.

27. CCD, 6:109, 161, 173, 178, 304; Stauffer, *Natural Selection*, 45–6, 73, 89.

28. TH to FD, 10 Oct. 1856, HP 15.74; 'knocked': TH to JH, 3 Sept. 1856, HP 2.19; *LTH*, 1:145–6; *LJT*, 50, 64–5, 342–4, 353; 'biggest': HAH's Reminiscences, HP 31.87–91; Ramsay Diary, 15 Mar. 1856, Ramsay Papers 1/24, Imperial College, London.

29. *LTH*, 1:143; HP 31.99; TH to FD, 10, 28 Oct. 1856, HP 15.74, 78.

30. CCD, 6:260; 'congenital': Owen, 'Affinities', 4–8; 'There': TH to FD, 3 Nov. 1856, HP 15.78.

31. HAH's Reminiscences, HP 31.91; *LTH*, 1:151.

13 EMPIRES OF THE DEEP PAST

1. TH to FD, [Jan. 1857], HP 15.80; Owen, 'Conclusion', 115; *LRO*, 2:60; Rupke, *Owen*, 93–5. Owen's title in the *Medical Directory*: TH to J. Churchill, 22 Jan. 1857, HP 12.194; reply, HP 12.195.

2. 'The Physiology of Sensation and Motion', Royal Institution, Jan.–Apr. 1857, HP 38.53, ff.146–7; 'fellows', 'I will': TH to FD, [Jan. 1857], HP 15.80; *LTH*, 1:138; HS to TH, 14 Jan. 1857, HP 7.102; Spencer, *Autobiography*, 2:11.

3. TH to FD, [Jan. 1857], HP 15.80; *LTH*, 1:137, 143.

4. Owen, 'On the Orders', 154–6; Owen, 'Conclusion', 115; Desmond, *Politics*, 254ff; 'Synopsis of a Course of Lectures on Fossil Birds and Reptiles', Museum of Economic Geology, Lectures 3 and 4, 25–6 Mar. 1858, in 'Richard Owen: Manuscripts, Notes, and Synopses of Lectures', Vol. 3 (1849–64), BM(NH); Meyer, 'Reptiles', 52, 55; Meyer, 'Reptilien'; Desmond, *Archetypes*, 65–71; Bowler, *Fossils*, 101–6.

5. Owen, 'Reptilian Fossils', 59–60. *Galesaurus* arrived in 1858; Owen read his paper on 20 April 1859, while Huxley was the G.S. Secretary. Bain, 'Discovery'; 'richer': A. G. Bain to R. Owen, 25 Sept. 1848, BM(NH) OC, 2.32; Owen, *Descriptive*, iii; Desmond, *Archetypes*, 195–6; Gruber and Thackray, *Owen*, 44–7. In 1858 Huxley was working on the Karroo two-

tusker *Dicynodon*: *SM*, 2:130; HM 2:96, and f.26 for his own later drawing of *Galesaurus*.

6. *SM*, 1:320; Buckle, *History*, 3:486; 'Buckle': TH to JT, [Mar. 1857], HP 9.22; Spencer, 'Progress', 450; *LHS*, 83; Spencer, *Autobiography*, 1:505; T. M. Porter, *Rise*, 60–5; Ruse, *Darwinian Revolution*, 145–6.
7. Portlock, 'Address' (1857), cvii, cxliv–v; (1858), lxxxii, clvii–iii; Murchison, 'Portlock', cxviii. Portlock recommended Huxley for the FGS: Huxley's admission form, 5 March 1856: Geological Society of London.
8. Colp, *To be an Invalid*, 59; *CCD*, 6:335, 366, 452; Stauffer, *Natural Selection*, 92–4, 134–8, 214, 223–4, 380; Kohn, 'Darwin's Ambiguity', 229–32; Ospovat, *Development*, chap. 9; F. Darwin, *Foundations*, 52.
9. *CCD*, 6:420, 424–8; Stauffer, *Natural Selection*, 275–9, 303–4; Ospovat, *Development*, chap. 7.
10. *CCD*, 6:456, 461–3; Darwin, *Origin*, 420; Winsor, 'Impact', 63–72; Di Gregorio, 'Order', 227–33.
11. Stauffer, *Natural Selection*, 379; *CCD*, 6:454; Huxley, 'Lectures', *Medical Times and Gazette*, 15 (1857), 238; *SM*, 1:311.
12. Cardwell, *Organisation*, 92–5; Harte, *University*, 107–12; A. W. Hofmann to TH, 20 June 1857, HP 18.208; CL to TH, 9 July 1857, HP 6.16; Linnean: A. Henfrey to TH, 13 Mar. 1857, HP 18.109; *LJH*, 1:410; Gage and Stearn, *Bicentenary History*, 53–5.
13. TH to JH, 3 Apr. 1857, HP 2.23; 'God': JH to TH, 2 Apr. 1857, HP 3.33; *CCD*, 6:451; *LTH*, 1:149. Diploma, 1 Oct. 1857: HP 32.4–7. He had already been elected to the Microscopical Society of Giessen on 7 Jan. 1857: HP 32.3.
14. Huxley's Deep Sea Soundings Notebook: HM 2:116; Pingree, *Huxley: Scientific Notebooks*, 48–9; Huxley, 'Chalk', 501; *CE*, 8:11–17; Rehbock, 'Huxley', 511–12; Rice, 'Huxley', 169–71. Darwin thought it 'the gravest of errors' that mid-oceanic mud could preserve remains as fossils: *CCD*, 6:506. Huxley disagreed: *Manual*, 79–82. Briggs, *Victorian Things*, 377; Young, *Portrait*, 16; Briggs, *Victorian People*, 23; Rolt, *Victorian Engineering*, 215–17; Paradis, *Huxley*, 75.
15. HAH to JT, 30 Aug. 1857, AD; 'on a': TH to JH, 16 Aug. 1857, HP 2.25; 'weary': TH to FD, 16 Sept. 1857, HP 15.86; 'rascally': JT to TH, [Jan. 1858], HP 1.221; Huxley's notebook: HM 3:126; *SM*, 1:482–501; TH to ES, 27 March 1858, HP 31.24; JT to TH, 19 July 1857, HP 1:21; TH to JT, 3 Sept. 1857, HP 8.29; *LTH*, 1:145–6, 159.
16. *CCD*, 6:419, 484, 7:58–9; Owen, 'Characters', 19–20; Wilson, *Lyell's Journals*, 86, 153. *SM*, 2:30, 51–6; 'Polemically': TH to FD, 10 Dec. 1857, HP 15.94.
17. Owen, 'Osteology', 343, 354–5, 370–2; Desmond, 'Owen's Reaction', 40–2.
18. Wilson, *Lyell's Journals*, 86, 157, 183; Lartet, 'Note'; Owen's marked copy of Lyell's *Supplement*, 14–15, BM(NH) Palaeontology Library; Owen, *On the Classification*, 86–7.
19. Owen, 'Osteological Contributions', 414–17; T. Savage to R. Owen, 24 Apr. 1847, BM(NH) OC, 23.103; Lamarck, *Philosophie Zoologique*, 1:349–57.
20. Desmond, 'Artisan Resistance'; Watts, 'Theological Theories'; Chilton, 'Geological Revelations'; 'Origin of Man', *London Investigator*, 1 (1854–5), 8ff. Wombwell's gorilla: T. J. Moore, 'Gorilla', 474; *LLL*, 2:358; S. S. Flower, *List*, 1:2; Barnaby, *Log Book*, 36–7; Barber, *Heyday*, 276, 310 n18.

21. W. Whewell to R. Owen, 3 Apr. 1859, BM(NH) OC 26.285.

22. Owen's Notebook 1 (Oct.–Dec. 1830), BM(NH), 27 Oct. 1830; Lankester, 'Flower', 254; *CCD*, 6:419; 'like': TH to JH, 5 Sept. 1858, HP 2.35; Gross, 'Hippocampus', 408, 413 suggests that Owen latched onto the ventricles because of their classical importance as body-soul interfaces.

23. Huxley, 'The Principles of Biology', Royal Institution, 19 Jan.–23 Mar. 1858, Lecture 10, 16 Mar. 1858, HP 36.97–100; Vevers, *London's Zoo*, 66.

24. *CCD*, 6:515; *LTH*, 1:143; Stauffer, *Natural Selection*, 10.

25. TH to FD, 27 Feb. 1858, HP 15.98; 'Hoorar': JH to TH, [26 Jan. 1858], HP 3.28; 'I had': RIM to TH, 26 Jan. 1858, HP 23.151; *LTH*, 1:150; *LJT*, 76; JT to TH, [Feb/Mar. 1858], HP 1.158; TH to JT, [March 1857], HP 9.22.

26. JT to TH, n.d., HP 1.158; 'corps': TH to JT, 20 Apr. 1858, HP 9.24; Bevington, *Saturday Review*, 277–80; Briggs, *Age*, 451; G. K. Clark, *Making*, 48; TH to JD, 20 Apr. 1858, HP 2.33; *LTH*, 1:139; *LJH*, 1:412.

27. TH to ES, 27 Mar. 1858, HP 31.24; HAH to ES, ibid.; *LTH*, 1:157, 159–60; 'travel', France: TH to FD, 18 Aug. 1858, HP 15.102; 'editor': TH to JH, 5 Sept. 1858, HP 2.35; 'Pon': JT to TH, 17 Feb. 1858, HP 1.22; fisheries: HP 43.76; also HP 20.23, 30.29.

28. Jensen, *Huxley*, 43; dinner guests in the 1860s: Watterson, *Marse*, 1:103.

29. TH to JH, 18 June [1858], HP 2.153; Spencer, 'Owen', 400, 415–16; *LTH*, 1:161; *LHS*, 87; Spencer, *Autobiography*, 2:24–5; Desmond, *Archetypes*, 95–9; Kennedy, *Spencer*, 72; *SM*, 1:571; Hall, 'Royal Society', 155–6; Stanley, 'Huxley', 121.

30. *CCD*, 6:290, 387–8, 457, 514–15, 7:107; R. Smith, 'Wallace', 178ff; Kottler, 'Darwin', 374; Durant, 'Scientific Naturalism', 35ff; Brooks, *Just Before the Origin*, chaps 1, 4; Wallace, *My Life*, chap. 6 et seq.

31. *CCD*, 7:116–25, 142, 507–11, 514, 520; Wallace, *Contributions*, 29, 42; Gage and Stearn, *Bicentenary History*, 57.

32. TH to JH, 5 Sept. 1858, HP 2.35; *LTH*, 1:159–60; *CCD*, 7:127, 137–8, 140, 161, 165, 222, 230, 270.

33. Owen, 'Presidential', li; Desmond, *Archetypes*, 61–4; Brooke, 'Natural Theology of the Geologists', 41, 56 n14. *LHS*, 81–97, 550–1; HS to TH, 31 Dec. 1858, HP 7.104; Spencer, *Autobiography*, 1:498–9, 503, 2:3, 8–16.

34. Dean, 'Through Science', 115, 121–4; Shatto, 'Byron', 151; Rudwick, *Scenes*, 80ff; Lightman, *Origins*, 6ff, on Mansel.

35. Huxley, *West. Rev.*, 64 (1855), 571–2; Hitchcock, 'Attempt', 250–1; Dean, 'Hitchcock's Tracks'; *London Quarterly Review*, 3 (1854), 238; Desmond, 'Designing'.

36. *LHS*, 91; *SM*, 2:112–13; notes on *Stagonolepis* and clippings on the GS meeting, HM 2:92; Geikie, *Life*, 2:120, 244, 311; Lyell, *Manual*, Postscript, x; CL to TH, 30 Nov. 1858, HP 6.18, for fears about dating; 'fairest': 'Death of the Rev. Dr Gordon', *Moray & Nairn Express*, 16 Dec. 1893; Desmond, *Archetypes*, 100, 171; Benton, 'Progressionism', 124–32; 'tooth': Collie, *Huxley*, 18–19, 30, 99–105.

37. HAH to ES, [Jan.–Feb. 1859], HP 31.29.

14 THE EVE OF A NEW REFORMATION

1. *LTH*, 1:161; 'bright': TH to ES, 28 Mar. 1859, HP 31.32; HAH to ES, [Jan.–Feb. 1859], HP 31.29.

2. TH to JH, 5 Sept., 2 Dec., n.d., 1858, HP 2.35, 39, 61; *LTH*, 1:133–4, 160; WBC to TH, 22 Oct. 1858, HP 12.94; also HP 3.36, 41, 43, 49, 10.302, 15.193, 17.143, 30.52; 'temple': Rupke, 'Road', 81–2; Rupke, *Owen*, 34–46, 97ff; memorial: HP 49.1–19.

3. *CCD*, 7:531; TH to JH, 29 Jan. 1859, HP 2.53; JH to TH, 22 Dec. 1858, 25 Jan. 1859, HP 3.45, 59; *LTH*, 1:165; 'Biologist': Huxley, 'Lectures', *Medical Times and Gazette*, 12 (1856), 429.

4. Huxley, 'Science and Religion', 35–6.

5. TH to FD, 30 Jan. 1859, HP 15.106.

6. TH to JH, [Apr. 1859], HP 2.43; 'By': JH to TH, [Apr. 1859], HP 3:47; *LJH*, 1:495–6; *LTH*, 1:165; *CCD*, 7:246–7, 252–4, 263–4, 270, 284–5; Colp, *To Be an Invalid*, 64ff.

7. *CCD*, 7:255–62, 272, 279, 299, 301–3, 308, 451.

8. CL to TH, 1 Oct. 1859, HP 6.27; TH to CL, 10 Oct. 1859, HP 30.33 (original APS); *LLL*, 2:325. Owen accepted the dating: 'On the Orders', 163; 'down': Collie, *Huxley*, 107–8. Huxley recognized *Hyperodapedon*'s similarity to the Triassic rhynchosaurs, the living Tuatara's ancestors, and this pushed him into a study of *Rhynchosaurus* itself in 1860 (Huxley's Diary, 22 Oct. 1860: HP 70.3; TH to CK, 4 Oct. 1860, HP 19.198). Other saurian studies: HM 2:89, 2:90–1; 2:94, 2:96; *SM*, 2:118–57; *LTH*, 1:154. Persistence: *SM*, 2:90; Huxley, 'Time', 144–6; Wilson, *Lyell's Journals*, 240; Desmond, *Archetypes*, 93–4, 102, 104, 171.

9. TH to CL, 26 June 1859, APS; *LTH*, 1:173; CL to TH, 17 June 1859, HP 6.20. Lyell was responding to Huxley's caricature of atoms flashing into elephants first mooted in his 'Lectures', *Medical Times and Gazette*, 12 (1856), 482–3; cf. *CCD*, 7:305–7; 'reptilian': R. Chambers to R. Owen, 6 Mar. 1849, BM(NH) OC 7.19; Darwin, *Origin*, 483; *CE*, 2:35–41, 53–4; Ospovat, 'Perfect Adaptation', 49.

10. *LTH*, 1:162, 164; *CCD*, 6:101; TH to E. Lankester, 1 Aug. 1859, Richard Milner Collection; TH to JH, 22 Apr. 1859, HP 2.49.

11. WBC to TH, 26 Sept. 1855, HP 12.82; 'Paradise': RIM to TH, 11 Oct. 1855, HP 23.147; *LTH*, 1:155.

12. JH to TH, [19 Nov. 1859], HP 3.63; *LJH*, 1:428; *CCD*, 7:328, 332, 336, 350–1, 362; Desmond and Moore, *Darwin*, 476ff.

13. *CCD*, 7:305, 340, 354; Wilson, *Lyell's Journals*, 227, 330–2, 335–6; 'race', CL to TH, 17 June 1859, HP 6.20; Bartholomew, 'Lyell'.

14. *CCD*, 7:368, 371, 375, 377, 392.

15. *CE*, 2:21, 24, 78–9, 448, 475; *CCD*, 7:383, 437; Irvine, *Apes*, 89; *LTH*, 1:170–1, 2:190–1; Bartholomew, 'Huxley's Defence', 529. Huxley's annotated copy of the *Origin of Species* with Darwin's covering letter is in the possession of the Huxley family.

16. Hull, *Darwin*, 114; *CCD*, 7:382–3, 387; *Athenaeum*, 19 Nov. 1859, 659–60.

17. *CCD*, 7:260, 390–1, 398–400, 404–5, 428, 434, 447; Carlyle, *Heroes*, 96.

18. *CCD*, 7:412–15; Hull, *Darwin*, 81–4, 93–4; Ellegard, *Darwin*, 37–8, 55, 367; D. Masson to TH, 10 Nov. 1859, HP 22.192; Huxley, 'Time', 145–6.

19. Haight, *Eliot and Chapman*, 102–4, 228–33, 237; TH to JH, [2 Jan. 1860], HP 2.59.

20. *CE*, 2:22–3, 51–3; Barton, 'Evolution'; Himmelfarb, *Darwin*, 216; Seaman, *Victorian England*, 144–5.

21. *CCD*, 7:356, 391, 398, 432, 434; *CE*, 2:34–49, 74–7; Bartholomew, 'Huxley's Defence', 529.
22. *CCD*, 7:379–80; 'startled': CK to TH, 7 Dec. 1859, HP 19.160; *LCK*, 2:66–7.
23. *CCD*, 7:324, 373, 413, 422–3.
24. Huxley, 'Darwin', cutting HP 41.1; cf. *CE*, 2:1–21; *CCD*, 7:457–8; 'I wrote': TH to JH, 31 Dec. 1859, HP 2.57; *LTH*, 1:176–7. The *Times* reviewer was Samuel Lucas: S. Lucas to TH, 9 Jan. 1860, HP 22.105.
25. *CCD*, 7:451, 458–9.
26. W. Elwin to J. Murray, 3 Dec. 1859, John Murray Archives; 'heard': TH to JH, [2 Jan. 1860], HP 2.59; TH on Elwin, HP 2.39, 2.43; Paston, *At John Murray's*, 174; *CCD*, 7:288–90, 359 n6.

15 BUTTERED ANGELS & BELLOWING APES

1. *CCD*, 7:396, 8:35, 81, 87, 97, 113, 119; Hull, *Darwin*, 138; 'stupid': TH to FD, 29 Feb. 1860, HP 15.110; *LJH*, 1:513; Mayhew, *London Labour*, 106–7.
2. RIM to TH, 14 Apr. 1860, HP 23.154; Geikie, *Life*, 2:321–2; *Athenaeum*, 19 Nov. 1859, 659–60; Secord, 'Geological Survey', 224, 260.
3. *CCD*, 8:97–8, 112–13, 176, 189 n7.
4. Mrs Dyster to HAH, 9 Apr. 1860, HP 15.108; *CCD*, 8:4–5, 25, 43. Huxley's 1860 diary lists 'Darwin' on 25 Jan., but arrows it to Thursday 26th (HP 70.3). E. Lankester, 'Lecture'.
5. TH to FD, 29 Feb. 1860, HP 15.110; Cunningham, *Volunteer*, 11, 113, 153.
6. *CCD*, 8:35, 52. Huxley's 1860 Diary on tickets: HP 70.3.
7. 'On Species and Races' MS, HP 41 ff.29, 30, 43–6, 49; cf. *SM*, 2:389, 391. The manuscript version (HP 41.9–56), which I have used, differs from the later printed abstract.
8. 'On Species' MS, ff.51–6; cf. *SM*, 2:392–4, quoting Tennyson, *Idylls*, 286; *CCD*, 8:80, 117 n11; 'I had', TH to FD, 29 Feb. 1860, HP 15.110; 'Professor Huxley at the Royal Institution', *Reasoner*, 25 (1860), 125; 'High': GR to TH, 13 Apr. 1860, HP 25.142.
9. *CCD*, 8:80, 84; TH to FD, 29 Feb. 1860, HP 15.110.
10. *CE*, 3:62; 2:59; *CCD*, 8:238; Dean, 'Through Science', 121. Huxley's failure to assimilate Darwin's 'selectionist' – or more accurately utilitarian – programme, while exploiting the *Origin* for ideological ends, has led Bowler (*Darwin*, 142–8) to call him a 'pseudo-Darwinian'.
11. *CCD*, 8:81, 109, 115, 124, 216, 320, 345, 405; Hull, *Darwin*, 201–2; D. Livingstone to R. Owen, 29 Dec. 1860, BM(NH), OC 17.415; Argyll to R. Owen, 2 Dec. 1859 and 27 Feb. 1863, OC 1.230.
12. TH to CL, 17 Mar. 1860, HP 30.34 (original APS); CL to TH, 16 Mar., 21 May 1860, HP 6.32–4; E. Richards, 'Huxley', 253–7; Harte, *University*, 122; Bibby, *Huxley*, 217; *LTH*, 1:211–12, 289, 310. Lyell shared Huxley's political view of Victorian women as conservative church-goers, and he feared that giving them the vote would 'delay educational reforms': *LLL*, 2:446.
13. *CCD*, 8:130, 150–4, 157, 160, 162, 190, 224, 247, 405, 490, 525; *CE*, 2:28, 61; Hooker, 'Reminiscences', 187; 'I have': GR to TH, 13 Apr. 1860, HP 25.142; Owen, 'Darwin', 500–1; Owen, *On the Anatomy*, 3:796 n6; Hull, *Darwin*, 177, 181–2; 'Palaeontology', *Athenaeum*, 7 Apr. 1860, 478–9.

14. G. Grote to TH, 23 Nov. 1860, HP 17.150; *SM*, 2:174; Schama, *Citizens*, 778; Huxley, *Lay Sermons*, 104–5, 117–18 (14 May 1860, not '1861']; *CCD*, 5:83, 8:474.

15. GR to TH, n.d., 13, 23 Apr., 13, 20 May 1860, HP 25.142–53; Pembroke dinner: TH to HAH, 27, 28 June 1860, AD; Rolleston on brains in HM 1.14.283–93; Rolleston, *Scientific Papers*, 1:ixff, 56, 61; *CE*, 2:61; Cunningham, *Volunteer*, 1.

16. Trains: Diary HP 70.3; A. Thomson to TH, 24 May 1860, HM 2:118:99; *SM*, 2:323–4, 400, 481; *LTH*, 1:179, 187; TH quotes: TH to HAH, 28, 29 June 1860, AD; 'So you': HAH to TH, 29 June 1860, AD; Jensen, *Huxley*, 79; *CCD*, 8:244–5; 265, 268, 270, 282; *Athenaeum*, 7 July 1860, 26; Ellegard, *Darwin*, 66. I assume Owen was responding to Huxley's comparison of apes and humans at the Royal Institution in 1858, but cf. Rupke, *Owen*, 272.

17. *Daily Telegraph*, 10 Apr. 1863, 4; 'finished': Gardiner, *Harcourt*, 1:247; 'to look', 'Vice': TH to HAH, 29 June 1860, AD; Gilley, 'Huxley–Wilberforce', 326–36; *LLL*, 2:335; Morrell and Thackray, *Gentlemen*, 395–6; *CCD*, 8:270; *LTH*, 1:181, 187; Wilberforce, *Pride*, 15–20; Desmond and Moore, *Darwin*, 348; Ellis, *Seven*. Huxley had openly castigated *Vestiges* only months before in 'Time and Life', 147.

18. TH to FD, 9 Sept, 1860, HP 15.115. Huxley was criticizing loose reports like the *Guardian*'s, which talked of the sad day 'when Professors lose their tempers and solemnly avow they would rather be descended from apes than Bishops': Ellegard, *Darwin*, 68. A. Wollaston, *Newton*, 119 for an eyewitness account that related the famous ape jibe to the Huxley–Owen clash on the preceding Thursday. Jensen, *Huxley*, 70–3, 76; Sedgwick, 'Natural History', 3; *LTH*, 1:183–4, 188; Lucas, 'Wilberforce,' 317, 327; Altholz, 'Huxley–Wilberforce', 315; Phelps and Cohen, 'Wilberforce–Huxley', 58–9; Sidgwick, 'Grandmother's Tale', 433; *LLL*, 2:335; *Athenaeum*, 14 July 1860, 65.

19. Wrangham, 'Wilberforce', 192; *CCD*, 8:270–1; 'position', TH to FD, 9 Sept. 1860, HP 15.115; Jensen, *Huxley*, 71–7; Gilley, 'Huxley–Wilberforce', 336–7; Lucas, 'Wilberforce', 323; Altholz, 'Huxley–Wilberforce', 315; Gould, 'Knight'; 'splendid': Gardiner, *Harcourt*, 1:247. Janet Browne reconstructs the Wilberforce-smashing legend in 'Darwin–Hooker Correspondence'.

20. TH to FD, 9 Sept. 1860, HP 15.115; 'slap': GR to TH, n.d., HP 25.150; *CCD*, 8:277, 280–1, 285, 306, 319; *LLL*, 2:335; *Athenaeum*, 7 July 1860, 19; Lucas, 'Wilberforce', 316; Himmelfarb, *Darwin*, 240; *LTH*, 1:188; Sidgwick, 'Grandmother's Tale', 434.

21. TH to JH, 27 Apr. 1861, HP 2.98; *LTH*, 1:191; GR to TH, n.d., 13 Apr. 1860, HP 25.142, 148, 150.

22. JH to TH, 4 Jan. 1860, HP 3.81; *LJH*, 1:414; *SM*, 2:471–2.

23. A. Thomson to TH, 24 May 1860, HM 2:118:104; di Gregorio, *Huxley*, 135–6; W. Sharpey to TH, 8 Nov. 1860, HM 2:118:116; Rolleston: HM 1.14.288–93; *CCD*, 8:171, 189; Gross, 'Hippocampus', 408.

24. G. Rorison to R. Owen, 25 Apr. 1860, BM(NH), OC 22.379; Rorison, 'Creative Week', 322; for more on this see Desmond, *Archetypes*, 79–80. Ellegard, *Darwin*, 294–5, 304.

25. Darwin's annotations on Wilberforce, 'Darwin's Origin', 239, 255, 259, Darwin Reprint Collection, R. 34, CUL; 'Article': JH to J. Murray, n.d., John Murray Archives; Paston, *At John Murray's*, 176.

26. *LJH*, 1:516; *CCD*, 8:294, 316, 516; Fawcett, 'Popular Exposition', 83. On the rector Henry Tristram's reconversion: Cohen, 'Three Notes', 598; A. Wollaston, *Newton*, 120–2.

27. JH to TH, [18 July 1860], HP 3.119; 'you': TH to JH, 17 July, 2 Aug., 1860, HP 2.67, 70; TH to P. L. Sclater, 16 Oct. 1860, APS; *CCD*, 8:294–6, 527; *LTH*, 1:209–10; *LLL*, 2:366; *LJH*, 1:413. At first Huxley really did want articles pro and con. He told the Oxford geologist John Phillips (20 Nov. 1860, OUM Loe/16) that if 'you or any one else with your knowledge & spirit, will favour us with the most anti Darwinian of articles, it shall receive the place of honour'.

28. *SM*, 2:446–7; *HM* 2:86–8 (Crossopterygians would come to be seen as the ancestors of the amphibians); 'more': TH to JH, 2 Aug. 1860, HP 2.70; *LTH*, 1:210, 215; *CCD*, 8:295; di Gregorio, *Huxley*, 73–4.

29. TH to FD, 9 Sept. 1860, HP 15.115; 'Honeymoon': TH to JH, [8 Aug. 1860], HP 2.74; 'deep', '99': TH to CK, 23 Sept. 1860, HP 19.176–7; *CE*, 2:59. Lightman, 'Pope Huxley', 150–2; Lightman, *Origins*, 7–10, 71ff.; *LLL*, 2:322–3; *LTH*, 1:212–13, 220; HS to TH, 11 Sept. 1860, HP 7.108; Harrison, 'Radicals,' 206; Turner, 'Victorian Scientific Naturalism', 334–9; Brown, *Metaphysical Society*, 139; Pevsner, *Buildings*, 328–9; Angela Darwin pers. comm.

30. TH to FD, 16 Sept. 1860, HP 15.119; *LTH*, 1:152, 213.

31. TH to CK, 23 Sept. 1860, HP 19.169–76; *LTH*, 1:151–2, 213, 217–22; 'up': HAH's Reminiscences, HP 31.92; 'stunned': JT to TH, 17 Sept. 1860, HP 1.32; *LJH*, 1:528; 'four': TH to FD, 16 Sept. 1860, HP 15.119; Huxley's Diary, HP 30.3 for 11 o'clock procession; grave: Angela Darwin pers comm.

32. CK to TH, 21 Sept. 1860, HP 19.162; 'Spinozaist': CK to TH, 16, 31 Oct. 1860, HP 19.193, 195.

33. TH to CK, 23 Sept., 4 Oct. 1860, HP 19.169, 191, 198; *LTH*, 1:217; Gilley and Loades, 'Huxley', 304.

34. *CCD*, 8:438, 475, 522–3, 527; 'coming': TH to E. P. Wright, 20 Nov. 1860, HP 29.102.

35. TH to CK, 4 Oct. 1860, HP 19.191, 198; *LCK*, 2:112–15; *LLL*, 2:336; 'useless': TH to CK, 23 Sept. 1860, HP 19.169; *LTH*, 1:217; 'Theology': CK to TH, 26 Sept. 1860, HP 19.180.

36. *LTH*, 1:214, 216, 222–3, 225; *LJH*, 1:536; *CCD*, 8:483; birth, travel: Huxley's Diary, HP 70.3; TH to JH, 19 Dec. 1860, HP 2.79; 'because': HAH's Reminiscences, HP 31.92. G. S. Jones, *Outcast London*, 45. It had been an emotionally turbulent year. Brother Jim had married Mary Anne Coleman after his first wife died.

37. JH to TH, n.d. HP 3.83; 'public': CL to TH, 5 Jan. 1860 [1861], HP 6.36; TH to S. Wilberforce, 3 Jan. 1861, HM 3:121.118; reply 30 Jan. [1861], HP 29.25; Blinderman, 'Oxford Debate', 126. 'What': CD to TH, 3 Jan. 1861, HP 5.155; 'mends': TH to JH, 3 Jan. 1861, HP 2.83; *LTH*, 1:224.

38. JH to TH, 4 Jan. 1861, HP 3.81; 'You': TH to JH, 3 Jan. 1861, HP 2.83; *LTH*, 1:223, 2:59.

39. TH to JH, 12 Feb. 1861. HP 2.91; also 6 Jan. 1861, HP 2.85; *LTH*, 1:224.

40. TH to HAH, 19 Mar. 1861, AD; 'suffering': E. Darwin to CD, [June 1861], DAR 210.10, CUL; 'dear': HAH to TH, 22 Mar. 1861, AD; 'House': CD to TH, 22 Feb. 1861, HP 5.157; Colp, *To Be an Invalid*, 69; *LLD*, 1:136; *MLD*, 1:460; Litchfield, *Darwin*, 2:176–7.

16 RESLAYING THE SLAIN

1. *CE*, 7:81; Cooper, *Immortality*, 15; Chilton, 'Geological Revelations'; Desmond, 'Artisan Resistance', 96, 100; Watts, 'Theological Theories'; *Reasoner*, 26 (1861), 62; R. D. N. , 'Place of Man'; 'Cook', 'My': TH to HAH, 'Friday' [15], 22 Mar. 1861, AD; *LTH*, 1:190; 'Rifle': Huxley's Diary, 13 Mar. 1861, HP 70.4.

2. *CE*, 7:79–81, 146, 153–5; Eng, 'Huxley's Understanding', 300; Desmond, *Archetypes*, 170; 'progress': Watts, 'Theological Theories', 134; 'absolute': TH to CK, 23 Sept. 1860, HP 19.169; 'cynics': TH to JH, 6 Jan. 1861, HP 2.85; *LTH*, 1:219, 224; Chilton, 'Theory'; Becker, *Scientific London*, 186; T. J. Parker, 'Huxley', 164. Secord, 'Geological Survey', 260–1; Geikie, *Memoir*, 276–7. Only workers could attend; they had to give their occupation on buying a ticket: J. P. A., 'Huxley', 2. According to this workers' source, the 'majority' at Huxley's lecture were freethinkers.

3. TH to HAH, [15], 19, 22 Mar., 1861; HAH to TH, 14, 20, 22 Mar, 1861, AD.

4. HAH to TH, 17 Apr. 1861, AD; CD to TH, 1 Apr. [1861], HP 5.162; *MLD*, 1:185. On du Chaillu and Owen: *LRO*, 2:115; J. Murray to R. Owen, BM(NH), OC 20.130–3. Owen, 'Gorilla', 395–6; Huxley, 'Man', 433. By now the argument had degenerated to Huxley's use of the word 'rudiment' to describe the ape's hippocampus. To Owen the idealist *philosophical anatomist* that was sloppy – a 'rudimentary organ' was a collapsed representation of the whole normal organ, like the human appendix; whereas Huxley the *transmutationist* meant the homological antecedent of the human hippocampus. Ideological differences cut to the very core of their neuroanatomical language.

5. JH to TH, [18–27 Apr. 1861], HP 3.86; *MLD*, 1:185.

6. TH to JH, 18 Apr. 1861, HP 2.95; 'ill': HAH's Reminiscences, HP 31.92–5.

7. Egerton, 'Monkeyana'; TH to JH, 18 Apr. 1861, HP 2.95; Huxley, 'Man', 498; *LTH*, 1:191.

8. TH to JH, n.d., HP 2.100; *LTH*, 1:192; CD to TH, 22 May 1861, HP 5.164. Within weeks Huxley was to visit Egerton's country seat in Chester to examine his Devonian fish (Huxley's Diary, HP 70.4: 31 July 1861).

9. *CE*, 7:71–2; Du Chaillu meetings 4, 8, 18 Apr., 4 July 1861: Huxley's Diary, HP 70.4; *Punch*, 14 Dec. 1861; Ellegard, *Darwin*, 43, 295; 'The Gorilla and the Mbouve', *National Reformer*, 1 June 1861, 4; 'relieve': TH to JH, 18 Apr. 1861, HP 2.95; HAH's Reminiscences, HP 31.92–5; *LTH*, 1:225. Du Chaillu (to R. Owen, 19 Aug. 1864, BM(NH), OC 10.173) caught a live gorilla.

10. Owen, 'Gorilla', 395; Huxley, 'Man', 498; Desmond, *Archetypes*, 75; Blake, 'Huxley', 563–4; Rolleston, *Scientific Papers*, 1:21, 52; GR to [*illegible*], 1 Oct. 1861, Wellcome Institute, London, AL 325619; Carlyle: Huxley's Diary, HP 70.4.

11. HAH to TH, 17 Apr. 1861, AD; Huxley, *Evidence*, 118; TH to HAH, 16 Apr. 1861, AD; *LTH* 1:191–2; *MLD*, 1:185.

12. TH to HAH, 16 Apr. 1861, AD; A. Stanley to TH, [15 Apr. 1861], HP 26.217; Moore, *Religion*, 26, 40; JH to TH, 11 Apr. 1861, HP 3.89; TH to JH, 18 Apr. 1861, HP 2.95. Powell, in *Essays*, 139; Corsi, *Science*, 283–4; Gilley and Loades, 'Huxley', 289; *LLL*, 2:351.

419

13. J. Lubbock to TH, 28 Feb. 1861, HP 22.61; A. Stanley to TH, 25 Mar. 1861, HP 26.218; Moore, *Religion*, 425, 435–7; *LJH*, 1:514, 2:54–6; *MLD*, 2:266–7; 'Memorial', HP 22.63; Ellis, *Seven*, 62.

14. TH to JH, 27 Apr., n.d., HP 2.98–100; 'cut': JH to TH, n.d. [after 18 Apr. 1861], HP 3.86; *LTH*, 1:191, 225.

15. TH to E. P. Wright, 11 May 1861, HP 29.107; *LTH*, 1:210, 231, 235; 'only': TH to FD, n.d. [early 1862], HP 15.113; brewery: Angela Darwin pers. comm.

16. Bynum, 'Lyell's *Antiquity*', 161, 171; Grayson, *Establishment*, 120ff; Boylan, 'Controversy', 174. TH to CL, 26 June 1861, HP 30.35; *LLL*, 2:341, 344; *LTH*, 1:174; Desmond, *Archetypes*, 83–6.

17. TH to CL, 25 Jan. 1862, HP 30.38; *LTH*, 1:197; K. Fuhlrott to CL, 13 Nov. 1861, 2 Jan. 1862, HM 3:121:68; *CE*, 7:169, 182, 184; CL to TH, 4 July 1862, HP 6.63. *LHS*, 102; Grayson, *Establishment*, 212; Rudwick, *Scenes*, 168.

18. CL to TH, 10 Jan. 1862, HP 6.53; *SM*, 2:558; *CE*, 8:158; 'If': TH to CL, 25 Jan. 1862, APS, also HP 30.38; Jenny Lind: Huxley's Diary 70.4; *LTH*, 1:197, 231; 'First': HM 2:58:76; 'mere': TH to FD, n.d., HP 15.113.

19. TH to FD, [early 1862], HP 15.113; *LTH*, 1:192–5; *Witness*, 11, 14 Jan. 1862; 'I told': TH to JH, 16 Jan. 1862, HP 2.112; 'sinners': JH to TH, 20 Jan. 1862, HP 3.98; *LJH*, 2:25; Himmelfarb, *Darwin*, 216; R. W. Clark, *Huxleys*, 66.

20. E. W. Cooke to TH, 8 Feb. 1862, HP 12.314; *SM*, 2:509–11; 'Neanderthal': TH to CL, 25 Jan. 1862, APS, also HP 30.38; CL to TH, 26 Nov. 1861, 10 Jan. 1862, HP 6.40, 53; *LTH*, 1:197; *CE*, 7:164, 168, 178–81, 192, 204.

21. TH to JH, n.d. [May 1861], HP 2.102; Secord, 'Salter', 67–8; TH to RIM, 17 May 1862, HP 39.60–3; TH to G. G. Leveson-Gower, [13 June 1861], HP 30.56; Bibby, *Huxley*, 114; Bibby, 'Huxley and University Development', 111.

22. ZSL Minutes of Scientific Meetings, 6 (1857–68), ff.237, 239–41 (cf Owen's more negative *public* pronouncement: 'Characters of the Aye-Aye'); Huxley's spider monkey paper was read on 28 May 1861, not 11 June as stated in *SM*, 2:493: ff. 213–16. Gross, 'Hippocampus', 409–10 on its importance in distinguishing the calcarine sulcus. Wallace: ZSL Minutes of Council, f.462. Huxley and Wilberforce were elected VPs on 15 May 1861: f.381. They worked together on at least five occasions during their 1861–2 term.

23. Bunbury, *Memorials*, Middle Life, Vol.3, pp. 204, 335–7; *LLL*, 2:356; *LTH*, 1:204; *CE*, 8:288ff; 'reconstruct': TH to W. J. M. Rankine, 18 Jan. 1862, HP 9.291; L. Horner to TH, 12 June 1861, 27 Feb., 21 Mar., 1862, HP 18.231–4. Despite Huxley's harping on 'persistence', when an out-of-sequence specimen did turn up, such as O. C. Marsh's supposed Carboniferous 'ichthyosaur' (a reptile associated with much later deposits), Huxley routinely suspected that it was a misidentified labyrinthodont: TH to CL, 5 May 1862, APS, also HP 30.40; O. C. Marsh to CL, 16 May 1862, HP 22.170.

24. CD to TH, 10 May 1862, HP 5.171; *LTH*, 1:205; *MLD*, 2:234; Desmond, *Archetypes*, 85–8; Lyons, 'Huxley', 556; *SM*, 2:530; *LLL*, 2:356. He went to Edinburgh looking for the fossil fish *Rhizodus* (on which he was working: Diary, HP 70.5; TH to W. J. M. Rankine, 18 Jan.–9 Dec. 1862, HP 9.291–

304) and ended up naming two new amphibians *Loxomma* and *Pholidogaster*.

25. Huxley's Diary, HP 70.5; *CE*, 7:147; TH to CL, 5 May 1862, HP 30.40; *LTH*, 1:199; *MLD*, 1:237.

26. *CE*, 7:204, 208; 'was': CK to TH, 28 Feb. 1862, HP 19.203; 18 July 1862, HP 19.205; Bowler, *Theories*, 65–6.

27. TH to E. P. Wright, [Feb. 1862], HP 29.111; Huxley's Diary, HP 70.5.

28. W. H. Flower, 'Introductory Lecture', 196, 199; Cornish, *Flower*, 43–6, 92–3; W. H. Flower, *Essays*, 43–7, 51, 133–4; 'Was': GR to TH, 1 Jan. 1865, HP 25.167.

29. Rolleston, *Scientific Papers*, 56, 61; Cornish, *Flower*, 100; *LTH*, 1:249; Desmond, *Archetypes*, 52–5.

30. W. H. Flower to TH, 11 July 1862, HP 16.117; *LTH*, 1:235–6; HM 2:58:15, 62; 2:97; *SM*, 2:546.

31. TH to CL, 17 Aug. 1862, HP 30.41; L. Playfair to TH, 29 Mar. 1861, HP 24.132; minutes: HP 43.3–49; *LTH*, 1:198, 201, 234; Huxley's Diary, HP 70.5.

32. TH to FD, 11 Oct. 1862, HP 15.123; Blake, 'Huxley', 563; Huxley, *Evidence*, 113–18.

33. CL to TH, 11 Oct. 1862, HP 6.76; CK to TH, 4 Aug. 1862, HP 19.207; *LTH*, 1:198; Ellegard, *Darwin*, 71–3. Flower went on to describe dissections of 16 ape and monkey brains at the Royal Society, using Huxley's terminology (e.g. of the calcarine sulcus): Gross, 'Hippocampus', 410; TH to W. Flower, 29 Aug. 1862, APS. A. Wollaston, *Newton*, 122–3, on Owen's indifference to the refutations. For a good account of the cerebral debate sympathetic to Owen, see Rupke, *Owen*, chaps 6–7.

34. Rupke, *Owen*, 295.

35. TH to FD, 11 Oct. 1862, HP 15.123; CL to TH, 9 Aug., [Oct.], 1862, HP 6.66, 70; TH to CL, 17 Aug. 1862, APS, also HP 30.41; *LTH*, 1:200; *LJH*, 2:32. Huxley also showed the proofs to Sir William Lawrence, who admitted their truth but advised him against publication to protect his reputation. Lawrence should have known: 40 years earlier, during the reactionary Regency, he had been accused of blasphemy and humiliated for his materialist *Lectures on Man*, but times were very different now: Agnosco, 'Huxley'; Desmond, *Politics*, 117–20.

36. TH to W. Sharpey, 13, 16 Nov. 1862, Sharpey Corres. MS. Add 227, Nos. 122, 124, University College London; E. Sabine to W. Sharpey, ibid., No. 121, UCL; Sharpey, 'Address'.

37. Bunbury, *Memorials*, Middle Life, Vol. 3, 276–7; 'And yet': HAH's Reminiscences, HP 62.1; Ellegard, *Darwin*, 51; Dyster, 'Evidence', 234.

38. TH to JH, n.d., HP 2.125; *LTH*, 1:206–7, 245; English, 'Hardwicke', 29–31, 35; Sheets-Pyenson, 'Popular Science', 567–9; piracy: Desmond, *Politics*, 163, 231, 412; 'confirming': J. P. A., 'Huxley', 2; Laurent, 'Science', 596. Huxley, *On Our Knowledge*, 51; Huxley's Diary, HP 70.5; Syllabus: HM 2.58.9; 'spirited': *British Controversialist*, 9 (1863), 300.

39. CL to TH, 23 Jan. 1863, HP 6.78; *LTH*, 1:207–8; CD to TH, 7 Dec. 1862, HP 5.179; *LLD*, 3:3; *MLD*, 1:215, 229; Huxley, *On Our Knowledge*, 126–30, cf. *CE*, 2:439–44; 'far', 'Professor Huxley's Lectures to Working Men', *Reader*, 1 (1863), 99–101; *Am. J. Sci.*, 36 (1863), 312 for a September 1863 listing of Appleton's edition.

17 MAN'S PLACE

1. CD to TH, 18, 26 Feb. 1863, HP 5.173, 191; *LTH*, 1:204; *MLD*, 1:238; *LJH*, 2:34; Himmelfarb, *Darwin*, 209; di Gregorio, *Huxley*, 153–4; Straus, 'Huxley's *Evidence*'; 'Evidence as to Man's Place in Nature', *Athenaeum*, 28 Feb. 1863, 287. Haight, *Eliot Letters*, 4:11. Industrial readers: Lyell's evidence before the Public Schools' Commission, in Tyndall *et al.*, *Culture*, 461; depression: CL to TH, 9 Sept., 11 Oct. 1862, HP 6.72, 76.

2. Watts, 'Man's Origin'; 'Man's Place in Nature', *National Reformer*, 14 Mar. 1863; 'best': TH to FD, 12 Mar. 1863, HP 15.125; Dyster, 'Evidence'; Torr, *Marx*, 141; Draper, *Marx*, 116.

3. R. Godwin-Austen to TH, 30 Mar. 1863, HP 10.183; 'astonished': TH to FD, 12 Mar. 1863, HP 15.125. *Athenaeum*, 28 Feb. 1863, 287–8; *LTH*, 1:201–3; Ellegard, *Darwin*, 165; GR to TH, 20 Mar. 1863, HP 25.163; 'find': H. Acland to TH, 22 Nov. 1863, HP 10.8; Moore, *Post-Darwinian Controversies*, 94.

4. R. King to TH, 8 July 1863, HP 19.155; casts: GR to TH, 20 Mar. 1863, HP 25.163, 159; G. Grote to TH, 16 June 1862, HP 17.152; Reeve: TH to FD, 22 Mar. 1864, HP 15.127; royals: J. Clark to TH, 25 Mar. 1863, HP 12.209.

5. CL to TH, 9 Aug. 1862, HP 6.66; Bartholomew, 'Lyell', 296.

6. 'Evidence as to Man's Place in Nature', *Athenaeum*, 28 Feb. 1863, 287–8.

7. Morris, *Heaven's Command*, 323–8.

8. T. Oldham to TH, 8 Apr. 1863, HP 23.236. Colenso presumably sat Huxley's first Hunterian lectures, on classification (17 Feb.–28 Mar. 1863: HM 2.58.11–37; Huxley, *Lectures*, 85, 100–1); Winsor, 'Impact', 72. By now Huxley had given the sea squirts primary status, and split his 'Annulosa' into echinoderms and arthropods. Coleman, 'Morphology', 155–60 on the break-up of typal divisions in this period.

9. J. W. Colenso to TH, 28 Mar. 1865, HP 12.274; GR to TH, 20 Mar. 1863, HP 25.163. Visits: Huxley's Diary, HP 70.6 (15 Feb., 18 June 1863). *Telegraph*, 10 Apr. 1863, 4. Huxley brought Colenso to the Athenaeum Club and forced a furious Lord Overstone to resign from the Visitors Committee: TH to S. J. Loyd, 12 Oct. 1864, HP 22.47–51; CD to TH, 22 May [1864], HP 5.174; *LLL*, 2:360.

10. 'Report of a Sad Case', HP 79.(6); 'Professors Huxley and Owen in the Police Court', *National Reformer*, 9 May 1863, 5. Kingsley's *Water Babies*, 172–3, parodied the 'hippopotamus major' debate for children.

11. R. Wagner to TH, 4 Jan. 1863, HP 28.88; R. Wagner to R. Owen, 30 Nov. 1860, BM(NH) OC 26.12; Wagner, 'Upon the Structure'; Gregory, *Scientific Materialism*, 32, 44; Dana, 'Evidence', 452; *MLD*, 1:236.

12. W. C. Thomson to TH, 26 Nov. 1863, HP 27.332; Melbourne *Argus* clipping, 'The Gorilla on its last legs', HP 40.249, also 40.251; C. S. Wood to TH, 24 Feb. 1864, HP 29.86; Butcher, 'Gorilla Warfare', 157, 159, 164. Mozley, 'Evolution', 422, 427 on old Macleay's view: he would only back Huxley's classification in so far as man was considered '*materially*'.

13. C. Vogt to TH, 23 Mar. 1863, HP 28.77; Vogt, *Lectures*, 378; 'contemptuous', *Reader*, 1 (1863), 99; Kelly, *Descent*, chap. 2.

14. L. Büchner to TH, 6 July 1863, HP 11.179; Montgomery, 'Germany', 82ff;

Gregory, *Scientific Materialism*, chaps 3, 5. The translation appeared as *Zeugnisse für die Stellung des Menchen in der Natur* (Braunschweig, Vieweg & Sohn, 1863).

15. Todes, 'Kovalevskii', 104–5; Todes, *Darwin*; Vucinich, 'Russia', 228, 235–6, 245–6; Vucinich, *Darwin*; Rogers, 'Reception', 496, 501–2; Bibby, *Huxley*, 101.

16. JT to HAH, n.d., 'Monday night', AD; Barton, 'Tyndall', 129–32; *LTH*, 1:231.

17. TH to CK, 30 Apr., 22 May 1863, HP 19.212, 229; *LTH*, 1:239, 242–3.

18. *CCD*, 6:184; Wilson, *Lyell's Journals*, 57–8, 94–8; Blake, 'Man', 153; E. Richards, 'Moral Anatomy', 376, 388–402, 410–19; E. Richards, 'Huxley', 264–6; Lorimer, 'Theoretical Racism', 412; Lorimer, *Colour*, 138, 143; Stocking, 'What's', 376–9; Rainger, 'Race', 60–4; Huxley, 'Negro's Place', 335; Mill, 'Mill on the Negro'; Paradis, *Huxley*, 64. According to 'Professor Huxley and the Anthropologists', *National Reformer*, 12 Mar. 1864, Huxley was offered the Presidency of the Anthropological Society in 1863 and declined it.

19. Blake, 'Huxley', 566–9; di Gregorio, *Huxley*, 154–5; d'Holbach's *System of Nature* had just been reissued: *National Reformer*, 2 Jan. 1864, 6. TH to C. C. Blake, 2 May 1863, HP 11.17; *LTH*, 1:274; GR to TH, n.d., HP 25.159.

20. E. Richards, 'Moral Anatomy', 421; E. Richards, 'Huxley', 262, 266ff; Stocking, 'What's', 375–9; Stocking, *Victorian Anthropology*, 248–56.

21. *LTH*, 1:210, 238, 245–6, 256n; HM 2:58:38; HM 2:58:10, 38–53; nights: HM 2:58:96; TH to E. P. Wright, 31 Dec. 1863, HP 29.122; 'appeal': TH to JH, 21 July 1863, HP 2.120; Huxley and Hawkins, *Elementary Atlas*.

22. TH to JH, 18 Aug. 1863, HP 2.123; 'been': TH to ES, 27 Mar. 1858, HP 31.24; Huxley's Diary HP 70.6 (earnings, 70.5); Clark, *Huxleys*, 73–4; Angela Darwin, pers. comm.; TH to the father of a boy engaged to Katy Huxley, 3 July 1874, HP 9.253; *LTH*, 1:248, 250. George died on 1 Aug. 1863.

23. *LTH*, 1:236, 244; Cornish, *Flower*, 75–6; Flower, 'Reminiscences', 284; HM 2:58:58, 63; 2:119; 1:14:166.

24. HAH to ES, 7 Mar. 1875, AD; 'Had': HAH to ES, 14 Aug. 1881, AD; 'eaten': TH to FD, 22 Mar. 1864, HP 15.127; *LLL*, 2:366; *LTH*, 1:202, 251; 'I wish', CD to TH, 5 Nov. [1864], HP 5.207; *LLD*, 3:3.

25. E. L. Youmans to TH, 9 Apr. 1864, HP 29.256; *LTH*, 1:247.

26. Lorimer, *Colour*, 168, also 12, 14, 55, 73, 76, 81, 107, 118, 124, 165, 171; *LHS*, 106–7; *LLL*, 2:360; *LLD*, 3:11.

27. *LTH*, 1:251; Angela Darwin, pers. comm.; McPherson, *Battle Cry*, chap. 22.

28. Taylor, *Huxley*, 8–13 (HM 1:16:88); Huxley, 'Professor Huxley's Lectures', 267–8; Huxley, 'Negro's Place'; TH to FD, 22 Mar. 1864, HP 15.127; GR to TH, 1 Jan. 1865, HP 25.167: Lorimer, *Colour*, 48, 140, 149; Craft: 'Science and Slavery', *National Reformer*, 9 Apr. 1864 (also 12 Mar. 1864 and 19 Sept. 1863).

The Colonel who commanded the 1st South Carolina Volunteers, the first regiment of freed slaves, wrote to confirm Huxley's observations that black ankles were normal. Not only could his troops stand to attention, but they fought like the best and earned their citizenship: T. W. Higginson to TH, 23 June 1867, HP 18.167; McPherson, *Battle Cry*, 564–5.

29. King, 'Reputed', 92, 96; Ellegard, *Darwin*, 165; *LLL*, 2:382–3; Stafford, *Scientist*, 148; 'midway': HM 1:14:170.

30. HP 31.158; Busk, 'Ancient Human'; *SM*, 2:589; Argyll, *Primeval Man*, 73; Gillespie, 'Duke', 44ff.

31. Best, *Mid-Victorian Britain*, 27; fisheries: V. H. Hobart to TH, 19 Sept. 1864, HP 18.184; TH to P. Wright, 3 Aug. 1864, HP 29.124; R. J. Coward to TH, 6 Apr. 1864, HP 12.324; HP 43.69ff.

32. After the ape-brain debate with Owen, Huxley had founded a 'Thorough Club' in 1862, for 'the propagation of common honesty', which pushed profundity towards the glib. It was a broad evolutionary coalition, and included Kingsley on one side and those cosmic theorists Spencer, Lewes and Chambers on the other. The club quickly withered. Haight, *Eliot Letters*, 4:66; *LTH*, 1:199; Huxley's Diary, 7 Oct. 1862, HP 70.5; HP 31.120–1.

33. Public Schools' Commission extracts in Tyndall *et al.*, *Culture*, 461; *LLL*, 2:359; Sir John Wrottesley consulted Huxley (23 May 1865, HP 29.250) as the Public Schools Bill passed through the Lords; 'Note of conversation with [Henry] Cole & [John] Donnelly', 30 Nov. 1864, HP 42.194; TH to JH, 6 Oct. 1864, HP 2.127; *LTH* 1:237, 254; 'concerns': JH to TH, 7 Feb. 1864, HP 3.105; 'have': TH to JH, 4 Dec. 1862, HP 2.114.

34. Brock and MacLeod, 'Scientists' Declaration', 41, 48, 50; Ellis, *Seven*, 109–11, chap. 4; Jensen, *Huxley*, 143; Huxley, 'Tyndall', 6.

35. Barton, 'Influential Set', 54, 58, 61–4; MacLeod, 'X Club'; *LJH*, 1:542; Jensen, *Huxley*, 143, 150; Spencer, *Autobiography*, 2:115–16; Huxley, 'Tyndall', 10; TH to GR, n.d., HP 25.180.

36. *LLL*, 2:369, 385; Geikie, *Memoir*, 284; *LJT*, 119, 125; Cornish, *Flower*, 79–87; Flower, 'Reminiscences', 281; A. P. Stanley to TH, 29 Nov. 1869, HP 26.226.

37. CD to TH, 5 Nov. 1864, HP 5.207; *LLD*, 3:5, 29; *LTH*, 1:254–5; *MLD*, 1:252–6, 258; MacLeod, 'Of Medals', 83; Bartholomew, 'Award'; Desmond and Moore, *Darwin*, 526; *LJH*, 2:75–6; *LLL*, 2:384; TH to JH, 3 Dec. 1864, HP 2.129; Barton, 'Influential', 61; *LJT*, 92.

38. TH to FD, 26 Jan. 1865, HP 15.129; Pearson, *Life*, 2:67–8; Roos, 'Aims', 162–5; Meadows, *Science*, 17–22; *LHS*, 117; Spencer, *Autobiography*, 2:118–20; 'heart', 'pig': T. Hughes to TH, 22 Nov. 1864, HP 18.326.

39. TH to FD, 26 Jan. 1865, HP 15.129; 'matured': *Times*, 25 May 1864, 8–9; Ellegard, *Darwin*, 168; *LLL*, 2:386; Chadwick, *Secularization*, 111; J. Moore, *Post-Darwinian Controversies*, 25; Ridley, *Palmerston*, 770; 'disgrace': TH to FD, 27 Feb. 1858, HP 15.98; Bradford, *Disraeli*, 254–5.

40. Huxley, 'Science and "Church Policy"'; Barton, 'Evolution', 263–4; Barton, 'X Club', 225; Moore, 'Deconstructing Darwinism', 376–7; Lightman, 'Pope Huxley', 158–9; *LHS*, 118; 'encyclical': TH to FD, 26 Jan. 1865, HP 15.129; cf. Roos, 'Aims', 164. Huxley's diatribe was more characteristic of overt secularist papers. Compare it to the hit at Wiseman in 'Science, and the Church of Rome', *National Reformer*, 25 June 1865.

41. GR to TH, 4 Jan. 1865, HP 25.171, 178; *LTH*, 1:265; *LJT*, 115.

42. TH to GR, n.d., HP 25.180.

43. CD to TH, 4 Jan [1865], HP 5.211.

44. TH to FD, 26 Jan. 1865, HP 15.129; 'hot': TH to HAH, 16 Apr. 1861, AD; HAH to TH, 17 Apr. 1861, AD; *LTH*, 1:265.

45. W. B. Clarke to TH, 6 May 1864, HM 1:16:181; C. Aplan to TH, 16 Dec. 1864 HM 1:16:143; E. Brown to TH, 10 Apr. 1865, HM 1:16:188–94; W. Turner to TH, 16 Nov. 1865, HM 1:16:32. Anthropometric studies: HM 2:105:50.
46. J. P. A., 'Huxley', 2; Bibby, *Huxley*, 100; Clark, *Huxleys*, 44; course: *LTH*, 1:264–5; J. Williams to TH, 5 Dec. 1864, HM 3:121:120; HM 2:102:1–13.
47. GR to TH, 1 Jan. 1865, HP 25.167.
48. Lewis, 'Japanese Connexion'; Lewis, 'Black'; Desmond, *Politics*, 36n; Lorimer, *Colour*, 56–7, 60, 68, 101, 113–14; *National Reformer*, 12 Mar. 1864; collection: Huxley, 'Government'.
49. TH to HAH, 17 Apr. 1861, AD.
50. *CE*, 3:66–7, 73; Harte, *University*, 114–15; E. Richards, 'Huxley', 260ff; Desmond, *Archetypes*, 159; Paradis, *Huxley*, 64–5.

18 BIRDS, DINOSAURS & BOOMING GUNS

1. MF to TH, 20 Aug. 1866, HP 4.157; Geison, *Foster*, chap. 3; Huxley, 'How to Become'; Mivart, 'Reminiscences', 990–1; Parker, 'Huxley', 161–5; Osborn, 'Memorial', 46; Fiske, 'Reminiscences'; A. Wollaston, *Newton*, 46; Block, 'Huxley's Rhetoric', 373; Gardner, 'Huxley Essay', 177.
2. St G. Mivart to CD, 22 Apr. 1870, 10 Jan. 1872, DAR 171, CUL; Mivart, 'Reminiscences', 985–8, 993; Gruber, *Conscience*, chaps 1–3; *CE*, 3:120; Howes, 'Mivart', 100.
3. E. H. Giglioli to TH, 4 Apr. 1865, HP 17.44; Corsi, 'Recent', 714; 'opposed': J. Young to TH, 14 July 1867, HP 29.271; 'tooth': TH to E. P. Wright, 30 Oct., 2 Nov. 1863, HP 29.116–18.
4. Bynum, 'Lyell's *Antiquity*', 178, 182; *LLD*, 3:39; *LJH*, 2:53; 'like': TH to JH, 12 June 1865, HP 2.131; *LJT*, 115; Harte, *University*, 114–15, 128.
5. *LLD*, 3:40; *LJH*, 2:47–8, 71; Hutchinson, *Life*, 1:74.
6. Tylor, *Primitive Culture*, 1:6; Burrow, *Evolution*, 229–30, 254–6; Lorimer, *Colour*, 140–60; Stocking, *Race*, 97–8; *LLD*, 3:40; 'really': JH to TH, 14 July 1865, HP 3.107; 'just': TH to JH, 15 July 1865, HP 2.134.
7. MF to TH, 1 July 1865, HP 4.151; 'out': TH to E. P. Wright, 4 Jan. 1866, HP 29.175.
8. TH to E. P. Wright, 4 Jan. 1866, HP 29.175; TH to CD, 4 Oct. [1865], HP 5.223; 'bound': MF to TH, 23 Oct. 1865, HP 4.153; TH to J. N. Lockyer, 22 Aug. 1865, HP 21.242; Roos, 'Aims', n16; Meadows, *Science*, 21–2; Pearson, *Life*, 2:69.
9. J. Lubbock to TH, 2 Aug. 1866, HP 22.65; 'Turkey': GR to TH, 1 Jan. 1865, HP 25.167; JH to TH, n.d., HP 3.85; 'scandal': TH to JH, 24 Jan. 1868, HP 2.140; '700': J. Crawfurd to TH, 6 Oct. 1866, HP 12.335; E. Richards, 'Moral Anatomy', 422–30; E. Richards, 'Huxley', 264–7; Stocking, 'What's', 380–5; Green, 'Huxley', 692; *CE*, 7:209; Lorimer, 'Theoretical', 412; di Gregorio, *Huxley*, 160ff. TH's 1865 ethnology notes, HM 1:16:119–41; HM 2:103.
   For Wallace's attempt to produce a mediating science see: Wallace, *Contributions*, 303–31; Durant, 'Scientific Naturalism', 40–5; R. Smith, 'Wallace', 179–80; Kottler, 'Darwin', 388; Schwartz, 'Darwin', 283–4.
10. A. R. Wallace to TH, 26 Feb. 1864, HP 28.91; *LTH*, 1:324; E. Richards, 'Huxley', 262–4.

11. *English Leader*, 13 Jan. 1866; *CE*, 1:37–40; TH to FD, 4 Jan. 1866, HP 15.131; flyer: HP 31.189; Draper, *Chronicle*, 120; Turner, *Between Science*, 18.

12. TH to JT, [Nov. 1867], HP 9.35; G. H. Lewes to TH, n.d., HP 21.220; Haight, *Eliot Letters*, 4:192, 214, 8:360; Jenny Marx, 29 Jan. 1866, in Lefebvre, *Marx–Engels* (Simon Schaffer's translation). Paradis, *Huxley*, 76–8 on the religious awe of infinite space and life's eternal flux which gave this lecture its impact.

13. Owen, 'The Reign of Law', Autograph Manuscripts of Sir R. Owen, BM(NH), Owen Coll. 59.1–2, 17; Huxley, 'To the Editor'; *English Leader*, 3, 24 Feb. 1866; *LTH*, 119.

14. CL to TH, 28 Nov. 1865, HP 6.192; E. P. Wright to TH, 1865–6, HP 29.128–237; HM 2:33:1–14, 2:89; W. Brownrigg to TH, 29 Nov. 1865, HP 11.125; *SM*, 3:180; *LTH*, 1:263.

15. Bibby, *Huxley*, 196; *LTH*, 1:275; Irvine, *Apes*, 242; W. C. H. Peters to TH, 3 July 1865, HP 24.109; *LJT*, 120–1.

16. *LTH*, 1:276; 1866 Hunterian Lectures HM 2:58:109; fellows: *English Leader*, 5 May 1866; 'What': G. M. Humphrey to TH, 22 Mar. 1866, HP 18.332; *SM*, 3:60–77; A. Wollaston, *Newton*, 133–5; O'Connor, *Founders*, chap. 11; *CE*, 3:79.

17. F. Burr to RIM, 19 Sept. 1866, HM 3:121:29; *SM*, 3:326–7; *LTH*, 1:276, 312; on *Toxodon*: CD to TH, 4 July [1866], HP 5.231. E. Lynn to TH, 11 Nov. 1868, HP 21.223; RI course on ethnology 3 May–9 June 1866, HM 1:16:171, 2:58:116, 2:60:1–93, 2:102:14; HP 33.74.

18. TH to ES, 18 Mar. 1866, HP 31.34; *LTH*, 1:273; Angela Darwin, pers. comm.

19. TH to ES, 18 Mar., 1 Dec. 1866, HP 31.34–6; *Times* notice, HP 9.243; Watterson, *Marse*, 1:97–9; Angela Darwin, pers. comm.; *LTH*, 1:273.

20. F. Burr to RIM, 19 Sept. 1866, HM 3:121:29; 'you': H. M. Hozier to TH, 20 June 1866, HP 18.314; V. Carus to TH, 15 Nov. 1866, HP 12.140.

21. The spread of liberalism gave the British a new European identity. The free-trader Richard Cobden even set up an International Education Society, planning parallel schools in Bonn, Paris and a London one in Isleworth. Modern languages and a liberal education were to ready the sons of professionals and businessmen for a new European role. Huxley and Tyndall became Governors of the London school in 1865 and planned its science teaching: HP 1.55, 1.57, 22.223–5, 34.35, 43.25, draft programme, 42.37, 42.46, 42.50, 42.51; *LTH*, 1:269–70, 308; Bibby, *Huxley*, 168–72.

22. *LTH*, 1:266–7; Weindling, 'Haeckel', 314, 317; E. Haeckel to TH, 17 May 1865, HP 17.170.

23. Gasman, *Scientific Origins*, 17–18; Weindling, 'Darwinism', 689, 694; Weindling, 'Haeckel', 311, 318–20; Bölsche, *Haeckel*, 133ff, 150; Kelly, *Descent*, 22; Coleman, 'Morphology', 150; Haeckel, *Generelle Morphologie*, 2:451; Haeckel, *History*, 1:1–2, 295; S. Gould, *Ontogeny*, 78, 170; E. Haeckel to TH, 4 May 1866, HP 17.174.

24. Marsh, 'Huxley', 182.

25. Grove, *Correlation*, 346; Ellegard, *Darwin*, 78–9; *LJH*, 2:102.

26. F. W. Farrar to TH, 24 Sept., 1 Oct. [1866], HP 16.21–3; HP 42.1–28; W. Smith to TH, 4 Dec. 1866, HP 26.129; *MLD*, 2:43; *LTH*, 1:277.

27. J. Hunt to TH, 6, 12 Oct. 1866, HP 18.334, 340; TH to J. Hunt, 9 Oct.

1866, HP 18.335; Stocking, 'What's', 382; E. Richards, 'Moral Anatomy', 426; J. Lubbock to TH, 2 Aug. 1866, HP 22.65; A. R. Wallace to TH, n.d., HP 28.93.

28. TH to CK, 8 Nov. 1866, HP 19.243; *LTH*, 1:279–82; HP 8.47; Jamaica Committee to JT, 12 Oct. 1866, HP 8.315; HP 8.331; Morris, *Heaven's Command*, 303–17; di Gregorio, *Huxley*, 172–3; Paradis, *Huxley*, 63–4; Lorimer, *Colour*, chap. 9; Bolt, *Victorian Attitudes*, chap. 3; Semmel, *Eyre*, chaps 4–5.

29. JH to JT, 13 Nov. 1866, HP 8.318 (also 'sight'); CK to TH, 6 Nov. 1866, HP 19.241; *LCK*, 1:3; '*naturally*': F. W. Farrar to JT, n.d., HP 8.342; HP 8.334; 'Professor Tyndall's Reply to the Jamaica Committee', HP 8.316; JT to HAH, n.d., AD; Spencer, *Autobiography*, 2:139; *LTH*, 1:279; *LJT*, 122–3; Huxley, 'Tyndall', 4.

30. Lorimer, *Colour*, 150–9, 195; Hunt's attack: W. B. Hodgson to TH, 3 Nov. 1866, HP 18.201; F. W. Chesson to TH, 20 Oct. 1866, HP 12.184. January 1867 Mechanics' Institute talks: *LTH*, 1:287; HM 1:16:142; 2:59:10; W. B. Carpenter to TH, 20 June 1866, HP 12.100; 'personally': TH to JH, 24 Jan. 1868, HP 2.140. M. Moore to TH, 9 Aug. 1867, HP 23.3, possibly having read of Huxley's May–June 1867 Fullerian course on Ethnology: HM 2:59:32; HP 33.73; di Gregorio, *Huxley*, 170ff. Stocking, *Victorian Anthropology*, 62 on 'Anglo-Saxon' self-imagery.

31. TH to ES, 1 Dec. 1866, HP 31.36; Briggs, *Age*, 492–7; 'denouncing' quoted in Collie, *Huxley*, 89 n59.

32. CD to TH, 12 Jan., 21 Feb. 1867, HP 5.235, 260; *MLD*, 1:281; HAH to ES, 20 Sept. 1869, HP 31.40; Becker, *Scientific London*, 248; Bibby, *Huxley*, 114–15.

33. Bölsche, *Haeckel*, 242; *MLD*, 2:350; Huxley, 'Natural History', 13–14; *LTH*, 1:289; E. Haeckel to TH, 12 May, 28 June 1867, HP 17.177–82; Haeckel, 'Huxley', 464–6.

34. Huxley, 'Natural History', 41; *LTH*, 1:288–90; 'German': CD to TH, 10 June 1868, HP 5.239, also 5.196; *MLD*, 1:274; Coleman, 'Morphology', 164, 171–3; di Gregorio, 'Dinosaur', 398, 415–16.

35. Benson, 'Naples', 332–3; *LTH*, 1:290–1; Groeben, *Darwin*, 10, 22; TH to A. Dohrn, 9, 22 Sept. 1867, HP 13.156–9.

36. *MLD*, 1:277–8; *LTH*, 1:288, 305; *LLD*, 3:69; Haeckel, *Generelle Morphologie*, 1:90, 173–4n; E. Haeckel to TH, 11 Aug., 21 Sept. 1868, 28 Feb. 1869, HP 17.187, 198. Nyhart, 'Disciplinary Breakdown', 374.

37. Huxley, 'Natural History', 40–2; Desmond, *Archetypes*, 89; *LLD*, 3:105.

38. *SM*, 3:238, 305; Workingmen's Lectures on 'Birds and Reptiles', 29 Oct.–3 Dec. 1866, HM 2:59:8.

39. *SM*, 3:241; cf. Seeley, 'Epitome', 326; Padian, 'Pterosaurs'; Hull, *Science*, 114, 348. (Huxley was in touch with Seeley, who sent him his book *Ornithosauria*: e.g. TH to H. Seeley, 20 July 1866, 27 Apr. 1870, APS.) Huxley's 1867 RCS syllabus HM 2:59:16. He had first mooted the 'Sauropsida' at the College of Surgeons in 1863–4: HM 2:58:94; Huxley, *Lectures*, 69; and his pupils were already using the word in 1864: W. Parker, 'Remarks', 57. For Owen's reasoning on the relationship of reptiles to *mammals*, based on his dinosaur and mammal-like reptile studies: Desmond, *Archetypes*, 119, 197–9, 246 n53–4.

40. *SM*, 3:238; interleaved copies: HM 2:36, HM 2:40; *LTH*, 1:285, 290. On

the response to his re-classification of birds, drawing in the clawed-wing hoatzins and mound-incubating megapodes, see HP 15.225, 22.237–9, 23.212–14, 24.35–7; A. Wollaston, *Newton*, 215.

41. HM 2:40:33, 43, 47; also volumes 41–3. The immediate cause of these avian classificatory trees, the first dated 22 Jan. 1868, was the need to respond to Newton's criticisms in the *Ibis*. (Newton, a Darwinian, liked to stir up controversy to keep his paper lively: A. Wollaston, *Newton*, 66.)

42. *SM*, 3:296, 365; Huxley, 'Reply', 361; interleaved 'Reply', HM 2:40:48; Allen, *Naturalist*, 190; O'Connor, *Founders*, 165; di Gregorio, *Huxley*, 79ff.

43. TH to RIM, 2 Oct. 1866, HM 2:33:15; *LTH*, 1:275; *SM*, 3:90, 198; G. Gordon to TH, 2 Nov. 1867, HM 2:59:45; 'incubus': TH to P. Sclater, 10 June 1867, ZSL.

44. Desmond, 'Owen's Response'; Desmond, *Archetypes*, 115–20; Padian, 'Pterosaurs'.

45. HM 2:93:70; *SM*, 3:465.

46. *CCD*, 7:409, 532. Only five years earlier, before Huxley had assumed his partisan role, he praised Phillips precisely for his avoidance 'of party prejudice': *West. Rev.*, 64 (1855), 565.

47. TH to MF, 26 Nov. 1867, HP 4.5; 'like': TH to A. Dohrn, 15 Jan. 1868, HP 13.160; *LTH*, 1:304.

48. TH to J. Phillips, 31 Dec. 1867, OUM 29.

49. Joan Evans, *Time*, 115–16; John Evans, 'Portions', 418–19; Mackie, 'Aeronauts'; Woodward, 'Feathered Fossil'; Owen, 'Archaeopteryx'; CL to TH, [Oct. 1862], HP 6.70; Rupke, *Owen*, 71–5.

50. *SM*, 3:345; Huxley, *American Addresses*, 241; notes on *Archaeopteryx*, 25 Dec. 1867, HM 2:40:7; Desmond, *Archetypes*, 124–30.

51. TH to J. Phillips, 28 Apr. 1870, OUM 29.1; Phillips, 'Cetiosaurus'; Phillips, *Geology*, 254–94; *SM*, 3:241, 311; Huxley, *American Addresses*, 65.

52. Huxley, 'On the Animals'; *SM*, 3:303, 366; HM 2:59:48; Di Gregorio, 'Dinosaur', 407–8. Huxley did not announce it that night, but he had another ancestor. Christmas 1867 in the British Museum had been celebrated with a turkey-sized dinosaur. Owen's so-called baby *Iguanodon* from the Isle of Wight was, Huxley realized, an adult of an unknown species, which he called *Hypsilophodon*. With an even more avian hip, it brought dinosaurs 'a further step towards the bird': *SM*, 3:482; Desmond, *Archetypes*, 144; HM 2:93:31; TH to J. Phillips, 31 Dec. 1867, OUM 29; *SM*, 3:458; TH to CL, 23 July 1868, APS, also HP 30.45.

53. J. Phillips to TH, 14 Oct., 19 Nov. 1869, HP 24.119, 121; *SM*, 3:466–70, 476–80. Huxley went on to amend dinosaur classification, rubber-stamping his ornithic product by uniting *Compsognathus* with the big dinosaurs in a new group, the 'Ornithoscelida' ('bird-leg'): *SM*, 3:487. Cf. Owen, *Monograph on the Fossil Reptilia*, 87–93. E. D. Cope to TH, 28 Nov. 1866, HM 2:33:21–2; Cope, 'Remains'; Osborn, *Cope*, 157; Leidy, 'Hadrosaurus'.

54. *LTH*, 1:303; Uschmann and Jahn, 'Briefwechsel zwischen', 15; E. Haeckel to TH, 27 Jan. 1868, HP 17.183. Haeckel (*History*, 2:226–7) interposed the beaked anomodonts (e.g. *Dicynodon*) between dinosaurs and birds. But Owen ('Description', 423) saw the anomodonts leading to mammals, showing that his and Huxley's divergence over the kinship of birds, reptiles and mammals was never as clear-cut as it later seemed.

19 EYEING THE PRIZE

1. Bibby, 'South London', 211; Hutton, 'Pope Huxley', 135–6; Lightman, 'Pope Huxley', 161.
2. Davies, *Heterodox London*, 1:111–12; G. S. Jones, *Outcast London*, 40, 85; Gilley and Loades, 'Huxley', 305; Gardner, 'Huxley Essay', 179–80; Stanley, 'Huxley's Treatment', 122; Paradis, *Huxley*, 58–9 offers the best analysis of the chess analogy. *CE*, 3:78–9, 82–3; Bibby, 'South London', 212; '*your*': W. F. Rae to TH, 6 Jan. 1868, HP 25.11. On Christian Socialism: TH to CK, 23 Sept. 1860, HP 19.169; *LTH*, 1:222.
3. JT to TH, 8 Jan. 1868, HP 1.45; Barnes and Shapin, *Natural Order*, 93; R. Young, *Darwin's Metaphor*, 190ff; *CE*, 3:88–9.
4. J. H. Titcomb to TH, 22 Nov. 1867, HP 28.25; Green, 'Huxley'; *CE*, 3:119–20; *LTH*, 1:302; Gilley and Loades, 'Huxley', 295–6.
5. *LTH*, 2:297; M. Kalisch to TH, 8 May 1868, HP 19.122; JT to TH, 22 Apr. 1869, HP 1.59.
6. Ellegard, *Darwin*, 82; *LJH*, 2:114–21; Holyoake, 'Priesthood', 1–3; J. V. Carus to TH, 30 July 1868, HP 12.142; *LLD*, 3:48–9; 'duty': JT to JH, n.d., HP 8.344; *LTH*, 1:301–2; 'out': TH to A. Dohrn, 7 July 1868, HP 13.166.
7. TH to W. C. Williamson, 16 Oct. 1869, APS; Rehbock, 'Huxley', 508–18; Rupke, '*Bathybius*', 54–6; Rice, 'Huxley', 171–3; Gould, '*Bathybius*', 198; *LTH*, 1:295–6; *SM*, 3:330; 3:454, and Fox, 'Skull', on his bird-like dinosaur *Hypsilophodon*.
8. Tyndall, *Fragments*, 92–3, 130, 163–4, 198, 441; Huxley, 'Tyndall', 4; Turner, *Between Science*, 25–7; *LJT*, 131, 148, 150; Mivart, *Essays*, 2:228. Ellegard, *Darwin*, 83; *LTH*, 1:297; Holyoake, 'Priesthood', 4–5.
9. Holyoake, 'Priesthood', 5–6; *CE*, 8:1–4, 7, 27, 35; *LTH*, 1:297. The prehistory of this talk can be seen in Huxley, 'Chalk', and in his London Institution lecture on cosmogony, 14 Oct. 1867, HM 2:59:40.
10. Baynes, 'Darwin', 505–6; Cockshut, *Unbelievers*, 91; Lightman, *Origins*, chap. 5; G. M. Young, *Portrait*, 96; Barton, 'Tyndall'; *CE*, 5:319–20.
11. E. M. Schmitz to HAH, 15 Nov. 1868, HP 26.43 (the eye witness); *CE*, 1:131–60; Geison, 'Protoplasmic Theory', 273–84; 'pouring': J. Young, 'Huxley', 242; Gardner, 'Huxley Essay', 182ff; Calderwood, 'Huxley's Sermons', 197; Weindling, *Darwinism*, 45–6; Gilley and Loades, 'Huxley', 298, 302; Morley, *Recollections*, 1:88, 90; Brown, *Metaphysical Society*, 51; J. Morley to TH, 31 May, 12 Nov. 1869, HP 23.14–15; J. Cranbrook to TH, 2, 23 Oct. 1868, HP 12.328–32; *LTH*, 1:299.
12. CD to TH, 19 Mar. [1869], HP 5.266; *LLD*, 3:113; HAH to ES, 7 Nov. 1869, HP 31.40; J. Morley to TH, 31 May 1869, HP 23.14; 'lunar': E. Frankland to TH, 16 Feb. 1869, HP 16.251; Geison, 'Protoplasmic Theory', 279, 284; J. Young, 'Huxley', 244; 'Protoplasm at the Antipodes', *Nature*, 1 (1869), 13.
13. St G. Mivart to CD, 25 Apr. 1870, DAR 171, CUL. Huxley, *Prove di Fatto Intorno al posto che L'Uomo Tiene Nella Natura* trans. Pietro Marchi (Milan, Treves, 1869). It also went into French as *La Place de l'homme dans la Nature* (Paris, Baillière, 1870).
14. HAH to ES, 7 Nov. 1869, HP 31.40; *LTH*, 1:307–10; syllabus, HM 2:63; MS, HM 2:64–5; Huxley, *Physiography*, vii; *CE*, 3:87, 111, 116, 129.

15. HAH to ES, 20 Sept.–7 Nov. 1869, HP 31.40; *LTH*, 1:305–6; 'definitely': TH to FD, [28 Sept. 1869], HP 15.133; 'I often': CD to TH, 10 June 1868, HP 5.239; TH on Jim's health problem: HP 9.253.

16. HP 31.101; CL to TH, 13 Feb. 1868, HP 6.126; RIM to TH, 18 Feb. 1869, HP 23.184.

17. Tait, 'Geological Time', 407, 422, 438; *MLD*, 1:314; Jenkin, 'Origin', 301; W. Thomson, *Lectures*, 2:64; *CE*, 8:306, 327–9; C. Smith and Wise, *Energy*, chaps 15–17; Burchfield, *Kelvin*, chaps 2–4; Jensen, *Huxley*, 171.

18. On 29 Apr., 5 May 1869: Huxley's Diary, HP 70.9; R. H. Meade to TH, 30 June 1869, HP 22.206; TH to G. G. Leveson-Gower (Granville), 12 Aug. 1869, HP 30.75; *SM*: 3,427; *LTH*, 1:306, 2:451; Stocking, *Victorian Anthropology*, 108. Later letters, e.g., HM 1:16:110, 168; HP 25.43, 28.192–4, 30.65.

19. P. M. Duncan to TH, 8 Sept. 1868, HP 15.26–8; also HP 10.267–9; 12.211–13; 15.26–35; 18.355–7; 21.29–38; 23.112; 27.261; 30.160; 33.1–31. Stocking, 'What's', 382–3; Rainger, 'Race', 68; purging: TH to D. W. Nash, 17 Nov. 1868, HP 23.196, also 23.98; E. Lynn to TH, 11 Nov. 1868, HP 21.223; E. Richards, 'Huxley', 269–75.

20. *LTH*, 1:292, 312; TH to MF, n.d., HP 4.3, 15.

21. Nobody had tried allegiances more than J. S. Mill with his call for black suffrage and Eyre's prosecution. But sympathies ran deep in this aristocracy of intellect. When Mill lost his Parliamentary seat, even though Tyndall reckoned he 'deserves what he has got', he added 'but if I had a pocket borough at my disposal he is the first man that I should choose to represent it': JT to TH, 19 Nov. [1868], HP 1.228.

22. JT to TH, 13 Mar. [1868], HP 8.345.

23. HAH to ES, 7 Nov. 1869, HP 31.40; Heyck, *Intellectual Transformation*, 178, 215–17; Roos, 'Aims', 165–71; *MLD*, 1:317; Huxley, 'Nature', 9; Meadows, *Science*, 25–31.

24. *LCK*, 2:214; Dockrill, 'Huxley', 470–3; Eisen, 'Huxley', 338–42; Lightman, *Origins*, 23ff; Paradis, *Huxley*, 80–5; 'hard': E. S. Beesly to TH, 8 Feb. 1869, HP 10.270; *CE*, 1:156; J. Morley to TH, 12, 13 Jan. 1869, HP 23.11–12; 'superstitious': Wollaston, *Newton*, 244; Huxley, 'Chalk', 500; Haight, *Eliot Letters*, 4:214–15; J. R. Moore, 'Theodicy', 173; Turner, *Between Science*, 22; nihilist: J. Young, 'Huxley', 257. Huxley echoed Carlyle, who was 'neither Pantheist nor Pottheist, nor any *Theist* or *ist* whatsoever, having the most decided contempt for all manner of System-builders and Sectfounders': Turner, 'Victorian Scientific Naturalism', 336–8.

25. J. Lubbock to TH, 16 Apr. 1869, HP 22.68; Huxley's Diary, HP 70.9; Brown, *Metaphysical Society*, 15, 21–7; J. P. A. , 'Huxley', 2.

26. Hutton, 'Pope Huxley', 135; Lightman, 'Pope Huxley', 155, 157; *CE*: 1:195, 5:238–9; J. R. 'Moore, 'Deconstructing Darwinism', 388–9, 394; Dockrill, 'Huxley', 464–9; J. R. Moore, 'Theodicy', 177–9; Cockshut, *Unbelievers*, 92; 'Professor Huxley's Doctrine', *English Leader*, 3 Mar. 1866, 101–2; Kottler, 'Wallace'.

27. JT to TH, [Sept. 1869], HP 1.60; TH to JT, 30 Sept. 1869, HP 8.75; *LTH*, 1:313; *Times*, 25 Aug. 1869, 6; 'repudiated': JH to TH, [Aug. 1869], HP 3.126; 'President Huxley', *Spectator*, 42 (1869), 1108–10; S. Northcote to TH, 19 Apr. 1869, HP 23.226.

28. 'President Huxley', *Spectator*, 42 (1869), 1108–10; Ellegard, *Darwin*, 65, 85;

'big wig': TH to HAH, 12 July 1851, HH 156; *LTH*, 1:89; 'like': TH to FD, [28 Sept. 1869], HP 15.133.

29. Ralph, 'MacGillivray', 185, 193; Collie, *Huxley*, 89 n59; 'President Huxley', *Spectator*, 42 (1869), 1108.

30. HAH to ES, 20 Sept.–7 Nov. 1869, HP 31.40; *LTH*, 1:231.

31. Hutton, 'Pope Huxley', 135; 'jacket': TH to HAH, 16 Feb. 1854, HH 262; Morris, *Heaven's Command*, 265–6; G. Young, *Portrait*, 72.

32. J. R. Moore, 'Theodicy', 173–4; G. Young, *Portrait*, 95; 'President Huxley', *Spectator*, 42 (1869), 1108; Morley, *Recollections*, 1:88–9; Cockshut, *Unbelievers*, 87.

33. HAH to ES, 19 Mar. 1873, AD; Heyck, *Intellectual Transformation*, 13, 138–9; J. R. Moore, 'Crisis', 68; J. R. Moore, 'Freethought', 308; '220': HAH to ES, 20 Sept.-7 Nov. 1869, HP 31.40.

34. *CE*, 1:270–1; Bibby, *Huxley*, 30–1; *LTH*, 1:16, 334–5.

Bibliography

Anonymous press articles are cited fully in the notes. Place of publication is London unless otherwise stated.

AMNH	*Annals and Magazine of Natural History*
ANH	*Archives of Natural History*
AS	*Annals of Science*
BFMCR	*British and Foreign Medico-Chirurgical Review*
BJHS	*British Journal for the History of Science*
CR	*Contemporary Review*
CUP	Cambridge University Press
ER	*Edinburgh Review*
HS	*History of Science*
JHB	*Journal of the History of Biology*
NC	*Nineteenth Century*
NR	*National Reformer*
NRRS	*Notes and Records of the Royal Society*
OUP	Oxford University Press
QJGS	*Quarterly Journal of the Geological Society*
QR	*Quarterly Review*
Report BAAS	*Report of the British Association for the Advancement of Science*
UCP	University of Chicago Press
VS	*Victorian Studies*
WR	*Westminster Review*

Agnosco, 'Professor Huxley', *Agnostic Journal*, 37 (1895), 1–2.

Allen, D. E., *The Naturalist in Britain: A Social History* (Penguin, 1978).

—, 'Huxley's Botanist Brother-in-Law', *ANH*, 11 (1983), 191–3.

Altholz, J. L., 'The Huxley–Wilberforce Debate Revisited', *J. Hist. Med. & Allied Sciences*, 35 (1980), 313–16.

Altick, R. D., *The Shows of London* (Cambridge, MA, Harvard UP, 1978).

Appel, T. A., *The Cuvier–Geoffroy Debate: French Biology in the Decades Before Darwin* (New York, OUP, 1987).

Argyll, Duke of, *Primeval Man* (Strahan, 1869).

Bibliography

Ashton, R., *The German Idea: Four English Writers and the Reception of German Thought 1800–1860* (CUP, 1980)

—, *G. H. Lewes, A Life* (Oxford, Clarendon Press, 1991).

Atkins, H., *Down, the Home of the Darwins* (Royal College of Physicians, 1976).

Audubon, M. R., ed., *Audubon and his Journals* 2 vols (Nimmo, 1898).

Backstrom, P. N., *Christian Socialism and Co-operation in Victorian England: Edward Vansittart Neale and the Co-operative Movement* (Croom Helm, 1974).

Bain, A. G., 'On the Discovery of the Fossil Remains of Bidental and other Reptiles in South Africa', *Trans. Geol. Soc.*, 7 (1854), 53–9.

Bainton, R. H., *Here I Stand: A Life of Martin Luther* (New York, Mentor, 1950).

Barber, L., *The Heyday of Natural History* (New York, Doubleday, 1980).

Barnaby, D., ed., *The Log Book of Wombwell's Royal No. 1 Menagerie, 1848–1871* (Sale, Cheshire, ZSGM Publications, 1989).

Barnes, B., and S. Shapin, *Natural Order: Historical Studies of Scientific Culture* (Sage, 1979).

Barrett, P. H., ed., *The Collected Papers of Charles Darwin* (UCP, 1977).

—, P. J. Gautrey, S. Herbert, D. Kohn and S. Smith, eds, *Charles Darwin's Notebooks, 1836–1844* (Cambridge, British Museum [Natural History]/CUP, 1987).

Barrow, L., *Independent Spirits: Spiritualism and English Plebeians 1850–1910* (Routledge & Kegan Paul, 1986).

Bartholomew, M., 'Lyell and Evolution: An Account of Lyell's Response to the Prospect of an Evolutionary Ancestry for Man', *BJHS*, 6 (1973), 261–303.

—, 'Huxley's Defence of Darwin', *AS*, 32 (1975), 525–35.

—, 'The Award of the Copley Medal to Charles Darwin', *NRRS*, 30 (1976), 209–18.

—, 'The Non-Progress of Non-Progression: Two Responses to Lyell's Doctrine', *BJHS*, 9 (1976), 166–74.

Barton, R., 'Evolution: The Whitworth Gun in Huxley's War for the Liberation of Science from Theology', in D. R. Oldroyd and I. Langham, eds, *The Wider Domain of Evolutionary Thought* (Dordrecht, Reidel, 1983), 261–86.

—, 'John Tyndall, Pantheist', *Osiris*, 3 (1987), 111–34.

—, '"An Influential Set of Chaps": The X-Club and Royal Society Politics 1864–85', *BJHS*, 23 (1990), 53–81.

Bassett, M., *Behind the Picture: H.M.S. Rattlesnake's Australia-New Guinea Cruise 1846–1850* (Melbourne, OUP, 1966).

Bayley, W. A., *Blue Haven: History of Kiama Municipality New South Wales* (Kiama, Kiama Municipal Council, 1976).

[Baynes, T. S.], 'Darwin on Expression', *ER*, 137 (1873), 492–508.

Becker, B. H., *Scientific London* (King, 1874).

Beddoe, J. , *Memories of Eighty Years* (Bristol, Arrowsmith, 1910).

Bell, S., 'George Henry Lewes: A Man of His Time', *JHB*, 14 (1981), 277–98.

Benson, K. R., 'The Naples Stazione Zoologica and Its Impact on the Emergence of American Marine Biology', *JHB*, 21 (1988), 331–41.

Benton, M. J., 'Progressionism in the 1850s: Lyell, Owen, Mantell and the Elgin Fossil Reptile *Leptopleuron* (*Telerpeton*)', *ANH*, 11 (1982), 123–36.

Berman, M., *Social Change and Scientific Organization: The Royal Institution, 1799–1844* (Heinemann, 1978).

Best, G., *Mid-Victorian Britain 1851–70* (Fontana, 1979).

Bibliography

Bevington, M. M., *The Saturday Review 1855–1868* (New York, Columbia UP, 1941).

Bibby, C., 'The South London Working Men's College', *Adult Education*, 28 (1955), 211–21.

—, 'Thomas Henry Huxley and University Development', *VS*, 2 (1958), 97–116.

—, *T. H. Huxley: Scientist, Humanist and Educator* (New York, Horizon Press, 1960).

[Blake, C. C.], 'Man and Beast', *Anthropological Review*, 1 (1863), 153–62.

[—], 'Professor Huxley on Man's Place in Nature', *ER*, 117 (1863), 541–69.

Blinderman, C. S., 'The Oxford Debate and After', *Notes and Queries*, 202 (1957), 126–8.

Block, E., 'T. H. Huxley's Rhetoric and the Popularization of Victorian Scientific Ideas: 1854–1874', *VS*, 29 (1986), 363–86.

Bölsche, W., *Haeckel: His Life and Work*, trans. J. McCabe (Unwin, 1906).

Bolt, C., *Victorian Attitudes to Race* (Routledge & Kegan Paul, 1971).

Bowler, P. J., *Fossils and Progress: Paleontology and the Idea of Progressive Evolution in the Nineteenth Century* (New York, Science History Publications, 1976).

—, *Theories of Human Evolution. A Century of Debate 1844–1944* (Oxford, Blackwell, 1986).

—, *Charles Darwin. The Man and His Influence* (Oxford, Blackwell, 1990).

Boylan, P. J., 'The Controversy of the Moulin-Quignon Jaw: The Role of Hugh Falconer', in Jordanova and Porter, *Images*, 171–99.

Bradford, S., *Disraeli* (New York, Stein and Day, 1982).

Briggs, A., *The Age of Improvement 1783–1867* (Longman, 1979).

—, *Victorian People* (Penguin, 1990).

—, *Victorian Cities* (Penguin, 1990).

—, *Victorian Things* (Penguin, 1990).

Brock, W. H., and R. M. MacLeod, 'The Scientists' Declaration: Reflexions on Science and Belief in the Wake of *Essays and Reviews*, 1864–5', *BJHS*, 9 (1976), 39–66.

[Broderip, W., and R. Owen], 'Generalizations of Comparative Anatomy', *QR*, 93 (1853), 46–83.

Brooke, J. H., 'Natural Theology and the Plurality of Worlds: Observations on the Brewster–Whewell Debate', *AS*, 34 (1977), 221–86.

—, 'The Natural Theology of the Geologists', in Jordanova and Porter, *Images*, 39–64.

Brooks, J. L., *Just Before the Origin: Alfred Russel Wallace's Theory of Evolution* (New York, Columbia UP, 1984).

Brown, A. W., *The Metaphysical Society* (New York, Columbia UP, 1947).

Browne, J., 'The Charles Darwin–Joseph Hooker Correspondence: An Analysis of Manuscript Resources and their use in Biography', *J. Soc. Biblphy Nat. Hist.*, 8 (1978), 351–66.

—, *The Secular Ark: Studies in the History of Biogeography* (New Haven, Yale UP, 1983).

—, 'Squibs and Snobs: Science in Humorous British Undergraduate Magazines around 1830', *HS*, 30 (1992), 165–97.

Buckle, H. T., *History of Civilization in England* 3 vols (Richards, 1903–4).

Bunbury, F. J., ed., *Memorials of Sir Charles J. F. Bunbury* 9 vols (Privately Printed, 1891).

Bibliography

—, ed., *Life, Letters and Journals of Sir Charles J. F. Bunbury* 3 vols (Privately Printed, 1894).

Burchfield, J. D., *Lord Kelvin and the Age of the Earth* (UCP, 1990).

Burkhardt, F., and S. Smith, eds, *The Correspondence of Charles Darwin* 8 vols (CUP, 1985–1993).

Burrow, J. W., *Evolution and Society: A Study in Victorian Social Theory* (CUP, 1966).

Burstyn, H. L., 'If Darwin wasn't the *Beagle*'s Naturalist, Why was he on Board', *BJHS*, 8 (1975), 62–9.

Busk, G., 'An Account of the Polyzoa, and Sertularian Zoophytes, Collected in the Voyage of the Rattlesnake', in MacGillivray, *Narrative*, 1:343–402.

—, 'On a very ancient Human Cranium from Gibraltar', *Report BAAS, Bath, 1864*, (1865), Notices 91–2.

Butcher, B. W., 'Gorilla Warfare in Melbourne: Halford, Huxley and "Man's Place in Nature"', in R. W. Home, ed., *Australian Science in the Making* (CUP, 1988), 153–69.

Bynum, W. F., 'Charles Lyell's *Antiquity of Man* and its Critics', *JHB* 17 (1984), 153–87.

Calderwood, H., 'Professor Huxley's Lay Sermons', *CR*, 15 (1870), 195–206.

Cardwell, D. S. L., *The Organisation of Science in England* (Heinemann, 1972).

Carlyle, T., *Critical and Miscellaneous Essays* 7 vols (Chapman & Hall, 1894).

—, *On Heroes, Hero-Worship, and the Heroic in History* (New York, Chelsea House, 1983).

Carpenter, W. B., *Remarks on Some Passages in the Review of 'Principles of General and Comparative Physiology* . . . (Bristol, Philip & Evans, 1840).

—, 'Dubois and Jones on Medical Study', *British and Foreign Medical Review*, 10 (1840), 175–203.

—, *Animal Physiology* 2 vols (Orr, 1843).

Carus, C. G., *The King of Saxony's Journey through England and Scotland in the Year 1844* (Chapman & Hall, 1846).

Chadwick, O., *The Secularization of the European Mind in the Nineteenth Century* (CUP, 1975).

Chandler, T., 'Rheumatism, with Periodical Fits of Delirium, Treated by Animal Magnetism', *Lancet* 2 (1837–8), 81–3.

—, 'Cures of Various Diseases with Mesmerism', *Zoist*, 2 (1844), 373–6.

—, 'Cases of Mesmerism', *Zoist*, 3 (1845), 189–95.

—, 'Extraordinary Effects of Mesmerism on a Gentleman, PERFECTLY BLIND for Eleven Years', *Zoist*, 5 (1847), 1–11.

Chesney, K., *The Victorian Underworld* (Penguin, 1972).

Chilton, W., 'Theory of Regular Gradation', *Oracle of Reason*, 27 Nov. 1841.

—, 'Geological Revelations', *Oracle of Reason*, 29 July 1843.

Clark, G. K., *The Making of Victorian England* (Methuen, 1962).

Clark, R. W., *The Huxleys* (Heinemann, 1968).

Clarke, J. F., *Autobiographical Recollections of the Medical Profession* (Churchill, 1874).

Coad, J. G., *The Royal Dockyards 1690–1850* (Aldershot, Scolar Press, 1989).

Cockshut, A. O. J., *The Unbelievers: English Agnostic Thought 1840–1890* (Collins, 1964).

Cohen, I. B., 'Three Notes on the Reception of Darwin's Ideas on Natural Selection', in Kohn, *Darwinian Heritage*, 589–607.

Bibliography

Coleman, W., 'Morphology between Type Concept and Descent Theory', *J. Hist. Med. & Allied Sci.*, 31 (1976), 149–75.

Collie, M., *Huxley at Work: With the Scientific Correspondence of T. H. Huxley and the Rev. Dr George Gordon of Birnie, near Elgin* (Macmillan, 1991).

Colp, R., *To Be an Invalid: The Illness of Charles Darwin* (UCP, 1977).

Cooper, R., *The Immortality of the Soul, Religiously and Philosophically Considered* (Watson, 1853).

Cooter, R., *The Cultural Meaning of Popular Science: Phrenology and the Organization of Consent in Nineteenth-Century Britain* (CUP, 1984).

Cope, E. D., 'Remains of a Gigantic Extinct Dinosaur', *Proc. Acad. Nat. Sci., Philadelphia* (1866), 275–9.

Cope, Z., 'The Private Medical Schools of London (1746–1914)', in Poynter, *Evolution of Medical Education*, 89–109.

Cornish, C. J., *Sir William Flower: A Personal Memoir* (Macmillan, 1904).

Corsi, P., 'Recent Studies on Italian Reactions to Darwin', in Kohn, *Darwinian Heritage*, 711–29.

—, *Science and Religion: Baden Powell and the Anglican Debate, 1800–1860* (CUP, 1988).

Cowherd, R. G., *Politics of English Dissent* (New York, New York UP, 1956).

Crosland, M., 'Explicit Qualifications as a Criterion for Membership of the Royal Society', *NRRS*, 37 (1983), 167–87.

Cunningham, H., *The Volunteer Force: A Social and Political History 1859–1908* (Hamden, Conn., Archon Books, 1975).

Dana, J. D., 'Evidence as to Man's Place in Nature', *Am. J. Sci.*, 35 (1863), 451–4.

Dante, *The Divine Comedy. Volume 1, Inferno*, trans. M. Musa (Penguin, 1984).

Darwin, C., *Journal of Researches into the Geology and Natural History of the Various Countries Visited by H. M. S. Beagle* (Colburn, 1839).

—, *A Monograph on the Sub-Class Cirripedia* 2 vols (Ray Society, 1851–4).

—, *On the Origin of Species by Means of Natural Selection, or the Preservation of Favoured Races in the Struggle for Life* (Murray, 1859).

—, *The Expression of the Emotions in Man and Animals* (Murray, 1872).

Darwin, F., ed., *The Foundations of the Origin of Species. Two Essays Written in 1842 and 1844* (CUP, 1909).

Davidoff, L. and C. Hall, *Family Fortunes: Men and Women of the English Middle Class, 1780–1850* (UCP, 1987).

Davies, C. M., *Heterodox London* 2 vols (Tinsley, 1874).

Davis, M., *Every Man his own Landlord: A History of Coventry Building Society* (Warwick, Coventry Building Society, 1985).

Dawson, W. R., *The Huxley Papers. A Descriptive Catalogue of the Correspondence, Manuscripts and Miscellaneous Papers of The Rt. Hon. Thomas Henry Huxley* (Imperial College, 1946).

Dean, D. R., 'Hitchcock's Dinosaur Tracks', *Am. Quart.*, 21 (1969), 639–44.

—, '"Through Science to Despair": Geology and the Victorians', *Ann. N.Y. Acad. Sci.*, 360 (1981), 111–36.

Desmond, A., 'Designing the Dinosaur', *Isis*, 70 (1979), 224–34.

—, *Archetypes and Ancestors: Palaeontology in Victorian London 1850–1875* (Blond & Briggs, 1982; UCP, 1984).

—, 'Robert E. Grant's Later Views on Organic Development: The Swiney Lectures on "Palaeozoology", 1853–1857', *ANH*, 11 (1984), 395–413.

Bibliography

—, 'Richard Owen's Reaction to Transmutation in the 1830's', *BJHS*, 18 (1985), 25–50.

—, 'The Making of Institutional Zoology in London 1822–1836', *HS*, 23 (1985), 153–85, 224–50.

—, 'Artisan Resistance and Evolution in Britain, 1819–1848', *Osiris*, 3 (1987), 77–110.

—, *The Politics of Evolution: Morphology, Medicine, and Reform in Radical London* (UCP, 1989).

—, 'Darwin, Huxley, and the Natural Sciences', *Isis*, 84 (1993), 594–5.

— and J. Moore, *Darwin* (Michael Joseph, 1991; New York, Warner, 1992).

Dickens, C., *The Posthumous Papers of the Pickwick Club* [1836–7] (Penguin, 1972).

—, *Sketches by Boz* [1839] (Mandarin, 1991).

—, *Bleak House* [1853] (Penguin, 1971).

Di Gregorio, M., 'Order or Process of Nature: Huxley's and Darwin's Different Approaches to Natural Sciences', *History and Philosophy of the Life Sciences*, 3 (1981), 217–41.

—, 'The Dinosaur Connection: A Reinterpretation of T. H. Huxley's Evolutionary View', *JHB*, 15 (1982), 397–418.

—, *T. H. Huxley's Place in Natural Science* (New Haven, Yale UP, 1984).

Dockrill, D. W., 'T. H. Huxley and the Meaning of "Agnosticism"', *Theology*, 74 (1971), 461–77.

Draper, H., *The Marx–Engels Chronicle, Volume 1* (New York, Schocken, 1985).

Duncan, D., ed., *The Life and Letters of Herbert Spencer* (Methuen, 1908).

Durant, J., 'Scientific Naturalism and Social Reform in the Thought of Alfred Russel Wallace', *BJHS*, 12 (1979), 31–58.

Durey, M. J., 'Bodysnatchers and Benthamites: The Implications of the Dead Body Bill for the London Schools of Anatomy, 1820–1842', *London Journal*, 2 (1976), 200–25.

Dyster, F. D. , 'Evidence as to Man's Place in Nature', *Reader*, 1 (1863), 234–5.

[Egerton, P.], 'Monkeyana', *Punch*, 18 May 1861, 206.

Eisen, S., 'Huxley and the Positivists', *VS*, 7 (1964), 337–58.

Eliot, G., *Middlemarch* [1871–2] (Penguin, 1985).

Ellegard, A., *Darwin and the General Reader: The Reception of Darwin's Theory of Evolution in the British Periodical Press, 1859–1872* (UCP, 1990).

Elliotson, J. , *Lectures on the Theory and Practice of Medicine*, ed. J. C. Cooke and T. G. Thompson (Moore, 1839).

—, 'More Painless Amputations and other Surgical Operations in the Mesmeric State', *Zoist*, 3 (1845), 490.

Ellis, I., *Seven Against Christ: A Study of 'Essays and Reviews'* (Leiden, Brill, 1980).

Eng, E., 'Thomas Henry Huxley's Understanding of Evolution', *HS*, 16 (1978), 291–303.

Engels, F., *The Condition of the Working Class in England* [1845] (Penguin, 1987).

English, M. P., 'Robert Hardwicke (1822–1875), publisher of biological and medical books', *ANH*, 13 (1986), 25–37.

—, *Victorian Values: The Life and Times of Dr Edwin Lankester M.D., F.R.S.* (Bristol, Biopress, 1990).

Epps, J., *The Church of England's Apostasy* (Dinnis, 1834).

Essays and Reviews, 4th ed. (Longmans, 1861).

Bibliography

Evans, Joan, *Time and Chance: The Story of Arthur Evans and his Forebears* (Longmans, 1943).

Evans, John, 'On Portions of a Cranium and of a Jaw, in the Slab Containing the Fossil Remains of the Archaeopteryx', *Nat. Hist. Rev.*, 5 (1865), 415–21.

Eve, A. S., and C. H. Creasey, *Life and Work of John Tyndall* (Macmillan, 1945).

Falconer, H., 'On Prof. Huxley's Attempted Refutation of Cuvier's Laws of Correlation, in the Reconstruction of Extinct Vertebrate Forms', *AMNH*, 17 (1856), 476–93.

Fawcett, H., 'A Popular Exposition of Mr. Darwin on the Origin of Species', *Macmillan's Magazine*, 3 (1860), 81–92.

Fayrer, J., *Recollections of My Life* (Edinburgh, Blackwood, 1900).

Fiske, J., 'Reminiscences of Huxley', *Ann. Rep. Smithsonian Inst.*, (1901), 713–28.

—, *The Personal Letters of John Fiske* (Cedar Rapids, Iowa, Torch Press, 1939).

Fletcher, J., *Rudiments of Physiology* 3 Parts (Edinburgh, Carfrae, 1835–7).

Flett, J. S., *The First Hundred Years of the Geological Survey of Great Britain* (H. M. Stationery Office, 1937).

Flower, S. S., *List of the Vertebrated Animals Exhibited in the Gardens of the Zoological Society of London, 1828–1927* (Zoological Society, 1929).

Flower, W. H., 'Introductory Lecture', *Medical Times and Gazette*, 1 (1870), 195–200.

—, 'Reminiscences of Professor Huxley', *North American Review*, 161 (1895), 279–86.

—, 'Richard Owen', *Proc. Roy. Soc.*, 55 (1894), i–xiv.

—, *Essays on Museums* (Macmillan, 1898).

Forbes, E., 'On the Mollusca', in MacGillivray, *Narrative*, 2:360–86.

—, *Literary Papers by the Late Professor Edward Forbes* (Reeve, 1855).

Fox, W., 'On the Skull and Bones of an Iguanodon', *Report BAAS, Norwich, 1868* (1869), Sections 64–5.

Gage, A. T. and W. T. Stearn, *A Bicentenary History of the Linnean Society of London* (Academic Press, 1988).

[Gallenga, A.], 'The Age We Live In', *Fraser's Magazine*, 24 (1841), 1–15.

Gardiner, A. G., *The Life of Sir William Harcourt* 2 vols (Constable, 1923).

Gardner, J. H., 'A Huxley Essay as "Poem"', *VS*, 14 (1970), 177–91.

Gaskell, E. , *Mary Barton* (Dent, 1967).

Gasman, D., *The Scientific Origins of National Socialism: Social Darwinism in Ernst Haeckel and the German Monist League* (Macdonald, 1971).

Geikie, A., *Life of Sir Roderick I. Murchison* 2 vols (Murray, 1875).

—, *Memoir of Sir Andrew Crombie Ramsay* (Macmillan, 1895).

Geison, G. L., 'The Protoplasmic Theory of Life and the Vitalist-Mechanist Debate', *Isis*, 60 (1969), 273–93.

—, *Michael Foster and the Cambridge School of Physiology* (New Jersey, Princeton UP, 1978).

Gillespie, N. C., 'The Duke of Argyll, Evolutionary Anthropology, and the Art of Scientific Controversy', *Isis*, 68 (1977), 40–54.

Gilley, S., 'The Huxley–Wilberforce Debate: A Reconsideration', in K. Robbins, ed., *Religion and Humanism* (Oxford, Blackwell, 1981), 325–40.

— and A. Loades, 'Thomas Henry Huxley: The War between Science and Religion', *Journal of Religion*, 61 (1981), 285–308.

Glick, T. F., ed., *The Comparative Reception of Darwinism* (UCP, 1988).

Bibliography

Godlee, R. J., 'Thomas Wharton Jones', *Brit. J. Ophthalmol.*, 93 (1921) 97–117, 145–56.

Golding, B., *The Origin, Plan, and Operations of the Charing Cross Hospital, London* (Allen, 1867).

Goodrich, E. S., 'Edwin Ray Lankester', *Proc. Roy. Soc.*, 106B (1930), x–xv.

Goodway, D., *London Chartism 1838–1848* (CUP, 1982).

Gould, J., 'On New Species of Mammalia and Birds from Australia', *Proc. Zool. Soc.*, 17 (1849), 109–12.

—, 'On New Species of Birds from Australia', *Proc. Zool. Soc.*, 18 (1850), 200–201.

—, 'On New Australian Birds in the Collection of the Zoological Society of London', *Proc. Zool. Soc.*, 18 (1850), 276–9.

Gould, S. J., *Ontogeny and Phylogeny* (Cambridge, MA, Harvard UP, 1977).

—, '*Bathybius* and *Eozoon*', in *The Panda's Thumb* (Penguin, 1983), 196–202.

—, 'Knight Takes Bishop?', *Natural History*, 95 (5) (1986), 18–33.

—, *Time's Arrow, Time's Cycle: Myth and Metaphor in the Discovery of Geological Time* (Penguin, 1990).

—, 'A Most Ingenious Paradox', in *The Flamingo's Smile* (Penguin, 1991), 78–95.

Grainger, R. D., *Observations on the Cultivation of Organic Science* (Highley, 1848).

Grayson, D. K., *The Establishment of Human Antiquity* (Academic Press, 1983).

[Green, J. R.], 'Professor Huxley on Science and the Clergy', *Saturday Review*, 24 (1867), 691–2.

Gregory, F., *Scientific Materialism in Nineteenth-century Germany* (Dordrecht, Reidel, 1977).

Groeben, C., ed., *Charles Darwin–Anton Dohrn Correspondence* (Naples, Macchiaroli, 1982).

Gross, C. G., 'Hippocampus Minor and Man's Place in Nature: A Case Study in the Social Construction of Neuroanatomy', *Hippocampus*, 3 (1993), 403–16.

Grove, W. R., *The Correlation of Physical Forces* (Longmans, 1867).

Gruber, J. W., *A Conscience in Conflict. The Life of St. George Jackson Mivart* (New York, Columbia UP, 1960).

— and J. C. Thackray, *Richard Owen Commemoration* (Natural History Museum Publications, 1992).

Haeckel, E., *Generelle Morphologie der Organismen* 2 vols (Berlin, Reimer, 1866).

—, *The History of Creation* 2 vols (New York, Appleton, 1876).

—, 'Thomas Huxley and Karl Vogt', *Fortnightly Review*, 58 (1895), 464–9.

Haight, G. S., *George Eliot and John Chapman* (New Haven, Yale UP, 1940).

—, *The George Eliot Letters* 9 vols (New Haven, Yale UP, 1954–6, 1978).

—, *George Eliot* (Penguin, 1985).

Halevy, E., *The Triumph of Reform, 1830–1841*, (Benn, 1950).

—, *Victorian Years, 1841–1895* (Benn, 1951).

Hall, C., *Memoirs of Marshall Hall* (Bentley, 1861).

Hall, M. B., 'The Royal Society in Thomas Henry Huxley's Time', *NRRS*, 38 (1983–4), 153–8.

Hardy, B., *The Exposure of Luxury: Radical Themes in Thackeray* (Peter Owen, 1972).

Harrison, J. F. C., *Early Victorian Britain 1832–1851* (Fontana, 1979).

—, 'Early Victorian Radicals and the Medical Fringe', 198–215, in W. F. Bynum and R. Porter, eds, *Medical Fringe & Medical Orthodoxy 1750–1850* (Croom Helm, 1987).

Hart, F., *The Roots of Service. History of Charing Cross Hospital 1818–1974* (Charing Cross Hospital Trustees, 1985).

Harte, N., *The University of London 1836–1986* (Athlone Press, 1986).

— and J. North, *The World of UCL 1828–1990* (University College London, 1991).

Hays, J. N., 'Science in the City: The London Institution, 1818–40', *BJHS*, 7 (1974), 146–62.

—, 'The London Lecturing Empire, 1800–50', in Inkster and Morrell, *Metropolis and Province*, 91–119.

Heyck, T. W., *The Transformation of Intellectual Life in Victorian England* (Croom Helm, 1982).

Hilton, B., *The Age of Atonement: The Influence of Evangelicalism on Social and Economic Thought 1785–1865* (Oxford, Clarendon Press, 1988).

Himmelfarb, G., *Darwin and the Darwinian Revolution* (Chatto & Windus, 1959).

Historical Account of the London Institution (1835).

Hitchcock, E., 'An Attempt to Discriminate and Describe the Animals that made the Fossil Footprints of the United States, and Especially in New England', *Mem. Am. Acad. Arts Sci.*, 3 (1848), 129–256.

Holloway, S. W. F., 'Medical Education in England, 1830–1858: A Sociological Analysis', *History*, 49 (1964), 229–324.

Holt, R. V., *The Unitarian Contribution to Social Progress in England* (Allen & Unwin, 1938).

Holyoake, G. J., *The History of the Last Trial by Jury for Atheism in England: A Fragment of Autobiography* (Watson, 1850).

—, 'The Priesthood of Science: Their Visit to Norwich', *Reasoner Review*, 1 Nov. 1868, 1–8.

Hooker, J. D., *Himalayan Journals. Notes of a Naturalist in Bengal, the Sikkim and Nepal Himalayas, the Khasia Mountains, &c* 2 vols (Murray, 1855).

—, 'Reminiscences of Darwin', *Nature*, 60 (1899), 187–8.

Howes, G. B., 'St. George Mivart', *Proc. Roy. Soc.*, 75 (1905), 95–100.

Hughes, R., *The Fatal Shore: A History of the Transportation of Convicts to Australia 1787–1868* (Pan, 1988).

Hull, D. L., *Darwin and his Critics: The Reception of Darwin's Theory of Evolution by the Scientific Community* (UCP, 1983).

—, *Science as a Process: An Evolutionary Account of the Social and Conceptual Development of Science* (UCP, 1988).

Hunter, W., *Historical Account of Charing Cross Hospital and Medical School* (Murray, 1914).

Hutchinson, H. G., *Life of Sir John Lubbock, Lord Avebury*, 2 vols (Macmillan, 1914).

[Hutton, R. H.], 'Pope Huxley', *Spectator*, 29 Jan. 1870, 135–6.

Huxley, Henrietta A., 'Pictures of Australian Life, 1843–1844', *Cornhill Magazine*, 31 (1911), 770–81.

Huxley, Julian, ed., *T. H. Huxley's Diary of the Voyage of H.M.S. Rattlesnake* (Chatto & Windus, 1935).

Huxley, Leonard, ed., *Life and Letters of Thomas Henry Huxley* 2 vols (Macmillan, 1900).

—, ed., *Life and Letters of Sir Joseph Dalton Hooker* 2 vols (Murray, 1918).

Huxley, Thomas Henry, 'On a Hitherto Undescribed Structure in the Human Hair Sheath', *Medical Gazette*, 36 (1845), 1340–1.

[—], 'Science at Sea', WR, 61 (1854), 98–119.

[—], 'Contemporary Literature: Science', WR, 61 (1854), 254–70, 580–95; 62 (1854), 242–56, 572–80; 63 (1855), 239–53, 558–63; 64 (1855), 240–55, 565–74; 65 (1856), 261–71; 67 (1857), 279–88.

[—], 'The Vestiges of Creation', BFMCR, 26 (1854), 425–39.

[—], 'Schamyl, the Prophet-Warrior of the Caucasus', WR, 61 (1854), 480–519.

[—], 'Owen and Rymer Jones on Comparative Anatomy', BFMCR, 35 (1856), 1–27.

—, 'On the Method of Palaeontology', AMNH, 18 (1856), 43–54.

—, 'Lectures on General Natural History', *Medical Times and Gazette*, 12 (1856), 429–15 (1857), 471 passim.

[—], 'Chalk, Ancient and Modern', *Saturday Review*, 6 (1858), 500–2.

—, 'Science and Religion', *The Builder*, 15 Jan. 1859.

—, 'The Government School of Mines', *The Builder*, 22 Jan. 1859.

—, *The Oceanic Hydrozoa* (Ray Society, 1859).

—, 'Time and Life: Mr. Darwin's "Origin of Species"', *Macmillan's Magazine*, 1 (1859), 142–8.

[—], 'Darwin on the Origin of Species', *The Times*, 26 Dec. 1859.

—, 'Man and the Apes', *Athenaeum*, 30 Mar., 13 Apr. 1861, pp. 433, 498.

—, *On Our Knowledge of the Causes of the Phenomena of Organic Nature* (Hardwicke, 1862).

—, *Evidence as to Man's Place in Nature* (Williams & Norgate, 1863).

—, *Lectures on the Elements of Comparative Anatomy* (Churchill, 1864).

—, 'Professor Huxley's Lectures on "The Structure and Classification of the Mammalia" at the Royal College of Surgeons', *Reader*, 3 (1864), 266–8.

—, 'The Negro's Place in Nature', *Reader*, 3 (1864), 334–5.

[—], 'Science and "Church Policy"', *Reader*, 4 (1864), 821.

—, 'To the Editor of the "Spectator"', *English Leader*, 24 Feb. 1866.

—, 'Reply to Objections on my Classification of Birds', *Ibis*, 4 (1868), 357–61.

—, 'Nature: Aphorisms by Goethe', *Nature*, 1 (1869), 9–11.

—, 'The Natural History of Creation', *Academy*, 1 (1869), 13–14, 40–3.

—, *Lay Sermons, Addresses, and Reviews* [1870] (New York, Appleton, 1882).

—, *American Addresses* (Macmillan, 1877).

—, *Physiography: An Introduction to the Study of Nature* [1877] (Macmillan, 1887).

—, *A Manual of the Anatomy of Invertebrated Animals* (New York, Appleton, 1878).

—, 'How to Become an Orator', *Pall Mall Gazette*, 24 Oct. 1888, 1–2.

—, *Collected Essays* 9 vols (Macmillan, 1893).

—, 'Professor Tyndall', NC, 35 (1894), 1–11.

—, *The Scientific Memoirs of Thomas Henry Huxley*, ed. M. Foster and E. R. Lankester, 5 vols (Macmillan, 1898–1902).

— and B. W. Hawkins, *An Elementary Atlas of Comparative Osteology* (Williams & Norgate, 1864).

Inkster, I. and J. Morrell, eds, *Metropolis and Province: Science in British Culture, 1780–1850* (Hutchinson, 1983).

Irvine, W., *Apes, Angels, and Victorians: Darwin, Huxley, and Evolution* (Cleveland, Meridian, 1959).

Jackson, P., *George Scharf's London. Sketches and Watercolours of a Changing City, 1820–1850* (Murray, 1987).

Bibliography

Jacyna, L. S., 'Immanence or Transcendence: Theories of Life and Organization in Britain, 1790–1835', *Isis*, 74 (1983), 311–29.

—, 'The Romantic Programme and the Reception of Cell Theory in Britain', *JHB*, 17 (1984), 13–48.

—, 'Principles of General Physiology: The Comparative Dimension to British Neuroscience in the 1830s and 1840s', *Stud. Hist. Biol.*, 7 (1984), 47–92.

[Jenkin, F.], 'The Origin of Species', *North British Review*, 46 (1867), 277–318.

Jenkins, M., *The General Strike of 1842* (Lawrence & Wishart, 1980).

Jensen, J. V., *Thomas Henry Huxley: Communicating for Science* (Associated University Presses, 1991)

Johnson, R., ' "Really Useful Knowledge": Radical Education and Working-Class Culture, 1790–1848', in J. Clarke, C. Critcher, and R. Johnson, eds, *Working-Class Culture* (Hutchinson, 1979), 75–102.

Jones, G. S., *Outcast London* (Penguin, 1984).

Jones, H. F., ed., *Samuel Butler. A Memoir* 2 vols (Macmillan, 1920).

Jones, T. W., 'Abstract of a Report on the Development of the Ovum of Man and the Mammifera', *Lancet*, 1 (1843–4), 258–62, 293–5.

—, 'Muscle a Neuro-Magnetic Apparatus', *Medical Gazette*, 33 (1843–4), 77–8.

Jordanova, L. J. and R. S. Porter, eds, *Images of the Earth* (Chalfont St. Giles, British Society for the History of Science, 1979).

J. P. A., 'Professor Huxley on Darwin's "Origin of Species" ', *NR*, 31 Jan. 1863, 2–3.

Kelly, A., *The Descent of Darwin: The Popularization of Darwinism in Germany, 1860–1914* (Chapel Hill, Univ. of North Carolina Press, 1981).

Kennedy, J. G., *Herbert Spencer* (Boston, Twayne, 1978).

Ker, I. and T. Gornall, eds, *The Letters and Diaries of John Henry Newman* (Oxford, Clarendon Press) Vol. 1 (1978); T. Gornall, ed., Vol. 5 (1981).

Keynes, R. D., ed., *Charles Darwin's 'Beagle' Diary* (CUP, 1988).

King, W., 'The Reputed Fossil Man of the Neanderthal', *Quart. J. Sci.*, 1 (1864), 88–97.

Kingsley, C., *The Water Babies* [1863] (Macmillan, 1883).

Kingsley, F., ed., *Charles Kingsley: His Letters and Memories of his Life* 2 vols (Kegan Paul, 1881).

Kirby, W., 'Introductory Address', *Zool. J.*, 2 (1825), 1–8.

Knight, C. , ed., *London* 6 vols (Knight, 1841–4).

Knox, R., 'Contributions to Anatomy and Physiology', *Medical Gazette*, 32 (1843), 463–7, 499–502, 529–32, 554–6, 586–9, 637–40, 860–2.

Kohn, D., 'On the Origin of the Principle of Diversity', *Science*, 213 (1981), 1105–8.

—, ed., *The Darwinian Heritage* (Princeton UP, 1985).

—, 'Darwin's Ambiguity: The Secularization of Biological Meaning', *BJHS*, 22 (1989), 215–39.

Kottler, M. J., 'Alfred Russel Wallace, the Origin of Man, and Spiritualism', *Isis*, 65 (1974), 145–92.

—, 'Charles Darwin and Alfred Russel Wallace', in Kohn, *Darwinian Heritage*, 367–432.

Lamarck, J. -B. -P. -A., *Philosophie Zoologique* 2 vols (Paris, Dentu, 1809).

Lankester, E., 'Dr. Edwin Lankester's Lecture on the Origin of Species', *NR*, 20 Apr. 1861, 8.

Lankester, E. R., 'William Henry Flower', *Nature*, 60 (1899), 252–5.

Lartet, E., 'Note sur un Grand Singe Fossile qui se Rattache au Groupe des Singes Supérieurs', *Comptes Rendus de l'Academie des Sciences*, 43 (1856), 219–23.

Bibliography

Laurent, J., 'Science, Society and Politics in Late Nineteenth-Century England: A Further Look at Mechanics' Institutes', *Social Studies of Science*, 14 (1984), 585–619.

Lefebvre, J. P., ed., *Marx–Engels: Lettres sur les Sciences de la Nature* (Paris, Editions Sociales, 1973).

Leidy, J., '*Hadrosaurus* and its Discovery', *Proc. Acad. Nat. Sci.*, Philadelphia (1858), 213–18.

Lenoir, T., *The Strategy of Life: Teleology and Mechanics in Nineteenth-Century German Biology* (UCP, 1989).

[Lewes, G. H.], *Ranthorpe*, [1847] ed. B. Smalley (Athens, Ohio UP, 1974).

[—], 'Goethe as a Man of Science', *WR*, 58 (1852), 479–506.

Lewis, A., 'Black Letter Day', *UCL Bulletin*, 7 (15) (1989), 18–19.

—, 'The Japanese Connexion', *UCL News* 1 (8) (1990), 4–6.

Lightman, B., 'Pope Huxley and the Church Agnostic: The Religion of Science', *Historical Papers* (1983), 150–63.

—, *The Origins of Agnosticism: Victorian Unbelief and the Limits of Knowledge* (Baltimore, Johns Hopkins UP, 1987).

Litchfield, H., ed., *Emma Darwin. A Century of Family Letters, 1792–1896* 2 vols (Murray, 1915).

Lloyd, C., *The British Seaman 1200–1800 A Social Survey* (Paladin, 1970).

London Medical Directory. 1845 (Mitchell, 1845).

Lonsdale, H., *A Sketch of the Life and Writings of Robert Knox* (Macmillan, 1870).

Lorimer, D. A., *Colour, Class and the Victorians: English Attitudes to the Negro in the Mid-Nineteenth Century* (Leicester UP, 1978).

—, 'Theoretical Racism in Late Victorian Anthropology, 1870–1900', *VS*, 31 (1988), 405–30.

Lubbock, A., *Owen Stanley R.N. Captain of the 'Rattlesnake'* (Melbourne, Heinemann, 1968).

Lucas, J. R., 'Wilberforce and Huxley: A Legendary Encounter', *Historical Journal*, 22 (1979), 313–30.

Lyell, C., *Principles of Geology* 3 vols (Murray, 1830–33).

—, 'Anniversary Address', *QJGS*, 7 (1851), xxxii–lxxvi.

—, *A Manual of Elementary Geology*, 4th ed. (Murray, 1852).

—, *Supplement to the Fifth Edition of a Manual of Elementary Geology* (Murray, 1859).

Lyons, S. L., 'Thomas Huxley: Fossils, Persistence, and the Argument from Design', *JHB*, 26 (1993), 545–69.

MacGillivray, J., *Narrative of the Voyage of H.M.S. Rattlesnake, commanded by the late Captain Owen Stanley, R.N., F.R.S., &c. during the years 1846–1850 including discoveries and surveys in New Guinea, the Louisiade Archipelago, Etc* 2 vols (Boone, 1852).

Mackie, S. J., 'The Aeronauts of the Solenhofen Age', *Geologist*, 6 (1863), 1–8.

Macleay, W. S., *Horae Entomologicae: Or Essays on the Annulose Animals* 2 vols (Bagster, 1819).

MacLeod, R. M., 'Science and the Civil List, 1824–1914', *Technology and Society*, 6 (1970), 47–55.

—, 'The X Club: A Social Network of Science in Late-Victorian England', *NRRS*, 24 (1970), 305–22.

—, 'The Royal Society and the Government Grant: Notes on the Administration of Scientific Research, 1849–1914', *Historical Journal*, 14 (1971), 323–58.

—, 'Of Medals and Men: A Reward System in Victorian Science 1826–1914', *NRRS*, 26 (1971), 81–108.

—, 'On Visiting the "Moving Metropolis", Reflections on the Architecture of Imperial Science', *Historical Records of Australian Science*, 5 (1982), 1–15.

—, 'Whigs and Savants: Reflections on the Reform Movement in the Royal Society, 1830–48,' in Inkster and Morrell, *Metropolis*, 55–90.

McMenemey, W. H., 'Education and the Medical Reform Movement', in Poynter, *Evolution of Medical Education*, 135–54.

McPherson, J. M., *Battle Cry of Freedom. The Civil War Era* (Penguin, 1990).

Manual, D. E., 'Marshall Hall, F.R.S. (1790–1857) A Conspectus of his Life and Work', *NRRS*, 35 (1980), 136–66.

Marsh, O. C., 'Thomas Henry Huxley', *Am. J. Sci.*, 50 (1895), 177–83.

Marshall, A. J., *Darwin and Huxley in Australia* (Sydney, Hodder & Stoughton, 1970).

Matthews, P., *Emigration Fields: North America, The Cape, Australia, and New Zealand, Describing these Countries, and Giving a Comparative View of the Advantages they Present to British Settlers* (Edinburgh, Black; Longman, 1839).

Mayhew, H., *London Labour and the London Poor* (Penguin, 1985).

Meadows, A. J., *Science and Controversy: A Biography of Sir Norman Lockyer* (Macmillan, 1972).

Meyer, H. von, 'The Reptiles of the Coal Formation', *QJGS*, 4, pt. 2 (1848), 51–6.

—, 'Reptilien aus der Steinkohlen-Formation in Deutchland', *Palaeontographica*, 6 (1856–8), 59–220.

Mill, J. S., 'John Stuart Mill, M.P. , on the Negro Suffrage', *NR*, 12 Nov. 1865, 723.

Mills, E. I., 'A View of Edward Forbes, Naturalist', *ANH*, 11 (1984), 365–93.

Minney, R. J., *The Two Pillars of Charing Cross* (Cassell, 1967).

Mivart, St. George, *Essays and Criticisms* 2 vols (Osgood, 1892).

—, 'Some Reminiscences of Thomas Henry Huxley', *NC*, 42 (1897), 985–98.

Monk, W., ed., *The Journals of Caroline Fox, 1835–71* (Elek, 1972).

Montgomery, W. M., 'Germany', in Glick, *Comparative Reception*, 81–116.

Moore, J. R., *The Post-Darwinian Controversies: A Study of the Protestant Struggle to Come to Terms with Darwin in Great Britain and America 1870–1900* (CUP, 1979).

—, 'Crisis without Revolution: The Ideological Watershed in Victorian England', *Revue de Synthèse*, 4 (1986), 53–78.

—, 'Freethought, Secularism, Agnosticism: The Case of Charles Darwin', in G. Parsons, ed., *Religion in Victorian Britain. Volume 1* (Manchester UP, 1988), 274–319.

—, ed., *Religion in Victorian Britain. Volume 3: Sources* (Manchester UP, 1988).

—, ed., *History, Humanity and Evolution* (CUP, 1989).

—, 'Theodicy and Society: The Crisis of the Intelligentsia', in R. Helmstadter and B. Lightman, eds, *Victorian Faith in Crisis* (Macmillan, 1990), 153–86.

—, 'Deconstructing Darwinism: The Politics of Evolution in the 1860', *JHB*, 24 (1991), 353–408.

—, 'Metabiographical Reflections on Charles Darwin', in M. Shortland and R. Yeo, ed., *Telling Lives: Studies in Scientific Biography* (CUP, 1995).

Moore, T. J., 'The Gorilla', *AMNH*, 10 (1862), 373–4.

Morley, J., *Recollections* 2 vols (Macmillan, 1917).

Bibliography

Morrell, J. and A. Thackray, *Gentlemen of Science: Early Years of the British Association for the Advancement of Science* (Oxford, Clarendon Press, 1981).

Morris, J., *Heaven's Command: An Imperial Progress* (Penguin, 1979).

Mozley, A., 'Evolution and the Climate of Opinion in Australia, 1840–76', VS, 10 (1976), 411–30.

Murchison, R. I., 'Major-General Portlock', *J. Roy. Geogr. Soc.*, 34 (1864), cxv–cxviii.

Murphy, H. R., 'The Ethical Revolt against Christian Orthodoxy in Early Victorian England', *Am. Hist. Rev.*, 60 (1955), 800–17.

Napier, M., *Selections from the Correspondence of the Late Macvey Napier*, (Macmillan, 1879).

Nicholas, F. W. and J. M., *Charles Darwin in Australia* (CUP, 1989).

Nordenskiöld, E., *The History of Biology* (New York, Tudor Publishing, 1942).

Norton, G., *Victorian London* (Macdonald, 1969).

Nyhart, L., 'The Disciplinary Breakdown of German Morphology, 1870–1900', *Isis*, 78 (1987), 365–89.

O'Connor, W. J., *Founders of British Physiology* (Manchester UP, 1988).

Osborn, H. F., 'Memorial Tribute to Prof. Thomas H. Huxley', *Trans. N. Y. Acad. Sci.*, 15 (1895), 40–50.

—, *Cope: Master Naturalist, The Life and Letters of Edward Drinker Cope* (New Haven, Princeton UP, 1931).

Ospovat, D., 'The Influence of Karl Ernst von Baer's Embryology, 1828–1859: A Reappraisal in Light of Richard Owen's and William B. Carpenter's "Palaeontological Application of 'Von Baer's Law'"', *JHB*, 9 (1976), 1–28.

—, 'Perfect Adaptation and Teleological Explanation: Approaches to the Problem of the History of Life in the Mid-Nineteenth Century', *Studies in History of Biology*, 2 (1978), 33–56.

—, 'Darwin on Huxley and Divergence: Some Darwin Notes on his Meeting with Huxley, Hooker, and Wollaston in April, 1856' (typescript).

—, *The Development of Darwin's Theory: Natural History, Natural Theology, and Natural Selection 1838–1859* (CUP, 1981).

Owen, R., 'On the Osteology of the Chimpanzee and Orang Utan', *Trans. Zool. Soc.*, 1 (1835), 343–79.

—, *Fossil Mammalia*. Pt. 1, *The Zoology of the Beagle Voyage of H.M.S. Beagle*, ed. C. Darwin (Smith, Elder, 1840).

—, 'Osteological Contributions to the Natural History of the Chimpanzee (*Troglodytes*, Geoffroy), including the Description of the Skull of a Large Species (*Troglodytes* Gorilla, Savage) discovered by Thomas S. Savage, MD in the Gaboon Country, West Africa', *Trans. Zool. Soc.*, 3 (1849), 381–422.

[—], 'Lyell – on Life and Successive Development', *QR*, 89 (1851), 412–51.

—, 'On Metamorphosis and Metagenesis', *Proc. Roy. Inst.*, 1 (1854), 9–16.

—, *Lectures on the Comparative Anatomy and Physiology of the Invertebrate Animals* (Longman, 1855).

—, 'On the Affinities of the *Stereognathus ooliticus* (Charlesworth), a Mammal from the Oolitic Slate of Stonesfield', *QJGS*, 13 (1857), 1–11.

—, 'On the Characters, Principles of Division, and Primary Groups of the Class Mammalia', *J. Proc. Linn. Soc.* (Zool.), 2 (1858), 1–37.

—, 'Presidential Address', *Report BAAS, Leeds, 1858*, (1859), xlix–cx.

—, 'Conclusion of the Twelfth Lecture of a Course "On Fossil Mammals"', *Proc. Roy. Inst.*, 3 (1858–62), 109–16.

—, *On the Classification and Distribution of the Mammalia* (Parker, 1859).

—, 'On the Orders of Fossil and Recent Reptilia, and their Distribution in Time', *Report BAAS, Aberdeen, 1859*, (1860), 153–66.

—, 'On Some Reptilian Remains from South Africa', *QJGS*, 16 (1860), 49–63.

[—], 'Darwin on the Origin of Species', *ER*, 111 (1860), 487–532.

—, 'The Gorilla and the Negro', *Athenaeum*, 23 Mar. 1861, 395–6.

—, 'On the Characters of the Aye-Aye, as a Test of the Lamarckian and Darwinian Hypothesis of the Transmutation and Origin of Species', *Report BAAS, Cambridge, 1862* (1863), 114–6.

—, 'On the Archaeopteryx of Von Meyer', *Phil. Trans. Roy. Soc.*, 153 (1863), 33–47.

—, *Monograph on the Aye-Aye* (Taylor & Francis, 1863).

—, *On the Anatomy of Vertebrates* 3 vols (Longman, 1866–8).

—, *Monograph on the Fossil Reptilia of the Mesozoic Formations* (Palaeontographical Society, 1874–89).

—, *Descriptive and Illustrative Catalogue of the Fossil Reptilia of South Africa* (Taylor & Francis, 1876).

—, 'Description of Parts of the Skeleton of an Anomodont Reptile (Platypodosaurus Robustus, Ow.) from the Trias of Graaf Reinet, S. Africa', *QJGS*, 37 (1880), 414–25.

Padian, K., 'Pterosaurs and Typology: Archetypal Physiology in the Owen–Seeley Dispute of 1870', in W. A. S. Sarjeant, ed., *Vertebrate Fossils and the Evolution of Scientific Concepts* (Reading, Harwood, 1994).

Paradis, J. G., *T. H. Huxley: Man's Place in Nature* (Lincoln, University of Nebraska Press, 1978).

— and T. Postlewait, eds, 'Victorian Science and Victorian Values', *Ann. N. Y. Acad. Sci*, 360 (1981).

Parker, T. J., 'Professor Huxley: from the Point of View of a Disciple', *Natural Science*, 8 (1896), 161–7.

Parker, W. K., 'Remarks on the Skeleton of the Archaeopteryx; and on the Relations of the Bird to the Reptile', *Geol. Mag.*, 1 (1864), 55–7.

Parssinen, T. M., 'Professional Deviants and the History of Medicine: Medical Mesmerists in Victorian Britain', in R. Wallis, ed., *On the Margins of Science* (Keele, University of Kent, 1979), 103–20.

Paston, G., *At John Murray's: Records of a Literary Circle 1843–1892* (Murray, 1932).

Paxton, N. L., *George Eliot and Herbert Spencer: Feminism, Evolutionism, and the Reconstruction of Gender* (Princeton UP, 1991).

Pearson, K. ed., *The Life, Letters and Labours of Francis Galton* 3 vols (CUP, 1914–30).

Peel, J. D. Y., *Herbert Spencer: The Evolution of a Sociologist* (Heinemann, 1971).

Pevsner, N., *The Buildings of England: London, except the Cities of London and Westminster* (Penguin, 1952).

Phelps, L. A., and E. Cohen, 'The Wilberforce–Huxley Debate', *Western Speech*, 37 (1973), 56–64.

Phillips, J., 'Cetiosaurus', *Athenaeum*, 2 Apr. 1870, 454.

—, *Geology of Oxford and the Valley of the Thames* (Oxford, Clarendon Press, 1871).

Pingree, J., *Thomas Henry Huxley. A List of his Scientific Notebooks, Drawings and Other Papers, Preserved in the College Archives* (Imperial College, 1968)

Bibliography

—, *Thomas Henry Huxley. List of his Correspondence with Miss Henrietta Anne Heathorn, later Mrs. Huxley, 1847–1854* (Imperial College, 1969)

Porter, R., 'Gentlemen and Geology: The Emergence of a Scientific Career, 1660–1920', *Hist. J.*, 21 (1978), 809–36.

Porter, T. M., *The Rise of Statistical Thinking 1820–1900* (Princeton UP, 1986).

Portlock, J. E., 'Anniversary Address', *QJGS*, 13 (1857), xxvi–cxlv.

—, 'Anniversary Address', *QJGS*, 14 (1858), xxiv–clxii.

Poynter, F. N. L., 'John Chapman (1821–1894) Publisher, Physician, and Medical Reformer', *Journal of the History of Medicine*, 5 (1950), 271–90.

—, 'Thomas Southwood Smith – the Man (1788–1861)', *Proceedings of the Royal Society of Medicine*, 55 (1962), 381–90.

— ed., *The Evolution of Medical Education in Britain* (Pitman, 1966).

Prest, J., *The Industrial Revolution in Coventry* (OUP, 1960).

Rachootin, S. P., 'Owen and Darwin Reading a Fossil: *Macrauchenia* in a Boney Light', in Kohn, *Darwinian Heritage*, 155–83.

Rainger, R., 'Race, Politics, and Science: The Anthropological Society of London in the 1860s', *VS*, 22 (1978), 51–70.

Ralph, R., 'John MacGillivray – His Life and Work', *ANH*, 20 (1993), 185–95.

Rasor, E. L., *Reform in the Royal Navy: A Social History of the Lower Deck 1850 to 1880* (Hamden, Conn., Archon Books, 1976).

Raumer, F. von, *England in 1835*, 3 vols (Murray, 1836).

Raven, C. E. , *Christian Socialism 1848–1854* (Cass, 1920).

R. D. N. , 'The Place of Man in the Animal Kingdom', *NR*, 29 June 1861, 6–7.

Rehbock, P. F., 'Huxley, Haeckel, and the Oceanographers: The Case of *Bathybius haeckelii*', *Isis*, 66 (1975), 504–33.

—, 'The Early Dredgers: "Naturalizing" in British Seas, 1830–1850', *JHB*, 12 (1979), 293–368.

—, *The Philosophical Naturalists: Themes in Early Nineteenth-Century British Biology* (Madison, University of Wisconsin Press, 1983).

Rice, A. L., 'Thomas Henry Huxley and the Strange Case of *Bathybius haeckelii*; A Possible Alternative Explanation', *ANH*, 11 (1983), 169–80.

Richards, E., 'A Question of Property Rights: Richard Owen's Evolutionism Reassessed', *BJHS*, 20 (1987), 129–71.

—, 'The "Moral Anatomy" of Robert Knox: The Interplay between Biological and Social Thought in Victorian Scientific Naturalism', *JHB*, 22 (1989), 373–436.

—, 'Huxley and Woman's Place in Science: The "Woman Question" and the Control of Victorian Anthropology', in Moore, *History*, 253–84.

Richards, R. J., *Darwin and the Emergence of Evolutionary Theories of Mind and Behavior* (UCP, 1987).

—, *The Meaning of Evolution: The Morphological Construction and Ideological Reconstruction of Darwin's Theory* (UCP, 1992).

Richardson, R., *Death, Dissection and the Destitute* (Penguin, 1989).

[Richmond, M.], 'Darwin's Study of Cirripedia', *CCD*, 4:388–409.

Ridley, J., *Lord Palmerston* (Panther, 1972).

Robertson, J., 'Dr. Elliotson on Life and Mind', *Medical Gazette*, 17 (1835–6), 203–10, 251–7.

Rogers, J. A., 'The Reception of Darwin's *Origin of Species* by Russian Scientists', *Isis*, 64 (1973), 484–503.

Rolleston, G., *Scientific Papers and Addresses* 2 vols (Oxford, Clarendon, 1884).

Bibliography

Rolt, L. T. C., *Victorian Engineering* (Penguin, 1988).

Roos, D. A., 'Neglected Bibliographical Aspects of the Works of Thomas Henry Huxley', *J. Soc. Biblphy Nat. Hist.*, 8 (1978), 401–20.

—, 'The "Aims and Intentions" of *Nature*', in Paradis and Postlewait, *Victorian Science*, 159–80.

Rorison, G., 'The Creative Week', in *Replies to 'Essays and Reviews'* 2nd ed. (Oxford, Henry & Parker, 1862), 277–345.

Rose, M., *Curator of the Dead: Thomas Hodgkin (1798–1866)* (Peter Owen, 1981).

Rowe, J. S., 'The Life and Work of George Fownes, F.R.S. (1815–49)', *AS*, 6 (1949), 422–35.

Rudwick, M. J. S., *The Meaning of Fossils: Episodes in the History of Palaeontology* (Macdonald, 1972).

—, *Scenes From Deep Time: Early Pictorial Representations of the Prehistoric World* (UCP, 1992).

Rupke, N. A., '*Bathybius Haeckelii* and the Psychology of Scientific Discovery', *Stud. Hist. Phil. Sci.*, 7 (1976), 53–62.

—, 'Richard Owen's Hunterian Lectures on Comparative Anatomy and Physiology, 1837–55', *Medical History*, 29 (1985), 237–58.

—, 'The Road to Albertopolis: Richard Owen (1804–92) and the Founding of the British Museum of Natural History', in N. A. Rupke, ed., *Science, Politics and the Public Good* (Macmillan, 1988), 63–89.

—, *Richard Owen: Victorian Naturalist* (New Haven, Yale UP, 1994).

Ruse, M., *The Darwinian Revolution: Science Red in Tooth and Claw* (UCP, 1979).

Saint-Pierre, J. -H. B. de, *Paul and Virginia*, trans. J. Donovan (Penguin, 1989).

Schama, S., *Citizens* (Penguin, 1989).

Schwartz, J. S., 'Darwin, Wallace, and the *Descent of Man*', *JHB*, 17 (1984), 271–89.

Schweber, S. S., 'Darwin and the Political Economists: Divergence of Character', *JHB*, 10 (1977), 229–316.

Seaman, L. C. B., *Victorian England: Aspects of English and Imperial History 1837–1901* (Methuen, 1973).

Secord, J. A., 'King of Siluria: Roderick Murchison and the Imperial Theme in Nineteenth-Century British Geology', *VS*, 25 (1982), 413–42.

—, 'John W. Salter: The Rise and Fall of a Victorian Palaeontological Career', in A. Wheeler and J. H. Price, eds, *From Linnaeus to Darwin* (Society for the History of Natural History, 1985), 61–75.

—, 'Darwin and the Breeders', in Kohn, *Darwinian Heritage*, 519–42.

—, 'The Geological Survey of Great Britain as a Research School, 1839–1855', *HS*, 24 (1986), 223–75.

—, *Controversy in Victorian Geology: The Cambrian-Silurian Dispute* (Princeton UP, 1986).

—, 'Behind the Veil: Robert Chambers and *Vestiges*', in Moore, *History*, 165–94.

[Sedgwick, A.], 'Natural History of Creation', *ER*, 82 (1845), 1–85.

Seeley, H. G., 'An Epitome of the Evidence that Pterodactyles are not Reptiles, but a New Subclass of Vertebrated Animal Allied to Birds', *AMNH*, 17 (1866), 321–31.

Semmel, B., *The Governor Eyre Controversy* (McGibbon & Kee, 1962).

Shapin, S., 'Phrenological Knowledge and the Social Structure of Early Nineteenth-Century Edinburgh', *AS*, 32 (1975), 219–43.

— and B. Barnes, 'Science, Nature and Control: Interpreting Mechanics' Institutes', *Soc. Stud. Sci.*, 7 (1977), 31–74.

Sharpey, W.,'The Address in Physiology', *Brit. Med. J.*, 2 (1862), 162–71.

Shatto, S., 'Byron, Dickens, Tennyson, and the Monstrous Efts', *Yearbook of English Studies*, 6 (1976), 144–55.

Sheets-Pyenson, S., 'Popular Scientific Periodicals in Paris and London: The Emergence of a Low Scientific Culture, 1820–1875', *AS*, 42 (1985), 549–72.

—, 'Horse Race: John William Dawson, Charles Lyell, and the Competition over the Edinburgh Natural History Chair in 1854–55', *AS*, 49 (1992), 461–77.

Shortland, M., 'Book Reviews: J. V. Jensen, *Thomas Henry Huxley*; M. Collie, *Huxley at Work*', *BJHS*, 26 (1993), 112–14.

[Sidgwick, I.], 'A Grandmother's Tale', *Macmillan's Magazine*, 78 (1898), 425–35.

Sloan, P. R., ed., *Richard Owen. The Hunterian Lectures in Comparative Anatomy. May and June 1837* (UCP, 1992).

Smith, C., and M. N. Wise, *Energy and Empire: A Biographical Study of Lord Kelvin* (CUP, 1989).

Smith, C. U. M., 'Evolution and the Problem of Mind: Part 1. Herbert Spencer', *JHB*, 15 (1982), 55–88.

Smith, F., 'Charles Darwin's Ill Health', *JHB*, 23 (1990), 443–59.

Smith, R., 'Alfred Russel Wallace: Philosophy of Nature and Man', *BJHS*, 6 (1972), 177–99.

Smith, T. S., *The Divine Government*, 5th ed. (Trübner, 1866).

Spencer, H., 'A Theory Concerning the Organ of Wonder', *Zoist*, 2 (1844), 316–25.

—, 'Progress: Its Law and Cause', *WR*, 67 (1857), 445–85.

—, 'Owen on the Homologies of the Vertebrate Skeleton', *BFMCR*, 44 (1858), 400–16.

—, *An Autobiography* 2 vols (Williams & Norgate, 1904).

Stafford, R. A., *Scientist of Empire: Sir Roderick Murchison, Scientific Exploration and Victorian Imperialism* (CUP, 1989).

Stanbury, P. and J. Holland, *Mr Macleay's Celebrated Cabinet* (Sydney, Macleay Museum, 1988).

Stanley, O., 'T. H. Huxley's Treatment of "Nature"', *J. Hist. Ideas*, 18 (1957), 120–7.

Stauffer, R. C., ed., *Charles Darwin's Natural Selection: Being the Second Part of his Big Species Book written from 1856 to 1858* (CUP, 1975).

Stocking, G. W., 'What's in a Name? The Origins of the Royal Anthropological Institute (1837–71)', *Man*, 6 (1971), 369–90.

—, *Race, Culture, and Evolution* (UCP, 1982).

—, *Victorian Anthropology* (New York, Free Press, 1987).

Straus, W. L., 'Huxley's *Evidence as to Man's Place in Nature* – A Century Later', in L. G. Stevenson and R. P. Multhauf, eds, *Medicine Science and Culture* (Baltimore, Johns Hopkins UP, 1968), 160–7.

Sutherland, J. A., *Thackeray at Work* (Athlone Press, 1974).

[Tait, P. G.], 'Geological Time', *North British Review*, 11 (1869), 406–39.

Taylor, P. A., *Professor Huxley on the Negro Question* (Ladies' London Emancipation Society, Tract 10, 1864).

Tennyson, A., *Idylls of the King* (Penguin, 1983).

Thackeray, W. M., *The History of Pendennis* [1850] (Penguin, 1972).

Bibliography

Thackray, A., 'Natural Knowledge in Cultural Context: The Manchester Model', *Am. Hist. Rev.*, 79 (1974), 672–709.

Thomson, D., *England in the Nineteenth Century* (Penguin, 1950).

Thomson, W., *Popular Lectures and Addresses* 3 vols (Macmillan, 1889–1894).

Tillotson, G. and D. Hawes, eds, *Thackeray: The Critical Heritage* (Routledge, 1968).

Todes, D. P., 'V. O. Kovalevskii: The Genesis, Content, and Reception of his Paleontological Work', *Studies in History of Biology*, 2 (1978), 99–165.

—, *Darwin Without Malthus* (OUP, 1989).

Torr, D., ed., *Karl Marx and Frederick Engels. Selected Correspondence 1846–1895* (Lawrence & Wishart, 1936).

Torrens, H., 'When did the Dinosaur get its Name?', *New Scientist*, 4 Apr. 1992.

Tristan, F., *Flora Tristan's London Journal: A Survey of London Life in the 1830s* (Prior, 1980).

Tugwood, D. T., *The Coventry and Warwickshire Hospital 1838–1948* (Lewes, Sussex, Book Guild, 1987).

Turner, F. M., *Between Science and Religion: the Reaction to Scientific Naturalism in Late Victorian England* (New Haven, Yale UP, 1974).

—, 'Victorian Scientific Naturalism and Thomas Carlyle', *VS*, 18 (1975), 325–43.

—, 'The Victorian Conflict between Science and Religion: A Professional Dimension', *Isis*, 69 (1978), 356–76.

Tylor, E. B., *Primitive Culture*, 5th ed., 2 vols (Murray, 1913).

Tyndall, J., A. Henfrey, T. H. Huxley *et al.*, *The Culture Demanded by Modern Life* (New York, Appleton, 1867).

—, *Fragments of Science*, 2nd ed. (Longman, 1871).

Uschmann, G. and Jahn, I., eds, 'Der Briefwechsel zwischen Thomas Henry Huxley und Ernst Haeckel', *Wissenschaftliche Zeitschrift der Friedrich-Schiller-Universität Jena*, Mathematisch-Naturwissenschaftliche Reihe, Heft 1/2, 9 (1959–60), 7–33.

Van Arsdel, R., 'The Westminster Review, 1824–1900', in W. E. Houghton, ed., *The Wellesley Index to Victorian Periodicals 1824–1900 Volume 3* (Toronto, University of Toronto Press, 1979), 529–58.

Vevers, G., *London's Zoo* (Bodley Head, 1976).

Vincent, D., *Bread, Knowledge and Freedom: A Study of Nineteenth-Century Working Class Autobiography* (Europa, 1981).

Vogt, C., *Lectures on Man*, trans. J. Hunt (Longman, 1864).

Vucinich, A., 'Russia', in Glick, *Comparative Reception*, 227–55.

—, *Darwin in Russian Thought* (Berkeley, Univ. California Press, 1988).

Waddington, I., *The Medical Profession in the Industrial Revolution* (Dublin, Gill & Macmillan, 1984).

Wagner, W., 'Upon the Structure of the Brain in Man and Monkeys, and its bearing upon Classification, with Special Reference to the Views of Owen, Huxley and Gratiolet', *Am. J. Sci.*, 34 (1862), 188–99.

Wallace, A. R., *Contributions to the Theory of Natural Selection* (Macmillan, 1875).

—, *My Life: A Record of Events and Opinions* 2 vols (Chapman & Hall, 1905).

Watterson, H., *Marse Henry* 2 vols (New York, Doran, 1919).

Watts, J. 'Theological Theories of the Origin of Man', *Reasoner*, 26 (1861), 102–4, 119–21, 132–4.

[—], 'Man's Origin and Nature', *NR*, 28 Mar., 4 Apr. 1863.

Bibliography

Webb, B., *My Apprenticeship* 2nd ed. (Longmans, Green, 1945).

Weindling, P. J., 'Darwinism in Germany', in Kohn, *Darwinian Heritage*, 685–98.

—, 'Ernst Haeckel, Darwinismus, and the Secularization of Nature', in J. Moore, *History*, 311–27.

—, *Darwinism and Social Darwinism in Imperial Germany: The Contribution of the Cell Biologist Oscar Hertwig (1849–1922)* (Stuttgart, Gustav Fischer, 1991).

Weiner, J. H., *War of the Unstamped: The Movement to Repeal the British Newspaper Tax, 1830–1836* (Ithaca, Cornell UP, 1969).

Whittell, H. M., *The Literature of Australian Birds: A History and a Bibliography of Australian Ornithology* (Perth, W. A., Paterson Brokensha Pty, 1954).

Wiener, M. J., *English Culture and the Decline of the Industrial Spirit 1850–1980* (Penguin, 1992).

Wilberforce, S., *Pride a Hindrance to True Knowledge* (Rivington, 1847).

[—], 'Darwin's Origin of Species', *QR*, 102 (1860), 225–64.

Wilson, G. and A. Geikie, ed., *Memoir of Edward Forbes* (Macmillan, 1861).

Wilson, L. G., ed., *Sir Charles Lyell's Scientific Journals on the Species Question* (New Haven, Yale UP, 1970).

Wiltshire, D., *The Social and Political Thought of Herbert Spencer* (OUP, 1978).

Winsor, M. P., *Starfish, Jellyfish, and the Order of Life* (New Haven, Yale UP, 1976).

—, 'The Impact of Darwinism upon the Linnean Enterprise, with Special Reference to the Work of T. H. Huxley', in J. Weinstock, ed., *Contemporary Perspectives on Linneaus* (Lanham, MD, University Press of America, 1985), 55–84.

Winter, A., 'Ethereal Epidemic: Mesmerism and the Introduction of Inhalation Anaesthesia to Early Victorian London', *Soc. Hist. Med.*, (1991), 1–27.

—, '"The Island of Mesmeria": The Politics of Mesmerism in Early Victorian Britain' (St. John's College, Cambridge, Ph.D Thesis, 1992).

Wollaston, A. F. R., *Life of Alfred Newton* (Murray, 1921).

Wollaston, T. V., *On the Variation of Species with Especial Reference to the Insecta* (Van Voorst, 1856).

Woodward, H., 'On a Feathered Fossil from the Lithographic Limestone of Solenhofen', *Intellectual Observer*, 2 (1862), 313–19.

Wrangham, R. W., 'Bishop Wilberforce: Natural Selection and the Descent of Man', *Nature*, 287 (1980), 192.

Young, G. M., *Portrait of an Age* 2nd ed. (OUP, 1989).

Young, J., 'Professor Huxley and "The Physical Basis of Life"', *CR*, 11 (1869), 240–63.

Young, R. M., 'The Development of Herbert Spencer's Concept of Evolution', *Congrès International d'Histoire des Sciences*, 11 (1965), 273–8.

—, *Darwin's Metaphor: Nature's Place in Victorian Culture* (CUP, 1985).

Index

Index

Index

Index

Index

obtaining a grant 151, 154, 156, 165, 167, 178, 180, 182, 183, 196, 198
Professional strategy:
Against privilege/patronage 12, 62, 83–4, 93, 108, 154–6, 158, 163, 169, 177, 262, 361; wants talent rewarded 12, 16, 31, 54, 62, 73, 84, 93, 169, 172, 180, 188, 202, 226, 242; ousts those with dual calling 283; confrontational strategy 298, 308; on science exams 327; absolute truth unattainable, 409 n37; imputes moral order to Nature 174, 200, 210, 288, 293, 345, 363; on value of zoology 200; on Nature's moral force, *see* full entries for Nature, Romanticism, Science. *See also* Materialism and Positivism
Science – Invertebrate anatomy:
Foundation membranes in coelenterates 83, 90, 208, 248, 254, 409 n30; new class 'Nematophora' 69, 83, 123, 167, 399 n24; human embryo homology of coelenterate membranes 90, 254
For individual groups, *see* separate entries
Invertebrate publications:
Papers 107, 123, 134, 145, 152; Men-of-war 61, 81, 152, 168; *Diphyes* 69, 69, 123, 152; jellyfish 82, 88, 152; *Trigonia* 73, 123; sea squirts 141, 161; molluscs 174, 176, 177, 188; cyclopaedia article 190; *Oceanic Hydrozoa* 178, 243, 248, 257, 259; dissecting technique 323
On embryology 83, 90, 235, 244, 260, 265, 271; archetypal-circular geometry of nature 176, 223, 399 n24, 411 n7; derides functional explanation of structure 200, 227; classification 208: five sub-kingdoms 208; seven primary groups 315
Palaeontology:
Moves into palaeontology 204, 218; view of geology 303; draws up 'Report on the Recent Changes in Level in the Bristol Channel' 229; disdains fossil

curation 201; fossil record has no Christian meaning 205; debates Owen on palaeontology 229; on School of Mines fossil catalogues 219; courses on fossils 232; fossil crocodiles 248, 275; changing views of fossil succession 264; fossil fish 284, 303, 321, 355; Crossopterygians 284, 355; *Pteraspis* 284; fossil amphibians 255, 300, 303, 321, 346, 355, 420–1, nn24–25; Marsh's 'ichthyosaur', 420 n23; *Galesaurus*, 412 n5; *Stagonolepis* 248; *Hyperodapedon Gordoni* 255, 515 n8; *Rhynchosaurus*, 415 n8; on *Dicynodon*, 412–3 n5; *Glyptodon* 306; evolution of horses 268 – *see also* separate entries
Anti-progressionist 176, 191, 204, 208, 215, 222, 248, 255, 258, 303, 305, 412 n5; on Agassiz, 412 n25; persistence of crocodiles 248; 'Persistent Types' 255, 259, 303, 358, 420 n23; attacks Carpenter's progressionism 219; origins 174; Palaeozoic man 192, 204, 248, 257; persistence of humans 257, 305; mankind an aberrant modification 191 – *see* entries for Beche, H. de la, Lyell, C., Murchison, R.I.
Birds/Dinosaurs:
Bird family trees 356, response to Newton, 428 n40; reclassifies birds 356, 427–8 n40; bird-reptile group 'Sauropsida' 355–6, 427 n39; College of Surgeons lectures on birds and reptiles 355; gives birds a dinosaur ancestry 357–60, 377; Royal Institution talk on origin of birds 359; *Archaeopteryx* 358; rebuilds dinosaurs as bipeds 358; *see* separate entry Dinosaurs
Deteriorating relations with Richard Owen – see also entry Owen, R.
Views on Owen 163, 175, 183; relations deteriorate 176–7, 193, 208, 213, 218; with Owen in Belfast 181; confronts Owen, 404 n10; attacks on Owen deliberate, 412 n25; attacks

parthenogenesis 226, 238; debates Owen on method of Palaeontology 229; slates Owen in *Vestiges* review 213; in his lectures 226; and Owen's lectures at the School of Mines 231; against Owen's classification 226; Platonic idealism 174, 218; *Lectures* 218; museum plans 251; archetype 273; creationist language 304; *Archaeopteryx* 358; on Royal Society Council 308; on rudimentary organs 419 n4; on skull 244; on unique human brain 238, 240, 276, 283, 295, 307
Religion and Theology:
3, 8, 63, 73, 75–6, 79, 81, 86, 104, 197, 252–3, 285, 331–2, 345, 372–3; evangelical 13, 285, 181; Calvinistic 'moderate' evangelicalism, 387 n24; Calvinism 75, 200; Puritan 8, 14, 280, 285, 340, 345, 366; scepticism 8, 75–6, 79, 86–7, 132, 154, 159–60, 165–6, 168–9, 185–6, 204, 210, 228, 252–3, 285–7, 293, 307–8, 319, 331–2, 345–6, 367, 373–5, 394–5 nn19–20, 403 n48; a Sadducee 166, 204; New Reformation 4, 253, 260, 270, 293, 367; military metaphor 104, 269, 331; against orthodoxy 169, 276, 403 n48 – *see* Disraeli, B., Wilberforce, S.; attacks 'Parsonism' 253, 269, 271; lectures clergy at Sion House 364; aims remarks at bishops in his audience 268; on Bible's moral truths 252; 'sin of faith' 184, 288, 340, 345, 346; on Genesis 253, 262; on biblical chronology 364; on immortality 288; on moral government of the world 288; on prayer 289; on Unknowable 285, 319, 332, 345, 374; visits Catholic seminary 341; on Jesuits 341; Cardinal Wiseman 331; Mivart 340–1, 368; Pope Pius IX 331; attacks spiritualism 192, 209; on true religion 331; a new rationale for belief 345; and atheism 285, 320, 346; avoids religion in class 340; liberal Anglican alliances:

Index

Index

Index

Index